DATE DUE			

Language in the USA

Language in the USA

Edited by CHARLES A. FERGUSON
Professor of Linguistics
Stanford University

SHIRLEY BRICE HEATH
Associate Professor of Anthropology and Education
Stanford University

with the assistance of DAVID HWANG

Foreword by DELL H. HYMES

CAMBRIDGE UNIVERSITY PRESS

CAMBRIDGE

LONDON   NEW YORK   NEW ROCHELLE

MELBOURNE   SYDNEY

Published by the Press Syndicate of the University of Cambridge
The Pitt Building, Trumpington Street, Cambridge CB2 1RP
32 East 57th Street, New York, NY 10022, USA
296 Beaconsfield Parade, Middle Park, Melbourne 3206, Australia

First published 1981

Printed in the United States of America

British Library Cataloguing in Publication Data
Language in the USA.
1. United States – Languages – History
I. Ferguson, Charles A II. Heath, Shirley
Brice III. Hwang, David
409'.73   P377   80-49985

ISBN 0 521 23140 X hard covers
ISBN 0 521 29834 2 paperback

Foreword

DELL H. HYMES

The United States is a more interesting country than it sometimes lets itself admit. One does not have to go to India or New Guinea for diversity of language. To be sure, it may sometimes seem that there are only two kinds of language in the United States, good English and bad. Only one kind, if some people are to be taken literally: English, surrounded by something else that cannot be called "English," or even perhaps "language." Yet within range of the broadcast in which such remarks are made may be households where there is knowledge of Spanish, Yiddish, Chinese, Korean, Vietnamese, Italian, German, Haitian, Ukrainian, Hebrew, and more. Driving through Arizona, the news on one wave length may be in Navajo. A church convention may be held partly in Finnish. Montana is the state of "big sky," and of fishing spots remote enough to find oneself alone, yet it is linguistically rich as well, as one chapter of this book reveals.

It is not that extermination of diversity has not had its advocates and successes. Many of the languages spoken in North America before Europeans came to its shores are dead. Many adults grew up in homes in which it would have been natural to become bilingual, but are monolingual today. Institutional policies and personal shame or fear of disadvantage have taken their toll. Whereas school children in Denmark and the Netherlands and elsewhere may grow up conversant with several languages, American school children usually pass through the stage of life in which it is easiest to learn languages without learning any beyond their first. Europeans see commercial, political, intellectual, and personal advantage in knowing the languages of other countries and cultures. Americans, somehow, seldom do.

Is it that we think the brain too small a place to hold more than one language at a time? That room for Spanish or Navajo will leave too little room for English? Is it that we fear that other ways of speaking will lead to an understanding of other ways of life, and so weaken commitment to our own? Is it perhaps that command of languages is assigned to a sphere of culture reserved for girls and women, something not suitable for boys and men?

Whatever the reasons, the United States is a country rich in many things, but poor in knowledge of itself with regard to language. That poverty has a cost. Laws and programs involving language are put into effect without much knowledge of the situations to be addressed. The civil rights movement stimulated attention to the educational needs of Black children. Lack of adequate knowledge of the actual language situation led to mistaken efforts on the part of many, liberal and conservative alike. Much more is now generally known about features that may be characteristic of some Black speech, about styles of verbal interaction, and about attitudes toward such things on the part of Black people. Yet the initial stimulus to research has not been well sustained. The full scope of the language experience of Black Americans would richly repay further study; there is need for a greater number of Black scholars to contribute to such knowledge. Commitment to these goals has seemed to wax and wane with the national political climate. It has not been well established as a purpose in its own right, one that will prove invaluable when the concerns that led to the civil rights movement once again crest.

The bilingual education of Spanish-speaking Americans has followed a similar course. Political mobilization and regard for equity have led to programs which had little in the way of precedent and basic research on which to draw. Courts have mandated tests which no one had experience in devising. Again, the efforts of many Native Americans to preserve and revitalize their languages sometimes can draw on existing knowledge and skilled assistance, sometimes not. There have been universities in the United States for two hundred years, but there is still not a single chair devoted to such languages.

In general, one sees a recurrent pattern of a surge of attention to a language situation, because of social and political concerns, and then a lapse. Research follows, not the flag, but political forces, and then fades away.

I paint the picture too bleakly, perhaps; a number of contributors to this book work steadily to make the picture less true. Yet this book derives importance from the degree to which the picture is correct. It is the first book to address the situation of language in the United States as something to be known comprehensively and constantly to be better known. That fact is bittersweet. It makes one doubly glad for the work of editors and contributors, yet sad that until now a concerned citizen could not find such a book.

The book is first of all an account of the country's linguistic richness, in relation to issues that concern many citizens. Its existence, and the future to which it points, depend on constancy of scholarly effort to obtain, sift, and interpret such information. The editors and contributors are to be thanked especially for showing so abundantly that usable knowledge of the current language situation of the country is worthy of such effort. The greater part of the attention of linguists in recent years has gone to models of language in general, neglecting languages in particular. Where the particular forms of language in the United States have been studied, often enough the concern has been with what has been, not with what is or is coming to be. Dialects of English have been studied in terms of geographical isolation and Old World provenience; European languages spoken in the United States have been examined in terms of their relation to the language in Europe; Native American languages have been studied in terms of what was aboriginal and oldest. The current life of language in a community has been neglected. It is to be hoped that this book will herald increased attention to that life.

It is especially important to note that most research, whether into formal grammar or past affinities, has tended to focus attention on a single form of a language – the "deepest" or most "basic," grammatically, or the oldest, historically. Seldom has attention gone to the full repertoire of a community, the full range of its varieties of language, the variety of purposes for which they are employed, the relations among those purposes. Where the education of Native American children is concerned, it may not be a Native American language that they bring to school, but their local variety of English. It can be of social importance to a Native American to be competent in the variety of Indian English spoken in his community; not to use it may imply that one is "putting on airs." Whatever the variety of English, traditional norms for taking the floor, for asking and answering questions, for all the verbal etiquette of daily life, may continue in force. Only recently has there been much serious attempt to describe the current life of English as a language of Indian communities. Again, the repertoire of many Spanish-speaking American communities is far more varied than the bare language names, "Spanish" and "English" would suggest. There may be more than one variety of both, reflecting regional identities and social networks. Yet, again, only recently has there begun to be description of the full life of language in such a community.

When we think of varieties of a single language, we may most readily think of a hierarchy, of varieties arranged vertically: standard, colloquial, substandard, or formal vs. informal. But, of course, there is a "horizontal" dimension to variation in language as well. A judge so impoverished verbally as to be unable to utter anything but Standard English sentences still would not speak the same in courtship as in court. At least one hopes he would not. Courtrooms, hospitals, churches and synagogs, and many other settings, have their own requirements as to speech. In becoming successfully a lawyer, doctor, priest, minister or rabbi, or any of a myriad roles in society, one comes to know how to speak in certain ways. From another point of view, there are a myriad activities which entail speaking in certain ways. From still another point of view, there are characteristics, subtle but perceptible, that go together with being of a certain age or interest, peer group or aspiration. One comes to be able to speak in a series of ways having to do with being certain kinds of person, doing certain kinds of things and not others. Some of these ways are of obvious consequence institutionally, involving, as they do, crime and punishment, sickness and health, salvation and spiritual ease. Others are of consequence in ways less easy to dramatize or define, yet evident enough when one complains of "having no one to talk to" in a crowded room. As we enrich our perception of the country, and move from "the language" to varieties of language, and to varieties of language use, we come ultimately to see the language situation in terms of voices. What kinds of voices are there and should there be? When and where and to what extent shall each be heard?

Perhaps it is in this context that questions of inequality can best be raised. The law of the land demands that equal educational opportunity not be denied because of language. "Language" has been understood most readily in terms of "languages," such as Spanish, and structurally definable varieties of a language, such as Black English Vernacular. If one defines "language," as I do, in terms of ways of speaking, as involving both structure and ways of using structure, there are even deeper implications, implications not yet legally explored. One's language affects one's chances in life, not only through accent, but also through action. Access to opportunities in the form of access to schools, jobs, positions, memberships, clubs, homes, may depend on ways of using language that one has no chance to master, or chooses not to master.

The concern of women for equality has drawn attention to features of language use that are not matters of gender alone, but tend to appear wherever differences of authority and status are established. There appear to be styles associated with differences of power, styles that recur in different situations, and that are found often enough, but not exclusively, among women. It is difficult to say in general, absolutely, just what features are part of such differences. Real life consequences are a consequence of an interaction among features of language itself, such as accent, and features of its use, some or both of which may vary with the person and circumstance. The accents of Lyndon Johnson, Henry Kissinger, and A. D. King, Sr., have been compatible with public esteem, yet have not been matters of indifference to all who have shared them. Clearly the interaction is complex, not something easily defined.

The difficulty of identifying the role of class in language in the United States may be due to the complexity of such interaction. Of course there are differences in speech, notably in cities, that can be calibrated in terms of a socioeconomic index, and it is important to do so; but class as an index of ongoing change in pronunciation or grammar is far short of class as an ingredient of identity. It is difficult to define or study class membership in the United States, as the disagreements of social scientists attest; yet a Trollope among us would be able to weave a tapestry of choices, as to where to live, where to drink, what to wear, what to eat, what to hope, whom to marry, how to talk, within the sphere of any city, that would leave its readers in little doubt as to the existence, not of tenants and landed gentry to be sure, but of distinguishable worlds that pass each other on the street. It is easier for Americans to think of distinct worlds in terms of region and ethnicity, but we must come to be able to articulate also what it is in voices that expresses and maintains the worlds of class.

A conception of the country as a country of kinds of voice speaks to any and all of the factors of origin and experience that condition personal speech. We can expect the great differentiation of occupation, the rapid changes of generational style, and other facets of our complex political economy, to continue to engender a plurality of actual voices amidst the homogenization of interchangeable voices employed on radio and television. With regard to ethnic accent, style and language itself, assimilation to a single English norm has clearly not occurred. The "melting pot" has not melted everything, and its contents are being renewed by the foreign policy of the country. Events since this book was first conceived, indeed, teach us that the United States is becoming, not less, but more diverse linguistically in the elementary sense of speakers of languages other than English. Cuban speakers of Spanish, Haitian speakers of Creole, Laotian speakers of Hmong, are cases in point.

A vital contribution of this book may be to draw attention to the need for accurate numbers on such matters. Despite the efforts of a few, there is much remaining to be done. It is striking that the considerable attention of social scientists and government to the establishment of social indicators, quantitative indications of the characteristics and quality of American life, has overlooked language, as a leading sociologist and sociolinguist, Allen Grimshaw, has pointed out. Many agencies, governmental and private, are involved with people who have a language other than English, but collection and organization of such information leaves much to be desired. What are the numbers, and the distribution in terms of age, geographic location, social origin and national provenience, occupation, and income, of persons who have no English or who have English and another language? What is the distribution of literacy, in English and in other languages, of such people? Surely these facts affect the concerns with national integration, educational effectiveness, productivity, delivery of social services, and the like, that are addressed by analyses and measurements of national characteristics. Numbers are not a substitute for knowledge of specific situations, but they are an essential cure for blindness. Some influential people are able to see multilingualism, differential literacy, and the like, only insofar as they have numbers attached to them. And to decide that something should be nationally measured is to decide that it is nationally important.

This much-needed book, then, is a resource to citizens, a spur to scholars, a challenge to those who shape policy and public life. Let the motto of our political life, one (government) from many, apply to our linguistic life as well. Just as federal unity does not erase the rights and obligations of states, linguistic unity need not entail obliteration of varieties of language. A national lingua franca and local richness can coexist. And, come to think of it, when the founding fathers of the country chose the motto, *E pluribus unum,* did they not show that they expected at least a little bilingualism from all of us? *E pluribus unum* – bilingualism is not so exotic after all. It is only as far as the nearest nickel.

Contents

Preface

The idea for this book came from several sources. One of the editors (Ferguson) had been associated with the five-nation Survey of Language Use and Language Teaching in Eastern Africa, financed by the Ford Foundation. That survey resulted in a series of volumes which described in some detail the language situation in each country, and it seemed reasonable to propose a volume which would do something similar for the USA. The other editor (Heath) had been collecting material for a number of years on the social history of language in the USA, and it seemed reasonable to propose a companion volume which would give a contemporary description with some historical depth. The editors decided to join their efforts in one book, even though Heath was then at the University of Pennsylvania and Ferguson at Stanford.

Encouragement for the volume came from the Committee on Sociolinguistics of the (American) Social Science Research Council. In 1976 the editors presented a trial prospectus to the other members of the Committee, at a meeting devoted to discussion of sociolinguistic projects, and received enthusiastic endorsement of the proposal, along with some suggestions on content and form of publication. Dell Hymes saw the volume as a means of stimulating public and professional interest in research on the ethnography of communication in the USA and kindly agreed to write a foreword to it. The editors are grateful to the Committee for its encouragement and suggestions, and in particular to the Co-Chairmen Allen Grimshaw and Dell Hymes for their personal interest in the project.

This book, in both its contents and the manner of presentation, is very much the product of the time in which it was written. During the period in which the book has become a reality, newspaper stories and television and radio programs have highlighted bilingual education, Plain English, legalese, and other language issues. Many of these media reports and public responses to them have been based on mythical notions of the language situation in the USA and have revealed a severe lack of reliable information about it. The book is an attempt to help fill that gap in knowledge for the general reading public in the United States and around the world.

In the preparation of the volume, the editors had the pleasure of extended conversation or correspondence with the contributing authors. In almost every instance the chapter author and the editors had somewhat different visions of what the chapter should contain, and the editors are deeply appreciative of the authors' patience and perseverance. The final result usually turned out to be better than either of the conflicting visions.

The audience envisioned for the book was, as already noted, the general reading public as well as college students not specializing in linguistics. David Hwang, a playwright and student of American literature, took three months out of his career to read the entire manuscript and assess its suitability for an audience of non-linguists. With unflagging patience he read and reacted to these essays, urging economy of expression and raising questions about ambiguous and contradictory points. Also, since the editors, busy with their academic tasks and usually separated by the width of a continent, could not complete the mechanical tasks of collating, verifying, and cross-checking, David did most of this work, and he even learned how to deal with a computer in order to consolidate the bibliography. On this bibliographical task, David Barton, a Research Associate at Stanford, assisted by producing the final print-out.

Barbara Kao typed the entire manuscript, often turning messy, edited typescripts into beautiful clean pages. Barbara never complained when she had to retype entire chapters because author or editors or both changed their minds, and she did a great deal to help the editors maintain consistency in presentation. Her performance went far beyond normal expectations and the editors are grateful for it. Penny Carter of Cambridge University Press was a model of editorial caring: after we thought we had completed our work, she showed us how passages could be clarified, inconsistencies lessened, and the readability and aesthetic appeal of text and illustrations heightened. To her treatment of hundreds of details she brought both sympathetic attention for the subject matter and a feeling for the intended style of the book. We thank her.

Finally, the editors acknowledge the support of a grant from the National Institute of Education to Heath for research on legal decisions relating to language policy. That grant contributed to the preparation of the volume directly since some of the research fed into chapters of the book. It also contributed indirectly by stimulating the investigation of related topics and by enabling the editors to be in the same city for a period of time and thus to make use of the services of David Hwang, Barbara Kao, David Barton, and the Stanford Computer Center. Finally, the contribution of Professor Clara N. Bush and the Department of Linguistics at Stanford is acknowledged for awarding Heath the status of Visiting Scholar, thus making the Stanford facilities doubly accessible.

C.A.F.
S.B.H.

Indian Republic Day, 1980
Osmania University, Hyderabad

The authors

James Beebe is a specialist in rural agricultural development of Third World countries, particularly interested in educational processes. During his five years with the U.S. Peace Corps in the Philippines he conducted training courses in the teaching of science in the schools and participated in a variety of agricultural programs. His doctoral dissertation at Stanford was a study of Filipino rice farmers. He has given lectures at universities in the Philippines and at Harvard University. In 1977–8 he was an assistant professor of Education at the Monterey Institute of Foreign Studies and also directed a community study of Filipinos in California. At present he is Human Resources Development Officer, USAID, Khartoum, Sudan.

Maria Beebe, a specialist in the study of language use and the language socialization of bilingual individuals, has had varied teaching, research, and organizational work experience in the Philippines and the USA. She has taught both Tagalog and English, has studied and taught Philippine dance forms and oral traditions, and served for two years in the U.S. Peace Corps. She has conducted research on language use in the classroom and in agricultural settings, and is currently completing her Ph.D. at Stanford University with a specialization in bilingual cross-cultural education.

Anthony F. Beltramo, specialist in Spanish linguistics, applied linguistics, and foreign language education, teaches at the University of Montana. His doctoral dissertation at Stanford investigated the linguistic acculturation of Mexican Americans in San José, California; he has published a number of studies of Mexican American Spanish, and he co-edited *El Lenguaje de los Chicanos*. For several years he has been studying the history of ethnic groups in Montana, and he has conducted a language survey of the state.

Courtney B. Cazden, specialist in the development of children's verbal abilities, author of *Child Language and Education* and co-editor of *Functions of Language in the Classroom*, has investigated many aspects of first and second language acquisition as well as educational problems related to language. Her recent experience includes a year of primary school teaching in California, observation of language in education in Great Britain, and participation in planning television programs for children. She is Professor of Education at Harvard University.

Aaron V. Cicourel, Professor of Sociology at the University of California, San Diego, has published books and papers on a wide variety of sociological topics, many of them reprinted in anthologies and translated into other languages. His studies of language have focused on the communication of the deaf, child language development, language in the classroom, and the language of doctor-patient exchanges. His *Cognitive Sociology: Language and Meaning in Social Interaction* is a path-breaking, controversial book which questions many established ideas. *Language Use and Classroom Behavior,* of which he is co-author, is based on extensive observations and recordings of classroom behavior and makes use of ethnomethodological techniques of analysis.

Jenny Cook-Gumperz is a specialist in children's acquisition of the social uses of language, and much of her research has dealt with child discourse in school and home settings. She received her doctorate at the University of London, where she was associated with the Sociological Research Unit. A shortened form of her dissertation appeared in book form as *Social Control and Socialization: A Study of Class Differences in the Language of Maternal Control.* Her published articles include "The child as a practical reasoner" and "Situated instructions: language socialization of school age children." Her concept of "situated meaning" has contributed to discourse analysis in both child and adult, bridging the fields of conversational analysis and linguistic semantics. Recent joint work with John J. Gumperz has treated the uses of literacy in school and home and interethnic communication.

Yole Correa-Zoli, Italian-American linguist and Associate Professor of Italian Language and Literature at the California State University, Hayward, has studied the characteristics of American Italian. Her doctoral dissertation at Stanford was an analysis of the Italian spoken in San Francisco. She has published several articles on American Italian, and is one of the founders of the Scuola di Lingua e Cultura Italiana in San Francisco.

Jerry R. Craddock, Professor in the Department of Spanish and Portuguese at the University of California, Berkeley, is known in the academic world both for historical philological studies and the investigation of all forms of Spanish used in the United States. His publications include many technical philological papers and reviews as well as "Spanish in North America," a review of the whole field, and "Lexical analysis of Southwest Spanish." He is co-author of the widely used annotated bibliography *Spanish and English of United States Hispanos.*

David K. Dickinson is a doctoral student in Human Development at the Harvard Graduate School of Education. He graduated from Oberlin College with a major in theology, has a master's degree in Elementary Education from Temple University, and taught for five years in public and private elementary schools in Philadelphia.

Charles A. Ferguson, Professor of Linguistics, Stanford University, is co-editor of *Language Problems of Developing Nations,* co-author of *Language in Ethiopia,* and a contributor to *Language and Linguistics in the People's Republic of China.* His studies on language in America include "Short *a* in Philadelphia English," "King James English as the language of American revelation," "Language planning in the U.S. and China," and "National attitudes toward language planning." He was the Director of the Center for Applied Linguistics, Washington, DC 1959–66, and he was a member of the SSRC Committee on Sociolinguistics from its formation and served as chairman 1964–70.

Joshua A. Fishman (Yeshiva University, New York) is an internationally respected scholar in bilingualism, ethnicity, language planning, and the sociology of language. His textbooks and readers on sociolinguistics are widely used, and his opinions are sought on language questions all over the world. He is the editor of the *International Journal of the Sociology of Language* and of an important series of sociolinguistic monographs. His volume *Language Loyalty in the United States* is the only general book on the language situation in the USA, and recently he has served as a consultant to the National Institute of Education on issues of bilingualism and education in America.

Glenn G. Gilbert, a sociolinguist, had graduate study in both Germany and France before receiving his doctorate in linguistics from Harvard University. He has specialized in German linguistics, the study of pidgin and creole languages, and language minorities in the USA. From 1963 to 1970, he taught at the University of Texas, and since that time has been at Southern Illinois University, where he is now Professor of Linguistics. He has published a book and numerous articles on German dialects in the USA, edited the two volumes *Texas Studies in Bilingualism* and *The German Language in America,* and co-edited *Problems in Applied Educational Sociolinguistics.* His current research is on the Pidgin German of foreign workers in Germany and on general issues of simplification and pidginization in language.

David L. Gold has been living in Israel since 1975, where he teaches courses in Jewish intralinguistics (the study of the speech and writing of Jews) at the University of Haifa. His special interests are Yiddish, Hebrew, Jewish English, and the Jewish languages of Romance stock. He has also published on lexicography, lexicology, translation, interpretation, linguistic geography, and language planning in *American Speech, Babel, Language Problems and Language Planning, Leuvense Bijdragen, Orbis, Word, Yidishe Shprakh,* and elsewhere.

John J. Gumperz (University of California, Berkeley) is a leading figure in sociolinguistics, having done field research in India, Norway, Austria, Great Britain, and the United States. A number of his concepts (such as ''verbal repertoire'' and types of code-switching) have become basic notions in sociolinguistic research. He is co-editor with Hymes of the classic *Ethnography of Communication* and the more recent *Directions in Sociolinguistics.* Many of his own papers have been collected in *Language in Social Groups* and a new volume of his essays, *Conversational Strategies.* Most recently he has studied problems in communication between different ethnic groups in England and in California.

Shirley Brice Heath, anthropologist and sociolinguist, author of *Telling Tongues: Language Policy in Mexico, Colony to Nation,* is especially interested in developing the field of historical sociolinguistics. She has done sociolinguistic research in Latin American countries and in minority communities in the USA, and she has made educational application of her findings in the schools of North and South Carolina. Her publications on language in America include ''National language academy: debate in the new nation,'' ''Colonial language status achievement: Mexico, Peru, and the United States,'' and ''Standard English: biography of a symbol.'' She was formerly Associate Professor of Education, University of Pennsylvania; she was a member of the SSRC Committee on Sociolinguistics, 1976–9.

Věra M. Henzl, Czech-American sociolinguist and specialist in language pedagogy, has studied register variation in Czech, English, and other languages and the characteristics of American Czech. Her doctoral dissertation at Stanford was on the maintenance of Literary Czech among Czech Americans. Her publications include ''Speech of foreign language teachers: a sociolinguistic analysis," "Foreigner talk in the classroom," and "Acquisition of grammatical gender in Czech." Currently she is studying ethnic differences in American children's narrative skills and linguistic correlates of successful doctor-patient communication. She developed a program in Czech instruction at Stanford and has been interested in the acquisition of English by American immigrants.

David Hwang is a Chinese-American playwright whose work concerns the experiences of Asian and Third World people in the USA. His plays have been presented in Los Angeles and San Francisco, and he was the youngest playwright invited to participate in the 1979 Eugene O'Neill National Playwrights Conference, where his *FOB* was performed. He has published poetry and critical pieces, taught classes in Asian American Studies at Stanford University, and is currently writing a play on the San Francisco State University Third World strikes.

Dell H. Hymes, distinguished anthropologist, past Chairman of the SSRC Committee on Sociolinguistics, has written and spoken tirelessly on the role of language in society and culture. His concepts of "communicative competence" and the "ethnography of speaking" have guided many researchers to new insights on the use of language. His anthology *Language in Culture and Society* has been a mainstay of courses in sociolinguistics and in language and culture, and his *Foundations of Sociolinguistics* is a basic book in the field. He edits the journal *Language in Society* and is currently Professor of Anthropology and Folklore and Dean of the Graduate School of Education at the University of Pennsylvania.

Braj B. Kachru, former Head of Linguistics at the University of Illinois and internationally recognized expert on the English of South Asia, has published linguistic studies of Kashmiri, Hindi, and English. His doctoral dissertation at Edinburgh was "An analysis of some features of Indian English: a study in linguistic method," and he has continued to investigate the differences between Indian, British, and American English. His publications include works on sociolinguistics, stylistics, and South Asian linguistics and literature.

William L. Leap became interested in the study of American Indian languages as a result of his doctoral studies with George L. Trager at Southern Methodist University. In 1972–73 and from 1974 to 1979 he coordinated the work of the Center for Applied Linguistics in areas related to American Indian education and Indian language maintenance. Currently, he is Associate Professor of Anthropology at the American University, Washington, DC. In addition, he serves as the bilingual education specialist for the Education Office of the National Tribal Chairmen's Association, while continuing his work with tribally sponsored language projects in the greater Southwest and the Pacific Northwest.

Patricia C. Nichols (San José State University), sociolinguist and teacher of writing, founding co-editor of *Women and Language News*, has studied linguistic change in Gullah and has published a series of papers on creole languages and the educational implications of linguistic variation, including "Ethnic consciousness in the British Isles," "Black women in the rural South: conservative and innovative," and "Complementizers in creoles." Dr. Nichols is particularly interested in the concept of "action linguistics" whereby a linguist doing field research simultaneously serves in a functional capacity in the community.

William M. O'Barr, Professor of Anthropology at Duke University, is a pioneer in the study of language use in both law and advertising. From 1974 to 1976, he directed the Law and Language Project at Duke University, which produced a wide-ranging series of articles on the language of the courtroom. He is currently completing a major research project on the language of advertising. He has also done research on communication in political and legal contexts in Eastern Africa and the USA. He and Jean O'Barr co-edited the volume *Language and Politics,* which deals mostly with Asian and African countries, including reports of their own research in Tanzania.

Christina Bratt Paulston, Swedish-American sociolinguist and specialist in second language teaching and bilingual education, has had professional experience in Sweden, India, Morocco, Peru, and the USA. She has written monographs, articles, and textbooks on the teaching of English to speakers of other languages, analyses of bilingual education goals and programs in the USA and other countries, and sociolinguistic studies of such topics as the pronouns of address in Swedish. At present she is Chairman of General Linguistics and Director of the English Language Institute, University of Pittsburgh.

Allan R. Taylor, linguist specializing in Native America, has published articles on a variety of languages, especially the Siouan languages, and a variety of topics, including nonverbal communication, word studies, comparative-historical linguistics, and systems of writing for Native American languages. He is currently completing a grammar and dictionary of Lakhota (Teton Sioux). His present position is Chairman, Department of Linguistics, University of Colorado.

Willard Walker, anthropologist interested in the history of American Indian communities and in the language and culture of contemporary Native America, has published linguistic and anthropological studies of the Zuñi and Cherokee peoples. He has also done field work among the Cree, the Yaquis, and the Passamaquoddies. He took part in an experimental Cherokee language project which resulted in the publication of a *Cherokee Primer* and a collection of *Cherokee Stories.* At present he is chairman of Anthropology at Wesleyan University.

Dorothy Waggoner is an applied linguist and specialist in bilingual education and language minority statistics. Her doctorate in linguistics is from Georgetown University and her professional career has been in the U.S. Department of Health, Education, and Welfare. Currently she is at the National Center for Education Statistics, where she is responsible for language minority statistics. Her published works include *Language and Demographic Characteristics of the U.S. Population* and "Non-English language background persons: three U.S. surveys."

Elizabeth Whatley received her doctorate in Elementary Education at the University of Pittsburgh with a dissertation on teachers' perceptions of the effects of Black vernacular on oral reading. Her professional teaching career has been in the area of reading, and her research has been chiefly on language use in Black communities. At present she is Professor of Reading at Cheyney State College, the oldest of the Negro Colleges in the USA. She is active in TESOL affairs and has completed a book entitled *Child Discourse in the Black Community.*

Walt Wolfram (University of the District of Columbia and Center for Applied Linguistics) is one of the most versatile sociolinguistic researchers on American English. He has published books on the English of Blacks in Detroit, Puerto Ricans in New York City, and on the English spoken in the Appalachian region. His publications range from research on glossolalia to articles on the teaching of English. He is co-author of *The Study of Social Dialects in American English* and *Field Techniques in an Urban Language Study*, and co-editor of *Black-White Speech Relationships*. His most recent works focus on the English of Native American Indians in the Southwest United States.

Ana Celia Zentella is a doctoral student in Educational Linguistics at the University of Pennsylvania. She is Director of the Puerto Rican Studies Program at Hunter College in New York City. Her research interest in Spanish-English code-switching has led to studies of this phenomenon in Philadelphia and in bilingual classrooms in New York. She has been active in the planning efforts of the National Institute of Education for a national center for research on bilinguals. Currently she is at work on a full-length ethnographic account of language use in a Puerto Rican barrio in New York City.

Notes on symbols

Glossary terms. Technical terms from linguistics and related fields have been avoided in this book. A number of specialized words and phrases are used, however, which may cause some confusion. About 120 such recurrent expressions are defined in the Glossary, pp. 527–33. In each chapter or other section of the book, the first time one of these expressions appears, it is printed in SMALL CAPITALS, indicating that it can be found in the Glossary.

Transcriptions. PHONETIC transcriptions are kept to a minimum in this book, and whenever possible the authors use ordinary English ORTHOGRAPHY. In a number of places, however, phonetic transcriptions or material in foreign writing systems appear. In these cases, the authors use the symbols usually employed in the appropriate language (e.g. Polish, Spanish) or specialized field (e.g. conversational analysis, Romance philology, American Indian linguistics). Thus the symbols are not used consistently throughout the book, and the list with notes given below is only a rough indication of the value of the symbols. For more precise explanations of symbols, items in the "Further reading" sections of the chapter should be consulted.

/. . ./	Slant lines enclose PHONEMIC or quasi-phonemic transcription.
[. . .]	Square brackets enclose phonetic transcriptions. They are also used in transcripts to enclose English translations of material in other languages.
[	A long bracket connecting lines of transcription indicates simultaneous speech.
→, ←	An arrow indicates change or derivation; the head of the arrow points to the outcome or derivative: A→B means "A becomes B" or "B is derived from A."
a: , a·, ā, á	Vowel length is indicated by a colon or a raised dot after the vowel letter or by a straight line or an accent mark over it.

ã, ē, ĩ etc. ạ, į, ụ, etc.	Nasalized vowels are represented by either a wavy line over the appropriate vowel letter or a hook under it.
à, ù, î, ô, á, é, etc.	Accented syllables are indicated by an accent mark (ˆˆ) over a vowel letter or by a raised vertical tick (')
wa'la	*before* the syllable. The accent marks sometimes indicate tones.
lo^h, a^e, g^w	A raised symbol indicates either a light pronunciation of the sound or a modification of the neighboring sound.
a, e, i, o, u	The basic vowel letters usually have their so-called "Italian" values, roughly as in: f*a*ther, r*e*in, mach*i*ne, n*o*te, r*u*de.

Other vowel letters have roughly the following equivalents in GENERAL AMERICAN ENGLISH:

æ	h*a*t
ɔ	c*o*re
ʌ	b*u*t
ɪ	b*i*t
ʊ	p*u*t
ɨ, y	A central vowel between ɪ and ʌ in quality.
ö, œ; ü, y	Front rounded vowels as in: French p*eu*, d*u*.
b, d, f, g, h, k, l, m, n, p, s, t, v, w, z	These usually represent their commonest English sounds.

The little wedge over a consonant letter indicates a PALATAL or PALATALIZED sound, as in:

š	*sh*ip
ž	a*z*ure
č	*ch*ip
ǰ	*j*ig
ṭ, ḍ, ṇ, ; etc.; c, ɟ	Palatalized consonants are also indicated by a small hook under the letter or by special letters such as c and ɟ for ky, gy.

The VOICED FRICATIVES are represented in two different ways:

ƀ or β	LABIAL
đ or ð	APICO-ALVEOLAR
ǥ or ɣ	VELAR

Other consonant letters have roughly the following equivalents:

θ	*th*ink
X	German Ba*ch*
ł	voiceless l as in Welsh *Ll*anfair
ŋ	si*ng*
ɲ, ń, ṇ, ñ	on*i*on

j, y	yes (note that "y" is used for the sound in English *yes*, a similar sound with fricative noise, or a front rounded vowel)
ʔ	Glottal stop, as in the middle sound of *oh-oh*, the exclamation of surprise.
r, r̄, ɹ, ɹ̱	The letter "r" is used to represent several different sounds, including trills and continuants; r̄ is a strong trill, upside down ɹ is a continuant or fricative, and ɹ̱ is a strong fricative.

Introduction

CHARLES A. FERGUSON and
SHIRLEY BRICE HEATH

The United States of America is a large and important country with a unique pattern of language use –the dominant English which is spoken just about everywhere, a number of Indian languages spoken by the original inhabitants of North America, several substantial remnants of colonial Spanish and French, and a host of diverse languages brought by successive waves of immigration from all over the world. One language, Spanish, is clearly second in importance to English, not only by number of speakers but by virtue of the special political relationship of Puerto Rico and the continuing interaction between the peoples of Mexico and the USA. American English is remarkably uniform considering the number of its speakers and the expanse of its territory, but it does show regional and social DIALECT variation as well as variation according to use. U.S. Spanish is also variable, depending largely on place of origin. The language situation in Australia is probably the closest parallel to that of the USA: English dominant, Aboriginal languages, and the languages of varied immigrant groups. But Australia has no counterpart to Spanish, the roles of colonial and immigrant languages are much less salient there than in the USA, and the nature of the social dialect variation in Australian English is quite different from that in American English.

Language is central to communication, and language differences are a major source of communication problems, whether the differences are variations within a language, such as in American English, or the use of different languages in communication events. In recent years a number of communication problems and language policy questions have reached unexpected prominence in American life. Language legislation and court decisions about language have made the headlines. Edwin Newman (1974) claims that current speakers and writers of English have moved away from the standard and that American English is in a state of decline. A current "crisis in education" centers around language and the apparent inability of many high school graduates to read English with comprehension and write it effectively. Permissive attitudes toward nonstandard varieties of American English in the classroom are blamed for declining test scores, and there is a corresponding call for a "return to the basics." Noel Epstein of the *Washington Post* points out a crisis he sees in the language diversity of the United States. In his view, and that of many others, bilingual education using the home language of students who have limited or no English fosters social and political divisiveness. Joey Dillard and other linguists introduce the American public to "Black English," "Red English" (of American Indians), and Southern Appalachian English, and many people interpret this diversity as evidence of the decline and splitting apart of American English. All these and other language issues are debated without an adequate historical and contemporary perspective on the whole linguistic situation of the country.

Also, the language situation in the USA affects language use in the rest of the world, especially by the spread of English to other nations, the activities of Americans and American institutions outside the USA, and the influence of American educational policies on education elsewhere. English has become the world's most important LINGUA FRANCA and is still spreading at a phenomenal rate across economic, political, and cultural boundaries as an international means of communication. The English of the USA is an important ingredient in this spread. Americans traveling or living outside their country have a reputation – in part deserved – for not learning local languages and for ignoring language aspects of national life in the host country. When Americans offer technical advice on communication satellites they are more concerned with the techniques of mass communication than with the languages required as means of communication in multilingual nations and regions. American educational innovations are often extended, at least on a trial basis, to other nations, and the strange spectacle unfolds of American methods of language teaching and bilingual education being applied in nations which already produce competent speakers of foreign languages and already make use of multiple language channels in schools. American research on reading is applied to other alphabets and functions of literacy far removed from the American research settings.

In short, the language situation in the USA is important for Americans and non-Americans to know about, yet in comparison with the great outpouring of books on almost all aspects of American life, very few books appear on language in the USA. Americans themselves, even otherwise well-informed, public-spirited citizens, have very little knowledge of the language situation in their nation. In fact, most Americans are unaware of the distribution of languages and the patterns of language use in their own local communities. People in the rest of the world also often have inadequate or distorted views of the language situation in the USA, and even when they visit America they may come in contact with only limited aspects of language use. This book offers some basic information as summarized by specialists in particular languages and language topics. It discusses some salient features of American English and how it varies, the Native American languages and New World Spanish and what is happening to them today, the maintenance of immigrant languages in different ethnic communities, the ways language is used in law, medicine, and education, and the options Americans have for national, local, and ethnic language policies in the future.

American myths about language

Like members of any other nation, Americans tend to share some beliefs about language in general and their own use of language. These beliefs, which we might call "myths," tend to reflect historical experiences Americans have had with language and doubtless serve useful social purposes in creating images about American national life. They are, however, only partly true, and in some instances they are actually false. For example, most Americans, if asked, would probably agree that English is the official national language of the country. Yet nowhere in American law is this stated, and a number of legal decisions, including Supreme Court cases, have acknowledged that English has no such status. Many nations spell out in their constitutions, or somewhere in their laws, the language or languages which are legal or official at the national level and the uses for which they are permitted or required, but the USA has never done so.

Some of the myths that are widely and strongly held among Americans are inconsistent with one another and represent basic ambivalences in American values. One of the most obvious of these conflicts is the tension between belief in correctness and pride in being free to speak without authoritarian control of the language. Many Americans have strong convictions that there *is* a correct way to speak and write English, even if they are not always sure what is is. They are often apologetic about their own pronunciation, grammar, and choice of words, and they approve the criticisms which appear in editorials, public speeches, and popular books against current "low standards" in English. American insecurity about correctness is notorious. Probably no other nation consults dictionaries so frequently to check on the pronunciation, spelling, meaning, and usage of words. Quite possibly no other nation buys so many style manuals and how-to-improve-your-language books in proportion to the population. In 1978 when a Midwestern American university opened a "hot-line" on correct grammar and punctuation, it received calls from all over the country and soon had a publisher eager to produce yet another style manual from the commonest queries and replies.

Yet many of these same Americans who are so concerned about correctness are also proud of the American freedom from authoritarian interference on language, and would bitterly oppose Congress passing a law about correct pronunciation, spelling, grammar, or vocabulary. They would ridicule the idea of a French Academy setting standards of language and be quite bewildered by the linguistic decisions of a Norwegian Parliament legislating the language of government correspondence or children's schoolbooks. Americans see no irony in rejecting language authority of the national government and private academic institutions but putting child-like trust in the authoritative lexicography of large-scale commercial publishers.

American attitudes toward languages other than English are equally con-fused. Many Americans regard the use of another language in the USA as a sign of inferiority and disadvantage – to be kept hidden in one's own case and educated away in the case of others. They view the study of foreign languages in school as not particularly useful in achieving a good education or preparing for a career. Yet some of these same Americans are proud of a President who can speak a few words of Spanish on a public occasion and are enormously impressed by a European visitor who speaks several languages. Although Americans tend to believe that English is hard for foreigners to learn, they often feel that educated foreigners "speak better English than we do."

American myths about variation in American English are a hodgepodge of evaluative judgments, beliefs about change, and a kind of anti-intellectualism. Brooklynites are believed to speak a crude form of English typified by *dese'n dose* for *these and those* or *Toity-toid Street* for *Thirty-third Street*. Bostonians are thought to have an affected form of English which has *hahf* and *cahn't* for *half* and *can't* and drops its *r*s as in *pahk the cah*, irritatingly also inserting some *r*s where they shouldn't be as in *idear* and *Cubar*. Southerners have a "drawl," New Englanders a "twang," and Chicagoans' pronunciation is "flat." These beliefs bear only a distant relation to the facts.

Americans tend to believe that the language is becoming homogenized because of the influence of the mass media, especially television. But there is no solid evidence of such across-the-board homogenization or – where DIALECT LEVELING is actually attested – that the mass media are the chief causal factor. On the contrary, there is considerable evidence that social dialect variation, especially in urban areas, is increasing and that the special languages of different occupational groups and followers of different life styles are proliferating.

A very widespread notion among Americans is that anything really worth saying can be said in "plain English." Almost everyone – including government bureaucrats – decries the use of the overwordy, needlessly obfuscatory style of governmental gobbledygook. In recent years, powerful movements have led to serious attempts at rewriting regulations, contracts, and public instructions to make them more intelligible. Although there have been successes in these attempts, some simplifiers have discovered to their surprise that complex messages sometimes cannot be expressed in short words and short sentences, and without the use of technical terms and complex modifying clauses. Although Americans generally share a belief in the value of "plain English," thus differing from people in some other cultures who have a high regard for elaborate language or for subtle layers of meanings, they have real ambivalences about intelligibility versus appropriateness. The very person who complains about the obscurities of legal language, when asked to draft a contract, may reach for legal-sounding words and constructions so that the language will be appropriate for the document. The young people who make fun of the pomposities and archaisms of religious language, when faced with the task of composing their own marriage vows, may turn to archaic pronouns and half-understood phrases to make the vows appropriately solemn. After all, the goals of maximal intelligibility and optimal stylistic appropriateness are not always compatible. Some years ago, when the Modern Language Association was revising its constitution, a distinguished literary scholar who bewailed the standardization and homogenization of American English styles, found himself arguing for an intelligible plain English wording of the constitution, which would rob it of its distinctive legal flavor and make it just like the homogenized nonliterary prose he so disliked.

Out of the large number of myths which could be examined, two are outstanding for their strength, pervasiveness, and essential wrongness: that the USA is a monolithic English-speaking nation in which other languages are only vestigial or transitory, and that the quality of English is declining sharply. It is certainly true that English is strongly dominant in the USA and that the pattern of linguistic assimilation of immigrant groups has been powerful throughout the nation's history. Also it is true and should not be forgotten that incalculable economic, political, and social benefits follow from the availability of a single means of communication over such a large and complex nation. But at the same time, these things are also true: about twenty-eight millions, or about 1 in 8, of the inhabitants of the USA have a language other than English as their MOTHER TONGUE or live in a household where such a language is spoken; two out of three of these people of non-English background are native-born Americans (i.e. were born in the fifty states, District of Columbia, Puerto Rico, or a U.S. territory). Scores of newspapers and radio programs are in languages other than English; hundreds of private schools around the country teach at least part of the day in a language other than English.

Language in the USA does not take sides on the issue of how multilingual the nation should or should not be, although most of the authors tend to favor one aspect or another of linguistic and cultural pluralism in the USA. It does try, however, to provide basic information about the use of different languages: which ones are disappearing, which are spreading, and what problems arise from the use and disuse of language under various circumstances. Throughout the volume, the authors give historical background on language use which can serve as a corrective to misperceptions and false beliefs about the languages of Americans. As a consequence, much of the volume is an examination of the widespread myth of American monolingualism, showing both the ways in which America impressively moves toward monolingualism and the wide range of situations in which non-English languages have been used and are still in use.

The myth of the decline of English is particularly interesting, because it is so old. Writers, teachers, public lecturers, and social critics have complained about the decline in English at least as far back as the fifteenth century, and often enough what the bemoaners of one century have seen as evidence of decline is regarded as excellence by the complainers of the next century, who see something else as decline. In some nations, the myth is of a Golden Age from which the language and literature have steadily declined, but in the English-speaking world, America included, the myth seems to be that the language has been doing well enough until recent decades, when dramatic decline has set in. The recent decades may, of course, be in the eighteenth century, when Samuel Johnson elevated the criticism to a principle in his often quoted phrase "tongues, like governments, have a natural tendency to degeneration." Or they may be in the nineteenth century, when the writings of Richard Grant White, an American journalist, were expounding on the horrors of the decline of American English. The "recent decades" are in our own century for Edwin Newman, who asserts firmly and indignantly "language is in a state of decline."

It is amusing to note that White offered as evidence of decline such monstrous usages as *demeaning* (= degrading), *jeopardize, presidential campaign*, and *standpoint*, all of which are freely and approvingly used by Newman, who is in turn worried about *hopefully* (= it is to be hoped), *ongoing*, and *quite a few* (= a considerable number), all of which will probably be used approvingly by the next generation's critics of decline. This is not to imply that what the critic disapproves always becomes accepted after a time. In the complex patterns of change which all languages – American English included – are continually undergoing, there may be reversals, shifts, and the persistence of unresolved problems. Whether to use *from*, *than*, or *to* with *different* has been debated for centuries and usage still fluctuates. White and Newman agree on proscribing *gubernatorial*, but neither offers a substitute and the word continues in regular use. White approved of *the house is a-building* but this construction seems to be (a-)disappearing. The efforts of the critics seem to have little effect on the changes in the language, and indeed the critics seem never to deal with the issues systematically, never to suggest means of reaching agreement on what constitutes decline and never to propose programs of action to arrest the decline. Their social function is apparently to reinforce the myth, to stimulate the insecure to intensify their efforts for self-improvement, and to stroke the egos of those who can feel with the critics that their own usage is superior to that of ordinary citizens.

Language in the USA does not attempt to solve questions of usage or provide direct assistance for readers who want to evaluate alternative ways of saying or writing their messages. It does not even try to give a general characterization of the changes taking place in American English. It does, however, offer the readers a chance to step outside the myth of language decline and learn some of the basic facts about language use in the nation. The facts are presented from various perspectives, but mostly with a linguistic or sociolinguistic orientation on the part of the authors. Some of the authors' own evaluations are apparent, but they are intended to show the opinion of some knowledgeable people rather than a uniform set of recommendations. We hope that the readers' own evaluations and judgments in the future will be affected by the information presented and stimulated by the opinions given.

The language situation in the USA

Every one of the major components of the language situation in the USA poses difficult questions about its present status and how it came to be the way it is.

When English was transplanted to the New World, what happened to it? In what sense is it dominant and how did its dominance come about? Is it becoming more uniform or splitting apart?

How diverse were the American Indian languages before the Europeans came and what are they like as languages? Will the 1980s see the extinction of the Native American languages or will a renaissance and a new range of uses emerge?

Where did the colonial languages other than English survive in the USA? How different is *their* submerged status from that of other minority languages and what effect has later immigration had on them?

Have immigrants to the USA been more willing to give up their languages than immigrants to other countries? What factors account for different patterns of language loyalty among immigrant groups? Does bilingualism build strength for the nation or does it divide and trouble it?

What are the most striking issues of language and public policy in the USA, and have the same issues been evident in the nation's history? How widely shared are American ways of talking? Do they cut across linguistic and cultural boundaries?

Full answers to these and scores of similar questions would be found in a comprehensive description of the language situation in the USA. Surprisingly enough, such questions often cannot be satisfactorily answered because the data have not been assembled and analyzed. The information we have available would fill many books, but it is fragmentary, specialized, and often lacking on the crucial points. Compared to many other nations, the USA has had poor census data on language use, little historical scholarship on the language situation, and few national institutions concerned with language issues on a broad scale. The United States is the world's leading producer of linguistic research as well as research on language acquisition, both first and second language, yet only a very small amount of research is devoted to the study of the language situation in the country itself. Hardly anyone is interested in establishing some kind of selected data base which could be used to compare changes in language use over time.

In the spring of 1976, the Bureau of the Census made a survey of language minorities in the USA, and the findings released from the National Center of Education Statistics in 1978 give a useful picture of the number and distribution of the principal language minority groups. Every state has a significant language minority population: in twenty-three states, it constitutes at least 10 percent of the population, and seven states have more than a million language minority persons. People of Spanish background, the largest group, number about 10.6 million, three-fifths of them in the southwestern states of California, Arizona, Colorado, New Mexico, and Texas. The top immigrant languages are Italian and German, then come French and Polish. Nearly two million speakers are of Chinese, Filipino, Japanese, Korean, or Vietnamese language background. The survey figures are a welcome contribution to the overall view of

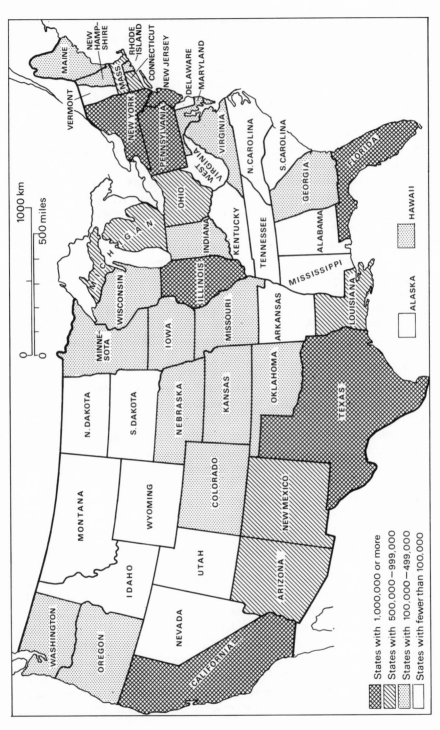

Figure 1. Location of language-minority persons (adapted from *National Center for Education Statistics Bulletin* 78: B-5)

States with 1,000,000 or more

States with 500,000–999,000

States with 100,000–499,000

States with fewer than 100,000

HAWAII

ALASKA

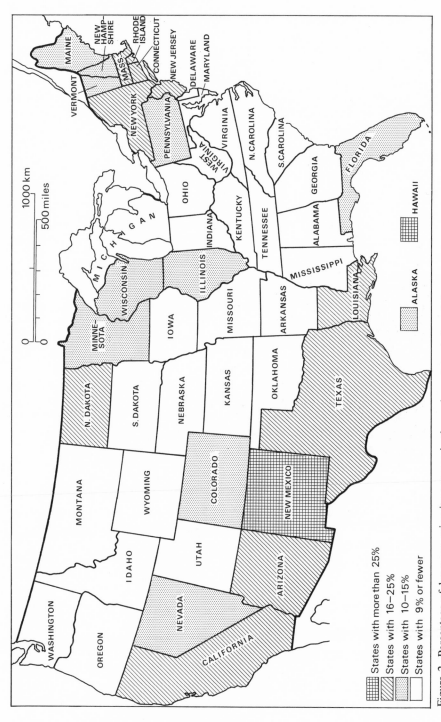

Figure 2. Percentage of language minority persons in the various states (adapted from *National Center for Education Statistics Bulletin 78: B-5*)

States with more than 25%

States with 16–25%

States with 10–15%

States with 9% or fewer

HAWAII

ALASKA

the language situation, and the accompanying maps (Figures 1 and 2) translate the figures into a helpful visual representation, but the survey does not begin to give the kind of detail about varieties of the languages, their nature and extent of use, literacy in the languages, and attitudes toward them which would be needed for rational consideration of the language resources of the USA.

Just as prudent policy makers collect information on other resources, it would seem desirable to collect information on language. Such information could help the nation as a whole as well as groups and individuals within it in coping with language problems. Resources can be squandered or lost, they can be carefully husbanded and tended, or they can be developed and invested in productive activities. The chapters of this volume present enough information to show how generally unknown the basic facts are, and to suggest that systematic investigation of language phenomena in the USA could "pay off" in more effective educational planning, more effective international communication, and more useful communication in the "helping professions," to name only three of the areas concerned.

The information that we have shows varied and changing patterns of language use in American Indian and non-English background immigrant groups as well as a general decline in the teaching of foreign languages in American schools and colleges. It also shows a new surge of activity in the teaching of English to speakers of other languages (TESOL), but a dramatic decline of American involvement in the teaching of English abroad. More information would be needed, as well as a highly sophisticated method of analysis, to gain an adequate understanding of the interrelationships of these and other language phenomena in the USA.

One example of an apparent relationship may indicate the possibility of social analysis of language use. From at least the time of World War I and possibly as far back as the Modern Languages movement of the 1880s, there has been a sharp distinction in attitudes toward non-English languages between the languages of immigrants and the foreign languages (FL) taught in school. The distinction has been shown in many ways. The use of the ethnic languages has been discouraged or even prohibited in school, and students who already speak the language are not encouraged to study it at school or major in it at college. The FL is taught as a subject to be learned, not a skill to be employed, and FL students typically do not use the subject language to communicate with fellow students who speak it naturally. For example, in a suburban school in the metropolitan area of Washington, DC where many children of Latin-American diplomats are in the student body, the Anglo students of Spanish typically do not communicate with them in their language.

In recent years, however, the strong attitudinal distinction between ethnic languages and FLs has shown signs of breaking down. For one thing, the enrollments in Spanish have held their own or risen as enrollments in French and German have declined, and Italian has shown a modest rise as well. As Spanish is becoming more visible and acknowledged on the American scene, it is studied more at school. Thus, the subject FLs are apparently now being elected to a considerable extent on the basis of use in the USA rather than because they are traditionally prestigious or associated with particular literatures and nations. At the same time, the use of the ethnic language at school is now often considered natural and even praiseworthy, and bilingual education programs may even use the ethnic language as the medium of instruction for serious content courses. Thus, two separate facts – the decline of FL enrollments and the appearance of bilingual education – which have resulted in large part from different causes, are related to each other in a larger pattern of change.

As might be expected from this changing pattern, the relevant language professions are divided and even hostile to one another. The FL teachers (themselves deeply divided by language loyalties) and the proponents of bilingual education generally see each other as adversaries in educational institutions, and neither group identifies with the TESOL specialists as colleagues. None of these three groups finds much in common with the regular teachers of language arts and English. These four major groups of professionals do not see one another as natural allies in a struggle for the strengthening and more rational deployment of the nation's language resources.

In the country's newly emerging sensitivity to language problems, even the question of language names can be a source of tension and disagreement. What should one call the languages and their speakers to be most informative and least offensive to others? To begin with, what should the English of the USA and its speakers be called? The problem of a name for the language stems in part from the fact that there is no single-word term for residents of the USA which is accurate and acceptable to residents of North, Central, and South America. All individuals in these areas are Americans, and though the term *American* has been used for 200 years to refer to U.S. residents, natives of other areas of the Americas have, in recent years, come increasingly to resent this exclusionist use of the term. The inaccuracy of applying the term *American* only to U.S. residents is further illustrated in the term *American Indian*. In general, this term refers only to the indigenous peoples of the United States, termed *Indians* first because early explorers mistakenly thought they had reached the East Indies. Today and throughout the centuries since discovery, indigenous populations of other areas of the Americas have been referred to as *Indians,* by their tribal names (Yaqui), or by the name of their predominant languages (Quechua). In the USA, the names for Indians have shifted over time. In the colonial and early national periods, the term *Indian* was used; in the early nineteenth century, *red man* became a common term. In the twentieth century, the term *American Indian* was predominant until the 1960s when *Native Americans* became the term preferred by many Indian groups who wished to stress their status as the true native Americans. In the 1960s the term *Red English,* formed analogously to Black English, returned the use of *red* to more general usage. In the 1970s, the terms *Native American, American Indian,* and *tribe* have acquired special meanings, because of federal programs for tribal Indians as opposed to Indians who have no tribal or reservation status. Currently, tribal names are used whenever possible by the Indians; and *American Indian* is the preferred general term for all tribal members in the United States, because this term is now used for certain federal programs designed for the indigenous of the United States. *Native Americans* is dropping out of favor, since Hawaiians and others were claiming to be Native Americans and thus to be eligible for such programs. *Alaskan Natives* is used to refer to the natives of Alaska, and they do not refer to themselves as *Indians*. Each of these terms is symbolic of membership at a different level: tribe, reservation Indians, Indians of the forty-eight states, or Alaska.

For some language groups, something so seemingly small as an accent mark, a hyphen, or a single letter can carry special signals of identity. In the 1960s, Hispanic students at San José State University viewed the placement of an accent mark on the letterhead of the university's stationery as a major symbol of the recognition of their presence in the student body. During this same period, Asian Americans began to insist the hyphen be dropped from "Asian-Americans." That preference has spread to other formerly hyphenated American groups, such as Italian Americans. Many Filipino Americans are coming to prefer "Pilipino" as their ethnic name, since the sound /f/ does not occur in Pilipino [Tagalog], the national language of the Philippines.

The speakers of American English have no single-word label to distinguish them from speakers of other varieties of English, but recently the term "Anglo" has become widely accepted as the name for speakers of English in the USA, as opposed to speakers of other languages in the same country. This brings us back to the language itself. Francis Lieber, a German American observer of language use and founding editor of the *Encyclopedia Americana* (1830), noted: "Much error would be avoided had we a totally different and compact term to designate *our common tongue*. Then we could fairly speak of Americanisms and Anglicisms, and would not confound matters of *taste*, of correctness of language, with matters of *right* [to speak as we choose]" (n.d.: II, 41–2). Ever since the colonial period, Americans and foreign observers – perhaps especially speakers of English from Great Britain – have commented on characteristics of the English spoken in the New World, comparing American English with that of England. The study of "Americanisms" began with John Witherspoon, who coined the word in the 1780s, and it has continued to the present time in dictionaries of Americanisms, books about them, and numerous articles on particular cases.

The general qualities attributed to American English are remarkably similar over the past 200 years, which suggests that some major characteristics of the language were set quite early and maintained, or at least that some myths about the language were established early. Observers noted that the geographical and social variation in English was much less in America than in Britain. The conditions of settlement and communication in the New World led rapidly to dialect leveling, which left no highly divergent local or class dialects of the British kind. John Pickering, an early statesman who published the first collection of Americanisms, observed: "it is agreed, that there is greater uniformity of dialect throughout the United States (a consequence of the frequent removals of people from one part of our country to another) than is to be found throughout England . . ." (Pickering 1816).

The same author noted what many other observers have commented on: there was good evidence that Americans "have a much stronger propensity than the English to add new words to the language." The scholars may note that Americanisms are of various sources. Some are archaic words preserved in the USA but lost from common usage in England (e.g. *fall* for 'autumn'). Others are responses to new objects and circumstances not found in England; these may be borrowed from American Indian languages or elsewhere (e.g. *squash*, the vegetable, from Narraganset) or created by English processes of word formation (e.g. the *cottonwood* tree). Some represent independent development of technologies in the two countries since the break (e.g. American railroad *switch* is the British *point*). Others refer to institutions and practices developed in connection with the political system of the United States: *Congressional*, *gerrymander*, and *gubernatorial*. In spite of the variety of sources for Americanisms, observers have repeatedly commented on the greater amount of innovation in the USA than in England.

These characteristics and others like them may be either admired or deplored. For example, the innovations may be regarded as corruptions or as examples of creativity, and the dialect leveling may be seen as democratic or as loss of vitality. Overall, the observers – with some notable exceptions – have tended to find that the Americanisms are undesirable, and this belief about Americanisms is a special case of the general myth of decline mentioned in the previous section.

A future-minded observer of American English, asked about the homogeneity and creativity of the language and its users, might have somewhat different comments. The homogenizing trends, especially in words and COLLOCATIONS, are spreading not only throughout the USA but to the English of the rest of the world, with American English the principal, although by no means exclusive, source of the trends. At the same time, however, regional and social dialect differences in the USA, especially in the sound system, are increasing. In the words of one of today's leading sociolinguistic researchers: "dialect diversification is continuing in the face of saturation by the mass media, and in spite of close contact among the social groups involved" (Labov 1972: 324). The innovative tendency of American English is also continuing, most obviously in words, but also in syntactic constructions. Yet here the growth of other centers of creativity outside the USA is a notable trend. New vocabulary and new slang appear in such different places as Britain itself, Australia, West Africa, the Philippines, or among second-language users of English on the European continent. The trends projected over a long enough period suggest a relatively uniform international English as a new Latin, with increasingly different local vernacular Englishes, and English-based, pidginized, informal lingua francas in a number of Third World countries. It is not possible to confirm or disprove prediction of this kind because of inadequate data, disagreements on methods of analysis, and a disinclination of scholars to work in this field.

The same is true for predictions about the language situation as a whole in the USA, and correspondingly for any policy recommendations in response to language problems in the nation that have reached the stage of public attention. Americans generally do not see the language situation in terms of resources to be managed, and for the most part they do not see language problems, or language aspects of larger social problems, as amenable to systematic, "scientific" investigation or as suitable areas for planning. Also, dealing effectively with language problems requires some understanding of national and local myths about language.

In short, it is difficult to produce a single book which will give enough data, analytic sophistication, and ideological leadership to affect the language situation in the USA. As noted before, few books even try to describe the language situation. Charlton Laird, whose book *Language in America,* tried to do both more and less than this one, complained in his Preface: "no one man living knows enough to write this book. Certainly I do not" (Laird 1970: ix). Equally certainly, twenty-five authors and two editors do not know enough to write this book, and by virtue of their variety of knowledges and viewpoints they may not provide as cohesive a book as a single author. But they offer a richness of perspective and a range of information which may stimulate the reader to think more about the language situation in the USA, how it came to be the way it is, how it may change in the future, and perhaps even how to intervene to affect the course of events.

Part I
American English

Introduction

The principal language of the USA is English, the language transplanted from the British Isles in the seventeenth and eighteenth centuries, molded by the subsequent history of the colonies and the new nation, and affected to some extent by interaction with English in the rest of the world and by contact with other languages. Americans have generally been satisfied to call their language "English," and when they need to differentiate it from other kinds of English, they are satisfied by adding their national adjective and calling it "American English." Occasionally, attempts have been made to name the language simply "American" as an entity distinct from the English of England, or Great Britain as a whole, or other parts of the English-speaking world, but these attempts have not succeeded, and it is only in a few foreign universities, in Germany, for example, where this distinction in name and subject matter is operative today.

The little question of the name of the language is symbolic of Americans' views on the language itself. Americans do not have a language ideology which identifies nation and language; they do not fight for their language as the symbol of their nationhood as many other nations do. They are content to be one of a number of nations speaking the same language. They find it hard to understand the ambivalence of the Spanish-speaking world which accepts its multiple nationhood, but tends to follow the language conventions of the Academy in Spain. They find it harder to understand the Arabic-speaking world which tends to deny its multiple nationhood and seek an ideal Arab nation. Hardest of all for Americans to understand are nations whose members talk eloquently of dying for their language or tie their language to their religion or their political independence or their destiny in the world.

This is not to say that Americans have not been concerned at all about their language. From the earliest days of independence, political leaders, academic spokesmen, journalists, and other writers have talked about the quality of language in the United States, the differences between British and American English, the place of English and other languages in the USA, and the role of English in the world. Chapter 1 follows some of these concerns through history, showing how American attitudes toward language diversity have changed over the years and how American norms of English have arisen and been codified. The whole area of language in the USA is one which historians have not treated, and the history of American language policies and language attitudes is a field that linguists and sociolinguists have hardly explored. This chapter breaks ground for research from both sides.

Americans give little thought to other kinds of English throughout the world, and university professors of English are usually just as poorly informed as ordinary citizens of the nation about the distinctive features of the language and literature of English-speaking countries other than Britain and the USA. Chapter 2 gives a unique view of American English from outside, and places the English of the USA among the other Englishes of the world. As English spreads across every continent as the most useful LINGUA FRANCA in the present-day world, it is important for us to understand its uses as MOTHER TONGUE, second language, and foreign language.

When English was transplanted to the New World, it was a language with deep DIALECT differences, reflecting the geographic divisions and social stratification of the British Isles and the differing influences of the Celtic languages spoken in Ireland, Scotland, Wales, and Cornwall, and the Danish and French spoken in Britain at different times and places. As is often the case with languages which spread fairly rapidly over language areas, the English of the American colonies underwent DIALECT LEVELING or homogenization. Early observers noted that American English lacked the highly divergent provincial and class dialects of Britain. Nevertheless, dialect variation developed in North America, derived from original British dialect differences, varied settlement patterns and demographic mobility, and the new geographical and social determinants. Chapter 3 outlines the major diversities of dialect variation in the contemporary USA and explains how linguists study the phenomena of variation. Strangely, the basic facts of regional and social variation are not discussed in traditional English language curricula in spite of the lively interest which Americans generally show in regional differences of vocabulary and pronunciation and in social differences of grammar. Recent popular publications and instructional units for high schools have begun to present some of this information, which is normally available only in professional journals and technical monographs. This chapter gives a balanced introduction to this material.

The languages of the western hemisphere are mostly indigenous Indian languages or TRANSPLANTED European languages. Some, however, are newly created CREOLES, which have arisen as a result of language contact and PIDGINIZATION processes. These creoles are especially evident in the Caribbean and the Guianan coast of South America, where English, French, and Spanish-based creoles are the mother tongues of substantial populations. In the USA, a few such creoles are spoken, most notably the English-based Gullah of the Sea Islands, Hawaiian Pidgin English, and the French-based creole of Louisiana. These languages are covered in Chapter 4, which gives basic information about the origin and present status of these languages. Another creole, the French-based language of the Metis, spoken in several northern states and in Canada, is discussed in Chapter 8 (Part II) on Native American lingua francas. Americans know little about these disappearing, unwritten languages which evolved in the New World to cope with communication problems in certain socially restricted multilingual settings. Chapter 4 helps to repair this lack of knowledge and appreciation.

The last chapter rounds out Part I by discussing the English used by the largest ethnic minority in the USA, the Blacks or Afro-Americans. In part this chapter connects with the preceding chapter on creoles because of the contribution which PIDGINS and creoles have made in the formation of the language of the American Black community. Unfortunately, the issue of the creole origin of Black English has become a point of controversy in American linguistics, drawing attention away from more productive questions. Whatley, however, gives space to the description of special ways of using language among Afro-Americans, letting us see the central role of language in the varied cultural expression of American Blacks. Her chapter gives some inkling of the riches a full description of the English of all the cultures of the USA would yield.

1

English in our language heritage*

SHIRLEY BRICE HEATH

The Constitution of the USA contains no reference to choice of a national language. Early national leaders chose not to identify one language as the official or national standard. The legacy of the colonial and Revolutionary periods includes tolerance of diverse languages and the absence of official selection of a specific language for use among the indigenous or a linguistic norm to be achieved by immigrants.

Some early national leaders, such as John Adams, proposed a national academy to regulate and standardize English, but these efforts were rejected as out of keeping with the spirit of liberty in the United States (Read 1936; Heath 1976c). Noah Webster's prolific and energetic writings on the language of America (1789) helped keep the goal of a national language in the public eye in the first half century of nationhood. His grammar, sold about the country in company with his blue-backed speller and the Bible, helped set the mood for the American public to embrace the commercially published dictionary as an authority on language correctness. The public schools promised to all an "English" education, understood to be the study of English grammar and spelling, and the achievement of skills in composition, reading, and mathematics. Public education promoted the vision of a Standard American English, which those who would mark themselves as social-minded and civic-conscious individuals should acquire.

The legacy of the language situation in the United States is, therefore, the rejection of an official choice of a national language or national institutions to regulate language decisions related to spelling, pronunciation, technical vocabulary, or grammar. Yet Americans overwhelmingly believe that English is the national tongue and that correctness in spelling, pronunciation, word choice, and usage, as well as facility in reading and writing English, are desirable goals for every U.S. citizen. Nevertheless, numerous diverse languages and varieties of English have been maintained in communities across the United States, and there has never been federal legislation to eliminate them.

---

* A longer and more fully referenced version of this chapter was originally published as "Our language heritage: a historical perspective" in Phillips 1977. Permission to use some of that material here has been granted by the American Council on the Teaching of Foreign Languages, Inc. and the National Textbook Company.

Government funding has in recent decades supported the teaching of foreign languages. These seeming contradictions have been played out in the past as well as in the present period, when BILINGUAL EDUCATION, the linguistic and cultural diversity of the USA, and cries for basic skills in teaching and writing English (see Chapter 20) seem to tug the future of English in the United States in different directions.

Linguistic diversity was not unusual in colonial and early national America. Classical and modern languages played critical roles in the social and political life of the early nation. Separate settlements within the United States maintained their native tongues in religious, educational, and economic institutions; newspapers, schools, and societies provided instructional support for diverse languages. The use of these languages was encouraged, and intellectual leaders valued different languages for both their practical and their symbolic purposes. Throughout the nineteenth century, a bilingual tradition existed in public and private schools, newspapers, and religious and social institutions. It was not until the late nineteenth century and the first half of the twentieth century that legal, social, and political forces strongly opposed maintenance of languages other than English. Only then was a monolingual English tradition mandated in some states and espoused as both natural and national. During the 1920s, legal and social forces restricted the use and teaching of foreign languages, especially German (see Chapter 12). Since the 1960s, linguistic minorities among widely varying ethnic groups have stressed the multilingual, multicultural nature of the national society. These minorities have pointed out the necessity of bilingualism in education, judicial matters, and the world of work (see Chapters 21 and 23). These efforts to revitalize the bilingual tradition in the United States have brought forth questions regarding the historic and current role of linguistic uniformity in national unity and the place of English in our language heritage.

Solutions to the contradictions?

In 1855, a London publication squarely faced the issue of the future language of the United States:

Does the supremacy of the English language in the United States run any serious risk? Considering the great, and every year increasing number of continental emigrants who bring with them their languages and associations – considering that the Americans of Anglo-Saxon descent do not exceed *one-third* of the whole population, if indeed, they amount to that – is there no danger that, in course of time, the English tongue may be compelled to yield a part of its ground, and be in some regions, at least, supplanted? And, may not present or future tendencies to widen the political separation of the two countries [England and the USA] have some further effect on this, their great common bond of union? (Bristed 1855: 75)

Early in the twentieth century, the possibility of language diversity leading to political separation was once again raised. However, this time the question centered not on the issue of England and the United States losing the bond of a common tongue, but on the possibility of a national split within the United

States. Numerous discussions of language and nation suggested that without a forceful language policy establishing English as the national language *and* restricting the teaching of other languages, the United States would be fragmented into linguistic minorities seeking to establish their own separate states.

A cleavage in the language now would mean to us a cleavage of the nation in its most vulnerable if not in its most essential part. That, no matter what our origin, no real American can desire; for it is not a question whether we are to be part German or part English. We might survive with the national spirit cut in two; but should our German born citizens be successful in making German co-equal with English in our public schools, the Bohemians, who hate the very sound of the German language, will demand a similar chance for the Czesch [*sic*] tongue, and they know how to fight for what they want. (Steiner 1916: 102–3)

The author further warned that Hungarians, Finns, Scandinavians, and other language groups would "clamor for the same privilege," and when that happened, "we may at once say good-bye to the unity of the United States." The purge of foreign languages was to extend from classrooms to concert halls; no teacher should instruct in a foreign tongue; no singer should perform in any language other than English.

Since the 1960s, the possibility of a linguistically divided nation has been discussed with great fervor and frequency. Not surprisingly, the solutions currently offered are similar to those made periodically over the past two hundred years. In response to the BILINGUAL EDUCATION ACT designed to provide bilingual education for children whose MOTHER TONGUE was a language other than English, and subsequent laws extending and amending this Act, numerous discussions pointing out the possibility of a divided nation have appeared in the press, in court cases, and on the platforms of local parent-teacher organizations. Editorials have suggested that the current encouragement of bilingual education will take the USA on a road to cultural, economic, and political divisiveness. Parents of children who come to school without English have been characterized as lazy, un-American, and undeserving of American citizenship (e.g. Cuneo 1975).

As is so often the case, easy interpretations from selected historical facts and rigid arguments such as those cited about equating linguistic and national unity do not bear up under comprehensive examination of the history of debates over language heritage. The question of the future of language as a national symbol and means of unification in the United States has been a frequent topic of debate with respect to one or another issue throughout the history of the country. In every case, language itself was not the central issue of debate, but became a focus of arguments made for political, social, or economic purposes.

During the colonial period, Latin, Greek, and Hebrew were debated as the languages of elitism, intellectual pursuits, and mental discipline. In 1743, an unknown citizen of the American colonies argued that English was in peril for those who knew "common sense in *English* only" (*American Magazine and Historical Chronicle* 1743–4: i). He felt exaggerated emphases on Latin and Greek and heavy Classical ornamentation of English threatened the future of language for the colonies' citizens. Those who felt that English and other modern languages were more practical often exaggerated the Classicists' arguments and led readers of early American periodicals to believe that those who favored the Classical languages proposed them as UNIVERSAL LANGUAGES to supplant all others. To this point, those who favored English and other modern languages made an argument familiar in pedagogical and linguistic circles today: "The only purpose of language is to convey ideas: if modern speech does this, it is complete: if it does not, it is no language" (*American Museum or Repository* 1798: iii). No doubt, fear of the over-zealous promotion of the Classical languages and their extension helped promote the legend that a legislator proposed the United States assert its linguistic independence by adopting either Hebrew or Greek as the national language. Attention to the pronunciation of Latin and modern Greek was an interest of Thomas Jefferson's, and some of his correspondence to scholars of Classical languages could be interpreted as favoring the extension of Greek in the USA (Wright 1943: 223–33).

Modern languages other than English also appear in debates and folk legends about a national language for the USA. Sir Herbert Croft, a British etymologist, reported in a letter of 1797 that Americans had proposed during the Revolutionary period the idea of "revenging themselves on England by rejecting its language and adopting that of France" (Croft 1797; Spurlin 1976). The most long-lasting and widespread legend is one which claims that German almost became the national language in 1794, and only one vote in the House of Representatives saved future generations from having to learn German instead of English. This "Muhlenberg legend" refers to a request from Virginia Germans that some laws of the United States be issued in German as well as English, as was done with many documents at the time. A Congressional committee favored the proposal, but when the issue came to a vote in the House, it was rejected 42 to 41. Frederick August Muhlenberg may have cast the deciding negative vote, but that cannot be determined from Congressional records (Lohr 1962; Kloss 1966). The legend was picked up by British and American journalists, passed on in a distorted and inaccurate form, and refurbished in the second half of the nineteenth century to remind Americans that Germans might once again muster sufficient power to turn around the language choice of the United States.

Social, political, and ideological factors

The centrality of language in social, political, and ideological issues accounts for both the frequency and intensity of language heritage debates. When Benjamin Franklin lashed out against the Germans in Pennsylvania in 1753, he feared their language would soon dominate the state. Of the Pennsylvania Germans, Franklin wrote:

Those who come hither are generally the most stupid of their own nation, and as ignorance is often attended with credulity when knavery would mislead it, and with suspicion when honesty would set it right: and as few of the English would understand the German language and so cannot address them either from the press or pulpit, it is almost impossible to remove any prejudices they may entertain. Their clergy have very little influence on the people, who seem to take pleasure in abusing and discharging the minister on every trivial occasion. Not being used to liberty, they know not how to make a modest use of it. (Franklin 1959: IV, 483–4)

Placing Franklin's pejorative statements in the context of political issues of the times indicates that they were motivated by his resentment of the Germans' domination of local elections and his fear that they would not support his choice for colonial governor. Franklin's comments also point out the willingness of speakers of one language to accuse speakers of other languages of immorality, unpredictability, and untrustworthiness. Throughout the history of the United States, whenever speakers of varieties of English or other languages have been viewed as politically, socially, or economically threatening, their language has become a focus for arguments in favor of both restrictions of their use and imposition of Standard English.

Ideological or political views about the status of a particular language may arise in response to issues which have no direct or necessary relation to language. Within these motivations, language may be considered a tool or a symbol, and politicians may not concern themselves with changing the language itself, but rather with promoting it for status achievement and extension to speakers of other languages. For example, within the United States, ideological adherence to English has been supported by the ideal of "a perfect Union," a coming together of diverse peoples in a creative force. Individuals, groups, and the national government have promoted the idea at different times throughout our history that speaking the same language would ensure uniformity of other behavioral traits, such as morality, patriotism, and logical thinking.

Roles for foreign languages

During the colonial and early national periods, foreign language maintenance was an issue for churches, local politicians, educators, and special interest groups. In urban areas, speakers of foreign languages formed societies to promote the use of their native language as they developed ways of caring for orphans, widows, and children of families who could not afford to send their children abroad for education (see Chapter 14). For example, the German Friendly Society of Charleston, South Carolina required that its members speak German in the late 1700s. Individuals were supposed to maintain their knowledge of foreign languages through individual study, or with minimal help from such primary associates as they could find. Colonial and early national newspapers abounded with advertisements placed by individuals who would give instruction in foreign languages in their home or in the home of the pupil. A typical advertisement read: "A Young Frenchman, who has been resident about seven months in this town, has a desire to make himself useful to the publick – and believes he can be so in no other way so well as in the instruction of the youth of both sexes in the French language'' (*Massachusetts Spy* April 19, 1772).

Arguments over the advantages of modern languages versus the Classical languages ran the gamut from the serious to the sublime and were often summarized in exaggerated terms by modern language instructors. One overly anxious tutor of German included in the advertisement of his services:

This being the original language of Europe, for which, as from the Celtic, its oldest dialect, the Greeks and Latins borrowed many hundreds of their words, as Sir Richard Steele observes in his English grammar; therefore, it is of greater antiquity than those of the Greeks and Romans – and as being the mother tongue, or the origin and source of the French and English, the radical knowledge, of these languages depend on it. (*Aurora General Advertiser*, Philadelphia, January 2, 1794: 9)

Bookkeepers who kept records in French advertised their services. Public brokers and translators were available for numerous languages.

There was, in addition, a keen interest among readers of early American periodicals in the language affairs of countries abroad. When the French circulated a petition asking that the language of public monuments be shifted from Latin to French, the petition was widely published in newspapers of the United States. Excerpts from the constitutions, scientific reports, and literature of the French were particularly widely distributed in American periodicals. General articles about language appeared frequently, and often asserted the equal value of all languages: ''Sense is Sense in all Languages'' and ''in Point of Invention, all Men are on a Par'' (*American Magazine and Historical Chronicle* 1743–4: vol.1, 1745: vol.2).

For some groups of the society, self-instruction in foreign languages was expected behavior; moreover, learning to read another language was viewed as a relatively simple task. Foreign languages were tools used to obtain knowledge not accessible in English. Many asserted both the ease and necessity of learning foreign languages. For example, Thomas Jefferson urged his daughter to read French daily, and he suggested to young correspondents that a speaking knowledge of French be acquired in Canada. He judged learning French ''absolutely essential'' and Spanish vitally important, because of both diplomatic interchanges and the history of Spanish influence in the New World. Jefferson himself learned Spanish by reading *Don Quixote* with the help of a grammar and dictionary. Self-education in foreign languages was also promoted for special vocational purposes. An 1834 grammar purporting to give in German and English colloquial phrases on every topic necessary to maintain conversation noted: ''The prevalence of the German language in many parts of the United States should form a powerful inducement for men in every situation of life to become, at least partially acquainted with it. To the man of business, especially, a knowledge of the German tongue is of the first importance, as it will greatly facilitate his intercourse with a very valuable part of our population'' (Ehrenfried 1834). Printers were recommended not only for their skills in printing, but also their knowledge of foreign languages. Most of the individuals learning modern languages other than English during the eighteenth and early nineteenth centuries were self-instructed and interested primarily in acquiring reading knowledge of the languages for either general information or specific career plans.

Institutions which provided instruction in languages other than English and the Classical languages focused primarily on retention of foreign languages for in-group maintenance or religious support. The family and religion were the primary institutions which supported use of the native languages of immigrant groups. Children learned to read from religious materials and were called on to display their school learning in understanding and contributing to aspects of church-related and community-centered activities. Children learned formal stylistic norms as well as characteristic features of the language used in religious settings – specialized vocabulary and formulaic utterances. They were expected to recognize differences between the style of language used in church services and that used in daily communications. Individuals and groups came to associate retention of their language with religious maintenance, and not until late in the nineteenth century was this connection broken for many religious groups. Some, such as the Hutterite and Amish, retain use of their language in worship services and community activities today. As churches began to realize the youth of their congregations would increasingly insist on the use of English in services, religious leaders sought other means to preserve their culture and language. Schools and newspapers gradually took over this service. Pastors and lay people feared that those who knew religious language in only their mother tongue would have no opportunities for meaningful worship if all churches went to English only. After 1900, shifts to English became more frequent, as children received catechism instruction in English, and national religious meetings allowed the use of English.

The language(s) of education

By the mid-nineteenth century, educators were calling for a common school system which would make education available to the youth of America. The social bases of education did not appeal uniformly to all Americans; the removal of education as a responsibility of the individual and his family, and the establishment of the power of the state to tax a citizen's property for school support caused numerous difficulties for the early schools. The society was not homogeneous, and establishment of nonsectarian, publicly supported schools open and free to all children raised almost immediately the question of diversities in the classroom. It was necessary during the decades of the 1860s, 1870s and 1880s to recruit students for schools. Opportunities for work and home responsibilities were more favorable and profitable settings for children of these decades than were schools. Political leaders and school personnel had to admit to the need to recruit students and to impress parents with the merits of compulsory attendance and public schooling.

Immigrants were thus looked upon during this period as potential clients to be courted and accommodated. In particular, the public schools wanted to draw children away from private academies where instruction was frequently given in languages other than English. A case study of Wisconsin's development of public instruction illustrates this trend (Jorgenson 1956). In 1847, the state convention heard requests that provision be made for free schools. A German-born member of the convention proposed that districts having large numbers of foreign-born settlers be allowed to offer instruction in languages other than English. The convention adopted the resolution. In a state where more than a third of the population was foreign born, such a concession seemed hardly necessary for specific notice. Each nationality group – Norwegians, Poles, Dutch, Swiss, or Germans – tended to establish its own community. In some of these, the mother tongue was used in public schools. What must have been merely nominal laws were passed in 1848, 1849, and 1854, stipulating that certain subjects in public schools were to be taught in English. Compliance with the laws was impossible in most settlements, and school personnel in communities worked without interference to ensure that the native tongue of their constituents was maintained in the schools. Proof of this practice is evidenced by reaction to the Bennett Law, passed in Wisconsin in 1889.

Proposed primarily to restrict child labor and to provide for compulsory school attendance annually for all children between the ages of seven and fourteen for not less than twelve weeks, the Bennett Law contained one section which stipulated that instruction be given in the English language. Passed without a dissenting vote, the law was received with severe hostility in German communities throughout the state. Parochial schools could no longer conduct their classes primarily in German, and public schools which had been doing so might now be more closely watched than before. The law was repealed in the legislative session of 1891. However, in Wisconsin, as elsewhere across the nation, in the next two decades, religious schools declined in number, and public schools increased in both enrollment size and influence (Billigmeier 1974).

In particular, in the middle decades of the nineteenth century, urban school systems were becoming more centralized and more conscious of their particular responsibilities to immigrants. Political leaders supported recruitment of immigrant children to public schools, and argued that education of the young would influence parents to make wise political choices. Moreover, there was ready recognition of the value of knowledge of multiple languages in education. In 1870, the U.S. Commissioner of Education stressed this point in his assessment of the national language situation: "the German language has actually become the second language of our Republic, and a knowledge of German is now considered essential to a finished education" (cited in Zeydel 1964: 345). Cleveland, St. Louis, and Milwaukee were among those urban school systems which provided for instruction in the students' first language or offered dual-language classes. Kluwin's (forthcoming) study of the Cleveland schools provides important data and interpretive analysis of school leaders' reasons for maintaining the languages of immigrant children in the elementary programs of the school system. Cleveland's superintendent during the 1870s was not afraid to announce that though certainly English was the "language of our country, it was only natural for German-speaking groups to keep their own language as a bond of common experiences, past and present." In 1871, Louis L. Klemm was appointed supervisor of German instruction in the elementary schools of Cleveland. Klemm focused on provision of kindergarten experience for immigrant children, teacher training, foreign language teaching methods, and organization of a network of German and German–English teachers for mutual exchange of materials and techniques. Klemm argued that society had the responsibility of enabling immigrants to recognize and avail themselves of educational opportunities for their children; he did not place blame on the immigrant for not assimilating solely through his own motivation.

Klemm advocated adoption of pedagogical methods used in Germany, and he imported books from Germany in order that elementary teachers might have ready access to sources of innovative instructional methods. He urged a comparative grammar approach in the teaching of English and German, and he recommended that attention to both languages be given in classes across the curriculum. The German language should not be reserved solely for basic literacy skills or social studies, but its use should be incorporated in the teaching of various subjects and across different functions of language usage. Regarding the relation between ethnicity and language, Klemm pointed out that the mixture of two peoples, Anglo-Saxon and German, would provide a creative force in the American society, and the bond of a common culture would be built while both languages were maintained. Klemm extended the German language into high schools, with the goal of better preparing German language teachers for the elementary system. Believing that foreign languages were best learned at an early age, Klemm proposed that only those native English speakers who had been part of the dual-language program at the elementary level be admitted to the high school classes of German.

By the 1890s, the public schools of Cleveland, San Francisco, and New York were beginning to meet their quotas for filling classrooms, and accommodation of the special needs of immigrant children no longer seemed as important as it had several decades earlier (Kluwin, forthcoming). Moreover, political forces were stirring up fears of "the foreign element" within the national population, and proposals were made to limit and restrict immigration. Language and literacy became foci for restriction. In 1897, President Grover Cleveland returned without approval to the House of Representatives a bill which excluded from admission to the United States "All persons physically capable and over sixteen years of age who cannot read and write the English language or some other language . . ." Cleveland viewed this restriction as "harsh and oppressive." Taft and Wilson vetoed similar bills (Davis 1920: 377) before one passed over Wilson's veto in 1917.

Concerns similar to the move to restrict immigration influenced changes in naturalization requirements. Before 1906, there was no prerequisite in naturalization laws that an alien either speak or be literate in English. However, the Nationality Act of 1906 required that an alien speak English in order to become naturalized. This requirement was codified in the Nationality Act of 1940 and extended to include demonstration of an ability to read and write English in the Internal Security Act of 1950 (Leibowitz 1976).

In the early decades of the twentieth century, educators and politicians included adults in their language teaching programs. Evening classes offered adults opportunities to acquire literacy and a speaking knowledge of English. Each city had its own policy, and in many cases private evening schools and individuals offered miraculous language conversion for immigrants at high prices. After 1915, licensing of evening schools and closer control of standards for the teaching of English and civics were accomplished in several cities. In addition, some individuals argued that adult immigrants should be able to study reading and writing through their native language. Jane Addams, the social reformer, pointed out that many older men and women never would learn English, but would need information in their own languages about coping with daily problems of living and managing families in American cities (Abbott 1917). Ironically, guides offering advice on many of these problems to immigrant populations were published *in English*. Public libraries in some cities supplied books in the languages of the immigrants, but information on specific problems such as the city's water and milk supply, sanitary regulations, or labor laws was not available in languages other than English during the first decades of the twentieth century.

Another approach to spreading English among the immigrant populations was the recognition that the school could not be the sole agent of Americanization. The superintendent of the Boston public schools pointed out in 1910 that out of the thirteen million immigrants in the United States, three million spoke no English. The majority of these were past school age, and linked use of their native tongue with practice of their religious freedoms. The superintendent noted that "Religious devotion and feeling are inextricably bound up with the native language, so that in spite of any lack of intention on our part, when we begin to propose compulsion about language, we probably seem to the foreigner to infringe upon religious rights" Davis 1920: 584).

In a remarkable effort at comparative social science inquiry, the superintendent reviewed the language policies of Switzerland and the Austro-Hungarian empire and concluded "the mere imposition of language cannot bring about automatically nationalization, a fact which uncompromising advocates of compulsion in this country should note" (Davis 1920: 586). He concluded that the language policy of the United States had, through its very inadequacy, been successful, because it had depended in the past on the motivations of the learners. Immigrants had been highly resourceful in hiring themselves out as groups working under an interpreter in foundries, stockyards, and construction projects. "Gang work" in employment and efforts to learn about city transportation systems, labor laws, and union practices had provided means by which immigrants were cushioned through group efforts to acquire English for necessary functions. The Boston school superintendent warned against forced subjugation of immigrants to a nationalize-through-language program; language is a "right which even *might* may not take away . . . a fundamental right which no constitution of men may remove" (Davis 1920: 587). The language policy choice for the United States in its program of Americanization was simple:

Shall we insist that the stranger who has joined our membership shall by law and compulsion acquire our language, conform to our major customs, become naturalized, renounce all prior allegiance, or shall we attempt to persuade him to adopt American customs and to use our language, by pointing out the moral obligation, by furnishing convenient means in the way of free instruction, and perhaps by granting privileges which may be withheld from the non-citizen? (Davis 1920: 588)

Language choice had to be in response to social, religious, and economic, as well as political issues. Americanization and the ideological role of English in political concerns were not nearly so important in a basic sense as socioeconomic issues. For example, industry was increasingly encountering difficulties with safety-first campaigns and problems of labor turnover. New state compulsory compensation laws were making employers liable for accidents which occurred as a result of immigrants' inability to read signs or understand instructions about machinery operations. Long-standing immunity from costs and damages based on the common law procedure involving the principle of contributory negligence had given way to unavoidable payments by employers. Laborers' knowledge of English and acquisition of minimal literacy skills became economic assets to employers. Furthermore, non-English-speaking employees moved from job to job rapidly, and companies began to emphasize the positive correlation between time on the job and knowledge of English among immigrant workers (Abbott 1917). Handbooks for immigrants warned:

English is absolutely indispensable to the workman. He needs it in order to find work. He needs it to take direction and have his work explained. He needs it unless he is willing to work for the smallest wages with no hope of increase. He needs it when he is in difficulties to avoid interested [exploitative] helpers. He needs it to protect himself without requiring the help of the law. He needs it to understand words of warning and keep out of danger, for every year hundreds of immigrants are hurt or killed in America; because they do not understand the shouts of warning, or do not know how to read danger signals, when a few English words might have saved their lives. (Carr 1912: 14)

Citizenship and Americanization as reasons to acquire English paled beside such realistic and basic reasons as personal safety, economic support, and social security. As industries became more involved with the need for immigrants to learn English, they also provided means. Newly arrived immigrants were established temporarily in the homes of English speakers who helped provide transition skills in coping with daily routines of city and factory life.

Labor unions actively recruited White immigrants in the hope of reducing rivalries among groups and of breaking down boundaries of ethnicity and language.

These practical measures came to be reinforced by the growing xenophobia of the period from 1920 through the 1940s, when repressive measures against German, Japanese, and Chinese speakers were supported by state and local institutions as well as laws. In the period from 1917 to 1923, states removed laws tolerating instruction in languages other than English from their codes and prohibited the teaching of foreign languages. Court cases challenged these laws, as in Meyer *v.* Nebraska (1923), when a teacher was convicted for giving German instruction in a private school. The Nebraska supreme court affirmed a fear of ethnic boundary maintenance and its relationships to use of languages other than English:

The legislature had seen the baneful effects of permitting foreigners, who had taken residence in this country, to rear and educate their children in the language of their native land. The result of that condition was found to be inimical to our own safety. To allow the children of foreigners, who had emigrated here, to be taught from early childhood the language of the country of their parents was to rear them with that language as the mother tongue. It was to educate them so that they must always think in that language, and, as a consequence, naturally inculcate in them the ideas and sentiments foreign to the best interests of this country. The statute, therefore, was intended not only to require that the education of all children be conducted in the English language, but that, until they had grown into that language and until it had become a part of them, they should not in the schools be taught any other language. (Meyer *v.* Nebraska, 262 U.S. 390: 397–8)

The Supreme Court overturned the conviction of the lower courts by ruling that a teacher's right to teach and a parent's right to engage him were protected by the Fourteenth Amendment. The attempt by the Nebraska legislature to interfere with the "calling of modern language teachers" and to spread fear of foreign tongues as perils to public safety were specifically rebuked. However, the Court stated that it did not question the power of the state to compel attendance in school and to require that instruction be given in English. With respect to several other state cases on school regulation in the 1920s, the Supreme Court ruled that requiring the language of instruction to be English in a state or territory of the United States was constitutional, but restriction of secondary language efforts by ethnic groups was unconstitutional (Leibowitz 1970, 1971, 1976).

With the Civil Rights Act of 1964 as background, federal legislators who debated the Bilingual Education Act in 1967 seemed to recognize the educational role of languages other than English for ethnic groups in the United States as had been the case occasionally in the early part of the century. Individual states, such as Massachusetts, California, New Mexico, and Texas also passed statutes favoring bilingual education. In the LAU *v.* NICHOLS case (1970–4), the courts had to face the issue of language with respect to whether or not Chinese-speaking students received equal educational opportunity when they were taught in a language they could not understand. Title VI of the Civil Rights Act of 1964 prohibited exclusion from participation in federally funded programs of any person "on the ground of race, color or national origin." The Bilingual Education Act of 1968 defined bilingual–bicultural education and established funding for programs for "children of limited English-speaking ability." By the early 1970s, most of the school districts of the United States were receiving federal monies, and control over language policies and other educational issues which had in the nineteenth century resided in local school boards, had shifted to administrators assessing districts' needs for federal funds. Therefore, as a condition for receiving federal aid, school districts had to take "affirmative steps to rectify the language deficiency of national-origin minority group students" unable to speak and understand English (Teitelbaum and Hiller 1977b).

Chinese students in San Francisco argued that they did not receive an equal educational opportunity in schools where they could not understand the language of instruction. Relying in part on Meyer v. Nebraska, the lower court ruled that uniform use of English did not constitute unlawful discrimination. The Supreme Court overturned the decision, ruling that under state-imposed standards which required school attendance, mandated use of the English language, and required fluency in English as a prerequisite to high school graduation, the Chinese students were not receiving equal treatment under Title VI of the 1964 Civil Rights Act. Ramifications of this decision and guidelines for compliance with it have increasingly raised the issue of ethnic boundary maintenance and relations between language and ethnicity. Discrimination has generally been identified in terms of differential treatment. In Lau v. Nichols, the failure to differentiate the language of instruction for Chinese students was judged to be discriminatory. Applications of the decision have most consistently affected educational policies for Spanish speakers in the Southwest, California, Florida, and New York. Other ethnic groups are now asking to be identified as "linguistic minorities" and to have public services and education made available to them in their own languages.

Implications of our language heritage

Currently, the majority of U.S. citizens do not seem to see the Bilingual Education Act as reviving a valuable tradition we have lost, but rather as an aberration in American history. Maintenance of the Anglo tradition and Americanization in language have seemed to most Americans both natural and national; most Americans view English as the "natural" choice, one which contributes to the national good. When particular groups now speak out for extensions of bilingualism in American society and emphasize the disparity of opportunities which exist between those who speak English and those who do not, many citizens become nervous over the possibility of political schisms. Historical accounts of the place of English in the language heritage of the United States should reassure those who believe language and ethnic maintenance in the United States has to lead to cultural or political divisions.

The language heritage of the United States is complex, and the status of English has been achieved through social and economic forces which shaped educational and labor practices and policies to promote English. Historical and literary accounts (e.g. Fairchild 1926) portray English as the implicit, if not the explicit, choice for the national language. National leaders have never considered in any concrete way such questions as the means for determining a standard norm of English, formulating policy with regard to tolerance or promotion of other languages, and implementing language choices in schools, business, law courts, and voting procedures. One observer has noted that this absence of attention to a specific language policy in the United States has created "one of history's little ironies": "no polyglot empire of the old world has dared be as ruthless in imposing a single language upon its whole population as was the liberal republic 'dedicated to the proposition that all men are created equal'" (Johnson 1949: 118–19). It has been proposed that the absence of compulsion is an indirect, but nevertheless strong, motivation for immigrants to learn English. For example, if Germans wished to speak German, they did so for internal group purposes; they broke no law in doing so. Therefore, if they rejected English and handicapped themselves economically, they did not have "the inner consolation of feeling that they defied tyrannous authority" (Johnson 1949: 119). Haugen (1966: 11–12) has noted that the lack of specificity regarding language choice and change at the national level and the emphasis on "individual enterprise" in these matters have effectively precluded either active opposition to the language attitudes and practices of those in power or proposals for legal reforms of U.S. language policy.

The place of English among other languages and the type of English to be used have been shaped by socio-economic forces in the United States. Without the force of law, institutions and individuals have alternately permitted, restricted, and promoted the use of languages other than English. Access to the wider society outside one's own primary group has, however, consistently been dependent on knowledge of English, and upward mobility in that society has called for facility in using a standard variety of English. The central themes of our language heritage have been the legal tolerance of other languages, a consensual high value placed on the ability to use English, and general recognition of Standard American English as a means and mark of socio-economic advancement.

FURTHER READING

The role of English in the language heritage of the USA is generally treated in one of two contexts: with respect to the history of language policies and bilingual education, or with respect to the evolution of American English as a viable language. Kloss 1977 is the most complete account of legal decisions, local policies, and state and federal legislation on the uses of languages other than English. Kloss opens to the scholar a multitude of primary sources, laws, town council meetings, and church records, etc. on the uses of languages other than English throughout U.S. history. General accounts of the history of bilingual education in the United States appear in Andersson 1969 and Andersson and Boyer 1978.

Books on American English have long been among those books on language with which the general reader is most familiar. H. L. Mencken's various editions and supplements (1919–48 and 1977) provide both substantive and humorous details on how American English came to be defined. C. Merton Babcock's reader, *The Ordeal of American English* (1961), consists of primary sources reflecting evolving views of a "standard" American English. Students in a variety of English courses have read Marckwardt's *American English* with pleasure since 1958. Laird's *Language in America* (1970) is a very readable, highly informative treatment of such topics as immigrant languages and the "linguistic growing pains" of American English. Dillard 1975 provides in his history of English in America treatment of these topics as well as discussion of the effect English in America has had on the use of English as a world language. Dohan 1974 and Dillard 1976a reflect the fascination Americans have always had with words, where they came from, and how they have developed meanings in their uses in the United States. Flexner 1976 presents the American language through American history in a book expressly designed for the lay reader. Notions of "good English" throughout the nation's history are traced in Finegan 1980.

2

American English and other Englishes

BRAJ B. KACHRU

The total number of languages in the world is large: say between 4,000 and 4,500. But, considering the total world population of 4 billion and 19 million, this seems to be a small number. If we divide this number by 4,500 languages, we have approximately one language for every 893,111 people, but that is not exactly how human languages are distributed. There are only five languages that can claim a really large number of speakers, namely, Chinese (811 million), English (363 million), Hindi–Urdu (271 million), Russian (240 million), and Spanish (219 million). Of these languages, only English can claim to have attained the enviable position of a more or less UNIVERSAL LANGUAGE. A universal language is one which, in its various forms and functions, is used by a large portion of the human population for easy communication between peoples of diverse cultural and language backgrounds. Attempts have been made toward developing a universal or international language since the 1880s. These attempts, however, have not been successful, though some artificial international languages have had partial success; for example, Esperanto. Other such attempts were much less successful, as was the case with Novial, Occidental, Interlingua, Volapük, Ido, etc. The reasons for their failure are many, but the fact is that they have less chance of general acceptance and survival than does a choice from among existing NATURAL LANGUAGES.

In the past, several natural languages have acquired widespread roles in ritual, diplomacy, literature, or fashion. One does not have to think hard to find examples: Latin for ritualistic uses and learned professions in Europe, French in diplomacy and fashion, and Sanskrit for ritualistic, religious, and literary functions in South Asia. However, in the last two centuries, the picture has completely changed. English, which was a minor language in the sixteenth century, has slowly but definitely gained an edge over other major languages as an international language. If we compare the present position of English with what the English poet John Dryden had to say about it in 1693, we can understand the extent of its diffusion and gain in prestige in the last three hundred years. Dryden complained, "We have yet no prosodia, not so much as a tolerable dictionary or a grammar, so that our language is in a manner barbarous" (cited in Baugh and Cable 1978: 255). The primary reasons for such development and expansion are not essentially linguistic, but political, social, and technological.

21

After all, linguistically speaking, or in terms of the communicative potential of a language, any human language has the potential of becoming an international language.

Let us briefly discuss what contributed to the attainment of such a status by English. The main reason was colonization, which brought major parts of Africa and Asia under the direct rule of English-speaking Britain. This initiated the diffusion of various types and degrees of BILINGUALISM in English. The introduction of western English-medium education resulted in the emergence of native elite groups in the far-flung areas of the empire, who in turn became the supporters of English and of western models of education. The diffusion of English as the language of colonial masters need not overshadow many positive aspects for which English was accepted and even demanded by the colonized people. The positive aspects of English include its long and rich literary tradition in various forms, its widespread use as a language of science and technology, and its proven capacity to absorb from various languages and cultures.

Englishes of the world

When we talk of the English language as an international language or as a universal language, we are talking of an abstract concept. Actually, there are a number of *Englishes* present in the world. The all-embracing concept of the English-using SPEECH COMMUNITY entails a strong generalization, since this speech community includes a number of subcommunities which may be divided in various ways. The first broad division may be in terms of the English-speaking nations of the world, for example, American English, Australian English, British English, Canadian English, Indian English, Jamaican English, and so forth. If we use ethnic criteria, we have, among others, Chicano English and Anglo-Indian English. On the other hand, if we are fond of color categories, we may use labels such as Black English, Brown English, White English, and Yellow English. The ways to cut the cake are limitless, and one can use a number of linguistic or functional criteria to do so.

There is, however, one distinction among the users of English which is useful and important to our present discussion. We must divide this speech community into three subgroups in order to see the roles and functions of the world Englishes in a realistic international context. The first group comprises those who use English as their first language – their MOTHER TONGUE – as do a large number of Americans, British, Australians, or English-speaking Canadians. These speakers may form culturally distinct groups, but they are *native* speakers of English. The second group uses English as their *second* language. In their case English is an acquired language which is learned after they have learned their mother tongue, which may be one of the languages of Asia, Africa, or the Philippines. The second language speakers of English must further be separated from those who use it as a *foreign* language, as for example in Iran for science and technology, in Japan for international commerce and tourism, or in Sweden where it has become the most popular foreign language in the schools. English as a second language has a distinct status in the language planning of a number of countries. In India, for example, it is treated as one of two associate OFFICIAL LANGUAGES in the Indian Constitution, the other being Hindi. However, this is not true of those countries where it is used basically as a foreign language. The members of the English-using speech community thus form a spectrum with reference to their competence in English: those who use English as their *first* language or mother tongue, as a *second* language – a medium of education, language of government, and the like – or simply as a *foreign* language. These distinctions are important since they separate these varieties in terms of their functions, the proficiency of their speakers, and the processes which are used to acquire each variety.

Speakers of the first language varieties of English number over 266 million, but they comprise only 73.3 percent of the total number of English speakers. The five largest groups are American English speakers (182 million), British English speakers (55 million), Australian and Canadian English speakers (13 million), and New Zealand English speakers (3 million).

American English and other colonial Englishes

The American variety of English has several special characteristics associated with its growth and development that offer an interesting linguistic case study for comparison with other varieties of English. On the one hand, it provides an example of linguistic pride and what may be termed a conscious effort toward establishing language identity. On the other hand, it has the unique characteristics of a TRANSPLANTED LANGUAGE. In this respect, then, it can be related to other Englishes which have been transplanted in various parts of the world. Mathews (1931: 9) was therefore correct when he said:

The fact should be borne in mind that the treatment given the English language in this country does not differ in kind from that given to the language wherever English colonists have gone. In India, Canada, Australia, and Africa the English language has been modified in very much the same way that it has in this country.

Other terms have also been used for transplanted English. Turner (1966) used the term "English transported" for Australian and New Zealand English; later Ramson (1970) also used this term as the title of his book, *English Transported: Essays on Australasian English.* Indian English fiction has been termed by Mukherjee (1971) *The Twice Born Fiction,* since as she says, it is "the product of two parent traditions . . ."

The attitude of British English speakers toward American English was not much different from their attitude toward other varieties of English. As an example, it is useful to read what the Very Reverend Henry Alford, D.D., Dean of Canterbury, had to say in his "Plea for the Queen's English" in 1863: "Look at the process of deterioration which our Queen's English has undergone at the hands of the Americans. Look at those phrases which so amuse us in their speech and books; at their reckless exaggeration and contempt for congruity . . ."

One way to show nationalistic pride against such an attitude of the "mother English" speakers was to proclaim American English distinct from the variety spoken by the cousins on the other side of the Atlantic. Therefore, initially some scholars preferred to call it the *American language* as opposed to *American English*. One might say that this was one way of getting even with the colonizers' linguistic superiority. This attitude is present in the well-known book by H. L. Mencken entitled *The American Language*. It was published in 1919 and embodies what Noah Webster (the "cracker-barrel lexicographer") had said over a century earlier about American English. The following words of Webster may not necessarily have proved correct, but they do demonstrate an attitude which cannot be ignored in understanding the genesis of American English.

Several circumstances render a future separation of the American tongue from the English, necessary and unavoidable. The vicinity of the European nations, with the uninterrupted communication in peace, and the changes of dominion in war, are gradually assimilating their respective languages. The English with others is suffering continual alterations. America, placed at a distance from those nations, will feel, in a much less degree, the influence of the assimilating causes; at the time, numerous local causes, such as a new country, new associations of people, new combinations of ideas in arts and science, and some intercourse with tribes wholly unknown in Europe, will introduce new words into the American tongue. These causes will produce, in a course of time, a language in North America, as different from the future language of England, as the modern Dutch, Danish, and Swedish are from the German, or from one another . . . (Webster 1789: 22)

We have introduced the term "transplanted language," and it is natural to ask what such a term implies and in what sense a language may be transplanted. A language may be considered transplanted if it is used by a significant number of speakers in social, cultural, and geographical contexts different from the contexts in which it was originally used. In this sense, then, there are several varieties of English which continue to be used as native languages by a majority of the people in Australia, Canada, the United States, and New Zealand which, as we know, were transplanted from the mother country, England. There are many other languages which have such transplanted varieties, for example, Spanish and Portuguese in Latin America; French in Canada and parts of Africa; Portuguese in Brazil, Sri Lanka, and Africa; Persian in India and Afghanistan; and Hindi in Fiji, South Africa, and the West Indies.

One might then say that a transplanted language is cut off from its traditional roots and begins to function in new surroundings, in new roles and new contexts. This newness initiates changes in language. It is these changes which eventually result in certain characteristic linguistic manifestations and are identified with labels such as the "Australianness" in one variety, the "Americanness" in another variety, or the "Indianness" in still another variety of English. These linguistic characteristics can be described with reference to the typical linguistically relevant "clue-marking" indicators such as those of social status, geographical origin, caste membership, or educational background, and in terms of the traditional linguistic levels. PHONOLOGICAL (and PHONETIC) clues show the differences in the way speakers pronounce words and use rhythmic or intonation patterns in a sentence. SYNTACTIC (or grammatical) clues show how words are combined in larger units, clauses, or sentences. MORPHOLOGICAL clues mark how words are formed from minimal meaningful terms. LEXICAL clues provide information about the vocabulary of language. SEMANTIC clues are concerned with what is generally known as "meaning." Thus, the "Americanness" in American English lies in the way Americans pronounce words, combine smaller units into larger units, and use the vocabulary. The same can be said about the "Australianness" in Australian English and the "Indianness" in Indian English. It is therefore appropriate that the modifiers of nationality (e.g. American, Australian, Canadian, Caribbean, Indian) are used to mark each variety different from the other varieties.

At this point, it should be noted that the concept of difference must not be taken too far. There are more similarities than differences between the various varieties of English; that is how an underlying Englishness is maintained in all these Englishes spoken around the globe. If it were not so, there would be serious problems in intelligibility between the speakers of various types of Englishes. Imagine the situation if Americans could not understand Australians, and Australians could not understand the British; or for that matter, if the educated non-native speakers of English, such as Indians and Nigerians, could not be understood by native speakers. But as we know, that is not generally the case. Any native speaker of English may have value judgments about varieties of English other than his own, i.e. an American may intuitively recognize the speech of Englishmen as "clipped, cold and rather effeminate"; an Englishman may speak of "the nasal twang" of an American, or "the sing-song" English of an Indian. However, in spite of these stereotypes of varieties of English, educated speakers of all these varieties generally understand each other. A native speaker of a language does not have to be a linguist to notice the individual, regional, or national speech characteristics of a person. After all, we often hear people say "he speaks a DIALECT," "he sounds like an Indian," "this person sounds Australian": such judgments are based on associating some features of a person's speech with a dialect, Indian English, or Australian English. The professional describes the differences for which non-linguists use cover terms such as "nasal twang" or "sing-song English" in a much more precise and technical way, but the fact of variation is recognized by both. Differences in speech are characteristic of the subgroups in speech communities.

The distinction which I mentioned earlier between the mother English of Britain and transplanted Englishes will, I think, be useful to us now. Mother English had a development and growth typical of a natural language. It was a historical development with various phases. English has done substantial pick-pocketing from other languages, such as Arabic (e.g. *alcohol, algebra, cork*); Dutch (e.g. *brandy, gin, golf*); French (e.g. *cavalier, garage, rapport*); German (e.g. *hamburger, wiener, bum*); Italian (e.g. *balcony, granite, sonnet*); Persian (e.g. *divan, shawl, spinach*); Greek (e.g. *barometer, idiot, tactics*);

Hindi (e.g. *shampoo, pajama, pundit*); Spanish (e.g. *alligator, mosquito, sherry*); American Indian languages (e.g. *chocolate, hominy, moose*), thereby enriching its word stock. But that is a different story and has been well documented in most of the histories of the English language, for example, Baugh (1935).

Let us now use the term "other Englishes" for those varieties of English which were spread and developed in areas other than the British Isles. As we noted, the speakers of mother English were not always tolerant and patient toward the growth and development of such varieties. On the contrary, they often had an attitude of arrogance and impatience toward transplanted varieties of English, since the speakers of such varieties did not conform to the patterns of Standard British English – what came to be called in the linguistics literature the RECEIVED PRONUNCIATION (generally abbreviated RP). RP is a type of acquired British speech generally considered as standard; it is the language of the famous old "public" schools and the universities of Oxford and Cambridge.

We might say that there is a bond which connects all the transplanted varieties of English, among them American English. This is perhaps as it should be. There are many reasons for it, one being that the processes which the speakers of these languages had to go through to establish their language identities have been more or less the same. The process of establishing an identity for a language can be as painful and as arduous as the struggle for political emancipation. In fact, that is part of the reason why some people attach so much importance to language in a political system or in nation-building activities. This is also the reason why language and nationalism are related and sometimes result in violent language conflicts, as for example in Belgium, Canada, Sri Lanka, and India.

The kinship among the transplanted varieties is historical, cultural, and linguistic. In historical terms the other Englishes have developed in two ways. The most stable and powerful centers of the other Englishes are those countries which were settled in by the British and have proportionately high populations from the mother country, i.e. Australia, Canada, the United States, and New Zealand. These countries were for a long time closely dependent on the mother country economically, culturally, and otherwise. As Laird (1970: 377) observes, "Until about the time of the 1914–18 war, the United States, well supplied with raw materials, imported almost everything else – human beings, religions, customs, education, science and technology, ideas, manufactured goods, books – in fact, most things that could bring language with them." If we add up the number of native speakers of English in the above-mentioned four countries, it is only 211.2 million, 58 percent of the total number of English speakers.

In addition to these transplanted varieties, the other Englishes that have significantly contributed to the diffusion of the English language are the result of Asian and African colonization which made Britain a world power of unparalleled strength and wealth for almost three hundred years. The contribution of colonialism to the countries in Asia and Africa has been a controversial and an

Table 2.1. *Enrollment in English in the top ten nations in which English functions as a second language*

Country	Students (millions)
India	17.6
Philippines	9.8
Nigeria	3.9
Bangladesh	3.8
Republic of South Africa	3.5
Malaysia	2.4
Pakistan	1.8
Kenya	1.7
Ghana	1.6
Sri Lanka	1.2

Source: Statistics based on Gage and Ohannessian 1974.

ongoing topic since the loss of the colonies. There are those who have only a critical or nationalistic attitude toward the colonial period, emphasizing the oppressive aspects of empire. There are also those who consider the British benign colonizers who, among other things, left the unifying legacy of the English language behind them. In the newly independent and formerly colonized nations, when hectic efforts are being made to remove marks of the colonial past with an upsurge of nationalistic pride, the English language is not necessarily considered a mark of that past: after all, it has been Africanized, Indianized, Caribbeanized, and has become a part of the living national traditions.

Therefore, it is not surprising that the non-native Englishes show a wide spectrum of uses – English in the former British colonies continues in the form of an "official" or "complementary" language or as a "library" language. The approximate overall total of those who study English as a non-native language in the schools, whether of former colonies or of other countries, is 1 billion and 15 million. In terms of geographical areas, these may be distributed as follows: Asia (excluding the USSR), 60 million; Africa, 20 million; Western and Central Europe, 15 million; Soviet Union, 10 million; western hemisphere, 10 million. Table 2.1 lists the ten countries with the largest enrollment in English in which English functions as a second rather than foreign language, and gives the total enrollment in each country.

In terms of numbers of users and the range of uses of English, one must specifically mention South Asian English. This variety of English is used on the South Asian subcontinent which includes Bangladesh (pop. 50.89 million), India (pop. 547 million), Nepal (pop. 11.7 million), Pakistan (pop. 61.96 million), and Sri Lanka (pop. 12.75 million). In India alone, if we accept the present language statistics, English is spoken by almost 3 percent of the total Indian population. This small percentage is rather misleading since in numerical terms it accounts for almost 18 million people, equal to 8.4 percent of the population of the United States, 139 percent of the Australian population, and 32.4 percent of the population of Great Britain. If we add to the Indian figure the number of English users in Bangladesh (3.8 million), Pakistan (1.8 million), and Sri Lanka (1.2 million), it totals 24.8 million.

Let us now consider in detail the Indian case to see how bilingualism in English was initiated on the subcontinent. It is a fascinating study in language imposition and language acculturation, and in many respects, it is similar to the cases of non-native World Englishes. Since the introduction of English on the Indian subcontinent and the development of South Asian English involves a span of over two hundred years, it will be useful to divide this period into several phases.

During the earliest period, missionary activity and colonial expansion were closely related in India, as in other parts of the world. The Christian missionaries went to India primarily for proselytization. Soon after that, the second phase started when there developed significant "local demand" from influential Indians such as Raja Rammohan Roy (1772–1833) to persuade the officials of the East India Company to introduce English education in India instead of continuing the traditional education by *pandits* and *mullas* in Sanskrit and Arabic respectively. Raja Rammohan Roy and others wanted the introduction of Western technology and knowledge through the vehicle of a Western language, namely English. In order to achieve this goal, Roy addressed a letter to Lord Amherst (1773–1857) urging him to use available funds for education in India for "employing European gentlemen of talent and education to instruct the natives of India in mathematics, natural philosophy, chemistry, anatomy, and other useful sciences, which the natives of Europe have carried to a degree of perfection that has raised them above the inhabitants of the world" (cited in Sharp 1920–2: I, 99–101).

The third phase of development of bilingualism in India was one marked by acute debate on the merits and demerits of the Oriental and Anglicist (Occidental) system of education for India. The Anglicists finally emerged victorious when the highly controversial and far-reaching Minute of T. B. Macaulay (1800–59) was passed. In this Minute, Macaulay aimed at forming a subculture in India which would include "a class who may be interpreters between us and those whom we govern, a class of persons, Indian in blood and color, English in taste, in opinion, in morals and in intellect" (cited in Sharp 1920–2: I, 116). This Minute finally received a Seal of Approval on March 7, 1835, from Lord William Bentick (1774–1839) when an official resolution approving Macaulay's Minute was passed. It is this resolution which initiated and seriously established English education in India. Some nationalists and orientalists have never forgiven Macaulay for the racial overtones of his statement, while others have simply overlooked it as exaggerated rhetoric.

The fourth phase begins with Indian independence, when English was given a position as the associate language of India. It is one of the fifteen languages recognized in the Constitution and shares with Hindi the status of a link-language.

On the African continent the missionaries had a deeper and greater impact on education and were more successful in the conversion of local people than they were on the Indian subcontinent. Their initial impact on African education started in the seventeenth century and did not stop with the end of Western colonization in Africa. The results in spreading Christianity in Africa are, therefore, more visible than elsewhere. Mazrui (1975: 12) correctly observes that "The Christian nations of the world are either white nations or black nations – there are almost no Christian nations in the intermediate colours of Asia." The colonial administrators also approached education differently in Africa. There the missionaries seem to have controlled education even after the European administrators began to pay attention to education. Knappert (1965: 99) notes:

When the European administrations began to think of education, they found that apart from the Coranic schools, all the education in Africa was being carried out by the missionaries. The government then gave the missionaries full responsibility for all education up to and including secondary level. That is how the number of languages taught at primary level rose to more than twenty in some countries and the governments encouraged diversity rather than unity.

The Asian, African, and West Indian varieties of English therefore have a clear colonial past. There are people in these countries who associate the English language with the colonial period and consider the supporters of English in those countries "Indo-Saxons" or "Afro-Saxons." Others in the now independent countries of Africa and Asia have a strong desire to establish identity with Great Britain and remain loyal to the British Standard (Kachru 1976a).

The colonial past of the not-so-colonial Englishes, such as American English or Australian English, cannot be equated with the colonial experiences of Asia and Africa. But in linguistic terms, these varieties demonstrate all the characteristics of a transplanted language. They also share an attitude of linguistic schizophrenia toward mother English, some wishing to be emancipated, others to remain loyal, considering British English the model and, therefore, an authority to be followed and imitated – "The standard writers of a language are, like the guardians of a well ordered state, its preservers from anarchy and revolution. They must be read – and as far as imitation is allowable must be copied . . ." (Beck 1830: 79).

Let us consider the earlier history of American English. At the beginning, the idea of a British model for American English was not actually relished by leaders of the American Independence movement. But there were some who felt a bond of "loyalty" toward it (see Heath 1977; Kahane and Kahane 1977). Those who supported the continuation of the linguistic bond felt a "language loyalty" toward Britain for cultural, humanistic, and literary reasons and, above all, to maintain "language solidarity." In opposition to this attitude of loyalty, there were those who wished to declare American English separate.

Linguistic "emancipation" was, in the United States as in other post-colonial nations, a natural consequence of political strife. In the United States, this attitude was behind suggestions to eradicate all symbols of the colonial past, including the English language. Attitudes favoring linguistic emancipation or loyalty in every nation are, however, most often caused by factors which are not linguistic. Desires to separate from or unify with a group motivate language loyalties. Ethnicity and or nationalism may cause groups to promote or decry English as a first or second language. In no case, especially for the now independent countries of Africa and Asia, is it possible to ascribe loyalty to or renunciation of English to single or simple causes.

Nativization of other Englishes

As I have mentioned, the other Englishes have more similarities to mother English than differences. Otherwise, it would be inappropriate to treat them as varieties of English. In *A Common Language: British and American English* by Marckwardt and Quirk (1964: 5) an attempt has been made to show that "the two varieties of English . . . have never been so different as people have imagined, and the dominant tendency, for several decades now, has clearly been that of convergence and even greater similarity." A study of Australian, Caribbean, Indian, Nigerian, or Filipino English will also show that in all these varieties there is an underlying Englishness. There is no need to elaborate on this point further.

However, I would like to discuss some typical characteristics of these other Englishes, which mark their distinct "Americanness," "Caribbeanness," "Indianness," or "Africanness." We will also see that the typical national or regional characteristics in each variety are, by and large, the result of the particular contexts. It is these linguistic, cultural, and ethnic contexts which provide the sources for what are termed Americanisms, Indianisms, Africanisms, or Caribbeanisms. Thus, the sources which result in the distinctiveness of these other Englishes are results of typical language-contact situations. In the new contexts, two or more languages come into contact for political, geographical, historical, or educational reasons; and the natural outcome of such contacts is linguistic innovation. The innovations specific to each variety can be regarded as deviations with reference to a norm. It is the sum total of these deviations in pronunciation, grammar and vocabulary which provides the framework for labeling various formations as Americanisms, Indianisms, Caribbeanisms, etc. Traditionally, the mother English of Britain has been considered the norm for marking the deviations; although in the case of certain second language varieties of English, as in the Philippines, Standard American English is treated as the norm.

Since we are focusing on the other Englishes primarily from a linguistic point of view, we should be able to account for the linguistic characteristics of each new variety, explained in terms of what the native context has contributed to it.

The contribution of the native cultural and or linguistic contexts results in what is technically called INTERFERENCE or transfer.

A quick glance at the dictionaries of other Englishes will show us many examples of such transfer. If a variety of English already has its own dictionary or other lexical studies, as American English, Australian English, Caribbean English, and Indian English have, it shows that the process of Americanization, Australianization, Caribbeanization, or Indianization of the English language has already taken place. In a variety-oriented lexicon we find several types of deviations. These may include words or compounds which are the result of the culturally pluralistic contexts of the New World, or of Asian and African colonies in which the English language was introduced. Also, these might demonstrate the new specialized uses to which the English language has been put in new contexts in administration, education, and politics.

One hundred and fifty years ago, in 1828, Noah Webster (see Sledd 1962: 32–3) presented the following arguments for a distinctly American lexicon of the English language:

It is not only important, but, in a degree necessary, that the people of this country, should have an *American Dictionary* of the English language: for, although the body of the language is the same as in England, and it is desirable to perpetuate that sameness, yet some differences must exist. A great number of words in our language require to be defined in a phraseology accommodated to the condition and institutions of the people in their states, and the people of England must look to an American dictionary for a correct understanding of such terms.

Webster's point regarding definitions of words suited to local circumstances is similar to the observation of Wilson (1940: i) about the uniqueness of certain terms in Indian English:

Ryot and *Ryotwar*, for instance, suggest more precise and positive notions in connection with the subject of land revenue in the South of India, than would be conveyed by cultivator, or peasant or agriculturist, for rent or revenue with the individual members of the agricultural clans.

The Englishman's terms, *cultivator*, *peasant*, and *agriculturist*, have to be replaced by *ryot* and *ryotwar* in the South Indian context. In their monumental and entertaining work, *Hobson-Jobson*, Yule and Burnell (1886: xxi) have pointed to the typical Indian characteristic of Indian English:

Within my own earliest memory Spanish dollars were current in England at a specific value if they bore a stamp from the English mint. And similarly there are certain English words, which have received in India currency with a special stamp of meaning: whilst in other cases our language has formed in India new compounds applicable to new objects or shades of meaning. To one or other of these classes belong *outcry, buggy, home, interlope, rogue (-elephant), tiffin, furlough, elk, roundal* ("an umbrella," obsolete), *pish-pash, earth-oil, hog-deer, flying-fox, garden-house, musk-rat, nor-wester, iron-wood, long-drawers, barking-deer, custard-apple, grass-cutter*, etc.

It is due to the typically Caribbean uses of English that Allsopp (1972: 5) has proposed "an authoritative lexicographical account of English *usage* in the Caribbean which must do more than give 'meanings' in isolation, but refer words and phrases to their areas and contexts of occurrence . . ." Such a Caribbean lexicon would account for the nativization of English in various forms; but it will also account for lexical variation (different names for the same item), for example, *golden apple* in Barbados has regional variants such as *pomme, cythere, jew plum, golden plum, box, meeting-turn, pardner, sousou, syndicate*; and it will explain the ethnic impact "in Caribbean culture from Trinidad and Guyana" and list Indic words such as *daru, holi, phagwa, anjuman, tajah*, which were introduced by the East Indian to Caribbean English. In the global context of English, as Allsopp (1972: 4) says, "Webster's or any other American dictionary, even when it calls itself 'International,' deals essentially with North American life, and fails, for Caribbean purposes . . ." Americanisms such as *bull-frog, razor-back, turkey-gobbler, egg-plant, jimsonweed, fox-grape*, and *apple-butter* listed by Mencken (1936: 113–21) are context-bound in the same way as the Indianisms such as *twice-born, dining-leaf*, or *caste-mark* are in Indian English. There is, as Spencer (1971a: 28) says, "certainly a sufficiency of terms and expressions to justify the term West Africanisms in English. Consider, for example, *cutting-grass, chewing-stick, head-tie, market-mammy, mammy-wagon*, and *fetish-priest*.

The best example of the influence of the multilingual settings of the new Englishes is provided by the process of hybridization. This process results in a number of formations which comprise lexical items from two or more languages and, in a sense, contextualize an item in a particular variety of English. Consider, for example, the following hybridized Indianisms listed in Kachru (1975): *lathi-charge, tiffin-carrier, tonga-driver, ahimsa-soldier*. Such formations may further be divided into those which have no grammatical constraints in the selection of the members of a hybridized item; for example, the four illustrations provided above, as opposed to others which have certain grammatical constraints. In such items we have a prefix from one language, as in *non-Brahmin*, and the noun from another language. On the other hand, we may have a suffix from one language and the preceding noun from another language as *-wala* in *policewala*, *-hood* in *Brahminhood*, *-dom* in *cooliedom*, and *-ism* in *goondaism*.

The nativization of English manifests itself in a much deeper form than merely in pronunciation and vocabulary. These two aspects are, of course, very obvious to any observant speaker of any variety of English. The aspect which has been least studied is the acculturation of English in various non-Western contexts. One can think of a number of contexts which have resulted in such acculturation. For instance, the caste system, in the typical Indian sense, is absent in those countries where English is used as the first language. Therefore, when the English language is used in typically non-English contexts, as in referring to the caste system or non-Western social roles, various linguistic

2 American English and other Englishes

devices are used to represent such contexts. These devices may include lexical borrowing from the local languages, extension of the semantic range of the English lexical items, or translation of native situation-dependent formations into English. The use of *forehead-marking* for the crimson caste mark which Hindus put on their forehead, or *nine-stranded thread* for the ritualistic thread worn after initiation called *yagnopvīt* by the Hindus, have semantic relevance only if viewed in the context of the Indian caste system (see Kachru 1965, 1966).

It is the use of English in non-Western social roles or speech functions in Africa or Asia which brings out its Africanization or Asianization. Let us consider the following examples which are used in the speech functions of greetings or personal interaction in Asian or African English.

(1) May we live to see ourselves tomorrow
(2) He has no chest
(3) He has no shadow
(4) Where does your wealth reside?
(5) What honorable noun does your honour bear?

If we consider these five examples from an American English speaker's point of view, they are contextually deviant and also deviant in the selection of words. One might say this is not the company which these words keep in such contexts in American English. In linguistic terms the Indian or African use of these words places them in a deviant COLLOCATION.

If seen from another point of view, we might say that their functional and formal appropriateness is doubtful, since they do not form part of the communicative repertoire of an American English speaker. On the other hand, let us consider (1) and (3) above from the point of view of an African English user whose first language is Ijaw, and for him, *May we live to see ourselves tomorrow* is roughly the equivalent of *Good night* in Western societies. Sentences (2) and (3) are the equivalent of *He is timid,* and as Okara (1963: 15) says, "Now a person without a chest in the physical sense can only mean a human that does not exist. The idea becomes clearer in the second translation. A person who does not cast a shadow of course does not exist . . ."

Sentences (4) and (5) are translations from Punjabi, an Indian language, and have been used in Indian English fiction by Khushwant Singh in his *Train to Pakistan*. These are culturally dependent polite forms for what would be equivalent to American English *Where do you live?* and *What is your name?* Many Indian English speakers will use these in normal speech only for comic effect, but in written English they are used by Singh for developing a character type in a plot, in which such use of English does not sound incongruous.

The process of translation, which is evident in the above examples, is not unusual in the history of the English language. It would be difficult for a modern-day native speaker of English to detect that *a marriage of convenience, I've told him I don't know how many times,* or *it goes without saying* were actually word-for-word imitations of French phrases.

As such formations gain wider currency, they become more acceptable – there is nothing intrinsically non-English about them. If we compare the idioms *a crocodile in a loin cloth* and *pin drop silence,* we notice that the first is more deviant in Indian English than is the second, the reason being that *pin drop silence* is heard and read more often than is *a crocodile in a loin cloth.* The device of translation is also used for creating local color. Consider, for example, the comparative constructions *lean as an areca-nut tree, helpless as a calf, as good as kitchen ashes,* and *as honest as an elephant* (Kachru 1976b). In Australian English (Ramson 1970: 52) what may be termed ''local color'' is similarly conveyed by formations such as *fit as a Malee bull, looking like a consumptive kangaroo, mean as a dishwasher, awkward as a pig with a serviette,* and *handy as a cow with a musket.* Quirk et al. (1972: 26) are right in saying that the English language has several ''interference varieties that are so widespread in a community and of such long standing that they may be thought stable and adequate enough to be institutionalized and regarded as varieties of English in their own right rather than stages on the way to a more native-like English.''

In the preceding paragraphs we have seen that each variety of English undergoes a process of acculturation in its new sociocultural context. In its new surroundings the transplanted English naturally becomes culture-bound. In order to make clearer what is meant by culture-bound, I shall present below two texts which can be properly understood and appreciated only if they are related to the cultural context of each variety. In *No Longer at Ease* (1960), Chinua Achebe, a West African English novelist, presents a blend of pidgin and educated English and provides a good example from West African speech of the functional use of CODE-SWITCHING, i.e. the switching from one language or language variety to another in the stream of discourse.

''Good! See you later.'' Joseph always put on an impressive manner when speaking on the telephone. He never spoke Igbo or pidgin English at such moments. When he hung up he told his colleagues: ''That na my brother. Just return from overseas. BA (Honours) Classics.'' He always preferred the fiction of Classics to the truth of English. It sounded more impressive.
    ''What department he de work?''
    ''Secretary to the Scholarship Board.''
    ''E go make plenty money there. Every student who wan' go England go de see am for house.''
    ''E no be like dat,'' said Joseph. ''Him na gentleman. No fit take bribe.''
    ''Na so,'' said the other in disbelief.

The use of code-switching in this text is a linguistic device used to introduce realism into the text.

Another way of contextualizing a text is to use the device of CODE-MIXING, i.e. the use of elements such as lexical items or larger units from another language or language variety in the stream of discourse (Kachru 1979a). In discussing South Asian music, to give one example, English lexical items are inadequate to present the technical concepts of Indian traditions of music. Consider the following example.

He set the pace for the recital with a briskly rendered Pranamamayakam in Gowlai a composition of Mysore Vasudevachar. One liked the manner in which he and his accompanying vidwan built up the kriti embellishing it with little flourishes here and there . . . Then came Kamboji Alapana for Pallavi . . . with Vedanayagam Pillai's Nane Unnie Nambinane in Hamsanandi the recital came to a glorious end. (*The Statesman,* December 14, 1969)

This excerpt is from a standard national newspaper.

Labels such as "West African" English, "Indian" English, and "American" English are useful to show that these varieties are not marked separately only in a geographical sense, but also in terms of their cultural component and language features. In order to adapt his discourse to a specific cultural context, an author may use a spectrum of Englishes – as does Achebe in the above passage – which vary from pidgin, regional, and national to international.

The national Englishes have essentially local uses in culturally and linguistically pluralistic societies. In turn, they have subvarieties which have varying degrees of intelligibility with the English of native speakers or with that of educated speakers of particular national varieties. Allsopp (1972) proposes several subvarieties of Caribbean English, namely "free vernacular," "vernaculars of subcultures," "elevated vernacular," "creolized English," and "formal Caribbean English." One might say that Indian English, too, has various subvarieties, ranging from almost complete intelligibility with native speakers of English to very limited intelligibility. These subvarieties are "educated Indian English," "Babu English," "Chee Chee English," "Butler English," and "Bazaar English" (see Kachru 1980).

It is, however, the pronunciation of a speaker which provides an index to the variety of his speech, or to a variety within a variety. As we know, one does not have to be initiated in phonetics or linguistics to identify, for example, a speaker of the American, British, or Indian varieties of English. Pronunciation seems to provide crucial clues toward marking a person as being within a particular group or outside it. By pronunciation we mean the use of segments, termed vowels and consonants, and equally if not more importantly, the way a person arranges syllables for the rhythm of language. It is well known now that rhythm plays an important role in intelligibility. We see that in English, as in other natural languages, some forms of pronunciation acquire prestige or become more acceptable. The two well-documented and generally acceptable forms of the native varieties of English are Received Pronunciation (RP), and General American (GA). There is no legal or official acceptance for these forms since, as mentioned earlier, English has no academy to regularize language use or prescribe language "etiquette." These standard forms develop by general acceptance or judgment, by looking up to some group, caste, or class for providing a language model, by accepting a model because it is spoken in a particular area, or by considering dictionaries, manuals, or certain types of educated people as "models" for linguistic etiquette. RP or GA are not necessarily "correct," but are more widely known. The radio has contributed to their acceptance. And, in the case of RP, the British Broadcasting Corporation gave it prominence; for a long time RP was identified with "BBC English." Recently things have changed, but that is another story. RP was also associated with the universities of Oxford and Cambridge, especially with those speakers who got their education from the "public" schools, as this term is understood in Britain. The term "General American" was suggested by Krapp (1919), mainly to refer to the variety of English spoken in the central and western United States and in most of Canada.

It is generally true that a standard variety of language is well documented and described by phoneticians, linguists, and language pedagogues. English has pronouncing dictionaries for both RP and GA. That was not, for example, true for Indian English or West African English until recently. Therefore, it was not uncommon to hear questions such as: What is Indian English? What is its "standard" or "educated" form? By form, of course, was meant DESCRIPTION, as this term is understood by linguists.

There is no doubt that the users of non-native Englishes found it more convenient to use RP, or a close approximation to it, as a pedagogical model. RP was well documented and teaching aids and materials were readily available. The well known British phonetician Daniel Jones had by 1918 made the job of teachers easier by his classic work *An Outline of English Phonetics* (*OEP*). It is not surprising that by 1956 it had already run into eight editions. Then appeared his *Everyman's English Pronouncing Dictionary* (*EPD*). What was more important, Jones stimulated a number of other young phoneticians to supplement his work. It was not long after Jones' *OEP* that John S. Kenyon published *American Pronunciation* (1924), followed by *A Pronouncing Dictionary of American English* (*PDAE*) (1944). Kenyon was unhappy to see that

there are few subjects on which educated Americans are so ready to pass judgment and give advice on the basis of so little sound knowledge as the pronunciation of the English we use. Influenced by certain types of teaching in the schools, by the undiscriminating use of textbooks on grammar and rhetoric, by unintelligent use of the dictionary, by manuals of "correct English", each with its favourite (and different) shibboleth, and, it would seem, by anybody or anything that has an air of cocksureness about it, we accept rules of pronunciation as authoritative without inquiry into either the validity of the rules or the fitness of their authors to promulgate them. (Kenyon 1924: 3)

These works on either side of the Atlantic opened the flood gates for such manuals. But it would be erroneous to say that Jones or Kenyon were the first to make such attempts. Since there is always demand for such books on language "etiquette," we find, for example, that in 1687 a phonetician named Christopher Cooper published *The English Teacher, or The Discovery of the Art of Teaching and Learning the English Tongue*. The aim of this book was to present rules of English pronunciation for "Gentlemen, Ladies, Merchants,

Tradesmen, Schools and Strangers . . ." We see here an attempt to produce an all-purpose manual for English. Over a century before Cooper, prescriptive statements about a standard variety were made. John Hart, another phonetician, wrote in 1569 that "the flower of English tongue is used" in the Court and London region. There are various attitudes which encourage prescriptivism in pronunciation and contribute toward a "standard" form. Pronunciation manuals or dictionaries are only the instruments which are used to fulfill such functions. After all, one function of a dictionary is to provide "standard" pronunciation and the variants. And when the users of other Englishes, Indian, West Indian, or West African, compile these dictionaries, they are aiming to show that they do recognize a standard pronunciation for the educated form of their variety, which may be different from RP or GA.

Pronunciation differences may be minor, and thus scarcely contribute to the problem of intelligibility, or they may create substantial problems. It may also be that the "educated" varieties of an English may be intelligible, but not some other varieties. It is possible that a speaker of GA might find educated Indian English more intelligible than, say, Cockney English.

But, small or large, the differences between RP and GA are such that the cousins on the two sides of the sea can be marked as separate. Some of the more obvious speech differences may be given as illustration. Americans tend to pronounce an *r*-sound in words if it follows a vowel; thus the vowel is "*r*-coloured." In British English this *r* is not pronounced. Consider the following sets of words which the RP speaker will pronounce in an identical way: *law, lore*; *paw, pore, pour*; *saw, sore, soar*; *maw, more*; *bawd, bored, board*. To a speaker of RP, GA speakers seem to pronounce the following words in the same way: *writer–rider*; *petal–pedal*; *catty–caddy*; *latter–ladder*; *utter–udder*. It is, however, the difference in the pronunciation of vowels that is a distinctive feature of GA, labeled by others "the drawl of Americans." The GA speaker tends to lengthen the vowels in strongly stressed syllables, while in RP these are "slightly lengthened." This "extra length" may be "drawl" to an RP speaker, but his reduced length is "clipped" for an American speaker. This would apply to, for example, first syllables of *after, daughter, terrible*, and the second syllables of *before, improve, control*. There are other differences, or what Daniel Jones called "mispronunciations" in Indian English, but we shall not discuss these here (see Kachru 1969, 1976b). But for intelligibility, it seems rhythm is more important than is pronunciation of individual speech sounds.

The grammatical differences between the educated *native* varieties of English are not significant. But there are some differences which may result in ambiguities. One of these, as Strevens (1977: 150) puts it, is "the have–have got–gets–gotten complex." The American use of *have* results in speech situations such as the following, when the other participant is British. American: "Do you have many children?" English woman: "No, only one a year" (see also Marckwardt and Quirk 1964; Foster 1976).

The search for a model: a dilemma in prescriptivism

The users of other Englishes who speak it as their second language generally tend to have as a model one of the native varieties of English. The choice of a model is not easy, since there are several established models from which one may select, for example, American, Australian, or British. There are also cases when people prefer a less well-known model such as Scottish English. What does one understand by the concept "model"? One might say, as in Kachru (1977:30), that model "implies a linguistic ideal which a teacher and a learner keep in mind in imparting instruction or in learning a language." In this sense then, model entails prescriptivism and provides criteria for codification of a language and recognition of a standard. In language acquisition one strives to acquire competence which approximates the model. But one does not always accomplish it, nor is it desirable to do so in all contexts of language acquisition.

Why certain models are preferred, as opposed to others, depends on historical, cultural, geographical, and attitudinal considerations. Languages which have academies for standardization, as is the case with French, may offer a clearer choice to a model seeker. English seems to have lost the opportunity of creating such an academy in the second decade of the eighteenth century, but according to some, it really was not such a serious loss. It was in 1712 that Jonathan Swift wrote a letter to "the Most Honourable Robert, Earl of Oxford and Mortimer, Lord High Treasurer of Great Britain," enclosing "A Proposal for Correcting, Improving and Ascertaining the English Tongue" in which Swift suggested that

The persons who are to undertake this work, will have the example of the French before them, to imitate where these have proceeded right, and to avoid their mistakes. Besides the grammar part, wherein we are allowed to be very defective, they will observe many gross improprieties, which, however authorised by practice, and grown familiar, ought to be discarded. They will find many words that deserve to be utterly thrown out of our language, many more to be corrected, and perhaps not a few long since antiquated, which ought to be restored on account of their energy and sound. (Swift 1907: 14–15)

This plea of Swift's did not suit the English temperament, and the proposal was abandoned with the death of Queen Anne who, with other influential people, was supporting the establishment of such an academy. The proposed English academy would have been modeled after earlier ones such as the Italian Academia della Crusca (1582) or the French Académie Française (1635).

It was only sixty-two years later that the United States became independent, and the question of an academy in America began to be debated. John Adams even put up a proposal before the Continental Congress in 1780 to set up a "public institution for refining, correcting, improving, and ascertaining the English language" (1856: VII, 249–50). This is exactly the echo of Swift. But as Heath (1977: 10) notes, pragmatism and universalism prevailed, and the United States disapproved of such a move, since "now the founding fathers believed the individual's freedoms to make language choices and changes represented a far more valuable political asset to the new nation than did a state decision to remove these freedoms from the individual.'' Therefore, a deliberate choice was made to have *"a policy not to have a policy."*

The debate about the merits and demerits of an American or a British standard continued. Those who supported the process of nativization had to argue with people like Pickering (1816: 67) who felt that ''we have in several instances deviated from the standard of the language, as spoken and written in England at present day . . . so many corruptions have crept into our English.'' The language debate in the new nation is a fascinating story and will provide a significant historical dimension to a student of language in the USA.

My aim in this chapter is not to discuss this debate in detail, but to draw certain conclusions from the two rather similar cases of Britain and America. In the absence of an official academy, other factors contributed toward providing a model of English to those who acquired it as a second or foreign language. A particular model was selected because of colonization, economic dependence, geographical proximity, or cultural impact. Why people prefer a certain model is difficult to ascertain. It involves attitudes which researchers find elusive. One does not always know how to separate people's attitude toward a model from their actual performance. The area is difficult to probe because one's perception of a norm and actual behavior do not necessarily correlate. In studies on attitudes toward models, one notices what may be called ''linguistic schizophrenia.'' In India, for example, the preferred model is British English, but in actual peformance, Indians speak Indian English with various degrees of competence – this is a difference between the norm (the attitude toward a preferred model) and the behavior of speakers.

As we will see in the following section, American English is slowly becoming today's world language, and its impact is all-pervasive on the English-speaking world. This new trend may therefore influence the choice of a model.

The growing impact of American English

Two hundred years ago on September 23, 1780, John Adams wrote in a casual way to a fellow American, prophesying that ''English will be the most respectable language in the world and the most universally read and spoken in the next century, if not before the close of this.'' Adams further proclaimed that English

is destined to be in the next and succeeding centuries more generally the language of the world than Latin was in the last or French is in the present age. The reason for this is obvious, because increasing population in America, and their universal connection and correspondence with all nations . . . force their language into general use . . . (cited in Mathews 1931: 42)

In these observations, although Adams uses the term ''English,'' what he actually meant was ''American English.'' At that time, naturally, Adams could not foresee all the reasons which later caused the diffusion and spread of

American English, but, by and large, his prophecy has come true in our life-time.

We must ask then: What is it that changed the picture? And why is American English no longer regarded as "a quaint, barbarous or amusing appendage to the British original" (Foster 1976: 18)? The reasons for this change in the position of American English are essentially non-linguistic, though there are some who believe that there is something intrinsic about the English language or the American variety of English which entitles it to this unique position. One has to make it clear at the outset that there is no validity in arguments that are based on ethnocentrism and linguistic ignorance. Consider, for example, Laird's speculation (1970: 480) that "the English language is spreading through the world partly because it is a good language with a simple grammar and a vast and highly flexible vocabulary . . ." An even more startling observation is found in Barnett (1964: 9) who smugly proclaims:

Contrary to popular supposition, languages evolve in the direction of simplicity. English, being a highly evolved, cosmopolitan, sophisticated language, has been refined and revised, planed down and polished through centuries of use, so that today it is far less complicated than any primitive tongue.

Then Barnett has a dig at "primitive" people and adds: "Some of the most difficult languages in the world are spoken by some of the world's most backward people – e.g. the Australian Aborigines, the Eskimos, the Hottentots, and the Yahgan Indians of Tierra del Fuego." One might ask: difficult for whom? The hypothesis that English is accepted abroad on the basis of its simplicity or its sophistication is not acceptable. It is therefore surprising that such a view was held even by a distinguished linguist, Jespersen (1905). In his view:

the English language is a methodical, energetic businesslike and sober language, that does not care much for finery and elegance, but does care for logical consistency and is opposed to any attempt to narrow-in life by police regulation and strict rules either of grammar or lexicon. As the language is, so also is the nation . . . One need not be a great prophet to predict that in the near future the number of English-speaking people will increase considerably. It must be a source of gratification to mankind that the tongue spoken by two of the greatest powers of the world is so noble, so rich, so pliant, so expressive and so interesting. (Cited in Fishman 1977f: epigraph)

This shows that Anglophile linguists can get as much carried away as do nonlinguists who know little about how language works.

What actually happens is that language and power go together. American English is accepted for the power and superiority which America as a nation has acquired in the areas of science, technology, commerce, military affairs, and politics since Adams wrote those prophetic words. After all, in the 1950s people started to learn Russian. This seemed a natural reaction after the phenomenal success of Sputnik I and the sudden evidence of the technological advance of the Russians. The USA has become the center of Western political, economic, and technological innovations and activities. Therefore, as we will see below, it is not surprising that even the speakers of mother English in

Britain have become tolerant of the encroachment of American English into their English, as have the Australians who earlier took mother English as the model. One notices this slow but definite encroachment in several semantic areas in British English. Let us consider the areas of film, television, theater, and advertising as typical examples. Foster (1976: 20) gives pride of place "to film as a vehicle of American linguistic influence . . . which has brought . . . transatlantic speech to the British hearth itself." Film, television, and theater have resulted in use of the language with American shades of meaning, for example, "when a film is said to *feature* an actor who has been *built up* by his company" (Foster 1976: 20). The theater has provided words such as *stooge* and *double-talk*. In advertising and salesmanship, Americans certainly excel and demonstrate "the transatlantic love of grandiloquence." American techniques are followed, and words which were exclusively American (e.g. *sales talk* or *sales resistance*) may be heard in Piccadilly Circus or Bond Street.

The British press is opening up to American innovations. The style of typically American news magazines like *Time* and *Newsweek* shows up in British newspapers; for example, the name of a town in the genitive is no more a typically American stylistic feature (e.g. *Newcastle's Central Station, London's Victoria Coach Station*). The same tendency is seen in the use of verbs such as *ban* 'prohibit', *crash* 'collide', *cut* 'reduce', *probe* and *quiz* 'investigate', and *sue* 'prosecute'.

It is not only in the use of single words that one notices this change; the conversation of the British is also spiced with set phrases which are considered to be of "American provenance," for example, *I wouldn't know, let's face it, simple as that, by and large, right now, way over (-down, -back), consult with, baby-sitter, round-trip*. There are idioms such as *to have a chip on one's shoulder, to scrape the bottom of the barrel*, and *out on a limb*.

This intrusion of American English into British English, or for that matter into Australian English, is slow but perceptible. One can correlate generational differences with the use of the American variety. John Wain, the British novelist, has very aptly captured this linguistic difference between two generations in his *Hurry on Down* (1959). In this novel a young man and his father are linguistically very dissimilar. The young man

talked a different language for one thing; it was demotic English of the mid-twentieth century, rapid, slurred, essentially a city dialect and, in origin, essentially American. By contrast it was a pleasure to hear his father whose speech had been formed, along with all his other habits, before 1914 . . .

The difference in speech and use of "American" is associated with a linguistic attitude toward American English in the new generation. In their minds American speech "is the hall-mark of the tough-guy and the he-man" (Foster 1976: 14). The changing British attitude and its acceptance of Americanisms is, of course, interesting for historical reasons. The linguistic wheel has turned full circle, and now the users of mother English are recognizing the legitimacy of the offspring.

In France, Spain, and Germany – in spite of puristic resistance to the American influence on French, Spanish, and German – one notices an intrusion of Americanisms in the press, at social gatherings, and on the radio and television. In a number of countries in Asia and Africa, the Englishization (or shall we say Americanization?) of the native languages has become a symbol of elitism and westernization, and for the vocal new generations, westernization represents modernization. In the last fifty years, America has become a phenomenon of envy and emulation for the new and emerging nations, for it combines technology, scientific progress, and, above all, power. The ubiquitous American tourist has contributed toward the spread of American English as much as Hollywood movies and student and faculty training programs. Even in the erstwhile British colonies, American English is having its impact. One can notice it in the newspapers from Ibadan, New Delhi, or Singapore.

Worldly success and elitism continue to be associated with westernization, and specifically with a knowledge of English. The refrain of a Ghanaian song succinctly sums it up. A person is successful if he has *been-to, Jaguar, fridgeful*. The term *been-to* (feminine, *beentress*) refers to a person who has been to England, indicating a status symbol; the possession of a *Jaguar* car shows prestige; and *fridgeful* marks class and affluence, indicating a refrigerator filled with food. In recent years *been-to* (or *beentress*) includes America too, and competence in American English. The Indianism *England-returned* is parallel to the Ghanaian *been-to*, but now it has less currency. The term *America-returned* is heard more often, conveying the same prestige, class, and status as did *England-returned* during the colonial days. Matrimonial advertisements also seem to prefer *America-returned* bridegrooms. And a person who is *America-returned* naturally comes with "Americanized" English.

It should not be inferred from the preceding discussion that an American traveling in the world will find, on various continents, American English used with the Midwestern or East Coast accent; far from it – the English language, American or British, will continue to be nativized and undergo changes in new contexts and new uses. Its uses will vary, as they do now, from an internationally understood "educated English," to several types of Englishes which are not necessarily meant for native speakers of English. These varieties have national and regional uses, developed because of the specific linguistically and culturally heterogeneous contexts of these societies: functionally, these "national varieties" are an essential tool of human communication. A monolithic universal English, therefore, is rather difficult to imagine. It would also be uninteresting to live in a society which used, as Firth says (1930: 196), "a shameful negative English which effectually masks social and local origin and is a suppression of all that is vital in speech."

FURTHER READING

There is no single volume which provides an introduction to English in its global context, its native and non-native varieties, and the diffusion of American English. The studies of international or universal languages concentrate primarily on *artificial* languages as opposed to *natural* languages. An introduction to international auxiliary languages is given in Guerard 1922 and in Jacob 1947. Part I entitled "International perspective on English" in Fishman, Cooper, and Conrad 1977 provides a detailed overview of the spread of English and its functions, with an exhaustive bibliography. Jones 1965 provides a survey of the "triumph" of English and "a history of ideas concerning the English tongue – its nature, use, and improvement – during the period 1476–1660." In the spread of languages, colonialism has played an important role. This aspect is discussed in Calvet 1974, Fishman 1977f, and Spencer 1971b.

There are, of course, several studies on the historical and linguistic aspects of the native varieties of English. The classic work of Mencken 1919 can still be read with pleasure and profit. A "corrected, enlarged, and rewritten" edition appeared in 1936, and two supplements were added to it in 1945 and 1948; an abridged edition appeared in 1977. Marckwardt 1958 is a more recent and shorter introduction to American English. Partridge and Clark 1951 is "an informal, not an academic, history of English since 1900." There is also a section on "Dominions English" with subsections on English in Canada, South Africa, Australia, New Zealand, and India. The differences and similarities between American and British English are presented in very interesting and informative conversations in Marckwardt and Quirk 1964, and Strevens 1972, 1977 discusses the main differences between the two varieties. In Pyles 1971 there is a very useful and detailed chapter on "Recent British and American English." A number of papers, especially the first two in Quirk 1972 discuss "linguistic bonds across the Atlantic." Foster 1976 (first published in 1968) has a long and informative chapter on the impact of America on British English. It is worth reading. An earlier paper by Foster entitled "Recent American influence on Standard English" (1956) provides numerous examples with detailed discussion. One can find a detailed treatment of Australian English in Morris 1898, Baker 1966, and Ramson 1966. A good treatment of Australian *and* New Zealand varieties of English is also presented in Turner 1966, and in the papers edited by Ramson 1970 which cover "Australasian" English.

The non-native varieties of English have been discussed mainly in individual papers published in scholarly journals or in chapters in books. Smith 1980 includes several studies on such varieties with an extensive bibliography. An overall view of the non-native varieties is given in Quirk "English today: a world view" (in Quirk 1972), Bailey and Robinson 1973, and Kachru 1976a, 1980. The following studies or collected works are recommended for specific non-native varieties. These studies also provide bibliographical references for further reading: Africa in general: Spencer 1963, Achebe 1973, McGregor 1971; West Africa: Spencer 1971a; Ghana: Sey 1973; Nigeria: Bamgbose 1971; India: Rao 1954, Gokak 1964, Kachru 1965, 1966, 1969, 1973, 1975, 1976b, 1978, 1979b, Nihalani, Tongue, and Hosali 1978; Malaysia: Tongue 1974; Singapore: Platt 1975, 1976, Crewe 1977; South Asia: Kachru 1969; Philippines: Llamzon 1969; West Indies: Ramchand 1973.

Attitudes toward various types of Englishes and their sociolinguistic motivations have been discussed in Kachru 1976a, Heath 1977, Kahane and Kahane 1977, and, most recently, Finegan 1980.

3

Varieties of American English

WALT WOLFRAM

> "I knowed you wasn't Oklahomy folks. You talk queer kinda – That ain't no blame, you understan'."
>
> "Ever'body says words different," said Ivy. "Arkansas folks says 'em different from Oklahomy folks says 'em different. And we seen a lady from Massachusetts, an' she said 'em differentest of all. Couldn' hardly make out what she was sayin'."
>
> (From John Steinbeck, *Grapes of Wrath*, quoted in Marckwardt 1958:131)

It takes little linguistic sophistication to recognize that there exist a number of varieties of American English. For as long as it has been spoken in the New World, variation in the English language of this continent has been a topic for comment. During the earliest periods, the difference between the English developing in the colonies and that spoken in England was the main focus of attention. In later periods, the distinct varieties of English spoken in various regions throughout the continent became the center of interest. And more recently, the social correlates of language diversity have become the object of considerable commentary. While the focus of attention on English varieties certainly shifts from time to time, the interest itself appears to be constant, affecting both professional scholars of the English language and lay observers.

For our concern here, there are both advantages and disadvantages to the widespread recognition of variation in American English. On the one hand, this recognition indicates a natural curiosity about the ways in which varieties of English might differ from each other. It is inevitable, for example, that a visitor from Chicago traveling along the coasts of South Carolina will note some aspect of language difference between the varieties spoken in these respective locales. A student of the English language who addresses these sorts of topics has only to stimulate this basic curiosity. More than one DIALECTOLOGIST has succumbed to the temptation to become an instant social success by answering the person who approaches him with the query "Can you tell where I'm from just by hearing me talk?" As we shall see later in our discussion, this is sometimes a question considerably more complex than the inquirer may anticipate, involving a number of dimensions.

On the other hand, the widespread recognition of variation in American English can give rise to a number of misconceptions about the nature of this diversity. Stereotypes and prejudices about language differences manifest themselves in folk notions about speech. A professional scholar of language variety in American English has to confront many misconceptions which have arisen out of this tradition of recognizing diversity. Popular myths concerning the supposed unsystematic, illogical, linguistically inferior status of nonmainstream varieties have been highly cultivated over the past several centuries, and the re-education of students to accept the systematic but different nature of these varieties requires a massive effort. (Although we shall not take up this issue again here, these premises must be kept in mind as we wind our way through the complexities of linguistic diversity in American English.)

Typically, differentiation in the varieties of American English has been recognized on several levels of language organization. First of all, there are differences in the vocabulary or LEXICON of the language. Differences on this level are probably most widely recognized, and there is a long tradition of noting these differences which goes back to the earliest travelers in the New World. In fact, some literary scholars in London were sufficiently conscious of new words arriving from this continent in the 1750s to suggest that a glossary of these items would soon be in order. This popular interest has persisted to the present day, and travelers who come from a visit to New England talking about how *tonic* is used, where one might refer to *soda pop* or *pop* in other regions, indicate a recognition on this level.

Another fairly obvious level of recognized differences concerns the pronunciation or PHONOLOGY of the language. A person who notices how a New Yorker says *chocolate* or how a person in the South pronounces *time* is recognizing a difference in the organization of the phonological system. A further level of organization on which differences between varieties are realized is the SYNTAX – the combinations of items as they are placed in sentences. Observations of different negative patterns such as *He didn't do nothing* in one variety as opposed to *He didn't do anything*, or different verb patterns such as *He was a-singin' and a-laughin'*, exemplify this level of differentiation.

Finally, there may be differences in language use, i.e., differences in how language forms are used in the context of speaking as opposed to differences in the forms themselves. Thus a Northerner who is familiar with the respect terms *sir* or *ma'am* might comment on the different set of social relationships and occasions in which these forms are used in some Southern areas.

A tradition of study

There is a long-standing tradition for collecting data on variation in American English. Some of the earliest collections were concerned with aspects of American English which set it apart from British varieties, particularly in vocabulary. Works such as Pickering's *A Vocabulary, Or Collection of Words and Phrases which have been supposed to be peculiar to the United States of America, to which is prefixed an essay on the present state of the English language in the United States* (1816) or Bartlett's *Dictionary of Americanisms* (1848) demonstrate such a concern motivating the collection of data. Although some early observers were impressionistic in their descriptions of differences, others were apparently quite meticulous in the collection of Americanisms, noting the setting, speakers, and context of usage for particular items which were recorded (Heath 1976b).

Differences between British and American English were not ignored in later concerns with language variation, but there was an increasing trend to focus on diversity within American English varieties themselves. Largely in connection with the study of settlement patterns, data on geographical distribution came into prominence. Thus, the American Dialect Society was formed in 1889 for "the investigation of English dialects in America with regard to pronunciation, grammar, vocabulary, phraseology, and geographical distribution." The initial hope of this society was to provide a body of data from which a DIALECT dictionary or a series of linguistic maps might be derived. Although a considerable amount of data on varieties of English was published in the society's original journal, *Dialect Notes*, it was not until 1928 that a large-scale systematic study of DIALECT GEOGRAPHY was undertaken, entitled *The Linguistic Atlas of the United States and Canada*. The primary purpose of the Linguistic Atlas was to trace the settlement history of the United States as reflected in the existent dialect patterning, although other objectives were also included, such as differences based on social levels, between spoken and written language, and so forth. The resultant works provided scores of articles on thousands of linguistic forms which could be differentiated across various sectors of American English, and the compilation of DIALECT ATLASES is still going on (Figure 3.1). Armed with a questionnaire designed to elicit particular items of phonology, syntax, and lexicon, fieldworkers could spend up to ten or twelve hours with one subject obtaining various forms. The fieldworker sought out locally rooted persons who were native speakers of English, some well-educated, others less so. Before addressing the specific questions from the manual prepared for fieldworkers (containing approximately 800 items designed to check points of pronunciation, grammar, and vocabulary), the fieldworker usually began the interview with broad questions on topics of general knowledge, for example, "Tell me about the house you grew up in" (McDavid, O'Cain, and Dorrill 1978). Figure 3.2 provides excerpts from the fieldnotes of Raven McDavid, completed in 1946 on the basis of an interview in Charleston, South Carolina with a white female, age 69. An artist and author, she was a member of the highest social class and had been drilled by her family on "correctness." She knew many archaic terms and pronunciations; she insisted on using these. The thought of a grammatical error in her speech was inconceivable to her; in her words, "Grandmother would turn over in her grave if she heard me say *ain't.*"

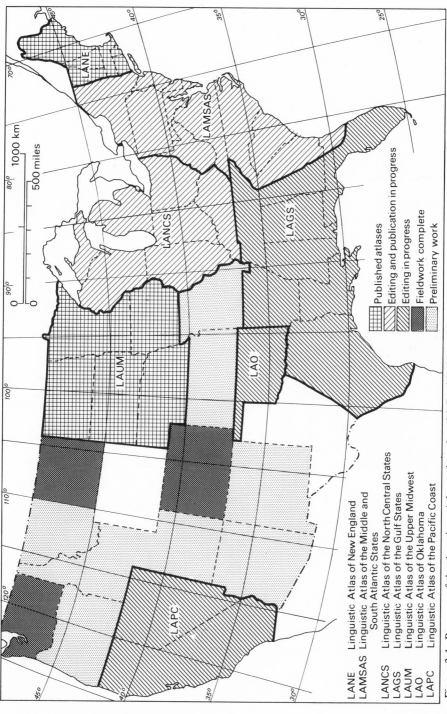

LANE   Linguistic Atlas of New England
LAMSAS Linguistic Atlas of the Middle and
        South Atlantic States
LANCS   Linguistic Atlas of the North Central States
LAGS   Linguistic Atlas of the Gulf States
LAUM   Linguistic Atlas of the Upper Midwest
LAO   Linguistic Atlas of Oklahoma
LAPC   Linguistic Atlas of the Pacific Coast

Published atlases
Editing and publication in progress
Editing in progress
Fieldwork complete
Preliminary work

Figure 3.1. Progress of the American Atlases (based on McDavid 1979a: 87)

Pronunciation

What are the two parts of an egg? One is the white; the other is ——
Variants: yok, yelk, yulk, yilk, yoke
Response: yulk; "heard": yelk

What color would you say the yolk of the egg is?
Variants: yellow, yallow, yillow, yollow, yeller
Response: yellow; "heard from grandmother, old-fashioned": yillow, yollow: "new
    way": yallow

When your skin and eyeballs turn yellow, you're getting ——
Variants: yellow jaundice, janders, yellow janders, jaundice
Response: jaundice, jandice "I say either"

Grammar

I wanted to hang something out in the barn, so I just took a nail and ——
Variants: drive, druv, driv, drove, droove
Response: drove a nail

The nail didn't get in far enough; you'd say, "It's got to be —— further."
Variants: driv, drove, droven, driven
Response: driven

A schoolboy might say of a scolding teacher, "Why is she blaming me,
I —— wrong."
Variants: ain't done nothing wrong, haven't done anything wrong
Response: I haven't done anything wrong. [Field worker noted informant never used
    double negatives except quotatively, e.g. "I never had no head for machin-
    ery."]

Vocabulary

Where did you keep your hogs and pigs? Did this have shelter or was it open?
Variants: hog pen, pig pen, hog lot, hog crawl, pig sty
Response: hog pen, pig pen; "old fashioned or obsolete": crawl, hog crawl, cattle crawl

harmonica (with reeds and blown, as distinct from a Jews' harp)
The thing you put in your mouth and work back and forth and blow on it. Do you
    remember any other names for it?
Variants: harp, breath harp, French harp, mouth organ, mouth harp, harmonica
Response: mouth organ

Figure 3.2. Samples from a dialect atlas worksheet. Included here are sample questions designed to
elicit certain points of pronunciation, grammar, and vocabulary; these questions were contained in
the manual used by each fieldworker. Listed below the question are possible variants of each item
provided in the manual for the fieldworkers' reference. Included in the response is not only the actual
response given, but also variants the informants mentioned as having "heard," extraneous comments
volunteered by the informant, and comments noted by the fieldworker from other portions of the
interview which related to this item. (Data provided by the editorial staff of the Linguistic Atlas of the
Middle and South Atlantic States, University of South Carolina)

Regional variation

Historically, probably more attention has been given to geographically correlated variation in American English than to any other type. The correlation of varieties of American English with geographical location is, of course, a reflection of underlying historical patterns which have led to a present-day pattern of regional variation. In some cases, regional variation can be traced to different patterns of settlement history where the migration of the early settlers is still reflected in the language. Some of the original differences may, of course, reflect the fact that settlers came from different regions of England where diversity was already existent; others may reflect the influences of another language where the settlers came from a non-English-speaking country. Patterns of population movement within the United States are also reflected in regional differences. Thus, a major shift in the White population has been from east to west, a pattern which is revealed in a number of language differences which parallel this movement.

When considering the regional aspects of variation in American English, the role of physical geography cannot be overlooked, since it, too, has exerted its historical influence on language differences. Although transportational obstacles are not generally considered to be a serious handicap with modern technological advances, separation of areas by rivers, mountains, and other natural boundaries has inhibited the spread of language in the past, because it restricted the mobility necessary for the diffusion of linguistic forms from one location to another.

Traditionally, the geographical distribution of differences in American English was traced by plotting particular linguistic items on maps. It was possible to draw ISOGLOSSES on a map (i.e., lines separating areas which used a particular item from those that did not). Major regional areas were defined, then, on the basis of a number of isoglosses which clustered in approximately the same way (i.e., an ISOGLOSS BUNDLE). An example of one type of map delimiting major regional varieties of American English based on the collection of Linguistic Atlas data, is seen in Figure 3.3.

While such a map might be useful in an approximative way, some qualification is necessary. Lines on a map such as this make it appear that the varieties are discrete entities exclusively possessing the territories in the area demarked by the lines. A careful examination of the isoglosses used to determine these areas would reveal that most often they do not coincide in a precise way. Thus, arbitrary decisions may be made in determining which isoglosses are to be considered most significant in determining varieties. In most cases, differences between varieties are not discrete, but relative in terms of a continuum of differences. Furthermore, some of the differences between varieties may be quantitative rather than qualitative. That is, two or more varieties may share a particular feature, but its relative incidence in one variety is greater than that in another. And there is often a transitional area between varieties where forms may be in considerable fluctuation.

When we examine the nature of regional variation, we find that it is most frequently the result of the spread of language changes through geographical

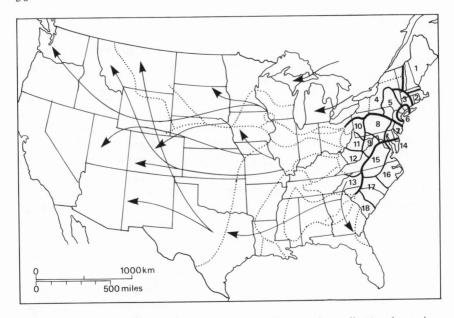

Figure 3.3. Dialect areas of the USA. Atlantic Seaboard areas (heavy lines) and tentative dialect areas elsewhere (dotted lines). Arrows indicate directions of migrations (adapted from Francis 1958: 580-1)

THE NORTH

1. Northeastern New England
2. Southeastern New England
3. Southwestern New England
4. Inland North (western Vermont,
   Upstate New York and derivatives)
5. The Hudson Valley
6. Metropolitan New York

THE SOUTH

14. Delmarva (Eastern Shore)
15. The Virginia Piedmont
16. Northeastern North Carolina
    (Albemarle Sound and Neuse Valley)
17. Cape Fear and Peedee Valleys
18. The South Carolina Low Country
    (Charleston)

THE MIDLAND

North Midland

7. Delaware Valley (Philadelphia)
8. Susquehanna Valley
10. Upper Ohio Valley (Pittsburgh)
11. Northern West Virginia

South Midland

9. Upper Potomac and Shenandoah
12. Southern West Virginia and
    Eastern Kentucky
13. Western Carolina and Eastern
    Tennessee

space over time. By analogy, this is likened to the effect of a pebble which is dropped in a pool of water. A particular change takes place at a given point in time and space and spreads from that point in successive waves or stages. The most concentrated existence of the linguistic item will be in the area where it was first introduced, and the outer periphery of the diffusion will evidence less concentration, since the change was later coming to that area. The outer boundaries, however, are not static but dynamic in nature, constantly undergoing change which makes the rigorous delimitation of geographically related boundaries a relative rather than absolute thing. Finally, there are other social factors which complicate the examination of differences in simple terms of geographical space. Variables such as social status, speaking style, ethnicity, and so forth might clearly transcend the simple geographical distribution of items. Recently, sociolinguists, students of language who focus on the social and cultural parameters of language differences, have attempted to reorient some of the theoretical and methodological aspects of the study of language variation. They consider linguistic variation to be essential in solving issues fundamental to the construction of an adequate linguistic model for describing a language, since variation is endemic to all languages. Methodologically, sociolinguists focus on the language of everyday conversation and go into the field to do their work armed with tape recorders to record conversation.

For the most part, data on social status as a variable in linguistic diversity come from the analysis of relatively spontaneous conversation. In this approach, particular variants are tabulated in relation to the number of times these variants might have occurred in actual conversation. For example, if we are tabulating an Appalachian English form such as *a*-prefixing, we count the number of times the *a*-prefix occurs in relation to the number of times it might have occurred. This is illustrated in the following passage, where the *a*-forms are in bold type and the cases where it might have occurred are italicized.

He was a retired Army man, and, we went up 'ere and John supposedly had a sack to put the coon in if we caught one. We's *gonna* try to bring it back alive, so we tromped through the woods 'til along about six o'clock in the morning. The dogs treed up a big hollow chestnut oak, and we proceeded to cut the thing down. It's about three or four inches all the way around. About four foot through the stump. We tied the dogs and cut the thing down. Well, we cut it down and turned one dog loose, and he went down in that thing, way down in the old hollow of the tree and it forked, and we couldn't get up in there so he backed out and he tied 'im. And we's **a-gonna** chop the coon out if it was in there, I's a kinda halfway thought maybe it just treed a possum or something. Well, I chopped in and lo and behold, right on top of the dang coon. Eighteen pounder, Jack Stern says, kitten coon. I run in with the axe handle down in behind him to keep him from getting out or backing down in the tree. He reached, fooled around and got him by the hind legs and pulled that thing out it looked big as a sheep to me. Turned 'im loose, he said "kitten, Hell." We had an old carbide light and he turned that over and the lights were . . . that's all the light we had. And, we had to hunt it then and the dogs took right after the coon right down the holler and the dogs caught it and Jack beat us all down there. Went down there and he's **a-holding** three dogs in one hand and the coon in the other hand. And they's all **a-trying** to bite the coon and the coon **a-trying** to bite Jack and the dogs, and

Jack pulled out a sack and it wasn't a dang thing but an old pillow case that Maggie had used, his wife, it was about wore out. So we fumbled around 'ere and finally got that coon in that sack and he aimed to close the top of it and the coon just tore the thing in half, in two, and down the holler he went again. With that sack on him, half of it and we caught that thing, and you know, E. F. Wurst finally pulled off his coveralls and we put that thing down in one of the legs of his coveralls and tied that coon up. He's *tearing* up everything we could get, we couldn't hold him he's so stout. And I brought that thing home and kept 'im about a month, fed 'im apples and stuff to eat so we could eat 'em. Well, I did I killed him and tried eat that thing, I'd just soon eat a tomcat or a polecat, I wouldn't make much difference. And, that's about the best coon hunt I believe I was on.

                                                     (Wolfram and Christian 1976: 181)

This passage, taken from the conversation of a retired coal miner who was a native of southeastern West Virginia, shows six constructions where the *a*-form might have been used, and in four of them it actually appears. Thus, we end up with a percentage (for this passage 67 percent) figure showing the incidence of a particular variant in relation to its potential usage. This approach to data is considerably different from the traditional Linguistic Atlas approach in which particular items were elicited in interviews based on a questionnaire.

If the multiple dimensions of diversity in American English are to be understood, it will be necessary to record, describe, and analyze language variation as it co-occurs with as many of these dimensions as possible. Sociolinguists, in examining language differences, also provide some explanations of patterned behavioral differences between groups of Americans. Different types of studies highlight particular factors, such as sex or age of speaker, functions of speaking, or ethnic membership of speaker and audience. However, it is ultimately the interaction of a number of variables which accounts for the observed diversity in language structure and use. In the following sections, we shall isolate some of the more essential social factors which must be recognized in explaining diversity in American English. It should be kept in mind that the discussion of these factors separately is an artifice of our description, and that ultimately these factors intersect with each other to account for the varieties of American English.

Social status

In a society where social status is an obvious aspect of its structure, it can be expected that there are essential dimensions of language variation which correlate with status differentiation. Naturally, this does not operate independently of other considerations, including the regional variation just discussed. We can speak of social varieties of American English as long as we realize that they do not exist in isolation from other factors. As it turns out, there are some aspects of variation in American English which may have social significance only within a given regional context, while others have a much broader geographical range. Thus, the absence of an upgliding vowel in an item like *time* (i.e., *tahm*) may not be particularly significant in some Southern contexts, whereas its use in some

Northern urban context might hold considerable social significance. On the other hand, the absence of a third person singular -*s* form in *He go* for *He goes* may be socially significant regardless of the particular locale.

Socially diagnostic items of American English may be either prestigious or stigmatized. Socially prestigious items are those used by high status groups as linguistic manifestations of social status, whereas socially stigmatized items are those associated typically with low status groups. In some varieties of American English, a slight raising quality of the vowel in items like *pass* or *fact* appears to have a prestige function. On the other hand, the pronunciation of *th* as a STOP in *that* (i.e., *dat*) or *the* (*duh*), or the use of the so-called double negative, such as *They don't do nothing*, may be a socially stigmatized rule. The absence of a prestige feature does not necessarily imply that its alternative is stigmatized, nor vice versa. For example, the pronunciation of the vowel in *pass* or *fact* without a raised quality is not necessarily socially stigmatized; by the same token, the pronunciation of *th* in *that* or *the* or the use of a single negative in *They don't do anything* is not necessarily prestigious. To determine the particular social significance of a linguistic item at a given point in time does not, of course, mean that it will necessarily stay that way. The social significance may change over time, for one reason or another. Thus, the absence of postvocalic *r* in New York speech (e.g., *fouh* for *four*) was socially prestigious at one time, but has since reversed its social significance for a younger generation of New Yorkers.

Among the varieties of American English, there are many more differences where the dimension of social diagnosis contrasts stigmatized and nonstigmatized variants as opposed to prestige versus nonprestige variants. This appears to match the observation that Americans tend to react more in terms of negative responses to socially stigmatized linguistic items than they do positively to socially prestigious items. On an informal level, mainstream or standard varieties of English might most practically be defined in terms of the absence of various socially stigmatized items as opposed to the presence of prestige items. While this might be an oversimplification, it does capture the relative importance of the stigmatized/nonstigmatized dimension compared with the prestige/nonprestige dimension.

The reactions that people have to socially significant items in American English have been classified into three main types (from Labov 1964: 102). First of all, there are social indicators, items which may objectively correlate with social status differences, but have little effect on a listener's assessment of an individual's status. One of the important clues to the existence of social indicators is their lack of sensitivity to style shifts in the language that take place in response to interlocutors, topics, situations, and so forth. If speakers are aware (on a conscious or an unconscious level) of a socially significant item, they will vary its frequency of usage as a part of their style shifting. That is, in a more formal occasion, they may use a prestige variant more frequently or a stigmatized variant less frequently. In the case of social indicators, however, this does not take place because of the relative unawareness that a particular form correlates with social status.

There are other features which show both social and stylistic variation; furthermore, they have a regular effect on a listener's reaction to a person in terms of social status. These have been called social markers. The sensitivity that these linguistic variables show to the stylistic parameter (i.e., more frequent use of a prestige variant in a more formal style) indicates that these forms are recognized on some level, whether conscious or unconscious. There appear to be many more social markers in American English than social indicators.

Finally, there are social stereotypes. Not only are these socially significant variants recognized on some conscious level, but they become the topics of overt comments from members of the community, or those who fulfill roles with respect to the perpetuation of the language norms in the society. Items such as *ain't*, the pronunciation of *dese*, *dem*, and *dose* for *these, them*, and *those* respectively, and the use of negatives such as *They don't do nothing* all appear to exemplify social stereotypes. There are few Americans, including those who may regularly use them, who have not heard comments about the social stigma which these items carry.

Socially diagnostic items in American English do not differ only with respect to the relative awareness that is indicated toward them. They may differ also with respect to how they correlate with social status. There are some items which may correlate with more finely differentiated social groupings, while there are others which reveal a more discrete break between fewer social status groups. For example, consider the distribution of two variables for the Black speech community in Detroit. In the case of postvocalic *r* absence in items such as *fouh* or *fathuh* for *four* and *father* respectively, we find a gradual increase in the relative frequency of "*r*-lessness." On the other hand, in the case of the grammatical absence of third person singular present tense *-s* forms, such as *he go* for *he goes*, we find a sharp demarcation between the middle classes and the working classes. The contrast between the correlation of these two socially significant rules for the Black speech community in Detroit is given in Figures 3.4a and 3.4b.

The picture indicated in these two types of correlation is probably reflective of the status system in America which makes it difficult to classify in any simplistic way. There are aspects of the social status system which appear to reflect a continuum much more than a discretely defined social class – GRADIENT STRATIFICATION, but there are other aspects of the social status structure which reveal a sharp demarcation between groups on the basis of status – SHARP STRATIFICATION. We may hypothesize that the sharper, more rigid the social boundaries in a society are, the sharper the stratification of linguistic features will be.

Ethnicity

Without a doubt, the most emotionally laden topic in the discussion of variation in American English is that of the relation between ethnicity and language differences. The essential debate here concerns whether varieties of American

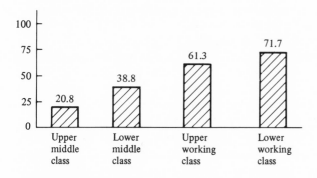

Figure 3.4a. Postvocalic *r* absence: an example of gradient stratification (adapted from Wolfram 1969: 110)

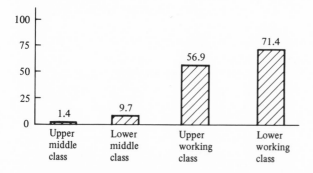

Figure 3.4b. Third person singular -*s* absence: an example of sharp stratification (adapted from Wolfram 1969: 136)

English correlate in a unique way with America's different ethnic groups, be they Black, Indian, Jewish, Italian, or any other group. Issues surrounding language and ethnicity have become highly charged for both lay and professional observers of language. For the layman, the possibility of distinct ethnic varieties has sometimes been associated with the supposed physical or mental attributes of the particular ethnic group. If, for example, it were admitted that some Black and White Americans spoke differently, then it might be a reflection of some inherent or physical difference between the two groups. For the professional student of language, the dispute concerning ethnic varieties of English centers around the historical origin of the varieties used in the United States and the dynamics of social patterns that affect speech. Language scholars take as axiomatic that the speech variety acquired by a given ethnic group has no relation to the physical or mental characteristics of that group. The supposed physical or mental basis of such a correlation is readily disproved by those situations where a person from one ethnic group is isolated from that ethnic group. In these types of situations, we find the individual speaking indistinguishably from those of the immediate social group. Thus, a Black who is socialized in an exclusively White group will speak as the others of that group, or a White American socialized in an exclusively Black cultural context will adopt the language of that group.

In recent years, the most hotly debated issue on ethnicity and language is that of Black – White speech relationship. In Northern urban areas, it is quite apparent that working class Blacks often use a variety of English which is considerably different from their White counterparts (see Chapter 5). The issue is, however, more hotly contested when comparable (or at least as comparable as American society will allow) socio-economic groups of Blacks and Whites are considered in the rural South, since most working class varieties of Black speech have had their origin in rural Southern varieties.

While some data must still be subjected to further analysis, recent studies indicate that even in the rural South, where the varieties are much more similar, there exist linguistic structures which distinguish Black and White working class speakers. For example, we have not been able to find consistent usage of the form *be* among White speakers in sentences such as *Sometime my ears be itching* or *She usually be here* meaning ''something happens or is true at various times.'' This form is, however, fairly common among working class Black speakers. Some of the differences are more subtle. Thus, both Southern Whites and Blacks may have the absence of *be* in a structure such as *You ugly* where the absence of the form corresponds to Standard English *are*, but typically only Blacks will extend its absence to correspond to Standard English *is* as in *He ugly*. Perhaps the most important differences are found in the combinations of structures which make up the varieties, rather than any one structure in particular. Reinforcement of our analysis revealing Black – White speech differences comes from various identification tasks in which listeners are asked to identify the ethnicity of a speaker from an audio-recording. In most structured research of this type, the accuracy of ethnic identification is well over 80 percent.

In most instances, the extent to which ethnicity correlates with language diversity is a function of the social distance between particular ethnic groups. With increased assimilation of ethnic members into the larger culture, we may expect the factor of ethnicity to be of minimal significance, but with ethnic isolation of one type or another, we may expect this variable to be of major significance. In reality, ethnic isolation occurs in varying degrees, depending on the social role of particular ethnic groups in American society. We may expect, for example, that a relatively homogeneous Jewish community will reveal some linguistic differences when compared with other groups (see Chapter 13), but we would predict that the differences will not be nearly as striking as that revealed for the Black community because of the relative social roles of these ethnic groups. Where an ethnic group speaks another language, the influence of this language may be exerted in differentiating the variety. The influence of German on the English of southeastern Pennsylvania is well attested in structures such as *The soup is all*. Similarly, the English spoken by some Indian groups in the Southwest may be influenced both directly and indirectly by the indigenous Indian language (see Chapter 6). With this added dimension, the factor of ethnicity and language variation in American English can indeed become very complex.

Sex

Although we may not typically think of varieties of American English being differentiated on the basis of sex, it can be demonstrated that particular aspects of language selection and usage are related to the sex of the speaker and/or hearer. If asked, for example, to guess the sex of a speaker who utters a sentence such as *Oh my, you shouldn't have done that, but you are a dear*, or *What an adorable package*, most of us would identify the speaker as a female. This is because the selection of vocabulary items in certain domains typically correlates with the sex of the speaker. In the first sentence, a difference in the type of expletives used by men and women is demonstrated, whereas the second case illustrates a disparity in descriptive adjectives. Similar types of differences might have been illustrated with reference to color terms, where it has been demonstrated that fine color distinctions such as *beige, lavender, mauve*, and so forth are more common to women than to men.

All the distinctions cited above relate to systematic differences in the selection of vocabulary items used by men and women. It is much more difficult to establish similar types of differences with respect to syntax and phonology. Some recent studies have suggested that certain types of syntactic patterns might be used more frequently by women than men (e.g. certain types of positive imperatives such as *Do come for dinner!* or tag questions such as *John is here, isn't he?*), but these claims have been disputed strongly by others.

Although sex differences cutting across the different varieties of American English may be difficult to establish for syntax and phonology, sex has been shown to be an important variable intersecting with other social variables such as region and social status. Various studies have, for example, indicated that males realize a higher incidence of socially stigmatized features than females of comparable socio-economic classes. Thus, working class females who use *-in'* for *-ing* (e.g., *sittin'/sitting*) would typically not be expected to use it as frequently as their male counterparts. Similarly, females who use socially stigmatized multiple negation (e.g., *He didn't do nothing*) would not be expected to use it as frequently as their male counterparts. The tendency of males to use more stigmatized variants in their speech is probably best seen as a reflection of different behavioral roles for men and women. There are clearly positive, if covert, values of masculinity and toughness associated with nonstandard speech for men (e.g. compare the stereotypic notions of how masculine heroes such as football players talk) which are not matched for women. Conversely, we expect females to have a higher incidence of prestige features than their male counterparts of comparable social status. Thus, if a particular vowel quality of the *a* in *bat* takes on a prestige value, we would expect its higher incidence among middle class women than men. The sensitivity of women to prestige norms makes them prime candidates for linguistic change, and studies of linguistic

change occurring across the United States indicate that females are often responsible for the initial adoption of new prestige variants in a given locale.

Age

Two aspects of age differences can be cited to account for some types of diversity
in the varieties of American English. First we have changes taking place in
American English which differentiate successive generations. In this case, a
change taking place in one generation of speakers in a particular locale would
typically not affect the older speakers of that region whose language system had
been firmly stabilized. Thus, older residents of Appalachia might use an *a*- prefix
on verb forms such as *He was a-singin' and a-dancin'* or pronounce *fire* and *tire*
something like *far* and *tar* respectively, whereas the current generation of
speakers in Appalachia is not nearly as inclined to use these forms. This is a
function of a language change taking place in which these particular items are
being lost or changed. From this perspective, different generations within a
population may be viewed as a reflection of American English varieties at
different time periods. The difference between the English brought from England
by the original English-speaking settlers and a given variety of English today is
thus a summation of the changes exhibited by the successive generations of
speakers.

The social significance of particular features can also change over time. Thus,
there is little social significance for the absence of *r* in words like *York* (Yohk) or
four (fouh) exhibited by New Yorkers over 50, whereas the absence of *r* may be
socially stigmatized for speakers under 50. It is interesting to note, in this regard,
that one of our shibboleths of nonstandard grammar, the ''double'' or multiple
negative (e.g. *There wasn't nobody nowhere*) was once the common and only
acceptable way of forming certain negative structures in the English language.

The other aspect of age differences relates to the life cycle of a particular
individual. Within this cycle, there are certain behavioral patterns that are
considered appropriate for various stages of life, and these include aspects of
speech. For example, certain vocabulary items, identified popularly as ''teenage
slang,'' may be quite appropriate for one age group, but would be quite inappropriate for other age groups. Terms such as *gig* for *job, wheels* for *car*, or *bread*
for *money* are associated with the teenage and early adult stage of life, but they
would seem quite inappropriate for a middle-aged person. For the most part,
these vocabulary items have a rapid life cycle, so that the expressions of today's
youth will not be carried over by the next generation of youth. Though the
particular items will change, the selection of a ''slang'' unique to the next
generation of youth will be perpetuated.

The most obtrusive aspects of age-graded language differences in American
English are probably found in certain vocabulary items, but there are also other
differences. For example, socially stigmatized variants are used more frequently
by adolescents than adults. During the adolescent period, the influence of peers
on speech is also maximized, and children learn the variety of their local peers as

opposed to the variety of their adults. It is quite typical to see a parent who moves from one region to another retain the variety of the original locale while the children adopt the new variety quickly. Aspects of this assimilation, which appears to be optimal from the ages of 5 to 12, are probably related to the acquisitional process as well as the influence of peers in forming the particular variety a child speaks.

Formal and informal styles

Most of us are well aware of the fact that written language style is expected to be somewhat different from that of spoken English, or that we talk to a casual acquaintance quite differently from how we speak to a respected authority. Style is obviously a dimension that intersects with other variables in accounting for diversity in American English.

One of the essential dimensions for viewing style in American English is formality – how formal or informal a particular style is. This dimension can be approached most clearly by defining formality in terms of the amount of attention paid to speech. The more attention paid to speech, the more formal the style. Formal styles are thus defined as those situations where speech is the primary focus, whereas informal styles are defined in terms of those situations where there is the least amount of audio-monitoring of speech.

In many cases, the relative usage of particular features of American English is clearly related to style, regardless of the social or regional variety used. For example, the use of -in' for -ing (e.g. *swimming, hunting*), which is found to some extent among all regional and social varieties of English, is typically used more frequently in more informal styles. Similarly, the use of *d* for *th* (*this, the*) will be more frequent in more informal styles, where the lessened attention to speech will allow the greater usage of stigmatized variants. We can expect that a stigmatized variant will show decreased usage, and a prestige variant will show increased usage, as we move from informal to more formal styles. Some variants, such as taboo terms and certain socially stereotyped stigmatized features may be totally absent from the more formal styles, while they persist in the informal styles.

The dimension of style appears to differ in its significance at various periods in the life cycle of an individual, although it is present to some extent at all periods. There is, however, less stylistic differentiation in the earliest stages of adolescence and the older stages of the life cycle. The reduced stylistic variation in the earliest stages is due to the acquisitional process, in which the sensitivity to the social significance of various styles usually precedes a full stylistic repertoire. During the later periods of life, adults have typically resigned themselves to their particular status and role in American society, and adaptation to particular situations becomes less variable. This is manifested in language by the reduction in the range of stylistic fluctuation. On the other hand, stylistic variation appears to be at its maximum during those periods in the life cycle when adults are establishing their own status and role in American society.

Stylistic variation also intersects with other social variables such as class. Intermediate social classes, such as the lower middle class, may be expected to show more stylistic variation than the upper middle class, which already "has it made," and the working class which basically has little contact with the upper middle class. The lower middle class, however, typically strives to emulate the middle class reference group with which it has contact, but by which it is not completely accepted. This creates a type of LINGUISTIC INSECURITY which results in the lower middle class sometimes using higher frequency levels of prestige features than the middle class itself when speech is in primary focus.

On the linguistic relationship between varieties of English

In the previous sections, we have attempted to set forth some of the regional and social parameters that are considered in accounting for the varieties of American English. At this point, we now want to turn to the nature of the linguistic relations among these varieties. As a preface to this discussion, it is necessary to recognize that there exists a large core of structures which is common to all varieties of English. The clear majority of syntactical, lexical, and phonological patterns are common to all varieties of American English. Granted this common base, however, we still want to know the nature and extent to which varieties differ from each other. We take as our underlying premise that the varieties of English will show structured, systematic relations to each other. While our notion of patterning may take us beyond some of the traditional notions of systematic patterning in linguistics, it can be demonstrated that there are sometimes intricate and subtle aspects of patterning to be found among the varieties of American English.

Differences between varieties may be either qualitative or quantitative in nature. In qualitative differences, linguistic forms found in one variety are categorically absent in another variety. For example, the use of so-called "distributive be" mentioned earlier (e.g. *He usually be upstairs*) as a characteristic of a Vernacular Black variety is a structure which is completely absent from the systems of many other varieties of English. Hence, we may speak of "distributive be" as a form which demonstrates qualitative differences among the varieties of English.

One of the most significant contributions of studies over the past decade has been the discovery that social varieties of English are often differentiated from each other not only by discrete sets of features, but also by variations in the frequencies with which certain forms or rules occur. This finding is in some ways at variance with popular perceptions of how the varieties of English are differentiated, since it is commonly held that certain low status groups always use particular socially stigmatized linguistic forms and high status groups never do. As it turns out, such "categorical" assessments do not match the actual language situation. In many cases, varieties of English are more typically differentiated by the extent to which a certain rule applies rather than the qualitative absence or presence of a rule. For example, consider the example of pronominal apposition

Table 3.1. *Relative frequency of pronominal apposition usage in four social status groups of Detroit speakers*

	Upper middle class	Lower middle class	Upper working class	Lower working class
Percentage of pronominal apposition	4.5	13.6	25.4	23.8

Source: Adapted from Wolfram 1969.

Table 3.2. *Relative frequency of -in' forms for four social groups of Detroit speakers*

	Upper middle class	Lower middle class	Upper working class	Lower working class
Percentage of *in'* forms	19.4	39.1	50.5	78.9

Source: Adapted from Wolfram 1969.

in a structure such as *My mother, she went to the store*. While such a construction is often thought of as restricted to lower status groups, its actual distribution among four different social classes in Detroit can be seen in Table 3.1. In each case, the percentage figure indicates how frequently the appositive pronoun form is used in relation to how frequently it might have been used.

While the use of this form does differentiate different social groups of speakers, the differences are on a quantitative, not a qualitative scale. Out of the thirty-six speakers used in the tabulations presented in Table 3.1, no speaker reveals the incidence of pronominal apposition in every case where it might have been used, and only one speaker reveals the complete absence of this form.

Similar types of observations can be made with respect to phonological systems. Popular perceptions might attribute the *-in'* of unstressed *-ing* forms (e.g. *swimming, laughing*) to lower status groups as an exclusive pattern and the *-ing* pronunciation to higher status groups as an exclusive pattern. Again, the careful examination of the actual incidence of the *-in'* pronunciation reveals a pattern of relative rather than absolute difference, as indicated in the frequency distribution of four social classes of Detroit speakers in Table 3.2.

Again we find a pattern of differentiation among social classes which is relative in nature. In fact all of the speakers in the sample cited here have some incidence of the *-in'* pronunciation.

That we observe variation between alternate forms, such as *-ing* and *-in'* does not necessarily mean that the fluctuation is completely random or haphazard. Although we cannot predict which form might be used in a given instance, there are factors which increase the likelihood that certain variants will occur. For example, the various social factors cited previously can all be important influences which affect the relative frequency of particular forms. Not all of the systematic effects on the variability of forms, however, can be accounted for by simply appealing to social factors. There are also aspects of the linguistic system itself which may systematically influence the likelihood of forms occurring. Particular types of linguistic context, such as surrounding structures or forms, may influence the relative frequency with which these forms occur.

The systematic effect of linguistic factors on the relative frequency of particular forms can best be understood by way of illustration. Consider the case of word-final CONSONANT CLUSTER reduction as it affects sound sequences such as *st*, *nd*, *ld*, *kt*, and so forth. In this rule, items such as *west, wind, cold*, and *act* may be reduced to *wes', win', col'*, and *ac'*, respectively. It is observed that the incidence of this reduction is quite variable, but certain linguistic factors influence the relative frequency of the reduction. These linguistic factors include whether the following word begins with a consonant as opposed to a vowel and the way in which the cluster has been formed. With reference to the following environment, we find that a following word which begins with a consonant will greatly increase the likelihood that the reduction process will take place. Thus, for example, we find reduction more frequent in a context such as *west coast* or *cold cuts* than in a context such as *west end* or *cold apple*. While some reduction may be found in both contexts, it is clearly favored when the following word begins with a consonant.

As mentioned above, we also find that reduction is influenced by the way in which the cluster is formed. To understand this relationship, we must note that some clusters are an inherent part of the word base, as in items like *guest* or *wild*. There are, however, other cases where a cluster is formed only through the addition of an *-ed* suffix, which is primarily formed phonetically through the addition of *t* or *d*. When the *-ed* suffix is added to an item such as *guess*, the form *guessed* is pronounced the same as *guest*, so that it now ends in an *st* cluster. Or, an item like *called* actually ends in an *ld* cluster as it is pronounced something like *calld*. In these cases, the cluster is formed because of the *-ed* addition, since neither *call* nor *guess* has a basic word form which ends in a cluster. When the degree of variation for base word clusters is compared with those formed through the addition of *-ed*, it is found that the former case clearly favors consonant cluster reduction. That is, we are more likely to find word-final consonant cluster reduction in an item such as *guest* or *wild* than in one like *guessed* or *called*. Again, we note that fluctuation can be observed in both types of clusters, so that the favoring effect of base word clusters on reduction is simply a matter of relative frequency.

When we compare different linguistic effects on the relative frequency of a variable reduction pattern such as word-final consonant clusters, we find that some will have a greater effect than others. In a sense, this is like the effect that social variables (e.g. class, sex, age, etc.) have on linguistic items where several different social factors influence the relative frequency of a form, but some social variables are more influential than others. Thus, the following linguistic context

Table 3.3. *Percentage of consonant cluster reduction in different regional and social varieties of English*

Language variety	Not -ed, followed by consonant (e.g. west/coast)	-ed, followed by consonant (e.g. guessed/ fast)	Not -ed, followed by vowel (e.g. west/end)	-ed, followed by vowel (e.g. guessed/it)
Middle class White Detroit speech	66	36	12	3
Working class Black Detroit speech	97	76	72	34
Working class White New York City adolescent speech	67	23	19	3
Working class White adolescent rural Georgia–Florida speech	56	16	25	10
Working class Black Adolescent rural Georgia–Florida speech	88	50	72	36
Southeastern West Virginia speech	74	67	17	5

Source: Wolfram and Christian 1976: 36.

of a consonant versus a vowel may have a greater influence than the effects of a base word cluster versus a cluster formed through the addition of -ed.

In many cases, the linguistic constraints on variation can be found to operate across different social variables, such as class, sex, and age. The regular effect of the linguistic constraints mentioned above for consonant cluster reduction can be seen in Table 3.3 which compares this process in different regional and social variables of English.

As we see in Table 3.3, all the varieties of American English represented here are systematically influenced by the following environment and the formation of the cluster. While the different groups reveal the same linguistic constraints, however, the relative effect of their influence may differ. For two of these groups (Working class Black and Working class White adolescent rural Georgia – Florida speech) the effect of the formation of the cluster is more important than the following environment, but for the others the following environment has a greater effect.

To understand the nature of differentiation among different varieties of English, it is necessary to appreciate the quantitative dimensions of some of these differences as indicated above. The actual relationships of the forms that differ-

Table 3.4. *Implicational relationship between* is *and* are *absence*

Language variety	*is* deletion	*are* deletion
Many standard varieties	0	0
Some Southern White varieties	0	1
Varieties of Vernacular Black English	1	1

entiate varieties are not nearly as simple as the categorical judgments people are sometimes prone to make, but are highly structured in some rather subtle ways. The systematic nature of the social and linguistic influences on fluctuating forms indicates one aspect of this detailed patterning.

Implicational relations between the varieties of English

In the preceding discussion, we have focused on the systematic aspects of the quantitative dimension of language differences in the varieties of English. This is not, however, the only way in which the relations between varieties of language may be viewed. Another way of looking at the relationship between varieties of English is through the consideration of various combinations of language structures. Varieties of English do not distribute themselves randomly in terms of the forms that may differentiate one variety from another. Instead, there are IMPLICATIONAL RELATIONS that hold between various forms in particular varieties.

An implicational relation in language variation holds when the presence of a particular linguistic characteristic in any variety of a language implies the presence of another characteristic in that same variety. When a form B is always present whenever a form A is present, we say that "A *implies* B."

As an example of an implicational relation, we can consider the case of COPULA deletion as it is called, i.e. the absence of a form of the verb *to be* in the present tense in such items as *You ugly* (cf. *You are ugly*) and *He ugly* (cf. *He is ugly, He's ugly*). Varieties of American English differ in the amount of copula deletion they show, and the absence of *is* implies the absence of *are*. In other words, if a variety of English shows absence of *is* in such sentences, it is sure to show also the absence of *are*, but not vice versa. This is another way of saying that some varieties of American English drop the *are* in such sentences, but do not drop the *is*.

Linguists represent implicational relations of this kind in charts where they generally use "1" to mean presence of a characteristic, "0" absence of a characteristic, and "X" variable presence of a characteristic. Table 3.4 represents the implicational relation of *is* and *are* deletion in some varieties of American English. It shows that there are varieties of English (many Standard English varieties) which have neither *is* nor *are* deletion, that there are also varieties (Black English Vernacular) which have both *is* and *are* deletion, and that there are still other varieties (some Southern White varieties) which only

Table 3.5. *Implicational array for different types of multiple negation in different varieties of English*

| English variety | | Multiple negative type | | |
	d	c	b	a
Standard English	0	0	0	0
Some Northern White nonmainstream varieties	0	0	0	X
Other Northern White nonmainstream varieties	0	0	X	X
Some Southern White nonmainstream varieties	0	X	X	X
Some varieties spoken in Appalachia	X	X	X	X
Some varieties of Black English Vernacular	X	X	X	1

have *are* deletion. Since we do not find a variety where *is* deletion is observed independent of *are* deletion we conclude that *is* copula deletion implies *are* copula deletion, but not the converse. Although we might extend the implicational table considerably beyond the one given here to represent many more details of copula deletion as it operates in a number of nonmainstream varieties of English, the basic relationship we have demonstrated here would still hold.

As we might expect, the implicational relationships that hold between the varieties of American English can sometimes be considerably more complex than our simplified illustrative case. To give a somewhat more extended picture, we can examine the case of so-called "double" or multiple negation as it is found in some varieties of English. We are essentially concerned with the syntactic pattern in English where a negative element is exhibited at more than one point in a sentence which contains an indefinite item of some type, such as a sentence like *He didn't do nothing because he was so lazy*. As it turns out, there are several different types of patterns which can potentially involve this type of negation. For our purposes we can identify four different types: (a) the realization of the negative element on all indefinites following the main verb (e.g. sentences like *He didn't do nothing because he was so lazy*), (b) the realization of a negative on an indefinite before the main verb and the placement of a negative within the main verb phrase (e.g. *Nobody can't do it because they're so dumb*), (c) the inversion of a negative of an auxiliary within the main verb phrase and an indefinite before the verb (e.g. *Can't nobody do it 'cause it's too hard*), and (d) the application of the negative element from one clause into the main verb phrase of another clause (e.g. *There wasn't much I couldn't do*, meaning something like 'There wasn't much I could do'). In Table 3.5 the three implicational symbols are used to indicate: the categorical operation of multiple negation, i.e. it is used in all cases where it might be used (1), the variable use of multiple negation, i.e. the rule may or may not apply to those cases where it could potentially apply (X), and the absence of the multiple negation, i.e. it categorically does not apply (0). Various varieties of American English are delimited in terms of the combinations of these rule applications, as indicated in the rows in Table 3.5.

One can see in Table 3.5 the detailed implicational relationships of the different negative types as typified in some representative varieties of English. If a variety has type *d* negation, then it will also have *c*, *b*, and *a*; if a variety has type *c*, then it will have both *b* and *a*; and if it has *b*, then it will necessarily have *a*. However, a variety will not have *d* but not *c*, or *b* but not *a*, and so forth.

The examination of implicational relations between various structures demonstrates two important dimensions with respect to language relationships. First of all, it gives a systematic basis for looking at the orderly relationships between varieties. Given the systematic implicational relationships, it is possible to determine the relative distance among different varieties of a language with respect to a given set of structures. For example, we may determine in Table 3.5 that the multiple negative structure in some Southern White varieties is considerably closer to that of Black English Vernacular than White Northern versions of this rule. By the same token, both Southern White varieties and Black English Vernacular are more distant from Standard English than White Northern nonmainstream varieties.

The second dimension added by implicational analysis relates to language change. Language change is an ongoing, dynamic process which takes place in a systematic way. One way of observing various stages in the process of change and which steps have preceded or will follow particular stages is to look at implicational relationships. For example, consider the case of the *h* in words such as *hit* for *it* and *hain't* for *ain't*, forms still found to some extent among speakers of American English in Appalachia and the Ozarks. At one point, *h* was found categorically for these items in both stressed and unstressed syllables. The presence of *h*, then, apparently became variable (i.e. sometimes it occurred and sometimes it didn't) in unstressed syllables while being categorically retained in stressed syllables. Next, the *h* was variably lost in both stressed and unstressed syllables, but more frequently in unstressed syllables where the change first started. If, however, it was variably lost in stressed syllables, it implied that it was lost in unstressed syllables as well, while the converse did not exist. Through time, the *h* was completely lost in unstressed syllables, while still retained variably in stressed syllables. And finally, it was lost in both stressed and unstressed syllables categorically. The stages of this change are summarized in Table 3.6. In this table 1 stands for categorical presence of *h* in *it* and *ain't*, X for variable presence, and 0 for categorical loss of the *h*.

Among American English varieties today, stages 3, 4, and 5 are still represented in some nonmainstream varieties and 5 is the Standard English usage where the loss of the *h* is complete. Ultimately, we would expect the varieties at stages 3 and 4 to carry through the change to stage 5, although we cannot predict how quickly this might take place. As found in this example, different varieties of American English may be seen to a certain extent as a reflection of ongoing language change at different stages in its progression. Based on the systematic nature of the implicational relations among forms, we can understand what steps have preceded and what steps are likely to follow in the dynamics of the change. With respect to some changes, a given variety may be ahead of others, whereas

Table 3.6. *Stages for language change in the loss of* h *in* hit *and* hain't *in American English*

	Unstressed syllables	Stressed syllables
Stage 1. Earliest stage of English, before undergoing change	1	1
Stage 2. Earlier stage of English, at start of *h* loss	X	1
Stage 3. Stages in full progress, still exhibited by some older speakers in Appalachia	X	X
Stage 4. Change progressing toward completion, exhibited by some speakers in Appalachia	0	X
Stage 5. Completed change, exhibited by most speakers of English outside of Appalachia and Ozarks and some younger speakers in Appalachia and Ozarks	0	0

with others it may be at an earlier stage. For this reason, we should resist the temptation to say that a variety spoken in some relatively isolated region such as the Appalachian or Ozark mountain range is simply a reflection of an earlier stage of English. While there are certainly retentions of older forms to be found in these areas, there are also aspects of these varieties which are more advanced in their language change than those of the surrounding mainstream varieties.

Dialect variation in American English is extensive, and is conditioned by – at least – the variables of the speaker's regional provenience, social status, ethnicity, age, and sex. Cutting across and intersecting with these variables are the dimensions of formality of style and occasion of use of the language (see Part IV of this volume). The research of dialectologists and sociolinguists has established some of the basic facts of variation in American English, but we are far from having an adequate picture of the present diversity or an adequate understanding of how the diversity is changing.

FURTHER READING

The regional aspects of diversity in American English are presented in the publications of the dialect geographers. Shuy 1967 and Reed 1977 provide summaries of this work intended for popular audiences. McDavid 1958 is an excellent account of the American dialect situation as known at that time, and McDavid 1979a, b provide articles which reflect the history of dialect geography in the United States. Originally conceived in 1929 as a comprehensive Linguistic Atlas of the United States, the atlas work has developed into a series of autonomous but interrelated projects. The results of investigations in different sections of the USA are available as follows: New England: Kurath et al. 1939–43, reprinted 1972; the Upper Midwest: Allen 1973–6; the Middle and South Atlantic states: Kurath et al. 1979; the North-Central states: Marckwardt et al. 1976–8; California and Nevada: Reed et al. forthcoming; Oklahoma: Van Riper et al. forthcoming; the Gulf states: Pederson et al. forthcoming. Work on many of the regional projects continues; for example, the Linguistic Atlas of the Middle and South Atlantic States, the largest and most comprehensive of the regional atlases, contains more than one million words and phrases, and is being prepared for publication in a tabular format. Interpretive summaries are available for some of the regional surveys; for example, Kurath 1949, Atwood 1953, and Kurath and McDavid 1961 for New England and the Middle and South Atlantic states, and Bright 1971 for California and Nevada. *The Dictionary of American Regional English (DARE)*, forthcoming, edited by Cassidy, will provide regional identification of thousands of lexical items, with examples of their uses from spoken and written sources.

The social aspects of diversity in American English are presented in several studies carried out in metropolitan areas in the 1960s and early 1970s. Labov's *The Social Stratification of English in New York City* (1966) was the pioneering work, followed by Shuy, Wolfram, and Riley 1967 and Wolfram 1969. Discussions of the language use in urban centers and the methodology of sociolinguists studying social variation in language appear in Labov 1972a, b.

Shopen 1980 provides an introduction to selected aspects of dialect diversity by actively involving the reader in the analysis of data. Traugott and Pratt 1980 is an introduction to linguistics with emphasis on the uses of linguistic analysis for studying literature; Chapter 8, "Varieties of English: regional, social, and ethnic," is the best coverage of literary dialect available. Wolfram and Fasold 1974 emphasizes the social dimensions of diversity, with a fairly comprehensive discussion of specific socially diagnostic structures. The collection of papers in Shores 1972, particularly Section I, looks at the regional and ethnic dimensions of variation through specific examples. Another collection, from a different perspective, is Williamson and Burke 1971. Brewer and Brandes 1976 provide discussions of issues related to controversies surrounding dialects.

Research on language variation by sex of speaker or addressee is presented in the collection of papers by Thorne and Henley 1975 (2nd edn. Thorne, Henley, and Kramarae 1980), which includes an extensive bibliography. Jespersen 1922, Chapter 13, provides the only extensive treatment of sex differences in language use in early general works on language. The most comprehensive and widely quoted articles are Key 1972 and Lakoff 1973a; both have been expanded into books, Key 1975 and Lakoff 1975, and both have been widely quoted (and sometimes loosely interpreted) in journalistic and popular treatments of sexism in language (e.g. Miller and Swift 1976). A popular source on sex differences in conversational interaction is Parlee 1979. A newsletter, *Women and Language*, produced by the Stanford University Department of Linguistics, links a network of scholars working on widely varying aspects of women's language.

4

Creoles of the USA*

PATRICIA C. NICHOLS

Three unique languages have developed in the United States and are spoken only there: Gullah, Louisiana Créole, and Hawaiian Creole. Few people have actually heard these languages spoken, and public awareness of them has come chiefly through dialect literature of the following kind:

WEGITUBBLE MAN

"Cucombuh! String-bean! Tettuh! Squash!
    Tuhmatuh! Tu'nip! Beet!
Whoa, dey, you mule! Ah yeddy woice
    Ub lady 'cross de street!
W'at, madam, is you wan' fuh day? . . .
    Tuhmatuh an' string-bean?
Some tettuh, too? . . . All right, mah Miss.
    Jes' lemme tote um een.

"Good medjuh? Yaas, ma'am, Ah is try
    Fuh alsway gib w'at right;
Ah ain' gwine cheat you; ent you know
    Ah nebbuh medjuh light?
De Good Book l'arn me w'at fuh do,
    An' w'en Ah claim by de't',
Ah wan' good medjuh gib tuh *me* –
    W'en dese ole eye be shet."
(Colcock and Colcock 1942: 7)

This narrative poem of the vegetable vendor peddling his goods and concerned with "good measure," both for his customers and ultimately for himself as well, is told in the Gullah of the Carolina low country. Interest in this language, as in the other two U.S. creoles, has been expressed chiefly through literature up until the present century. In the past two decades, linguists, as well as social scientists and educators, have become interested in these languages for what they might tell us about universal and social processes which are exemplified through language. Policy planners have begun to consider these creoles as national resources. As

---

* Several scholars have contributed bibliographic information and critical comments on material in this chapter: Charles W. Joyner and William A. Stewart on Gullah, Raleigh Morgan, Jr. on Louisiana Créole, and Richard R. Day on Hawaiian Creole. None of them is to be held accountable for its final form.

representations of unique responses to language problems facing settlers in a new land, the three creoles represent both a gift from the past and a problem for the future. They are indigenous to the American scene, but bring with them no clues as to how best to incorporate them into the linguistic and cultural plurality that is now a prime characteristic of that scene.

Definitions

The term CREOLE is used here in the linguistic sense of a language which develops from a PIDGIN or contact language. As such, it is a general term which refers to a language type and not just to a particular language. Many creoles exist throughout the world; some present world languages which are widely used in both commerce and scholarship were once creoles. A pidgin typically arises in trade or contact situations where speakers do not share a common language. It is a spoken language, reduced in both function and structure from the full language on which it is based. Typically, it will have no INFLECTIONS which mark grammatical categories like number, gender, and tense, as in the following example from West African Pidgin English of Nigeria:

i kom fo wi haos
'he/she/it came/comes to our house'

The vocabulary used in the pidgin will be based on the language of speakers having the superior social status in the social situations in which it is spoken. The grammar will be drastically reduced from that of either of the first languages known to its speakers. A creole is structurally more complex than a pidgin, though some scholars have noted that the pidgin/creole dichotomy represents an idealization, in that no definite point of transition from pidgin to creole can be identified. A creole characteristically develops when the children of pidgin speakers hear the pidgin spoken frequently by parents and other relatives who do not share each other's native languages. Such families adopt and adapt the pidgin as their home language, expanding it in form and function to meet the need for a full language which is adequate for a whole range of communicative needs. In the process, a creole evolves as a separate language, recognizably different in important respects from any of the source languages of the pidgin.

One cautionary note on the definition of creole as used by linguists: this definition differs from an earlier colonial use of the term to refer to children of European parents born in the colonies, and later extended to cover all non-European peoples in colonial settings (see Chapters 9 and 10). In Louisiana the term "creole" is still often used to refer both to descendants of French and Spanish colonists and to the variety of colonial French still spoken in some parts of the state, as well as for the pidgin-derived Créole French originally spoken only by descendants of West African slaves. The literature on the language varieties spoken in Louisiana is often confusing on this point. A recent government publication on bilingual schooling in the USA differs crucially from the definition used here; Mizrahi (1970) uses the older meaning of creole to refer to the regional varieties of French spoken by Acadian and French descendants primarily. These varieties of French are the standard DIALECT of Louisiana French (probably near extinction and spoken chiefly near New Orleans) and the Acadian or Cajun dialect (originally spoken in rural areas of upper Louisiana settled by Canadian immigrants in the eighteenth century). Being substantially similar in PHONOLOGY, grammar, and vocabulary to varieties of French spoken in other parts of the world, both the colonial standard French of New Orleans and the Cajun French of the countryside are dialects of French. The Créole French (originally spoken by West African slaves and their descendants on plantations in the Louisiana colony) is structurally very different from these other two varieties of French, and is the only language variety spoken in Louisiana which is considered a creole in the linguistic definition of the term.

Since the beginning of the twentieth century, serious scholarly attention has been devoted to pidgins and creoles. A considerable body of scholarship now exists and has been catalogued in an excellent annotated bibliography (Reinecke, Tsuzaki, De Camp, Hancock, and Wood 1975). A quarterly newsletter keeps scholars and an interested public aware of more recent publications and ongoing research (Reinecke and Tsuzaki 1977).

Early work on pidgins and creoles was done in relative isolation from similar work conducted elsewhere. Perhaps as a reflection of this isolation, earliest theories on the origins of pidgins and creoles emphasized the "simplified" nature of pidgins and posited that the trade or colonial situation had given rise to a crude, makeshift medium of communication each time the need arose. The similarity between such makeshift languages and "baby talk" was often noted. Called the POLYGENETIC theory of pidgin origins, these early views maintained that each creole and its antecedent pidgin represented individual developments which were repeated in parallel situations all over the world. More recent work on baby talk and child language indicates that all languages have such a REGISTER, which shows important universal trends of language and language change. In this light, the early descriptions of pidgins as similar to "baby talk" point to a more important generalization, missed by the polygenetic theory of pidgin origins. This early theory fails to explain the widespread similarities noted in the structure of pidgins and creoles throughout the world. A later MONOGENETIC theory takes into account the striking structural similarities found between these languages in different geographic locations. In one version of this later theory, a single original pidgin – probably Sabir of the middle ages – is seen as the ancestor of all creole languages. As this pidgin was introduced into new trade situations where unknown languages were spoken to the pidgin speakers, it was successively "relexified" with new vocabulary from the newly encountered languages, while retaining most of its original grammatical structures. This monogenetic theory fails to account for successful transmission on the basis of very limited contact, especially in language situations like that of Hawaii. More recently, work on linguistic universals, stimulated by the pioneering work of Joseph Greenberg (1966), has led some scholars to look for the origins of pidgins and creoles in universal potentials of fundamental attributes which exist across languages neither genetically nor geographically related. The

72 PATRICIA C. NICHOLS

Figure 4.1. Coastal South Carolina and Georgia (based on an original map by Frank H. Nichols, Jr.)

LANGUAGE UNIVERSALS theory overcomes problems inherent in both the monogenetic and polygenetic theories. It has also stimulated new study of pidgins and creoles as potential sources of insight into linguistic universals. To take only one example, the absence of a COPULA, or verb *to be*, has been widely noted for a variety of pidgins. The hypothesis is that all languages which normally use such a copula will tend to omit it in varieties of simplified speech. This hypothesis has led, in turn, to insight into the potential relationship between simplified registers across languages and the development of pidgins. Ferguson and Debose (1977) speculate that simplified registers are addressed to people whose knowledge of the community's language is felt to be less than normal: babies, foreigners, deaf people, etc. BROKEN LANGUAGE, or imperfect approximations of a language by speakers of another language, is used by those speakers in the process of learning a new language. When both simplified register and broken language are used in the same communicative situation, a pidgin typically results. Scholars working within the language universals theory have noted processes of language change common to both developing pidgins and creoles and to early child language acquisition and have begun to develop a theory of natural SYNTAX. The potential impact of the language universals view of pidgins and creoles extends beyond the study of such languages in and of themselves, and promises to expand our understanding of all language as dynamic and continually subject to systematic variation.

Gullah

Of the three U.S. creoles, Gullah and Louisiana Créole French were probably contemporaries. Known also as Geechee or Sea Island Creole, Gullah is indigenous to the coastal South Carolina strip between Georgetown and Beaufort (see Figure 4.1), where the early colony's rice plantations existed in the 1700s. Some scholars argue for an earlier origin on the upper Guinea Coast of West Africa before the colonial settlement of South Carolina, maintaining that Gullah was brought to the colony as a fully developed creole rather than as a pidgin. Today the creole is spoken primarily by Black inhabitants of coastal South Carolina and Georgia, portions of lower North Carolina, and northern Florida. The number of speakers at present is unknown, though estimates as high as 300,000 have been made. There are no purely creole speakers, but only those who show greater or lesser use of creole features along a continuum of language use ranging from creole to a dialect of English. The following sample of Gullah speech was collected in the South Carolina Sea Islands in the early part of this century:

wɛn dɪ yaŋkɪ kʌm tru, ɒɪ bɪn ʌp dɪ kʌntrɪ. an i ɟɪt dɪ
fɒɪə n sɛt dɪ hɐus fɒɪə – sɛ̃t dɪ bɪg hɐus əfɒɪə. an i tʌk ɐut ɛwɪtɪŋ
ɐut dɪ hɐus. i dʌn ɪt; dɪ yaŋkɪ dʌn ɪt – tʌk ɲut ɛwɪtɪŋ
ɐũt dɪ hɐus, n ca əm owə dɪ ʌɽə sɐɪd ɒn dɪ strɪt n ɟi
əm sʌmbɒɽɪ dɛ. bət i sɛ̃t dɪ hɐus əfɒɪə. an dɛn ɪf yu kɒl,
"yɛs, sʌ; yɛs, mɒsə," i sɛ̃: "hu ɪz yu kɒlɪn mɒsə? tu gɒt no
mɒsə. ɒɪ kʌm tu fri yu, an doncu lɛ mi – lɒj ɪz ɒɪ yɛ, dõ lɛ mi
yɛ yu kɒl ɛm mɒsə."

'When the Yankee come through, I been up the country. And he get the fire and set the house afire – set the big house afire. And he took out everything out the house. He done it; the Yankee done it – took out everything out the house and carry it over [to] the other side on the street and give it [to] somebody there. But he set the house afire. And then if you call, "Yes, sir; yes, master," he say: "Who is you calling master? You got no master. I come to free you, and don't you let me – long as I here, don't let me hear you call him master." '

("The Yankee" by Rosina Cohen, Edisto Island, South Carolina, transcribed and translated in Turner 1949: 280–1)

In the 1970s the following sample was obtained from a 9-year-old girl in Georgetown County, South Carolina:

CHRISTMAS

When Christmas come I had gone to my Aunt —— house. Then my aunt say have to beat my little sister 'cause she had, she had broke a glass, with the cocoa in um. And then we had gone up to we other cousin house name ——. And then we had see–then we–then that night we had gone up to Jerome. Then when we come from there, the dog had come and bite my little sister and my little sister say, "Owww, Ooooo." And then ee say, "Unnn." And then she–and then after that–Monday, we–I had gone to my aunt house fuh see my baby sister. And then we had gone and play. And then I had ride her bicycle. And she bicycle had broke. And —— say, "Oh, ——, see what you done do: broke that girl bicycle."

   I say, "I ain't do um; you do um 'cause you want me fuh tote you."

(Transcription based on standard orthography)

Typically the speech of those in their seventies and eighties who had no formal schooling and the speech of children who have not yet been to school will show greater use of creole features, in most social situations, than will the speech of others in the same households who have had more exposure to schooling. There is great variation in language use along the continuum, both on the part of entire speech communities and on the part of the same speaker in different speech situations. Children by the age of 8 or 9 years can switch from creole to more standard usage for the benefit of their teachers in the schools, who frequently do not understand the creole. Sometimes an older child will caution a younger sibling about talking that "country talk" in front of an outsider.

   Structurally, Gullah shows important differences in the nominal and verbal systems from the English to which it is related. In its nominal system, the third person singular pronouns were probably originally *ee* and *um*, forms which give no indication of gender and distinguish between only objective and "all other" cases:

ee must-a hide in them-wood or something	[he]
he took *ee* mother long with um	[his]
Miss Hassel had – *ee* had all kinds of flowers	[she]
and *ee* was foggy, and they couldn't see	[it]
but I ain't see she fuh tell *um* nothing	[her]
I ain't know fuh get *um* off	[it]

Today usage is highly variable, with *he* often used to refer to females and *she* sometimes used in object position:

if *he* see me, *he* blow ee car	[she]
but I ain't see *she* . . .	[her]

Nouns show no inflections for number and possession; word order is used to indicate both:

there was this big snake with *two horn*
we go in our *cousin car*

In the verbal system, tense marking is greatly reduced from that of English. One verb form can be used to indicate both past and present tense:

P —— *get* up when the chicken crowing	[past]

The copula, or verb *to be*, is generally not required in equative clauses:

he ugly

ASPECT is expanded from that characteristic of English, with the addition of habitual aspect:

this summer, when my daddy *be* work*ing*,
they always have lot of peaches   [habitual]

Progressive aspect, or on-going action, can be indicated by *duh*, while perfective aspect, or completed action, can be indicated by *done*:

Gregg *duh* hide   [progressive]
I *done* know   [perfective]

The number of basic prepositions of place is smaller than that of English, with *to* being used to indicate both "position at" and "movement toward."

can we stay *to* the table?

This reduction is similar to that found in other English-related creoles in the Caribbean, except that in those creoles *at* is the form chosen to indicate both meanings. The *fuh*-complementizer, used to introduce infinitive clauses in Gullah, is similar to that found in Hawaiian Creole and other English-related creoles in the Caribbean:

I come *fuh* get my coat

Multiple negation is common, with *ain't, not,* and *don't* used as the principal negators:

I *ain't* want to leave this sunshine-world
these books must be *don't* like me *no* more

In phonology, there are similarities between the vowels of Gullah and those of certain West African languages, which are almost certainly the ones serving as source languages for the pidgin ancestor of Gullah. There is a smaller vowel inventory than exists for English. Earlier in this century a number of West African vocabulary items could be found in Gullah, but these have largely passed out of use. A few West African plant and animal names can still be heard (*goober* 'peanut,' *cooter* 'turtle'). One of the personal pronouns is occasionally used in its original form (*yunna* 'you' (pl.)), as is the term for outsiders (*buckra* 'white man').

There is more known about Gullah than about either of the other two U.S. creoles. Its existence in the United States dates back to the original thirteen colonies, and an extensive popular literature utilizes features of both the language and style of West African stories. The stories of Ambrose Gonzales (1969) have probably circulated most widely, and the novels and Gullah sketches of Pulitzer Prize winner Julia Peterkin (1970) are perhaps the best written. We have considerable knowledge of the linguistic characteristics of Gullah because of the work of

76 PATRICIA C. NICHOLS

Lorenzo Dow Turner in the early part of this century. A Black linguist familiar with several West African languages, Turner studied Gullah in the Sea Islands for a period of fifteen years. His provision of Gullah narratives at the conclusion of his analysis of Gullah vocabulary and phonology allows for comparisons with the language as it is spoken today (Turner 1949).

Despite the body of popular stories and linguistic studies which exist for Gullah, there has been virtually no recognition of the creole within public policy. With the provision of public schools for all Black children in the state of South Carolina in the 1950s, in anticipation of integration, many Gullah-speaking children received the opportunity for education for the first time. Instruction and instructional materials, however, were totally in English. Because segregated schools were still the norm during this decade, all of their teachers were Black and many understood the creole. Such teachers could and did provide help for the children in making the transition from the creole to a dialect of English; all such help was strictly informal, however, and totally unsupported by the educational establishment of the state. When integration became a reality in the 1960s, Gullah-speaking children often found themselves under the instruction of teachers who had never heard the creole, had been given no instruction in its systematic differences from English, and had to resort to the use of other children as "interpreters" for their Gullah-speaking classmates. This situation still obtains today in areas where Gullah is spoken. The high levels of illiteracy in the region are regularly bemoaned in educational circles and an extensive adult education program has been under-way in South Carolina since the mid-1960s, but there is little official recognition of the basic language differences which might be the source of widespread reading problems among the Black population.

There are a few indications that public awareness of the creole is growing in ways that might affect public policy. In 1975 the Charleston County School Board asked William A. Stewart to draw up a program to instruct teachers in Gullah, an indication that at least some public officials are aware of the educational implications of having teachers assigned to instruct students whose language they do not understand and who, in turn, do not understand the teacher's language and communicative expectations. Stewart observes that acceptance and recognition of Gullah varies in individual schools and that lack of comprehension between Gullah and English speakers is widespread throughout the school system. In 1976 an annual symposium on Language and Culture was begun at the University of South Carolina, focusing on the rich linguistic and cultural heritage of that state and including scholarly input from throughout the nation. In late 1977 a Reading Conference was held at The Citadel, one of the leading colleges in coastal South Carolina, with one of its major sessions devoted to instructional techniques for the Gullah-speaking child. One recent project funded by the U.S. Department of Labor deserves mention as the kind of public recognition of Gullah which may well be on the horizon in educational policy. In the South Carolina port of Beaufort, the Sea Island Language Project was established in 1976 to teach English as a second language to Gullah-speaking adults in order to enhance their job opportunities. Though the project was a small one, with only forty students, its impact may be significant if it and similar projects attain widespread community support.

In the public schools, a few individual teachers have begun to use the language experience approach to reading in order to incorporate some measure of the children's language into the curriculum, but no officially sanctioned materials based on Gullah have been used by the public schools to date. That creole-speaking children may not be receiving equal educational opportunities in classrooms where a dialect of English is the medium of instruction is potentially a subject for consideration under provisions for BILINGUAL EDUCATION (see Chapter 21).

Louisiana Créole

The Créole French of Louisiana developed about the same time and under similar conditions as Gullah in South Carolina. Also known as Gombo or Negro French, it evolved as the native language of descendants of West African slaves brought to southern Louisiana by French colonists (see Figure 4.2). Senegal is reported to have been their major country of origin. Today the number of creole speakers is unknown and the status of the creole itself is uncertain. Louisiana Créole co-exists with two dialects of French and a regional variety of English; in this situation a certain amount of leveling has taken place, and all language varieties show influences from the others.

The following sample of Louisiana Créole was collected by Raleigh Morgan in Saint Martin Parish during the 1950s. It consists of the opening lines of an animal tale about Compere Lapin and his dupe, Compere Bouki:

ɛ̃ fwa lapɛ̃ di: buki anɔ̃ fɛ rekɔl
buki di: nu va gɛ̃ pu travaj
lapɛ̃ di: nu sape travaj pu nu mɛ̃m
buki di: sa nu va plãte
lapɛ̃ repɔ̃n: nu va plãte mai
buki: sa nu va fɛ avɛk mai
lapɛ̃ repɔ̃n: nu va mule mai-la pu fɛ djigrij e lafarin mai
nu va fɛ kuškuš pu mwɛ̃ e twa mãže
sa va ãpɛše nuzɔt vɔle
sa fɛ e plãtɛ mai. jɛ fɛ jɛ mai
kã jɛ mai tɛ fɛt, lapɛ̃ kɔnɛ̃ buki t alɛ vɔle

'Une fois le lapin dit: Bouki, allons faire la récolte. Bouki dit: Il nous faudra travailler? Le lapin dit: nous travaillons pour nous-mêmes. Bouki dit: que'est-ce que nous allons planter? Le lapin répond: nous allons planter du maïs. Bouki: qu'est-ce que nous allons faire avec ce maïs? Le lapin répond: nous allons mouler le maïs pour faire du gru et de la farine de maïs. Nous allons faire du couche-couche pour nos repas. Ça va nous empêcher de voler. Ils font ça: et ils plantent le maïs. Quand le maïs est prêt, le lapin sait que Bouki allait le voler.'

(Morgan 1975: 23–4)

A brief account of the settlement history of the Louisiana territory helps make clear the great complexity of the present language situation there. For the greater

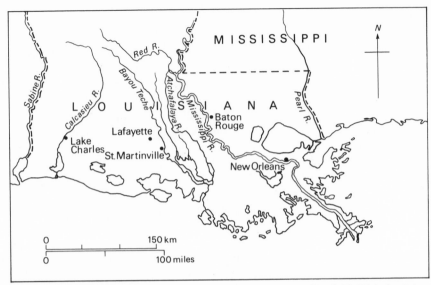

Figure 4.2. Southern Louisiania (based on an original map by Frank H. Nichols, Jr.)

part of the eighteenth century, Louisiana was a colony of France, and its settlers
spoke a colonial dialect similar to the French of Touraine or Orléans. The
common practice of wealthy families was to send their sons back to France for an
education, a practice which helped maintain the standard features of the dialect.
Slaves from a variety of West African countries were brought to work the indigo
plantations, speaking several West African languages. Cut off from their home
countries, they needed a language of mutual intelligibility; a French-related creole
developed among them. In the latter part of the eighteenth century, large numbers
of Acadians immigrated to Louisiana from Nova Scotia; these immigrants spoke a
less prestigious dialect of French than the original settlers, which was similar to the
"patois" of Normandy, Picardy, and Saintonge. At about the same time, the
colony was sold by France to Spain and received some Spanish settlers and
officials (see Chapter 9). Widespread intermarriage between the original French
colonists and the Spanish, as well as the established influence of French, ensured
the continued use of French until the colony was retroceded to France in 1800.
Shortly after the turn of the century, France sold the Louisiana Territory to the
United States, opening the door to the influence of English. The famous battle with
the British at New Orleans at the close of the war of 1812 asserted U.S. interest in
the territory, and many settlers from other southern states migrated to Louisiana
and established plantations of sugar and cotton. By 1840, more than half the
population was Black, though it is not known what portion were speakers of
Créole French. It is even possible that many were Gullah speakers, brought from
eastern states to work the new plantations. For forty years after Louisiana became
part of the United States, French was used along with English in public transactions (see Chapter 12). Three varieties of French were spoken: the original

standard dialect of the early colonists, the Créole French of their West African slaves, and the Cajun dialect of the Canadian immigrants. Little English was studied in schools; a French-English interpreter was used in the legislature; both French and English were used in the courts. As late as the 1880s laws were still published in both French and English, but the use of French apparently declined after the war of 1860, which required the southern states to find a common ground and to minimize their differences. In 1864 the Louisiana constitution decreed that English was to be the language of instruction in public schools, and the use of French in official places gradually diminished. By 1959 the prestigious colonial dialect had practically disappeared, though the Acadian dialect was still widely spoken. Today, Acadian French and Créole French often coexist, particularly in rural areas where schooling has been limited. Often both are spoken by Blacks and Cajuns, though with certain differences for each ethnic group. Great variation exists and a certain amount of DIALECT LEVELING has taken place in such a language contact situation. DIGLOSSIC situations exist in which families use a dialect of French or English with outsiders, but Créole French with each other.

Although the structural description of Louisiana Créole French which follows will be based primarily on older accounts, it should be recognized that the language as it is spoken today shows great influence from the language varieties with which it coexists. As early as the 1930s, the tendency to mix "Negro-French" and "standard" Louisiana French was noted, especially as Black and White speakers conversed together. Today, with the increasingly rare use of the original colonial dialect, contact is more likely to be between the creole and the Acadian dialect.

Though it is a French-related creole and primarily French in vocabulary, Louisiana Créole shows important structural similarities to the English-related creoles. In its nominal system, gender is not marked; *li* is used as the third person singular pronoun for both masculine and feminine gender:

li viṇi pu-mõte āho-la
'she/he managed to climb up there'

Personal pronouns are *mo, to, li, nu, vu, ye*. Like Gullah, Louisiana Créole has both singular and plural forms for the second person pronoun. *La* is the definite article for either gender:

mo met mua sarše apre ti-košõ-*la*　　　　　[masc.]
'I set myself to looking for the little pig'
li kup *la*-kɔrd kup li kup *la*-kɔrd　　　　　[fem.]
'he cuts the string'

For nouns and adjectives, the masculine form is generally used exclusively. In the verbal system, one form can be used to indicate both past and present; the particle *te* can also indicate past tense:

mo kup
'I run'

mo *te* kupe
'I ran'

The future is formed by adding the particles *a* or *ale* before the verb:

m'*a* kupe; m*ale* kupe
'I will run'

The particle *ape* can indicate progressive aspect:

m'*ape* kupe
'I am running'
mo te'*pe* kupe
'I was running'

At the earlier stage of the creole, no copula (or verb *to be*) was used in equative clauses. Also like Gullah, Louisiana Créole does not regularly use a passive construction. Other structural features include the use of *pas* as a negator (compare the *ne . . . pas* of French), *en* to mean both 'en' and 'sur,' *au ras* to mean both 'dans' and 'près,' omission of *a* and *de,* and the use of *pu* for 'pour' or the expression of purpose.

In the most complete description of the creole's phonology, Morgan (1959) reports the use of four front and four back vowels, with no SCHWA or front rounded vowels except in borrowings from English or Acadian French. Consonant clusters occur, but many are unstable; both final consonants and final syllables can be lost. Often the definite article is compounded with the noun which follows it:

lɔm
'the man'

Throughout the literature on Louisiana Créole the use of African vocabulary items is often noted, but the basic vocabulary is derived from French.

Our knowledge of this creole comes primarily from brief articles appearing in scholarly journals since the late nineteenth century. There is no full-scale treatment like that of Turner for Gullah and Reinecke for Hawaiian Creole. Popular literature is represented by Fortier's collection (1894) of a few folktales; there also are reports of oral "Gombo" versions of the Brer Rabbit stories, similar to the ones told by Joel Chandler Harris in English and Gullah. A linguistic description of Louisiana Créole was published by Fortier (1884–5), but modern scholarship dates from Lane's study of Saint Martin Parish in 1935. The same parish has been studied by Raleigh Morgan since the 1950s; most recently he has undertaken a study of variation in the creole copula. It is hoped that a broad study of linguistic change in Louisiana Créole will be undertaken before the opportunity is lost. Scholars have noted the importance of such an investigation to French dialectology and to linguistic theory generally.

Recognition of Louisiana Créole in public policy appears to be nonexistent. Recent descriptions of the language situation in Louisiana indicate that many Black and White speakers in rural areas understand both Créole and Acadian dialect, and that the creole and the dialect may in fact be merging. The degree of mutual comprehension is not known, nor is it known how many monolingual speakers of creole still exist. Bradley (1976) reports that in the parish of Lafayette, over 30 percent of the Black population above the age of 25 have had no formal education. Since Blacks who have had no schooling are almost certain to be creole speakers, there must be a substantial number of families for whom the creole is the primary home language. Children from such homes would enter school as monolingual creole speakers. In bilingual programs instituted by the state and federal governments since 1968, the creole receives no recognition. According to Bradley, bilingual programs funded by the federal government are geared primarily to children whose first language is Acadian French, while those funded by the state and directed by the Council for the Development of French in Louisiana (CODOFIL) are concerned with teaching standard French as a second language to English-dominant students. The state has provided money since 1972 for a pilot program which brings teaching assistants from France to teach in selected elementary schools. In such classrooms, the variety of French used and taught is similar to that of the colonial dialect which has almost disappeared from use in Louisiana. In such a climate, the creole is ignored and the Acadian dialect may sometimes be disparaged. To remedy this lack of recognition, a study of the extent to which Louisiana Créole is spoken by children entering Louisiana schools is particularly needed. Only with such information can steps then be taken to ensure that creole-speaking children receive equal educational opportunities as those children who are instructed in their own first language. As should be clear from the structural description above, the creole's differences from both French and English are substantial.

Hawaiian Creole

Hawaiian Creole arose much later than either Gullah or Louisiana Créole – in the nineteenth century according to most accounts or in the early twentieth century in the view of some recent scholars. Known to many inhabitants of the islands as Pidgin English or simply as Pidgin, the language is not considered to be a creole by all observers. As the description which follows will indicate, however, it shows distinctive structural characteristics and variation characteristics of a language which has evolved from a pidgin. What is referred to as "Pidgin" by local Hawaiians is here considered a creole. The lack of unanimimity in its characterization may reflect its recent origins, as well as the great variation in use among speakers from a variety of ethnic groups. Like Gullah, it is an English-related creole with a vocabulary which is basically English. Unlike either Gullah or Louisiana Créole, the source languages of the antecedent pidgin had no West African roots.

The need for such a language in the Hawaiian Islands (see Figure 4.3) arose in the latter half of the nineteenth century, when they became a plantation colony dominated by English speakers from the U.S. mainland. To work the plantations, a system of contract labor was used to supplement that of the indigenous Hawaiian population, and workers were brought from parts of East Asia, the

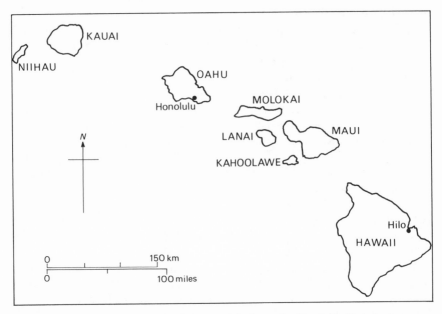

Figure 4.3. Hawaiian Islands (based on an original map by Frank H. Nichols, Jr.)

South Pacific, and southern Europe. The highly unstable pidgin which serves as the source of Hawaiian Creole received input from Hawaiian, Japanese, Chinese, and Portuguese, as well as English. In recent years, Filipino languages such as Ilocano have also had some influence. According to recent estimates, somewhat less than half of Hawaii's present population of 788,000 are now habitually creole speakers. Most inhabitants of Hawaii speak a dialect of English which is similar to other varieties of mainland American English. Probably less than 5 percent continue to speak an English-related pidgin in addition to their first language, and these speakers are primarily elderly immigrants.

The following sample of Hawaiian Creole speech was obtained from a recording made by William Labov of a conversation between three teenage boys from the island of Oahu.

TRANSCRIPTION	TRANSLATION
B: aᵉ tɛl yu dis##	I tell you this.
hæd wʌn fɛsɪn ɪn dea	Had one pheasant in there
H: o əp baᵉ da rænč ɪn molokaᵉ	Oh, up by the ranch in Molokai
mi æn buli æn maᵉ kʌsɪn	me and Buli and my cousin
go æh##ɛvⁱ taᵉm wi wɛn go	go, eh. Every time we wen go
fo kɛč da čɪkɪn sʌmbʌdi hæda	for catch the chicken somebody
stat da kah##	hadda start the car.
æh yu go tə græb hə	Ah, you go to grab her,
dɛn da fɛsɪn flaᵉ we	then the pheasant fly away.
A: fɛsɪn čɪkɪn fak##	Pheasant, chicken, fuck.
yu tɛl yu go fo græb	You tell you go for grab

da čikɨn da fɛsɪn rʌn   the chicken the pheasant run
we##yu min yu gaᵉz waz   away. You mean you guys was
kɛčɨn fɛsɪn   catching pheasant?
H: da fɛsɪn   The pheasant.
B: yæ   Yeah.
H we laᵉk it əm   We like eat it.
A: izi fo kɛ̃č   Easy for catch?
H: izi   Easy.

(Day: 1972a: 34–5)

     Several approaches have been used to describe the range of variation character-istic of language use in Hawaii. Reinecke described a "continuum of mastery" in his 1935 study (published in 1969). Such a continuum ranged from the poorly pronounced and greatly simplified speech of the uneducated laborer at the one end of the scale, to the speech of the exceptional immigrant or descendants of immigrants at the other end who use fluent and adequate English but whose speech reflects a touch of the foreign accent and idioms peculiar to the primary language group. Tsuzaki (Hymes 1971) has described Hawaii's language situa-tion in terms of three coexistent systems – a pidgin, creole, and dialect of English – none of which occurs in unadulterated forms but only in combinations of different proportions. More recently a study under the direction of Derek Bickerton at the University of Hawaii has begun to describe the linguistic continuum in terms of a series of *lects,* or varieties of language, ranging from the most conservative speech spoken on the islands of Kauai and Hawaii to the most highly decreolized varieties used on the main island of Oahu, which contains three-fourths of the state's population and where the university and state gov-ernment offices are located.

     Reinecke (1969) provides a comprehensive history of the language interaction which has taken place in the islands since the latter part of the eighteenth century, when Hawaii became a stopping place for trade vessels. At this early period a few foreigners of European background settled in the islands and learned the indigenous Hawaiian language. Hawaiians themselves shipped as sailors on European vessels and learned the languages of their crews. During the early nineteenth century when the sandalwood trade and whaling industry flourished, interpreters were available in the islands for trading purposes. The coming of the Protestant missionaries from the U.S. mainland in the early nineteenth century influenced language change extensively. With their emphasis on reading the Christian scriptures in one's own native language, these missionaries quickly learned the Hawaiian language and devised an alphabet to represent it in writing. They established schools to teach reading and writing, and formal literacy became almost universal, with the native language used as a carrier of European ideas. By 1839 the Bible had been translated into Hawaiian. Government documents were written in Hawaiian for some years, and also translated into English. Later English was used exclusively for these documents, as English-speaking advisers to the Hawaiian monarch gained in influence and power. Foreign immigration grew, much money was invested in large sugar cane plantations, and the native population was diminished by disease and through intermarriage with the foreigners. The plantations were worked initially by native laborers, but in 1852 the first contract laborers were imported from China and this system continued until the end of the century. The contract laborers who came were usually young bachelors, some of whom married native women or women from other ethnic groups. They lived isolated lives on rural plantations, not free to leave as long as their contracts were in effect. As soon as their term of labor was up, however, many moved into other occupations in less isolated settings. Besides the Chinese, other large groups who came were the Japanese, Koreans, Filipinos, Puerto Ricans, and Portuguese. Minor groups included Spanish, Germans, Norwegians, Russians, Galician Poles, and South Sea Islanders.

Reinecke points out that the servile conditions which obtained for contract laborers in Hawaii were similar to those which had existed earlier for West African slave laborers in South Carolina, Louisiana, and other parts of the Americas. Crucial for language development, contact with the homelands was broken, and speakers of many diverse languages were thrown together in situations necessitating a common medium of communication. Assimilation with the dominant population was not possible for groups which had significant cultural and racial differences from the dominant group. In Hawaii, where so many different cultural groups have come together, those groups with a European heritage have been more easily assimilated into the dominant mainland population and have risen to positions of power and prestige much faster than those of non-European heritage. The need for a makeshift language among nonassimilated groups who communicated with each other and with the dominant group precipitated the rise of a pidgin soon after the arrival of the Chinese and Portuguese laborers in the mid-1800s. Reinecke maintains that the early Pidgin English was historically related to the *hapa haole* ('half stranger') speech of the earlier whaling days. Bickerton and Odo (1976) disagree on this point, suggesting that the early *hapa haole* was a Hawaiian pidgin, not English. They argue that a true Anglo-Pidgin did not develop before the twentieth century. Studies now underway on the language situation in Hawaii should shed more light on this and other questions about the early pidgin which preceded Hawaiian Creole. What should be clear from the social and historical conditions outlined here is that conditions were favorable for the development of an English-related pidgin and creole at some point.

After the close of the nineteenth century, when the Hawaiian monarchy was overthrown and sovereignty was transferred to the United States, the status of English as the dominant language was assured. Thereafter, the native Hawaiian language was essentially confined to the home, with English used in most spheres of public life. A colonial dialect of English began to develop in some segments of the population, simultaneously with the creole spoken by second and third generation descendants of immigrants in some ethnic groups. The formal schooling which has been widespead in the island since the coming of the Protestant missionaries has favored the merger of the two language varieties. Since 1898,

English has been the primary language of instruction in the schools, and education has been widely available. The development of a homogeneous people for whom English is the only language of citizenry has been a stated goal of educational policy since 1898. In 1976 Bickerton and Odo reported that persons who had had no schooling at all appeared to be nonexistent in Hawaii. Since the variety of English used in schools is a standard dialect, few purely creole speakers remain; most speakers command varying numbers of higher lects along a creole continuum. Regional variation can be found among the different islands. The language used on Oahu is most like that of the mainland variety of English; here is where most recent immigrants from the mainland settle and where the media and centers of higher education are located. At the other extreme, the more isolated islands of Hawaii and Kauai show the most creolized speech. The islands of Maui and Molokai are somewhere in the middle. Odo (1970: 234) characterizes the present language of the state as "Hawaiian English," which is "neither standard nor creole but a mixture of both language varieties whose features are used almost interchangeably and side-by-side."

The description of the structural characteristics of Hawaiian Creole is based primarily on early descriptions of the language, supplemented by modern speech samples. From the available descriptions, the status of gender marking in the nominal system is not clear. Gender is reported to be occasionally troublesome, with *his* often used for a female referent. Either *om* or *um* is used for the third person object pronoun (English *it*), as well as a variable vowel plus *m* or complete deletion of the pronoun:

we like eat *um*
'we like to eat it'

We might suspect that gender is unmarked, as it is for both Gullah and Louisiana Créole, from these sketchy reports. Use of object pronouns in subject position is reported, indicating that case marking is different from that of English. One of the most striking features of the Hawaiian Creole nominal system is the absence of articles, or the variable use of *wan* and *a* before nominals:

I go see *wan* movies
'I went to see a movie'

The -*s* inflection for marking the plural is often missing, or used variably with a -*dem* marker after the noun. Likewise, the possessive -*s* inflection on nouns is also absent.

In the verbal system, one form can be used to indicate both past and present tense, as in both Gullah and Louisiana Créole:

my cousin *go,* eh
'my cousin went, eh'

The past tense can also be indicated by the use of *wen* before the verb:

as what *wen* fuck up the thing
'that's what fucked up the thing'

Future tense is indicated by *gon*:

I *gon* see wan movie

Stay is a nonpunctual marker used to indicate both progressive and habitual aspect:

us *stay* playing basketball over here

The copula is not required in the present tense:

George different
'George is different'

Never is the general negator used for past tense; *no* or *not* are used for nonpast descriptions:

he *never* go
'he didn't go'
I *not* joking
'I'm not joking'

The complementizer is often omitted before infinitive clauses, or *for* or *fo* is used, similar to the *fuh* of Gullah:

ask him *for* iron my shirt

The basic number of locative prepositions may be smaller than that of English, with *at* used to mean both ''in'' and ''at'' in the creole. As all descriptions of the Hawaiian language situation indicate, use of these creole features is highly variable and the same speaker may use both creole and Standard English forms in the same stretch of discourse.

With the heavy influx of Haoles, or mainland Whites, after World War II and the granting of statehood in 1959, public policy has been strongly supportive of Standard English, at the expense of the creole, in all spheres of public life. Prior to 1971 the Department of Education in Hawaii held to a policy of complete eradication of the creole in the speech of island children. This policy has been a recognized failure. Reinecke long ago noted the existence of strong peer pressures within some youth groups *not* to speak the standard dialect. For some ethnic and social groups, the creole serves as a mark of identity and holds high value. For youths who continue to speak the creole, more standard English holds connotations of being ''high and mighty.''

Since 1971, official policy of the educational establishment toward the creole has entailed recognition of it as a valid language variety, but one which calls for ''improvement.'' Day (1972b) cites a 1971 curriculum guide issued by the department, which maintains that ridding the child of ''sub-standard'' English should not be the target for instruction. The same document labels creole-speaking children as ''language-deficient'' and in need of pattern drills in the standard dialect designed to correct their deficiencies. Day's own research calls into question the need for such drills, since the children give evidence of knowing much more about Standard English than their everyday speech indicates. The attitude conveyed by such a policy is that the standard dialect used in the classroom is somehow "better" than the creole which is the home language of many children.

In the state's official bilingual program, the creole is not overtly recognized as a language "other than English." Instructions for scoring the Language Facility Test included in the plan are such that creole speakers would score low: "If auxiliary verbs are omitted (He riding, she sitting), credit should not be given for a sentence" (Hawaii 1976: 56). Since lack of a present tense copula is characteristic of the creole, judgments about "complete sentences" are likely to be biased against creole speakers, with the use of such scoring criteria. Throughout this plan there is no discussion of the complex pidgin–creole–dialect continuum which is the most striking characteristic of the language situation throughout the state of Hawaii; no overt provisions are made for dealing with the language differences which obtain between the creole-speaking child and the teacher in the classroom.

Gullah and American English

While all three of the U.S. creoles are undergoing significant changes under pressures of modernization and expanded educational and job opportunities, we have relatively more knowledge about the nature of these changes in Gullah. In addition, questions have been raised in recent years about the possibility of a creole origin for some of the features which characterize dialects of English spoken by Blacks throughout the United States (see Chapter 5). Because of the intrinsic interest of such questions for language history and policy, the possible relationship between Gullah and Black English will be discussed in some detail.

A recent sociolinguistic study of a rural community in coastal South Carolina reveals some of the linguistic stages in the transition from Gullah to dialects to English. Using speech samples from speakers who interact with each other daily, we can distinguish three distinct stages in the evolution of the third person neuter pronoun:

Gullah
(1a) *ee* ain't quite no place over here fuh put you house at
      'There's hardly any place over here to put your house'
(1b) *ee* much cooler
      'It's much cooler'

Black English
(2a) *it* was more old people
      'There were more old people'
(2b) *it* not like it is now
      'It was not like it is now'

Standard English
(3a) *there* was no really form of communication
(3b) *it* was kinda tough

The stages in development can be represented as follows:

$$
\begin{array}{ccc}
\text{I} & \text{II} & \text{III} \\
ee \longrightarrow & it \longrightarrow & \left\{ \begin{array}{c} there \\ it \end{array} \right\}
\end{array}
$$

The examples reveal a development from a subject form *ee*, used in both equative and existential clauses, to the dialectal *it* for both types of clauses, to the separation of two clause types by the pro-form *there* and the neuter *it* of the standard dialect. As as added bonus, recognition of such a developmental pattern within Gullah gives us greater insight into a parallel development in the history of English.

The probable pattern through which gender marking develops can be seen in the variable usage of a single speaker, a woman of 88 years who had had no formal education:

(4) I ain't see *she* for tell *um* nothing
    'I haven't seen her to tell her anything'
(5) I hadn't seen *her* since *ee* bury *ee* brother
    'I haven't seen her since she buried her brother'

In these examples, the feminine pronoun appears in all possible positions. The stages of development seem to be something like the following:

$$
\begin{array}{ccc}
\text{I} & \text{II} & \text{III} \\
ee\ (\text{Subj}) \longrightarrow & \left\{ \begin{array}{l} she\ (\text{Subj}) \\ ee\ (\text{Poss}) \end{array} \right\} \longrightarrow & \left\{ \begin{array}{l} she\ (\text{Subj}) \\ her\ (\text{Poss}) \end{array} \right\} \\
um\ (\text{Obj}) \longrightarrow & she\ (\text{Obj}) \longrightarrow & her\ (\text{Obj})
\end{array}
$$

The forms of the middle stage posited here would be like those which are still occasionally noted in some varieties of Black English, while those of the first stage would be characteristic of a very early stage of the creole. As examples (4) and (5) indicate, usage at present is highly variable, even for those speakers who use creole forms most frequently.

A final illustration of the relationship between Gullah and Black English comes from the marking of aspect, or quality of action, in the verbal system. This grammatical category is not overtly marked in other dialects of American English. In the creole, an older *duh* particle is the form used to indicate ongoing or habitual action:

(6) But now she *duh* work now to Brookgreen
    'But now she's working at Brookgreen'

Occasionally schoolchildren can be heard using the *duh*-form in similar contexts, but more often a form characteristic of Black English is used:

(7) This summer, when my daddy *be* working, they always have lots of peaches
(8) I been to Georgetown; you have to always *be* going

The use of the invariant *be* form to mean "object or event distributed intermittently in time" for speakers of Black English is discussed in Chapters 3 and 5, along with other characteristic features of that dialect.

The foregoing examples provide only a small sample of forms characteristic of the creole and of Black English dialects which coexist in the speech of both community and individual in rural South Carolina. Gullah itself may not be the only source of those features which distinguish Black English from other dialects of American English; parallel creole developments may have taken place in other parts of the United States where West African speakers of an English-related creole were concentrated. For example, in southwestern Texas a community of mixed Native American and African background speaks a language sometimes referred to as Seminole Language, Texas Seminole, or Brackettville Gullah, which has important syntactic similarities to the Gullah of South Carolina. It is entirely possible that several language varieties similar to Gullah existed in those states of the Deep South where large numbers of Blacks were concentrated. If that were indeed the case, they have now disappeared and Gullah remains as a living example of how the transition from a creole to a dialect of English is made. As such, it merits our respect and study as a linguistic forerunner of the distinctive dialects of English spoken by many Blacks in the United States.

Who now speaks Gullah? A quantitative study (Nichols 1978) of selected creole forms indicated that older women who had never been to school used such forms most frequently. Among adults who had once had some schooling, males were more likely to use creole speech than females in their age groups. Young and middle-aged women used more standard forms than any other members of their speech community, and led the movement of the entire community toward a more standard dialect of English. Social factors influencing the different responses of the sexes appear to be related primarily to job opportunities. The jobs increasingly available to Black women in the region entail use of a standard variety of spoken and written English. The top five occupations engaged in by Black men, in contrast, call for no language-related skills – though these jobs invariably pay more than those open to women. Other factors influencing language choice are peer pressure and available role models. Observation of schoolchildren in the region suggests that many children who enter school as creole speakers have acquired some competence in the use of more standard forms by the age of 9 or 10. Boys were found to change more slowly than girls. By the age of 11 many girls had sharply curtailed their use of creole forms in the classroom where standard English is the medium of instruction, while boys their age continued to use creole forms both inside and outside the classroom. At home, young adolescent males often use more creole forms than their fathers. Since prestige is gained among male peers through use of verbal skills associated with the use of creole, the school dialect is in competition with the home language among young males. They frequently have more incentive to use creole speech patterns in which they are highly proficient than to use a dialect which seems to have little relevance in their daily lives. For different members of a speech community, then, social factors work both to maintain the creole and to modify it in the direction of a dialect of English. Within the same family and within an individual at different life stages, these pressures can be observed to operate with different effects. The same household may contain a very old member who is uneducated and little traveled, middle-aged adults who have varied contact with a wide range of language in their daily jobs, and an assortment of children of all ages, including one or two preschool children who are cared for daily by the oldest family member. The language used in such a family will encompass a continuum ranging from the highly creolized speech of the oldest and youngest members at one extreme, to the mixture of Black English and standard dialect forms used by the mother and her high school daughters at the other extreme. In such a setting, the family unit serves as a living bridge between Gullah and other varieties of American English.

The future

Although the three creoles unique to the United States (for discussion of Michif, a creole spoken in North Dakota and parts of Canada, see Chapter 8) represent significant developments in the country's social and linguistic history, they have received relatively little popular notice outside their immediate geographic regions. Even locally, where the creoles are known to be "different," they are held in low esteem – by speaker and hearer alike. Part of the reason for their low prestige is the competition from more widely spoken languages. Gullah and Hawaiian Creole, both English-related, developed and survive in areas where English is the major language. The French-related creole of Louisiana exists where two regional varieties of French, as well as English, have long been spoken. The prestige of the creoles is also affected by the low socio-economic status of their speakers. In Louisiana and the states of South Carolina and Georgia, creole speakers are primarily descendants of West African slaves. In Hawaii they are descendants of contract laborers from Hawaii itself, as well as other countries of Asia and the South Pacific.

That the creoles have been maintained as viable home languages into the latter part of the twentieth century in one of the most highly industrialized countries, despite the low esteem in which they are held, indicates something of their continuing vitality and importance for their speech communities as living languages. Under pressures from formal education now widely available, the creoles may function primarily as markers of group identity in the future. Both Gullah and Louisiana Créole may well serve as symbols of ethnic consciousness among Blacks, as Hawaiian Creole may serve to unite peoples of diverse non-European backgrounds in the pluralistic setting of Hawaii.

Given such forces at work, public policies which seek to eradicate the creoles are doomed to failure. More tragically, educational policies which fail to recognize the creoles as language varieties which are substantially different from those used in most classrooms may doom creole-speaking children to failure with academic subjects in large numbers. The experience of British schools with creole-speaking children from the West Indies in recent decades can be held up as an example of the consequences of such policies (Townsend and Brittan 1972).

It is entirely possible to construct public policies which will both support the home language of a given population group and simultaneously introduce a language of wider communication. Current bilingual programs in some classrooms may serve as examples of such evolving policies within U.S. education. For the creole languages of the United States, recognition of their "differentness" from languages of the classroom would seem to be an essential first step in developing a viable policy which will include them as well.

FURTHER READING

The briefest and most readable, yet well-informed and scholarly, introduction to pidgins and creoles is Todd 1974. R. A. Hall, Jr. 1966 also provides a useful overview and Reinecke et al. 1975 contains an annotated bibliography to the general subject of pidgins and creoles. Recent studies can be found in Hymes 1971, Valdman 1977, and Day 1980. Reinecke and Tsuzaki 1977 provide updated information on current research.

For Gullah, Turner's 1949 work is the most accessible description; it has been reprinted in paperback. W. A. Stewart's 1967 article on the historical development of American Negro dialects has been reprinted in several collections. Traugott 1976 provides an excellent discussion of the relationships between pidgins, creoles, and dialects. Other work is largely unpublished to date. Cunningham's 1970 dissertation is the best available analysis of Gullah syntax. Nichols' 1976 dissertation deals with processes of change in Gullah; Joyner's 1977 dissertation places the language in its cultural context.

Broussard's 1942 study of Louisiana Créole is based on his memory of the language as heard in his youth. Most of the research on this creole remains in journals; articles by Lane 1935 and a series by Morgan 1959, 1964, 1970, 1975 are especially good. Conwell and Juilland's 1963 study of Acadian French is useful also.

For Hawaiian Creole, Reinecke's 1935 study (published in 1969) is the most comprehensive. Research currently underway promises to provide new insight into the processes of creolization. Bickerton and Odo 1976 provide a preliminary report, and the dissertations of Day 1972a and Perlman 1973 examine important portions of Hawaiian Creole syntax.

5

Language among Black Americans

ELIZABETH WHATLEY

The Afro-American experience in the USA has been different from that of any other group, and the language situation of Black Americans is correspondingly different. Unlike other groups who came to America, almost all Africans were brought over as slaves, and up until the Emancipation Proclamation, the overwhelming majority of Blacks in the USA were still slaves. During the period of slavery, as well as in the modern period, the patterns of communication between Blacks and other Americans reflected the social distance between them. Also, the Africans who reached American shores spoke many different African languages and were, on the whole, unable to maintain viable speech communities based on the use of their MOTHER TONGUES.

Thus, it is no surprise that Black Americans speak varieties of American English rather than African languages, and that the language of Blacks will tend to differ from the language of other Americans in any community. Strong assimilatory forces have been at work and in some contexts are becoming stronger, so that in many instances Blacks may speak to all intents and purposes the same way as their neighbors. Just as complete linguistic assimilation takes place with immigrant groups, so it can and does with Blacks. On the other hand, several historical events have reinforced the tendency to differ. One was the early use of English-based PIDGINS and CREOLES among slave populations. This had a tremendous effect on the kind of English which Black Americans have come to speak, not only in the surviving creole of the Sea Islands (see Chapter 4), but also in varieties of speech which have been called Black English Vernacular (see Chapter 3).

Blacks in urban life

Another powerful historical event was the great exodus of Blacks from the Southeast to the Northeast and other parts of the country in the early twentieth century. This movement of people brought varieties of southern, often rural, Black English to urban areas of the North, where quite different kinds of English were spoken. The juxtaposition of northern and southern features made the separation of White and Black speech all the more evident and incontrovertible in these northern communities. The development of these speech com-

92

munities was the result of a series of factors which created situations conducive to language maintenance on the one hand, and the development of a distinctive DIALECT on the other.

The evolution of predominantly Black urban areas in northern cities is traceable by an examination of the migratory patterns of Blacks from southern regions of the United States. From the 1790s to the early 1900s, 90 percent of the Black population lived in the South. In 1910, 89 percent continued to live in the South, but the percentage began to decrease in each succeeding decade to 85 percent in 1920, 77 percent in 1940, and 60 percent in 1960. Precise causes of the migration of Blacks to the North are unknown; however, certain social and economic factors influenced the movement. The first was the severe devastation of southern cotton by the boll weevil following on a series of bad crop years. The second was the development of labor needs in factories of the North. With the onset of World War I, the immigration of Europeans to the United States was abruptly curtailed. Industry, which previously provided hundreds of thousands of jobs each year for new immigrants, now had its labor supply curtailed during a period of great demand for labor. Many firms sent recruiters to the South to encourage Blacks to come North. Many Black southerners who migrated North later encouraged friends and relatives to join them, and the move became easier for those with someone at the other end to help find a job and a place to live. After World War I, immigration from Europe resumed, only to be curtailed permanently by restrictive legislation in the early 1920s. Black Americans then established a secure position in the northern industrial scene.

Most Blacks who migrated during this period were crowded into the ghettoes of New York, Detroit, Chicago, and Philadelphia, where reasonable housing was in extremely short supply. Initially, Blacks moved into neighborhoods inhabited by European immigrants who had not made sufficient economic gains to move out of these areas. But the increasing influx of Blacks created a major problem for northern inhabitants: competition for both living space and jobs. The slum areas of major cities absorbed thousands of Blacks between 1900 and 1914; however, the saturation point was reached shortly thereafter, and the demand for houses and living space produced dramatic increases in rents.

Every large city experienced a similar housing shortage as Blacks moved into previously White areas, took over the parks and playgrounds, and transformed White and mixed communities into solidly Black areas. It became quite clear that the territory of Black areas had to expand. The line was drawn. Urban Whites had nowhere to go in this presuburban period, and they attempted to create legally defined residential districts for Whites only. The courts struck down this attempt, and expansion of Black residential zones was halted through restrictive covenants and gentlemen's agreements between White homeowners and realtors. Explicit geographical boundaries were reinforced by explicit social boundaries in recreation, worship, and education. There were limited contacts between the diverse ethnic groups of the cities. The restricted social environment of Blacks fostered continuation of features of Black speech brought from the South and promoted the development of linguistic traits distinctive to urban life. The absence of sustained social and cultural contact with mainstream America created a linguistic situation in which Black speech was relatively free from White American English influences. By the end of the great Black migration, the speech forms of Blacks had changed considerably from southern variations.

Contributing to this change was the increasing participation of Black performers in public entertainment. In New York, Chicago, and Detroit, Black musicians played to White audiences whose responses helped promote the growth and development of blues and jazz. A network of entertainers traveled across the country, hitting small towns occasionally and giving distinctive character to portions of large cities: the French Quarter of New Orleans, Louisiana became synonymous with jazz and certain of its stars. The personnel connected with the entertainment world developed widespread communication networks connecting segments of Black populations in northern and southern cities. Innovations in music, dress, and language spread rapidly among these Blacks.

The constant contact among performers and agents and back-up personnel in the diverse locations led to some degree of homogenization of terms and styles of talking among Blacks in certain situations. Copping a plea and shucking, language performances used to get out of compromising situations with persons of authority, became familiar to Whites in their effects, if not their internal structures, as Black entertainers worked to provide themselves minimal comforts and opportunities in cities which allowed them highly restricted access to hotels and restaurants. Jiving, a style of talking in which both performer and audience know that the performance and not the content of the language is what counts, became widely recognized as a specialized language performance of Blacks. Increasingly included as a humor form in comic interludes in musical performances and in vaudeville, jiving, shucking, and copping a plea became language styles expected of Blacks by Whites. Radio helped make the stylization of Black speech and language performances known to an even wider audience of Americans than that of the live entertainment circuit. Amos and Andy, and Rochester, Jack Benny's butler, helped develop stereotyped notions of the speech styles of Blacks and the ways they presented themselves to the world. Blacks were often forced to recognize it was to their advantage economically and socially to play to the images of them and their speech perpetuated through the entertainment world.

The result was some degree of homogenization in at least the speech structures and styles used by those who had roles which put them in daily association with Whites. Thus, the in-group communication of entertainers and the extension of some of these forms and styles promoted through the public media had a leveling and homogenizing influence on some styles of speech spoken by urban Blacks. Another homogenizing factor was the continuation of ties from northern urban communities to their home communities in the South. Funerals, homecoming celebrations at churches, and family reunions took northerners "down home" at least annually. In many urban centers, there developed communities in which a majority of members were from a particular southern state; for example, Philadelphia, in the 1970s, still had many neighborhoods whose residents maintained strong ties to South Carolina.

Ironically, widespread expectations of some language uses typical of interactions outside the community helped promote their maintenance within the community as well. In addition to those widely recognized aspects of language behaviors performed primarily for Whites were the highly distinctive language styles used almost exclusively within Black American communities. Black preaching styles, verbal games, and ritual insults of Black children, and vivid and allusive styles of street talk among adults had long been a part of Black community life. However, these speech styles used only among Blacks for in-group interactions were not displayed for public entertainment until the 1960s, when Black families were featured in television, theater, music, and cinema. For example, only after the Civil Rights movement of the 1960s did television situation comedies feature Blacks who ritually insulted family members and poked fun at each other for copping pleas, jiving, and using nonstandard language structures and ''Black-only'' styles of manipulating language. Even middle class Blacks who had made it out of the ghetto were portrayed in situation comedies as occasionally ''reverting'' to the ''talk and tricks'' characterized as typical of ''street talk.''

Yet many aspects of expressive language use maintained by Black communities have not been flaunted for the entertainment of mass audiences. Many of these uses are certainly less distinctive but perhaps more significant in revealing the ways language is transmitted and evaluated in Black communities. Day-to-day interactions across community members of different age, sex, and status relations do not depend on the stylized speech performances which have been presented in the entertainment world. Workaday transactions within families and among friends are critical because they help maintain the social structure of the community as a whole. For communicative purposes, the eldest adults are the highest status members of the Black community. They have the privilege to initiate and maintain any or all types of communication with others regardless of their age. They can praise, fuss, tease, lie, joke, or preach. Other adults are high status members and can, without sanction, initiate almost as many types of communicative acts as can their elders. Nevertheless, they are restricted from using particular language behaviors with the elderly; a daughter may not fuss, preach, or lie to her 'mamma' or any elder citizen. Both elders and other adults have nonreciprocal communicative rights when interacting with children. That is, there are many language behaviors which children cannot engage in with adults, yet they must acquire competence in these behaviors, because their power and prestige as adults depend on their facility with a wide range of styles and communicative acts. The age of conversational partners determines, in large part, the kind of language used. In this chapter a number of examples of verbal interaction will be given. They are all actual recorded events and they are transcribed here in a slightly modified form of ordinary ORTHOGRAPHY.

In the communicative event called fussing (a type of dispute or argument), whether a speaker fusses *at* or *with* another depends upon age and status relations. A fussing episode may be brief:

A: I told y'all not to do that!
B: Oh, stop fussing!

It can also be a more lengthy interaction. When speakers alternately state their disagreements, they are *fussing with* each other:

A: See what y'all did now, I told y'all 'bout messin' with stuff don't (be)long to y'all.
B: I ain't do it. He did.
C: No I didn't! You always sayin' I do stuff. You did it.
B: Yeah, I saw you, I saw you.

A *fussing at* interaction occurs when (a) two or more speakers talk simultaneously or (b) when a speaker directs disagreements to an interlocutor who either will not or cannot respond, because rules of language use related to age and status relations prevent doing so.

Among Black Americans, the eldest members of the community are given the widest latitude in the use of language. They can engage in all types of communication unless restricted by communicative norms related to the sex of the speaker. A female grandparent would not, for example, engage in ritual insults, toasts (epic-like tales), or other male-dominated communicative events. Preschool-age children are also given wide latitude in language use. They too are permitted to engage in most communicative events with few exceptions. Latitude given to the very young provides the widest possible spectrum of communication for modeling. Adults can *fuss with* or *at* other adults of equal or comparable age. They can *fuss at* children but never *with* them. Similarly, adults do not *fuss with* or *at* elder members of the community. Children can engage in fussing interactions with peers or with younger siblings or relatives. They cannot engage in any type of *fussing with* adults or with the elders of the community.

Fussing is an example of one of the ways Black Americans structure the community for communicative purposes. Children are low status members of the community and engage in communicative events primarily with other children. They are constrained by language use rules from initiating and maintaining certain types of interactions with adults. Interaction rules also require children to engage in particular kinds of language use; among these are formulaic greetings and other politeness forms, such as verbal responses to directives.

Children initiate greetings when they encounter familiar adults or when introduced to new ones. When accompanied by adults, they greet after adults have greeted each other. Community ways of interacting require equal status members to greet each other first followed by greetings from high status members (e.g. adults) to low status members (e.g. children). When unaccompanied by adults, children are required to initiate the greeting when the addressee is a familiar or known member of the community. If children fail to offer a greeting, adults remind them of community expectations. They may offer a greeting, sometimes with INTONATION to show indignation; or they may accuse children of lacking knowledge, "You forgot how to speak?!" These verbal signals function as directives and compel children to assume their responsibility for initiating greetings.

A typical greeting is illustrated in the following interaction which occurred between three adults, A, B, and C, and two children, D and E. Speakers A and B are adults of equal age and status. Speaker C is an elder member of the community and the mother of A. Speakers D and E are 12 and 13 years of age, respectively. Speakers B and E enter the home where A, C, and D are waiting for them.

Adult A: I saw you drive up. Come on in.	A $\xrightarrow{\ 1\ }$ B
Adult B: Hey, y'all, what's going on?	A $\xleftarrow{\ 2\ }$ B
Adult A: Ain't nothin' to it.	A $\xrightarrow{\ 3\ }$ B
Hi E, how are you? (kisses E)	A $\searrow^{4}$ E
Child E: Fine.	A $\nwarrow^{5}$ E
Adult B: Hello Miss C. How are you?	C $\searrow^{6}$ B
Adult C: Jus' fine.	C $\searrow^{7}$ B
Hello, E.	C $\searrow^{8}$ E
Child E: Hello.	C $\nwarrow^{9}$ E
Adult B: (to D) Aren't you gonna speak?	D $\nearrow^{10}$ B
Child D: (to B and E) Hello.	D $\rightleftarrows^{11}$ E, B

Neither simultaneous greetings (i.e. one greeting exchange between the children and another among the adults) nor a generalized greeting to all is acceptable; the relative status of each member and acknowledgement of that status by greeting rituals must be marked. In groups of mixed ranks, such as the one illustrated here, exchanges between equals both open and close the greeting routine. Close analysis of the set of rules operating in this interaction reveals an unexpected complexity in the order of turn taking. The sequencing of the utterances is indicated by numbers; the directions of arrows indicates the relative rank of speakers. Several related rules are demonstrated in this interaction. First, the language used by speaker B to greet speaker C is less casual than the language used to greet speaker A; speaker C is high status, speaker A equal status. Secondly, both children maintained appropriate boundaries of language use and interaction rules. Whether accompanied or alone, children are not required to exceed the briefest form of greetings. "Hi," "Hello," or "Morning" are sufficient and appropriate forms of language use by children. Attempts to engage in an elaborate greeting – "Hello, Miss C. How are you? Nice day isn't it? How are your plants?" – is considered inappropriate for children. It is the act of greeting which carries communicative value in child–adult communications, not the extent of the verbal routine.

What may be a culture-specific form of politeness is the way in which children are required to show adults they are attentive listeners and they value adults' communications. One of the ways children indicate recognition of adults is to respond verbally when given directives or called. For example, if an adult tells a child to go downstairs and get the newspaper, the child must immediately respond verbally to the directive. Carrying out the task is not sufficient; a verbal acknowledgment of the directive is needed.

In child–child interactions, a wide range of the culture's rules of language use occurs. Interactions prohibited between children and adults or between adults take place among children. And, while these interactions are directly and importantly influenced by adult patterns of language use, there are aspects of language use which occur only in child–child interactions. The rules of language use are highly structured and follow intricate patterns of operation. They are rarely explicit, yet children learn what they are and when to apply them. Moreover, they learn how to punish those who break the rules and do not consistently mark their knowledge of how to keep boundaries.

For example, in boasting interactions, children use language skills to declare their achievements, attributes, and superiority over others. A boast may be a spontaneous speech act or a preplanned communicative event. Spontaneous boasts occur during children's everyday conversations and are usually outgrowths of immediately preceding utterances. Furthermore, they do not result in argumentative interactions between the speakers.

A: Your mother feed you too much.
B: Yeah, she feed me a whole lot and then she say "See how big I am." My mother's big.
A: My mother's bigger.
B: Yeah, well I guess I'll be going since I can't get in the door.

Spontaneous boasts show children's knowledge of appropriate ways of using language to interact with peers. Preplanned boasts indicate the strategies children know they will use when interacting. The goal of preplanned or purposeful boasting is to complete a sequence and win by receiving a closure from the other child. To fulfill this goal, the child must plan an entire series of responses to possible utterances from the opponent. Strategies used are frequently the result of collecting and organizing information into systematic and logical arguments. Most important, the underlying purpose of the interaction (i.e. to boast) must be disguised, often hidden behind an apparently innocent question.

A: Do you know 'bout factors and all that stuff?

B: Yea, I know all that.

A: Well, how come you only made a 50 on that test?

B: That test was tough – she ain't no good teacher anyway.

A: But you been in the other Math class, the one dat ain't done factors like we have.

B: We did too.

A: No, you didn't. You only up to page 130. We on 165. You can't do factors. You can't do none of that stuff.

B: Yea, but I can do spelling – and you can't.

It is clear in this boasting episode that child A had collected highly specific information to support his boast, and he set child B up to a challenge by a seemingly innocent question. The strategies and information to support these were planned out in advance. Child A wins this sequence, because child B must shift topic and begin another boast.

The boundaries of the primary SPEECH COMMUNITY, which includes those recognized as members of the Black community, are marked by the situations and participants for these and other communicative events reserved for in-group associations. The means, purposes, and patterns of selection of all these events, those used by adults only and those used by children only, are reflections of the social structure. They are learned by children who listen to and observe adults and other children, practice these events among themselves, and thus gradually become competent language users by their community's standards. With the exception of works such as Labov, Cohen, Robins, and Lewis (1968), Mitchell-Kernan (1971), Kochman (1972), and Labov (1972a), relatively little scholarly attention has been devoted to description of these uses of language (and their contexts) in Black communities. Instead, much greater attention has been given to describing the structure and history of the language.

Black English: a variety of American English

In the early 1970s, the publication of *Black English: Its History and Usage in the United States* (Dillard 1972) brought to the attention of the American public a major question regarding the system of language used by Black Americans. Was it a separate system or was it part of the same system as other Englishes? The work of Labov *et al.* (1968) had shown that the VERNACULAR (sometimes referred to as street talk) of Blacks had distinct rules of its own and was not, as had been the common misconception, a mass of random errors committed by Blacks trying to speak English. Labov (1972a), examining systematic relations between the rules of Black English Vernacular (BEV) and others and between different BEV rules, showed that the rules of BEV and Standard English did indeed form a single system for BEV speakers. Therefore, BEV could most accurately be considered a "subsystem within the larger grammar of English" (Labov 1972a: 64).

BEV has, therefore, come to be widely accepted as a rule-governed linguistic system (see Chapter 3). However, some parts of its PHONOLOGY, MORPHOLOGY, and SYNTAX and ways of speaking are neither produced nor fully understood by speakers of other English dialects. However, as a dialect of American English, many of its features and patterns are quite similar to those of Standard English. Some of the different or unique structural characteristics of BEV can be seen in the language used by two children engaged in a conversation with an adult in their neighborhood. Jimmy and David are 10 years of age.

Jimmy: Hey Ms. Smith, d'ya evvah watch Kung Fu on TV wif dat dude . . . wha's his name?

David: He have my name, Jimmy. He David, too.

Jimmy: Yeah, dat's right. Dat's duh dude's name.

Ms. Smith: Yes, I've watched it a few times. It's really an exciting show.

David: Did you evvah see how he throw all dose dudes aroun', an' how he use his legs?

Jimmy: Yeah. You know what? He can really fight. He don't fight to be mean dough [though]. He fight to be good, and he'p people. An' he always duh good guy.

David: You know what? He one of dose pries' or somefin'. Hey Ms. Smith, what is he? I can't remembah what dey call'.

Ms. Smith: Have you ever heard of the word 'monk'?

Jimmy: No, what dat?

David: It's one dose pries', I think, ain't it? Yea, it one dose pries' dat live wif ovvah pries', dose monks. He live in a convent like.

Jimmy: In wha'? Wha's dat?

David: Ah man, ain't you know what dat is? It's where dey have people dat . . . people like pries' an' nuns live' dere.

Jimmy: No, but ain't he live in duh desert? He always be walkin' on a desert on TV.

David: No, but he ain't live in duh desert. He don't walk dere all duh time. He don't live dere. He jus' be walkin' dere sometime'. He move aroun' a lot, you know. He travel all different places.

Jimmy: I'm wonderin' where he learn everyfin'.

David: He learn' in duh convent when he young, I think. Dat's where dey say on TV one time.

On the phonological level, several features of Black English are evident in this interaction. One of the most obvious is the use of *duh, dat, dose, dere,* and *dey.* Jimmy and David consistently use a *d* sound for the voiced Standard English *th* sound at the beginning of words such as *the, that, those, there* and *they.* The use of *d* for the voiced *th* (as in *that*) is heard in other varieties of American English as well; for example, it is common among New Yorkers. BEV differs from these other varieties in having the *d* mostly at the beginning of words, but otherwise *v* for the voiced *th*. For example, in this conversation David says *ovvah* for *other*, where a white New Yorker might say *uddah*.

Another phonological characteristic of Jimmy and David's conversation is "*r*-lessness" or the dropping of *r*'s after vowels. This is not shown consistently in the spelling used here, but at the end of words, where it is especially noticeable, it is indicated by the spelling -*ah*, as in *evvah* 'ever' and *remembah* 'remember'. This dropping of the *r* is common in many parts of the English-speaking world, and the prevalence of *r*-lessness in the English of Black Americans in part reflects the southern origin of many varieties of Black English.

A more characteristic feature of BEV is the simplification or weakening of CONSONANT CLUSTERS at the end of words. All speakers of English tend to reduce word-final consonant combinations such as -*st*, -*sk*, and -*nd* by pronouncing the last consonant weakly or not at all (e.g. *las'* for *last*, *des'* for *desk*, *han'* for *hand*), and the more informal, rapid, and casual the speech is, the stronger this tendency is. In BEV the tendency is even stronger, and some words are regularly pronounced without the final consonant, such as *jus'* and *roun'* in this conversation.

Sometimes this weakening of final consonant clusters results in BEV plural forms which differ from the usual English plurals for particular words. Nouns that end in a cluster such as -*st*, -*sk*, or -*sp* may lose the final consonant and then make the plural as though the singular ended in -*s*. Since nouns ending in a sibilant in English add an extra syllable, spelled -*es*, to make the plural, as in *glass: glasses*, these BEV plurals will have an extra syllable. For example, many speakers of BEV will say *desses* as the plural of *des(k)*. In the sentence *Sometime' dey even have contesses to see who bettah*, the plural *contesses* is based on the singular *contes'* in which the final -*t* has been dropped completely. In the conversation between Jimmy and David, the word *priest* is pronounced without the final -*t*, but some feeling of the final -*t* apparently persists because David seems to say *pries'* and not *priesses* for the plural. We cannot be completely sure, however, because the use of the plural ending is optional in BEV, and David may simply be using the singular.

The optionality of the plural is a grammatical feature of BEV, and another similar feature is the optionality of the past tense. Speakers of BEV sometimes use the same form of the verb for both present and past. Also, because of the weakening of final clusters as just described, it is often impossible to decide whether a verb form is the present tense used for the past or a past tense form with the final -*d* or -*t* dropped in pronunciation. In the last exchange of the conversation, when the boys use the verb *learn*, it is not clear whether it is the present tense or the past tense without the final -*d*.

Another grammatical feature characteristic of BEV is the omission of the -*s* ending which marks the third person singular in verbs. In place of Standard English *he learns*, the speaker of BEV often says *he learn*. This is not just the weakening of a consonant cluster, because the ending is also omitted after vowels, and in the case of words like *have* and *do* that have special forms for the third singular (*has, does*), BEV does not just drop the final -*s* of these forms but uses the full *have* and *do*. There are a number of examples of this phenomenon in the Jimmy and David dialogue: *He have my name. He throw all dose dudes aroun'. He fight to be good. He live in a convent. He move aroun' a lot. He travel all different places.*

One of the most often discussed grammatical characteristics of BEV is the use of the verb *to be*. It is often absent where Standard English would have it, the forms are different from those of Standard English, and there is at least one use of *be* in BEV which has no equivalent in Standard English. Omission of the verb *to be,* or "COPULA deletion," as it is usually called by linguists, is very characteristic of BEV. In all varieties of American English, speakers contract forms of *be* in some sentences; for example, in ordinary conversation, almost everyone would usually say *She's married,* instead of *She-is-married.* BEV takes the process a step further and lets the *is* be omitted completely. The boys' conversation has examples of both contraction and deletion.

Contraction	Deletion
Wha'*s* his name?	He—David, too
Dat'*s* right	He—always duh good guy
Dat'*s* duh dude's name	He—one of dose pries'
Wha'*s* dat?	What—dat?

In sentences where the *is* or other form of *be* is not contracted in general American English usage, it is not deleted in BEV. There are several examples in the dialogue:

What *is* he?
You know what dat *is*?

The special use of *be* which is found almost only in the English of Black Americans is illustrated toward the end of the boys' conversation. Jimmy says *He always be walkin' on a desert on TV,* and David in his rejoinder says *He jus' be walkin' dere sometime'.* This use of "invariant *be*," as it is often called by linguists, refers to repeated actions over a considerable extent of time, and the distinction between *he walk, he walkin'*, and *he be walkin'* has no exact parallel in Standard English. Incidentally, these three verb forms typically have different negatives.

He walk	He don't walk	[momentary]
He walkin'	He ain't walkin'	[progressive]
He be walkin'	He don't be walkin'	[habitual]

Another grammatical feature which has had a good deal of attention is the pattern of negation in BEV. Standard English generally requires just one negation in a clause, but BEV prefers the pattern of multiple negation where negation keeps being repeated throughout the clause or sentence. For Standard English *I didn't see anything like that anywhere,* BEV may have *I ain't see nothin' like dat no place.* Multiple negation was the rule in Old English, and examples are still common as late as Shakespeare, but the spread of the rule of single negation has gradually restricted multiple negation to nonstandard varieties of English. One factor in the change in English was the influence of Latin, which allows only single negation. Ironically, the modern Romance languages, such as French, Spanish, and Italian, which are the descendants of Latin, have all developed multiple negation as standard. Multiple negation, while typical of BEV, occurs in other dialects and registers of English, and is generally understood by speakers of Standard English. Some uses of the negative contraction *ain't* are, however, distinctive of BEV. For example, the use of *ain't* as a single past negative, as in the sentence just cited *I ain't see* for *I didn't see,* is pretty well limited to BEV, although the use of *ain't* for *isn't* or *hasn't* (*He ain't gonna do it, he ain't done it*) is common to many kinds of nonstandard English.

A number of other interesting phonological and grammatical features of BEV have been studied and several of them appear in our sample conversation (see Further reading), but one overall characteristic is apparent: the amount of fluctuation in forms and constructions which occurs in Black English. Almost every statement about BEV includes a qualification such as "may occur," "sometimes," "often," or "generally." Fluctuation of forms in the speech of the Black community tends to be greater than in other varieties of American English. The same speaker on one occasion will pronounce a plural ending and on another occasion will drop it. One sentence will have *ain't* for the past negative and the next one may have *didn't* or *ditn't*. The most plausible explanation for this fluctuation is the existence of two poles of language usage in the community – the most extreme form of creole-like English, what has been called BASILECT, and the model of educated Standard English, the ACROLECT. The fluctuating intermediate forms may represent different degrees of formality and different levels of competence in the polar forms. Someone who controls Standard English very well may prefer to relax into a more informal style or someone who is not very competent in Standard English may try to speak more formally. The fluctuation need not depend on the individual speakers' efforts to move back and forth between the extremes, since most American Blacks probably grow up in communities where they hear fluctuations in use on all sides, and the community has no well-codified norm of its own apart from the mainstream standard language.

One consequence of the considerable distance between basilect and acrolect and the great fluctuation in sounds and forms is that professional people in the Black community generally have a broader range of styles of speaking in their verbal repertoire than their White mainstream counterparts. A middle class Black preacher in an urban church must be able to move back and forth among different levels of language use and different styles of preaching to maintain effective communication with his parishioners and his colleagues (Mitchell 1970). Unfortunately most of the linguistic research on Black English has been concerned with the varieties most divergent from Standard English and has paid little attention to the varieties of English spoken by educated Blacks in the varied settings and occasions of life in Afro-American communities. An earlier generation of dialectologists was interested in the continuity between British and American English and played down the distinctions of Black English (McDavid and McDavid 1971). The current generation of sociolinguists is interested in the linguistic analysis of the most informal and distinctive varieties of Black urban vernacular. Some ethnographers of communication are beginning to study the functional uses of different varieties of language in the daily life of Black American communities to give a balance to this perspective.

The origins of Black language

Coordinate with research on the uses and structures of the language of Black Americans has been an interest in the history of these speech forms. Where did they come from? How have they evolved? Current researchers generally agree that both structural and functional patterns have their roots in African traditional culture and in the social adjustments of the slave trade, and that they have taken their distinctive form in the evolution of Black American culture and social organization in New World settings, both rural and urban. There are, however, divergent views on the history of language contact situations which contributed to the development of particular structures or dialect features. During the period of Black migration and extending to the early 1960s, dialectologists believed that the language of Blacks was a direct descendant of the standard British regional dialects that existed in the colonial era of American history and that their language was largely the result of the influence of contact with southern White speech.

The views of dialectologists were seriously challenged by a group of scholars who proposed that the dialect spoken by Blacks is a pidgin-derived language, and not solely British and White in origin (see Chapter 4). Stewart and Dillard have been the leading proponents of this view. W. A. Stewart (1967) pointed out the need for African slaves to learn some kind of English and expressed his conviction that in almost all cases what they acquired was a pidginized variety of English. He and Dillard (see especially Dillard 1972) adduced historical evidence to show that a pidgin English existed in many places in West Africa in the sixteenth century. They both have tied the development of a pidgin English in Africa to the transformation of an earlier Romance-language-based pidgin by relexification, i.e. the replacement of the original Romance vocabulary by words taken from English. Although the exact origins of West Africa Pidgin English are still controversial, there can be no doubt of its existence at the time of the slave trade, and it is highly probable that many slaves acquired some kind of pidgin English either before they left Africa or in the course of their transportation to the New World and first experiences after arrival. The more interesting question is how much remained of their African mother tongues. Apparently very little remained of active use of the African languages comparable, for example, to the vestiges of Yoruba and other languages in Cuba, Brazil, and elsewhere. But Africanisms persisted in the English they spoke, some are still apparent in varieties of Black English, and a few have even entered the mainstream of American English.

An important early study which tends to support the maintenance of features of African languages is Turner's (1949) study of the communities of Blacks located on the Sea Islands and mainland of coastal South Carolina and Georgia. Prior to the 1801 Slave Trade Act nearly 100,000 slaves were brought directly from Africa to the Charleston, South Carolina region. It is assumed that these slaves had little or no knowledge of the English language and that the relative isolation of the Sea Islands allowed for the development of a language which was not of direct British descent. Turner found Africanisms in the sounds, morphology, syntax, vocabulary, and intonation of the region's dialect, and hypothesized numerous similarities between Gullah and the African languages. Turner's findings were originally rejected by dialectologists as an isolated phenomenon of "selective cultural differentiation" (Dillard, 1972: 117). Hall (1950), Dalby (1969, 1972), and Hancock (1970), however, supported Turner's thesis and showed additional instances of the spread and influence of Africanisms in languages, arts, music, and dance. Thus a number of scholars have come to agree that the creole of the Sea Islands is not an aberrant phenomenon of Afro-American language, but rather a remnant of speech situations which were probably widespread in the early days of slavery. There is little doubt that the language of Black Americans did and still does, to a certain extent, reflect aspects of the West African languages. Some scholars have posited retention of particular vocabulary items, some used exclusively by Black Americans, others widely known in other American English dialects (Dalby 1972; Dillard 1976a). *Bad* (often pronounced *ba-a-ad*) is an example often cited as showing the influence of West African languages. The use of negative terms to express positive values occurred in West African languages and appears today in the street or jive talk of young Black Americans in particular. Words common to other dialects of English, such as *banjo, tote* (for 'carry'), *okay, jazz,* and *jam* (as in *jam session*), are also posited as being of West African origin, though there are debates surrounding each of these items. Somewhat less debated is the influence particular speech events or styles of talking developed by Blacks have had on the talk of young adults using almost any dialect of English. The words of American popular music sung by Whites and Blacks alike have double (sometimes multiple) interpretations; negative terms carry positive meanings; White and Black American teenagers, church organizations, and business executives have *rap* sessions. The latter, a term first used by BEV speakers to mean 'greet, speak to, flirt with, con or fool,' has been extended in meaning to convey a 'down-to-earth talk.'

The language of Black Americans, has, as have other dialects of American English, features unique to its subsystem as well as features of the general system of English grammar. In their communities and other primary groups, Black Americans have unique styles of talking and ways of structuring and communicating social relationships through particular uses of language, such as greeting and fussing. Likewise, many members are competent in engaging in speech events expected of them in interactions with outsiders and in exchanges with members of their own age and sex. In many ways, the Civil Rights movement of the 1960s and publicity over the educational crisis of Black students have helped to promote linguistic research on the language of Black Americans and to cause this variety's existence to be widely discussed by educators, journalists, and politicians. Such promotion has fostered two major misconceptions: the first is the view that Black English is entirely unique among dialects of American English. The second is that there are two major dialects of American English, that spoken by Whites and that used by Blacks. Neither of these views is accepted by linguists, but both have widespread acceptance by the man on the street. Research within communities of speakers of other varieties of American English, as well as continuing attempts to learn more about the similarities and differences of language structures and functions among Black Americans, may someday provide both a comprehensive and an accurate picture of the varieties of English in the United States.

FURTHER READING

In the past decade, there has been a proliferation of works on the language of Black Americans. Some are polemic case studies of unjust treatments of Blacks because of their "language deficiencies." Others are attempts to explain and/or justify the language of Blacks to educators and other nonlinguists; still others are highly technical studies of the language structures of members of certain social classes in urban areas of the United States. The bibliography by Brasch and Brasch 1974 is the most comprehensive guide to the wide range of writings available on the language of Black Americans (but see Algeo 1974). For both language and culture in general, several collections prepared for use as textbooks make accessible "classic" articles and papers published in obscure places (Whitten and Szwed 1970; De Stefano 1973).

Dillard's *Black English* (1972), portions of his general works on American English (1975, 1976a), as well as his treatment of Black names (1976b), have provided laymen with a history of Black speech which gives special attention to pidginization and creolization (but see Wolfram 1973). The writings of W. A. Stewart 1968, 1970 greatly influenced Dillard's views of the history of language contact between Blacks and Whites. The research most relevant to the history of Black speech published before the 1960s was that of Turner 1945, 1949.

Labov's work among Black speakers in New York (1966, 1972a, b) and that contributed primarily by Shuy, Fasold, and Wolfram (Shuy, Wolfram and Riley 1967; Fasold 1969; Wolfram 1969) in Detroit were the earliest technical linguistic studies. The findings of these studies have been reported in a wide variety of other sources, many of which were oriented toward educators (Baratz and Shuy 1969; Fasold and Shuy 1970; Labov 1970). Burling 1973 is intended for a more general public. Wolfram and Fasold 1974 gives a comprehensive treatment of sociolinguistic research including Black English.

Studies of the folklore of Blacks were available much before studies of the structures of language in use among Black Americans; one of the best known is Abrahams 1970 (first published 1964). Children's folk games and stories are collected in Jones and Hawes 1972. A comprehensive summary of these works and historical treatment of the music of Blacks is given in Levine 1977. Lomax 1950 and Keil 1966 are excellent accounts of the music and entertainment world of Blacks.

Ethnographic studies of the culture of Black Americans provide some insight into the general contexts of speech activities. Urban studies include Hannerz 1969 and Stack

1976; rural studies, Young 1970 and Martha Ward 1971. Kochman 1972 is a collection of papers on language use in urban Black America. There is no comparable collection on the language use of Black children in their communities; Mitchell-Kernan and Kernan 1977 and Whatley, forthcoming treat speech events such as directives, narratives, boasts, jump-rope jingles, and fussing episodes. Heath, forthcoming compares the uses of language in the community with those of the classroom and other institutional settings, such as medical clinics, social service offices, etc.

Part II

Languages before English

Introduction

When European explorers and settlers came to North America they found a population of Native Americans here, speaking their own languages and living their own cultures. Descendants of these Native Americans, or "Indians" as Columbus called them, have maintained some aspects of their languages and cultures, although some have disappeared and all have been affected by the ways of life and forms of language used by the new Americans around them. The language situation of the Native Americans of the USA is not well known and understood by the general population of today. Uninformed though Americans may be about colonial languages and immigrant languages of their nation, they are even less well informed about American Indian languages. Unfortunately, the ignorance is compounded by misinformation and widespread stereotypes that are often far from the truth. Native Americans themselves are sometimes unfamiliar with the relationships among their languages and the history of their languages and cultures in North America.

In Part II of this volume, we try to clear away some of the misinformation, give an overview of the Indian languages today, and present material from the language history of Native Americans, including the writing systems they have used and the means of communication they have employed between speakers of different languages. In this Part we also deal with Spanish, one of the colonial languages, apart from English, which survived in the USA. In the Southwest, Spanish preceded English, was at times closely connected with Indian languages, and now constitutes a large component of the Spanish language in the USA.

Four erroneous ideas about Indian languages frequently appear in discussions about Native Americans. A little thought given to these ideas and some attention paid to a few well-known events in American history would suffice to show their distortion or denial of facts. Many Americans no longer hold such ideas, but they are sufficiently widespread to affect the actions of educators, legislators, and the general populace. They are:

1. There is only one Indian language, and it makes sense to ask whether someone "speaks Indian."

2. The Indian language is a primitive kind of language, having strange sounds, limited vocabulary, and undeveloped grammar, and it is not suitable for modern communication.

3. The Indian language is dying out and will soon be totally forgotten.

4. Most Indians cannot speak English properly and use a broken kind of English that includes the greeting "How!", the exclamation "ugh!", and the word "heap" as a multipurpose quantifier and intensifier.

At the time the Europeans began to arrive, the language situation in North America was one of great linguistic and cultural diversity, with well over 200 different, i.e. mutually unintelligible, languages belonging to about fifteen LANGUAGE FAMILIES. In the nearly five centuries between Columbus and the present, some languages disappeared, many SPEECH COMMUNITIES were displaced from their traditional locations, and patterns of interlanguage communication changed drastically, but roughly the same amount of language diversity exists today as was evident in pre-Columbian times. The Native Americans themselves had no cover term for "Indians" in their languages, and a sense of pan-Indian unity had no reason to emerge before non-Indians appeared.

No present-day language used as the primary means of communication in a fully functioning speech community is "primitive" in the popular sense, and American Indian languages, like all other full, NATURAL LANGUAGES in the world, have their finely structured sound systems and grammatical systems, and have large vocabularies of tens of thousands of different LEXICAL items. Many Indian languages are "undeveloped" in the sense that they lack one or more of the following: widespread written use of the language, a well-established "standard" form of the language, and extensive terminology for modern science and technology. Apart from such features, the Native American languages are full-fledged human languages, and they show an astonishing variety of grammatical systems. In fact, the analysis of Indian languages by American linguists has been one of the most important factors in the development of linguistic science in the USA. Franz Boas' treatment of the grammatical categories in the indigenous languages of North American (Boas 1911) has remained a classic demonstration of the range of diversity possible in the organization of human language, and most of the prominent names in the history of linguistics in the USA are associated in one way or another with the study of Indian languages: William Dwight Whitney (1827–94), Edward Sapir (1884–1939), Leonard Bloomfield (1887–1949).

The great linguistic diversity of North America meant that the Indians had to find ways of communicating between speakers of different languages. When European languages were added to the American scene, the Indians had further problems in communicating with speakers of these non-Indian languages. The Plains Indian sign language is the best known among the LINGUA FRANCAS used by Native Americans – it is even taught, in simplified form, in many Boy Scout troops as part of the lore of the outdoor life. Many other lingua francas were utilized in different settings, and modern scholarship is just beginning to trace these AUXILIARY LANGUAGES, some of them in pre-Columbian use, some of them PIDGINIZED varieties of European languages. Since the situations that called forth these lingua francas are no longer the same, they have mostly died out of use, and the PHILOLOGICAL task of reconstructing them from contemporary records, modern oral tradition, and linguistic comparison is a demanding one, recounted in Chapter 8.

The notion that American Indian languages are dying out is partly true, in that some languages have vanished and some now have very few remaining speakers, but it is also false in several important ways. In general, Native Americans have maintained their languages in spite of extraordinary pressures from government, churches, and the mass of the American people. They have maintained their languages longer and more effectively than the non-English-speaking immigrants to the country, and some Indian languages have more speakers now than they have ever had in their history. Navajo, now spoken by more than 175,000, is the most outstanding example, but other smaller communities can also be named. Native Americans in the USA recognize the importance of English in the nation as a whole, and the majority of them speak English either as a MOTHER TONGUE or as one of the languages in their repertoire, but every ''tribe'' or speech community has its own unique language situation. Some of these situations and the efforts being made to extend the uses of Indian languages are described in Chapter 6.

The full story of writing in the autochthonous languages of the western hemisphere has never been told, and it is a neglected area of research for the Indian languages of the USA. Writing, i.e. the visual representation of language by sequences of characters or letters, was invented in the New World presumably in complete independence of its invention at several times and places in Asia, and scholars are still struggling with the full interpretation of some of the American writing systems, especially the Mayan hieroglyphs. In pre-Columbian times, it was only in the Aztec empire of what is now Mexico that writing had definitely begun to fill the wide range of functions that writing had assumed in the civilizations of Southwest Asia, India, China, Europe, and North Africa. In the Americas, as in sub-Saharan Africa, federations and empires flourished, sometimes on a very large scale, without the use of writing. Examples are the Iroquois Confederacy in what is now central New York state and the vast Inca empire in the area of present-day Peru, Ecuador, and Bolivia. After the coming of the Europeans, however, the idea of writing spread fairly rapidly among Native American groups, either at the initiative of Europeans or by stimulus diffusion among the Indians. Under the Spanish colonialists, Classical Aztec (Nahuatl) and Classical Mayan (Yucatec) were written in roman letters and a vast number of local legends, plays, administrative reports, chronicles, and literary pieces were copied or newly produced. Most Americans are surprised to learn that the total written output in these two languages comprises a body of literature equal in extent and variety to the whole corpus of Classical Latin and Greek.

Further to the north, in what is now the USA, writing had not been in traditional use; it received less encouragement from the colonial authorities, and it spread more slowly. Yet writing came into use also among the Native Americans of the USA, and Chapter 7 gives an account of a number of the Indians' experiences with written forms of their languages, some now forgotten, others still alive and functioning. The accomplishment of Sequoyah, the Cherokee who created a SYLLABARY for his people, is perhaps the best known of these experiences, but many other less famous episodes are equally significant.

The fourth erroneous notion about the use of language by Native Americans has probably been the most subtly and insidiously damaging. The stereotype is all too familiar: the taciturn Indian who expresses himself, when he deems it necessary, in a pidginized form of English that may demonstrate his loyalty, cunning, knowledge of the lore of woods and plains, and occasional nobility, but shows his lack of intellectual potential and inability to master the proper use of English. This caricature of Indian English became firmly entrenched in American folklore, especially in the folklore of children, where it remains as a substratum of adult attitudes toward Native Americans. This stereotype form of language even spread to works about American Indians in other countries, and successive generations of Germans, for example, have read Karl Mey's cowboys-and-Indians novels of the American West, in which the Redman speaks in a distorted and pidginized German modeled on the American stereotype. Even now, at a time when there is greater consciousness of ethnic stereotypes and new respect for the Native Americans, this representation of Indian English continues in comic books, movies, and reruns of the Lone Ranger and Tonto.

The truth is almost the exact opposite. Many Indian tribal groups placed a high value on oratory of various kinds, and subtle and sophisticated uses of the Indian languages were practiced and respected. The metaphors and appeals based on *ethos, pathos,* and *logos* resemble closely those of classical writers of antiquity (Washburn 1975). Moreover, the Indians' errors in mastering English were probably less severe on the whole than the Europeans' errors in learning to speak Indian languages. One area of communication between Native Americans and new Americans which constitutes a fascinating, neglected by-road of early American history, is the pattern of verbal performance which evolved in treaty-making negotiations. Different traditions of public oratory and means of reaching agreement among the various Indian groups and between Indians and Europeans contributed to a more or less uniform style of negotiating in which principals and interpreters acted out a kind of performance new to all the groups represented.

The first Europeans to share the North American continent with the Native Americans in any substantial numbers were the Spaniards, and their national language, Castilian, soon became naturalized in the New World. The language policies of Spain encouraged the use of Indian languages, particularly the lingua franca Nahuatl, but they also encouraged the teaching of Castilian. Castilian Spanish spread from the top down, and the growing middle layer of *mestizos,* between the *peninsulares* from Spain and the local Indians, increasingly became Spanish-speaking. BILINGUALISM between Spanish and Indian languages was added to the bilingualism between local languages and the Indian lingua franca, and throughout a large part of Mexico, Spanish gradually took over the lingua franca functions of Nahuatl. The area of Spanish language presence ultimately included a large part of what later became the Southwest of the USA as well as parts of Florida and elsewhere on the Gulf of Mexico. When English entered those territories as a result of the political changes of purchase, conquest, and annexation, it was added to this varied picture of monolingual Spanish speakers, bilinguals in Spanish and one or more Indian languages, bilinguals in various

Indian languages, and monolingual speakers of Indian languages. New patterns of English monolingualism and various kinds of bilingualism involving English became more prominent in the area. Although the numbers of people following the various patterns have changed, all these basic patterns still exist in the Southwest. In the state of Arizona, for example, there are monolingual English speakers, monolingual Spanish speakers, monolingual speakers of Indian languages, and many kinds of bilingualism. For instance, the Yaqui speech community employs English, Spanish, and Yaqui in various proportions depending on the age, sex, and life styles of its members.

The history of Spanish in the USA is thus partly the continuation of a colonial language, and the use of Spanish in the Southwest is based on the spread of Spanish there before the arrival of English, even though it has repeatedly been reinforced by immigration from Mexico and, to a lesser extent, by the coming of people from other parts of the Spanish-speaking world. The colonial role of Spanish in North America is largely ignored in the teaching of American history, and few Americans are aware, for example, that the first university in North America was not English-speaking Harvard, but the Spanish-speaking University of Mexico, or that there were some forty colleges and seminaries in operation in New Spain by the end of the Spanish regime. The influence of colonial Spanish language and culture on the Native Americans was also greater than is usually recognized. The Indians of the American Southwest had their first contact with European culture from the Spaniards, and their languages all have Spanish loanwords which reflect that contact, especially names of domestic animals and food plants, words relating to political and military administration, and to religion. Chapter 9 gives an account of some aspects of this New World Spanish, particularly Mexican-American Spanish, and its influence on other languages in the region.

Spanish in the USA is also an immigrant language, as a result of the later arrival of Hispanic populations originating in Cuba and other Spanish-speaking countries. The special case of Puerto Rican Spanish is discussed in the first chapter of Part III. Thus the complex national role of Spanish in the USA which is in the process of working itself out, is reflected by its double treatment here, spanning colonial and immigrant status.

6

American Indian languages

WILLIAM L. LEAP

No discussion of language in the USA could hope to be complete unless it pays careful attention to the languages spoken by this country's first inhabitants. The fact that languages (and *not* a single language, with many DIALECTS) are at issue here must be emphasized from the outset. For there are, by present estimate, over 200 distinct Indian language traditions currently attested within the Indian tribes and communities of the fifty states. These languages have long been a significant (even if frequently overlooked) component of the nation's cultural resources. They are certainly not "limited" in their descriptive power, nor are they "primitive" in their potential for expressiveness. The structural details of Indian languages reflect profound appreciation for the physical world and its natural order. European colonists depended on this understanding as a means for their own survival on numerous occasions during the contact period. Reflexes of that dependency, and of the various forms of interaction which subsequently came to replace it, have become commonly attested in American English usage. Words of Indian-specific cultural items (teepee, wampum, kachina), foodstuffs (succotash, maize), place names and geographical terms (Tallahassee, Mississippi) along with phrases ranging from the most esoteric (*Gitchee Gumee, Nokomis*, and other items from Longfellow's poetry) to the most trivial of purposes (*kemo sabe* of Lone Ranger and Tonto fame) are all familiar vocabulary to most of the nation's citizenry.

Of interest here, however, is the fact that America's native languages exist in more stable forms than such context-specific usages might seem to imply; 206 different American Indian languages are currently spoken, are being learned, and are being retained within the national Indian community. In instances where ancestral language fluency is gone, efforts are being mounted to correct the situation to the extent that comparative data, archival records, and personal recollection will allow. The interest in the maintenance of Indian language fluency must be taken as a measure of the importance associated with that fluency by tribes and community members. Indian languages offer more than a casual badge of cultural solidarity for their speakers. Fluency in the language ancestral to a person's tradition helps establish that person's place within his own tribe or community, much as control over Standard English helps the person secure his position within the society outside of the Indian-specific domain. While any number of questions can be raised about the authenticity of contemporary expression which some Indian groups have given to traditional culture, questions have never been raised about the legitimacy of cultural details conveyed through, or accompanied by, Indian language terms.

Indian language fluency offers Indian people some real and viable complements to the proficiency in English which Indians, like all U.S. citizens, are expected to maintain. This chapter will examine the contributions to American language pluralism which have been, and continue to be, made by America's native languages. First, the richness of the nation's Indian language inventory will be developed by reference to the diversity and relatedness which crisscross the Indian language traditions attested at the present time. Next, the impact of the contact experience on the precontact language traditions will be explored, noting the inroads which the introduction of English fluency has made on the continuity of those traditions. This will set the stage for a more detailed review of the efforts toward Indian LANGUAGE MAINTENANCE currently being undertaken by tribes and Indian communities throughout the United States. Comments on the prospects for success of these efforts will be offered at the close of the chapter.

American Indian language families

The richness of America's Indian language traditions can be described in terms of any number of characteristics. Yet contemporary interest in Indian language maintenance and language revival can best be understood only if the *diversity* contained within those traditions has first been clarified. To do this, comments on the classification of Indian languages must first be made. Through the development of accurate classifications of language relationships, historical connections between Indian languages (and by extension, between their speakers) can be determined, and thus the range of similarity and diversity within these languages can likewise be ascertained.

Classifications of Indian languages in such terms have been made by any number of linguists over the past 100 years. In some cases – e.g. the Tanoan languages of the Rio Grande pueblo communities, or the Dakota, Lakota, and Nakota Sioux "dialects" – the fact of relationship has remained as apparent as are the historical ties linking French, Spanish, Portuguese, and Italian into a single, Romanic language family. A glance at the data displayed in Table 6.1 will show how easily a close historical relationship between two of the Tanoan languages (Taos and Isleta) could be identified. These common terms show striking similarities in form and structure. The relationship between Tewa and this Tiwa unity (Taos and Isleta) is less immediately clear, but can be supported through more carefully developed comparisons. The terms from Keresan, in contrast, appear to be so dissimilar to the data from the other languages that no historical connection between them need be posited within this argument. But the status of Towa and Piro remains less clear. In this as well as other instances in American Indian historical linguistics research, the evidence available for comparative purposes only hints at the relationships which might (or might not) exist between single Indian languages or more inclusive LANGUAGE FAMILIES.

Table 6.1. *Some southwestern Indian language relationships*

	Taos	Isleta	Tewa	Towa	Piro	Keresan
1. 'head'	p'inema	p'i	p'o	ts'oc	pi-nem	-násgái
2. 'hair'	phaena	pha	pho	fwola	sana-e	-há.zanɨ
3. 'forehead'	p'aphoena	p'aphoa	tsigo	wape	tsi-kia-nem	-pɪ
4. 'ear'	t'aɬoana	t'aɬua	oye	watye	tah-so-hem	-yúpɪ
5. 'eye'	tsinema	tci	tšii	se	tsi-hia-ne	-hụwaná?ani
6. 'mouth'	ɬamua	ɬamu	so	tyekwa	sa-na-e	-kʌ
7. 'neck'	k'oanem	k'oa	k'e	to	youl-wa-hem	-wi
8. 'body'	tuwata	tuu	tuwa	kwalo	el enkwerpo	dápʌcɪ
9. 'bone'	ununa	un	phekhun	honc	ou-an-em	hásgəni
10. 'spring time'	tanwiena	tanwin	taandi	tondakiw	halepun-a	tí·çʌ
11. 'white'	p'atho	p'athu	ts'a	kwidjulo	na-atzay-e	-šé
12. 'red'	phaɬ	phaimo	p'i	unculo	na-u-e	kɔ́-anɨ
13. 'yellow'	ts'u	tc'u	ts'e	olculo	na-sawa-e	činɪ
14. 'blue/green'	tsa	tcu	tsonwa	watsaculo	na-tzeu-e	-wisk3

Source: Comparative recordings in Harrington 1909. Keresan words from Davis 1964.

In such instances, the decision to establish historical connections or to posit independent linguistic traditions usually depends on the individual scholar's attitude toward the process of language classification itself. American Indian linguists have tended to fall into one of two camps: the "lumpers," who emphasize common traits shared by more inclusive sets of relatable languages; and the "splitters," who tend to set up independent language groupings on the basis of identified linguistic contrasts. A review of the major attempts to classify Indian languages will show the continuing influence of both positions. J. W. Powell, for example, established the presence of fifty-eight different Indian language families in the area north of Mexico, on the basis of comparative vocabularies submitted to the Bureau of American Ethnology by missionaries, army officers, and other persons with interests in America's native languages (Powell 1891). Edward Sapir, some thirty-eight years later, regrouped Powell's families into six more inclusive linguistic "phyla" using grammatical processes and word structure as the primary index for his classification (Sapir 1929). Fifteen years later, Harry Hoijer returned to Powell's original statement and reviewed what had subsequently become known about their interrelationship (Hoijer 1946). Identification of such "possible relationships" seems an appropriate way to introduce the reader to the "linguistic structures of Native America," especially since, as Hoijer noted, none of the families established by Powell's analysis had become discredited by more recent investigation. Trager and Harben (1958), on the other hand, used the phylum-level distinctions from Sapir's analysis to systematize their interpretation of these same relationships. Morris Swadesh (1960) has likewise worked with Sapir's analysis, but in precisely the opposite direction. In several places he has cited evidence which demonstrates, in his opinion, that "the great bulk of American languages form a single genetic phylum going far back into time."

Clearly, differing purposes in the treatment of diversity are being served in each analysis. In the present case, the need is simple – to establish the fact of Indian language diversity. Recognizing this, a middle-ranged attempt at classification seems appropriate, one which recognizes family-level language groupings but does not disregard more widely ranging language relationships as well. Applying this perspective to the language traditions currently attested within the United States yields the following classification of American Indian languages. The accompanying map, Figure 6.1, gives an approximate idea of the probable location of the various language families. Note, however, that several families (Tlingit and Haida, Wakashan, Sahaptin, and Kiowa-Tanoan) do not appear on the map; their distribution is either too limited or too interspersed with larger language families for them to be represented on the map, which shows only a rough outline of Native American languages.

1. *Eskimo.* Spoken along the Arctic coast and immediately adjacent islands of Greenland, Canada, and Alaska. Formerly it was believed that this family consisted solely of two very closely related languages, one in western Alaska, the other in the remainder of the Arctic area. More intensive research, sponsored in the main by the Alaska Native Language Center at the University of Alaska,

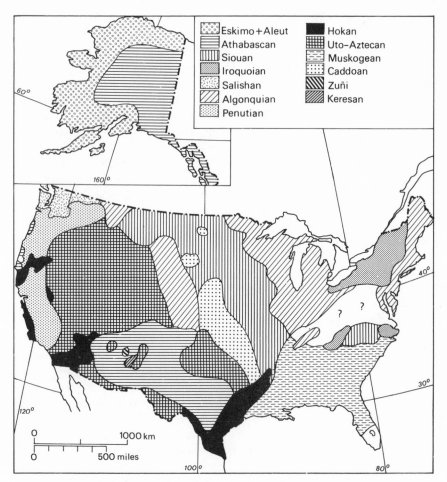

Figure 6.1. American Indian language families (adapted from the frontispiece map by
Ronald F. Abler in Spencer, Jennings et al. 1977. Copyright © 1977 by Harper and Row,
Publishers, Inc. Reprinted by permission of the publisher)

has now shown that there may be as many as *five* distinctive Eskimo languages
spoken in Alaska alone. Here as elsewhere in this list, the level of fluency is not
uniform across the given area. Thus while Eskimo remains the first language of
persons in rural Alaska ("the bush"), regardless of age level, larger settlements
(e.g. Bethel) and urban areas within the state report that many of the children
entering school for the first time are not fluent in Eskimo.

2. *Aleut.* Spoken in the Aleutian island chain, which extends off the southwestern corner of Alaska to separate the Bering Sea from the Pacific Ocean.
Aleut and Eskimo languages are believed by some to comprise a larger, more
inclusive super-family, although the similarities could be due to close historical
contact and not common linguistic origin. Archaeological settlements in the
Aleutian islands do appear to predate the earliest attested Eskimoan settlements
by several thousand years.

3. *Tlingit* and *Haida*. Spoken along the coast and adjacent islands of southern Alaska and northwest corner of British Columbia. Speakers' tradition reports that both Tlingit and Haida are distantly related to the various Athabaskan languages of interior Alaska and, by extension, to Navajo and Apache languages of the U.S. Southwest (see 5 below). Even if this is true, the degree of relationship reflects such great time depth that each language deserves its own treatment in this listing.

4. *Wakashan*. Spoken on Vancouver Island and the adjacent coastal mainland of British Columbia, Nootka and Kwakiutl are the more familiar Canadian members of this family. Makah, the ancestral language of Neah Bay and surrounding areas on the northwest corner of Washington's Olympic peninsula, is the only Wakashan language spoken on the U.S. mainland.

5. *Athabaskan*. Languages within this family are found within an enormous area of the interior of Alaska and western Canada (e.g. Kuchin, Eyak); in scattered sections of Washington, Oregon, and northern California (Hupa, Tolowa); and in large sections of the U.S. Southwest (Navajo and the several Apache languages). Many of the Athabaskan languages have been the focus of intensive analysis by linguists and anthropologists. Practical benefits have been evidenced in many instances. A writing system is available for use by Hupa speakers, for example, which gives a unique symbol for each of the contrastive sounds of the spoken language. This system departs in significant ways from the alphabetic principles and spelling conventions common to American English, where a number of letters and groups of letters can represent the same sound. The distinctive "Indian" quality can be associated with written Hupa and the written language is said to have become a point of pride for many members of the tribe because of it.

Navajo is the most widely spoken of the Athabaskan languages, primarily because the Navajo nation is the largest single tribal entity in America. (By some estimates, in fact, there may be more speakers of the Navajo language than there are of all other American Indian languages combined.) Even though English fluency continues to expand within the tribal membership, Navajo has remained the language of the home and the language preferred for communication for most persons on the reservation. Navajo is also the only native American language which has had a commercially prepared typewriter keyboard designed especially for its speakers' use.

6. *Salishan*. These individually distinctive languages are found in southern British Columbia and the Puget Sound area, though related languages also extended across northern Washington state, northern Idaho, and into western Montana. American members of the Salishan family include: Lummi, Quinault, upper and lower Chehalis; Okanagon, Lake, and other Salishan languages on the Colville reservation; Spokane; Kalispel; Coeur d'Alene; and Flathead. Kutenai is an isolated language probably distantly related to the Salishan family. In most cases, fluency in these languages has been retained only within the older segments of each reservation's SPEECH COMMUNITY, though persons in many families can still be found to use descriptive phrases and idioms particular to their tribe's ancestral language during daily English conversations.

7. *Penutian*. The Penutian languages spoken in the USA are found primarily in California (e.g. Yokuts, Miwok, Maidu) and in Oregon (Klamath, Upper and Lower Chinook). While most speakers of Tsimshian are found in British Columbia, some Tsimshian speakers live in southern Alaska, as well.

8. *Sahaptin*. This grouping includes the fifteen or more dialects spoken on the Yakima reservation and the Sahaptin portion of the Indian speech community on the Colville reservation (Washington state) as well as the Sahaptin dialects spoken on the Warm Springs and Umatilla reservations (Oregon) and by the Nez Perce (Idaho). Sahaptin itself is often classified as a unit within the Penutian language family, given the evidence for historical relationship which can be identified through linguistic comparison. On the other hand, an extreme amount of intercommunity intelligibility still sets Sahaptin apart from the other Penutian languages. This aggregate autonomy has been recognized by the Sahaptin speakers themselves. One consequence of this has been a three-state, five-tribe Sahaptin Language Consortium, established in 1976 to assist member tribes in addressing their common interests in Sahaptin language maintenance and cultural retention. Separate status is given to Sahaptin in this listing for these reasons.

9. *Hokan*. As is the case for the Salishan, the Hokan grouping is composed of a large number of diverse languages, including Karok, Shasta, Pomo, and Washo (in California); as well as Hualapai, Havasupai, Mohave, Diegueno, and other Yuman languages of Arizona, southern California, and northern Mexico. The rural location of many of the Hokan speech communities has helped retain ancestral language fluency into the twentieth century. Recent ties of cooperation between dedicated linguists and trained native speakers have resulted in highly successful, tribally based language maintenance projects accompanied by significant advances in linguistic scholarship as well.

10. *Uto-Aztecan*. Like Hokan, languages in the Uto-Aztecan family are found on both sides of America's southern border, for only half of the languages in this family are native to the United States. The grouping includes Luiseño, Serrano, and other languages of southern California; Hopi, spoken within the cluster of mesa-topped villages which constitute the pueblo of Hopi in northern Arizona; Pima and Papago, spoken in southern Arizona and northern Sonora; a number of languages whose speakers were traditionally found within or near the Great Basin (Mono, Paiute, Shoshone, Ute, Chemehuevi); and Comanche, one of the languages of the southern plains. Yaqui, formerly spoken only in Mexico, is now spoken in southern Arizona – primarily within the area called Pascua, a barrio of metropolitan Tucson.

Recent missionary-based efforts at language research have assisted in the maintenance of Uto-Aztecan fluency in some instances, especially within southern Arizona. Other Uto-Aztecan tribes remain strongly traditional and have resisted efforts toward cultural assimilation throughout their contact history. These factors, along with the rural location of many of these speakers' homesteads, have facilitated a continuity in native language expression still evidenced within most of the communities to this day.

11. *Kiowa-Tanoan.* This family includes Kiowa, one of the languages of the southern Plains; as well as Tiwa, Tewa, and Towa, three of the six languages spoken within the puebloan Southwest. Traditionally, the Tanoan languages were associated with Rio Grande pueblo communities. But during the aftermath of the Pueblo Indian revolt of 1680, a group of Tewa speakers moved from their home in central New Mexico, to set up a colony on the second mesa of Hopi pueblo, Arizona. Today, members of that colony are often fluent in both Indian languages (and in English and Spanish as well). Many anthropologists are said to have gotten their "authentic information" about traditional Hopi culture from persons of Tewa background so that distinctions between the two groups sometimes become blurred in social science accounts.

12. *Zuñi.* Zuñi is a single language, spoken at the pueblo of the same name in western New Mexico. It may be relatable to the languages of the Penutian family (7 above), but the time-depth associated with that relationship suggests that Zuñi people have had their own, autonomous cultural history for a considerable period of time.

13. *Keresan.* The language is spoken within seven of the pueblo communities of central New Mexico: Acoma, Laguna; Santa Ana, Zia; San Felipe, Cochiti, and Santo Domingo. As may be the case for Zuñi, Keresan can be termed a linguistic isolate, meaning that close relationships with other languages common to the region cannot be readily demonstrated. But in this case, the totally unique structure of Keresan grammar makes it unrelatable to *any* other language in native North America. And even if it were relatable, the connection would lie at so great a time-depth as to make the fact inconsequential for historical analysis. This implies that Keresan speakers may have been among the first (or at least, the earliest of the currently known) inhabitants of the puebloan Southwest, a fact receiving increasing support from recent archaeological research in the area.

14. *Siouan.* This family constitutes a large grouping of languages which were spoken primarily in the Plains areas at the time of European contact. Several internal divisions within the family are recognized. These include: Ponca, Quapaw, Omaha, and Osage (in Arkansas and the southern Plains); Winnebago (Wisconsin, and now Nebraska as well); Mandan, Hidatsa, and Crow (in the northern Plains); and the three commonly identified "Sioux" languages – Dakota, Lakota or Teton, and Nakota or Assiniboine (in Minnesota, Montana, and North and South Dakota). Members of the Siouan family were also attested in the lower Mississippi valley – Biloxi, Ofo; in the Carolinas – Santee, Catawba; and in Virginia – Tutelo. Most analyses now accept the historical relationship between Siouan, Iroquoian, and Caddoan, though a Siouan-specific period of internal language divergence is also accepted by those scholars.

15. *Caddoan.* Originally spoken in southwestern Louisiana and eastern Texas (Caddo proper), speakers of what became known as Arikara, Pawnee, and Wichita appear to have moved onto the Plains, where they were at the time of European contact. Today, Arikara speakers are found on Fort Berthold reserva-

124   WILLIAM L. LEAP

tion in North Dakota; the other tribes of the Caddoan language family reside in Oklahoma. Ancestral language fluency is not extensive within any of these contexts, though Fort Berthold Arikaras are now involved in a language maintenance effort involving three Indian languages (Arikara, Mandan, and Hidatsa) to correct the situation within that community.

16. *Muskogean.* These languages appear to have been members of the largest language family in the southeastern United States; the remaining languages in that area, other than the members of the Siouan family, are commonly viewed as language isolates. Familiar members of this family include: Creek, Choctaw, Alabama, Koasati, Seminole, and Miccosukee. Attempts were made to remove the Muskogean tribes into "Indian country" during the 1830s. The diverse locations of their descendants today attest to the only partial effectiveness of that policy – Choctaw speakers are found in Mississippi and eastern Oklahoma; Creek speakers in Florida, Alabama, Texas, and Oklahoma; Seminole speakers in south-central Florida and Oklahoma, and so on.

During the early years of the nineteenth century, Protestant missionaries administered schooling programs serving the Muskogean tribes. In those schools, children's ancestral languages played critical roles within the instructional process. The long-standing tradition of Choctaw language literacy, which continues within the Mississippi and Oklahoma communities to this day, has been only one of the by-products of those efforts.

17. *Iroquoian.* This family includes Huron and the languages of the League of the Iroquois – Seneca, Cayuga, Onondaga, Oneida, and Mohawk, all of which were originally spoken in the southern Great Lakes region; as well as Tuscarora and Cherokee, originally spoken in North Carolina and Virginia. Tuscarora speakers moved (back?) to the southern Great Lakes region and were admitted to the League around 1715. A major portion of the Oneida tribe was removed to Wisconsin in the nineteenth century. Senecas, Cayugas, and Wyandots were relocated from New York state to Oklahoma. Such also became the case for many of the Cherokees. The development of the Cherokee SYLLABARY by Sequoyah (see Chapter 7), and its acceptance and use by Cherokee people as a whole, may have contributed greatly to the retention of Cherokee language fluency in spite of the "trail of tears": children in some sections of Oklahoma still enter school with Cherokee as their first language, not English. The flourishing continuation of the Longhouse religion in Iroquois communities in New York state may likewise have assisted in the retention of ancestral language fluencies in those contexts.

18. *Algonquian.* Members of this language group show widespread geographic distribution, both during the precontact period and at the present time. Algonquian languages originally spoken in the northeastern states include Cree, Micmac, Passamaquoddy, Shawnee, and Delaware. Ojibwa (Chippewa), Menominee, and Potowatomi were spoken by Algonquian tribes in the Great Lakes Region. Speakers of Shawnee and Delaware were subsequently moved into Oklahoma, where fluency is attested primarily within the older segments of the communities. Fluency level for other of the Northeastern and Great Lakes Algonquian languages is not so severe, but in only the exceptional case (e.g. Red Lake, Minnesota) is the language known by the majority of community membership.

In the pre- and early contact periods, Cheyenne-, Arapaho-, and Kickapoo-speaking tribes moved out of the Great Lakes region and onto the Plains. Speakers of Blackfoot (Siksika) may have done likewise, but at an earlier point in time. Today these tribes have been settled on reservation lands in eastern Montana and Oklahoma; Wyoming; Kansas and Oklahoma; and western Montana, respectively. Fluency varies from household to household within each tribe. Some speakers of Kickapoo are also found in northern Mexico; there it is not uncommon to find families maintaining trilingual fluency – English, Spanish, and Kickapoo.

Additional, and more temporally remote, connections have also been posited, to link the Algonquian language family with the Ritwan languages of California (Yurok and now extinct Wiyot) and with the languages of the Wakashan family discussed in 4 above.

Several of the languages and language families cited in the preceding listing were referred to as language "isolates." This term is used to indicate that a particular language or language grouping has no immediately recognizable relatives within or beyond its speakers' geographic area. Such language isolates are attested within numerous locales – Etruscan, the antecedent of Latin in ancient Italy; Euskera, the language of the Basques of northern Spain and southern France; the language of the Sumerian civilization in the Near East; Burushaski, spoken in several villages in the mountains north of Kashmir. In most instances, linguists assume that the speakers of these languages are descendants of the earliest (or earliest known) inhabitants of the given area. Such observations, as George Trager (1967) demonstrated numerous times, are useful in establishing relative chronologies of the peopling of particular regions. The correlation previously discussed, linking the status given Keresan language, and the extreme archaeological time-depth now assigned to Keresan culture, is only one illustration of this phenomenon in native America.

Other recognized linguistic isolates in the United States include: Tunica, Chitimacha, and Natchez in the Southeast; Tonkawa and Karankawa in Texas; Yukian (a family with two members – Yuki and Wappo) in California; and Chimakuan (a family with two members – Quileute and the now extinct Chimakum) in Washington state. The presence of Indian language isolates in all parts of the United States reminds us of the extreme amount of time-depth at issue in any discussion of American Indian language relationships or language history. While Muskogean speakers seem in the statistical majority in the U.S. Southeast today, the presence of Tunica, Chitimacha, Natchez, and other pockets of unrelatable Indian languages in that area demonstrates conclusively that speakers of other native language backgrounds must have been present in the Southeast as well. Add to the list of Indian language isolates, those languages no longer spoken in Indian America: Piscataway, Miami, Serrano, Pecos, Piro, Yana, and others. Some of these are also language isolates. Others are members of more inclusive language families discussed in the preceding listing. Today all such languages are known only through missionaries' journals, explorers' records, and other archival sources. In fact, in many cases, a casual reference to an otherwise unidentified tribe may constitute our only record of a language's existence.

Table 6.2. *Mother tongue of Indians by sex, age, and whether living on identified reservations*

United States	Population		Sex		Age (years)					
	Number	Percent	Male	Female	Under 6	6 to 15	16 to 24	25 to 44	45 to 64	65 and over
TOTAL All Indians	760,572	100.0	373,514	387,058	111,414	198,268	129,570	173,226	104,459	43,635
Indian mother tongue	242,967	31.9	119,854	123,113	30,569	56,493	41,041	62,495	36,518	15,851
Algonquian	18,079	2.4	8,876	9,203	1,456	3,214	2,361	5,675	3,702	1,671
Athabaskan	106,566	14.0	52,039	54,527	17,880	30,783	19,385	23,376	10,918	4,224
Navajo	89,749	11.8	43,708	46,041	15,364	26,539	16,384	19,248	8,800	3,414
Caddoan	647	0.1	304	343	4	6	83	248	246	60
Iroquoian	17,571	2.3	8,983	8,588	1,217	2,566	2,745	4,942	4,030	2,071
Muskogean	16,507	2.2	8,243	8,264	1,452	2,889	2,599	4,614	3,570	1,383
Piman	11,311	1.5	5,691	5,620	1,515	2,890	1,861	2,510	1,696	839
Pueblo	11,289	1.5	5,479	5,810	1,560	3,030	1,713	2,779	1,430	777
Keresan	3,435	0.5	1,636	1,799	384	738	518	891	633	276
Tanoan	3,041	0.4	1,429	1,612	340	761	520	881	294	245
Zuñi	4,813	0.6	2,414	2,399	836	1,531	680	1,007	503	256
Salishan	1,377	0.2	629	748	51	161	170	448	352	195
Sahaptin	1,258	0.2	524	734	111	252	173	383	220	119
Shoshonean	14,174	1.9	6,810	7,364	1,393	3,026	2,528	3,829	2,215	1,183
Siouan	20,221	2.7	10,179	10,042	2,119	4,078	3,355	5,611	3,523	1,535
Yuman	2,201	0.3	1,145	1,056	252	503	320	560	398	168
Uto-Aztecan	32	–	8	24	6	–	8	12	6	–
Not specified	21,734	2.9	10,944	10,790	1,553	3,095	3,740	7,508	4,212	1,626

Table 6.2. (cont.)

United States	Population		Sex		Age (years)					
	Number	Percent	Male	Female	Under 6	6 to 15	16 to 24	25 to 44	45 to 64	65 and over
Other mother tongues	465,991	61.3	227,975	238,016	72,719	128,918	79,401	99,581	61,004	24,368
English	383,764	50.5	187,300	196,464	64,720	114,142	64,976	74,982	46,500	18,444
Spanish	24,621	3.2	12,474	12,147	2,919	5,104	4,728	7,051	3,396	1,423
French	8,387	1.1	3,961	4,426	540	1,138	1,258	2,483	2,093	875
Aleut and Eskimo	1,699	0.2	1,016	683	115	176	362	782	204	60
Other	47,520	6.2	23,224	24,296	4,425	8,358	8,077	14,283	8,811	3,566
Mother tongue not reported	51,614	6.8	25,685	25,929	8,126	12,857	9,128	11,150	6,937	3,416
ON IDENTIFIED RESERVATIONS										
All Indians	211,843	100.0	103,860	107,983	36,199	64,501	32,277	41,687	25,413	11,766
Indian mother tongue	123,255	58.2	60,360	62,895	18,503	34,289	18,774	26,781	16,806	8,102
Algonquian	8,721	4.1	4,397	4,324	853	1,881	995	2,179	1,912	901
Athabaskan	69,059	32.6	33,440	35,619	12,075	21,103	11,194	14,076	7,555	3,056
Navajo	58,409	27.6	28,193	30,216	10,127	18,031	9,453	11,829	6,383	2,586
Caddoan	33	–	22	11	–	–	–	27	6	–
Iroquoian	3,780	1.8	1,956	1,824	331	729	482	986	771	481
Muskogean	413	0.2	221	192	64	86	59	90	106	8
Piman	7,690	3.6	3,882	3,808	1,042	1,972	1,165	1,510	1,292	709
Pueblo	9,374	4.4	4,580	4,794	1,361	2,683	1,310	2,074	1,261	685
Keresan	2,503	1.2	1,191	1,312	259	574	362	542	545	221
Tanoan	2,447	1.2	1,179	1,268	287	669	374	659	238	220
Zuñi	4,424	2.1	2,210	2,214	815	1,440	574	873	478	244
Salishan	577	0.3	278	299	6	68	50	187	164	102
Sahaptin	676	0.3	240	436	81	167	58	175	102	93

Table 6.2. (cont.)

United States	Population		Sex		Age (years)					
	Number	Percent	Male	Female	Under 6	6 to 15	16 to 24	25 to 44	45 to 64	65 and over
Shoshonean	7,722	3.6	3,711	4,011	938	1,988	1,292	1,704	1,142	658
Siouan	11,636	5.5	5,757	5,879	1,417	2,836	1,685	2,916	1,825	957
Yuman	1,131	0.5	624	507	148	235	111	293	212	132
Uto-Aztecan	6	–	–	6	6	–	–	–	–	–
Not specified	2,437	1.2	1,252	1,185	181	541	373	564	458	320
Other mother tongues	73,588	34.7	36,182	37,406	14,675	25,621	10,979	12,479	7,018	2,816
English	54,592	25.8	26,953	27,639	12,173	21,005	8,180	8,080	3,882	1,272
Spanish	596	0.3	280	316	107	123	76	179	58	53
French	655	0.3	321	334	3	63	10	166	221	192
Aleut and Eskimo	59	–	25	34	–	–	9	42	8	–
Other	17,686	8.3	8,603	9,083	2,392	4,430	2,704	4,012	2,849	1,299
Mother tongue not reported	15,000	7.1	7,318	7,682	3,021	4,591	2,524	2,427	1,589	848

Source: Adapted from U.S. Bureau of the Census 1973: Table 18 (data based on 15 percent sample. Data on identified reservations include only those Indians living on 115 reservation areas identified by the Bureau of the Census on the basis of information from the Bureau of Indian Affairs).

The picture of Indian language diversity currently attested by the tribal Indian communities merely reflects the tip of the proverbial iceberg. If there are over 200 different Indian languages spoken in America today, there may have been over 500 different Indian languages spoken in America at the time of European contact. Yet even though specific data on many of these languages have been lost, archival research, language family comparisons, and other techniques of historical linguistics (see Haas 1969) can be combined with accurate descriptions of the structures and usage patterns associated with the Indian languages still spoken within Indian America to yield an accurate picture of the general richness of this precontact linguistic heritage. Some idea of the numbers of speakers of Indian languages can be obtained from Table 6.2 which gives estimates based on a 15 percent sample survey conducted by the Bureau of the Census in 1970.

The diversity of Indian languages

The fact of Indian language distinctiveness and overall language diversity must be underscored. Sapir and Swadesh in a now classic article discussing grammatical categories in American languages (1946) provided some contrastive data to illustrate the point quite succinctly by translating the English sentence 'He will give it to you' into six American Indian languages. The resulting sentences are:

Wishram (Penutian family)
ačimlúda

a-č-i-m-l-ud-a
'will-he-him-thee-to-GIVE-will'

Takelma (Penutian family)
ʔòspink

ʔòk-t-xpi-nk
'WILL GIVE-to-thee-he or they in future'

Southern Paiute (Uto-Aztecan)
maγavaaniak'aŋa'mi

maγa-vaania-aka-aŋa-ʔmi
'GIVE-will-visible thing-visible creature-
thee

Yana (Hokan)
ba·jamasiwaʔnuma

ba·-ja-ma-si-wa-ʔnuma
'ROUND THING-away-to-does or
will-done unto-thou in future'

Nootka (Wakashan)
ʔoyi·ʔa·qχateʔic

oʔ-yi·-ʔa·qχ-ʔat-eʔic
'THAT-give-will done unto-thou art'

Navajo (Athabaskan)
neido·ʔá·ɬ

n-a·-yi-diho-ʔá·ɬ
'thee-to-transitive-will-ROUND
THING IN FUTURE'

Note that English translation correlates for each of the grammatical components within the verbs have been provided in each instance. Some of the most

Table 6.3. *Punctual and segmentative verbs in Hopi*

ha'rï	'it is bent in a rounded angle'	harï'rïta	'It lies in a meandering line'
pa''ci	'it is notched'	paci'cita	'It is serrated'
ca'mi	'it is slashed inward from the edge'	cami'mita	'It is fringed'
wa'la	'it gives a slosh'	wala'lata	'It is tossing in waves'
yo''ko	'he gives one nod of the head'	yoko'kota	'He is nodding'
ro'ya	'it makes a turn'	roya'yata	'It is rotating'

Source: Whorf 1936: 127–30.

immediately noticed contrasts are: the initial occurrence of the 'give' reference in Takelma versus the apparent absence of a 'give'-related element in the Navajo expression; classification of the reference by shape in Yana versus by visibility in Southern Paiute; the numerous ways in which the fact of future reference is marked. All of these suggest areas within which grammatical expression, and presumably the speaker's perspective on the action itself, can be expected to vary.

Since the linguistic work of Whorf, scholars with interests in American Indian languages have made much of the cultural implications of such distinctions. In most cases, scholars have been able to link the uniqueness of the forms of expression in any given Indian language with the particular interests, needs, situational demands, and cultural priorities of the tribe(s) using that language in daily conversation. This is not to argue, necessarily, that the Indian cultural experiences gave deliberate shaping or structure to Indian language grammars. However, there are some instances, such as that reflected in the Hopi verb forms in Table 6.3, where the correlation between grammatical process (the reduplication of the final syllable in the first column, before the *-ta* suffix is added to form the items in the second column) and language reference seem too coincidental merely to be the product of chance. And it certainly is safe to point out, based on the comparative evidence, that speakers of Indian languages give formal expression to their classification of the universe and the things within it, through the sentence forms and word-level structures generated by those languages' grammars.

Mathiot (1962), for example, shows how Papago speakers are able to identify certain salient facts about the organization of their natural environment through the use of contrasts between grammatical categories. By her analysis, Papago language places "quail" and "deer" within one grammatical class, while placing "woodpecker" and "antelope" within a second, distinctive category. On the face of it, "quail" and "deer" appear to have little in common, "woodpecker" and "antelope" even less so, and thus the "logic" underlying each grammatical category does not seem clear. Yet as Mathiot sees it, it is not the noun class of the individual item, but the contrast in reference between pairs of items provided by the respective classifications which is at issue here. Through the contrast just cited, for example, the speaker is able to make a formal

distinction in his speech between birds which remain close to the ground and
birds which actually fly – a bit of information which might be of importance in
discussions of hunting strategies or other traditional activities.

Hage and Miller (n.d.) have shown, in a separate discussion, how the Shoshone
language maps out its own ornithological classification using a totally different
linguistic technique. In Shoshone, varying levels of specification for a given
variety of "bird" can be made, by contrasting its reference label with *kwinaa*
(for a larger bird) or *huittsuu* (for a smaller one). *Kwinaa* itself is the Shoshone
word for 'bird' in general; 'large bird'; all eagles, hawks, and falcons; and, most
particularly, 'golden eagle' – depending on the level of contrast and, in the final
instance, accompanying descriptive material. Thus to refer to a bird in Shoshone
language as a *hai* (as opposed to a *kwinaa*) shows that the bird is not an eagle,
hawk, or falcon, and places it within the category "crow or raven." To refer to a
bird as a *pia kwinaa,* on the other hand, shows that the bird is an eagle (as
opposed to certain kinds of hawks), yet this leaves the relative age of the bird
open for further detail.

Recall that Papago and Shoshone are related languages, in that they both are
members of the Uto-Aztecan language family. The presence of a common,
historically defined basis for these classifications might therefore be expected.
Yet the principle and process of classification is distinct in each instance: Papago
makes its identification by contrasting grammatical categories, Shoshone by
contrasting on the level of the individual term. Here then is an example of the
ways in which languages, even given common historical backgrounds, can
become adapted to the reference needs of their speakers, and of their speakers'
immediate environment. Whether such divergent adaptation is the by-product of
the long-term experience of each tribe in its current locale, or the result of a
deliberate shaping of one or both grammars to meet more immediate needs, is not
so much at issue. Much of the distinctiveness which characterizes a particular
Indian language has come to highlight its speakers' culturally salient, socially
significant reality.

Recognizing this, it becomes difficult to make generalizations about "Indian
language expressiveness" which will be found to be valid for all of the languages
of Native America. Far too often, we find Indian languages making quite
different uses out of what appear at first to be quite similar structural principles.
Haas (1944) shows, for example, that within the Koasati (Muskogean family)
speech community of southwestern Louisiana, "the speech of women differs in
certain well defined respects from that of men." She cites such evidence as the
following, to illustrate the nature of these differences:

Women	Men	
lakawtakkó	lakawtakkós	'I am not lifting it'
lakawwîl	lakawwís	'I am lifting it'
lakáw	lakáws	'He is lifting it'
lakawčin	lakawčî.s	'Don't lift it!'
lakawhôl	lakawhós	'Lift it!'

observing that the speech of the women appears to be more archaic (i.e. closer to the historical pattern common to the Muskogean family as a whole) than is the speech of the men. Of interest here, however, is the fact that the marking of sex of speaker in Koasati occurs in the suffix of the verb form. And while, by Haas' analysis, younger women have begun to use the men's, not the women's, verb forms, men and women are nonetheless expected to be familiar with both sets of forms, traditionally correcting the usage of children of either sex, and using the constructions appropriate to the sex of specific characters when telling stories.

Men and women's speech differences are attested in other Indian languages (see Chapter 8). Among the Tiwa-speaking pueblos of the Rio Grande, specific etiquette-related terms will differ, depending on speaker sex: thus Isleta language distinguishes *hawá* 'thank you (man speaking)' from *hárkem* 'thank you (woman speaking),' but the grammar does not appear to have the extensive differences of Koasati.

An analysis of sex-related speech differences among the Gros Ventres (Hidatsa) by Regina Flannery (1937) offers another variant on this theme. There, as within the Tiwa pueblos, men and women's speech centers on specific lexical items, though some instances of suffix-related contrasts are also cited. There, however, in contrast to Koasati or Isleta, much greater segregation in usage was identified, so much so that – according to the comments reported for one member of the tribe – younger people expressed reluctance to speak the language in front of their elders for fear of using expressions of grammatical forms of the opposite sex and then being ridiculed publicly for doing so.

That sex-related differences are found in Indian languages is not all that needs to be said on the matter. A closer look at the sex-related distinctions employed in tribal speech, and at the rules of DISCOURSE which govern their occurrence, provides insight into the cultural interpretation of male and female complementarity appropriate to each context. Indian languages do not so much define sex differences as they mark and maintain them. And not surprisingly, other kinds of social facts are also marked in Indian languages, including generational position, as noted for Kwakiutl by Boas (1932) and for Sandian Tiwa by Brandt (1970, 1975); distinctions between the sacred and secular components of the natural order, as shown for Zuñi language by Newman (1955) and in Western Apache by Greenfield (1973); the possibility of formal marking of rank, as noted by Drucker (1939) and numerous others on the Northwest coast; even social "class" – cf. Mishkin (1940) in reference to the Kiowa and other Plains tribes.

Given that each Indian language is functionally well-suited and appropriate for the cultural contexts in which its speakers employ it, it comes as no surprise to find that, as a general rule, Indian speech communities were multilingual, not language unique, in their verbal repertoires. Older members of tribal communities within the U.S. Southwest and on the Pacific coast still evidence sufficient fluency in several of the Indian languages in their region, as well as their own ancestral tongue, so that – as they now explain it – guests who come to the community from other tribes can be made to feel at home more easily. Intertribal marriages, adoptions, trade networks, ceremonial activities, and other such factors may likewise have helped to structure and maintain tribal multilingualism in the precontact period.

Certainly it was within the capability of precontact Indian peoples to learn as many languages, or develop as many other means of intertribal communication, such as PIDGINS and sign languages (see Chapter 8) as their circumstances might have dictated. Far from being a casual component of the precontact Indian experience, Indian languages appear to have given the tribal membership a readily available means through which they could invest in the continuing vitality of the tribal life style and its cultural and social uniquenesses. Here may rest the reason why Indian language fluency was so often a prime target for the work of missionaries, educators, members of the federal Indian administration, and other persons seeking the eradication of the ''Indian problem'' through one strategy or another. The languages were, and remain, important parts of the tribes' cultural inventory. And as English became a more visible part of the daily life of Indian peoples, even greater importance came to be placed on the maintenance of the ancestral language tradition within many communities. The reasons underlying this importance can be summarized in terms of two specific points.

First, and perhaps most importantly, Indian languages are clearly a part of the cultural heritage of local Indian communities. Daily life, personal interaction, political decision making, and ceremonial responsibilities were carried out in ancestral language terms before the time of European contact. For many of the tribes who survived the contact period, the language continued to be used for these purposes. The maintenance of ancestral language fluency helps guarantee further continuation of these traditions, and adds a sense of authenticity to that which is designated as ''Indian'' within the contemporary life style. The loss of fluency, in contrast, creates a break with the past and its cultural roots, producing a barrier which is difficult, if not impossible, to overcome by alternative means.

Second, the language of the community is an *expression of the cultural traditions*. Frequently, where Indian language expression is concerned, the reference contrasts quite markedly with the reference perspective allowed by the language of the surrounding society. The English sentence, *I am growing corn*, for example, cannot be given a literal translation in many Indian languages. Their grammars give formal marking to the fact that the corn, and not the gardener, does the growing. Sentences like *The Xerox machine made me a copy* or *The Coke machine did not give me my change* are equally ''nongrammatical'' in these languages. Machines, not being animate, cannot do anything for anyone under their own power. For members of many Indian communities, the power of the Indian language to give highly specific culture-based reference perspectives is important, especially if much of the day's conversation must be carried out in English. Under such circumstances, Indian language fluency reminds the speaker that no single language has a monopoly over truth, logic, or precision of expression; for any reference given in English, or given by an English speaker, there is always another way to say it, and another reference perspective which can be brought to the discussion.

The contribution of a viable Indian language tradition to the community member's sense of personal and social identity should now be clear. As one Cherokee educator has written:

For most Indian tribes, the most symbolic thing to them is their language. The Cherokee talk their language and by this they are able to define the tribe. . . There was a time when we lost most of our people over sixty. If we did not have our rituals written down, we would not have them today. Young people in urban areas do not know how to speak their native language and I think it is critical that they learn. If they don't, they will be in a bind because you cannot be an Indian and go home and not know how to speak your language.

Indian language maintenance: historical perspectives

The sentiments expressed by this Indian educator are certainly not unique to the Cherokee community, nor are they a product of Indian experiences in twentieth-century America. Most non-Indians forget that the schools founded in Indian communities by missionaries at the time of initial European occupation of America provided their instruction by using local Indian languages as well as the mother tongue of the missionary group. Choctaw and Cherokee people, among others, placed high value on the boost to language maintenance which these schools provided. When they took over responsibility for their own tribally based schooling programs, they continued using their own tongues until federal policy forbade the teaching of Indian students in any language other than English. The creation, acceptance, and use of syllabaries in Cherokee, Cree, and Ojibwa communities, and the popularity of the English-based alphabets used in the Sioux communities emphasize the same point: Indian people have never neglected any sensible opportunity which promised to preserve ancestral language skills (see Chapter 7). In instances where formalized ancestral language instruction or the acceptance of a written form of the language has been de-emphasized, community sensitivity toward other, more traditional maintenance strategies is found to be quite strong. The rejection of innovations proposed by outsiders often means that the community members in question continue to prefer their own techniques of language preservation. To this writer's knowledge, there have been no instances, either historical or contemporary in context, where an Indian community has intentionally allowed ancestral language fluency to disappear. In the past, particular institutions, such as the Bureau of Indian Affairs (BIA) schools, exerted strong and incessant pressures against use of the Indian tongues. In addition, the absence of economic opportunities in Indian communities and apart from English monolingual environments made it mandatory for many Indians to exchange their indigenous languages for English in order to survive economically. Many American institutions and policies have denied Indians the right to their linguistic and cultural heritage.

This insensitivity has been expressed in several guises since the beginnings of European occupation. First, there was a full-scale destruction of many Indian tribes either through deliberate genocide or through more subtle processes such as the removal of Indian people into "Indian country," the formation of the reservation system, and now the continual pressures to move into the mainstream presented by the surrounding society. The BIA and other Indian authorities within federal and state governments have had long-standing commitments to assimilationist policies. Such agencies have tended to react to any expression of Indian identity through Indian culture as a move toward cultural pluralism and separatism, and away from goals preferred by the larger society. The language policies of the federally controlled Indian schools have been particularly critical in this process. At one time, the use of any language other than English for instructional purposes within an Indian classroom was expressly forbidden by federal policy, thereby bringing over 100 years of tribally based bilingual schooling in many communities to an end. Children were punished for speaking their ancestral language on the playground or in other informal contexts. Education of students in off-reservation boarding school, especially for secondary level education, forced the separation of Indian youth from their parents. Always located far from the home community, the boarding schools guaranteed a lengthy separation of the student from the influence of his ancestral culture. The thorough mixing of tribal backgrounds in the dormitories helped ensure the choice of English as the only common language among the student population.

Such policies had a massive impact on ancestral language maintenance, including some results which their advocates may not have predicted. Parents who went through the boarding school experience vowed never to subject their children to such humiliation. To guarantee this, in some instances, parents deliberately stopped speaking the ancestral language to their children and insisted on a monolingual, English-only home environment. This, they felt, would make certain that no language "handicap" would cripple their children's educational betterment.

In recent years, particularly after World War II, policies of out-migration began to move Indian people from the reservation into the urban context. Where many members of the same community made such a move, it was possible to transplant some sense of community life into the city, and fluency in the ancestral language could remain viable in the alien environment. More frequently, however, the move to the city was made by individuals or by single families. The practical necessity of family-focused English fluency could not be ignored under those circumstances, and unless strong ties could be maintained with the home community, language loss was inevitable.

The role of Head Start and other child care programs in the decline of Indian language fluency also needs to be assessed. This is not to disregard the important benefits which early childhood intervention programs have had in areas of health and personal welfare; in some instances (notably, Acoma and Choctaw), these programs have been integrated into the community's efforts at native language maintenance. In most cases, however, the programs are run by outsiders and staffed by younger adults from the community, whose fluency in the ancestral language may not be as strongly grounded as that of their grandparents, who took charge of the family-based, day-care effort in traditional times. The young adults could not provide as effective a language model for the children, especially when working with lesson plans based on non-Indian views of child development.

There is one final reason why language loss has been a common part of the Indian language experience in America: the assumptions and stereotypes which the society at large brings to any consideration of Indian language fluency. Rank-and-file Americans know little about Indian people and even less about Indian cultures. Indian people were viewed as primitives and as savages until recent times and we still see reflexes of this attitude in contemporary society, most noticeably in the tendency to group all Indian peoples into a single social category ("the" Indians) who speak the same (Indian) "dialect." It is still widely assumed that if Indian people want to better themselves, they need only shift from "Indian" to "English."

Indian language maintenance: current expression

It seems somewhat ironic that the federal government, for so long the basis of so much repression of Indian languages and cultures, should now become a primary focus for assisting local communities in their efforts to maintain or regain their ancestral language fluency. People in some communities are made uneasy by this shift in policy and view with suspicion the policy makers who support the efforts towards greater community-based fluency. They prefer, in most instances, to keep ancestral language instruction out of the (BIA or public) schools and strictly within the context of traditional community institutions where it has remained for hundreds of years. But the fact that Indian communities are bicultural societies is difficult to ignore, and many people are willing to find ways to draw on the opportunities which surrounding society makes available to them, without having to compromise ancestral principles in the process. "To be able to receive an education and still remain an Indian is of value to an Indian child," writes one pueblo Indian teacher candidate in New Mexico. The development of educational programs which provide necessary life skills without destroying personal identity is a current priority in all Indian communities. In general terms, we best view these efforts as expressions of the principle of community control, which argues that the local or tribal membership is in the best position to make decisions concerning the content and direction of services to Indian children. Community control has received great impetus from the provision of Public Law 93-638, the Indian Self-determination and Education Assistance Act. This allows tribal authority the option to contract directly for any number of services, under BIA funding, from whatever source the tribe finds to be most appropriate.

The move toward self-determination, especially in the education area, creates additional needs for a variety of technical and managerial skills at the local level (for a discussion of these skills in interethnic communication, see Chapter 19). Community-controlled schools, for example, mean that qualified Indian staffing must be found, people who can meet both the standards of excellence set by the community membership and the standards of certification of the Department of Public Instruction in the state in which the school is located. Such doubly certified staff are necessary if Indian education programs are to provide necessary life skills without destroying the students' personal and community-based sense of identity, which has been the consequence of the Anglo-dominated, English-speaking schooling programs for Indian students in previous years.

The impact which the move toward self-determination in all forms of social services will have on the ancestral language question has already become clear. Two general directions of language maintenance efforts are emerging on the national Indian scene. The first are interests in restoring familiarity and fluency in the ancestral language to the community membership as a whole. This includes instances where only the older members speak the ancestral code, and there is interest in expanding speaker skills into the other generations, as well as cases where the language is no longer spoken by any community member at all save for those who recall "a few words and phrases."

Second are interests in retaining existing fluency within the community membership. This includes instances where the children are fluent in the ancestral code, and the concern is to keep that fluency when and as English skills are added to their repertoire, as well as cases where the children are fluent in both the ancestral code and English, and the community wishes to retain that balance without compromising either set of language skills.

Note that both concerns specifically focus on *children's* language needs. In all communities known to this writer, while the question of adult-level fluency is not being disregarded, the children are viewed as the primary focus for any intensified efforts at language maintenance. This is so for a very valid reason. If the children do not gain fluency, there is no way to assure continuity of verbal expression. If fluency cannot be stabilized within the children's generation, there is no way to assure continuity of verbal expression into the next generation.

Taken in this sense, the overriding concern with language maintenance in all communities, regardless of the state of current language fluency, needs to be described as community-based and tribally focused. The concern is expressed in several ways within contemporary Indian communities. First, there are the possibilities of language instruction (and continuing language use) offered through existing traditional institutions. The religious and ceremonial life of a community, for example, may allow important opportunities for concentrated language instruction. Initiation rites often involve the learning of terminology, songs, and other verbal lore necessary for responsible and meaningful participation in these activities. In communities where the native religion is gaining increased acceptance once again, extensive language (re)learning is also beginning to be evidenced. As long as community leaders have retained ceremonial knowledge in the ancestral language, traditional institutions provide invaluable resources to the local maintenance effort, in a fashion consistent with the overall style of teaching and learning also traditional in the community.

Similarly, opportunities afforded by traditional or more recently imposed government structures function indirectly toward language learning ends. In communities where the tribal council or community-wide meetings are conducted in the ancestral language, or where the use of English on those occasions, while permissible, is not preferred, young people who remain on the reservation and participate in these affairs are expected to become fluent in the language of these activities. Specialized vocabulary in English as well as traditionally based terminologies are therefore required, and attendance at these meetings, reinforced by opportunities for practice in the home or other less formal contexts, produces a growth in necessary language skills, noticeable soon after the young person begins his involvement in these aspects of community life.

Both of these examples underscore the importance of the home as a language learning center in the Indian community. Homes where fluent grandparents reside have always given these children a natural advantage over children who come from family units containing only parents, and not grandparents. But with the increase in day- and wage-labor and the growth of single-family residence units on the reservations, opportunities for intensive, daily contact with grandparents have begun to decline. Families with parents from differing tribal groups may add further complication to the picture.

Some work is now being done, through Parent–Child Development Programs, Head Start, and other early child-care efforts, to develop home-based (or day-care centered) language-related teaching materials for use by preschool students in these contexts. Ancestral language instruction is basic to programs at Acoma pueblo and in the Mississippi Choctaw communities. This approach assumes, however, that there are fluent speakers supervising the activities of the children who can assume responsibility for the instruction-related components of these activities. Where this is the case, and where adult literacy in the ancestral language can be developed, supplying the home or day-care center with reading materials in the native language has been found to have positive impact on the children's language skills and language-related interests. Yet a definitive set of guidelines for encouraging language training as a part of early childhood efforts has yet to be developed; at present, home-based initiatives depend on the interests of the child-care program authorities, and on the willingness of parents or grandparents to work within such a formalized instructional framework. Here, as elsewhere, success depends on local-level initiatives.

Home-based instruction has become increasingly important within the urban Indian context. The diversity of Indian language backgrounds represented in any urban community or school district is often used by non-Indian educators as an excuse for taking no action, since (as it is argued) each language must have its own instructional curriculum. That such efforts need not be costly is being demonstrated by several Indian educators in the Chicago area, who are developing sets of home-based materials which can be used as activity-sheets for children placed in grandparents' care during the working day. The model for these work-sheets comes from materials prepared by the Quileute tribe of Washington state (Jensen and McLaren 1976), to reintroduce familiarity and fluency on the K-3 level in their community. Ponca tribal authorities are planning to use similarly designed materials, to address the ancestral language question in their communities, under a project through the Oklahoma Indian Affairs Commission, funded in part by the National Endowment for the Arts.

The basic question in the design of such home-based materials is, of course, what to teach. Well-meaning parents often assume that if the child learns sets of vocabulary words today, tomorrow he will become a fluent speaker. Without providing adequate examples of sentence formation to the child, such a personal transformation from passive to active skill is not likely to occur – unless, as sometimes happens, the child combines English grammar and Indian vocabulary to meet his conversational needs. Some of the more "acculturated" Indian speech styles used in urban and reservation communities today may well have their origins in such a process of reanalysis. While the end-product may not be aesthetically pleasing, such codes do underscore the point that Indian children will work with whatever linguistic resources are provided to them, to develop a linguistic entrée into their cultural heritage. The introduction to Leap (1977) reviews critical facts about these "Indian English" codes.

Thus, just as institutional opportunities for linguistic reinforcement require input and support from the home context (a critical factor in the several communities where the ceremonial life is also almost gone), language teaching and learning in the home require additional reinforcement as well. Parents, like sympathetic classroom teachers, may need adequate programs for staff development to undertake language instruction in a meaningful way. Recognizing this, formalized efforts at Indian language maintenance often develop into community-wide programs where the total membership gives support to the teaching effort. In some instances, the tribal government has contracted with an outside language specialist or research organization, to develop an instructional package which the community can use for language-related purposes under its own auspices, through evening classes at the community center or other means. Coeur d'Alene people (Idaho) recently developed *Snchitsu'umshtsn: The Coeur d'Alene Language*, a textbook for a course in their ancestral language (Nicodemus 1975). Accompanying cassette tapes and a highly sequenced set of lesson plans allow individualized instruction, though some efforts to hold formal classes using the materials are also intended. The Quileute language materials mentioned above are also the product of a similar arrangement among community, native speaker, and qualified consulting linguist.

In other instances, community preference leads to the development of a native language component within the local school, a so-called BILINGUAL EDUCATION program (see Chapter 21), where educators and community personnel share the responsibilities of the language teaching effort as part of each classroom day. To gain an effective picture of the concerns of these programs, we have to distinguish between the developmental and implementational stages of such efforts. At the present time, most attention seems to lie in the areas of basic research, ORTHOGRAPHY development, planning of instructional materials, and the necessary staff training appropriate to the teaching tasks. Until such efforts are well underway, any attempt to begin extensive native language instruction is recognized as premature.Thus in recent years, the opportunities allowed by summer workshop programs have become increasingly popular: workshops allow staff training, language research, and materials development to occur under qualified

professional leadership, within a concentrated period of time. The summer
program of the Native American Linguistic Institute offers training in linguistic
analysis at beginning and advanced levels to fluent community members and
affirms the right of native speakers to serve as their own community's language
specialists.

University programs in some states have begun making responses to these
needs, either by sending faculty members into the community for purposes of
on-site instruction (e.g. the University of New Mexico under contract to the
Sanostee and Toadlena schools), or by setting up degree or training opportunities
within the university curriculum for more intensive student training (e.g. the new
Linguistics program at the University of Arizona), or by developing research
components (e.g. the Alaska Native Language Center at the University of
Alaska) which can undertake basic research and development tasks on behalf of
the area's Indian communities. The resource, materials development and dissemination centers, funded under amendments to the BILINGUAL EDUCATION ACT, also
offer possibilities for securing qualified personnel for on-site staff training and
development. Several of these centers, including the Native American Materials
Development Center in Albuquerque and the Midwest Resource Center, Arlington
Heights, Illinois, have made significant attempts to direct their resources toward
the language needs of Indian people.

The important avenues toward career development as well as responsible tribal
service which are being created through the development of school-based Indian
bilingual programs need to be noted here. In instances where young people are
fluent speakers of the ancestral language, the possibility of serving community-
related language interests as a member of the school staff (teacher or teacher
aide) are immediately apparent. BIA-mandated Indian preference hiring policies
guarantee that, where qualified candidates from within the tribal community can
be identified, teaching positions for those candidates will be found within the
staff of the BIA school, vacancies permitting. The Department of Health,
Education, and Welfare (DHEW) Office for Civil Rights' requirements, as
mandated under the U.S. Civil Rights Act of 1964, often lead to the same goal
within the public school context. In several areas state colleges and universities,
recognizing these needs, have already made provisions for the training of Indian
teacher candidates to serve as teachers of bilingual–bicultural education. "Eminence credentialing," certifying the candidate on the basis of the skills he or she
already possesses, is being used in Minnesota and other states as a way to speed
up the certification process.

In instances where young people are not fluent speakers, the absence of
fluency does not necessarily exclude them from language-focused, school-related
employment. Here the Oneida Language Project (Wisconsin) is perhaps the best
example of what can be done. Only a small number of the older people are fluent
speakers. So, to carry out an Oneida-as-Second-Language program in the four
schools serving the community, a two-step program has been established. Young
people receive instruction from fluent speakers on a particular topic or lesson
plan on day 1, then they go into the classroom and provide the instruction to the

students on day 2. Success is evidenced in the growth of language skills and interest in language learning at all levels of the Oneida program. Some argue, of course, that having nonfluent speakers assume so critical a role in the instructional process could weaken the quality of instructional content. The Oneida program has a built-in feedback mechanism to alleviate the problem in this instance: children go home, share their new language skills with grandparents, who can cross check on day 3 the information originally provided on day 1, completing the cycle and continuing the program dynamic.

There are instances where community members resent the inclusion of native language maintenance bilingual education programs within the local school, viewing these as an additional intrusion of Anglo society into the private affairs of the tribal community. The Miccosukee people (South Florida) have reached an intriguing compromise in this regard. Four days a week, instruction is carried out in English-related content subjects, using English as the language of instruction. One day a week is set aside for Indian-related education, and community members, rather than "teachers," assume responsibilities for student instruction. To underscore this point, the classroom is moved from the school to a nearby, out-of-doors locale, so that traditional topics can be dealt with freely, without fear of outside interruption.

San Juan Pueblo's day school (New Mexico) has achieved a second solution to this issue. The language of the school is English, but time is reserved for Tewa language arts in each classroom. As the students' Indian language fluency becomes more secure, instruction in content subjects through the ancestral language as well as English may be provided to reinforce the practical uses of Tewa fluency which the program is seeking to provide. Public schools on the Yakima reservation, and the community-controlled school at Rocky Boys (Montana) have comparable programs underway.

In instances where the students come into the school already fluent in the ancestral language, a different set of classroom-related language initiatives is required. The common tactic now finds instruction beginning in the native tongue, gradually adding English until both languages can be used in a complementary way to meet the goals and objectives of the instructional curriculum. The community-controlled schools on the Navajo reservation provide our best example of this approach to Indian education. As the following statement of objectives suggests, the direction of the language instruction is quite consistent with the overall focus of the school's commitment to education:

Upon graduation from high school, students should demonstrate the following competencies: (1) fluency in both English and Navajo; (2) communicativeness; (3) the ability to understand the speech behaviors, values, and attitudes of Navajo elders; (4) the ability to demonstrate appropriate clan membership, privileges, and protocols; and (5) the ability to discuss Navajo tribal government, current issues, organizations, accomplishments, and anticipated future developments. (Pfeiffer 1975:137)

In the case of the community-controlled Navajo schools, we are dealing with a language situation quite opposite to that at San Juan, Yakima, Rocky Boys, or

Oneida. In the Navajo schools, it is English, and not Indian, language arts which require concentrated attention.

The federal role in Indian language maintenance

Once again, the fact of Indian language diversity appears. For while it can be said that all of the school-related language maintenance programs which have been reviewed here are providing instruction in two languages – the students' ancestral code as well as English – the particular style in which the two directions for language instruction become coordinated within the school curriculum appears to vary widely. No single approach to the Indian language maintenance question can ever expect to be uniformly effective within Indian America for this reason, unless that approach affirms and facilitates the rights of tribal authorities to make meaningful educational decisions in response to locally defined educational needs.

The appropriate relationship between the educational efforts of the federal government and the educational concerns of tribes and Indian communities always becomes difficult to define for these reasons. It has become increasingly clear over the past decade that the models for bilingual education as put forward by federal policy (see Chapter 21) do not address the needs of Indian students or the concerns of Indian communities, where language maintenance or language preservation is concerned. Instead of viewing the Indian language-related instruction as a legitimate end in its own right, something which should be part of all Indian children's educational experiences, federal priority views the Indian language merely as a means to bridge the gap until facility in English has been obtained. This fact helps explain why so few Indian communities have received federal support for their language maintenance efforts.

There is, moreover, a built-in deterrent to the creation of any school-related native language teaching effort which will rely on federal funding as the primary source of its support. Federal funds must be sought anew each year. Support cannot be guaranteed beyond the close of the fiscal year in which the funds were granted. Numerous times, funds have been granted to initiate a language effort, but funds to continue the effort are then (for any number of reasons) not forthcoming. Weaknesses in the arguments presented in the proposal are not the only reasons for such cut-offs.

Faced with such a development, the local community has a limited number of options. First, it can rely on community monies from tribal sources to continue the effort, though few tribes have sufficient funds in their treasury to absorb what may be extensive program costs. Second, the community may redirect monies from other, more stabilized sources of outside assistance toward language-related purposes, though sometimes this requires extensive redefinition of the purposes of these funds within the school budget, and usually this leaves other critical areas of student instruction less adequately supported. Third, the community may try to secure additional monies from a previously untapped source.

The numerous problems related to proposal writing also serve as a deterrent to the use of federal (or other external) funds for language maintenance purposes. Some school officials report that their primary task each year becomes grantsmanship, and not the education of the students placed in their charge. Federal funding also requires provision for program evaluation, to document proof of success and positive impact – ignoring the fact that native language instruction may be a future-oriented investment, showing "pay-off" in school success in the later years, the presence of fluency in subsequent generations, or in any number of other, nonimmediate ways.

Recognizing these factors, some communities have decided not to participate in the "funding game," relying on local resources or well-meaning but unstructured local initiatives to carry out the school-related language effort. Yet a wide range of tasks have to be undertaken if any native language maintenance effort is to be implemented, including:

1. basic research in the language, to provide effective sequence to the instructional effort and guidance for decisions about spelling conventions;
2. development of a functional writing system which does not ignore community preferences and gives adequate representation to the structural features of the language;
3. staff training, to provide fluent speakers with the basic skills in language pedagogy and curriculum development, so that the instruction they provide will be of the highest possible caliber;
4. the availability of teaching materials;
5. an evaluation plan, to monitor the progress of each student according to his abilities and strengths.

It is therefore doubtful that tribal communities, regardless of their commitment, can find sufficient resources to be able to underwrite the costs of these efforts independently. Other local priorities – adequate housing, employment, health care, and so on – cannot be neglected. Existing resources can be used to cover only so many tasks.

To find a solution to this problem, we must return once again to the nature of the language learning and language maintenance processes. People learn languages for reasons. As long as opportunities for speaking are made available to the speech community, fluency in the language appropriate for those opportunities will continue to be maintained. Federal funding, dynamic school-based language arts initiatives, technical assistance from colleges, universities, and private agencies, and other forms of "enabling assistance" cannot take the place of the responsibilities which the community members must *themselves* assume – if languages from their own ancestral tradition are to be learned, used, and retained within their local membership.

Tribes and Indian communities are showing increasing evidence of their ability to assume such responsibilities. In earlier times, the tasks could be handled as part of the normally occurring teaching and learning activities within the home and community. Within those contexts, individuals found numerous opportunities for acquiring and perfecting language skills which full participation in community life would require of them. Since the time of the European occupation, however, outside factors and influences have come to interfere with the continuation of Indian traditions in their many forms. What had formerly been treated as a normal part of community life now required special, formalized community efforts and intensified tribal commitments to obtain. Thus the success of current Indian struggles for language maintenance depends on the extent to which such efforts are able to formalize what had previously been automatic and spontaneous cultural activities.

FURTHER READING

Linguistic Structures of Native America (Hoijer 1946) contains technical descriptions of eleven of the native languages of the USA and can be read to gain an impression of the ways in which the grammars of Indian languages may differ. The Indian language component of the *Handbook of North American Indians* (a Smithsonian Institution publication to appear in 20 volumes; see Heizer 1978) contains additional such sketches, many of which describe languages which are spoken by only small numbers of speakers, or languages not widely discussed in other, more accessible volumes. Two journals – the *International Journal of American Linguistics* and *Anthropological Linguistics* – frequently contain articles specifically devoted to Indian language structure or some culturally related topic of Indian language interest. In addition to the references on language classification already cited, Zisa's 1970 classification and listing may prove useful especially to the person with nominal familiarity with Indian language diversity.

Szasz 1974 outlines many of the critical phases in the provision of educational services to Indian tribes by the Bureau of Indian Affairs (BIA). References to the BIA's changing approach to Indian language questions are made throughout the volume. Prucha 1973 provides a collection of primary sources, including some on language policies in the ''Americanization'' of American Indians. Missionaries' programs and the role of language are recounted in Berkhofer 1972. Fuchs and Havighurst 1973 provide information, some of which is superseded by more recent data, on the language-related educational needs of American Indian students.

A fully detailed history of the Indian language maintenance movement has yet to be written. A picture of current needs and interests can be found in the published record of the Oversight Hearings on Indian Education Supplemental Programs, held before the Subcommittee on Elementary, Secondary, and Vocational Education of the House Committee on Education and Labor, September 16, 20 and October 7, 1977. Statements from Indian educational authorities, tribal leaders, as well as federal officials are contained in those proceedings; their arguments profile the diversity of the Indian language maintenance movement in all its forms. The numerous citations in Evans, Abbey, and Reed 1977 inventory materials used from 1965–74 for Indian language arts instruction within the schools serving Indian students. History and current need are also reviewed in the opening pages.

7

Native American writing systems

WILLARD WALKER

The invention of writing systems for Native American languages and the subsequent spread of literacy in certain native speaking communities is a forgotten chapter in American intellectual history. The GRAPHIZATION of Indian languages has taken place in a variety of ways. Sometimes it was an outsider, often a missionary, who studied the language and adapted the ORTHOGRAPHY of a European language to its sound system. This was the case with Ivan Veniaminov, who adapted the CYRILLIC alphabet of Russian to the needs of Aleut speakers in the first half of the nineteenth century, and with Jotham Meeker, who adapted the roman alphabet to a variety of languages in Indian Territory (now Oklahoma) at roughly the same time.

Other Native American orthographies were created by native speakers who modified a writing system they had learned from a European source, as in the case of Pablo Tac's Luiseño orthography, or modified one associated with another Indian language, as in the case of the Winnebago syllabary, which was adapted from a Fox writing system in the 1880s.

Still other systems were developed by native speakers who, like Thomas Wildcat Alford, a Shawnee intellectual, modified earlier systems associated with their own languages. There are several well-documented instances, however, in which a Native American, after seeing others read and write his own or some other language, has grasped the idea of writing and has succeeded in inventing a writing system without prior experience in reading or writing any language. Thus Sequoyah, early in the nineteenth century, devised a writing system for Cherokee in the southeastern USA and Uyakoq, a century later, devised a system for Yupik Eskimo in Alaska, although neither was literate in any language. There is also the case of Qiatuaq, another Yupik-speaking Eskimo, who invented an entirely new writing system after seeing Uyakoq demonstrate that literacy in Yupik was possible; and it may have been under very similar circumstances that speakers of Central Algonquian languages in the Midwest developed a whole series of different, but structurally related, writing systems in the nineteenth century.

Before turning to the particular writing systems to be dealt with, I should stress certain points that are rarely made or considered. First, the Native American languages spoken in the USA far outnumber those derived from Europe. Second, a remarkable number of these Native American languages have remained viable, despite the regularly recurring predictions of their demise made by successive generations of Euro-Americans (see Chapter 6). Third, some of these languages, including a few that are native to Atlantic seaboard states, for example, Passamaquoddy in Maine and Miccosukee and Muskogee Seminole in Florida, are read by substantial numbers of native-speaking children as well as adults. Fourth, due largely to certain changes in federal policy and the availability of funds and expertise, many traditional native writing systems seem to have become more widely used in the past decade, and a great many new writing systems have recently been adopted by native-speaking communities with no prior tradition of literacy. The long-term implications of these developments are difficult to assess; but it is at least clear that Native American writing systems will be used, and hence will probably evolve, for a long time to come and that, as a consequence, no account of these writing systems written today can fail soon to be outdated.

In this chapter I hope to provide a survey of the writing systems associated with American languages native to the United States together with some information on their various histories, the social and cultural contexts in which they have been produced, modified, and used, and some evidence indicating historical relationships between certain of them. I will emphasize writing systems which have been developed and/or used by native speakers rather than those devised by Euro-Americans for the use of native speakers. As a consequence I will have to ignore a number of well-known and relatively "important" languages with viable traditions of literacy, such as Navajo, for example, in order to allow space for certain writing systems associated with such little known and relatively "unimportant" languages as Mahican, which indeed is not even spoken today.

I should also note that, by limiting myself to the languages native to the United States, I am excluding from consideration all the writing systems associated with the native-speaking populations of Canada and Latin America. These include some, like the Micmacs of eastern Canada and the Yaquis of Sonora, which are represented by substantial immigrant populations in the United States which continue to speak their respective languages and preserve some measure of their traditions of literacy.

Sequoyah and the Cherokee syllabary

The Cherokee writing system was invented by a monolingual, illiterate Cherokee named Sequoyah who perfected a syllabic writing system (SYLLABARY) and gave a public and conclusive demonstration of its effectiveness before influential Cherokee leaders at New Echota, Georgia, in 1821. According to Mooney,

The syllabary was soon recognized as an invaluable invention for the elevation of the tribe, and within a few months thousands of hitherto illiterate Cherokee were able to read and write their own language, teaching each other in the cabins and along the roadside. The next year [1822] Sequoya visited the West, to introduce the new science among those who had emigrated to the Arkansas . . . On account of the remarkable adaptation of the syllabary to the language, it was only necessary to learn the characters to be able to read at once. No school houses were built and no teachers hired, but the whole Nation became an academy for the study of the system, until, "in the course of a few months, without school or expense of time or money, the Cherokee were able to read and write in their own language". (Mooney 1900: 110, quoting an article in *The Cherokee Phoenix* printed in 1828)

The fact that, within the space of a few years, thousands of Cherokee speakers accepted Sequoyah's innovation and actually became literate is no less remarkable than the innovation itself. People wrote letters, kept accounts, and copied sacred songs and curing formulas. A weekly newspaper, *The Cherokee Phoenix*, was printed by the Cherokee national press as early as 1828; and "Between 1828 and 1835 the press . . . issued a number of portions of the Bible, copies of the laws passed by the National Council, various political pamphlets, 4 editions of a Cherokee Hymn Book, temperance tracts, and religious documents" (White 1962: 511).

The New Echota press was confiscated by the Georgia Guard in 1835, acting under orders from Reverend John F. Schermerhorn and the Cherokee agent and with the assistance of Stand Watie, a Cherokee who advocated compliance with Georgia's insistence on "removal" of the Cherokees to Indian Territory (Foreman 1938:15). A new Cherokee national press was established in Indian Territory, now Oklahoma, in 1835, however; and between 1835 and 1861 "this press printed 13,980,000 pages of books, tracts, pamphlets and passages from the Bible . . . An Annual *Almanac* . . . *The Cherokee Messenger*, a bi-monthly religious magazine . . . as well as numerous tracts, primers, spelling books, arithmetics, Bible passages, a complete New Testament, hymn books, and other miscellaneous publications" (White 1962: 511–12). In the period between the Civil War and 1906, when the Cherokee press was again confiscated, this time by the U.S. government, a newspaper, *The Cherokee Advocate*, and a number of religious and educational books were printed. More recently, Cherokee language publications have been made available by the American Bible Society and, in the 1960s, by Cherokee Phoenix Publications, the Carnegie Corporation Cross-Cultural Education Project of the University of Chicago, the Laboratory of Anthropology of Wesleyan University, and the Original Cherokee Community Organization (see Walker 1975). A large proportion of the existing Cherokee literature, however, consists of manuscripts. These are, for the most part, church records, curing formulas, unpublished Christian songs, and personal correspondence. The largest collections of these manuscripts are probably those of the Smithsonian Institution and the American Philosophical Society.

Figure 7.1 shows two versions of the Sequoyah syllabary thought to have been written by Sequoyah himself, perhaps for John Howard Payne who met Sequoyah in 1840 in the "cockloft" of John Ross' log house in Indian Territory (Foreman 1938: 42–3). The characters are arranged in Sequoyah's order of presentation rather than the "systematic" arrangement used by the Reverend Samuel Worcester in his table of characters published in the first issue of *The Cherokee Phoenix* on February 21, 1828. Each syllable is written in two radically different forms. The lefthand member of each pair of characters probably represents a form used by

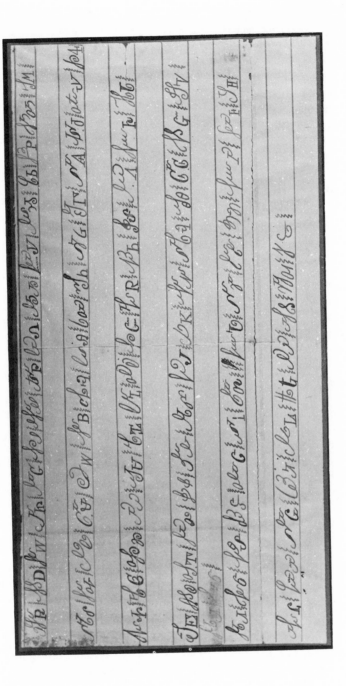

Figure 7.1. Two versions of the Cherokee syllabary, apparently written by Sequoyah himself for John Howard Payne, who interviewed him in the Cherokee Nation, Indian Territory, in 1840 (reproduced by permission of the Thomas Gilcrease Institute of American History and Art, Tulsa, Oklahoma)

Figure 7.2. A reproduction of a painting, now lost, believed to have been painted by Charles B. King when Sequoyah traveled to Washington, DC in 1828 as a representative of the Arkansas band of Cherokees to negotiate a land treaty (reproduced by permission of the Smithsonian Institution National Anthropological Archives)

Sequoyah prior to 1827. The righthand forms are, for the most part, very similar to the printed characters designed by Worcester in 1827 "after the model of [Sequoyah's] alphabet at the foundry of Messrs. Baker and Greene, Boston" (Foreman 1938: 13). Note that the portrait of Sequoyah (Figure 7.2) shows him holding a card with characters arranged in Sequoyah's order but in the forms of Worcester's type font. Such a card was printed at New Echota in 1828, the same year in which Sequoyah sat for his portrait. Had he, himself, written the characters he is holding in the portrait, they would have resembled the characters in Figure 7.1, probably the lefthand members of each pair, rather than Worcester's printed forms.

KEY TO SEQUOYAH'S SYLLABARY

Ꭰ [a, ʔa]	Ꭱ [e, ʔe]	Ꭲ [i, ʔi]	Ꭳ [o, ʔo]	Ꭴ [u, ʔu]	Ꭵ [ɨ, ʔɨ]
Ꭶ ga	Ꭸ ge, ke	Ꭹ gi, ki	Ꭺ go, ko	Ꭻ gu, ku	Ꭼ gɨ, kɨ
Ꭷ ka					
Ꭽ ha	Ꭾ he	Ꭿ hi	Ꮀ ho	Ꮁ hu	Ꮂ hɨ
Ꮃ la, ła	Ꮄ le, łe	Ꮅ li, łi	Ꮆ lo, ło	Ꮇ lu, łu	Ꮈ lɨ, łɨ
Ꮉ ma	Ꮊ me	Ꮋ mi	Ꮌ mo	Ꮍ mu	
Ꮎ na	Ꮑ ne, hne	Ꮒ ni, hni	Ꮓ no, hno	Ꮔ nu, hnu	Ꮕ nɨ, hnɨ
Ꮏ hna	Ꮐ (not used)				
Ꮖ gwa, kwa	Ꮗ gwe, kwe	Ꮘ gwi, kwi	Ꮙ gwo, kwo	Ꮚ gwu, kwu	Ꮛ gwɨ, kwɨ
Ꮜ s					
Ꮝ sa	Ꮞ se	Ꮟ si	Ꮠ so	Ꮡ su	Ꮢ sɨ
Ꮣ da	Ꮥ de	Ꮧ di	Ꮩ do, to	Ꮪ du, tu	Ꮫ dɨ, tɨ
Ꮤ ta	Ꮦ te	Ꮨ ti			
Ꮬ dla	Ꮮ dle, tle	Ꮯ dli, tli	Ꮰ dlo, tlo	Ꮱ dlu, tlu	Ꮲ dlɨ, tlɨ
Ꮭ tla					
Ꮳ [ja, dza] [ca, ča]	Ꮴ [je, dze] [ce, če]	Ꮵ [ji, dzi] [ci, či]	Ꮶ [jo, dzo] [co, čo]	Ꮷ [ju, dzu] [cu, ču]	Ꮸ [jɨ, dzɨ] [cɨ, čɨ]
Ꮹ wa, hwa	Ꮺ we, hwe	Ꮻ wi, hwi	Ꮼ wo, hwo	Ꮽ wu, hwu	Ꮾ wɨ, hwɨ
Ꮿ ya, hya	Ᏸ ye, hye	Ᏹ yi, hyi	Ᏺ yo, hyo	Ᏻ yu, hyu	Ᏼ yɨ, hyɨ

Sequoyah's Cherokee syllabic characters with phonetic values for each. All sequences which are not enclosed in square brackets are phonemically distinct. The letter Ꮙ (gwo, kwo) is often used in place of expected Ꮚ (gwu, kwu). Note that many of the characters represent more than one sequence of phonemes. Note also that the phonetic values of characters bear no relation to those of similar letters of the English alphabet.

Figure 7.3. Key to Sequoyah's syllabary (Walker 1975: 191. Reprinted from *Studies in Southeastern Indian Languages* by permission of the University of Georgia Press. Copyright © 1975 by University of Georgia Press)

Since the Cherokee nation was dissolved and incorporated into the state of Oklahoma at the end of the nineteenth century, the ability to read Cherokee syllabics has been functional in only two major aspects of Cherokee life: participation in religious activities and the practice of Indian medicine. To participate fully in a Cherokee church congregation, one has had to be able to read aloud from the Bible. In a Sunday School class, for example, each participant is required to read a verse from the New Testament or, if illiterate, is expected to repeat after someone who reads for him. Each Sunday School class, then, is a test of each participant's ability to decode written Cherokee into spoken Cherokee.

A large number of adult Cherokees in each generation have been semi-professional Indian doctors, and the practice of Cherokee medicine entails the ability to read. Unlike the church member, who reads materials printed for general public use, the doctor records his curing practices in handwritten Cherokee for his own future reference. He reads these materials in privacy rather than in public, and reads for content, as opposed to reading aloud without necessarily understanding the text.

Cherokee society has had a long tradition of literacy, in part perhaps because Cherokees associate literacy with knowledge, and knowledge has been a prerequisite to the full acceptance of individuals as mature and responsible members of Cherokee communities. Twentieth-century Cherokees, then, have been motivated to learn to read Cherokee to participate more fully in church activities, to become competent doctors, to acquire generalized knowledge, or for some combination of these three objectives. Since young people are relatively unconcerned with religion, medicine, and knowledge, most Cherokees have not become literate in their native language before becoming adults. Thus the fact that most contemporary readers of Cherokee are over 30 does not necessarily mean that Cherokee literacy is declining.

Sequoyah's writing system includes eighty-five letters, of which one represents the sound of English *s* and six others represent vowel sounds, or sequences of GLOTTAL STOP plus vowel. The remaining seventy-eight letters represent combinations of consonant plus vowel. (See the key to Sequoyah's syllabary in Figure 7.3.) Originally there was an eighty-sixth character which was deleted by Worcester when Sequoyah's characters were modified for printing in 1827. There was also a set of characters used to represent numerals; but these have long since been discarded in favor of Arabic numerals or written versions, spelled out in the syllabary.

Many of Sequoyah's syllabic characters, or more precisely the characters as modified by Worcester for the 1827 type font, resemble English capital letters; others seem to have been borrowed from Greek or the Cyrillic alphabet; still others appear to have no precedent in other writing systems. Those which resemble English capitals stand for sounds which are quite unlike the sounds they stand for in English. Thus A, B, C, D, E, for example, are pronounced go, yi, tli, a, gi, respectively. The fact that Sequoyah used such traditional European letters for such quite different sounds clearly indicates that he was ignorant of their PHONETIC values in the European languages and was in no sense literate in English or any other European language.

To become fully literate in Cherokee, it is necessary to learn certain spelling conventions as well as the phonetic values of the eighty-five letters. Most words consisting of alternating vowels and consonants can be spelled in the syllabary without difficulty. The word /uujiilįįʔii/ 'cotton,' for example, is written with a sequence of letters representing /u/, /ji/, /li/, and /i/, respectively. In syllabic writing, the long vowels, represented in the transcription above as doubled vowels, are not distinguished from the corresponding short vowels; and the four pitches, represented above by arabic numerals ([1] for lowest, [4] for highest, etc.), are not marked at all. A few words are identical in spoken Cherokee except that they differ as to vowel length and/or pitch, which cannot be marked in syllabic writing. Thus /ám(àá)/ 'water,' with short vowel and pitch [2], contrasts with /áam(àá)/ 'salt,' with long vowel and pitch [3]; but these words are identical in syllabic texts. This is not a serious problem, however, since Cherokees reading a text will usually know from the context which word is meant. Many writing systems in the world ignore differences in vowel length and tone in this way.

A somewhat more troublesome problem is the spelling of consonant combinations. Since the syllabary letters represent either a vowel (e.g. /a/) or a sequence of consonant plus vowel (e.g. /ma/), there is no obvious way to represent a sequence of consonants with no vowel between them. Some combinations can be written by the use of the letter for /s/, the only letter in the syllabary which stands for a single consonant instead of a syllable. Words with consonant combinations consisting of /s/ followed by another consonant, such as /hisgii²⁴³/ 'five,' are easily spelled, since the letter for /s/ may be inserted between the syllabic letters for /hi/ and /gi/²¹²³⁴³. Problems arise, however, in spelling a word such as /diineełdii/ 'dolls' which has a combination of consonants other than /s/ without an intervening vowel (in this case /łd/). Consonant sequences such as this one must be written as though a vowel were present, and which of the six vowels must be chosen is often dictated by convention. The word for 'dolls' is written with the syllabics *di-ne-lo-di*, in that order, with the syllabary character for /lo/ representing the /ł/.

Other problems arise in spelling such words as /koogaa³³⁴³/ 'crow,' for there is no letter used specifically for the syllable /ko/ or for a number of other low frequency syllables. A single letter, resembling English A, is used to represent both /ko/ and /go/, which are VOICELESS and VOICED counterparts, made at the same place of articulation. Likewise, other letters are assigned to both /to/ and /do/, /kʷe/ and /gʷe/, /kị/ and /gị/, etc. In reading, of course, it is necessary to choose between alternative phonetic values in order to pronounce such words as /koogaa³³⁴³/ 'crow' correctly. A few letters have as many as four phonetic values, for example, the letter resembling an English K, which represent /jo/, /čo/, /dzo/, /tso/.

The spelling conventions of Cherokee are, however, much easier for a fluent speaker of the language to acquire than are the spelling and reading conventions of English for English-speaking Americans. English has many more examples of the same spelling for different sounds (e.g. *meat, bread, great*) than does Cherokee. English also uses different spellings for the same sound (e.g. *I, eye, aye*). Cherokee has nothing like the *-ough* problem in English; the *ough* in *bough, cough, dough, rough, through*, and *thorough* is pronounced differently in each case. The Cherokee conventions are relatively few in number and are quite easily learned. Many of them may be ignored without adversely affecting communication.

A Cherokee manuscript often contains a variety of clues as to the geographical, religious, or occupational background of its author. It normally contains considerable evidence as to his mastery of the spelling conventions and also reflects the vagaries of his penmanship; but, more importantly, it may contain words, or forms of words, which are associated with regional dialects. If, in a manuscript from Oklahoma, /h/ is indicated where one would expect a glottal stop, the document may have originated in the vicinity of the present Oklahoma–Missouri border. If, on the other hand, the glottal stop is indicated where one would expect /h/, the writer may have grown up near Porum, in Muskogee County. When words ending in /a/ are spelled as though the final vowel were /ị/, a dialect such as that spoken south of Stilwell, in southern Adair County, is indicated. Special orthographic conventions may also be significant, for example, the letters representing /no/ or /hno/ and /gʷa/ or /kʷa/, which in print and in most manuscripts appear as Z and Ꮿ, respectively, are sometimes written ·/· and :|:, most often, perhaps in Delaware County. Particularly significant is the appearance of a redundant *s*, i.e. when such a word as /sakoonigeeʔii²²³³⁴⁴³²/ 'blue' is spelled *s-sa-ko-ni-ge-ʔi*. This spelling convention dates from the earliest days of written Cherokee; for Sequoyah, himself, signed his name not *si-gʷo-ya*, but *s-si-gʷo-ya*, with a redundant *s* at the beginning. In later times, as when Worcester and Boudinot translated the New Testament and printed it in Cherokee, the redundant *s* was omitted; and for this reason many generations of Christian Cherokees have learned, by reading the Bible, the more recent (and more streamlined) tradition of indicating *s*-plus-vowel with a single letter. The redundant *s* persists, however, in manuscripts written by native doctors and others associated with pagan (Nighthawk) communities, for theirs is a manuscript tradition that dates from before the removal of the Cherokees to Oklahoma, one which has maintained its redundant *s* down to the present time.

Iroquoian and New England writing systems

For the Indian languages of the Middle and New England states, there is no story of literacy comparable to that of the Cherokee. No Indian leader created a writing system; all writings in the Indian languages were in the roman alphabet, and all were inspired by missionaries, either English or French.

The languages of the Six Iroquois nations of New York (Mohawk, Oneida, Onondaga, Cayuga, Seneca, and Tuscarora) are distantly related to Cherokee but are not mutually intelligible with it. There is an extensive published literature in these languages, particularly Seneca, and these and related Canadian languages have been written in the roman alphabet since as early as Cartier's first voyage in 1534. Books and public notices in the roman alphabet are still very much in evidence on the New York and Ontario reservations.

According to Postal (1964: 270), the Reverend Jean-André Cuoq, a nineteenth-century missionary, "used largely what has come to be the traditional orthography of Mohawk, and except for systematic lacks (failure to note stress, the falling tone, vowel length, post vocalic /h/, and glottal stop, and transcribing [the nasal vowels] ʌ and u as *en* and *on* respectively) this representation is PHONEMIC . . ." That is to say that, subject to these reservations, there is a one-to-one correspondence between Cuoq's letters and native Mohawk categories of sounds. Nasalized vowels, which are of very high frequency in all Iroquoian languages, continue to be written in the manner of Cuoq (and standard French practice) as sequences of vowel plus *n*, although Cuoq himself carefully distinguished between nasalized vowels and vowels plus the consonant *n* by writing the former as vowel plus *ñ* (or *n'*) and the latter simply as a vowel plus *n*.

Though publications also exist in a number of the Algonquian languages of New England, including Massachuset (around Massachusetts Bay) and Narraganset (in present-day Rhode Island), they are relatively few in number and consist primarily of religious tracts and vocabulary lists. The most readable and informative publication is surely Roger Williams' *A Key into the Language of North America*, a seventeenth-century book written in English and Narraganset by the founder of Rhode Island. Despite its title, the book is concerned with the beliefs and customs of the Narragansets and the Puritans and their interrelationships.

The popularity and enduring interest of this book is suggested by the fact that it has been reprinted in every century since its original appearance in 1643.

A word list and ''Pater Noster'' in Mahican (Stockbridge) were published by Jonathan Edwards (1788), who became fluent in the language after moving to Stockbridge, Massachusetts at the age of six. Two native residents of Stockbridge, John Quinney and Captain Hendrick Aupaumut, translated *The Assembly's Shorter Catechism* into Mahican, probably in 1818; and, according to Jones (1854: 120), Aupaumut ''sent a speech,'' presumably written in Mahican, to his people at New Stockbridge in New York inviting them to join him on the White River in Indiana, where some of them found him when they migrated west in 1818.

Abiel Holmes published a list of eighty Mahican words (1804a: 26–7), several of which were procured from John Konkapot Jr., ''a young and intelligent Indian of the Stockbridge tribe . . . The spelling is chiefly according to the mode adopted by the present secretary of the Grand Council of the tribe (who was educated at Dartmouth College) in their public records; and the vocabulary was in fact . . . mostly written by the young Indian himself, in order to preserve as much accuracy as possible.'' A shorter vocabulary, together with a text and translation by Konkapot, can be found in Holmes (1804b); and a ''translation of the 19th Psalm into the Muh-he-con-nuk [Mahican] language, done at the Cornwall School,'' is included in Morse (1822: 359–40). The last Mahican text was recorded with an English translation at Red Springs, Wisconsin by J. F. Estes, ''an educated Dakota Indian . . . in the Dakota system of orthography,'' and may be found, together with a key to this orthography, in Prince (1905).

All the New England writing systems tend to reflect English spelling conventions except in northern New England, where French priests had a pervasive influence until relatively recent times and perhaps among certain southern New England tribes which migrated westward and made contact with German-speaking Moravian missionaries. It may well be that in the Algonquian northeast, literacy has been, until very recent times, largely confined to a small elite group of adult political leaders identified with church organizations. The bulk of the native population was probably semi-literate at best, which may account for the apparently widespread practice of writing spaces (or hyphens) between syllables, rather than spaces between words,a practice that has long been used in the area by English speakers in writing the exotic names of summer camps and cottages.

In the present decade a number of Passamaquoddy readers have been published by the Wabnaki Bilingual Education Program, Motakmiqewi Skulhawohsol, Indian Township, Maine in an orthography based on a modern grammar (Teeter 1971).

The Meeker orthographies and the Shawnee alphabet

During the same period in which Sequoyah established a writing system for the Cherokees, Jotham Meeker, an English school teacher and missionary, performed a similar task for the Potawatomis, Ottawas, and Chippewas (Ojibwas). In the period 1827–33, at three mission stations in what are now southern, central, and northern Michigan, Meeker learned something of all three languages and is said to have become fluent in Ottawa. After learning the printer's trade and being transferred to Sault Ste. Marie in 1832, he began to devise an orthography for Ojibwa and successfully taught two young Ojibwa boys to read "after a few days' instruction" (McMurtrie and Allen 1930: 26). In the following year he went to Indian Territory and established the Shawanoe Mission Press, which was to print over fifty books and pamphlets in various Indian languages and at least one newspaper (in Shawnee) during the next twenty years. Publications included primers, portions of the Bible, etc. in Choctaw, Unami Delaware, Iowa, Kansa, Muskogee Creek, Osage, Oto, Ottawa, Potawatomi, Shawnee, and Wea (Miami); and they were printed in Meeker's "new system of writing and reading" which "wholly excludes spelling" and "enables the learner to paint his thoughts on paper, with precision, as soon as he acquires a knowledge of a number of characters about equal to the English alphabet" (McCoy 1840, quoted in Pilling 1891: 353).

It is not clear that many Indians learned to read the Meeker orthographies, although some apparently learned in an amazingly brief time, and Chief Charles Journeycake of the Delawares is said to be the author of a hymnal in the Meeker–Blanchard Delaware orthography (Ira D. Blanchard was an associate of Meeker's who published a primer in Delaware). Significantly, perhaps, some Indians who learned the Meeker orthographies from missionaries passed on their skills to other Indians who were not taught literacy directly by White missionaries. Regardless of how many Indians learned to read the Meeker orthographies, however, the Shawanoe Mission Press must have had a considerable impact, for its publications were frequently read aloud by missionaries to groups of Indians who evidently listened and comprehended what was said.

The Meeker orthographies make use of English (roman) letters; but the phonetic values assigned to some of these letters vary from one orthography to another. The letter *b*, for example, represents a stop consonant /b/ in Potawatomi, but a SPIRANT /θ/ in Shawnee and a vowel /u/ in Delaware. Details of the orthographies used for Potawatomi, Ottawa, Delaware, and Shawnee are presented in Table 7.1.

In the present century, Thomas Wildcat Alford, a native speaker of Shawnee, used a writing system similar to one used by Johnston Lykins in an 1834 publication of the Shawanoe Mission Press (Table 7.1, last column). Like the orthographies of Meeker and his associates, it uses the roman alphabet and assigns the letter *r* to a vowel. Unlike the Meeker orthographies, however, Alford's system distinguishes between long and short vowels. "The vowels only has each two length [*sic*] of the same sound which are a, e, i, o, r, u and v; and are divided into long and short vowels, representing the long and short length of the same sound" (Alford 1929: 199). Alford's vowel letters, then, each represented always and only one of the mutually contrasting vowels in the spoken language, including the short and long vowels. There was, however, one exception.

Table 7.1 *Phonetic value of letters in the Meeker orthographies used for Potawatomi, Ottawa, Delaware, and Shawnee*

Letters	Potawatomi	Ottawa	Delaware	Shawnee
e	[i]	[i]	[i]	[i]
o	[o]	[o]	[o]	[o]
a	[a]	[a]	[a]	[e]
i	[i]	[i]	[i]	[a]
u	[ə]	[ə]	[ə]	
r	[ɛ]	[ɛ]	[e]	
w	[u]	[w]	[u]	[u]
y	[ay]		[ay]	
b	[b]		[u]	[θ]
c			[ɛ]	[č]
h	[č]	[č]	[č]	[h]
l	[š]	[š]	[l]	[l]
j			[š]	
v			[h]	
p	[p]	[p]	[p]	[p]
t	[t]	[t]	[t]	[t]
k	[k]	[k]	[k]	[k]
s	[s]	[s]	[s]	[s]
m	[m]	[m]	[m]	[m]
n	[n]	[n]	[n]	[n]
f		[ŋ]	[ŋ]	
d	[d]			
g	[g]			
q			[kʷ]	
x			[x]	
ɔ	[ʔ]			

Source: Pilling 1891: 354–5.

Following Lykins perhaps, Alford used the letter *a* to represent both short /e/ and long /ee/. The other long vowels /ii, uu, oo/ were written *e, o, r*, respectively; and the other short vowels /i, u, o/ were written *i, u, v*, respectively. Since the letter *a* represented both short /e/ and long /ee/, Alford was forced to distinguish the voiced and voiceless variants of certain consonants which occur predictably, according to his statement, before long and short vowels, respectively. "B," he says, "is sounded same [*sic*] as in English, and is always followed by long vowels . . . ," whereas "P . . . is always followed by short vowels . . . " (Alford 1929: 199–200). Thus the letters *b, p, d, t, j, c*, and perhaps *g* and *k*, representing the predictable variants of /p, t, č, k/, might have been reduced by half if the system had distinguished /e/ from /ee/. Lykins wrote only *p, t, c, k*; but failed also to mark vowel length. Alford wrote nine other consonants /m, n, l, w, y, d, kʷ, h, s/ and one cluster /ks/ as *m, n, l, w, y (i* before short vowels), *f, q, h, s,* and *x,* respectively. Although this system seems to be derived from that of Lykins or some other Shawnee alphabet in the Meeker tradition, it is clear that Alford's system was better adapted to the Shawnee sound system than any of its predecessors and, indeed, was only a whisker away from being a perfectly phonemic transcription. Therefore, though Alford did not *invent* a writing system for his native language, he was able to take one devised by non-native speakers and improve it to better suit his language.

The Fox syllabary and related systems

Mystery surrounds the origins of a native writing system associated with speakers of three Central Algonquian languages: Potawatomi, the Mesquakie, Sauk, and Kickapoo dialects of Fox, and formerly the Ottawa dialect of Ojibwa. According to Huron Smith (1933:12), the Potawatomi version was devised by Joe Ellick, a Forest Potawatomi of Soperton, Wisconsin in about 1878 "so that absent members of the tribe could write home to their people." The Fox version probably dates from about the same time, since Alice Fletcher was told by "a party of Sauk and Fox Indians" in the winter of 1883–4 "that one of their tribe had invented an alphabet, and that many of the Indians could by its use write their native language" (Fletcher 1890a: 299, 1890b: 354). None of those whom Fletcher met on this occasion had learned the system, however, so it may have been a quite recent innovation. As for the Ottawa version, we know only that Mack-aw-de-be-nessy, an Ottawa of Arbre Croche, Michigan, who died in 1861, believed it to have been used since about 1827.

The orthography of all three variants of the system is based on a European cursive form of the roman alphabet, and possibly a French source since vowel letters have continental, rather than English, phonetic values and the system lacks a symbol for /h/. Although the orthography is essentially phonemic, it is learned and taught as a syllabary. Syllables, but not letters, are named, and each syllable is written either as a vowel letter or as a connected sequence of letters representing consonant plus vowel and is divided by a space from the following sequence. The system is currently used in all the Fox communities and among the Potawatomis; a derivative of the system is also used by the unrelated Siouan speaking Winnebagos.

Mesquakie Standard Orthography (MSO) and Kickapoo Standard Orthography (KSO) have been fully described by Voorhis (1972). A syllabary recorded by Jones (1906: 90) and reproduced in Figure 7.4 illustrates MSO. Kickapoo phonology differs from Mesquakie chiefly in that pitch accent is phonemic and Kickapoo /θ/ and /s/ correspond to Mesquakie /s/ and /š/, respectively. Accordingly, KSO writes lower-case cursive *d* for /s/ and lower-case cursive *s* for /θ/. It also writes lower-case cursive *a* or *u* for all instances of /a, aa/. Otherwise it is identical to MSO, although the Kickapoos living in Cahuilla have acquired some Spanish spelling conventions: *cu* for /kw/, *ll* for /y/, etc.

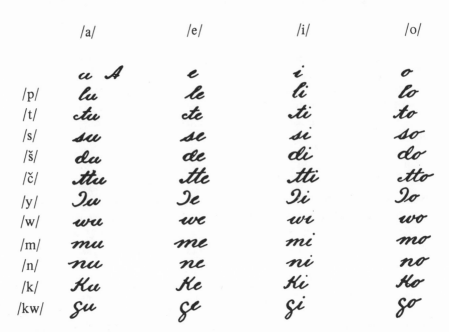

	/a/	/e/	/i/	/o/
	a *A*	*e*	*i*	*o*
/p/	*lu*	*le*	*li*	*lo*
/t/	*tu*	*te*	*ti*	*to*
/s/	*su*	*se*	*si*	*so*
/š/	*du*	*de*	*di*	*do*
/č/	*ttu*	*tte*	*tti*	*tto*
/y/	*Ɔu*	*Ɔe*	*Ɔi*	*Ɔo*
/w/	*wu*	*we*	*wi*	*wo*
/m/	*mu*	*me*	*mi*	*mo*
/n/	*nu*	*ne*	*ni*	*no*
/k/	*Ku*	*Ke*	*Ki*	*Ko*
/kw/	*8u*	*8e*	*8i*	*8o*

Figure 7.4. The Mesquakie syallabary (reprinted from Jones 1906: 90). Vowels and consonants have been added in phonemic notation to identify the phonetic values of the rows and columns

	/a/	/e/	/i/	/o/
/p/	l	$l.$	$l^\bullet$	$l..$
/t/	t	$t.$	$t^\bullet$	$t..$
/s/	λ	$\lambda.$	$\lambda^\bullet$	$\lambda..$
/š/	α	$\alpha.$	$\alpha^\bullet$	$\alpha..$
/č/	tt	$tt.$	$tt^\bullet$	$tt..$
/y/	9	$Ɔ.$	$Ɔ^\bullet$	$Ɔ..$
/w/	w	$w.$	$w^\bullet$	$w..$
/m/	m	$m.$	$m^\bullet$	$m..$
/n/	n	$n.$	$n^\bullet$	$n..$
/k/	K	$K.$	$K^\bullet$	$K..$
/kw/	8	$8.$	$8^\bullet$	$8..$

Figure 7.5a. Mesquakie syllabary variant: dot notation (reprinted from Jones 1906: 90). Vowels and consonants have been added in phonemic notation to identify the phonetic values of the rows and columns

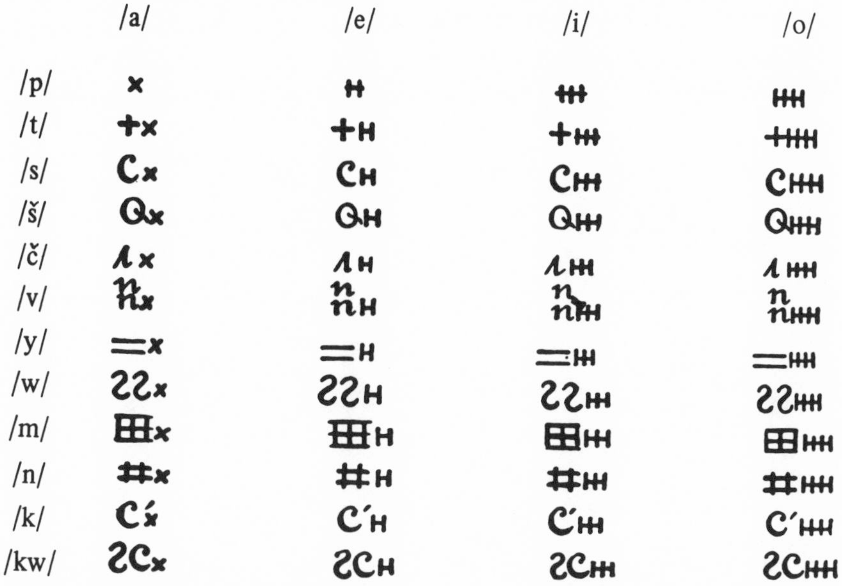

	/a/	/e/	/i/	/o/
/p/	x	H	HH	HHH
/t/	+x	+H	+HH	+HHH
/s/	Cx	CH	CHH	CHHH
/š/	Qx	QH	QHH	QHHH
/č/	ʌx	ʌH	ʌHH	ʌHHH
/v/	𝑛x	𝑛H	𝑛HH	𝑛HHH
/y/	=x	=H	=HH	=HHH
/w/	22x	22H	22HH	22HHH
/m/	⊞x	⊞H	⊞HH	⊞HHH
/n/	#x	#H	#HH	#HHH
/k/	C′x	C′H	C′HH	C′HHH
/kw/	2Cx	2CH	2CHH	2CHHH

Figure 7.5b. Mesquakie syllabary variant: x- and scored-line notation (reprinted from Jones 1906: 91). Vowels and consonants have been added in phonemic notation to identify the phonetic values of the rows and columns

Several other Fox orthographies have been reported. One in which /e, ee/, /i, ii/, and /o, oo/ are marked by a dot, a raised dot, and a double dot, respectively, and /a, aa/ is unmarked is shown in Figure 7.5a. Another variant marks /a, aa/ with an *x* and /e, ee/, /i, ii/, and /o, oo/ with a horizontal line crossed by two, three, or four vertical lines, respectively; consonants are written with a special set of symbols (see Figure 7.5b). Michelson (1927) describes two additional variants, one of which consists entirely of "our ordinary Arabic numbers."

A fragment of a note spontaneously composed in 1968 and written in MSO to Paul Voorhis is reproduced below in MSO, dot notation, crossed line notation, phonemic transcription, and English translation.

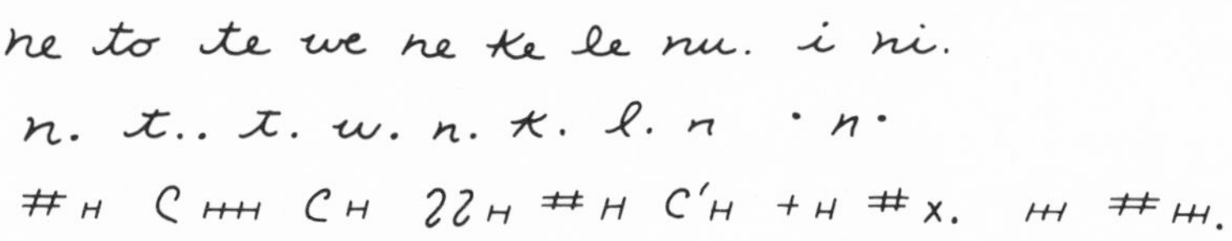

ne to te we ne ke le nu. i ni.

n. t.. t. w. n. k. l. n ⋅ n⋅

#H C HHH C H 22H #H C′H +H #x. HH #HH.

netooteewenehkeepena lini
'We went to town. That's all'

A chart of the Potawatomi version of the syllabary is reproduced in Figure 7.6.

Current	Traditional	Hockett
b	*ℓ*	p
p		p˙
d	*ƚ*	t
t		t˙
j	*tt*	c
ch		c˙
g	*k*	k
k		k˙
gw	*ʒ*	kw
kw		k·w
z	*ⅉ*	s
s		s˙
zh	*sh*	s
sh		s˙
m	*m*	m
n	*n*	n
ng	*ʒ*	nk [word-initial position only]
w	*w*	w
y	*y*	y
'	[unmarked]	ʔ
i	*i̇*	i
e	*ℓ*	u
ē		e
a	*a*	a
o	*o*	o

Figure 7.6. Potawatomi letters and phonemes (reprinted from Nichols 1974: 1). The middle column shows letters used in the traditional Potawatomi orthography. The right-hand column shows the corresponding symbols in a phonemic transcription, and the lefthand column shows the symbols in the orthography currently used by the Wisconsin Native Languages Project

Andrew J. Blackbird describes the origin of the Ottawa version of the syllabary as follows:

When I was a little boy, I remember distinctly his [father, Mack-aw-de-be-nessy or Black Hawk] making his own alphabet, which he called ''Paw-pa-pe-po''. With this he learned how to read and write: and afterwards he taught other Indians to read and write according to his alphabet. He taught no children but only grown persons . . . many Indians came there [to Mack-aw-de-be-nessy's summer wigwam near Arbre Croche, Michigan] to learn his Paw-pa-pe-po and some of them were very easy to learn, while others found learning extremely difficult.(Blackbird 1897: 19–20)

Blackbird included the Ten Commandments, the Creed, and the Lord's Prayer transcribed in ''Ottawa and Chippewa'' with hyphens between syllables and spaces between words. He also indicated that the letters *a, e, I* represented /a, e, i/, respectively, that /o/ was evidently written *au, aw*, or *ah*, that prevocalic /y/ was written *i*, and that /č/ was written *tch*, as in *tchiman* 'boat.'

When Alice Fletcher learned of the existence of the Fox writing system from a party of Sauk and Fox Indians in 1883–4, both she and they were visiting among the Siouan-speaking Winnebagos in Nebraska. Thus the Nebraska Winnebagos also learned of the Fox syllabary in 1883–4; and when some of them went to Iowa in the following year to return the visit, one of them, according to Fletcher (1890a: 299), ''acquired the alphabet, and became before long quite expert in its use, to his own amusement and that of his friends.'' Thus in the space of a few days or weeks a writing system adapted to Fox, an Algonquian language, came to be used by the Siouan Winnebagos. In this new environment it quickly established itself. ''The knowledge spread rapidly among the Winnebagos of Nebraska, and also to that part of the tribe living in Wisconsin, so that at the present time the principal correspondence of the tribe takes place by means of these characters'' (Fletcher 1890a: 299).

A letter from the Winnebago Indian agent written to Fletcher in 1885 reads as follows:

The tribe have suddenly taken to writing their own language, and people who have never learned English have acquired this art. The people claim they took the basis of it from the Sauk and elaborated it themselves. It is a very suggestive sight to see half a dozen fellows in a group with their heads together working out a letter in these new characters; it illustrates the surprising facility with which they acquire what they want to learn.(Fletcher 1890b: 355)

Winnebago literacy evidently declined after Fletcher's time, however. In 1912, according to Paul Radin (1954:21), the Winnebago syllabary ''was known to very few Indians and was used only for the writing of letters.'' The syllabary is used today, but apparently by only a small and dwindling group of elderly Winnebagos in Wisconsin. I have no information as to whether it survives in Nebraska. No text seems ever to have been published in Winnebago syllabics, save for a few brief fragments, but the system has been described by Fletcher (1890a, b), Susman (1940), and Walker (1974). Many of the Winnebago texts published in phonemic transcription and English translation by Radin were based on manuscripts in syllabics. Sam Blowsnake's classic *Autobiography of a Winnebago Indian* (Radin 1920), for example, is a translation of a manuscript originally written in Winnebago syllabics on lined, grade school, tablet paper.

According to Susman (1943), spoken Winnebago has five oral vowels /i, e, a, o, u/ and three nasalized vowels /i̧, a̧, ẉ/. There is also a distinction between short and long and between stressed and unstressed vowels. There are twenty consonants. Six are voiced /b, g, ǰ, z, ž, ɣ/; six more are voiceless counterparts of the preceding /p, k, č, s, š, x/; and there are eight additional consonants /m, n, w, t, r, y, h,ʔ/. In adapting the Fox orthography to their own language, therefore, the Winnebagos were faced with the problem of writing eight vowels (leaving aside the distinctions of length and stress) and twenty consonants with an orthography that distinguished only four vowels and ten consonants. With regard to the vowels, their solution was to disregard, not only length and stress, but also the distinctions between oral and nasal vowels and between /o/ and /u/. The voiced series of consonants /b, g, ǰ, z, ž, ɣ/ were written as lower-case cursive *ℓ ₖ tt ʜ d* and *℀* , respectively. Of the eight miscellaneous consonants, /m, n, w/ and /t/ are written, as in MSO, with lower-case cursive *m n ⱳ* and *t* , respectively. The consonant /r/, however, is written with an upper-case cursive *ℒ* ; and /y/ is written with a lower-case cursive * y* . The letter which represents /h/ after vowels also marks a preceding consonant as voiceless, thus accounting for all six of the voiceless consonants. Voiceless /k/, however, is sometimes written with a special symbol resembling an upper-case cursive *𝒳* . The glottal stop is not overtly represented but is inferred before the letter *a* or before any sequence of two identical vowel letters.

A fragment of a syllabic text written by Sam Blowsnake is reproduced below from Susman (1940) together with her phonemic transcription and translation.

ʔé:ja	ni̧géreže	jo·bá̧ha̧
there	somewhere-it-is	four-times
hakewehášge	na̧i̧resʔaže	
six-times-perhaps	sleep-they	

'Somewhere over there they slept four or perhaps six times'

Uyakoq and the Alaskan Eskimo orthographies

Five Eskimoan languages are spoken in Alaska: Aleut, in the Aleutian chain, Pacific Yupik, in the Alaskan Peninsula area, Central Alaskan Yupik, Siberian Yupik (on St. Lawrence Island), and Iñupiak, a dialect of Iñuit, which is spoken across the arctic coast from eastern Alaska to Greenland.

A phonemic orthography for Iñupiak was devised by Roy Ahmaogak, a native speaker, and others in the 1940s and modified by Ahmaogak and Donald Webster in the 1960s. This latter version of the orthography, with the substitution of the letter *q* for *k*, was accepted as the standard Iñupiak writing system by a conference of Iñupiak speakers at Fairbanks in 1972. Another phonemic orthography was devised for Siberian (St. Lawrence Island) Yupik by the Alaska Native Language Center at the University of Alaska in 1972. Yet another phonemic orthography was developed in 1972 for Pacific Yupik (also called Suk, Supik, Gulf Yupic, Sugcestun "Aleut," etc.).

The most interesting Alaskan Eskimo writing systems, however, are those associated with Central Yupik, because, like the Cherokee and Winnebago syllabaries, they were devised by native speakers who were unable to read any second language.

The first native syllabic orthography for Central Yupik was invented by a speaker of the Kuskokwim dialect named Uyakoq shortly after 1900. Prior to that time he wrote the language with an IDEOGRAPHIC system, apparently based on traditional PICTOGRAPHS to which, however, he began to add qualifying signs to generate words which his ideographs could not otherwise specify. The first eight pages of Uyakoq's notebook document a gradual shift from a purely ideographic system to a system in which some words are represented by ideographs for phonologically similar words but are further specified by additional symbols for syllables, most often in word-final position. A ninth page is blank; but the remainder of the notebook is in a completely syllabic orthography which became more and more consistent and refined through time. The earlier form of the orthography was adopted and used by two other men, Kavaraliaq and Wassilij; and the fully developed syllabary was learned by several younger Yupik men and continued to be read as late as the early 1970s. A second syllabic orthography, based on the same principles as Uyakoq's but with radically different symbols, was devised by Qiatuaq after a visit to Uyakoq's village during which he saw Uyakoq's manuscript while it was read to him. At least one other Central Yupik orthography, used by elderly women in the Kotzebue Sound area, may be derived from an early version of Uyakoq's system.

Uyakoq was exposed to English cursive writing through his son, Hermann, who learned to write English at the Bethel Mission Station some time before his death in 1905–6 at age 16. Hermann taught his father to write a few words, such as *Jesus*, in cursive English script; but Uyakoq did not learn the significance of individual letters. He later told the Reverend John Hinz that he felt incapable of learning the alphabet, perhaps because he believed that a knowledge of spoken English was prerequisite to learning the English orthography. It is evident from his manuscript that he used words in English script to represent, not words in spoken English, but corresponding words in Yupik, since they appear together with symbols representing Yupik inflectional suffixes. Not knowing the English orthography, he invented his own; or, as he told Hinz, "Because I was so stupid, God gave it to me" (Schmitt 1951: 105). Qiatuaq also described his own orthography, derived from Uyakoq's, as a sudden gift of God.

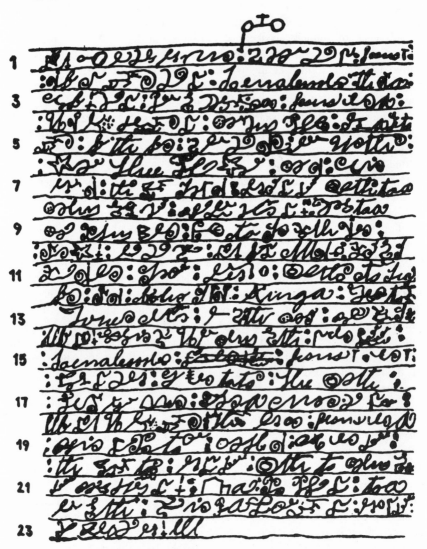

Figure 7.7. A passage from the "Passion of Christ" written by Uyakoq shortly after his divine revelation (reprinted from Schmitt 1951: table 10)

Figure 7.7 shows a passage from the "Passion of Christ" written by Uyakoq shortly after his divine revelation (after the blank ninth page of his notebook). Signs resembling colons are used to mark word boundaries. The fourth word on line 12, which resembles a cursive *Kinga*, consists of two components: *King-*, which Uyakoq evidently learned from his son and used to write /ata/ 'father'; and

-*a*, representing the syllable /im/ and also the partial syllable /m/. The two symbols combined represent /atan'rim/, a form glossed as 'Lord' by Schmitt.

Veniaminov and the Aleut alphabet

Both Cyrillic and roman orthographies are currently used in Aleut native literacy programs associated with both the Atkan and Eastern Aleut dialects. The traditional system is a modified Cyrillic orthography, essentially that of Ivan Veniaminov, a Russian priest who arrived at Unalaska in the 1820s. Some of the earliest literature printed in Aleut Cyrillics was translated by native Aleuts. According to Krauss (1973: 803),

The nineteenth century Aleut priests (Tikhon for Fox Island or Eastern Aleut Netsvetov and Salamatov for Atkan) under Veniaminov translated the Gospels and other religious material, and established the foundation for written literature in Aleut, in a Slavonic alphabet which they adapted very well to the needs of Aleut . . . This written tradition was attacked with a vengeance by the American schools: it was in the wrong alphabet, it was the wrong language, and perhaps (above all) it represented the wrong religion. The American school system has struggled for three generations to eradicate this literacy, and has by now achieved almost complete success.

The Aleut Cyrillic system maintains a one-to-one correspondence between letter and native sound categories except that /h/ is marked by a diacritic and the sequences /ya/ and /yu/ are written, in accordance with Russian convention, as the single letters я and ю . Veniaminov's н‍г used to represent /ŋ/, was a particularly appropriate innovation since it is composed of Cyrillic н and г, representing /n/ and /g/, respectively in both Aleut and Russian.

The history of Aleut literacy dates from the 1820s, when Veniaminov developed his Cyrillic orthography, produced a printed literature, and trained male, native "readers" to read sacred texts in church services. Prior to the acquisition of the Aleutians by the United States, native literacy was taught in boys' schools associated with each of the Russian Orthodox churches on the islands. The orthography was used, however, in both sacred and secular contexts, principally by men, who traditionally passed on this skill to their male *anáqisan* (godsons) in the next generation. After the United States purchased Alaska, native literacy was suppressed by the churches and by federal authorities until the 1970s, by which time the number of native Aleut speakers had dropped "well below 1,000" (Krauss 1973: 803).

Prior to the 1970s there was no secular Aleut literature in print, although there was an extensive manuscript literature on secular topics. According to Ransom (1945: 340),

Among the Aleut, where the whole life of the community gradually came to center about the Russian Church, writing had a chance to break away from restricted doctrinal usage through the custom of the priest issuing ukases, manifestos, or simple bulletins . . . posted on some centrally located bulletin board protected from the elements by a wooden hood, and sometimes by cleverly fashioned swinging doors . . . Today [1945] the bulletin post is the most important feature in the community. On it are posted as required the bulletins of the Church, the Church-sponsored organizations of the Brotherhood and the Sisterhood, notices sent out from the United States Commissioner relating to fishing practices, the control of liquor, etc. Even regional laws may be posted, when the chief or one of the Brotherhood, or the priest, has had time to translate such material into Aleut . . .

Ransom speaks also of the practice of letter writing which was widespread among the Aleuts as late as the 1940s:

The advent of the white man and trading brought into being regular trade routes and a system of mail distribution, unofficial in regions lying beyond regular mail routes, but a regular part of transportation facilities over recognized sea lanes. (1945: 342)

A fragment of an Aleut text written in Cyrillic by Afenogin Ermeloff at Nikolski in 1949 is reproduced below, courtesy of Gordon H. Marsh and William S. Laughlin.

akaɣariuub	Наᴎь	akaka	šaĭakaub
then	this-one	came-back	he-came-here

aɾaɾáнь	Kанɡɾàkaнь	ucxáĭiɾuʞ
after	he-was-sick	in-bed

The Cyrillic Aleut orthography became the basis for a native semaphore system invented by Afenogin Ermeloff and others after a U.S. Coast Guard base was established at Unalaska in World War I. An account of this system, which was allowed to lapse after two-way radios became common on the islands, may be found in Ransom (1941).

The symbols of Silas John

One of the most unusual writing systems in the world is the set of symbols developed by Silas John Edwards of the Fort Apache reservation in 1904. The system is unusual in the shapes of the symbols, in its limitation to a very restricted religious use, and in the fact that the symbols may represent not only spoken words of Western Apache, but also body movements and ritual gestures to be performed. The writing system is associated with a religion founded by Edwards as the result of a dream which he had when he was 21 years old. In the dream he was taught prayers and a writing system with which to record them. "There were," he says, "sixty-two prayers. They came to me in rays from above . . . They were presented to me – one by one. All of these and the writing were given to me at one time in one dream . . . " (Basso and Anderson 1973: 1015).

Silas John, as he is usually called, was literate in English as a young man and was much influenced by an early association with Lutheran missionaries on the Fort Apache reservation. In 1916, according to Basso and Anderson,

. . . Silas John publicly proclaimed himself a messiah and began to preach. At the same time, he wrote down each of his prayers on separate pieces of tanned buckskin, using paints made from a mixture of pulverized minerals and the sap of yucca plants. By 1925, however, prayer-texts were written in ink on squares of cardboard. Today, many (and possibly all) of the original painted buckskins have been lost or disposed of, and Silas John's script is preserved in paper 'prayer books' (*sailiš jaan biʔokǫǫhi*) belonging to Apaches living on the San Carlos and Fort Apache Reservations.

By 1920, it was apparent to Silas John that his acceptance as a religious prophet was assured, and he then selected twelve 'assistants' (*sailiš jaan yiłnanałseʔhi*) to circulate among the Apache people, pray for them, and encourage them to congregate. The assistants were taught to read and write and, after demonstrating these skills, went through an initiation ritual in which they were presented with painted buckskins of their own. Thus equipped, they were placed in charge of carefully prepared sites known as 'holy grounds' and were urged to perform ceremonials on a regular basis, using their buckskins as mnemonic aids. As time passed and members of the original group of assistants began to die, Silas John appointed new ones, who, in turn, were taught the script, formally initiated, and given the texts of prayers. This process, which has continued unmodified up to the present, accounts for the fact that, even among Apaches, knowledge of Silas John's writing system is not widespread. From the very beginning, access to the system was tightly controlled by Silas John himself, and competence in it was intentionally restricted to a small band of elite ritual specialists. (Basso and Anderson 1973: 1015–16)

The writing system, together with its associated rituals, has survived into the 1970s on both the Fort Apache and San Carlos reservations. Silas John texts were also recorded on the Mescalero reservation by Harry Hoijer in 1931.

The Silas John writing system has been used only to record the sixty-two prayers acquired in the vision of 1904. These prayers are of three varieties: *ʔidaʔan biʔokǫǫhi*, therapeutic prayers; *ʔindee keʔistsane biʔokǫǫhi*, prayers with which to avoid or resolve marital discord; and *ʔindee biʔokǫǫhi*, prayers for health, longevity, and social harmony. Some, if not all, of the prayers in any one of these three categories are very similar, their texts differing in only a very few symbols. Prayers of different categories, however, differ substantially, and their texts differ accordingly. It can scarcely be coincidental that the Western Apaches have exactly sixty-two clans and that all but a few of these are grouped into one of three phratries (clan clusters). All sixty-two prayer-texts consist of sets of symbols (*keʔeščin*) "arranged in horizontal lines to be read from left to right in descending order," as in Figure 7.8 (Silas John's "Prayer for Life"). Each symbol represents a single line of prayer, i.e. a word, phrase, or one or more sentences. Some symbols have not only a linguistic referent, i.e. a prayer-line, but also a KINESIC value, inasmuch as they direct the reader to perform certain nonverbal acts, which are, of course, along with the prayer itself, integral parts of the Silas John rituals. Thus the symbol "*she ℐ*," for example, represents the prayer-line *šii šihadndinihi* 'mine, that which is my sacred pollen', but it also instructs the reader to "Face toward the east. Extend fully the right arm, fold the left arm across the chest, and bow the head. After remaining in this position for a few moments, drop the left arm and trace the sign of a cross on one's chest." Symbols which have kinesic as well as linguistic referents are

1. _⌐   *ni⁇aʸolzǫǫnǫ⁇* 'when the earth was first created'

2. ε   *⁇iiyaa⁇ ⁇aʸolzǫǫnǫ⁇* 'when the sky was first created'

3. ♂   *daitsee dagoyǫǫnǫ⁇ ni⁇⁇iɬdįįže⁇* 'in the beginning, when all was started in the center of the earth'

4. ᴜ⁴   *yoosn bihadndin* 'God's sacred pollen' (Take a pinch of sacred pollen in the right hand and place a small amount on each item of the ritual paraphernalia.)

5. ✝   *hadndin ⁇iɬna⁇aahi* 'a cross of sacred pollen'

6. ⋒   *hadndin hidaahi* 'living sacred pollen'

7. ✠   *hadndin ⁇iɬna⁇aahi dįįyo nadiyooɬ* 'a cross of sacred pollen breathing in four directions' (Take a pinch of sacred pollen in the right hand and place a small amount on each arm of the ceremonial cross that marks the eastern corner of the holy ground.)

8. ⚬⚬   *yoosn bihadndin ⁇iɬna⁇aahi hidaahi* 'God's cross of living sacred pollen'

9. ↲⁴   *šii šihadndinihi* 'my own, my sacred pollen' (Face toward the east, extend fully the right arm, fold the left arm across the chest, and bow the head. After remaining in this position for a few moments, drop the left arm and trace the sign of a cross on one's chest.)

10. ↲⁴   *šii ši⁇okǫǫhi* 'my own, my prayer'

11. ≋   *šilagan hadǫǫžę⁇ dįįgo bihadaa⁇istįįgo* 'like four rays, power is flowing forth from the tips of my fingers'; *šilagan hadǫǫžę⁇ biha⁇dit⁇įįgo* 'power from the tips of my fingers brings forth light'

12. ᴜ→   *dašižǫ⁇ beišgaaɬ č⁇idii* 'now it is known that I go forth with power'

13. ⋒   *nagostsan biʸalatažę⁇* 'on the surface of the world'

14. ××××   *nagowaahi nagoščǫǫdi nagoɬdiihi behe⁇gozini* 'sinful things are occurring, bad things are occurring, sickness and evil are occurring, together with harmful knowledge'

15. ⅏   *dįįžę⁇ biɬhadaagoyaa* 'in four directions, these things are dispersed and fade away' (Take a pinch of sacred pollen in the right hand and place a small amount on each arm of the cross that marks the eastern corner of the holy ground.)

16. ⑂   *biɬ⁇anabǫǫžę yoosn biyi⁇ sizįįhi* 'following this, God came to live with man'

17. ⑁   *yoosn binadidzooɬhi* 'the breath of God'

18. ⑂   *yoosn bihadndin* 'God's sacred pollen' (Take a pinch of sacred pollen in the right hand and trace four circles in the air directly over the ritual paraphernalia.)

19. ᴜ   *yoosn* 'God Himself'

20. ⋒   *hadndin hidaahi* 'living sacred pollen'

Figure 7.8. Silas John's "Prayer for Life" (adapted from Basso and Anderson 1973: 1020. Copyright © 1973 by the American Association for the Advancement of Science). Kinesic instructions are given in parentheses

called *keʔeščin hantʔe ʔanleʔ* 'symbols that tell what to do.' Those which have only linguistic referents are called *keʔeščin hantʔe ndii* 'symbols that tell what to say.' Different symbols may share identical linguistic referents or identical kinesic referents. No symbol, however, shares both its linguistic and its kinesic referent with any other symbol.

The Silas John symbols are also classified according to their relative complexity into two groups: unitary symbols, *keʔeščin doɬeedidildaahi* 'symbol elements standing alone'; and compound symbols *keʔeščin ɬeedidilgoh* 'symbol elements put together.' A symbol is classed as unitary if it has no component which is, itself, meaningful. Thus a symbol which consists of a horizontal row of four *x*s is a unitary symbol, since a single *x* or a horizontal row of two or three *x*s has no meaning. The symbol " U→ ," however, is classed as compound because both of its constituents are meaningful signs. Some, but not all, unitary symbols occur together with other elements, of which some may themselves be unitary symbols when not so combined. The compound symbol Ü, which occurs near the end of the text in Figure 7.8, consists of the unitary symbol U *yoosn* 'God' plus a second component ∵ *hadndin* 'sacred pollen', which occurs only as a component of compound symbols. The compound symbol Ü represents the prayer line *yoosn bihadndin* 'God's sacred pollen' and the instruction to take a pinch of sacred pollen in the right hand and trace four circles in the air directly over the ritual paraphernalia.

The linguistic referent of a compound symbol may be more than the sum of the referents of its two constituent parts and hence cannot be inferred from a knowledge of the constituents' referents in other contexts. Thus " U " is a unitary symbol with the linguistic referent *yoosn* 'God' and " → " is an element, which occurs only as a constituent of compound symbols, with the linguistic referent *ʔintin* 'path, trail, road'; but the compound symbol " U→ " has the linguistic referent *dašizǫʔ beišgaaɬ čʔidii* 'it is known that I alone go forth with this power.'

Pablo Tac's Luiseño orthography

The Indian people traditionally associated with the mission of San Luis Rey, in what is now San Diego County, California, have come to be known as Luiseños, and their language as Luiseño. Although native literacy has never been widespread among these people, a Luiseño orthography was invented by one of their number, Pablo Tac. Tac was born in 1822 at the mission of San Luis Rey and was a student in Rome from 1834 until he died at age 19 in 1841. Before his death he wrote several manuscripts, including a grammatical sketch and a fragment of a Luiseño–Spanish dictionary. These were published long after, and a brief "dialogue" in Luiseño with Spanish translation was reprinted with phonemic transcription, English translation, notes, and analysis by Kroeber and Grace (1960: 214–15, 221–37). Tac's orthography was based on Spanish, the five vowels of Luiseño /a, e, i, o, u/ being represented as in Spanish. Doubled vowels were sometimes written to indicate vowel length; and doubled consonants seem to have been used, as in written Italian, to indicate that a preceding vowel was short and accented. The Luiseño distinctions between /k/ and /q/, /s/ and /š/, and /n/ and /ŋ/, none of which is indicated in Spanish orthography, were neatly and efficiently preserved by Tac's device of writing a superscript dot over c (before a, o, u) and qu (before i or e) to indicate the backed velar stop /q/, over s to indicate the backed fricative /š/, and over n to indicate the velar nasal /ŋ/, as distinct from /k/, /s/, and /n/, respectively.

Although Pablo Tac's writing system for Luiseño never became the basis for a viable tradition of literacy, his achievement merits a place for him in the history of Native American literacy along with Sequoyah, the Cherokee; Joe Ellick, the Potawatomi; Mack-aw-de-be-nessy, the Ottawa; Thomas Wildcat Alford, the Shawnee; Uyakoq and Qiatuaq, the Eskimos; Silas John, the Apache; and the pioneer Fox and Winnebago scribes whose names are unknown.

Native American literacy

It is not difficult to document the fact that certain Native Americans have, at various times and places, invented writing systems, that some of these have been adopted by the relevant language communities, and that enduring traditions of literacy are well established in several Native American societies. It is much more difficult to make generally valid statements about the nature of Native American literacy or identify the factors that have encouraged or discouraged Indian literacy in the United States over the last two centuries. One learns to read a language only at the expense of a great deal of time, effort, and aggravation. We are told that a very large minority of American high school graduates who speak English as a native language are "functionally illiterate" (see Chapter 20). That is to say that millions of native speakers of English in the United States are unable to read their own language adequately despite twelve years of instruction in literacy skills and growing up under the constant bombardment of printed English in the form of headlines, traffic signs, neon signs, television subtitles, and a whole range of printed notices. This being the case, it is remarkable indeed that Americans whose first language is not English and who have received no support whatever from the American educational system have nonetheless contrived somehow to preserve their own traditions of literacy. In the case of some American Indian societies this feat has been accomplished by people who, for several generations, were forbidden to use their native language at all in Federal Indian Schools. Krauss' statement that the American school system "has struggled for three generations to eradicate [Aleut] literacy" is valid for all of the Native American societies mentioned in this chapter as having persistent traditions of literacy, for all of them have been subjected to systematic and prolonged efforts on the part of educators to stamp out their languages and their traditions of literacy and substitute the English language and English literacy.

The crusade against native languages seems to have been predicated on three widely held assumptions. First, English-speaking educators tend to assume that English is "better" than any other language, particularly, perhaps, any Native

American language. Many monolingual English-speaking educators actually seem to think that English is the only language appropriate for rational discourse. A second assumption is that *all* Americans should speak, read, and write English, despite the fact that no generation of Americans has as yet conformed to this ideal. A third assumption is that, in order to gain full control of spoken and written English, one must assiduously divest oneself of competence in any language other than English (see Chapter 21). Although this last assumption is patently false, generations of educators have endorsed it, even to the point of prohibiting the temporary use of native languages as vehicles for teaching English, the "target language," to children with no prior knowledge of the English language. Although demonstrably false, this view remains popular among teachers who are reluctant to permit the use of native languages in their classrooms.

The Native American groups which, despite all obstacles, have developed traditions of literacy in their own languages seem to share certain characteristics. All of them, of course, have preserved some sort of social organization, at least at the local community level. It would seem that such groups have also found one or more functions for their own literacy. Thus the spread of Fox, Winnebago, Cherokee, and Mahican literacy occurred at the same time that these several tribes were divided by migrations. In all four cases it seems reasonable to suppose that the first individuals to become literate were motivated by a desire to communicate with relatives who had departed for the west or, as the case may be, had lingered behind in the east. The Aleuts and Yupiks were never forcibly "removed" or broken into separate reservation communities; but their dispersed settlements and frequent hunting and fishing expeditions made the ability to read and write letters a useful skill. Motivation for literacy is not always based on the need to correspond with absent friends and relatives, however. The Cherokee syllabary, for example, has long been used in the context of religious services and religious instruction where those to whom messages are read are all present in the same room with those who are reading. Likewise, the Cherokee medical practitioners who record curing formulas in the syllabary do so primarily for their own reference, not for unspecified readers at some remote place and time. The factors that tend to perpetuate native literacy, then, need not include a felt need to communicate with distant members of a tightly knit society; but they do seem to include the perception of literacy as a useful skill which enables the literate to achieve some worthwhile objective.

The Oklahoma Cherokee communities suggest other ways in which Native American literacy may differ from the conventional literacy associated with middle class, English-speaking Americans. We have historical evidence that Cherokees can learn to read both Cherokee and English, that in the nineteenth century most of them did so, and that in the twentieth century most of them have ceased to do so. Literacy in this society, if not in all other Native American societies, would seem to be a function of four variables: traditional learning patterns, the teaching patterns of the instructor, incentives to learn, and the social definition of the principal learning contexts. Unlike most middle class Americans, the Cherokees do not expect all members of their communities to become literate. What seems to be important is that each community should have a few responsible people in key roles (preachers, church secretaries and treasurers, medical practitioners, etc.) who are literate. It usually turns out that, in fact, virtually every household either has a member or has ready access to some neighbor who is literate in Cherokee. Such people tend to be middle-aged or elderly. There is no pressure on children to become literate while they are still children; nor is there any tendency to withhold instruction from the elderly on the ground that they have, for many years, failed to learn and are therefore classified as proven failures.

Cherokee learning patterns are probably similar, in many respects, to those of many other Native American societies. The members of any given Cherokee community do most of their learning in the home, the homes of neighboring kinsmen, the church, and the school. Cherokees usually learn a skill by watching others practise it for some time before trying it themselves. There is, in other words, a long period of prelearning in which the prelearner watches, passively, his kinsmen exercise the skill. Typically, this prelearning is done in the natural, routine context of the home or church and of the family or kinsmen. Ordinarily, prelearning is done informally in the course of the everyday business of Cherokee life.

In Cherokee society there are few authority figures and very little coercion. The proceedings at a church service are normally initiated by a rotating committee of elders; and church-goers feel free to get up and go out the door at any time. Although the male head of a family has considerable authority within the household, the extended family provides many refuges for the coerced, and the members of a given household are frequently to be found in the nearby homes of relatives. Thus escape routes are built into Cherokee social structure, such that undue pressure on an individual or group is almost certain to result in withdrawal.

When formal, coercive instruction does occur, it often involves a father instructing one or more of his children, and the subject matter is typically the Cherokee Bible and the techniques necessary to read this Bible. The child typically resists coercion passively or rejects it by withdrawal. Significantly, however, Cherokees seem to do much of their prelearning of the Sequoyah writing system in this coercive type of situation. In the native view, this prelearning is not considered a part of learning. If remembered at all, it is thought of as a period of failure to learn, which is quite unrelated to the subsequent attainment of literacy. This ultimate achievement often comes later in life and generally in a noncoercive context. It is thought of as a sudden revelation. A Cherokee will say, for example, that it is easy to learn to read Cherokee, that he learned in two days, in a day, or even in an afternoon, stretched out under a tree alone with the Bible. Under questioning, however, he concedes that his father had previously instructed him, without success, night after night at the kitchen table. Ultimately, his father gave up; and the venture is remembered only as an abortive experiment that "didn't work."

In general then, Cherokees conceive of literacy and other skills as coming to them almost instantaneously, as a kind of revelation. They tend to discount the long period of exposure to a skill and the successful prelearning of fragments of relevant information. Significantly, they also conceive of knowledge as a gift from God, and modern Cherokees say that literacy can never be universal, since God would not give the gift of literacy to everyone. If he did, bad Cherokees would have power with which to conjure the innocent. In traditional theory then, only the just are given the ability to read; and the extent of one's opportunity and effort to learn appear quite unrelated to achievement.

Much conventional education in the United States is impersonal and coercive, predicated on the assumption that students are motivated to learn fragments of skills in a fixed sequence through concentrated effort, responding favorably to success in mastering these fragments, and sustained throughout their ordeal by a constant faith in the utility of the skill ultimately to be acquired. As I have already mentioned, however, Cherokee motivation varies and is principally, perhaps, a function of age; learning is typically nonfragmented and nonsequential; achievement is not conceived as a result of effort expended; and the utility of literacy and other skills is, for large segments of the population, highly questionable.

Since the federal government took over the Cherokee school system in 1898, Cherokees have viewed the school as a White man's institution which Cherokee children are bound by law to attend, but over which their parents have no control. Most Cherokee speakers drop out of school as soon as this is legally possible. While in school, they learn relatively little due in part to the language barrier, but also due to this unfortunate, but accurate, definition of the school as a White man's institution. As a further complication, Cherokee parents are well aware that educated children tend to leave the community, either geographically or socially. To them, the school threatens the break-up of the family and division of the community, precisely those consequences which no genuinely viable and integrated community can tolerate.

It seems clear that the startling decline during the past seventy-five years of both English and Cherokee literacy in Cherokee society results, in part at least, from the limited utility of Cherokee literacy and from the fact that learning to read English has been associated with coercive instruction, particularly in the context of an alien and threatening school presided over by English-speaking teachers and controlled by English-speaking superintendents and PTAs which conceive of Cherokee as a "dying" language and Cherokee school children as "culturally impoverished" candidates for rapid and "inevitable" social assimilation. Indians and Whites alike are constantly equating competence in the school with assimilation into the White middle class. Likewise, Indians and many Whites equate the prelearning and fragmentary learning of skills with failure to learn.

For the Cherokee community to become literate in English once again, Cherokees must be convinced that English literacy does not imply the death of their society and that education is not a clever device to wean children away from their communities and kin. This is not a uniquely Cherokee or even a uniquely Indian situation. Identical attitudes toward education and the school can, no doubt, be found in Appalachia, in urban ghettos, and, indeed, in all societies where the recruitment of individuals into the dominant society threatens the extinction of a viable social group. From the experience of the Cherokees with literacy, we may infer that the persistence of literacy in their own language in a minority group is a consequence of the fact that literacy in that language has some utility for its speakers. Moreover, literacy in the minority language does not have the negative connotations which literacy in the dominant language acquires through its association with the school and all that that implies.

FURTHER READING

Goody 1968 and Fishman 1977a offer wide perspectives on the creation and modification of writing systems, the spread of literacy in many parts of the world, and the functions of literacy in different societies, and the articles in them provide extensive bibliographies. Unfortunately, there are no general works on the graphization of Native American languages in the USA and the functions of literacy in different American Indian communities. A thoughtful, informative article on Canadian Cree orthography, Burnaby and Anthony 1979, gives an account of alternative orthographies (including traditional syllabaries) and the psycholinguistic implications of using one or another of these in language programs for Cree children.

For information on literacy and writing systems associated with specific North American languages or language stocks mentioned in this chapter, see the following:

Algonquian languages: Hanzeli 1969 discusses early French missionary efforts in the description and graphization of American Indian languages. Pilling 1891 lists all the early works published in Algonquian languages, along with examples of writing systems.

Cherokee: The most recent account of Cherokee literacy is Walker 1975. Feeling 1975, a Cherokee–English dictionary, contains a grammatical sketch. Holmes and Smith 1976 is on spoken Cherokee. The *Journal of Cherokee Studies*, published since 1976 by the Museum of the Cherokee Indian in cooperation with the Cherokee Historical Association, provides readable and lively historical and literary studies.

Winnebago: Walker 1974 is the most recent, detailed treatment.

Eskimoan: Schmitt 1951 gives an account of Uyakoq and his Central Alaskan Yupik syllabary, but it is available only in German. Krauss 1973 gives an overview of Eskimoan and Aleut writing systems. Ransom 1945 discusses the effects of literacy among the Aleut.

Luiseño: Kroeber and Grace 1960.

Western Apache: Basso and Anderson 1973 is an excellent account of the symbols of Silas John; it is also available in Fishman 1977a.

8

Indian lingua francas

ALLAN R. TAYLOR

When persons speaking mutually unintelligible languages are in more or less permanent contact, some means is always found to bridge the communication gap. The most straightforward solution is for some or all of the parties to learn the language of the other parties to the contact. In this case, communication is effected through the BILINGUALISM of some or all of the participants.

Many American Indian groups solved their problems of communication at tribal and language boundaries through the mediation of bilingual persons. Often such bilingualism resulted from accidental factors such as intermarriage or a period of residence in a foreign tribe. There have also been instances where bilingualism was deliberately cultivated either by individuals or by entire communities who maintained intimate political and social contact across tribes for many generations. Outstanding examples of societal bilingualism are the Tewa-speaking Hano of New Mexico, almost all of whom also speak Hopi, and the Yurok and Karok of California, most of whom could understand (if not speak) each other's language. The nineteenth-century traveller Stephen Powers was much impressed with the extent of this Yurok-Karok bilingualism: "two of them will sit and patter gossip for hours, each speaking in his own tongue. A white man listening may understand one, but never a word of the other" (Powers 1877: 44). Certain closely associated Cree and Assiniboine bands in the Canadian prairie provinces are said to be largely bilingual even today. Bilingualism was particularly high in California and on the Northwest Coast. The same was probably true in the Southeast.

Speakers of mutually unintelligible American Indian languages also often either adopted or developed a third language used largely or only to mediate contact. Such a language is called a LINGUA FRANCA. A lingua franca may be a NATURAL LANGUAGE, such as English, French, or Cree, or it may be a pidginized language or PIDGIN, such as a simplified form of English, or Mobilian, a pidginized form of Choctaw. It may also be a pidginized language which has come to be the MOTHER TONGUE of a group, i.e. a CREOLE (see Chapter 4), such as the language of the Métis. When a lingua franca is essentially a hybrid speech form, put together on the spot from numerous sources, it is called a JARGON. A nonverbal language, such as Plains Sign Language, may also be used as a lingua franca.

175

Pidgins and jargons should not be identified, however with the "broken" form of a language as it is spoken by individual foreigners. BROKEN LANGUAGE represents (usually) a foreigner's best efforts to speak the language, and the broken form is not ordinarily transmitted to other learners of the language, such as the foreigner's children. Moreover, broken speech is not restricted, as a rule, to particular situations, as are pidgins and jargons.

The subject of lingua francas in North America before contact with Europeans presents an interesting paradox. Judging from the situation after the Europeans came, they were certainly rare; yet one of them, the Plains Sign Language, represents the most sophisticated of its kind in the entire world. Precontact use of lingua francas, like precontact bilingualism, is largely unresearched. Postcontact lingua francas, on the other hand, especially pidgins and jargons, have received considerable attention during the 1970s. This chapter will deal entirely with postcontact lingua francas, and will give special attention to those which were pidgins or jargons.

European languages as lingua francas

Eight European languages were introduced into North America by European powers: Danish, Dutch, English, French, German, Russian, Spanish, and Swedish. The Swedish and Dutch colonies disappeared before these languages gained any importance as colonial languages in North America, although Dutch LOANWORDS have survived in some American Indian languages such as Delaware. German, unsupported by a colonial administration, had little chance to become prominent in North America, although it, too, may have had minor lexical impact on contiguous Indian languages. Russian served as a lingua franca in the Aleutian Islands and the nearby Alaskan mainland between approximately 1750 and 1867, and a legacy of Russian loanwords is found in Aleut, Eskimo, and several Alaskan Indian languages. A few Russian words are also found in the Pomo language called Kashaya, which was spoken at the mouth of the Russian River north of San Francisco, California. Russian loanwords reached Kashaya through the Russian and Aleut personnel at Fort Ross, the Russian outpost located at the river's mouth between 1812 and 1841. Danish has had no impact outside of Greenland, but it is the language of administration and urban culture in Greenland, and many native Greenlanders know it in addition to their Eskimo mother tongue.

French was an important lingua franca during the colonial period and even later, reflecting the early dominance of France in the Laurentian region of Canada and in the Mississippi Valley. English eventually replaced French as the lingua franca in all French territory except French-speaking Québec. Expansion of the United States, continuing the successful expansion of British North America, carried English further and further westward, where it served as the principal lingua franca on all frontiers. Spanish was used as a lingua franca in early Florida and later in Texas and the Southwest, including California, and left a substantial legacy of loanwords in Indian languages (see Chapter 9).

In most cases, European languages which became lingua francas began as the property of a few (often mixed-blood) individuals, who served as interpreters between the native community and Europeans. One of the earliest (and most famous) examples of the pivotal role of such individuals is that of Squanto, the Wampanoag Indian friend of the Pilgrims. Squanto was captured on the Massachusetts coast in 1615 and subsequently sold into slavery in Spain. By unknown means he arrived in England in 1617, where he lived until his return to North America in 1619. His ability to be an intermediary between the Plymouth colonists and the Massachuset tribe thus derived from the knowledge of the English language and culture which he had gained as an accidental exile in Europe. From 1620 until his death in 1622 he played a crucial role in relations between the Massachusetts Bay colony and the neighboring Indians; there is a considerable body of evidence that he exploited his position to the maximum possible extent for his own gain.

With the advent of significant cultural assimilation, however, individual bilingualism was replaced by societal bilingualism, with a decided trend toward obsolescence of the native languages. It is true that English, for example, is a lingua franca between members of historical Indian tribes, but English can scarcely be called a lingua franca today, when it is the only language of many Native Americans. In many cases the state of societal bilingualism was preceded by a period of use of a PIDGINIZED variety of the European language. A special section below is devoted to pidginized European languages.

Native American languages as lingua francas

A few Native American languages are known to have been used as lingua francas, but probably more were used than we know. It is also impossible to know in many cases whether the language so used was pidginized, since early records of Native American languages are deficient in both quality and quantity.

The Muskogee or Creek language enjoyed wide use as a lingua franca during the period when most tribes in the Southeast belonged to the Creek Confederacy. This political affiliation, which included seven language groups, Muskogean as well as others, lasted from pre-European times (possibly as early as the sixteenth century) until 1836-40, when most of the Indians in the Southeast were removed to Indian Territory (Oklahoma). Creek continued to be used as a lingua franca in Florida into the twentieth century between Indians there (''Seminoles'') who had different tribal languages.

Similarly, a Virginia Algonquian language may have been the lingua franca of the Powhatan Confederacy, which briefly united a number of tribes with different languages in the Virginia and Maryland tidewater during the early seventeenth century. This confederacy collapsed shortly after the arrival of the English in Virginia, and details on the language situation are lacking.

One of the earliest mentions by Europeans of a native lingua franca is that by the Virginia historian Beverley (1722, republished 1947), who named the language of one of the Southeastern Siouan groups, the Occaneeches, as the "general language" of the Virginia–North Carolina region. His statement refers to the early eighteenth century. No details on the structure of the language, and no sample, were given by Beverley, so it is impossible to know whether this was natural language, or a pidgin or jargon. A vocabulary from 1716 of another Southeastern Siouan language, labeled "Sapoñey," looks very much like a jargon, and this vocabulary may be, in fact, a sample of the Occaneeche lingua franca. Most of the items in the vocabulary are Siouan, except the numerals, which are of Algonquian and Iroquoian origin.

Ojibwa (Chippewa) served as an "outside language" for most of the tribes around the Great Lakes during the late seventeenth, eighteenth, and early nineteenth centuries. Many of the tribes were Algonquian in speech, but some, for example, Winnebago and Dakota, were not. According to an eighteenth-century English visitor, Ojibwa was in his day "universally spoken in council by the chiefs who reside about the great lakes, to the westward of the banks of the Mississippi, as far south as the Ohio, and as far north as Hudson's Bay; notwithstanding many of the tribes, within the space of territory I have described, speak . . . a different language" (Long 1904: 28). This claim is a slight exaggeration, at least insofar as the northern extent is concerned, unless Long is not distinguishing Cree from Ojibwa. The two are actually quite closely related, and virtually mutually intelligible at their borders. Long also observes (p. 30) that the Ojibwa, "as spoken by the servants of the Hudson's Bay Company, is somewhat different, though not essentially so, and is called by them the *Home-Guard Language*." This statement could mean that the company employed a pidginized form of Ojibwa, or that it used a slightly different DIALECT than that known to Long. It is certain that Ojibwa became a lingua franca thanks to its use by the fur companies, whose employees were often native speakers of some Ojibwa dialect (Chippewa, Algonkin, Saulteaux) and whose local officials, as often as not, had Ojibwa wives.

South of the Ohio River, the "Illinois" (Peoria) language, another Algonquian language, seems to have been used in the seventeenth century along the Mississippi as far down as the confluence of the Arkansas. Early French explorers such as Marquette and La Salle had no difficulty finding interpreters between the Peoria language and the local language until they reached the northern border of the present state of Louisiana. The use of Peoria as a lingua franca faded out during the eighteenth century (it was probably replaced by French), but the Algonqiuan elements in the Mobilian trade language used around the mouth of the Mississippi probably reflect the early importance of Peoria further upriver.

In the Canadian prairies the lingua franca of the fur trade seems to have been Cree, an Algonquian language closely related to Ojibwa. The use of two lingua francas reflects the seventeenth-century rivalry between Britain and France: the French trade was through Québec, and used Ojibwa; the English trade was from posts ("factories") on Hudson Bay, and used Cree. In each case, the lingua franca was the language of the most prominent local native group. British traders from the eighteenth and early nineteenth centuries note the use of Cree in trade by Northern Athabascan groups such as the Chipewyans, Beavers, and Sarsis.

Regarding the Sarsis, one observer wrote: ''Most of them have a smattering of the Cree language, which they display in clamorous and discordant strains, without rule or reason'' (Coues 1897: 2.737). This statement may indicate that a Cree-based pidgin, rather than Cree proper, was used in trading with these people.

A French exploring expedition into the Northern Plains in 1738–9, led by the Sieur de la Vérendrye, used Assiniboine to communicate with the Mandans, a tribe they found living in permanent villages on the Missouri River in what is now southern North Dakota. Communication with the Mandans was through an Assiniboine-speaking Cree, whose desertion later caused severe difficulties. This use of Assiniboine reflects the role of the Assiniboines, who, with the Crees, lived in the southern Canadian prairies and served as middle men in the distribution of European trade goods to the tribes beyond the reach of the Hudson's Bay and French Canadian traders. It is significant that de la Vérendrye did not find the Plains Sign Language in use among the Mandans at that time.

The missionary, Charles L. Hall, found in the late nineteenth century that many Mandan and Hidatsa Indians knew Dakota, probably the *l*-dialect of that language spoken by their former enemies, the Teton Sioux. Teton Sioux was known by a number of individuals from Northern Plains tribes during most of the nineteenth century. In the Southern Plains, Comanche was often used as an outside language in the early nineteenth century. The use of Teton Sioux in the Northern Plains and Comanche in the Southern Plains reflects the similar political roles and general importance of these two tribes in their respective regions.

Navajo appears to have been used rather frequently in the Southwest, perhaps as early as the eighteenth century. A late nineteenth-century visitor to the Hopi, Alexander Stephen, used Navajo in speaking with Hopis and Hopi Tewas (Hano), and he heard Hopis using Navajo with visiting Zuñis. Many Hopi Tewas still speak excellent Navajo, but today only with Navajo people.

Another Athabascan language, Hupa, was reported as in wide use in the late nineteenth century between unrelated tribes in northern California. This reflected the political importance of the Hupas, who dominated a number of weaker tribes and compelled the latter to use Hupa with them. Some of these tribes gave up their own language and adopted Hupa.

Pidginized European languages

In addition to use of either European or Native American languages as lingua francas, many tribes developed or adopted pidgins and jargons. Both European and Native American languages were pidginized in the sporadic but continuing contacts among Native American groups for which no natural language served as a lingua franca. Since many such contact situations arose before and during the conquest of North America, there is relatively little remaining evidence of pidginized lingua francas, and we can guess that a number disappeared without a trace. For example, it is now clear that European fishermen frequented the rich fishing grounds of the North Atlantic off the coast of North America for a considerable period before the permanent settlement of North America by Europeans. Contact of some sort between European fishermen and Native Americans goes back at least to the beginning of the sixteenth century, probably earlier, and pidginized forms of Breton, Portuguese, Basque, French, and English (Irish?) may have been used for communication.

Pidginized French and English are well attested in other regions and for later periods. Numerous examples of a pidgin English in use by Native Americans have been recorded from the seventeenth century through the nineteenth. Leecham and Hall (1955), Dillard (1972), and Goddard (1977) give various samples of Pidgin English as used by Indians in New England and elsewhere. (Many of the examples – all recorded by Whites – are certainly not completely correct renditions of Indian Pidgin English, since standard English spelling is used, and some expected simplifications in grammar do not appear.) An East Coast variety of Pidgin English was transmitted by White traders and runaway slaves to Indians elsewhere on the continent, so that the form of the pidgin was quite uniform throughout the period of its use, roughly 1600–1900.

Two short examples from a source not cited by the above authors – *Remarkable Adventures in the Life and Travels of Colonel James Smith*, first printed in Lexington, Kentucky, in 1799 – are illustrative of Indian Pidgin English. In 1755 the 18-year-old Smith was captured in western Pennsylvania by a war party of Iroquois and Delaware Indians. He remained with the Indians four years. Smith was captured just before the famous defeat of General Braddock in the so-called French and Indian War. The first example comes from a passage about the defeat: "I asked him (an English-speaking Delaware) what news from Braddock's army. He said the Indians spied them every day, and he showed me, by making marks on the ground with a stick, that Braddock's army was advancing in very close order, and that the Indians would surround them, take trees, and (as he expressed it) *shoot um down all one pigeon* (shoot them down like pigeons)."

The other example comes from a later conversation between Smith and the same Delaware interlocutor: "On my return to camp I observed a large piece of fat meat; the Delaware . . . observed me looking earnestly at this meat and he asked me, *'What meat you think that is?'* I said I supposed it was bear meat; he laughed and said, *'Ho, all one fool you, beal now elly pool'* (Ho, you're a complete fool; bears are very poor [i.e. thin] now.)" (Kephart 1915: 18, 27).

Leecham and Hall (1955) list a number of characteristics of Indian Pidgin English, several of which Smith accurately reproduces in his narrative: the use of nouns in their singular form only and the omission of articles, omission of the verb *be*, the use of *um* to mark a transitive verb, the use of *all one* to mean *like* and *completely*. Smith also indicates that the Delaware speaker replaces English *r*, which Delaware lacks, with *l*, a sound which occurs in Delaware. Notice also that he drops the *v* of *very; v* is a sound foreign to Delaware. Presumably the Delaware would also have replaced the *th* sounds *(think, that)* with *t* and *d*, and possibly *f* (fool) with *p*, although no examples appear.

Pidginized French also began to be noted in the seventeenth century. An early instance is the French-based jargon observed in 1606–7 in use between French fishermen and the local Micmac population in Nova Scotia. The pidgin purportedly included a large Basque element (Lescarbot 1907: 3.125). Details on the jargon are completely lacking. French PATOIS served (and still serves) as the outside and, in some cases, only language of a large number of mixed blood persons who resulted from French exploration and trade in the interior of North America. In Canada these persons are called Métis. The Indian parentage of these people came from most of the tribes of North America except those of the Southwest; the French parentage is from the French population of eastern Canada. As long as the Métis were in contact with Indian nations, their primary language was a Native American one (Ojibwa, Cree, Dakota, Osage, etc.). It became French (and often eventually English) after the frontier moved further west and left them stranded among a European majority.

A nineteenth-century American observer of the Métis of the Red River Valley of Manitoba, V. Havard, compared the speech of the French Métis to that of the "poorer classes" of Québec, but with important differences in pronunciation, vocabulary, and grammar. He characterized their patois as clearly a pidginized form of French: the pronunciation as "defective" and "grotesque" when compared with the cultivated French of his day; the vocabulary as "not comprehensive"; the grammar as simplified. "The Métis avoids grammatical difficulties in the use of verbs and pronouns by using as few tenses as possible, and these preferably in the third person singular; for instance *çã dit çã* 'they say so' . . ." (Havard 1880: 326).

One of the most fascinating surviving offshoots of the pidginized French of the Métis is a creole spoken on the Turtle Mountain Reservation in northern North Dakota. The Métis speakers of this language call it Michif. A great many nouns in it are of French origin, as are other grammatical elements which are tied closely to nouns in syntax, including articles, adjectives, possessive pronouns, and prepositions. The verbs of Michif and elements tied to verbs, including some noun forms incorporated into verbs, are of Algonquian (Cree) origin. Some examples of Michif phrases and sentences will indicate the extent of the integration of pidginized French into the language: a noun phrase completely of French origin, *æn pčit mæzõ blãš* 'a little white house' (cf. French *une petite maison blanche*); a verb phrase completely of Cree origin, *kiše pe·kičiče·w* 'he washes his hands' (where *ičiče* 'hands' is incorporated into the verb in Algonquian fashion); a mixture of French noun phrases with Cree verbs, *æn om ke·yayo· si žvu ewaniha·t* 'there was a man who lost his horses' (cf. French *un homme* 'a man' and *ses chevaux* 'his horses'), *la fãm mičimine·w li pči (wa)* 'the woman is holding the child' (cf. French *la femme* 'the woman', *le petit* 'the child') (Rhodes 1977; personal communication from John C. Crawford 1978).

Pidginized Spanish was probably used in Florida, Texas, and the Southwest, since Spanish administration often brought diverse language groups together, most of whom were thenceforth in some contact with the Spanish language. A sample of pidgin Spanish used by Indians is available from the Bodega Bay area north of San Francisco. Use of a Spanish-based pidgin is reported for that area by Vancouver in 1792–3, and an aged Bodega Miwok woman who had learned some of the pidgin from her parents was able to recall some examples in the early 1960s (personal communication from Catherine A. Callaghan 1978). The pidgin, according to the informant, was called Chileno. The few examples of Chileno show a largely Spanish lexicon, but with virtually no attention paid to such requirements of Spanish grammar as gender agreement and personal forms of verbs. For example, the third person singular indicative was used regularly with all persons in all tenses and moods. Compare:

Chileno	Spanish
Yóo no entyende ustée	*Yo no le entiendo a usted*
'I don't understand you' [Note: *entiende*	
'he, she understands']	
Nosóotros tiyéene ?áamre	*Nosotros tenemos hambre*
'We're hungry' [Note: *tiene* 'he, she has']	
Biyene kon nosotros	*¡Venga con nosotros!*
'Come with us!' [Note: *viene* 'he, she	
comes']	

As with many pidgin languages, however, the speakers of Chileno apparently varied in their use of forms like this, and some verbs in correct personal forms were collected. These may show that the whole expressions were learned as fixed phrases or that the pidgin was undergoing some DECREOLIZATION in the direction of normal Spanish grammar. Examples are: *yóo no sée* 'I don't know' *(yo no se); no pwéedo ?ír* 'I can't go' *(no puedo ir)*. The past tense was sometimes indicated by an auxiliary verb, a form of the verb *dar* 'give': *?éste día nosóotros dáa múy áamre* 'we were very hungry today' ("this day we gives very hunger"). Yet, in other cases, a correct imperfect verb form was used: *yóo stáawa akíi* 'I was here' *(yo estaba aquí)*. The masculine form of the adjective was used for both genders; thus *wéenu mučáača* 'good girl' *(buena muchacha)*.

A number of questions about Chileno will probably remain permanently unanswered. For example, why was the pidgin called Chileno? Is it typical of the Spanish contact vernaculars which grew up in the multilingual mission societies? Did it originate in the northern California missions, or was the pidgin transplanted to California from other areas (Mexico, South America)? What percentage of the vocabulary and grammar were Spanish? Why did the pidgin survive well into the twentieth century, long after the collapse (*c.* 1840) of the mission society which spawned it? A possible answer to the last question is the biography of Callaghan's informant: her parents had different Indian native languages.

Pidginized Native American languages

Several pidginized Indian languages are also well attested. It is interesting to note that both Indian and European users of these speech forms were often unaware that they were speaking pidgins rather than natural languages. The missionary Paul Le Jeune, writing in 1633, described the use of jargonized Montagnais as follows: "when the French use it, they think they are speaking the Savage Tongue, and the Savages, in using it, think they are speaking good French" (Le Jeune 1897: 5.113–14).

A pidginized form of the Unami dialect of the Delaware language was used during most of the seventeenth century in parts of what are now New Jersey, Delaware, New York, and Pennsylvania. The pidgin originated in trade between Europeans and the Delawares, and it was used successively by the Swedes, the Dutch, and the English. A Swedish Lutheran minister, Johannes Campanius, translated the Lutheran catechism into the pidgin (published 1696), and the samples of Delaware found in the writings of William Penn are also Pidgin Delaware. The most extensive record of the pidgin is the so-called "Indian Interpreter," a trader's vocabulary of words and phrases found early in the twentieth century among deeds and other documents dated in the 1680s from Salem County, New Jersey. The entire list was published, with commentary, early in this century (Prince 1912; see also Thomason 1980).

The vocabulary of the pidgin is largely Delaware in origin, although words from other sources are also present. For example, two Dutch words for coins appear in the Interpreter, as does a Spanish-derived term for horse, *copy* (from *caballo*). Several words from related Algonquian Indian languages of southern New England are also listed: *papouse, nietap* 'friend,' and *squaw*. English contributed *me* 'I': *me mauholumi* 'I will buy it,' *me matta wingeni* 'I don't care for it'. Semantic areas represented most heavily are those dealing with trade, making inquiries, and diplomatic functions. The complex MORPHOLOGICAL structure of Delaware is largely eliminated; Delaware words, or parts of words, are strung together in English word order, more or less without grammatical concord. Pidgin Delaware probably passed out of use sometime during the eighteenth century, quite likely through replacement by English (or pidginized English). There was also a pidginized form of Massachuset used with Indians in southern New England, and pidginized Powhatan is preserved in vocabularies collected by Captain John Smith and William Strachey.

An Eskimo jargon, perhaps several, was used during the nineteenth century in northwest Alaska between Eskimos and visiting ships. The famed Arctic explorer Vilhjalmur Stefánsson collected and published a "ships' trade jargon" which he encountered early in the twentieth century at Herschel Island (Stefánsson 1909). The same jargon was used at Point Barrow and around Kotzebue Sound. The lexical base of the jargon was Inupik Eskimo, with "a few English words, a few from the South Sea Islands (and especially the Hawaiian), a word or two from Spanish and from Danish" (Stefánsson 1913: 355). Stefánsson's own description is succinct and worth repeating here: "The jargon vocabularies of different men vary from probably 300 to 500 words. There being no inflection, this language is easy to learn. It can be picked up in a week and will serve for the expression of the ordinary simple ideas concerning the everyday life of the North. The jargon is, however, quite incapable of expressing any fine shades of thought, and those who know it only, get the impression of the Eskimo that their minds are more impoverished and their thoughts cruder than is really the case."

Examples given by Stefánsson show the grammatical clashes which are expected in jargons: *īla kaktunga* 'he I-am-hungry' (= 'He is hungry'); *ōmīakpûk alaktok pishuktok awonga* 'the-ship he-goes he-wants I' (= 'I want to go on shipboard'). (The spellings given here have been changed slightly from those used by Stefánsson.) Another Eskimo-based contact vernacular was used between the Mackenzie River Eskimos and the neighboring Loucheux Indians.

One of the more interesting instances of a restructured Native American language is still in actual use. This speech form has been called "Trader Navajo" by its chief student, Oswald Werner. Since large numbers of Navajos prefer to use only Navajo in reservation contexts, resident traders must acquire at least a smattering of Navajo in order to do business with them. Usage is not uniform from trader to trader, but all have greatly simplified the enormously complex grammar and PHONOLOGY of Navajo. Since the Navajos themselves do not use pidgin in speaking to the traders, this speech form might better be regarded as "broken Navajo" rather than as pidgin Navajo. To the extent that it is similar among the various traders, it may represent a kind of incipient pidgin.

Most of the pidgins and jargons used in North America have been local and ephemeral. Three, however, are of great importance in terms of their areal spread and length of use. These are Mobilian, the Chinook Jargon, and the Plains Sign Language.

Mobilian (French *Mobilienne;* also called the Chickasaw trade language, and Yama by some present-day Indians) was spoken by members of most of the tribes throughout the territory now constituting the southeastern United States, from western Florida to the Texas Gulf Coast. It was also known for a considerable distance up the Mississippi River.

Mobilian probably dates from the arrival of the French on the Gulf Coast late in the seventeenth century. It is first mentioned specifically in 1704, when the French traveler Pénicaut asserted that Mobilian was understood by all of the "nations," an observation which was often repeated by the eighteenth-century French writers, and again by the first American Indian agent in New Orleans, John Sibley. Mobilian was studied briefly at the end of the nineteenth century by the Swiss–American anthropologist and linguist, Albert Gatschet, but he published virtually nothing on the language.

After a century of silence, interest in Mobilian has seen an upsurge during the 1970s. A small body of texts in Mobilian was collected during the summer of 1970 among Choctaw and Koasati Indians living in Louisiana and East Texas. Since then the collector of this material, James M. Crawford, has published a monograph on Mobilian (Crawford 1978), and a doctoral dissertation by Emanuel J. Drechsel on the structure and functions of Mobilian is in progress at the time of writing.

According to tradition, Mobilian is a pidginized form of Choctaw-Chickasaw; examination of new samples of Mobilian by an expert in Muskogean languages entirely confirms the tradition (Haas 1975). There are, however, elements in the pidgin (chiefly LEXICAL) which come from other sources. The principal contributors to the pidgin, apart from other Muskogean languages (e.g. Alabama), are

Algonquian (probably Peoria, but possibly also Shawnee and Delaware), and the colonial languages French, Spanish, and English.

The sound system of Mobilian is simple: syllables tend to have single consonants between vowels. The only sound which is unusual for the European contact languages of the area is a voiceless *l*. French and English speakers regularly replace the voiceless /ł/ with the sequence *shl* /šl/. The result is that words containing /ł/ always have a doublet form with /šl/: *łało* or *šlašlo* 'fish,' *tałape* or *tašlape* 'five.' Mobilian represents a simplification of Choctaw in its grammar. For example, the complex affix system of Choctaw verbs has largely been replaced by separate words with the same meaning: Choctaw *oki sabanna* 'I'm thirsty,' Mobilian *oki inu bana*; Choctaw *ikfala·yo* 'not tall,' 'short,' Mobilian *falaya ekšu* or *falayakšu*. The simple sentence normally has the order: object (or adverbial), subject, verb. There is no linking verb equivalent to English *be*. *Šunak išno banna?* 'Do you want money?' (money you want); *Bašpo eno bašle* 'I cut it with a knife' (knife I cut); *Elton eno aya* 'I go to Elton' (Elton I go); *Šunak čukma* 'money is good' or 'good money' (money good). Word order is not rigid, however, as is shown by the fact that alternate word orders used by French and English speakers cause no difficulty; compare *eno aya čuka* 'I go home' to the similar sentence *Elton eno aya* 'I go to Elton.'

The Chinook Jargon of the Northwest was quite different from Mobilian in origin and structure, and much more is known about it, thanks to over a century of publication in and on the Jargon, including dictionaries, grammatical studies, and texts. Chinook Jargon was spoken along the Northwest Coast from Oregon to the Alaska Panhandle and inland along the great rivers, chiefly the Columbia. Some kind of trade language may have existed on the Northwest Coast before European contact, in view of the sophistication of the societies in that area. The Chinook language itself (as opposed to the Jargon) might have been used in this way, given the strategic location of Chinookan speakers on the lower Columbia and at the mouth of that river. This area was certainly one of the main crossroads of trade up and down the coast into the plateau hinterland.

Chinook Jargon was first noted early in the nineteenth century. Fort Astoria was established at the mouth of the Columbia in 1811, and one of the original party, Alexander Ross, correctly noted the difference between Chinook proper and "another lingo, or rather mixed dialect, spoken by the Chinook and other neighboring tribes, which is generally used in their intercourse with whites. It is much more easily learned, and the pronunciation more agreeable to the ear than the other . . ." (Ross 1849: 348–9). Even earlier the explorers Meriwether Lewis and William Clark recorded some Indian terms in 1805–6 which occur only in the Jargon (Coues 1965).

With the arrival of European and American traders, settlers, and missionaries at the end of the eighteenth century and during the nineteenth century, the use of the Jargon expanded rapidly, eventually reaching deep into the interior (eastern Washington, Oregon, Idaho, western Montana) as well as south into California and north into British Columbia and Alaska. In its heyday (roughly 1860–1900) there were probably as many as 100,000 speakers of the Jargon. There is no

186 ALLAN R. TAYLOR

recent statement on the present number of persons knowing some of the Jargon, but Samuel Johnson, a student doing doctoral research in the late 1970s, located thirty-one persons in British Columbia and Washington who were sufficiently versed in Chinook Jargon to supply him with lexical and textual materials.

The LEXICON of the Jargon comes from five major sources: Nootka, (Lower) Chinook, Chehalis, French, and English. There are also a number of Algonquian words, most apparently from Ojibwa. The Nootkan elements were probably introduced by Whites, who themselves used broken Nootka in the late eighteenth-century coastal trade. Chehalis, Algonquian, French, and English elements were added as the territory (and users) of the Jargon expanded northward and inland. In time, English came to be the dominant source. Estimates of the number of roots used in the Jargon vary between 500 and 1,000. The inevitable result is that each root has a broad range of meaning which is sharpened and clarified by the context. Widespead root compounding also extended the size of the lexicon. For example, the term *mamuk* 'to make, to do' could be compounded with a variety of verbal, adjectival, and nominal roots to create a host of meanings: 'to bring; to boil; to begin; to think, to correct; to twist; to finish; etc.,' to name only a few. The speaker of Chinook Jargon also used the nonlinguistic context to the maximum possible extent: tone of voice, look, gestures.

The sound system of the Jargon was apparently not constant. Speakers of various languages tended to use the phonetics of their own language when speaking the Jargon, although the basic system was a severe simplification of the phonology of Lower Chinook proper. Hence, the same expression might be pronounced in a number of somewhat differing ways, depending on the language background of the speaker.

Michael Silverstein (1972) finds that the grammar of the Jargon, though ostensibly Chinook, actually represents a system which is neither Chinook nor English (nor anything else). It is, instead, what remains after wholesale dropping of elements which have no analogs in the donor languages (e.g. Chinook dual number and neuter collective; English articles and auxiliary verbs). Chinook Jargon thus has a ''grammar'' by default.

Although the Chinook Jargon is now almost totally extinct, it survives in part in place names and lexical contributions to American English, especially the English of the Northwest. It is a curious fact that most of the Chinookisms which have been adopted on a broad scale are derogatory; this is probably a reflection of the well-attested racial and cultural arrogance of frontier Whites. Probably the best known word of this type is *potlatch,* a word whose primary meaning in the Jargon is 'gift.' In contemporary American English this refers to an ostentatiously expensive party which is characterized by its vulgar display of wealth and the basic vulgarity of the host and guests. The Northwest Coast analogs of this were the lavish feasts given by prominent individuals and clans, one of whose functions was to impress the guests (and embarrass rivals) with the opulence of the occasion. Another such word, *chéechako,* was popularized around the turn of the century by the writer Jack London. The literal meaning of this term is 'newcomer,' but it quickly acquired the meaning of 'greenhorn, tenderfoot,' derisive terms which imply naiveté and ineptitude in unfamiliar and challenging circumstances.

Still another example is the expression *siwash*. In Chinook Jargon, *siwash* (from French *sauvage*) meant 'Indian,' but it evidently had a derogatory connotation even in the Jargon, and the term is avoided today by the handful of remaining Jargon speakers. In the local English of the Northwest, the term is used as a noun meaning "Injun," and as a verb (*to siwash it*) meaning to eke out a miserable existence under slipshod conditions. In general American English, the expression "old Siwash" is used in reference to a small, insignificant, rural or "rustic" college.

Possibly also of Chinook Jargon origin is the slang expression *high muckymuck* (also *high muckamuck* and *high mucketymuck*). This expression is used of arrogant and petty public officials and bureaucrats who are overstepping their authority. A few other terms occasionally used specifically in the Northwest are *chuck* 'water; creek,' *muckamuck* 'food, chow, grub,' *klootchman* (or *klootch*) 'squaw' or 'squaw man.' Some Chinookisms which have acquired an aura of regional identity are exploited commercially. Examples of this are *tyee* 'chief,' which is often used as a motel name in the state of Washington. Another is the greeting *klahówya* (usually *klahówya tílakum* 'how are you, friend') which is the name of a local brand of deodorant soap (Johnson 1980). Probably only Chinook Jargon place names will ultimately remain a permanent part of English, however. One example of this is Skookumchuck Creek, British Columbia. In the Jargon *skookum* meant 'powerful, big, important.' *Skookumchuck* meant 'strong current, rapids, whitewater.'

Plains Sign Language

The Plains Sign Language is the most sophisticated aboriginal sign language known. Moreover, in its resources and versatility it can be compared favorably with any known sign language, including sign language varieties consciously invented by Europeans in recent times to permit communication by the deaf.

It is not known where or when the Plains Sign Language originated. Several factors could have conspired to bring it into existence, including the need to communicate in silence in hunting or war situations, and the need for means of communication by the deaf and by people of different language backgrounds. Signing with the hands and body is apparently a pan-human response to situations of this kind, as anyone knows who has found himself in a position where verbal communication was impossible.

The Plains Sign Language probably originated somewhere in the Southern Plains or in a nearby region of the continent. This assumption is based largely on the fact that the Sign Language was clearly spreading north and northwest during the nineteenth century, and continues to do so in the twentieth.

Given its complexity and wide intertribal use, the Plains Sign Language must be several centuries old. The earliest probable observations of the Sign Language by Europeans are reported by sixteenth-century Spaniards. Núñez Cabeza de

188   ALLAN R. TAYLOR

Vaca and three other explorers survived the ill-fated Narvaez expedition to west
Florida and spent eight years (1528–36) wandering among Indians between the
Texas Gulf Coast and Mexico. During this period they learned a good deal about
the geography and contemporary native peoples of south-central North America,
including a smattering of their languages. In his *Relación* (1542), Cabeza de
Vaca mentions the use of signs with and between Indians somewhere inland in
the Southern Plains. He indicates that communication was easy and complete.
The expedition of Francisco Vásquez de Coronado (1540–2) also penetrated the
southern and central plains, reaching, it is assumed, territory which is now in the
state of Kansas. In the account of the expedition, Indians called Querechos
(probably Tonkawas or Plains Athabascans) were twice reported as communicating in signs so effectively that no interpreter was needed.

Recent Indian testimony on the origin of the Sign Language is, understandably, vague. Many nineteenth-century Indians believed it had been
invented, with the Kiowas mentioned most often as the inventors. This may
reflect the fact that the Kiowas were among the most proficient users of the Sign
Language in the Southern Plains in the last century. The Kiowas could not have
invented the Sign Language, however, since they were latecomers to the area,
having arrived there only in the eighteenth century.

During the nineteenth century, the Sign Language was used throughout the
Plains, but also in areas contiguous to the Plains. The area of heaviest use was
the Central Plains, from the Texas panhandle to the Missouri River and its
tributaries in North Dakota, Wyoming, and Montana. Sign use was also prominent outside of this area, wherever tribes belonged wholly or partially to the
Plains culture, or were in regular contact with such tribes through trade or
warfare. This broader area included the northern portion of Mexico east of the
Sierra Madre Oriental, the U.S. Southwest as far as the upper Rio Grande Valley
of New Mexico, the plateau region of Colorado, Wyoming, and Idaho, and the
northern fringes of the Plains in southern Canada. Sign use did not extend very
far east of the Mississippi River, but many Indians belonging to tribes originally
from that part of North America (e.g. Delawares, Kickapoos) learned the Sign
Language and used it with western Indians such as the Comanches and Kiowas.
Sign Language use also spread, evidently in the twentieth century, into the
woodland fringe beyond the northern edge of the Plains in Alberta, Saskatchewan,
and Manitoba.

During the period when the Sign Language was an ongoing lingua franca, not
all tribes using it were recognized as equally proficient. There was, in the
nineteenth century, a decided south-central Plains center of gravity for skilled
use of the Sign Language by numerous individuals of several tribes. The Kiowas,
Comanches, Cheyennes, and Arapahos were especially noted. It may be significant
that the Kiowas and Comanches, on the one hand, and the Cheyennes and
Arapahos, on the other, were more or less permanent allies until they were finally
subdued by the U.S. army. What is suggested is that there was a strong political
motivation for their knowledge and use of the Sign Language. It is certainly
significant also that these tribes were among the most nomadic.

Reliable nineteenth-century testimony on sign proficiency in the Northern Plains is lacking. The Crows are credited with disseminating the Sign Language into the plateau region to the north and west. In 1956 (West 1960: II, 65), the Crows were regarded by other Northern Plains Indians as exceptionally proficient, with high esteem also for Northern Cheyennes and Blackfeet. Excellent individual signers were found also among the Nez Perces, Flatheads, Gros Ventres of the Prairie (Atsinas), Oglala Sioux, and Hidatsas. West found, somewhat unexpectedly, that the Sioux tribes, Oglalas excepted, were rather undistinguished sign users.

Adult men played the dominant role in public life, and were, therefore, often characterized as the primary users of the Sign Language. However, the fact that women did know and use the Sign Language is attested by several nineteenth-and twentieth-century observers. An especially picturesque example is that of the "sign dance":

A woman, after dancing around alone, will take up a man, lead him into the circle, place him opposite to her, both dancing. She will then say to him in the "Sign-Language", "Here I am, ready to be made love to; what do you think of me?" He answers in the same language, as his wit or discretion prompts. This special figure is one of the greatest favorites, the conversations being a collision of wits, every sally of which is received by the spectators with uproarious laughter and unbounded applause. (Dodge 1959: 374-5).

There can be no doubt that the issue here is one of the opportunity for sign use or the appropriateness of sign use by women, not their possession of the capability. For example, in West's 1956 survey of sign use in the Northern Plains, 19 percent of the signers (twenty-three individuals) were adult women. West did experience difficulty in locating women who were willing (and able) to use the Sign Language: "Plains Indian women . . . do not and are not supposed to know the Sign Language as well as their husbands" (West 1960: II, 78).

Sign use in 1956 was almost entirely confined to elderly persons: four out of five were past 60. Middle-aged and younger signers were hard to find everywhere except among the Crows, Northern Arapahoes, and Northern Cheyennes. The informants of General Hugh Scott two decades earlier were also elderly men. It is thus possible that, until very recently, the advanced age of signers was not the result of obsolescence of the sign language so much as a cultural function: older men were those entitled to demonstrate proficiency in sign knowledge and use. Younger persons are now interested in the Sign Language as an ethnic symbol, but it is too early to know whether any of these younger persons will actually join – or create – communities of signers.

Learning of the Sign Language has traditionally been by observation, individual practice, and through long and intimate contact, although outsiders have sometimes received instruction. But even at the time of its ascendancy, not all Plains Indians learned the Sign Language. Even in tribes known to be expert in sign talk, some persons did not learn signs well enough to communicate in the Sign Language. No doubt persons in a position to enjoy political and social benefits were principally the ones who became masters of the Sign Language.

One of the main uses of Sign Language was, of course, conversation. The Sign Language was used primarily between interlocutors of different language background. The astonishing thing is, however, that it also enjoyed widespread use between individuals of the same language, tribe, and even family. It is thus clear that in the nineteenth century (and probably before), the Sign Language was regarded as an alternative communication channel which speakers could use whenever they wished. The conversational use of the Sign Language has largely lapsed today, although it has been reported recently for both Crows and Northern Cheyennes. This appears to be an isolated local phenomenon, since the present writer has not noticed comparable use of signs among contemporary Blackfeet, Kiowa, and Sioux Indians.

Apart from conversational and related uses, several other functions for the Sign Language are well attested. The use of signs for entertainment in the "sign dance" has already been mentioned. Public story telling in signs was also frequent, and this use survives into the present. Indeed, northward diffusion of the Sign Language in this century may be attributed to this use. Signing was also used for oratory, largely before multilingual audiences. Probably the last instance of this was the grand council assembled by General Hugh Scott at Browning, Montana, in 1930, so that a filmed record of signing could be preserved.

A few remarks are in order about the nature of the structure of the Sign Language and of the signs themselves. Any representational system such as a language, pairs *signs* with *referents*. That is, some sort of symbol is associated with a particular meaning in the minds of initiated persons. The association of the symbol and the meaning may be arbitrary, or it may be based on some kind of resemblance between the symbol and its meaning. In most sign systems the relationship is arbitrary: the symbol has the understood meaning only because learners are taught to associate that meaning with that symbol.

The Plains Sign Language, as is true of most sign languages, makes heavy use of portrayal of meanings by descriptive gesture or body stance. Insofar as this is so, the Sign Language can be said to be pantomimic. However, some notions, by their very nature, cannot be physically represented. Even when physical representation is possible, there is normally a choice in precisely how the representation is to be done and what particular trait or aspect of the referent is to be represented in the sign. Thus, arbitrariness can be found even in a pantomimic sign system. The Plains Sign Language is, then, a mixed system varying from gestures whose reading is obvious to gestures whose meaning has to be learned.

The production of signs can be described in much the same way as articulate speech is described. In sign language articulation, the analog of the tongue is the hand or the hands. These may adopt several basic shapes; West (1960: I, 42) posits eighteen such basic shapes: open, clenched, one or more fingers extended with the others closed, one or more fingers curved, etc. No other part of the body is used as an articulator: even the rare full arm motions are accompanied by a distinctive hand gesture, and signs for actions characteristic of the feet such as walking and dancing are made with the hand. The hand(s) may be used in a stationary position, moved up, down, forward, back, to the left, to the right, in concert, parallel to each other or crossing over each other. Motion may be distinctively rapid and tense, slow and lax, or neither (i.e. neutral); distinctively far out from the body, close in, or neither; proceeding, again distinctively, in straight lines, through curves, in circles, trembling, or wagging from the wrist.

The analog of the place of articulation in verbal speech (for example the palate or the upper teeth) is the point at which a gesture is made, or to which the hand moves during the gesture. West suggests that there are at least forty of these. In most cases the place of articulation is a place on the signer's own body: head, hair, forehead, ear, eye, nose, upper lip, mouth, chin, chest (heart), lower arm, leg, etc. Utilization of the back of the body as a place of articulation is rare, both due to its general inaccessibility to the articulator and to its invisibility to the interlocutor. When this part of the body is used, as in the sign for 'tail,' the signer must turn so as to present his profile while signing. The place of articulation is often not actually touched; instead, the hand is only brought into close proximity to the relevant body part. When the place of articulation is not a part of the body, it is somewhere in the space nearby, as in indicating a height in front of the body in the sign for 'child.'

Signs are generally formed in a continuous flow, but sentences and longer segments of DISCOURSE may be set off by brief pauses, when the hands and arms are dropped to the speaker's sides or lap, or used for some other (nonsignaling) purpose. When signing is done at a distance, movements are exaggerated in various ways to make the sign more "readable." For example, movements are increased in scope, slowed down, and clear the body more widely when this is appropriate. Some highly visible object may be held in the hand so that the eye of the interlocutor follows it rather than the less visible hand. In earlier days, a blanket, a shield, a lance – even a firebrand – were used in this way.

All of the signs are built from around eighty mutually contrasting basic gestures. Each sign usually includes three or four of these basic gestures. A few examples of individual signs are given in Figure 8.1; these illustrate both the mechanics of the formation of signs and their conventional or representational nature. The prose descriptions of the signs which follow are based on those given in Clark (1885).

'Among.' Bring left hand in front of body about height of neck, thumb and fingers extended, separated and pointing upwards, hand slightly compressed; point right index finger downward, other fingers bring it up to left hand and mix it in with fingers of left hand by moving it about among them.

'Bad.' Conception: suddenly thrown away. Hold both closed hands, back up, in front of body, hands at same height and equidistant from body; move hands outwards, downwards, and simultaneously open them with a partial snap, terminating the movement with fingers extended and separated. This sign is frequently made with one hand.

'Buffalo.' Conception: horns of buffalo. Bring hands, palms towards and close to side of head, index fingers partially curved, others and thumbs closed; raise hands slightly and carry a little to the front.

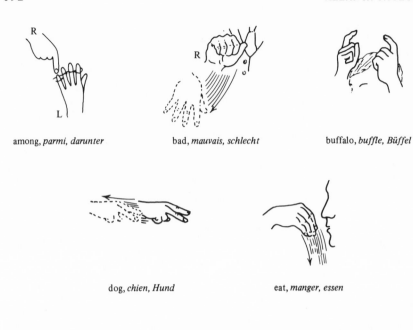

among, *parmi, darunter*   bad, *mauvais, schlecht*   buffalo, *buffle, Büffel*

dog, *chien, Hund*   eat, *manger, essen*

perhaps, *peut-être, vielleicht*   question, *question, Frage*   wolf, *loup, Wolf*

Figure 8.1. Examples of signs used in Plain Sign Language (reprinted from Tomkins 1929)

'Dog.' Conception: dog drawing tepee poles. Bring right hand, back up, in front of and little lower than left breast, first and second fingers extended, separated, and pointing to left; draw hand to right several inches, keeping index about parallel to front of body. Some Indians only indicate the height of the animal, and make a barking sound.

'Eat.' Bring tips of fingers of nearly compressed right hand, in front of, close to, and a little over mouth, back of hand to left and front, fingers pointing towards face and a little downwards; by wrist action move hand downwards, tips passing a little below and close to mouth. To represent eating rapidly, or eating a great deal, as at feasts, or many people eating, both hands are used, left being fixed similarly to right, hands passing round each other by rotary motion.

'Perhaps.' Conception: two hearts. Bring side of right hand, at base of thumb, against breast over heart, back of hand up, first and second fingers extended, separated, pointing to left and front, other fingers and thumb closed; by wrist action, turn the hand, so that back of hand will be about to front; then back to first position, repeating motion. Both hands may also be used. When it is desired to express many doubts, all the fingers and thumb of right hand are extended and separated, held in the above-described position and the hand turned in the same way.

'Question.' Hold right hand, palm outwards, well out in front of body, about height of shoulder, fingers and thumb extended, separated, pointing upwards. If addressee is close, turn hand slightly, by wrist action, two or three times, moving it also a trifle to right and left. If addressee is distant, hold hand higher, and move well to right and left.

'Wolf' (also means 'Scout' and 'Pawnee'). Conception: the erect ears of the wolf. Hold the right hand, palm out, near right shoulder first and second fingers extended, separated, and pointing upwards, others and thumb closed; move the hand several inches to front and slightly upwards, turning hand a little, so that extended fingers point to front and upwards. Sometimes both hands are used, left being similarly fixed to right and held opposite left shoulder. A slightly modified form of this sign was adopted early in the twentieth century as the sign for 'scout' in the Boy Scout movement.

Almost all signs have lexical rather than syntactic meaning. Lexical meanings are understandable in isolation (e.g. *tree, run*); grammatical meanings are understandable only in the context of a sentence (e.g. *of, 's*). Only one sign in the Sign Language appears to have exclusively grammatical meaning – the sign which indicates that the utterance to follow is a question. Other notions often expressed in the grammar of spoken languages (tense, gender, possession, number, command) are expressed by signs which have basic lexical meaning. Tense, for example, is indicated by words equivalent to time adverbs (tomorrow, yesterday); gender, by words for male and female; possession by the sign for 'possess' between the sign for the possessor and the sign for the thing possessed.

When words are composed of more than one sign, it is characteristic that each succeeding sign narrows the meaning of the preceding sign. This process continues until the desired meaning is specified. As examples of this process, take the notions *Negro, sister-in-law,* and *bachelor*. Negro: Whiteman + black; sister-in-law: brother + possess + wife; bachelor: man + marry + no.

The order of words in a signed sentence is fairly free, and the same thing can usually be said with a number of alternate word orders, though in some cases a particular word order is preferred. In general, subjects precede verbs, modifiers follow the element modified.

A short passage from a sign dictionary will give an idea of both the syntax and the flavor of sign discourse. Signs are represented by English words separated from each other by a hyphen.

I-arrive-here-today-make-treaty.   My-hundred-lodge-camp-beyond-Hills-Black-near-river-called-Elk.   You-chief-great-pity-me.   I-poor.   My-five-child-sick-food-all-gone. Snow-deep-cold-strong.   Perhaps-chief-great-above-see-me.   I-go.   Moon-die-I-arrive-there-my-camp.

("I arrived here today to make a treaty. My one hundred lodges are camped beyond the Black Hills, near the Yellowstone River. You are a great chief, pity me. I am poor. My five children are sick and have nothing to eat. The snow is deep and the weather is intensely cold. Perhaps God sees me. I am going. In one month I shall reach my camp.") (Clark 1885: 17–18)

Signing was often accompanied by verbal language; usually the verbal speech had the same meaning as the signed message. Perhaps because of this, some have assumed that signed messages are a translation of a spoken analog. A further deduction from this assumption is that the grammar of the Sign Language is based on, and subordinate to, the grammar of a spoken language. Grammatical transfers from verbal to sign language are hard to prove, however, since both spoken and signed language are guided in general by logical possibilities. Qualifiers in any language, for example, may either precede or follow the word which they qualify. Questions are normally marked as questions either at the beginning or the end of utterances, etc. Thus the range of choices is so narrow that arbitrary choices would often yield the same result as those made deliberately and with a patterned relationship in mind.

The case is not so with vocabulary, especially where metaphor is involved. Sign neologisms were sometimes sign translations of spoken words and there must also have been some translation of signs into verbal language. Indeed, the heavy use of descriptive compounds in word coinage in the Plains languages may go back to the use of such compounds in the Sign Language.

The preceding rapid survey of American Indian lingua francas has had to deal most extensively with those which date from the conquest of North America by Europeans. The amount of treatment accorded each varies in direct proportion with the extent of knowledge about the speech form. This, in turn, is a function of history: in general, the more recent, the more knowledge we have about the lingua franca. More will undoubtedly be learned in coming years about some, but others are literally lost forever.

In describing each known lingua franca, an effort has been made to give a sample of the speech form and some information about its origin, evolution, use, and continuing impact (if any) on American civilization. Much more could have been said, in some cases. In particular, the social contexts in which the contact vernaculars arose have been slighted. A number of scholars are now at work on these aspects, and we can expect that their findings will soon become a part of general American awareness.

FURTHER READING

There are few general works on lingua francas, but Samarin 1968 gives a brief useful introduction to the topic. There are even fewer works on American Indian lingua francas. Two substantial historical studies of language use among American Indians give some attention to the use of lingua francas. These articles, to appear in volumes XV and XVI of the *Handbook of North American Indians* (a Smithsonian Institution publication to appear in 20 volumes, see Heizer 1978), are: Wick R. Miller, "Ethnography of speaking" and Michael Silverstein, "Dynamics of recent linguistic contact" (titles not final).

Drechsel 1976 is a summary of pidginization and creolization among American Indian languages. For Indian Pidgin English, the first serious article was Leecham and Hall 1955, which is still worth reading. Dillard 1972: Ch. 4 includes treatment of it along with other pidginized forms of English in America, and Dillard 1976a: Ch. 1 gives additional information – especially on vocabulary items that came from it into general American English. Goddard 1977, 1978 are also informative.

For the Mobilian trade language the only complete treatment is J. M. Crawford 1978. Among the many treatments of Chinook Jargon, those of Silverstein 1972 and Johnson 1977, 1980 are the most recent, and include the most valuable information from earlier works. For Chinookisms in North American English, a good source is Avis 1967.

The Plains Sign Language also has an abundant literature, part of it popular. The best sign dictionary is Clark 1885, but picture dictionaries such as Tomkins (1929; several subsequent editions) are very useful, though less comprehensive than Clark. A good general discussion of the Sign Language can be found in Taylor 1975, part of which is summarized here. For technical description, the reader should refer to Mallery 1881 or West 1960. Umiker-Sebeok and Sebeok 1978 contains a large number of the technical publications on the Sign Language which have appeared during the past century, including the works of Mallery.

9

New World Spanish*

JERRY R. CRADDOCK

This chapter by the nature of its subject, provides a fitting conclusion to Part II, but also constitutes an appropriate introduction to Part III, for Spanish was well established in the New World when the first English-speaking settlers arrived here. Florida, Louisiana, and especially the Southwest have been termed the "Spanish borderlands" because they formed the northern frontier of Spain's far-flung American dominions.

The linguistic impact of the Spanish borderlands

The English colonies of the Atlantic seaboard were, in the middle of the eighteenth century, little more than an enclave hemmed in by the French to the north and west and by the Spanish to the south and southwest. In the course of a century, from the Peace of Paris in 1763 to the Gadsden Purchase of 1853, the English-speaking populations wrested control from the French and the Spanish (including the Mexican "successor state") over continental North America down to the Rio Grande, the Gila and the Colorado rivers. Colonial establishments may evolve into new nations, or they may in their turn undergo a second colonization that results in a transfer of political and economic power to another colonizing people. Thus the English colonies in North America became the United States and Canada, and these two entities have absorbed the dominions of Spain and France in North America, exclusive of present-day Mexico. The colonial Hispanic establishments of the Spanish borderlands of Florida, Louisiana, and the Southwestern states have undergone the three principal stages which can be distinguished in the process of secondary colonization. These are: (a) the exploration and settlement of the primary colonists; (b) the first contacts with the secondary colonists and the transfer of political power; (c) the integration of the primary colonists into the political structure erected by the secondary colonists.

In stage (c) for the Spanish borderlands, the original Hispanic colonists did not, of course, simply disappear. Some emigrated back to the mother country or

* The editors subjected my original draft to an extremely searching revision, and added a section on Spanish loanwords in the Native American languages of the Southwest, as well as a passage on the origin and socio-economic situation of the Louisiana *isleños;* for all of which I am grateful. My good friend and colleague Richard V. Teschner, University of Texas at El Paso, was kind enough to read the first draft and forward to me some opportune recommendations.

196

to other colonies still under the sway of their homeland, and some were driven away by the new settlers. But many stayed on, seeking to maintain their homes and livelihoods under the Anglo-American political regime. Those who remained have succeeded in retaining their cultural identity for many years. They have also gradually become assimilated into the dominant culture, by volition, by inertia, and sometimes by force. Even when assimilation has occurred for the primary colonists, they and their descendants have, nevertheless, exercised a profound influence on the culture that has enveloped them.

The Spanish borderlands first entered the current of western history as the northernmost fringes of the Spanish exploration and conquest of the Americas. For more than three centuries, their history is inseparable from that of Spain and Mexico. Our chief source of knowledge about the Spanish spoken in the borderlands derives from historical documents dating from the first permanent settlements until the end of the Spanish empire. They are often of inestimable value to the investigator wishing to catch at least occasional glimpses of everyday life, and may also afford the linguist scattered hints at the development of local varieties of language. Written documents, both historical and literary, constitute the only direct evidence for the language of bygone ages. In addition, the written language has functioned as an important vehicle for the generalization of linguistic influences; therefore, the historical and literary materials are essential to place the linguistic data in their proper context.

The Spanish colonies left a rich historical record, abundant both in connected narratives and in original documents, and the interpretation of this material has been carried forward by gifted historians, who more than anyone else have made the Spanish borderlands an indelible part of the nation's collective awareness. The nonhistorical learned literature of the Spanish borderlands is relatively meager but this meagerness is counterbalanced by an extraordinarily rich folklore. Lyric and narrative poetry, tales, and, most remarkably, theater, have been cultivated in a predominantly oral fashion since the founding of the first outposts down to the present day. Also, the Spanish borderlands have inspired modern-day English-writing authors, who have made the Hispanic tradition one of the enduring values of American literature.

The commerce, industry, trades, crafts, agriculture, architecture, customs, and laws of the borderlands have continued to bear the imprint of Hispanic civilization long after their political integration into the Union. In these institutions, the face-to-face interactions between Spanish- and English-speaking settlers over the centuries have led to numerous mutual influences. One of the most noticeable of these in the English language of the United States is the large number of Spanish LOANWORDS. These loans are most evident in southern and western TOPONYMY, i.e. the names of geographical features, towns, villages, and every sort of political and administrative division; in the terminology relating to the cattle industry, mining and farming; in the designations of myriad flora and fauna; in the words for the favorite alimentary and culinary products adopted from the Spanish settlers. The peculiar flavor of southwestern English is due in large part to contact with southwestern Spanish.

198   JERRY R. CRADDOCK

The single most prolific source of Hispanic place names has been the liturgical
calendar of the Catholic Church. The day a town was founded, a landmark was
sighted, a crisis was overcome, could be conveniently memorialized by applying
the name of the appropriate saint or holy day. One well-known example is Point
Reyes ('kings') in California, named for the Three Kings of the Epiphany, who
are so important in the Hispanic celebration of the Christmas holiday season. To
give the reader some idea of the number and variety of Southwest place names of
Spanish origin, let me cite instances from my own experience, as one who has
spent most of his life in the region. Born in *Pueblo* ('town, village, settlement'),
Colorado (for *Rio Colorado* 'Red River') I often traveled with my brothers and
parents over Monarch Pass to Montrose to visit my grandparents. Heading west
from Pueblo, we could see the mountains of *San Isabel* ('Saint Elisabeth')
national forest to the south; the first large town along the way is *Canon* City,
pronounced [kǽnyən], that is, from Spanish *cañón* 'gorge, ravine', a name that
presumably refers to the nearby Royal Gorge. Further along, the impressive
Sangre de Cristo ('blood of Christ') range comes into view, while the entrance to
Monarch Pass is guarded by a town, named *Salida* ('exit'),a reflection, no doubt,
of the geographic perspective of Hispanic explorers and settlers. Beyond Gunnison
lies the small village of *Cimarron* ('wild, fugitive'; probably referring here to
'big horn sheep') in the environs of Blue *Mesa* ('table [mountain]'); the last rise
before our destination is *Cerro* Summit ('hill').

In the summer of 1977, my family's pilgrimage to our native state took us
along the more intensely Hispanized southern edge: from *Mesa Verde* ('green
table [mountain]') – we spent the night in *Mancos* (masculine plural adjective
'one-armed, maimed') – through *Durango* (compare the Mexican city of the
same name), *Álamosa* (feminine singular adjective derived from *álamo* 'pop-
lar'), over *La Veta* Pass ('the [mineral] vein') and on to Pueblo via Walsenburg,
center of an important coal-mining district. After moving to *California* (fabulous
realm of Amazons in a sixteenth-century Spanish romance of chivalry), we
eventually settled in a suburb named *El Cerrito* ('the little hill'); the through
street nearest our home is *Potrero* ('colt pasture'), which leads to the major
artery *San Pablo* ('Saint Paul') Avenue.

The Spanish speaker finds some of these names disconcerting since they seem
so inappropriate as toponyms. For the Anglo-American settlers, Spanish words
were more or less SEMANTICALLY opaque. They felt no discomfort at christening an
administrative division (*Colorado*) with a Spanish adjective derived from the title
of the principal river that flowed through it; compare also *Nevada*, extracted from
Sierra Nevada ('snowy range'). *Pueblo*, as a generic term, makes as poor a sort
of place name by Spanish standards as would the word *town* in isolation for the
English speaker, but the latter finds the designation Pueblo perfectly specific and
adequate to its purpose. Many current Spanish street and subdivision names are,
of course, the spurious and often ungrammatical creations of real estate developers. Spanish *vista* 'view' enters into many un-Spanish combinations as a replica
of English *view*. In Colorado, the possibly authentic *Buena Vista* ('good view')
embodies a normal adjective + noun construction, but it seems to have inspired

the coining of *Monte Vista* ('mountain view'), which involves an inadmissible noun + noun sequence. In my experience, two of the most absurd examples are the street name *Estabueno* ('it's good') in Orinda, California, and the El Cerrito apartment house christened *Bayo Vista*, a "Spanglish" (see Chapter 10) rendering of 'bay view'.

There has been LEXICAL influence of Spanish on American English even beyond the direct borrowing of loanwords. For example, a Spanish word may be taken into the English language, and the original Spanish meaning changed as the word takes on a meaning used only in the United States. Let me describe just a few well-known examples. *Arroyo* has in the Southwest the specialized meaning 'dry creek' or 'dry wash' which cuts a rather sharply defined and deep crevice into the ground. After a cloudburst, a deep torrent roars down between the often narrow walls; most of the time, however, only infrequent stagnant pools and cracked mud bear witness to the occasional presence of a 'running stream,' the Spanish meaning of the word. Other Spanish words are borrowed even when there is an existing English word with the same general meaning as the Spanish term. *Burro* 'donkey' seems at first glance an unnecessary importation, but the Mexican animal must have struck the Anglo-American settlers as generically different from the Yankee *donkey*. Proof of the term's naturalization in English, if any is needed, are the noun + noun constructions formed with it: *burro bush, burro weed, burro deer* and *burro school*.

Some loanwords undergo remarkable grammatical transformations in the borrowing language. The Spanish first person singular HORTATORY imperative *vamos* 'let's go' spawned the second person command *vamoose!* 'beat it!' In the Spanish, *vamos* includes the speaker; in English, *vamoose* is usually an imperative addressed to others. Whether *vamoose* gave rise to *mosey*, originally 'to move swiftly, scram,' a meaning that fits the supposed source, is a matter of controversy. Certainly the most common current meaning denotes a slow, dawdling movement, as in *to mosey along*. One should note that many Hispanisms nowadays have a rustic or archaic flavor; not a few have been kept current by their use in Western movies.

Isleño and New Mexican Spanish

Another perspective from which to view the linguistic aspects of the Spanish borderlands is to study the surviving Spanish-speaking communities themselves. Within the present borders of the United States, there exist two principal Hispanic speech communities which are living sources for colonial borderland Spanish, direct survivors of the Spanish colonial era. These are the Isleños ('Islanders') of Louisiana and the Spanish settlements in northern New Mexico and Southern Colorado (referred to hereafter as simply colonial New Mexico). Elsewhere in the Southeast and Southwest, the Spanish-speaking colonies either abandoned their language and cultural identity or were overwhelmed by more recent immigration from the Caribbean and Mexico. In the southern reaches of the Southwest border states, there never occurred, however, any interruption of

continuous Hispanic settlement. The two Spanish-speaking communities mentioned
have lived into the twentieth century in almost complete isolation from the
centers of Hispanic and Anglo-American civilization. This isolation helped them
preserve numerous features of their language and culture and promoted their
survival as identifiable cultural entities.

The history of the Isleños is sparse, and relatively few accounts of their
language and culture exist (Fortier 1904: II, 60ff.; Gayarré 1903: III, 115–29).
During the Spanish domination (1764–1803) of what is now Louisiana, the
Crown and local governors supported immigration. Incoming farmers were given
small parcels of land to encourage commercial agriculture. One group of these
peasant proprietors was from the Canary Islands and settled along the small
waterways of Saint Bernard Parish (a parish is the local civil division of
Louisiana which corresponds to a county in other states). The Isleños remained
in this parish, farming, working on neighboring sugar plantations, and occasionally selling their produce in New Orleans. Living in relative social isolation from
outsiders, the group maintained the identity of its culture and language. Well into
the twentieth century, they have continued to live with no formal municipal
government and to find marriage partners within their own group. MacCurdy, a
linguist and folklorist who worked among the Isleños intermittently from 1941
through 1947, estimated the population numbered about 2,500 (MacCurdy 1950;
see also Kammer 1941). During the 1940s, there were four elementary schools in
the parish; all taught in English and some forbade the speaking of Spanish on the
school grounds. Illiteracy was extremely high, though the rich folklore of the
group contained themes and heroes from Classical Spanish literature. The material for their folklore has been periodically replenished by new immigrants from
both Spain and Latin America. The occupations of the Isleños – trapping,
fishing, and shrimping – provide numerous occasions for sharing riddles, stories,
and lore in general.

The dialect shows a strong affinity to the colloquial speech of the Antilles,
especially Santo Domingo, with which Louisiana had numerous contacts during
the colonial period, and to Andalusian Spanish, since the Spanish of the Canary
Islands, from which the Isleños originally came, is fundamentally a variety of
that particular dialect group. The vocabulary is remarkable in that it contains,
alongside some more or less typical archaisms, loanwords of Louisiana Créole
provenience, and, of course, a generous portion of English loans, all fully
adapted to Hispanic phonological and morphological patterns. To provide a brief
indication of the features of this Hispanic dialect, I offer an annotated sample as
recorded by an Isleño speaker, in a somewhat simplified transcription taken
from MacCurdy's dissertation (1948a: 23). A Standard Spanish version follows
with an English translation:

[nosótro disímoʰ árgoleʰ / sí / áy algúno akí / no áj múčoʰ pórke áj máʰ
    plería ke naḍa / péro ay alúnoʰ árgoleʰ por akí / tinímos beyotéro /
    bimbéra / kōŋkunū / kopáj / yalgúnoʰ máʰ ke áj]

Nosotros decimos "árgoles" [for *árboles*]. *Si, hay algunos aquí. No hay muchos porque hay más pradera que nada, pero hay algunos árboles por aquí. Tenemos encina, vimbrera, almez, copal y algunos mas que hay.*

'We say "árgoles." Yes, there are some here. There aren't many because there is more prairie than anything else, but there are some trees around here. We have oak, willow, hackberry, sweet gum, and some others that there are.'

Analysis of the Isleño passage shows that the syllable-final *s* is weakened to *h* or occasionally lost completely, for example, *muchos* 'many' → [mučoʰ]; *nosotros* 'we' → [nosótro]. Also, the VOICED FRICATIVE sounds of /b, d, g/ are sometimes interchanged or are weakened and lost, for example, *árboles* 'trees' → [árgoleʰ]; *algunos* 'some' → [alúnoʰ]. In verb forms, some of the stem vowel alternations of standard Spanish are regularized, for example, *dice* 'he says': *decimos* 'we say' → [díse]: [disímoʰ]. Such traits crop up in popular dialects all over the Hispanic world.

As for the LEXICON, I will mention only three items of interest. The Standard Spanish word for 'oak' (*encina*) has yielded to *bellotéro* 'acorn bearer,' derived from *bellota* 'acorn.' The Créole French influence is illustrated by *concunú*, a form that goes back ultimately to the local French name of the 'hackberry,' *bois inconnu*, literally 'unknown tree.' Isleño *plería* 'plain, prairie' reflects French *prairie* with DISSIMILATION of the first of two successive *r*s. These Créole French loanwords constitute the single most distinctive feature of the Isleño dialect.

The other living source for colonial borderland Spanish is New Mexican Spanish. The language of this SPEECH COMMUNITY, like that of the Isleños, contains numerous archaic verb forms, words, and turns of phrase, as well as a heavy lexical influence from English. The former trait no doubt reflects the state of the Spanish language as it existed during the colonial period; the latter, of course, arose from contact with the later Anglo-American settlers.

To illustrate New Mexican Spanish, I have taken the following jest from Espinosa (1930: 303), given first in New Mexican Spanish, then Standard Spanish, and finally English.

[ũŋ kúra le díxwa su sakrihtáŋ ke le kosjéra gwéɓoz ɓländítus / el sakristá lus ečwá kosér i los irɓjó por un óra / el kúra ya känsáw de sperár / xuónde stáɓal sakristán i le díxo / kése loz gwéɓos / ke twaɓía no stán yel sakristá le ɹehpõndjó / yásjun óra ke stäŋ kosjédose péro taɓía no staᵐ blädítus]

Un cura le dijo a su sacristán que le cociera huevos blanditos. El sacristán los echó a cocer y los hirvió por una hora. El cura, ya cansado de esperar, fue donde estaba el sacristán y le dijo: "¿Qué es de los huevos? Que todavia no están?" Y el sacristán le respondió: "Ya hace una hora que están cociéndose pero todavía no están blanditos."

'A vicar asked his sexton to cook him some soft-boiled eggs. The sexton began to cook them and boiled them for an hour. The vicar, tired of waiting, went to the sexton and said to him: "What's with the eggs? Aren't they ready yet?" And the sexton replied: "They've been cooking for an hour but they're still not soft." '

Among the many phonological characteristics one could mention, I will point out only the most interesting; none, however, is unique to this dialect. Unstressed *e* and *o* adjacent to another vowel regularly become the semivowels [j] and [w] : *ya hace un* → [yásjun]; *dijo a* → [díxwa]. This may occur as well when INTONATIONAL stress overrides lexical stress: *echó a* → [ečwá]; or when the two vowels come into contact through loss of a consonant: *todavia* → [twabía]. Word-final unstressed *a* is lost if the following word begins with a vowel: *una hora* → [un óra]. Vowels are strongly nasalized before syllable-final nasal consonants: [xuõnde]; in this situation, the nasal consonant at times ceases to be articulated: [kosjédose].

The adverb *onde* 'where' is an authentic archaism preserving the earlier form replaced in the Standard Spanish by *donde*, which stems from the medieval construction *de onde* 'from where, whence.' The phrase *huevos blanditos*, literally 'soft eggs' with a DIMINUTIVE suffix attached to the adjective *blando* 'soft,' whose ordinary meaning provides the point of the jest, may show the influence of English *soft-boiled*; Standard Spanish for 'soft-boiled eggs' is *huevos pasados por agua* 'eggs passed through water.'

In both Isleño and New Mexican Spanish one finds scores of English loanwords. For my present purposes, I will mention only one type of adaptation. The phrase *pátrás* = Standard Spanish *para atrás* 'backwards, to the rear' appears in numerous CALQUES of English verb + particle constructions involving the adverb *back*, for example, *to go back, to give back, to bring back*, and so on. Thus in Isleño one reads: *Le dijo que trugiera los ojos de Marie patrás* (standard = *le dijo que volviera con los ojos de María*) 'He told him to bring back Maria's eyes.' This construction has turned up in many areas of Spanish – English contact in the United States, and represents one of the few instances where such particles carry over into the Spanish replicas.

These communities provide opportunities for the study of colonial Spanish maintained through the years as the major language. Yet there are other colonial Spanish influences in evidence today as loanwords in Native American communities of the Southwest.

The impact of Spanish on Native American languages of the Southwest

For many Americans, the influence of Spanish on Southwestern American Indian languages is even less well-known than is the history of colonial Spanish-speaking communities. Yet, in the Southwest, Yaqui, Keresan, Taos, Tewa, Zuñi, and Hopi all show the influence of Spanish. Their initial contact with western culture in the 1500s was with Spanish speakers, and that contact has persisted in many ways into the current period. Loanwords are only symbols of that contact, but symbols which are relatively prominent and provide evidence of the types of culture contact Indians and Spanish have experienced. Shepherd (1975) provides an analysis of the types and percentages of Spanish loanwords retained by each group.

In parts of the Southwest, following the initial years of military contact by Coronado and other Spanish explorers, the mission was the frontier institution and Jesuit and Franciscan missionaries the primary frontiersmen (Bolton 1917). The Jesuits lived among the Yaqui after 1617 and refashioned the already tightly knit Yaqui communities into even more cohesive units. Teaching in the Indian language, the Jesuits were able to use persuasion rather than force to influence the religion, social organization, and material culture of the Yaqui. Only interference from governmental and military forces broke the early pattern of peaceful acculturation. In the 1880s, when Mexico established military and political control over their territory, the Yaqui were dispersed and the majority settled in Arizona, where they maintained both their tightly knit communities and intermittent contact with Mexican Americans of the area (Spicer 1961). The linguistic influence of the Spanish remained such that in the 1940s, for the Arizona Yaqui, an estimated 65 percent of words related to social organization, religion, and material culture were derived from Spanish (Spicer 1943). Unlike other groups in contact with Spanish, the Yaqui do not use loan translations and rarely combine Spanish and Yaqui roots. Instead, Spanish terms are borrowed. The majority of Yaqui Indians are today bilingual in Yaqui and Spanish. Spanish borrowings used in Yaqui have Yaqui phonetic patterns; the same speaker using these words in Spanish retains Spanish pronunciation (Spicer 1943; Fraenkel 1959). Many Yaqui are trilingual in Spanish, English, and Yaqui, using each language for particular functions (see Chapters 6 and 8).

The languages of other Southwestern Indian groups, for example, the Eastern or Rio Grande Pueblos, show much less Spanish influence and reflect the different history these groups had with the Spaniards. Military expeditions and demands for submission characterized early Spanish contact with the Eastern Pueblos. Franciscan missionaries were not established among the Indians until 1630, and the Franciscans used harsh measures to eradicate indigenous religious practices. The Pueblo Revolt of 1680, and the ensuing repressive measures of the Spaniards further alienated these Indians from Spanish religious habits, material culture, social organization, and language. It is estimated that the percentage of Spanish loanwords in Keresan, Taos, and Tewa is less than 5 percent. All make use of loan translations, but rarely borrow directly or compound Spanish and native roots (Trager 1944; Spencer 1947; Dozier 1951, 1956; Kroskrity 1978). Today many Eastern Pueblos speak Spanish and/or English for particular purposes or occasions involving outsiders, and maintain their native tongue for functions within their primary groups.

The Zuñi maintained what might be termed passive resistance to the Spaniards during the seventeenth century. Located on the fringes of the area the Spanish hoped to colonize, their contacts with Spanish religious and political personnel were infrequent. The Hopi also maintained passive resistance to the Spaniards

204   JERRY R. CRADDOCK

and received most of their influence from the Spanish through the Eastern Pueblos. Less than 2 percent of the vocabulary of either Hopi or Zuñi are Spanish loanwords, and most of these came from the Eastern Pueblos (Dockstader 1955; Newman 1958). Spanish cultural influence has also been slight, and today, though there are some individuals who are bilingual in Hopi or Zuñi and Spanish, the majority prefer English as a second language.

Shepherd (1975) has identified five major semantic areas into which Spanish loanwords in American Indian languages tend to fall: religious terminology, military and governmental terms, terms for domestic plants and animals introduced by the Spaniards, items of material culture, and words denoting measurement. In religious terminology the Yaqui have /líos/, later /díos/, from Spanish *Dios* 'God,' /'áanimam/ from Spanish *ánima* 'soul.' The Keresan use /kahón/ = Spanish *cajón*, meaning 'box' in Spanish but 'coffin' in Keresan. The Taos have /kum:ayliʔ'ina/ from Spanish *comadre* 'godmother of one's child,' a relationship which has been incorporated by the Taos. The Tewa use /santùh/ from Spanish *santo* 'saint.' The Zuñi use /santu/ to mean 'doll,' a meaning which probably developed in connection with figurines of saints. The Hopi use /pavóya/ from the Spanish *polvarear* 'to sprinkle with pollen,' an event which takes place in a native ceremony. Perhaps the most well-known of all Spanish loanwords in Southwestern Indian languages is *caballo*, traced by Kiddle (1978) in numerous languages. The lexical borrowing in all the languages is a significant indicator of the Spanish impact and influence which has maintained itself for nearly three hundred years in the Southwestern portion of the United States.

Immigrant Spanish

In turning from colonial Spanish and its influences to the Spanish of twentieth-century immigrants, one leaves, in a certain sense, the often romantic world of history and literature and enters the somewhat mundane realm of the social scientist. There are, to be sure, a history and literature associated with each group of Hispanic immigrants, but in quantity they cannot compare to the avalanche of sociological, economic, and political writings on Hispanic immigrants that has rumbled off academic presses in the current century. Though the relevant linguistic work cannot match either in quality or quantity the production of the other social sciences, it too has achieved a bulk of unwieldy dimensions. Here, I will limit myself almost exclusively to considerations of a purely linguistic nature.

During the twentieth century, three powerful streams of Hispanic immigration have flowed into the United States, to wit, in order of their relative chronology and numerical importance, Mexican, Puerto Rican, and Cuban. These immigrations have had the effect of re-Hispanizing to a certain extent the parts of the country that once were the Spanish borderlands. In the latter portion of the nineteenth century, there had occurred a significant reduction of the Hispanic presence in most of those regions (for the case of California, see Pitt 1970); in the 1970s, the significance of the Hispanic elements in the United States population has never been greater. The Hispanic immigrants have not, however, settled only in the former Spanish borderlands. From urban focal points like Miami, New York City, and Los Angeles, they have established themselves in every state of the Union, wherever economic opportunities beckoned (see Chapters 10 and 21). Of the three immigrations, the Cuban is the most recent and least studied (Smith 1968). Though some immigration from Cuba occurred before 1958, for instance in Tampa, Florida (Pizzo 1968), it was in the wake of the Castro revolution that hundreds of thousands of Cubans sought political refuge in the United States. Though many remain concentrated in Miami and the state of Florida, many others have moved elsewhere. As a group, the Cubans have been helped in their adaptation to the new environment by several factors. The Cuban refugees were predominantly middle class, could count from the first on the political sympathies of the host population, and have not had to confront the intense prejudice that has hindered the progress of Puerto Rican and Mexican immigrants.

Large-scale Puerto Rican immigration to the mainland began after World War II. Strictly speaking, the Puerto Ricans are not immigrants since they possess U.S. citizenship; however, their migration, to use the more accurate term, involves a movement from a Hispanic to an Anglo-American environment as drastic and abrupt as any experienced by the other Hispanic immigrants. Again, though large Puerto Rican barrios exist in New York City, they too have chosen many other parts of the country for permanent residence (Fitzpatrick 1971; Chapter 10, this volume).

The physical circumstances of Mexican immigration are quite different from those attendant upon Puerto Rican and Cuban immigration, in that a long land border joins Mexico and the United States. Likewise, U.S. citizens of Mexican descent living along the border provided from the beginning a transition the Puerto Ricans and Cubans lacked. Nevertheless, with the rapid industrialization of the Southwest which took place after 1900, that region increasingly presented a human environment as foreign to the Mexican immigrant as that of any other part of the United States.

Though unsettled political conditions in Mexico during the first decades of this century spurred some emigration from the homeland, the primary motive for coming to the United States has been economic. However ruthlessly Mexican immigrants have been exploited in agriculture and industry by U.S. standards, the wages they received constituted a gain over their economic possibilities at home. Indeed, in the vast majority of cases, the purpose of the immigrant worker was not to resettle in the United States but to return home with all he could manage to save from his wages (this is still the case with illegal immigrants; see Critchfield 1977). In the course of time, however, many have remained to become U.S. citizens. Like the Cubans and Puerto Ricans, the Mexican immigrants did not confine themselves to the neighborhoods of the ports of entry, but fanned out over the entire country, especially the Middle West, eventually to the East Coast and as far south as Florida (Grebler, Moore, and Guzman 1970). In all three immigrations, there has occurred a diaspora of impressive dimensions;

yet the relative density of immigrant population remains higher near the favored ports of entry, Miami for the Cubans, New York City for the Puerto Ricans, and the Southwest urban centers for the Mexicans.

Only certain generalizations may be made concerning the Spanish of immigrants. In each case, the immigrants possess the linguistic system prevalent in their homeland, with characteristic phonological and lexical properties which distinguish each Spanish-speaking nation's VERNACULAR from all other varieties of Spanish. If the immigrants belong to economically deprived social strata, their Spanish is not likely to be that of the standard norm of their homeland, while middle class immigrants by and large do conform to Standard Spanish, i.e. that typically spoken by educated urbanites. All immigrant dialects have in common a fundamental trait: the powerful influence of English. The nature of that influence varies according to several factors. In the first place, immigrants are exposed to differing types of English, depending on the geographical region in which they settle, the Cubans meeting at least initially the Deep South vernacular (or just as often the displaced mid-Atlantic parlance of vacationers and retirees), the Puerto Ricans finding themselves in close contact with the urban Black English of New York City (Wolfram 1974), and the Mexicans encountering the rural dialects of the Southwest and Midwest. One pervasive English influence, affecting all, however, is that exercised by the entertainment and news media, especially television. Since those sources propagate a relatively homogeneous standardized variety of English, they contribute to a certain DIALECT LEVELING of the English adopted by Spanish-speaking immigrants.

Secondly, where and how well each of the two languages concerned has been acquired determines to a large extent the characteristics of English influence. Adult immigrants arrive with a completely formed native language, and often learn imperfectly the language of their adopted country. Normally their Spanish betrays little English influence beyond sometimes numerous loanwords, fully adapted to Spanish phonological and morphological patterns. Very young immigrants and immigrants' children born in the U.S. may acquire a native command of English, and it may happen that their Spanish is not as fluent as their English, a situation that can become more and more frequent in later generations, depending on the cohesiveness of the local Hispanic community, the individual's desire to assimilate to the dominant culture, or to preserve his Hispanic heritage, and so on. However well-developed the Spanish competence of such persons may be, their native command of English almost inevitably leads to a more profound influence of that language on their Spanish. Beside loanwords and calques, in the Spanish of these bilingual speakers, one is likely to find quite subtle SYNTACTIC deviations from normal Spanish sentence structure, and at least the beginnings of phonological influence, most immediately in stress and intonation, though specific sounds may also be affected. Moreover, bilinguals find it both convenient and expressive to use both languages among themselves in the same conversation, switching smoothly and instantaneously from one to the other. Of course, with interlocutors they know to be basically monolingual in Spanish or English, bilinguals most often refrain from this CODE-SWITCHING.

These generalizations must be qualified by the realization that each of these speech communities contains many speakers possessing an extremely broad repertoire of styles, ranging from formal Spanish and/or formal English to informal Spanish, with many intermediate varieties, some of them interlingual, i.e. involving code-switching and CODE-MIXING.

In addition, some particular linguistic features may characterize the type of Spanish linked to one group, i.e. Cuban, Puerto Rican, or Mexican, and not another. Conversely similar changes may have occurred in each variety in its contact with English. A few examples will illustrate. In Mainland Cuban Spanish, contact with English manifests itself first and foremost in the lexicon. Loanwords are adapted to Cuban phonology: *troba* 'trouble' (Fernández 1973: 48) seems orally transmitted, as opposed to *trubles* (Varela de Cuéllar 1974: 16), a form that betrays the influence of the written word. Both conform fully to phonological patterns of Cuban Spanish. Some adaptations achieve a remarkable shape in the borrowing language: *gúlgor* 'Woolworth' and *sagüesera* 'southwest area.' A systematic study of the phonological equivalences that speakers establish between the two languages can be quite revealing of specific phonological traits. For instance, *rula* 'ruler' and *corna* 'corner' suggest that English word-final syllabic *r* is not perceived as a consonant or that the corresponding English forms are pronounced with final SCHWA, a vocalic sound that Spanish speakers most often transmute into *a*. However, note that *corna* preserves the *r* of the first syllable. *Cuora* 'quarter' and *jira* 'heater' illustrate the identification of the voiced flap articulation of American English *t* with the very similar flapped *r* of Spanish. Both traits, syllabic *r* → Spanish *a* and flapped *t* (or *d*) → Spanish *r*, appear wherever Spanish and English come into direct contact.

Grammatical adaptation in general follows established patterns, for example, *flirtear* 'to flirt,' *lonchar* 'to lunch.' Adverbial particles do not normally enter into the adapted form, thus 'to hang around' becomes simply *janquear,* but recall the important exception noted aboved, involving *pátrás* ← *back.* Varela de Cuéllar (1974), in the most complete study of Mainland Cuban Spanish available, analyzes the gender of borrowed nouns, each of which must be assigned to the categories of masculine or feminine. Her observation that the gender of English loanwords may reflect the gender of the Spanish words being displaced raises a curious question: is there perhaps an extended period of time in which the two forms, loanword and Spanish equivalent, coexist in the purely Spanish lexicon of individuals? If so, one would wish to determine the conditions governing the use of the two competing forms. The final -*a* (← English syllabic *r*) of *cuora, rula, corna* and *jira* has determined their feminine gender, since most Spanish words in -*a* are feminine; but there may be no other way of explaining the feminine gender of *estorma* 'storm' and especially of *güindo* 'window' (whose -*o* would normally provoke identification as a masculine) than by taking into account the gender of the corresponding Spanish words: *tormenta* (fem.) 'storm' and *ventana* (fem.) 'window.'

LOANBLENDS, forms that involve a merger of English and Spanish lexical stock, are uncommon. Most scholars improperly include among loanblends, loanwords that have undergone normal morphological adaptation such as *flirtear*. Even *yonquero* 'junkman,' in my view, is not a true loanblend; it is modeled after the type *zapatero* 'shoe-maker' from *zapato* 'shoe' on the basis of a presumptive loanword *yonque* 'junk,' though this last item is lacking in Varela de Cuéllar's word lists.

Perhaps the most common species of lexical influence produces LOANSHIFTS, words already existing in the borrowing language whose meaning changes to match more closely that of the corresponding words in the loaning language. Very often the words involved in the two languages are formally similar, but that is not a necessary condition for loanshifting to occur. Varela de Cuéllar cites *largo* with the meaning 'large' rather than 'long'; it is evident that *largo* cannot be a phonological adaptation of *large*, i.e. a loanword. On the other hand, *carpeta* 'carpet' may be no more than a loanword, unless it can be established that the Spanish word meaning 'table cover, portfolio' belongs or belonged to the active part of the immigrants' vocabulary.

A special form of loanshift is the calque, the word-for-word translation of entire idiomatic phrases. Such calques are normally unintelligible to the mono-lingual Spanish speaker: *Está para arriba de tí* 'It's up to you.' Sometimes phrases are calqued for humorous effects; at any rate I suspect such may have been the case with *maquillarse la mente* 'to make up one's mind,' cf. *maquillarse* 'to make up (the face with cosmetics).'

Syntactic departures provoked by English interference typically belong to a more developed stage of BILINGUALISM where the language of the adopted country becomes more native to the bilingual speaker than the language of his parents. Fernández (1973: 71) records the utterance *Lo que Uds. estaban haciendo no fue estudiando* 'What you were doing wasn't studying' for standard *Lo que Uds. hacían no era estudiar*. The English influence is most evident in the use of *estudiando*, since bilinguals tend to associate the Spanish gerund in *-ndo* with the English verbal noun and adjective in *-ing*. There exist a number of syntactic environments where the two forms function in similar fashion, but the Spanish gerund cannot normally serve as a verbal noun, as in *corriendo es buen ejercicio* 'running is good exercise' (Fernández 1973: 70) for standard *correr es buen ejercicio*.

If Mainland Cuban Spanish has had scant attention from linguists, one cannot say the same for Mexican Spanish spoken in the U.S. Linguistic study of Southwest Spanish boasts a long and distinguished tradition, while recent de-cades have witnessed the flourishing of a distinctive ethnic literature (see, for example, Castañeda Shular, Ybarra-Frausto, and Sommers 1972). Chicano language and literature are now widely taught academic subjects, while South-west Spanish is the primary research mission of the Cross-Cultural Southwest Ethnic Study Center (El Paso, Texas) and its associated Southwest Areal Lan-guage and Linguistics Workshop, which recently celebrated its eighth annual meeting (Arizona State University, April, 1979).

For the purpose of illustrating Mexican Spanish spoken in the U.S., I have chosen a passage from a tape recording made in El Paso, Texas (January, 1971) by Ms. Ellen Muller for Professor Jacob Ornstein, founder and guiding spirit of the just-mentioned Cross-Cultural Study Center (see also Ornstein 1975, 1976).

[mi famílja aɓla espaɲól en la kása pórke kjéren ke sépamos aɓlar espaɲól bjén/ kon mis amígos yo áɓlo iɲglés pero kon únos espaɲól/ kon los ke áɓlo espaɲól kási es distinto del koɾekto/ lo áɓlo komo éyos lo áɓlan pa: entendernos/ si stój en la kláse un amígo kj áɓla espaɲol me íse/ wáča la profesóra es más mḗnsa ke la moská kestá ayí]

Mi familia habla español en casa porque quieren que sepamos hablar español bien. Con mis amigos yo hablo inglés pero con algunos español. Con los que hablo español casi es distinto del [español] correcto; lo hablo como ellos lo hablan para entendernos. Si estoy en la clase, un amigo que habla español me dice: "Mira a la profesora; es más estúpida que la mosca que está allí."

'My family speaks Spanish at home because they want us to speak Spanish well. With my friends I speak English but with some [I speak] Spanish. With those I speak Spanish to it's almost different from correct [Spanish]. I speak it the way they speak it so we can understand each other. If I am in class, a friend who speaks Spanish says to me: "Look at the teacher; she is stupider than the fly over there." '

This transcription has been considerably edited to remove hesitation phenomena, repetitions and corrections. The phonology of this specimen is a close approximation to standard Mexican Spanish, with only a few minor differences: glide formation evident in [kj ábla], suppression of the initial consonant of the verb *dice* [íse], and the loss of initial *e-* after a word ending in a vowel [stój]. The deviant subjunctive [sépamos] for standard *sepamos* is of widespread occurrence in colloquial Spanish on both sides of the border.

This passage fails to reveal any notable English influence; suffice it to say that the broad patterns are similar to those described for Cuban and Puerto Rican Spanish. Most interesting and characteristic of Southwest Spanish are the slang words [wáča] and [mḗnsa]. They pertain, at least originally, to the argot commonly known as *pachuco*; it is a form of speech called *tirilí* or *tirilongo* in El Paso, involving massive lexical substitution within a Spanish phonological and morphological base. It is as incomprehensible to uninitiated Spanish speakers as it is to English speakers. The *pachuco* lexicon comprises substantial elements from the international underworld jargon of the Gypsies (*caló*, or less appropriately, *germanía*), novel morphological and semantic restructurings of Spanish words, and numerous Anglicisms.

In 1970, I provided a survey of linguistic work dealing with Spanish spoken in the United States (Craddock 1973). Since that time, there has been an exponential growth in the quantity, and often the quality, of such work. More and more linguists now provide careful phonetic transcriptions of speech, and place lexical data in the contexts in which they were recorded. In addition, Spanish-speaking communities have greatly increased their bilingual participation in domains outside their homes, especially in education. Bilingual materials covering such topics as Chicano history are now available. Numerous programs of Chicano and Puerto Rican studies, in particular, are training students not only to be sensitive to their cultural and linguistic heritage, but also to provide accurate social science and linguistic descriptions of their communities. It is perhaps in such efforts that the best hope lies for avoiding the integration paradox: the social, economic, and political integration of minority language groups seems in the past to have brought with it, or to have been accompanied by, an almost complete cultural assimilation with attendant displacement of the minority group's original language in favor of English. This loss is surely unnecessary and a waste of a precious cultural heritage; it is, after all, monolingual speakers who should be regarded as culturally deprived.

FURTHER READING

The classic account of the Spanish borderlands remains Bolton 1921, which can be supplemented by Bannon's more recent survey (1970); excellent bibliography on pp. 257–87. Bolton and Marshall 1920 wove the stories of the three European colonizations, English, French, and Spanish, into a single narrative. One may wish to compare Toynbee's curious pages (1934–54 [1962]: II, 65–73) on "The struggle for North America." There exist two useful Spanish efforts to assess the total impact of Hispanic civilization on the United States: Fernández Flórez 1965 (in English) and Fernández-Shaw 1972. The colonial Southwest continues to inspire major historical efforts such as John 1975 and Jones 1979, just to mention a couple of the most notable titles to have come to my attention in the past few years.

The chief poetical monument of the colonial borderlands, Villagrá 1610, treats a historical theme (Pedro de Oñate's expedition into New Mexico); it has been rendered into English by Espinosa 1933. Concerning the rich folk literature, the best available bibliography is Tully and Rael 1950, limited to New Mexico; see also Paredes 1966.

For the impact of the Spanish borderlands on Anglo-American literature, two fine guides have been prepared: Williams 1955, comprehending all facets of Hispanic influence, and Major and Pearce 1972, restricted to literature of Southwestern inspiration. Robinson 1969 provides particularly valuable insights into the collision of Mexican and Anglo-American values as reflected in literary works.

The most abundant sources for place names of Spanish origin are Barnes 1960 (Arizona), Pearce 1965 (New Mexico), and Gudde 1969 (California). To place the Southwest in perspective, one now has the excellent collection of G. R. Stewart 1970, as well as his earlier, more discursive treatment (1967). Though antiquated, Bentley 1932 still offers the most comprehensive survey of Spanish loanwords in English. With regard to the Southwest, Adams 1968 is extremely useful, while Mathews' 1951 dictionary contains thousands of well documented Hispanisms.

The only general treatise on the language of the Louisiana Isleños is MacCurdy 1950 (a Spanish version appeared in 1975). Folklore texts are available in Fortier 1894: 197–210, MacCurdy 1948b, 1949, and Claudel 1955. New Mexican Spanish is the subject of one of the classics of Hispanic dialectology, by the native son Aurelio M. Espinosa (1930–46; translated by Alonso and Rosenblat from the 1909–13 English original).

Most of the studies of Spanish influence on the American Indian languages of the Southwest were done in the 1940s and 1950s; one of the best known is Dozier 1956. Kiddle's more recent paper (1978) surveys just the spread of the Spanish word *caballo* 'horse,' but also has useful references.

For both the colonial and immigrant varieties of U.S. Spanish, Teschner, Bills, and Craddock 1975 constitutes a comprehensive bibliographical introduction (with 1977 supplement). The language of Cuban immigrants is the least studied; Varela de Cuéllar 1974 is the best published work one can cite on the subject. Puerto Rican Spanish in New York City inspired the methodologically important study of Ma and Herasimchuk 1971 (see also Chapter 10, and the references and Further reading there). The classic works on Mexican immigration, Gamio 1930 and McWilliams 1949, include important chapters on language. Some of the most significant contributions on Mexican Spanish spoken in the U.S. remain unpublished (e.g. Bowen 1952, Beltramo 1972, Sánchez 1974, and Elías-Olivares 1976). Perhaps the most accessible introduction is that of Sánchez 1972, and the finest recent lexicon belongs to Galván and Teschner 1975. On the intriguing subject of code-switching, consult Valdés Fallis 1976, 1978a, b, as well as Gumperz and Hernández Chavez 1972. The study of Southwestern *caló* has moved beyond Barker's outdated treatement (1950) in the unpublished dissertations of Katz 1974 and Webb 1976. The reference works of Coltharp 1965 and Trejo 1968 continue to be indispensable. Hernández-Chavez, Cohen, and Beltramo 1975 gathered together under one cover a representative selection of linguistic readings in the field.

Part III

Languages after English

Introduction

"You people are always asking for an explanation when a group keeps its language instead of shifting to English; in India it is the reverse: we ask for an explanation when a group loses its language and shifts to another one." With this observation the late P. B. Pandit, distinguished linguist from India, intervened impatiently in a 1971 conference discussion of language surveys in the USA and other countries (Ohannessian, Ferguson, and Polomé 1975). His words changed the tone of the discussion. The basic point was not the difference in attitudes between India and the USA but the difference in attitudes between IMMIGRANT LANGUAGES and languages which have spread by other means. Everywhere in the world the language outcome of immigration tends to be different from language spread that comes from colonization, conquest, internal migration, or the activities of traders or missionaries. When a population more or less voluntarily leaves its home country to settle for a lengthy period or permanently in a country of a different language, its language loyalty is modified by the very decision to emigrate. The members of the group realize, even if they do not consciously articulate it, that their use of language will be different from what it was. The change is likely to mean, at the very least, that some of them will have to add some control of another language and, at the other extreme, the group may even be eager to have their children shift completely to the new language. On the other hand, the immigrant group, in its need to maintain psychological strength under the new circumstances, may cling to its language all the more strongly, especially in connection with traditional occasions of celebration and familiar institutions of religion and group identification.

The history of immigrant languages in the USA is a complex story of differing patterns of language loyalty. The overall trend is undoubtedly to language loss and assimilation to English, even when other ethnic characteristics persist or are strengthened, but within this trend every immigrant group has had its unique experience of change in language use and language loyalty. Some maintain a wide range of uses for their MOTHER TONGUE generation after generation, reinforced by new immigrants and by return visits to the "old country" (e.g. many Greek American communities); others "lose" their language almost immediately (e.g. many Dutch American communities). For one group the

215

maintenance of written exchange (letters, books, magazines) is an important tie to the old speech community (e.g. many Czech American communities) while for another, literacy in the mother tongue plays no role at all (e.g. the ''Assyrians'' who came to California from the Middle East). The chapters of this Part give some idea of the great range of immigrant language experiences in the USA, but they cannot do justice to the deep feelings involved and the wrenchings of the changes in cultural values and ways of life which can come with changes in language use.

The top immigrant languages in terms of the numbers who claim mother tongue or primary use are all treated one way or another in these chapters. Spanish, which is both colonial and immigrant, is discussed here as an aspect of Puerto Rican life on the mainland. French and German are dealt with in a comparative study which notes the similarities and differences between the immigrant language experiences of these two prominent Western European speech communities. Italian has a chapter to itself, while the stories of Polish and Yiddish are told as parts of more comprehensive chapters on Slavic languages and Jewish languages in the USA. These ''top'' languages are ones all of us have heard about, even though we may be only vaguely informed about them, but each of the dozens of other immigrant languages has its story and only a few could be included.

The Scandinavian languages are not covered here in spite of their importance and ''visibility'' on the American language scene. This is partly because the use of these languages has been better described than most immigrant languages; indeed Haugen's *The Norwegian Language in America* (1969) is one of the classic treatments of languages in contact and has served as a model for studies of other immigrant languages. Full coverage of Swedish, Norwegian, Danish, Icelandic, and the unrelated Finnish would illustrate such general questions as the difference between rural and urban immigrant languages, the carryover of old language rivalries to the New World, the role of the church in language maintenance, and language conservatism among immigrants in contrast to language innovation in the parent nations.

Another obvious omission is the treatment of Chinese and Japanese, languages strongly represented in Hawaii and on the Pacific Coast and with significant numbers of speakers in many Eastern and Midwestern cities, including New York and Chicago. In 1942 Japanese Americans on the West Coast had the unique experience in the USA of being removed as an entire ethnic group to ''relocation centers,'' but by the 1970s their number included mayors, U.S. senators, and leaders in business and the professions. The Japanese language is now widely taught in American colleges and universities, and in parts of the country where Japanese Americans are an important ethnic minority, it is taught as a foreign language in high schools. Nevertheless, Japanese Americans, with the exception of those living in Hawaii, are steadily shifting to English.

The language situation of Chinese Americans is much more complicated. The national language of China is the Mandarin variety of Chinese (now called *Putonghua* 'common speech'), but most Chinese immigrants to the USA speak

Cantonese. This is very different from Mandarin and the two varieties are not mutually intelligible. Since most modern written Chinese is based on Mandarin, the dialect difference raises problems of LANGUAGE MAINTENANCE and educational policy. Even the kind of Cantonese which the Chinese Americans speak causes difficulties, because most of them have come from the rural Seiyap districts southwest of Canton and speak dialects of that region rather than the Standard Cantonese of the city, which is used by more recent immigrants from Hong Kong. The language experience of Chinese Americans deserves a book in itself.

The original languages of Asian American communities differ in striking ways from the European languages that most immigrants brought with them. They are mostly written in "exotic" alphabets or nonalphabetic writing systems, and the traditional cultures which they reflect contrast sharply with the cultures of European ethnic groups. The only Asian American group whose language is examined in this Part is the Filipino Americans. Their number has been growing steadily, and they have become a substantial ethnic minority at least in Hawaii and California. Their language situation is not typical of Asian Americans, but Filipino multilingualism, the search for a national Philippine language and the existence of a Philippine English are further examples of the diverse configurations of language use among immigrant groups in the USA.

It may be a cliché to call the USA a laboratory for social scientists interested in interethnic relations, but it is clearly a laboratory of languages in contact which has never been seriously utilized by specialists in the language sciences. The six language chapters of this Part give some indication of the phenomena to be studied, and the final language profile of Montana gives an inkling of the sociolinguistic complexities just below the surface. All the chapters show the need for additional data from language surveys, ethnographic studies, and sociolinguistic investigations, if we are to understand the sociohistorical realities of the USA and if the people are to have an informed basis for national and local policies affecting language.

10

Language variety among Puerto Ricans

ANA CELIA ZENTELLA

Puerto Rico is a small, densely populated island in the Caribbean Sea east of Haiti and the Dominican Republic; 3,400 square miles in area, it has a population of over 3 million. It was conquered and settled by Spaniards at the beginning of the sixteenth century and remained under Spanish control until 1898 when it was taken over by the United States. Since 1952 it has been an *estado libre asociado* 'free associated state' or 'commonwealth' which is theoretically self-governing internally. As early as the late nineteenth century, Puerto Ricans began migrating to the United States, and since World War II, the migration has been increasingly heavy, although fluctuating from year to year in accordance with the economic conditions. By the end of the 1970s, there were over half as many Puerto Ricans off the island as on it.

Unlike the other immigrant groups who preceded them, such as the Italians, Russians, Germans, and Irish, or those who followed the years of heaviest Puerto Rican migration, such as the Dominicans and Cubans, Puerto Ricans were subject to U.S. laws before they arrived on the mainland from the island. U.S. citizenship was conferred on Puerto Ricans a few weeks before the United States entered World War I in 1917.

Through their periodic waves of migration, Puerto Ricans represent the most significant wave of immigrants to the Northeast of the United States in the twentieth century. Approximately 2 million Puerto Ricans live in the USA today, and although the majority live in the north (57 percent in New York City), over thirty cities have Puerto Rican communities of 5,000 or more persons. In Newark, New Jersey, Philadelphia, Pennsylvania, Cleveland, Ohio, and other large cities across the United States, there are Puerto Rican communities. Spanish is the dominant language of these communities; according to the 1970 census, Spanish is the mother tongue of more than 83 percent, and 72 percent speak Spanish at home. The forces which led other immigrant groups to replace their mother tongue with English have not taken effect on Puerto Ricans in the same ways. The figures, however, tell us little about the complex interrelationships among the different varieties of Spanish and English, their forms and functions, and attitudes toward them in the daily lives of Puerto Ricans. The languages Puerto Ricans speak, and how they speak them,

218

are the ever-evolving result of Taino Indian ancestry, over 400 years of Spanish rule, the African slave trade, U.S. policies on the island since its invasion in 1898, and experiences on the U.S. mainland since the first thousand Puerto Ricans were recorded in the U.S. census of 1910.

The earliest known inhabitants of the island were the Taino Indians, an Arawakan group who lived on a number of Caribbean islands. The majority of the Taino Indians were exterminated, fled, or were assimilated during the first sixty years after Ponce de Leon's first settlement in 1509, and only a small number of Indian terms remain in the Spanish of Puerto Ricans. The African contribution was greater, but, to date, only some 125 words have been traced to specific African languages, and little is known about the African contribution to Puerto Rican PHONOLOGY, SYNTAX, and ways of speaking. The limited information on Taino and African vestiges in today's Puerto Rican Spanish may be due more to methodological limitations and racial prejudices than to a dearth of influence. Indians, Africans, and Spaniards contributed to the formation of the Puerto Rican *criollos*. The term *criollos* was used to designate those who, by the second half of the last century of Spanish rule, were recognized as distinct in language variety, culture, and physical characteristics from the *peninsulares*, residents who had come to the island from Spain.

U.S. language policy in Puerto Rico

Puerto Rico rebelled against Spain in 1868, was granted autonomy in 1897, and was invaded by the U.S. in 1898. Between 1898 and the present, three periods of language policy roughly parallel the stages of the island's economic development:

1. 1898–1948: The semi-feudal agricultural economy became an agricultural capitalist economy based on sugar plantations
2. 1949–68: Cheap labor costs attracted light industry
3. 1969–present: Intensive industry largely controlled by U.S. corporations dominated the island's economy (Language Policy Task Force, hereafter LPTF, 1978a)

The United States set out to Americanize Puerto Rico with a vengeance during the first fifty years of its occupation. Policy makers in Washington, DC believed in the bond between culture and nation, and saw as one of their first tasks to wrench Puerto Rico's ties from Spain and Latin America and to replace them with allegiance to the USA. Victor Clark, an early Commissioner of Education, summarized the government's view: "if the schools became American and the teachers and students were guided by the American spirit, then the island would be essentially American in sympathies, opinions, and attitudes towards government" (Figueroa 1972a: 40). Language, the vehicle through which all people learn about and identify with their culture, was the primary target. In the view of U.S. officials, the Spanish of Puerto Ricans had to be replaced by a more legitimate language.

Their language is a patois almost unintelligible to the native of Barcelona and Madrid. It possesses no literature and has little value as an intellectual medium. There is a bare possibility that it will be nearly as easy to educate these people out of their patois into English as it will be to educate them into the elegant tongue of Castile. (Osuna 1949: 324)

Through the imposition of English and the concomitant negation of Spanish, the colony was supposed to come to terms with North American values. Symbolically, the spelling of the island's name became anglicized; *Porto Rico* replaced *Puerto Rico* as the dominant term during this period of U.S. influence.

The USA was aided by some of the island's landowners and merchants, who, twelve days after the 1898 invasion, constituted themselves as an assembly of "representative Porto Ricans." They requested that a copy of the U.S. school system be established on the island. Ironically, only six months before, on February 11, 1898, Spain had decreed that Puerto Rico had the right to establish its own educational system. By contrast, on January 19, 1899, Governor Guy Henry decreed that all teachers had to learn English, that openings would be filled first with those who knew English, and that all high school, normal school, and Collegiate Institute graduates had to be examined in English. Practically overnight, all subjects had to be taught in English, and all court proceedings were conducted in English. Initially, some Americans reported the amazing success of the English-only policy. The first Commissioner of Education under the American flag reported after only one year's efforts "the average Puerto Rican child already knew more about Washington, Lincoln, Betsy Ross and the American flag than the average child in the U.S." (cited in Hanson 1962:115–16). A sobering contrast to this hyperbole was a 1925 Columbia University study which showed that 80 percent of the students failed both English and Spanish and dropped out of school (International Institute of Columbia Teachers College 1926). Puerto Rican teachers (many of whom had lost their jobs), intellectuals, political representatives, high school students, and workers attempted to fight back with legislation, pickets, and strikes, but for fifty years, from 1898–1948, "English only" was the dominant policy. Perhaps even more serious were the constant changes in the language policy; during those years the policy changed more than eight times – three times during the first year – as colonial officials alternately reacted to either political directives or demands of the people.

In response to growing resistance and the documentation of increasing failure in the schools, U.S. President Herbert Hoover appointed a Puerto Rican, José Padín, as Commissioner of Education in 1930. Padín allowed instruction in Spanish up to the eighth grade, with English as a compulsory subject in these grades and the medium of instruction in secondary schools. At the time, Puerto Rican workers were organizing for independence under the influence of Pedro Albizu Campos' Nationalist Party. They rallied around the issues of language and culture, in addition to the economic ones exacerbated by the stock market crisis. On Palm Sunday in 1937, Nationalist marchers were attacked by the police and more than 200 were injured, twenty killed. The retaliation of the

Nationalist Party against the North American commanding officer for what is known in Puerto Rican history as the Massacre of Ponce caused the head of the Senate Committee on Insular Affairs to visit Puerto Rico. After an extraordinary trip through the countryside during which he asked everyone "Do you speak English?", the senator correlated the unrest of the people with the fact that they did not know English. Upon his return to Washington, he instituted a new "get tough" policy in respect to English that forced Padín's resignation, and stipulated that any and all of his successors had to commit themselves in writing to a strong English policy as a prerequisite for senatorial endorsement. As a result, in 1936–37 and again from 1945 to 1948 (after another Commissioner, José Gallardo, was forced to resign because he had reinstated Spanish), there was no Commissioner of Education because every major educator knew there would be strong public disapproval for anyone in the office. In 1948, Mariano Villaronga, the first Commissioner under a Puerto Rican governor, overrode a Truman veto against teaching in Spanish and administratively ordered it. The teaching of Spanish finally became law as part of the Commonwealth Constitution of 1952.

During stage 2, 1948–68, the ruling party under the colonial government was the Popular Democratic Party (Partido Popular Democrático, hereafter PPD). During its administration, the PPD gave ideological support to the supremacy of Spanish, but the actual program supported a policy of extending the English language through use of new instructional methods (LPTF 1978a: 25). Textbooks, curriculum design, teacher training, USA–Puerto Rico exchanges, and audio-visual equipment and materials all stressed English and neglected Spanish.

After twenty years of PPD management, factionalism within the party and the lack of resolution of the island's political and economic problems helped to strengthen opposition parties, among them the New Progressive Party (Partido Nuevo Progresista, hereafter PNP), linked to the U.S. Republican Party, and pro-statehood. Its members, led by millionaire industrialist Luis Ferré, believed that Puerto Rico could be the first Spanish-dominant state in the Union, although their legislative efforts favored the supremacy of English. Under the PNP, private schools were allowed to teach in English, and their enrollment doubled in fifteen years from 8.4 percent of the student population in1960 to 16.9 percent in 1975; this figure was expected to rise to 25 percent in 1980. The public schools also devoted time and money to the teaching of English, and a 1960 study revealed that public school students wanted more English classes than their private school counterparts (Epstein 1970).

Attitudes towards English reflect the ambivalence often found in colonial territories and newly independent nations. On the one hand, the colonial language, in this case English, enjoys great prestige, many parents are eager for their children to acquire it, and many students want more and better instruction in it. It is seen as the language of the wealthy, the most educated, the most powerful. In Puerto Rico, it is the language of U.S. businessmen and Puerto Rican managers in business and industry. The local language enjoys less prestige: the poor speak it, less powerful countries speak it, the USA does not speak it. On the other hand, the colonial language is in many quarters bitterly resented, and school failures and high drop-out rates are attributed to the role of the colonial language in the schools (see Chapter 21).

If the 1960 survey was accurate and still holds true, the pattern of attributing high prestige to English and low prestige to Spanish seems to be more true for public school students than for private school students. This may be because the poor see their only hope for survival, on an island with approximately 50 percent unemployment, as linked to English, and they see the schools as the only place they might learn it. The children of the middle class are apparently more secure, both economically and linguistically. Neither group considered more contact with English threatening to the national identity. Whether or not it is necessary to speak Spanish to be a Puerto Rican is a hotly debated question in some circles, and one which has been further underscored by the arrival of over 20,000 English-speaking children of return migrants from the USA to Puerto Rico in the period between 1974 and 1979.

Throughout the last eighty years, despite confusing policies and bitter struggles, Puerto Ricans have continued to speak Spanish. As the decade of the 1980s begins, every student must study English for two hours each day for the first six grades, then daily throughout the junior and senior high school, and for four semesters throughout college. Nevertheless, unless they have lived on the mainland of the USA (estimates are that one-third of all students in Puerto Rico have been to the mainland), few public high school or even university graduates speak fluent English. Yet, statistics have shown a continual increase in the percentage of the population speaking English (proficiency level not specified): 3.6 percent in 1910, 27.8 percent in 1940, and estimates project the 1980 figure will exceed 50 percent.

Advocates of independence repudiate the imposition of English and stress Puerto Rico's Indian–African–Spanish roots and ties with Latin America. This does not mean that *independentistas* repudiate the English language; in fact, its leaders speak English fluently. They believe it is positive to learn as many languages as possible, but mastery of one's own must come before learning others. Thus, all shades of the political spectrum claim to support BILINGUALISM, but may differ in their definition. For many nonindependence supporters (generally viewed as assimilationists by the *independentistas*), bilingualism is a façade for English domination. A recent analysis of the language question in Puerto Rico by U.S. Puerto Rican independence supporters summarizes the problems and offers a solution:

In the Puerto Rican case, as elsewhere, anti-colonial and anti-imperialist forces must make the difficult choice between defending the national language in the face of the growing economic power of the colonial language, or the democratic demand that everyone share the economic pedagogical benefits of bilingualism. Multi-functional bilingualism is clearly the best choice in such a situation; it offers both links to family and traditional culture, and also the resources of the economically more powerful language. (LPTF 1978a: 29)

To resolve the problem through this solution requires institutional and societal changes which will set aside the long years of ambiguity over language policy and its links to cultural and social membership.

Puerto Rican Spanish

The language situation in Puerto Rico has not only created political and social shifts, but it has also affected characteristics of the language itself. The Spanish of Puerto Rico has been the subject of much debate and strongly held views. Unfortunately, most of the research on Puerto Rican Spanish is in the form of either fragmentary analyses of abstract phonological and grammatical systems or early twentieth-century DIALECT studies and commentaries on vocabulary items. The most complete work on the structure of Puerto Rican Spanish, particularly the geographical distribution of PHONETIC variants, is based on data collected in 1928 by the dean of Spanish DIALECTOLOGY, Tomás Navarro Tomás (Navarro 1966). There has been no research based on the concept of a SPEECH COMMUNITY sharing rules for both the linguistic and social uses of a variety of codes in its linguistic repertoire. This concept, central to recent work in sociolinguistics and the ethnography of speaking, would be an indispensable framework for the true picture of language use in Puerto Rico.

The issue which has received most attention is the debate about Puerto Rican Spanish and its asserted deterioration from earlier Spanish through heavy influence from English. As in most colonial societies, purists defending the native language have been concerned over vocabulary borrowed from English. They have pointed to the apparent proliferation of English words as evidence of the deterioration of Spanish. Some purists have attempted to expunge every English word from the vocabulary of Puerto Ricans, refusing to accept *jet, sandwich,* or *bar,* words which are internationally acceptable.

Rubén del Rosario, a Puerto Rican philologist and recently retired professor of Hispanic Studies at the University of Puerto Rico, classified the prevalent anglicisms on the island into three major categories:

I. General use, for example, sport, show, ticket, bar
II. Localisms and archaisms: baking (powder), ciodí (C.O.D.), freezer, fudge, la high (high school), marshal, panty, postmaster, rush, size, teacher, brown (color)
III. False anglicisms, for example, clerk, pyjama (Rosario 1970: 17–18, 20)

The first category includes words that are current in the speech of educated people throughout Latin America and in other countries with extensive North American contact; they also appear in foreign language dictionaries and are not considered substandard. Rosario claims that only the twelve English words of category II are unique to the Spanish of Puerto Rico. False anglicisms, the third category, are words he claims are incorrectly attributed to English, for example, *clerk* (French) and *pyjama* (Hindustani). However, although these words may not have originated in English, they were borrowed by Puerto Ricans from English, not from French or Hindustani.

Rosario maintains that the phonology of the language has not been affected by English. It falls perfectly within the framework of Latin American Spanish (see Chapter 9), specifically the Spanish of the Antilles, i.e. the islands of the Caribbean. It has the eighteen consonants of Antillean Spanish, i.e. it differs from the Castilian norm of Spain in lacking the PALATAL LATERAL, spelled *ll*, the *th* sound, spelled *c* (before *e* and *i*) or *z*. These two sounds are replaced by a *y* and an *s* sound respectively, and the *j* sound of Castilian is reduced to a simple *h*. Also, like much of Caribbean Spanish, Puerto Rican Spanish tends to drop syllable-final *-s* in some styles of speech. When the *-s* is dropped, it may be replaced by a light aspiration *-h*, or disappear altogether, and Rosario claims that a preceding *e* or *o* is lower or more open in pronunciation so that it contrasts with final *-e* or *-o* not followed by *-s: Dios > dio(h)* 'God' versus *dió* 'gave,' *pies > pie(h)* 'feet' versus *pie* 'foot.' Other researchers question whether the loss of *-s* is signaled by this vowel difference.

There are only three aspects of the Puerto Rican pronunciation of Spanish, besides its INTONATION patterns, that are particularly distinctive; none is the result of English interference. In addition to the APICO-ALVEOLAR version of the trilled *rr* (written as double *rr* in the middle of a word, but single *r* at the beginning of a word), two other varieties exist in Puerto Rico. Both are VELAR; one sounds like the French *r*, and the other devoices and approximates the *j* of Castilian. The second distinctive characteristic of Puerto Rican pronunciation of Spanish is the reduction of final unaccented vowels, especially after *ch* and other VOICELESS consonants. The final vowels of *lech(e)* 'milk,' *noch(e)* 'night,' *cop(a)* 'cup,' etc. have been found to be reduced by 25 percent in length (Rosario 1970: 9). The third characteristic, substitution of *-l* for syllable-final *-r*, for example, *paltil* for *partir* 'divide,' is limited to nonstandard speech; it was noted as a characteristic of *jíbaro* 'peasant' speech over one hundred years ago in *El Jíbaro* (Alonso 1949, first published 1849).

The debate over the influence of English on Spanish can therefore not focus on pronunciation. Instead, the question of the degree of MORPHOLOGICAL and syntactic convergence of Puerto Rican Spanish with English has generated the most heated debates. In 1968, a professor from Spain, Germán de Granda, spent one year as a teacher in Puerto Rico and then attempted to analyze the language and society of Puerto Rico from 1898 to 1968. His blistering portrayal of a language and culture in decay was applauded by some *independentistas* at the time because he attributed this deterioration to the colonial status of Puerto Rico. He claimed that a process of "impoverishment and simplification of Spanish," "convergence with English," and "dialectalization" (by which he meant the speech of a middle class that was formerly lower class becoming the standard) was rampant from 1940 to 1968. He characterized this period as one of permissive acculturation in contrast with the first period (1898–1939) when forced acculturation was rejected by both the intellectual elite and the poor masses. He characterized the Spanish of this earlier period as:

Rich in forms, abundant in lexicon and lively expression, exact and detailed in aspects of nature and daily life, full of words emotionally conditioned, generally conservative as regards lexicon, moderately so as regards phonology, and attentive to propriety, beauty, and correctness of expression. (Granda 1969: 125–6)

However, he characterized the current Spanish of technicians, administrators, and other members of the small middle class as full of "vulgarisms, slipping of the norm, and preeminence of local forms" (Granda 1969: 175).

The portrayal of Puerto Rican Spanish by Granda was severely attacked by Rubén del Rosario and others on theoretical and scholarly grounds (Rosario 1969). Although Granda's book contained approximately 1,000 footnotes, 135 in the first thirty pages, it did not report any fieldwork or contemporary research. Rosario charged Granda with magnifying the "problem" by looking through the distorting prism of *España, madre patria,* 'Spain, the motherland.' The Spaniard contended that Puerto Ricans were erring and off the track, but his track apparently led to Madrid, not to an Antillean or Latin American standard.

His proof of severe English INTERFERENCE rested on nine syntactic points; the book did not touch upon phonology, and accepted Rosario's description of the vocabulary. No data and no specific examples were given for any of the nine points, but the author maintained they were all rampant in Puerto Rico. Without examples, readers cannot ascertain the syntactic features to which he referred or "the correct Spanish" forms he preferred. For example, Granda claimed that Puerto Ricans say *en* 'in' instead of *a* 'to' and *de* 'of, from.' But when? They certainly do not say *el libro en José* for *el libro de José* 'Jose's book' or *voy en la tienda* for *voy a la tienda* 'I'm going to the store.' Of the remaining eight items, Rosario attacks four as having nothing to do with English interference, because they occur in the Spanish of both Spain and Latin America, and he insists the other four, although influenced by English syntax, are not heard frequently in Puerto Rico (Rosario 1969). Unfortunately, his refutation is vague and without substantial data. The eight points are the following.

I. Show no English influence
1. Redundant use of the pronoun, for example, *yo vivo, tú vas,* instead of *vivo* 'I live,' *vas* 'you go.' Spanish does not require the pronoun.
2. Replacement of the simple present tense with the present progressive, for example, *Está comiendo* instead of *come* for 'He is eating.' Spanish present tense includes both a simple statement of present tense "he eats" and the act of doing X "he is eating"
3. Preference for the passive voice over the active, for example, *La carta fué mandada* 'The letter was sent' instead of *Mandó la carta* 'He sent the letter.' Spanish prefers the active voice
4. Substitution of *aquel, aquella* 'that' and *aquellos, aquellas* 'those' for *ese, esa* 'this/that' and *esos, esas* 'these/those,' for example *aquella gente* instead of *esa gente* for 'those people'

II. Not common in Puerto Rico

1. The redundant use of possessive adjectives, for example, *Me lavo mis manos* instead of *Me lavo las manos* 'I wash my hands.' Spanish employs the definite article instead of the possessive adjective with parts of the body, articles of clothing, etc.

2. The redundant use of indefinite *uno* 'one.' This term is unclear; neither Granda nor Rosario gives an accurate example, but Pérez Sala (1973) explains it as including *uno* unnecessarily, for example, *Ese problema es uno de suma importancia* 'That problem is a very important one'

3. The placement of an adverb between *haber* (auxiliary 'to have') and a past participle instead of before or after them, for example, *he a menudo notado* instead of *he notado a menudo* or *a menudo he notado* 'I have often noticed'

4. Use of equivalents for English *who, well, how,* where Spanish does not use them, for example, *Cómo te gustó Puerto Rico?* instead of *Te gustó Puerto Rico?* for 'How did you like Puerto Rico?'

We are caught between Scylla and Charybdis, the voice of doom of Granda who interprets every modern linguistic variation as an imitation of English models, and the almost absolute complacency of Rubén de Rosario who does not fear change. He believes every language is in constant flux and adapts to the pressure of the era, without necessarily implying any drastic change in the psyche of the people. He quotes a 1921 statement by the guru of Spanish philology, Ramón Menéndez Pidal:

si un idioma no es el reflejo del alma del pueblo es una síntesis de la historia del desenvolvimiento de esa alma colectiva, es un reflejo del desarrollo intelectual del pueblo que lo habla. Innumerables son los pueblos que en un momento de su vida han cambiado de idioma y este cambio no nos quiere decir que hayan cambiado de alma, ni que hayan alterado su íntima psicología, lo que sí nos revela es que entonces aquel pueblo cambió totalmente en su orientación en la cultura.

['if a language is not the reflection of the soul of a people, it is a synthesis of the history of the unfolding of that collective soul, it is a reflection of the intellectual development of the people who speak it. There have been innumerable cases of peoples who at one point in their lives have changed languages, and this change does not mean that they have changed their souls, nor that they have altered their intimate psychology; what it does reveal to us is that then those people totally changed their cultural orientation.'] (Rosario 1970: 29)

It is precisely the change in cultural orientation that most Puerto Ricans cannot face with complacency, especially when the change is not voluntary, but imposed. In the absence of a strong Indian or African tradition, distinctive dress, or political autonomy, the Spanish spoken in Puerto Rico has served as a banner for national unity and distinctiveness. Puerto Rican Spanish helps to shape and reflect Puerto Rican nationality and to transmit Puerto Rican culture. Therefore, whether a Puerto Rican speaks only Spanish or only English or some combination of the two is sometimes interpreted as a comment on allegiance to the national culture. Some of the younger generation are expressing much of the same reality in English, especially the Nuyo-ricans, as New York/USA Puerto Ricans are sometimes called.

Sociolinguistic research on language attitudes and language in use is not available to provide an accurate picture of how language and culture allegiances are being played out in communities of Puerto Ricans on the island and on the mainland. Most of the published work from Puerto Rico sets out to prove that Spanish is intact, and depends on questionnaires and formal interviews. The basic premise of one study that attempted to provide data with which to refute Granda is that "the Puerto Rican has not reneged on his tradition, . . . he wants to continue being Latin American and even more important, he wants to speak Spanish" (Pérez Sala 1973: 131–2). His study of the speech of sixty-five Puerto Ricans of different socio-economic classes found only three anglicized syntactic structures in general use in the classes represented in his sample:

1. *el drogadicto* (instead of *adicto a drogas*) 'the drug addict'
2. *¿Cómo te gusta Puerto Rico?* 'How do you like Puerto Rico?'
3. *¿Cómo te gustó la película?* 'How did you like the film?'

Numbers 2 and 3, essentially the same structure, are the same feature cited by Granda and rejected by Rosario as rare (II, 4 above).

The sample collected by Pérez Sala includes two other examples of interference cited by Granda:

1. the redundant *uno* (see II, 2), one of sixteen anglicisms found only in the speech of the most educated subjects
2. *habían pronto llegado* 'they had soon arrived' (see II, 3) instead of *habían llegado pronto,* one of the twenty-one utterances he calls sporadic anglicisms

Pérez Sala classifies most of the other features cited by Granda as false anglicisms, i.e. not traceable to English.

Although Pérez Sala decries the lack of scientific investigation in the area of syntax, his own study uses only sixty-five subjects, the great majority of them between the ages of 40 and 60. Fifteen are public figures whose speech was recorded while they were on television, obviously a formal situation. The other fifty informants were allowed to speak freely on any subject. The lack of control for formal and informal styles, the older age of the majority, and a slight preponderance of highly educated speakers probably had a significant effect on the results.

The work of North American linguists in Puerto Rico, although somewhat less fraught with partisan judgments, also does not make use of recent advances in sociolinguistic theory and methodology. Dillard (1975) and Nash (1970) both maintain the existence of a mixed Spanish–English, or "Spanglish," on the island, based on isolated examples from the media, commerce, and students, and residents in San Juan, the major metropolitan area. Neither offers much beyond "hybrid" as a definition of Spanglish. Nash considers it a mix of

Spanish morphology and syntax with English-derived vocabulary of three types: unadapted LOANWORDS, adapted loans, and loan translations (Nash 1970). Dillard includes examples of grammatical convergence, for example *Tengo dos cheeseburgers trabajando* 'I have two cheeseburgers working,' and claims the hybridization process is a natural continuation of the development of Puerto Rican Spanish from a Spanish Caribbean creole that is yet unattested (Dillard 1975). It has also been suggested, although not substantiated, that Puerto Rican Spanish is a more developed mixture of English and Spanish, a CREOLE, but one that never passed through a PIDGIN stage (Lawton 1971).

Spanish and English on the mainland

Many of the island arguments are reiterated on the mainland, often based on even less research. The 1970 census found that Spanish is still the first language for the majority of Puerto Ricans in the USA, but the census does not include the third generation of migrants. Spanish is primarily maintained by those who were born in Puerto Rico, but that percentage has continually decreased: it represented 70 percent of the U.S. Puerto Rican population in 1960 and 55 percent in 1970. Moreover, the Puerto Rican population is a very young one. The median age is 19, compared to the U.S. median of 28.6, and the proportion of preschoolers is double the national average.

The language and culture of Puerto Ricans have come under heavy attack in the schools and on the blocks of the ghettoes in which the majority live. At home Puerto Ricans must communicate in Spanish, but schools and jobs require spoken and written Standard English, and survival on the street often demands a knowledge of Black English. Language problems plague the school systems. Of the 260,000 Puerto Rican schoolchildren in New York City, for example, approximately 30 percent have severe or moderate language difficulty in English. The statistics that graphically depict Puerto Rican failure are becoming well known: approximately three to five years behind the average in reading, math, and verbal tests; 55–80 percent drop-out rates across the nation; 75 percent of the Puerto Rican population without a high school diploma; and a 60 percent drop-out rate in the first two years of college (Aspira 1976). Spanish helped build a strong identity for some of the few Puerto Ricans who "made it," but others left the ghetto and Spanish behind them. The experience of other non-English-speaking migrations suggests that it is nearly impossible for immigrant groups in the USA to maintain their first language much beyond the second generation. The political status of Puerto Rico, the proximity of the island, the availability of fast, modern travel, the class background and racial mixture of Puerto Ricans, and their participation in social and educational movements may, however, alter the usual historical pattern of linguistic assimilation for immigrants to the USA.

The great majority of Puerto Rican parents want their children to know Spanish and want to help them as much as their limited education, time, and energy allow (Zirkel 1973). Their experiences in Puerto Rico and the reality of their harsh existence in U.S. cities have also taught them the importance of English. A few may be more proud of their children's English than of their Spanish, as was the mother who boasted *Mi hijo es americanito, sólo habla inglés* 'My son is a little American, he speaks only English.' This mother and others learned their lesson well after having been turned away from jobs, apartments, and polling booths (English literacy was required of voters until 1965 in New York City), because they spoke only Spanish. On the other hand, life in the extended family household and segregated communities, and visits to the island, demand at least a passive knowledge of Spanish.

School experiences are crucial in shaping language attitudes. Perhaps the most obvious pressure to conform to U.S. patterns is in the transformation of Spanish names. If the child's name is Ana Celia, Ana may be spelled with two *n*'s and Celia dropped completely. The written accents are omitted from María and Raúl Hernández's names. Wilfredo and Magali Quiñones (/kiñónes/,something like Kee-nyó-ness) become Willie and Maggie Quinones (/kwinóniz/, Quee-nó-nies), although the pupils are expected to learn to pronounce and spell their teachers' names correctly. If they speak only Spanish, they may be put into a class for retarded children or slow learners, or forced to sink or swim in an English-speaking class. It is not unusual to find Spanish-speaking children, tagged "NES," i.e. non-English speakers, incorrectly placed in classes for the handicapped or emotionally disturbed. When children speak Spanish to their friends, they may be chastised.

In junior and senior high schools, Puerto Ricans who want to study Spanish are often encouraged to take French instead ("after all, you already know Spanish"), but in Spanish classes they are told that they do not speak "real Spanish," but a dialect, and "dialect" becomes an epithet (but cf. Valdés Fallis and García Moya 1976; Valdés Fallis and Teschner 1978; Valdés, Lozano, and Moyda, in press). No one ever explains to them that everyone speaks a dialect of his/her language meaning that specific vocabulary items, pronunciations, intonation contours, and grammatical features distinguish each geographical region, class, ethnic group, and race from the others (see Chapter 3).

Some of the worst critics are other Latin Americans in the USA who help propagate the myth of the inferiority of Puerto Rican Spanish without recognizing that it is essentially a class question. The majority of Latin Americans in the USA are from the small sector of the upper class of their countries; the class background of most Puerto Rican migrants is quite different. The critics tend to judge Puerto Rican Spanish by the speech of those who have had little or no formal education in the language; they forget the many nonstandard forms in the Spanish of their less educated compatriots. Unfortunately, some Puerto Ricans join in the attack.

Almost 600 years after colonization by Spain, these critics still attempt to impose a Castilian standard, or some other South American notion of correctness. In Spanish classes, Puerto Ricans are told not to say *abrigo*, but *sobretodo* for 'overcoat,' that *sombrilla* is incorrect for *paraguas* 'umbrella.' They must say *impermeable* instead of *capa* for 'raincoat.' Their anglicized forms are considered barbarisms. Many attempts are made to "correct" Puerto Rican pronunciation. Some even try to insist on the pronunciation of the Spanish *ceceo*, i.e. written *c* (before *e* and *i*) and *z* are pronounced [θ] as in *thing*, although over 200 million Latin Americans and many Spaniards pronounce these as /s/. An analogous situation for English speakers in the United States would occur if English teachers demanded the British word *lift* instead of *elevator*, and insisted upon "shedule" as the correct pronunciation for *schedule*. When Puerto Rican students want to major in Spanish, they may be criticized for choosing "a snap course." No one makes the same comment about English speakers who major in English, although both courses of study focus on literary genres, not on the ability to speak colloquially. An incident which happened in the 1950s in New York illustrates this double standard. A junior high school Spanish medal was given to a student whose average did not measure up to the 98 percent average of a Puerto Rican student, because it was felt the Puerto Rican had an unfair advantage. On the other hand, the English medal was given to a native English-speaking student with the highest average, although the same Puerto Rican student had an English average in the high 90s.

Many of the 1.6 million foreign-language-speaking children in the USA experience similar injustices. Speaking another language is not considered an asset for the poor, but a handicap. Bilingual programs are new and very limited, and most of them have been designed as TRANSITIONAL BILINGUAL EDUCATION programs whose main purpose is to teach English, not to produce bilinguals (see Chapter 21). In 1973, five years after the passage of the federal BILINGUAL EDUCATION ACT, bilingual programs reached only 3 percent of the children in New York City who needed them. After two years of litigation between the Puerto Rican educational agency, Aspira, and the New York City Board of Education, a consent decree was signed on August 29, 1974, because "the city school system had failed to meet the needs of Spanish speaking children causing high truancy and drop out rates among these youngsters." It also stated the obvious, i.e. that "low reading scores [in English]by Spanish speaking children were the result of their inability to understand English" (*Bilingual Review* 1974: 1).

The decree stated that all children whose English language deficiency prevented them from effectively participating in the learning process and who could more effectively participate in Spanish should receive: (a) intensive instruction in English; (b) instruction in subject areas in Spanish; (c) the reinforcement of the pupil's use of Spanish and reading comprehension in Spanish *where the need is indicated* (emphasis added). Since the decree cites only those children who cannot speak English well, it eliminates from the program the other 165,000 (out of 200,000) students who could strengthen their Spanish. If it were meant to be a truly bilingual program, it would include them, and the rest of the Hispanic and other non-English speaking children presently excluded. The message of the schools is that Spanish is inferior and the variety learned by Puerto Rican children from their parents is particularly unacceptable.

What are the features of the Spanish passed on to their young by Puerto Ricans in the United States? A study carried out by Casiano Montanez in 1964 (published in 1975) focused on phonology, and found that island-born Puerto Ricans spoke Spanish in New York with a "typical" Puerto Rican accent. Their phonological system was like the one described above for Puerto Rico except for very slight changes in the speech of the more educated who used American English pronunciations of *r* and *l* and had minor variations in vowels. Otherwise, even those who had lived in New York for twenty years or more maintained Puerto Rican Spanish pronunciation even when adopting English words.

As in Puerto Rico, the adoption of English words is most often cited as "proof" that Puerto Ricans "cannot speak Spanish" and as the basis for the theory of the existence of Spanglish, presumably a new language, a pidgin, created from a mixture of English and Spanish with denuded grammar. Spanglish, supposed to be characteristic primarily of Puerto Ricans in the USA, is defined imprecisely in both Puerto Rico and the United States. The only "rule" of Spanglish as popularly referred to in the media is that any word in English can become a Spanish word by adding a final *-a* or *-o*. A list of forty-five words published as a glossary of Spanglish terms (Fernández 1972) was given to 186 Puerto Ricans in New York (approximately 55 percent of whom were raised in the city and the other 45 percent in Puerto Rico), and they were asked to report on their use of these terms (Zentella 1973). Only twenty-four were used by more than 50 percent of those interviewed. These included terms such as *la boila* 'the boiler,' *la factoría* 'the factory,' *el elevador* 'the elevator,' *la carpeta* 'the carpet,' *lonchar* 'to lunch,' *el super* 'the superintendent,' *el londri* 'the laundry,' and *el bloque* 'the block.' Of those born and raised in New York City, 99 percent could not give a Spanish-origin word for terms such as: subway, superintendent, truck, raincoat, mop, laundry, boiler, lawn, factory, token, hijack, and dime. On the other hand, only one-third of those born and raised in Puerto Rico produced a Spanish-origin term for: mop, dime, factory, boiler, token. In a similar study, U.S. Puerto Rican bilingual college students considered 67 percent of fifty Spanglish terms acceptable Spanish and could provide only 35 percent of their formal Spanish equivalents (Acosta-Belén 1975).

There is little value in this type of approach, i.e. word lists cannot give a true picture of the linguistic competence of the speakers interviewed, because the words are out of context and elicited in a formal situation. The only way to ascertain whether or not these words are common in U.S. Puerto Ricans' Spanish, and, more important, to understand the different social situations or communicative needs that elicit them, is to record large samples of informal speech and some structured situations. Nevertheless, it is of some importance that several words were known only in English, from which we may assume that they could never appear in the Spanish of those speakers in any context. We can make some tentative suggestions as to why these particular words are adopted in their English form. Almost all of them seem to depict a different cultural and/or psychological reality, one specific to life in the USA, and new or foreign to Puerto Ricans. Laundries and apartment superintendents are recent for most of the poor; boilers and subway tokens are unknown in Puerto Rico. Blocks, factories, and lunches are not the same in Puerto Rico as in the U.S., and the adoption of the English words for them may reflect the need to communicate the specific North American reality, for example, *almuerzo* means a long, heavy lunch, but *lonchar* implies a quick sandwich or a hot dog. But not every borrowed word can be attributed to different cultural/situational demands. The length of the word may be a factor, and/or matters of innovation or prestige. Historically recurrent varieties of word borrowing constitute three of the five features of what Milán originally called Spanglish, but now prefers to call New York City Spanish (Milán 1976):

1. Semantic reassignment: a Spanish word takes on a new meaning because of its similarity to an English word, for example *carpeta* 'folder' comes to mean 'carpet'
2. Large-scale word borrowing – see examples above.
3. Loan translations and literal translations from English into Spanish: for example, *Tome Ud. ventaja de X* 'take + you + advantage of ' instead of *aprovéchese de X* 'take advantage of X'

The other two characteristics Milán noted in New York City Spanish are:

4. Syntactic readjustments: for example, the pronoun is placed before the verb instead of after it in questions, for example, *¿Que Ud. piensa?* ("What you think?") for *¿Que piensa Ud.?* 'What do you think?' ("What think you?")
5. Phonemic distinction: open final *-e* and *-o*. This feature, also mentioned in Rosario's vowel inventory (above), is challenged by recent research (Poplack 1977)

In the late 1970s, Milán urged all researchers and practitioners to avoid the term Spanglish:

As a scientific term attempting to designate a particular phenomenon, it is hopeless since it fails to capture the broader context wherein the phenomenon occurs. As a label, it is grossly misleading, since it does not even come close to describing either the structure or the nature of its pretended designatum. (Milán 1976: 22)

Languages throughout the world, often those of a minority culture, have undergone changes as a result of close contact with the majority language. These changes, however, do not necessarily produce a third language. Often, the minority language dies out as succeeding generations learn the language of the majority. Historically, certain social and linguistic conditions have been correlated with the processes of PIDGINIZATION and CREOLIZATION (see Chapter 4). Given these criteria, there is no pidgin "Spanish" in Puerto Rican communities.

Some researchers suggest that the nature of the Puerto Rican experience in the USA may challenge the traditional definitions of language change (LPTF 1978a). They cite the fact that some 25,000 Puerto Rican children tested in New York City in compliance with the consent decree failed both the English and the

Spanish tests. Although the exams themselves have come under heavy attack for both their content and administration (Santiago 1978), the fact that so many youngsters were evaluated as lacking dominance in either language is interpreted as an indication that these children may be in the process of evolving new linguistic codes. Although this may be a premature conclusion (given the inadequacies of the exam in question and the state of knowledge of language proficiency testing in general), an important fact often overlooked is that linguistic change is an inevitable result of cultural change, and purist attitudes cannot stem the tide.

In addition to words from American English, Puerto Rican language behavior also includes CODE-SWITCHING, i.e. a shift from Spanish to English or vice versa for entire sentences or parts of them. Although it is clear that speakers will often switch to another language if they are at a loss for a particular vocabulary item, or are having trouble with certain grammatical constructions, recent research indicates that code-switching is not always the result of a lack of linguistic knowledge nor is it an *ad hoc* mixture. What makes a bilingual speaker who is equally at ease in both languages switch codes? In many ways they do so for the same reasons a monolingual speaker switches from a formal to an informal style (e.g. by choosing a colloquial word or dropping the *-g* of *-ing* verbs) or vice versa.

Gumperz and Hernández Chávez point out that Chicanos may switch between Spanish and English even if they do know the words or grammar in both languages for any of the following reasons:

1. to express the meaning more effectively
2. because the experience or the item referred to is typical of the other language's culture
3. to establish the social identity of the referent or speaker
4. to embellish a point
5. to reflect confidentiality or privateness (Gumperz and Hernández Chávez 1975)

Others suggest that linguistic features such as trigger words, for example, homophones and proper nouns, prompt the transfer to another code (Clyne 1967). All of these features were found in the code-switching of bilinguals in Puerto Rican households in Philadelphia (Marlos and Zentella 1978), and in New York Puerto Rican bilingual classrooms (Zentella 1978a, b). Lavandera (1978) has suggested that bilinguals may feel constrained in a monolingual setting in either of the languages they know. Research on code-switching by Puerto Ricans corroborates the fact that code-switching is part of the full linguistic repertoire of fluent bilinguals and is predominantly directed at ingroup members only (Marlos and Zentella 1978; Poplack 1978a.) Fluent code-switching is not indiscriminate mixing; code-switches are subject to syntactic constraints, the rules for which are shared by all competent switchers in the speech community (Pfaff 1975; Timm 1975), and some rules may be shared by all switchers in all bilingual situations (Gumperz 1976b).

In many speech communities, this type of code-switching is seen as a verbal skill, i.e. one more communicative tool at the disposal of the bilingual person. The rules are acquired at an early age. Five- and six-year-old Puerto Rican children in a New York City bilingual first grade demonstrated the ability to switch languages according to social situation and the addressee's language dominance, although less than 1 percent of their egocentric speech, i.e. talk to themselves, included code-switches (Centro 1976). In another study, third and sixth grade students (56 students, ages 8–13) used language-switching as a stylistic device (Zentella 1978b; cf. Dearholt and Valdés Fallis 1978; Valdés Fallis 1978b, 1980). They were also able to make accurate judgments of their own and fellow students' language dominance. At a young age, children learn which languages they should speak, and to whom, and how to alternate languages for stylistic purposes. They are aware of particular family dyads, i.e. they report that they speak Spanish to adult monolingual Spanish speakers and to their younger sisters and brothers, but that they speak both languages to older sisters and brothers, and sometimes to their fathers. They essentially play follow-the-leader in the choice of language if they are confident of their knowledge of the language chosen by their addressor: in the Zentella (1978b) study 74 percent of the children interviewed (23–31) followed the interviewer's unexpected switch in language, and almost half switched immediately. The others switched within two to ten questions. Of the eight children who never switched in the interview, five were recent immigrants for whom it would have been impossible to handle the exchange in English. The varieties of code-switching that exist within the boundaries of the sentence range from what may be termed "crutching," for an unknown word or expression, to virtuosity, i.e. the juxtaposition of varied grammatical units that observe syntactic constraints. The most adept code-switchers in these bilingual classes were girls, and this may be correlated with research in Norwich, England (Trudgill 1974), Panama (Cedergren 1973), and New York (Labov 1966) that documents how women in these cities are more sensitive to issues of appropriate language behavior and language change than men. In the New York Puerto Rican bilingual classes studied, sentence internal code-switching tended to be an informal speech style that appeared more often in game situations than in classroom recitations (Zentella 1978a). Although the Puerto Rican community voices negative attitudes toward code-switching, its continued use by students, teachers, and the rest of the bilingual community suggests that covert norms do in fact value the dual USA–Puerto Rico identity conveyed by the code-switched speech. For U.S. Puerto Ricans, as for Chicanos in East Austin, Texas (Elías Olivares 1976), adept code-switching is a marker of proficient bilingualism.

The definition of a bilingual person may vary for each bilingual speech community or segment of it. Some Puerto Ricans may consider themselves bilingual if they can understand both languages, although they may speak only one well. Others feel they cannot claim to be bilingual because they speak a nonstandard variety of Puerto Rican Spanish. Fishman's well-known study of Puerto Ricans in Jersey City, based mainly on interviews with forty-three people, defined six language styles and four linguistic subgroups (Fishman, et al. 1971). Current research on a block in the barrio in New York City has found similar styles, and different styles are produced by the same speakers in different situations, or at different points within the same speech situation (LPTF 1978b). For example, young Puerto Ricans' control of Spanish syntax and vocabulary may be much better when limited to home and neighborhood topics. They may feel insecure and ill-equipped in Spanish when discussing school work (e.g. homework, compositions) or in formal settings (e.g. filling out applications), since the only contact with many of the vocabulary items will have been in English. Furthermore, they may have a general level of insecurity in formal situations which even restricts the use of Spanish skills they have in other settings. For example, students who use the Spanish subjunctive correctly with their friends in the halls of schools become painfully hesitant in the classroom or in a formal meeting and insist on reverting to English. The extent to which linguistic insecurity impedes U.S. Puerto Ricans' performance in Spanish remains to be studied. The expressive ability of adolescents and others is probably also severely hampered by their impression of the status of Spanish as low, and its correlation with being, in their terms, "uncool" or "hicky." There is some recent evidence, however, that the "nearly unanimous linguistic insecurity" (Fishman et al. 1971: 353) of ten years ago is being replaced by an affirmation of and pride in Spanish and bilinguality (LPTF 1978c). The future of Spanish in the community and the varietie(s) spoken will depend on innumerable socio-economic and political factors.

Another factor in the changing pattern of language use is the similarity of the English of some Puerto Ricans to the English of many North American Blacks. A 1973 analysis of the English of twenty-nine Puerto Rican adolescents indicated what many nonlinguists had long observed, namely, that the English of these youngsters assimilates to Black English, especially if they have extensive Black contacts (Wolfram 1974). It is nearly impossible to distinguish some Puerto Rican speakers from Black speakers, and although the first language of many may have been Spanish, there is little or no Spanish interference in their English. As in Black English (see Chapter 5), the Puerto Rican adolescents studied omitted the off glide in [aɪ] so that the word 'I' sounded like *ah,* they dropped the postvocalic [r], *(car → ca),* reduced final consonant clusters of *test* → *tess,* substituted [t] for [θ] in words like *think,* and replaced [θ] with [f] in words such as *mouth, tooth.* These phonological features were found in the speech of all the teenage subjects, but syntactic features of Black English, such as negation patterns, for example, *Didn't nobody do it,* or invariant *be,* for example, *He be botherin me,* were assimilated primarily into the speech of those Puerto Ricans with Black friends.

Puerto Rican English is similar to the English of those with whom they live and work in closest contact, or wish to emulate. The influence of Black English is the logical result of close ties with Afro-Americans in the schools, apartment buildings, and streets of northern ghettoes. However, young Puerto Rican children in Philadelphia with no Black contacts used Black English features in informal speech, but had features characteristic of White Philadelphians in their formal speech (Poplack 1978b). In addition, the majority of Puerto Ricans who speak fluent English can be recognized as Puerto Rican because of certain phonological features not found in surrounding dialects. Syllable-timing, characteristic of Spanish, as opposed to stress-timing, characteristic of English, has been isolated as one of the features that contributes to the distinctive sound of Puerto Rican English (Anisman 1975).

Future prospects

On the basis of his 1969 research, Fishman predicted that Puerto Ricans would maintain their mother tongue longer than some other national minorities had, because each language dominated a particular domain, for example, Spanish in the home and English in the school (Fishman et al. 1971). However, increasing numbers of U.S.-born Puerto Ricans who are English-dominant speak English to their siblings at home, and island-born Spanish-dominant Puerto Ricans in bilingual programs can speak Spanish to their teachers. If it is true that stable bilingualism depends on distinct domains for each language, bilingual programs, even the few that are not designed as transitions to English, may aid in the loss of the mother tongue instead of its maintenance. Fishman et al. (1971) suggested that in comparison with other language groups, Puerto Ricans in New York City were not yet language conscious or organized on behalf of language use and maintenance; he found their language loyalty and purity "foreign ideologies," and few members were involved in maintenance efforts. The history of Puerto Rico and the story of the language policy struggle, outlined above, now provide some evidence to the contrary. There is also some evidence of Puerto Rican efforts to organize around language issues in the USA, particularly in New York City. The struggle for community control of the public schools, for bilingual–bicultural programs, bilingual licenses, community paraprofessionals, and the right to vote in Spanish, among others, were taken up by grass roots groups, such as the United Bronx Parents, as well as Puerto Rican agencies, and community professionals. Together they crushed the New School of Social Research's attempt to offer Spanglish courses in 1970 (Varo 1971), and they participated actively in the struggle to establish courses and departments of Puerto Rican Studies in the universities. Puerto Rican students who were able to enter City University under the now defunct Open Admissions program flocked to the language courses in the Spanish departments. Songs, plays, and poetry in both languages are flourishing, and *salsa* music with its Spanish – and sometimes English – lyrics is increasingly popular. In the area of research, students and faculty helped to establish the Centro de Estudios Puertorriqueños, whose Language Policy Task Force (LPTF) is conducting extensive research in el Barrio, the East Harlem Puerto Rican community. The Centro, United Bronx Parents, the Puerto Rican Educator's Association, Aspira of America, the Puerto Rican Legal and Educational Defense Fund, the Puerto Rican Forum, the first director of the New York City Board of Education Office of Bilingual Education (Hernán La Fontaine), and many others, have publicly stated their commitment to bilingual and bicultural education, and the right of national minorities to maintain their linguistic and cultural traditions.

The National Puerto Rican Task Force on Educational Policy (NPRTFEP), in which most of these organizations are represented, has the following goals as an "agenda for discussion":

1. Full bilinguality beyond the first generation
2. Spoken and written command of Standard Spanish and English without downgrading nonstandard dialects and code-switching
3. Language(s) of instruction based on sensitivity to the community's needs and usage
4. School involvement in language events of the artistic, professional and organizational life of the community (NPRTFEP 1977: 30–2)

Not only are these groups beginning to take the lead in the formulation of language policy for their community, they also recognize the need for, and several have begun to undertake themselves, research on Puerto Rican language varieties and language attitudes. Until that research is carried out, all assertions concerning the disappearance of Spanish, the existence of a pidgin that is distinct from Spanish and English, or the non-Puerto Rican identity of a monolingual English third generation, are premature. The appropriate framework for the analysis of a speech community encompasses a variety of subgroups, codes, DISCOURSE settings, and styles, and incorporates the community's view of the role of language in its society (Hymes 1974; Heath, in press). A complete ethnography of speaking would integrate the results of such an analysis within the larger context of the community's reality. We might expect, for example, that the rules for appropriate speech behavior in the Puerto Rican community would have cultural correlates in the changing notions of Puerto Rican identity, the roles of women, men, and children, and the concept of *respeto* 'respect,' among others. In addition, specific social and economic variables – choices of marriage partners, employment opportunities, and accessibility to education in Spanish – will have important effects on Puerto Rican speech communities. Independence or statehood for the island will affect the general climate of acceptance of Spanish. Morever, the number of years and types of education to which they are exposed and the number of years in the USA and frequency and extent of visits to Puerto Rico are major factors to be considered in a thorough analysis of the language use of Puerto Ricans. The presence of 2 million Puerto Ricans in the USA and a total of 11 million Hispanics (see Chapter 22) affords an extraordinary opportunity to study at close hand the linguistic repercussions of colonialism, mass migration, cultural conflict, assimilation to surrounding class, ethnic and regional dialects, and contrasting models of bilingual education. The results of such research could make an important contribution to the general body of linguistic knowledge. Even more significant, perhaps, would be its contribution to our acceptance of linguistic and cultural diversity in the USA as essential to the development of its language minorities and the nation as a whole. The Puerto Rican experience should offer some insight into the indispensable components of a working national language policy in a democratic nation.

FURTHER READING

The best analyses of the history and/or culture of Puerto Rico are written in Spanish. Fernández Méndez 1970 is a comprehensive cultural history of the Indian, African, and Spanish contributions, and of U.S. colonization. The most extensive research on the linguistic contributions of the Indian and African culture to the Spanish of Puerto Rico is reported in Alvarez Nazario 1961, 1977. Alvarez Nazario's most recent work (1979) is on the dialect of the *jíbaro* or country folk. In addition, the Instituto Lingüístico of the University of Puerto Rico in Río Piedras is an excellent source for linguistic analyses of the Spanish spoken in Puerto Rico today, including dialectal studies of several towns, all written in Spanish.

The following books are suggested for those who want to read more about Puerto Rican history and culture in English. Wagenheim 1970 is a readable general introduction and includes chapters on the island's history, economy, education, culture, and the diaspora. Figueroa 1972b provides a detailed account of the early period of Puerto Rico's history, from pre-Columbian times until the U.S. invasion in 1898. Excellent analyses of the socio-economic reality of the island in the twentieth century are contained in Lopez and Petras 1974.

On the topic of language in education, Negrón de Montilla 1975 documents the linguistic policies of the seven Commissioners of Education during the first three decades of U.S. control of the island. A variety of views on the language question on the island as it relates to pedagogy and political issues are presented in Epstein 1970.

The best statistical profile and general overview of the Puerto Rican community in the United States is the 1976 report of the U.S. Commission on Civil Rights. A critical listing of most of the studies available on the languages Puerto Ricans speak on the continent is included in Teschner, Bills, and Craddock 1975. The most recent research on language questions in the New York Puerto Rican community is being conducted by the Language Policy Task Force of the Center for Puerto Rican Studies, City University of New York.

The language of Italian Americans*

YOLE CORREA-ZOLI

Italian Americans are the largest language-sharing ethnic minority in the United States except for the Hispano-Americans, who are divided among Mexican Americans, Puerto Ricans, Cubans, and others. Yet, the Italian American community is less "visible" on the national scene than some others; the Italian language is not taught very widely in American schools and colleges, and the Italian Americans themselves, at least until recently, have not shown great interest in encouraging the maintenance and spread of the Italian language. Some of the reasons for the surprising position of Italian in the USA lie in the situation of Standard Italian and DIALECTS in Italy; other reasons may be found in the patterns of Italian immigration to the New World.

Standard Italian and Italian dialects

The Italian language represents the evolution of spoken Latin on the Italian peninsula over a period of centuries. Like most other European languages, Italian has a standard variety which exists side by side with, and in many ways is added on top of, a host of regional and local dialects.

Natural geographical aspects of the peninsula as well as the lack of political unity from the fall of the Roman empire until the unification of modern Italy in the late nineteenth century resulted in the flourishing existence of many distinct dialects, originally separate developments of spoken Latin. The Spezia–Rimini ISOGLOSS divides the peninsula into two major dialect areas: the Northern dialects and the Central-Southern ones (see Figure 11.1 and Table 11.1). The Northern area is further differentiated into the Gallo-Italian groups (Ligurian, Piedmontese, Lombard, and dialects of Emilia-Romagna) and the Venetian group. To the south of the Spezia–Rimini line, the Central Italian variety covers the regions of Tuscany, Umbria, and Rome as well as northern Latium and the northern Marches. Its Tuscan, or more precisely, Florentine variety formed the

* I would like to acknowledge the editorial help of Ruggero Stefanini, University of California, Berkeley, and my Colorado and Bay Area informants. Very special thanks are due to Professor Robert Di Pietro who shared with me his recent studies, and whose perceptive insights into the Italian language in the USA have for some time been for me a source of inspiration.

239

240

Figure 11.1. Map of Italy showing the Spezia–Rimini isogloss

Table 11.1. *Selected samples of dialects in the Italian peninsula and Sicily*

Milano (Lombardy)	*Standard Italian*
gh'hô daa ôn pügn sott el barbòzz che l'hô indôrmentaa.	gli ho dato un pugno sotto il mento che l'ho addormentato.
el padrôn l'e padrôn perchè s'el gh'ha tort el vol rezôn.	il padrone è il padrone perchè se ha torto vuol ragione.
Romagnolo (Romagna) (fragment of a local poem)	
da là sò os ved l'êlba matutena os respira on'êria frizantena pura fresca, senza inquinament respira sò pu fört tranquillament.	da lassù si vede l'alba mattutina si respira un'aria frizzantina pura, fresca, senza inquinamento respira dunque forte, tranquillamente.
Neapolitan (Campania)	
Chi mm' 'o ffa fa? Meglio farse na passiáta a Pusilleco!	Chi me lo fa fare? Meglio fare una passeggiata a Posillipo!
E che fiura faccio c' 'a gente ca mme vede accatta 'u biglietto?	E che figura faccio con la gente che mi vede comprare il biglietto?
Vide Napule e po' muore!	Vedi Napoli e poi muori!
Calabrese (Calabria) (fragment of a local poem)	
Cumpagna di li scoli elementari quandu era picciriddu e tu fighiola nnucenti non sapivamu chi fari iocávamu e parravamu di scola.	Compagna della scuola elementare quando io ero raggazzo e tu bambina innocenti non sapevamo cosa fare, giuocavamo e parlavamo della scuola.
Sicilian (Sicily) (fragment of a regional song)	
Non cantu nè p'amuri e nè pp'amanti picchì mancu mi passi ppi la menti ma pè l'amuri miu ca nun mi voli ma pè l'amuri miu can nun mi senti.	Non canto nè per gli amori ne per gli amanti perchè nemmeno mi passa per la mente ma per l'amore mio che non mi vuole ma per l'amore mio che non mi sente.

backbone of Standard Italian which then evolved in its own way. These Central dialects present a multitude of traits which link this group with those in the North and in the South, the latter presenting the greatest divergence from northern varieties of the language.

Degrees of intelligibility vary among dialects: that of Romagna (North) and that of Apulia (South), for example, exhibit such striking linguistic differentiations both from each other and from Standard Italian that they would barely be intelligible between speakers who have little or no knowledge of the standard language.

The "Questione della Lingua," or what is or ought to be the standard, was initiated by Dante Alighieri in his *De Vulgari Eloquentia* and has been debated for centuries. While the Florentine-based language enhanced by the prestigious works of Dante, Petrarch, and Boccaccio became the most widely accepted standard, a number of other dialects have frequently been the vehicle of literary expression in poetry, fiction, and the theatrical arts. The Roman VERNACULAR (Romanesco), for example, has been used by distinguished contemporary writers such as the poet Trilussa and the fiction writer Carlo Emilio Gadda; the Neapolitan dialect by the poet Salvatore di Giacomo and the great playwright Eduardo de Filippo. In the eighteenth century, playwright Carlo Goldoni, reformer of the Italian theater, had several of his characters speak in Venetian dialect. Since World War II, Standard Italian has increasingly been influenced by the language of science and technology, and by the centripetal force of Rome, center of the administrative and political life of the country, as well as of the motion picture industry.

Throughout all socio-economic groups, increased reliance on mass media and the spread of education are making Standard Italian the exclusive, or at least the dominant, language for most Italians, especially the young. Active use of the dialects is being lost while a passive ability to understand them persists. Although they are being pushed into more restricted settings, the dialects have by no means been annihilated. Many, if not most, speakers exhibit some dialectal PHONETIC carry-overs of varying degrees in their speech. It is not uncommon even for a public speaker, actor, or announcer to display slight phonetic departures from the standard which will announce to the trained ear the region of the speaker's origin. Generally, we can speak of "regional varieties" of Standard Italian which are a type of compromise between the standard and the dialects.

Although possibly less intense during the last thirty to forty years, definable attitudes and value judgments regarding dialects are still a reality. These were shaped by socio-economic and cultural differences among the regions. In general, Southern dialects enjoy less prestige nationally than the Central or Northern ones.

Finally, Italian is the language of 61 million persons, 56 million of whom have been counted by the latest Italian census. In terms of world status, Italian occupies seventh place among the European languages spoken in the world.

The Italian immigrants and their language

While my grandmother was alive, I spoke Italian [up to age 7]; after she died, my grandfather insisted we speak English [much to be regretted now – as he grew older he couldn't figure why none of the grandchildren could speak Italian]. My father, born in Italy, would speak to us in Italian, but never insisted we answer in Italian.

Felt strongly discrimination with a feeling of embarrassment when my father spoke to us in front of our playmates and friends. We lived in a mainly Irish community.

I was told in school not to speak Italian so as to develop my English.

Yes. In order to keep culture and language alive. ["Why English?":] In order to be able to work and communicate with others around us.

My parents spoke limited Italian and they did not speak to their children because they felt that they would not be able to command the English language well.

Attitudes on my mother's [non-Italian] side of the family were always neutral, but on the Italian side, the absence of the language in the home is seen as an unfortunate loss. As kids we were taught a few things *about* the language, and some phrases. However, circumstances did not allow frequent enough a contact to lead to oral control. To continue studying seriously the language now, would be to fill a gap that has existed as far back as I can remember.

These comments are in reply to the question: "As you were growing up, were you ever given any reasons why you should/should not speak Italian, or learn Italian?" This question forms Part II of a questionnaire circulated in the mid-1970s among second and third generation Italian Americans in the San Francisco, California Bay Area. Further attitudes about dialects and Standard Italian are revealed by the following statements:

I did not speak Italian at home but understood both Italian and dialect. My parents never forced us to learn because at that time, they were interested in learning English and studying English in order to pass their citizenship. They spoke in Italian – and we answered in English. Because we were now in this country – we should be Americans – was the attitude.

Always encouraged to speak Italian, although especially after my grandparents passed away I had fewer people to speak with and going to school. Before I entered grammar school I only spoke the Genoese dialect, never English.

Even though we spoke dialect in the family I was always encouraged to learn Standard Italian.

How widespread are the negative attitudes mentioned above? Have acculturation and evolution of traditional family patterns resulted in the disappearance of the ancestral language? Some recent studies seem to indicate the contrary. Waggoner (1976; see also Chapter 22, this volume) reported that in 1975 nearly 3.9 million people (aged 14 and older) claimed Italian as their mother tongue, and these constituted nearly one in seven among all claimants of non-English mother tongues in the United States. Of those who spoke a language other than English (in households where a non-English language was used), 8 percent spoke only Italian, 76 percent of the Italian–English bilinguals usually spoke English, and 16 percent usually spoke Italian. There are approximately 20 million people of Italian ancestry in the U.S. today, 1.5 million of whom are found in and around New York City. This projection includes *first generation* U.S. residents born in Italy, *second generation* American-born children, and the *third generation* Americans who claim one or both grandparents born in Italy.

Political events and economic conditions in Italy, and U.S. immigration laws were some of the factors determining the timing and numbers of immigrants. Earliest immigration, prior to 1880, included political exiles, intellectuals, artists, and adventurers. East of the Mississippi and north of the Ohio, communities of Northern Italians predominated until 1880 when the mass migration began, rising to a peak in 1900–10 when over 2 million Italians arrived, the majority from southern Italy. Their settlements, most numerous in the Northeastern states, laid down the basic distribution affecting the flow of future immigration (Velikonja 1970). This flow fluctuated along reduced lines until 1920 when the Immigration Quota Law of 1924 slowed it considerably without, however, putting a stop to it. Italian settlements, frequently referred to as "Little Italies," continued to receive a fresh influx of immigrants, the highest number of which was in the 1960s, with a total of 211,717 (Miranda 1977); 93,151 were admitted in the five-year span 1971–5. The total Italian immigration to the U.S. from 1820 to 1975 is 5.3 million, the second largest group of immigrants (cf. Germany with 7.0 million, the largest single block, and Great Britain with 4.9; U.S. Bureau of the Census 1976).

The result is that now every state has an identifiable Italian American community, most frequently urban. All these communities seem to continually regroup and be in a constant state of flux (Nelli 1967). U.S. census figures reveal that the "Foreign Stock" (first and second generation) are concentrated in the Northeastern states (69 percent), followed by the North and Central states (14 percent), the West (10 percent) and the South (7 percent). In the West, a steadily increased flow of preponderantly Northern and Central Italians has been registered for California since 1910. Some few states, Washington, for example, have experienced a decrease.

A great deal of literature, much of which has appeared since 1960, has focused on the history, sociology, and psychology of these immigrant groups. Frequent topics have been the stigma of crime, the hostilities and prejudices, and the stereotypes in the minds of many Americans who

retain an extraordinary image of the Italian immigrant and his descendants as cultural aberrations who sing tenor, and peddle fish, and who are romantic, oily, prudish, devious, faithful, sexy, clannish, open-minded, tolerant, intolerant, brilliant, anti-intellectual, unambitious and industrious, all at the same time. (Cordasco 1974: v)

Essentially many of these studies demonstrate that the culture of the Italian Americans is an accommodation between American urbanization and various elements from the Old World. Herbert Gans (1967:6) has pointed out that, judging from currently available evidence, Italian immigrants were acculturated but not really assimilated. Campisi (1948) observed that as a result of such acculturation, the Southern Italian family in America has shifted from a peasant and patriarchal type toward the contemporary American type. This shift produced conflicts and disorganization in the first and second generations, which diminished in second and third generation families patterned after the contemporary urban American family, except for a strong emphasis on maintenance of affectionate bonds with immigrant relatives.

The data supplied by the National Center for Education Statistics do not, of course, specify what kind of Italian is being spoken in these households and by individuals, whether standard or dialect, with or without American English borrowings. In the case of Italian, this is not a simple issue, since the distribution and status of Italian dialects in the USA have been scantily studied and seldom in any systematic way. Some information can be gleaned indirectly from observations of groups studied for some other specific reason, be this linguistic description or, more frequently, folkloristic research. Personal observations and experiences are both limited in scope and tend to be linked to specific goals. However, immigration records and other historical data lend support to the general view that Southern dialects prevail in urban communities of the Northeast, and Central and Northern dialects in the West.

In an investigation of the acquisition of syntax in bilingual children, Kessler (1971) reported a prevalence of Southern Italian dialects (such as Calabrese, Sicilian, and Abruzzese) in South Philadelphia. In this study, parents and children categorically endorsed the value of BILINGUALISM. A linguistic approach to the acculturation of Italians in New York City by Tofani (1951) also showed a strong pattern of preference for Southern dialects. A variety of Southern dialects were similarly found in Boston's North End by Biondi who investigated the linguistic development and socialization process of monolingual and bilingual Italian American children in this area. In this community, in which 89 percent of the residents were of Italian descent, immigrant parents apparently demanded quite vigorously that Italian continue to be spoken within the home (Biondi 1975), while well-defined social contexts provided Italian American children with guidelines for choosing either Italian or English.

Studies not strictly linguistic but meant to amuse or to shock have concentrated on the New York area, commenting upon "Italo-American" speech, the basis of which is frequently Neapolitan or Sicilian (Livingston 1918 and Prezzolini 1939, among others). Though studies of dialects in the West are very rare, investigations undertaken in the San Francisco Bay Area in the 1970s supported previous general observations regarding the preponderance of Northern and Central Italian dialects (Radin 1935; Simoncini 1959; Correa-Zoli 1970). In 1927, it was reported that the largest percentage of Piedmontese immigrants were in California, and New York, Pennsylvania, and Colorado had the next greatest numbers (Zallio 1927). Studies of Italian immigration as a social phenomenon confirm these reports (Rolle 1968). Until new findings oppose them, these observations should be interpreted as confirming the predominance of Northern and Central Italian dialects in California and the West in general.

Within this broad framework showing the preponderance of a certain dialect or dialects in a specific area, Italian language communities seldom displayed a homogeneous picture, but instead formed a series of "islands" determined by economics and *campanilismo,* literally 'bell-tower-ism,' referring to identification with a city or region as opposed to a nation.

A concrete example from a recent study will illustrate the distribution pattern of speakers by regions of provenience in the city of San Francisco since the 1850s, patterns which are still somewhat discernible (Gumina 1977). Sicilian fishermen lived near the fishermen's wharves, Calabrians and Neapolitans in other identifiable districts, such as Filbert, or Bernal Heights and Excelsior districts. The Piedmontese and Tuscans occupied the Russian Hill area and later moved into the fashionable residential district around the Marina. While the heart of Little Italy was to be found in North Beach, an almost insular community of truck farmers was expanding in the Outer Mission hills – mostly Ligurians, Tuscans, and Neapolitans, and some Italian Swiss dairymen. On the opposite coast, New York, at the turn of the century, also offered a picture of regional "islands" (Rolle 1972): Neapolitans and Calabrians in the Mulberry Bend district, Ligurians on Baxter Street, Sicilians on Elizabeth Street, Piedmontese and Lombards west of Broadway, Ticinese Italians near the Hudson River and 69th Street.

The linguistic consequence of these islands in a proximity not previously experienced in the mother country is a certain DIALECT LEVELING. In 1932 a language community in Nevada was described as having "a Babel of dialects striving toward the Standard as a common denominator for communication" (Turano 1932). Standard Italian is used exclusively by the educated speaker, and greater reliance upon the standard is required in the U.S. than in Italy in former years. Standard Italian is now needed by dialect groups all of which are termed "Italians" by Americans. Recently, two persons from virtually opposite dialect backgrounds, Lombardy and Sicily, remarked that since living in San Francisco they had to use consistently the standard language and to relegate the dialect to family usage. The former resident of Lombardy remarked: "Se si gira, il nostro dialetto non lo capiscono, quindi bisogna parlare l'italiano" ('If we get around, our dialect is not understood, so we must speak the standard').

Apart from English borrowings of various types discussed below, San Francisco Bay Area speakers of today seldom lapse into stretches of speech which could be identified as Venetian, Genoese, or Sicilian, but maintain a variety of Standard Italian characterized by ample phonetic carry-overs, and at times features of other Italian dialects. It could be argued that the fairly high percentage of speakers from Central Italian regions, Tuscany in particular, is influencing this Standard Italian base. In other areas of the country where Southern dialects predominate, a Southern dialect base of American Italian speech is the norm, as illustrated in:

> *Avimm' fatto un bel pari e dopo simm' iuti a veder un piccio. Che bello sciò.* 'We had a good party and then went to see a movie. What a good show.'

In a more standard-like KOINÉ as in the San Francisco area, the equivalent might be:

*Abbiamo fatto un bel pari e poi siamo andati a vedere un muvi. Che bello
sció.* (American Italian: *pari* 'party,' *muvi* 'movie,' *sció* 'show')

All speakers, however, even those who primarily use dialect at home and in the
language community where a certain dialect or koiné prevails, have some
competence in Standard Italian, even though it may seldom be used.

Robert Di Pietro has effectively described five linguistic stages of forms and
performances characterizing the Italian American language codes which function as markers in stages of ethnicity. These languages include Standard Italian
(or dialect) and English. Stages 1, 2, and 3 follow the Italian immigrant in
various steps of adjustment and acculturation as English is being acquired, and
the Italian koiné is being developed. Stage 4 applies mostly to the second
generation ethnic who may be a receptive bilingual only; stage 5 includes those
ethnics who have little or no receptive knowledge of the koiné and who speak
Standard Italian only if they have studied it in school. Individuals may move
through several stages in their lifetime or several generations may remain in the
same stage (Di Pietro 1976a: 214).

In the San Francisco Bay Area, the language of the Italian American is often
characterized by stretches of Standard Italian or dialect interspersed by the
following kinds of American English influence. The degree of this influence is
frequently an indicator of the stages of ethnicity identified by Di Pietro. The
variables determining the extent of their use include formal education (English
or Italian medium), length of residence in the USA, and individual tendencies
to accept or resist borrowing from English.

1. English LOANWORDS adapted MORPHOLOGICALLY and PHONOLOGICALLY, such
   as the nouns *la raída, lo sciáuro, il bisinísse, il troblo, il gioncáccio, la
   paipétta (ride, shower, business, trouble, junk, pipe)* and the verbs *drai-
   vare, frisare, pintare (drive, freeze, paint)*
2. Various types of LOANSHIFTS from English. Those promoted by interlingual similarity of sound and meaning are in distinct prevalence, such as
   *Scuola Alta, guardare bene, prendere vantaggio, carta cittadina, rendi-
   tare* (modeled on *High School, look well, take advantage, citizenship
   paper, rent*)
3. CODE-SWITCHES, frequently interjections, for some individuals almost a
   mannerism, displaying various degrees of phonetic adaptation, such as
   ainó, orráite, sciuro, ezzó (I know, all right, sure, that's all) or strings of
   English words, frequently unnoticed by the speaker

A few archaisms, such as *scudo* 'dollar,' are of particularly wide usage, persist-
ing even in the speech patterns of those who have become or remained proficient in Standard Italian.

PIDGINIZATION often appears as a transitional phenomenon in Italian American
communities, but there is no evidence of a stable English or Italian-based pidgin
maintaining itself in community use. Nevertheless, stereotypes of uneducated
Italian immigrants using a hybrid mixture of Italian and English persist in spite

of evidence from linguistic studies. Observations in the San Francisco Bay Area in the 1970s did not yield either an English- or an Italian-based PIDGIN, i.e. a hybrid merger of the two languages characterized by simplified grammar and mixed vocabulary. This situation is undoubtedly determined by the location, which receives a moderate but steady flow of speakers who, regardless of regions of provenience, are better educated and less underprivileged than in former years. In this connection, it must be observed that language accultura-tion today appears to be much less painful than in former years, since bilingual children can and do acquire English in school, and yet, as a result of the recent climate of acceptance for ethnic group identification, continue Italian at home. In the North End of Boston where 89 percent of the population is of Italian descent of first, second, and third generations, the dominant language spoken is English. Both monolingual and bilingual children identify themselves as Italian Americans and are requested "quite vigorously" by their parents to continue speaking Italian in the home in both parent–child and sibling–sibling interac-tions (Biondi 1975: 130).

Cases of pidginization have been reflected in the *Macchiette Coloniali* ('Co-lonial Skits') which delighted Italian immigrant audiences in the early part of the century. The creative aspects of the Italian American koiné, or English-based pidgin, dealing artistically with situations arising in practical life in the "melt-ing pot," are well discussed by Livingston (1918).

American Italian speech influenced by English has had its share of outraged purists, as well as amused observers. It has been characterized as *ristrettezza e grossolanitá* (a jargon still untutored and mechanical, limited and gross) (Pre-zzolini 1939) and "curious speech . . . peculiar patois of Little Italy" (Turano 1932). Luigi Barzini's amusing reference to the Biblical flavor of the New York expression *sciabolatori del Re Erode* 'the saber warriors of King Herod', a rendition of "shovelers of the railroads," is notorious among cultivated Italian Americans (Barzini 1930: 265).

A large number of such *americanismi* as they are called in Italy, have pene-trated the local speech of certain areas in Italy; these were introduced by Italian immigrants returning from the USA for either temporary or permanent resi-dence in Italy. Not infrequently, these loanwords have permanently entered the local lexicon and are used by Italians who have never been to the USA.

Maintenance and attitudes

Ascertaining, even on a modest scale, the attitudes and life experiences of Italian ethnics regarding their ancestral language is a difficult task, the results of which evidence ambiguities toward Standard Italian and English and Italian. Surveys by questionnaire in the southwestern Colorado coal-mining area and the San Francisco Bay Area illustrate some of the attitudes and life experiences which condition these ambiguities. The Colorado survey (Correa-Zoli 1977) was carried out in an area of approximately 3,000 dialect speakers, primarily second and third generation, with Calabrian, Sicilian, and Piedmontese dialects prevailing. These Italians claimed little knowledge of Standard Italian, reported dialects were used to a limited extent in homes, and traveling was mostly from Colorado to Italy. Apparently, interest in maintaining the Italian language has grown weaker in recent years, but the reverse is true regarding the preservation of the culture and traditions. In this community, use of the ancestral language was not felt to be a necessary component of ethnic identity.

To the questions: "With whom/on which occasions did you speak dialect or Standard Italian as you were growing up in the USA?" "Has this situation changed today?" Colorado informants' responses included the following.

Most of the old timers who spoke Italian and did not understand the English language are now deceased. It is very unfortunate that this has happened.

I wish I had paid more attention as a child.

Most of the people whom I spoke with have passed away and left this part of the country.

Everyone understands English.

In the San Francisco Bay Area, 149 replies to the same two questions on language use noted above were received, mostly from second and third generation ethnics of Italian or mixed parentage (only thirty-one were foreign-born) (Correa-Zoli 1978)

Even with relatives who are living mainly in Italy, I try to use the Standard Italian and not the dialect [Genoese]. I try to use very little dialect now. We visit the relatives in Italy about every two to three years.

Do not use Italian anymore. Can understand but I do not speak it.

Most people with whom I conversed in dialect have either adopted the English language, died, or speak with a mixture of both English and dialect [Sicilian]. Also, I moved away from the contacts.

Due to continued study of Standard Italian, I have become more fluent and use it with more Italian-speaking friends.

No, I should learn in order to understand better and be able to communicate more fully with family and not lose my cultural heritage.

No, my parents are Italian, and they wanted me to learn, and I'm glad I did. Now I can communicate with many people. My parents encouraged me also to learn English so I could speak right.

Yes, I did and I still do, for knowledge, for business, for family, for honor of ancestry.

Further data on receptive and/or productive knowledge of Standard Italian or dialects yielded by the San Francisco Bay study (total 149)are given in Table 11.2.

Table 11.2. *Use of Italian in San Francisco Bay Area, 1978*

No knowledge whatsoever	24
Comprehend	125
Dialect only	33
Standard only	30
Both	62
Speak	91
Dialect only	42
Standard only	29
Both	20
Receptive *only* in either standard or dialect (i.e. reply in English).	34

The dialect speakers claiming not to understand Standard Italian were frequently second or third generation offspring who heard the dialect at home and had not had formal language study. The number of those informants who could speak only dialect included six elderly first generation immigrants. (The dialects used are shown in Table 11.3.) Those who claimed no knowledge of either standard or dialect included many third generation offspring in their twenties living in households where Italian was seldom or never spoken. Nearly all of those who were proficient in Standard Italian, both receptively and productively, had received some type of formal schooling either in the USA or in Italy, although a few were the offspring of Tuscan-speaking parents who considered this variety of Italian to be a form of the standard language.

Proficiency as self-evaluated by these individuals seemed to be fairly equally divided between "good" and "fair." Eleven estimated their capacity as "excellent."

Speech settings involving Standard Italian or dialects were primarily at home with the immediate family, or with other relatives, and friends. Other settings given, in order of decreasing frequency, were: with Italian monolingual visitors to the USA, shopkeepers, professionals, and church members. The number of second and third generation ethnics in whose homes Italian was used as they were growing up was almost four times as large as the number exposed to the language infrequently or not at all. Specific reasons for the decrease in the frequency and extent of communication in Italian since their childhood were the adoption of English by parents and grandparents, and/or death of these and other relatives. The single most frequent cause of increase was the intervention of formal instruction in Standard Italian which permitted them to interact with more friends, Italian visitors to the USA, customers and clients, and professionals.

The survey did not reveal a widespread use of Italian media. Only about 18 percent availed themselves of Italian media in each category here reported;

Table 11.3. *Italian dialects used in San Francisco Bay Area, 1978*

Northern Italy	46
Liguria (Genoa)	26
Trentino-Alto Adige	4
Friulia	2
Lombardy	6
Piedmont	8
Central Italy	10
Tuscany	5
Marches	5
Southern Italy	37
Naples	4
Apulia	12
Basilicata	2
Calabria	7
Sicily	12

frequently the same persons gave an affirmative answer to several categories. Preferences in decreasing order were: Italian films, Italian American television programs, Italian newspapers, Italian magazines, Italian radio, Italian books. (See below for discussion of the Italian American media.)

Comments were received from 132 informants, some brief and some detailed, regarding family attitudes toward using Italian as they were growing up. A weakening of interest in maintenance is clearly displayed by third generation parents.

Second Generation		*Third Generation*	
Encouraged	74%	Encouraged	48%
Neutral	26%	Neutral	42%
Discouraged	–	Discouraged	10%

Further elucidation on attitudes was revealed by answers to the question: "As you were growing up, were you ever given any reasons why you should/should not speak Italian or learn Italian?" Reasons for maintenance by the second or third generations were, in order of decreasing frequency:

1. interpersonal relationships with friends and relatives either here or in Italy. Immediate family closeness, immediate family ties, grandparents in particular;
2. culture and heritage;
3. to learn Standard Italian after having been exposed only to dialect;
4. desirability of being bilingual.

Reasons for lack of maintenance, also ranked by frequency, were:

1. to learn English quickly and be Americans;
2. to please and help parents who wanted to learn English themselves;
3. to avoid feelings of discrimination and embarrassment from non-Italian peers.

A third generation 25-year old women summed up three generations of attitudes:

My parents' generation were told to speak English at home in order for their parents to learn and understand spoken English. My father learned English in school and was completely bilingual [Genovese/English] up until High School. My mother understands the Italian dialect, speaks a few words, tutored by grandfather, but was never fluent. My parents' generation grew up "undercover" so to speak, trying to discourage any traces of their heritage, poverty, ignorance, whatever became associated with their nationality. I and those of my generation have been made aware of this and are progressing and successfully reversing this situation.

Tofani (1951) pointed out that the third generation Italian Americans favored maintenance of their language; he concluded the Italian language in the USA was "far from dead" in spite of the fact that Italians did not maintain separate schools for the propagation of their language as did some other groups.

It appears that maintenance of Italian has taken place primarily in the home environment, while the value of formal instruction in Standard Italian is being increasingly recognized by Italian Americans, frequently of the third generation. To understand this current phenomenon, it is necessary to consider the interest in Italian ethnicity which is gaining momentum and to examine the role and extent of Italian language instruction in the USA.

Italian ethnicity and language instruction

The 1960s and 1970s witnessed a rediscovery of an Italian American identity derived in part from the rising consciousness of other ethnocultural groups. The Italian Americans who traditionally prided themselves on their rapid assimilation into the "melting pot" began to re-evaluate their American experience and their ethnic identity.

A number of books by eminent scholars focused on the Italian American experience in the United States. Earlier literature, including Italian American fiction, was re-evaluated (e.g. Basile Green 1974). Fictional accounts of Italian American life, most notably and notoriously Mario Puzo's *The Godfather*, appeared on national best-seller lists. New periodicals such as *Italian-American Identity*, a monthly magazine focusing on Italy as well as Italians in the USA, and *Italian Americana*, a journal carrying articles on history and sociology, book and motion picture reviews, short stories, poems and memoirs, appeared in the 1970s. The role of Italian Americans in politics was also marked by the *Washington Newsletter*, issued in January, 1977 by the Italian American Foundation of Washington, DC.

Italian American media, which had generally been declining over the years, are showing some evidence of a revival. In the late 1970s, *Il Progresso Italo-Americano* of New York was the only daily newspaper. Independent weeklies were found in California (Los Angeles, San Francisco), Connecticut (Middletown), Michigan (Madison Heights), New Jersey (Paterson), Rhode Island (Providence). Many others appeared less frequently, and included a number of publications covering religion, fraternal organizations, politics, education, labor, and Italian culture. The case of San Francisco might illustrate the rather typical rise, fall, and revival of the Italian press. In 1965, *L'Italia,* printed mainly in Italian, ceased publication after seventy-five years of existence. It had served the dual purpose of Americanization of immigrants as well as affirming cultural heritage and giving news of the mother country. In 1966, prompted by the void felt by the Italian American community in San Francisco, *L'Eco d'Italia* appeared and still exists, the second of the Italian language weeklies on the West coast, the other one being *L'Italo-Americano* of Los Angeles. The San Francisco weekly reaches first, second, and third generation Italian Americans throughout California, Nevada, Oregon, and Washington (Sodo 1977).

Radio audiences have declined as well, although Italian remains among the big five in terms of stations and listeners, the others being Spanish, Polish, French, and German, in decreasing order. There have been sharp increases in television viewing since 1950. There are three major locations for Italian American television programs in the USA: New York, Chicago, and San Francisco. The last will serve, once again, as an illustration of the significant rise in popularity of the medium. There are four separate weekly Italian television programs in San Francisco. The Italian language is used in two hours of programming dedicated to Italian movies, drama, opera, music, religious presentations, news from Italy, and contributions of Italian Americans in the USA. Commercial advertising in Italian by local merchants and firms occupies a portion of the time.

The American Italian Historical Association (AIHA) was founded in New York in 1966 by historians, educators, sociologists, and interested laymen whose aim was to "remedy the serious lack of accurate knowledge concerning the history of the Italians in the U.S." AIHA members are found in New York State, the mid-Atlantic states, New England, and the Midwest. A Western Chapter was established in San Francisco in 1974.

Increased interest in an Italian ethnic identity is also verifiable in higher education students' organizations, attracting many nonethnics interested in the Italian culture. Names of students' organizations such as Il Quartiere Italiano and The Italian Folk Arts Group (California State University, Hayward) are revealing. Stanford University's Casa Italiana came into existence in September, 1976.

Against this renaissance of interest in Italian ethnicity among Italian Americans is their puzzling indifference toward the Italian language as a research topic. A compilation of doctoral dissertations on the Italian American experience completed in U.S. and Canadian universities from 1908 to 1974 reveals a total of only ten dissertations with linguistic or partially linguistic content, out of a total of 148 (Pane 1975). Published books (Kessler 1971; Biondi 1975; Di Pietro 1976a) and scholarly articles (Fishman 1966; Di Pietro 1976b) are equally scarce.

It is tempting to find parallels between this apparent scholarly neglect and the invisible or "status-less" situation of Italian language maintenance in the USA. Are Italian Americans linguistically apathetic? Fishman et al. (1966) believe this to be the case, at least with respect to organized efforts under their own auspices and control. Traditional regionalism, strong identifications with family, people, foods, and celebrations and less with cultural and nationalistic aspects are cited as causes for this apathy.

It is also reasonable to assume that for many Italians, acculturation effectively wiped out the ancestral language, since the society at large gave no rewards for Italian–English bilingualism. Some of those who felt bilingualism desirable perhaps turned to another more culturally prestigious language such as French, or a more "practical" one such as Spanish. This is probably yet another aspect of the same acculturative process by which some Italians anglicized or gallicized their Italian surnames so that *Lorenzi, Martini,* and *Olivieri* became *Lawrence, Martin,* and *Oliver,* and *Esposito, Passalacqua,* and *Di Michele* became *Esposite, Passalacque,* and *Dichele* (Fucilla 1949). Being an Italian immigrant in the USA has been neither glamorous nor easy. Yet, all evidence currently available points to the fact that the Italian language was not wiped out, but that it remained ethnically infused, in homes and Italian neighborhoods scattered throughout the country.

From 1959 to 1968, reports on the teaching of modern foreign languages showed consistently wide gaps between the places held by Spanish, French, German, and Russian on the one hand, and Italian on the other. Italian decreased, or at best, had very modest increases at all levels, from elementary to college, while other languages were growing rapidly in the aftermath of the National Defense Education Act, which gave governmental financial support to the teaching of foreign languages. In the fall of 1961, Italian experienced a 12 percent rate of increase against a total increase in language study of 13.2 percent; still, the representation of Italian among the other major languages was only 1.9 percent. Causes cited for this lag include: the longstanding prestige of Spanish, French, and German; administrative indifference and opposition; prejudiced advice of counselors who refer to Italian as having "poor market value"; persistent immigrant status; and teacher apathy.

However, current efforts of Italian American organizations, which are culturally, if not linguistically, attached to their country of origin may help turn this trend. Evidence points to a steady if nondramatic growth for all levels of instruction of Italian, during the late 1960s and early 1970s when all modern languages, with the exception of Spanish, experienced various degrees of decline. From 1969 to 1971, Spanish and Italian stood alone in showing a significant rate of growth in higher education, at both the undergraduate and graduate levels (Lange 1972). The number of higher education institutions offering

Table 11.4. *Italian Bilingual Education Programs in New York*

	1973–4	1974–5	1975–6
Districts	7	6	9
Elementary schools	9	17	21
Junior high schools	5	8	8
High schools	–	1	3

Source: Valenti 1976: 6.

Italian in California, for example, more than doubled, from twenty-three in 1965 to fifty-two in 1968, according to the American Association of Teachers of Italian (*Britannica Review* 1968). A detailed report in 1970 on the status of Italian Studies in the USA and Canada indicated a growth from 304 institutions of higher learning offering Italian in 1960 to 519 in 1969 (Pane 1970). In the late 1970s, the Foreign Language Association of Northern California reported that nationwide enrollment in Italian in grades 7–12 increased more than 50 percent from 1968 to 1974; the increase in the West was 83 percent in the six-year period (AIHA March, 1977). In addition, adult education courses in Italian were more numerous, and there had been a marked increase in the number of books directed to the learner of Italian language and Italian culture.

The San Francisco Bay Area has seen the steady growth and expansion of a Saturday school, the Scuola di Lingua e Cultura Italiana, in South San Francisco. A nonprofit organization founded in 1970, the school has offered the Italian American communities of the Bay Area instruction for children and adults in the Italian language, history, culture, cooking, and regional folk-dancing, and has employed an average of eleven teachers each year.

Italian Bilingual Education programs in New York date from 1973. Table 11.4 indicates their expansion. Until 1976, Chicago had one Italian Bilingual Program; since then, seven additional ones have been implemented, and three more were planned in 1977.

What can we conclude from all these data? Is the Italian language finally achieving a place among the major foreign languages taught in American schools? Fishman et al. (1966) predicted that Italian would eventually "arrive" dignified and appreciated as the other three major foreign languages have been, but at the price of increasing de-ethnicization. As the self-image of the former immigrant becomes more positive, others as well as Italian Americans them-selves, may study Italian and see it as critical to an understanding of the millions of people of this descent whose ethnic identity has not totally dis-appeared, as well as to the more effective interaction with Italy and its people of today. Predictions and considerations, however, do not alter the facts that the gains made in formal instruction in Italian are still too modest to fill the gap existing between it and the three major languages. Paradoxically, scholarly interest in Italian ethnicity has not taken account of language maintenance even though Italian, or its dialects, is the third most widely spoken "other language" in U.S. homes, and Italian American communities and organizations have lent only weak support to educators at all levels. The recent expansion of formal instruction in Italian in the USA, except possibly in the New York area, must be interpreted as generated by the equally recent ethnicity interest of Italian Americans rather than by organized efforts on behalf of the language *per se*.

FURTHER READING

Among the many excellent works on Italian Americans, four deserve to be singled out for mention. Gambino 1974 is a very readable, full-scale study, offering a blueprint for "creative ethnicity." The author is the chairman of Italian American Studies at Queens College, New York, the first such program to be established. Rolle 1968 treats Italian immigrant experiences in the American West. Vecoli 1978 offers an extremely compact and informative overview of the Italian experience in the USA; Cordasco 1974 is a comprehensive bibliographical guide.

The academic journal *Italian Americana*, mentioned in the chapter, appears twice a year under the co-sponsorship of Queens College and the State University of New York at Buffalo. It covers all aspects of Italian participation in American culture, both historical and contemporary. Two newsletters provide current information on Italian American activities nationwide: the *Newsletter* of the American Italian Historical Association (AIHA), issued at the University of Florida, Gainesville, and the *Washington Newsletter* of the Italian American Foundation in Washington, DC.

There are fewer publications on the language of Italian Americans. A valuable early study, Vaughn 1926a,b gives precise information on Italian dialects in the USA, but it is now outdated. The doctoral dissertations of von Raffler Engel 1953 on Italian American bilingualism and Correa-Zoli 1970 on the Italian of San Francisco remain unpublished. Von Raffler Engel 1961 is a useful short article. Probably the best place to start for contemporary information on American Italian are articles published by Di Pietro 1976a,b, 1977 and Correa-Zoli 1973, 1974. Di Pietro 1976a is perhaps the most valuable of these. Biondi 1975, on the sociolinguistic acculturation of the Italian American child, has broader interest than the title suggests.

On the place of Italian in American education, Fucilla 1975 gives a recent historical perspective on the teaching of Italian, and Valenti 1976 provides useful information on the establishment of Italian bilingual education in New York.

12

French and German: a comparative study

GLENN G. GILBERT

The French and German languages have played a long and important role in the history of the United States. In this chapter I propose to treat the two languages together so as to highlight their common historical development and future prospects in this country. The main focus will be on patterns of immigration, the location of areas of concentrated settlement with substantial language retention, and the analysis of enrollment trends both in BILINGUAL EDUCATION and in the teaching of French and German as foreign languages to English-speaking students.

French and German immigration

The vast majority of immigrants who came to the United States from French- and German-speaking parts of Europe and from French Canada spoke primarily a regional or local DIALECT (a "lower" or L FORM of the language) that differed substantially from Standard French and Standard German (the "higher" or H FORM of the language). At the time emigration to America began, France had been a highly centralized country for many centuries and had a standard form of the language based on the speech of Paris. Germany was split into numerous competing territories and principalities; but it, too, possessed considerable historical and cultural unity and had a standard language which represented a compromise among regional dialects. Both France and Germany made use of H languages occupying similar sociological positions. The H forms were used in the domains of government, religion, education, and interregional trade. The L dialects were reserved for family, friendship, work, and local trade. During most of the period of emigration, only the minority of adults who could read and write had even a passing acquaintance with the H form of their language. The majority of emigrants used L dialects only.

Surprisingly little is known about the exact origins of the immigrants. Estimates for the year 1790 show that there were about 17,600 persons with French surnames and 176,400 persons with German surnames in the United States. This represents, respectively, 0.6 percent and 5.6 percent of the total population.

The Germans were highly concentrated in southeastern Pennsylvania where they made up 26.1 percent of the population (based on an estimated 110,000

Table 12.1. *Immigrants to the USA likely to have been speakers of French or German, 1820–1975, listed by country of last residence*

Country	Number of immigrants to the USA (000s)
France	742
Canada	4,048[a]
Belgium	201
Switzerland	346
Germany	6,954
Austria and Hungary	4,312
Poland	503
Czechoslovakia	136

[a] Of which an estimated one-third (1,349) were French Canadian.
Source: U.S. Bureau of the Census, 1976. The figures for French- versus English-speaking Canadians are estimated from the U.S. Census reports 1890–1950, when these groups were distinguished.

persons with German surnames). The Pennsylvania German group has been much better investigated than most, and historical records show that most of the immigrants were from the Palatinate, Baden, Württemberg, and Switzerland. There were also German settlers in New Jersey, Maryland, Virginia, and North Carolina, but all of these states combined had scarcely one-half of Pennsylvania alone. All other states had insignificant numbers.

Although French help was essential in the founding of the United States, and its virtual gift twenty years later of the Louisiana Territory was hardly less valuable, there were very few actual immigrants from France in colonial or early republican times. The census of 1790 indicates that only in New Jersey did they form as much as 2 percent of the population (based on 3,560 people with French surnames). There were a few in South Carolina and in the band of states stretching from Virginia to New York, but the numbers involved were very small. The proportion of Protestants (Huguenots) among them was high, and they were rapidly absorbed.

In the nineteenth and twentieth centuries, the number of German immigrants far exceeded the French (see Table 12.1). Most of the immigrants from Belgium and Switzerland were not French-speaking; on the other hand, the number of German (and Yiddish) speakers from Switzerland, Austria, Czechoslovakia, Poland, and further east was substantial.

The acquisition of Louisiana in 1803 did swell the numbers of French speakers to some extent. The census of 1810 shows the future state of Louisiana with 77,000 inhabitants; Mississippi had 31,000, Missouri 20,000, and Illinois 12,000 (all figures rounded to the nearest thousand). The proportion of those who were French-speaking is unknown, although one estimate places the number of French speakers in all of Louisiana in 1803 at 20,000 (Abernethy 1961: 253). This figure is most likely too low.

Most French spoken in Louisiana today (the 1970 census lists 572,262 persons of French mother tongue) is either "Cajun," a type of French introduced after 1755 from Canada, or Louisiana "Créole," a descendant of the plantation pidgin and creole French used by Black slaves (and by Whites) in the French Caribbean islands (see Chapter 4). The census of 1970 reports only 2,869 non-White speakers of French, a ridiculously low figure. It is said that both types of French are spoken by both races, but there is little reliable information on actual language use.

When settlers from different regional dialects mingle in a colonial setting, the distinguishing features of the dialects tend to be modified or lost, so that the resulting variety of the language is "leveled out," and this happened to some extent in Canadian French, which thus differs systematically from both H and L varieties of European French. The French language in Upper Louisiana (i.e. present-day Missouri and Illinois) is of predominantly Canadian extraction, representing a LEVELED COLONIAL LANGUAGE whose sources were in the northern and north-central dialects of the French provinces of Normandie, Perche, Picardie, Maine, Brie, Champagne, Beauce, and l'Ile-de-France.

It is this type of French which immigration statistics show to have been predominant in the United States. Basing ourselves on the statistics of Table 12.1, if we assume that there were 50,000 French-speaking immigrants from Belgium and Switzerland (and probably even this figure is too high), it will be seen that the French Canadians outnumber the European French by almost two to one. In addition, the French Canadians tend to be concentrated in New England and in other states bordering Québec or the Great Lakes, which heightens their impact in those areas (see Figure 12.2 below).

The immigrants from Germany are even more difficult to localize, both with regard to their origins and their ultimate destination. On the question of origins, John Hawgood, the gifted British historian of the German element in the United States, reaches the conclusion:

It is true that certain regional trends can be discerned. Thus up to 1848 and to a lesser extent up to 1866, emigration tended to be more brisk from western and southern Germany (and particularly from the south-western corner) than (if the Polish areas can be excepted) from the east and north-east . . . it may be generally claimed that those parts of the United States which received Germans in large numbers, received them from all parts of Germany. We do not have mainly Prussians in New York, mainly Bavarians in Wisconsin, mainly Rhinelanders in Missouri, mainly Hessians in Texas, mainly Pomeranians in California, or mainly Hamburgers in Chicago; rather do we find a *gemischtes Aufschnitt* in each. (Hawgood 1940: 74–75)

Unfortunately, Hawgood bases his claims more on shrewd guesswork than on actual immigration statistics. More exact information can be gleaned from the pages of Heinz Kloss' monumental *Atlas of 19th and Early 20th Century German-American Settlements,* where there is mention of additional unanalyzed source material:

In 1920, all foreign-born persons who listed as their country of birth a country which had been affected by the boundaries set up by the Treaty of Versailles were asked for their precise place of birth. This made it possible to ascertain, for instance, the number of people born in Alsace-Lorraine, Danzig, and the Saar area. If these lists have been preserved (which is extremely doubtful), they would provide unique information on the place of origin of those born in the Reich. (Kloss 1974: 5, n. 24)

A counterexample to Hawgood's view is found in recent studies of immigration to Central Texas, a favorite destination of German immigrants in the two decades before the Civil War (Gilbert 1977). The immigration was *gemischt*, to be sure, but then again there were almost no settlers from southern Germany – Austria, Bavaria, and most importantly, Switzerland, Baden, and Württemberg. The leveled colonial language which developed in Texas consequently turned out very differently from Pennsylvania German.

Language in German and French communities

A noted feature of Pennsylvania German grammar is the merger of the nominative and accusative cases. (Standard German has a nominative, accusative, dative, and genitive.) Texas German, on the other hand, has merged the dative and accusative, a process which, interestingly, parallels a similar change in Old English some 1,200 years ago. Still, the effect on language structure of the grammatical simplification in both forms of American German has been very much the same. During a sojourn of one, two, or three centuries in America, these varieties of American German have undergone grammatical changes similar to those taking place in some European dialects of German. Of even greater interest, the changes have been of roughly the same type and in the same direction as those experienced by Old English in the 700 years from its beginnings in England to the close of the Old English period (*c.* 1066). The same process has simply been speeded up.

Immigration, foreign stock, and MOTHER-TONGUE statistics all attest to the massive presence of the German ethnic element in the United States. Even so, the language never rose above what could be called an "immigrant status," politically subordinate to English. True, many frontiersmen were German-speaking and often occupied virgin lands to the west of the Anglo-Americans, but the settlements were invariably laid out under the political dominance of Great Britain and later of the English-speaking United States. Neither Prussia nor any of the other German states attempted to establish a colonial empire in North America. The nearest thing to a German "colony" was southeastern Pennsylvania and adjoining areas; but this was peopled by religious dissenters. They were outcasts from the home country, not colonial representatives of it.

Because of their initial political subordination, the Germans were psychologically prepared – sooner or later – to accept English in place of Standard German as their H language. During the one-hundred-year period from 1820 to 1920, the bulwarks of the German language H, the church, schools, and press, were progressively converted to an English language H. This tendency, although hastened by World Wars I and II, had been present in germinal form from the earliest days of settlement. People might have dreamed of a New Germany on American shores, but no one really expected it to happen.

Table 12.2. *Increase of French speakers in Québec and Louisiana, and of German speakers in Pennsylvania, 1790–1970 (population figures in 000s)*

	Québec	Louisiana	Pennsylvania
Total population in 1790[a]	128	77	434
Estimated number of French or German speakers	128	77	110
Percentage of ethnic speakers in total population	100	100	25.3
Total population in 1970[b]	6,028	3,641	11,794
Ethnic mother-tongue speakers (natives of natives only)	4,867	559	269[c]
Percentage of the latter in total population	80.7	15.4	2.3
Percentage increase of speakers 1790–1970	3,802	726	245

[a] The figure for Louisiana is from 1810; in Québec, only Catholics are included in the figure given.
[b] For Québec, 1971.
[c] Includes "Dutch."
Sources: United States Censuses of Population; Henripin 1968: 5.

In contrast with German, French enjoyed a much stronger position, at least initially. French-speaking settlers arrived under the auspices and protection of an official plan of French colonization designed to establish a New France in North America. The colonists were reliably Catholic and often deeply conservative. Progressives, liberals, and Huguenots who wanted to go to America were obliged to emigrate to the English-speaking colonies, where they were quickly absorbed. Political and religious conservatives were steered to New France.

Even after the loss of Canada to the British, and Lower and Upper Louisiana to the Americans, the Standard French language (in its Canadian-Louisiana form) continued to fulfill the н function in religion and education. Memories of New France died hard.

Québec, Louisiana, and Pennsylvania form a kind of continuum of ethnic language retention. Table 12.2 indicates the percentage of absolute increase of French or German speakers from the end of the eighteenth century to 1970. Even if we inflate the number of French speakers in Louisiana in 1810 by assuming that all 77,000 inhabitants (of whom 42,000 were Black) spoke the language – which has the effect of lowering the percentage of increase from 1810 to 1970 – French in Louisiana has obviously been maintained far better than German in Pennsylvania.

The historical and attitudinal factors leading to these disparities of retention deserve further detailed study. Just what are the social and linguistic determinants that lead to a Québec-like outcome as opposed to, say, the language situation in Pennsylvania or Louisiana? In late colonial and early republican times, contemporary observers could have easily predicted eventual nonassimilation and separatist tendencies in the latter two areas. Indeed, numerous writers and politicians voiced deep misgivings concerning the large German immigration to Pennsylvania and the annexation of Lower Louisiana, but the formation of separatist enclaves did not happen.

French and German in classrooms

In addition to their role as ethnic languages, French and German have, of course, been important as courses of study by Anglo-Americans, but only in the past century. The Classical languages took precedence over modern languages in all levels of education until after the Civil War. By 1883, there was enough support for modern language teaching for the Modern Language Association to be formed. Initially, the Association adopted the methods and objectives of the Classicists, emphasizing the discipline of the mind such study provided and stressing grammatical analysis and the translation of prestigious literature in a two-year course. In addition to changing emphases in education on modern language study, the ups and downs of instruction in French and German have been closely linked with such factors as: the attitude of Americans toward France and Germany, the real or imagined value of the language to the learner or the society, and the numerical strength and concentration of French and German ethnic groups in the United States.

France was a deadly enemy in the middle 1700s; consequently, despite its obvious value and the secret admiration of many, the language was officially treated like the plague, especially in New England. Germany came to occupy a similar position after 1917, and enrollment figures plummeted incredibly. In the eighteenth century, French made a healthy recovery after France's assistance to the Colonies during the Revolutionary War, something which German in the twentieth century has not been able to do. Viewed over the long run, German's demise in the last sixty years has coincided with the decline of French as well. Both languages are in serious trouble at all levels of education.

Table 12.3 indicates the wild variation in enrollments in these languages over the last eighty-five years in grades 9–12 in American high schools. The statistics of declining German instruction in the years 1915–22, and thereafter, are especially dramatic. The cultural loss to the United States was incalculable, and a trend was set in motion which worked against *all* foreign language study, the principal victim being French. The concerted and speedy action to drop German, which was taken in unison by independent local and state school boards across the country, is truly frightening. An educational decree issued from a centralized dictatorship could have hardly done it better. Worse still, the damage has not been repaired to any significant degree in the ensuing sixty years. The only winner in the debacle seems to have been Spanish, but it, too, is now standing on shaky ground (high school Spanish enrollments, grades 7–12, have declined since 1970). If it were not for the continuing massive influx of Puerto Ricans and Mexicans into the continental United States, we would already have

Table 12.3 *Enrollments in modern foreign languages with percentages of total high school population, grades 9–12, 1890–1974*

Year	Total HS pop. (9–12)	MFL enrollment	% MFLs in HS pop.	French enrollment	% French in HS pop.	German enrollment	% German in HS pop.
1890	202,963	33,089	16.3	11,772	5.8	21,311	10.5
1895	350,099	62,685	17.9	22,757	6.5	39,911	11.4
1900	519,251	114,765	22.1	40,503	7.8	74,252	14.3
1905	679,702	199,153	29.3	61,852	9.1	137,299	20.2
1910	915,061	313,890	34.3	90,591	9.9	216,869	23.7
1915	1,328,984	477,110	35.9	116,957	8.8	324,272	24.4
1922	2,230,000	611,025	27.4	345,650	15.5	13,385	0.6
1928	3,354,473	845,338	25.2	469,626	14.0	60,381	1.8
1934	5,620,626	1,096,022	19.5	612,648	10.9	134,897	2.4
1948	5,399,452	740,800	13.7	253,781	4.7	43,195	0.8
1958	7,897,232	1,298,687	16.4	479,769	6.1	93,054	1.2
1959	8,155,573	1,556,745	19.1	602,366	7.4	123,312	1.5
1960	8,649,495	1,867,358	21.7	744,404	8.6	150,764	1.7
1961	9,246,925	2,192,207	23.7	908,082	9.8	184,820	2.0
1962	9,891,185	2,391,206	24.2	996,771	10.1	211,676	2.1
1963	10,750,081	2,781,737	25.9	1,130,987	10.5	260,488	2.4
1964	11,075,343	2,898,665	26.2	1,194,991	10.8	285,613	2.6
1965	11,611,197	3,067,613	26.4	1,251,373	10.8	328,028	2.8
1968	12,721,352	3,518,413	27.7	1,328,100	10.4	423,196	3.3
1970[a]	18,406,617	4,286,570	23.3	1,562,598	8.5	462,407	2.5
1974[a]	20,989,804	3,853,265	18.4	1,253,696	5.8	441,367	2.1

[a] For 1970 and 1974, the "total high school population" includes grades 7 and 8. Although this obviously increases the absolute figures, the percentages are roughly the same, e.g. for 1968, total public high school enrollment in grades 7–12 was 17,543,239, total modern foreign language enrollment was 4,357,786 (24.8 percent), French enrollment was 1,685,822 (9.6 percent), and German enrollment was 475,951 (2.7 percent). Clearly, the trend, 1968–74, is strongly downward in all categories.

Sources: Childers 1959–61: 33; Kant 1970: 403; Foreign Language Annals 1977: 116.

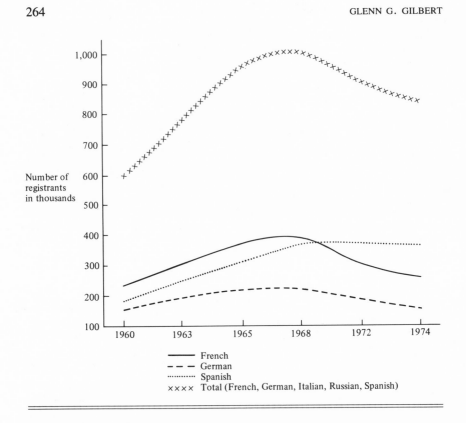

Year	French	German	Spanish	Total registrations for the five most commonly taught modern foreign languages (French, German, Italian, Russian, Spanish)
1960	228,813	146,110	178,689	595,324
1963	302,226	182,609	246,673	781,920
1965	371,625	213,901	310,340	952,496
1968	388,096	216,263	364,870	1,040,284
1972	293,084	177,062	364,531	904,398
1974	253,137	152,139	362,151	832,077
Percentage change 1960–74 (1960 is 100.0)	110.6	104.1	202.7	139.8

Figure 12.1. Foreign language registrations in U.S. institutions of higher education, 1960–74. Combined totals for junior colleges, four-year colleges, graduate schools. *Sources:* Kant 1969; Foreign Language Annals 1976: 90

achieved the dubious distinction of being the largest block of one-language speakers in the world, with various dying ethnic languages forming only tiny exceptions in an otherwise uniform sea of monolingualism.

The increasing relative strength of Spanish in secondary education is now making deep inroads into French and German instruction at the junior college, four-year college, and graduate levels. Figure 12.1 indicates the seriousness of recent declines (1968–74) in French enrollments in higher education. Since total college enrollment has increased rapidly in the period 1960–74, the percentage of students in the total student body studying French and German has actually declined, German very rapidly, French on a more shallow curve. Only Spanish has held its own.

Public and parochial bilingual schools, where German, French, and other languages were a medium (or co-medium), as well as an object of instruction, were once quite widespread in the United States. French/(English) schools once flourished in Louisiana and New England, German/(English) schools in various locations in Pennsylvania, Cincinnati, Baltimore, Indianapolis, and many other cities (see Chapter 1). The German/English bilingual school system reached such proportions, both in quantity and quality, that it came to exert a pervasive influence on the methods and goals of *all* American education. By the end of the nineteenth century, Germany and the German language were considered by many Americans to be foremost in education in the world, from kindergarten through graduate school.

The intensity and location of the non-English medium schools is a direct reflection of attempts to retain Standard German and Standard French in their H function and to retard or totally prevent English from replacing them. Even before 1917, however, it had become clear to many ethnics that these schools, by temporarily slowing the advance of English in the H function, were simply making easier the transition to ultimate English monolingualism. Any lingering hope of creating and maintaining a stable German/English or French/English bilingualism vanished when all bilingual schools were abolished in the hysteria of 1917–18.

The unconstitutionality of the English-medium laws was later confirmed by the Supreme Court in decisions handed down in 1923 and 1927. But the damage was such that public bilingual schooling was not attempted again until 1963 (Spanish/English in the Coral Way School, Miami, Florida).

The BILINGUAL EDUCATION ACT, passed by Congress on January 2, 1968, went far beyond any previous national language legislation by providing federal sanction and funding for the use of ethnic languages as a medium of education, especially at the elementary school level. In 80–90 percent of the projects funded in the first two years of the program, the ethnic language involved was Spanish. The comprehensive survey made by Andersson and Boyer (1970) showed only eight French/English programs as of 1970: two in Maine, one in New Hampshire, one in Massachusetts, two in New York City, one in Washington, DC, and one in San Francisco. (Significantly, none was in Louisiana.) This represented 6 percent of all programs for 1968–70. Ironically, there was none at all in Ger-

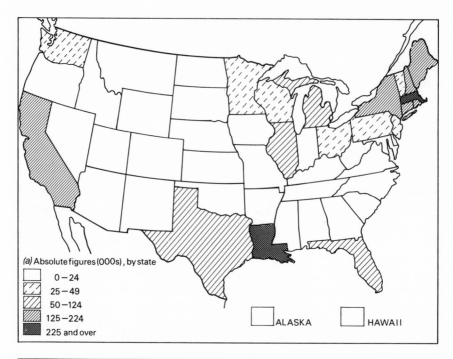

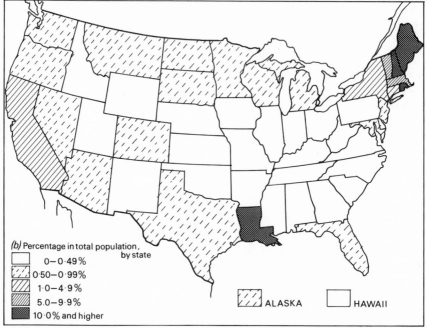

Figure 12.2. Mother-tongue speakers of French 1970. Combined foreign born, foreign stock, natives of natives. *Source:* United States Census 1970

man/English, even though three-quarters of a century earlier, German bilingual programs far outnumbered all other languages combined.

In 1973–74, a tabulation of the languages involved in Title VII bilingual/ bicultural education projects showed Spanish with 124,275 students enrolled, equivalent to 96.5 percent of all students in the Title VII program. Although there were still no projects for German, French programs existed for 2,628 students (2 percent of the total). There were also 1,473 students enrolled in trilingual French/Spanish/English programs.

Although *any* bilingual French/English programs may be counted as better than none, clearly the effort up to now has been hardly more than token. Resistance to non-English medium education in Louisiana has been notable; in New England, less so. As of 1974, Louisiana had three projects with 1,355 French-speaking students (see Chapter 4); Maine, two projects with 761 French-speaking students; New Hampshire, one project with 220 students; and New York City, four projects with approximately 292 French-speaking (creole) students. Interestingly, the latter are almost exclusively from Haiti, an important new source for French speakers, where a variety of Standard French is the H language and the French-based Haitian Creole is the ordinary spoken L variety. However, only a small fraction of Haitian children living in New York City have been reached by these programs.

German and French are still spoken over wide areas of the United States by Americans of native parentage, although the actual numbers involved are generally small. Figure 12.2 maps the location of French mother-tongue speakers by state, in absolute numbers and as a percentage of total state population. Figure 12.3 gives the same information for German. As expected, French shows its greatest strength in Louisiana (including an extension of the Louisiana enclave in southeastern Texas) and New England. The percentage map reveals further traces of French in all states bordering Canada (except Idaho), the Middle Atlantic states (except Pennsylvania and Delaware), Florida, the Southwest, and the West Coast.

German is more uniformly distributed, with focal areas, in absolute numbers, north of the Mason–Dixon Line and the Ohio River (except New England), the Midwest, Texas, and California. On Figure 12.3, the focus shifts to Wisconsin, the Dakotas, and surrounding states, much of the area consisting of ranches and dry farming with a currently declining population. Moderate traces of German are indicated in almost all the other states as well, with the exception of the Southeast. This attests to the geographic spread and great numerical strength of the German element in the American population.

If we project to 1975 the figures that Faust calculated for 1900 (Faust 1927: II, 27), the German ethnic heritage group would today number around 50 million persons, or 27 percent of the White population. This estimate, which is probably not too far off the mark, gives an idea of the enormous human contribution made by Germany to the United States. Only the English/Scottish/Irish component was greater, and that by a ratio of 34 to 18.

The 1970 census mother-tongue figures also provide a breakdown into foreign-

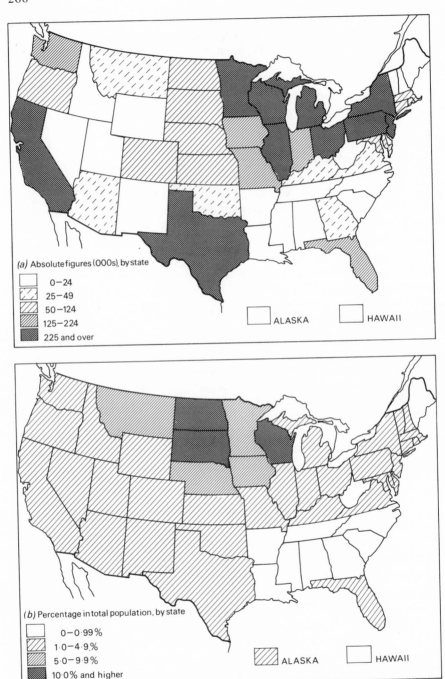

Figure 12.3. Mother-tongue speakers of German, 1970. Combined foreign born, foreign stock, natives of natives. *Source:* United States Census 1970

born, foreign stock (one or both parents foreign-born), and natives (native-born parents), "natives of natives." A national language retention index for French and German was calculated by dividing the number of "natives of natives" by the total number of mother-tongue claimants. This yielded a retention of 56 percent for French and 41 percent for German. A separate index for each state was calculated and compared with the national index. Figure 12.4 shows how far above, or below, the national average each state fell.

French retention is very high in Louisiana and surrounding states, including the whole Southeast (except Florida). Surprisingly, it is not very high in New England, although this may be an effect of relatively large numbers of first generation French Canadians still living in that area. Conversely, in Louisiana, since there has been virtually no French-speaking immigration in this century, retention figures would tend to be magnified by the virtually 100 percent native-born American population.

German shows high retention in Texas and adjoining states and in the band of states stretching west from Pennsylvania as far as South Dakota and Kansas. North Dakota, Nebraska, Illinois, and especially Michigan stand out from this cluster as being relatively nonretentive.

Since the 1970 census defines mother-tongue claimants as persons who either spoke the language themselves *or* who simply grew up in a household where someone else spoke it (such as grandparents or other older relatives), the figures can easily lead to a vast overestimation of the current use of these languages. A special census survey conducted in July, 1975, by the National Center for Education Statistics (see Chapter 22) estimated the French ethnic heritage group to number about 2.8 million persons. 2.24 million native-born Americans, over 14 years of age, claimed French as their mother tongue, but only about 268,000 still actively spoke the language in households where French was used in preference to English. The corresponding figures for German are 13.69 million persons of German ethnic heritage (which, in light of the projection of 50 million given above, is undoubtedly much too low), 4.23 million mother-tongue claimants, and 129,000 active German speakers in households where German is spoken in preference to (i.e. more than) English. Unfortunately, a state-by-state breakdown of these figures is not yet available.

The survey indicates that only 12 percent of the 1975 French mother-tongue claimants still use French as their own individual language in French-speaking households, while another 38 percent live in households where the mother tongue is spoken, but where the individual's own usual language is English. The remaining 49 percent live in households where only English is spoken. The corresponding percentages for German show an even more rapid switch to English: 3 percent, 26 percent, and 71 percent, respectively.

Estimated numbers of *foreign-born* persons, over 3 years of age, in households with languages other than English, show an astonishingly rapid shift from German to English. In July, 1975, out of the approximately 974,000 persons born in Germany living in the United States, only 70,000, or 7.2 percent, used German as their usual individual language.

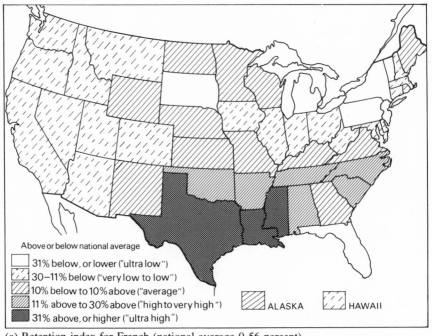

(a) Retention index for French (national average 0.56 percent)

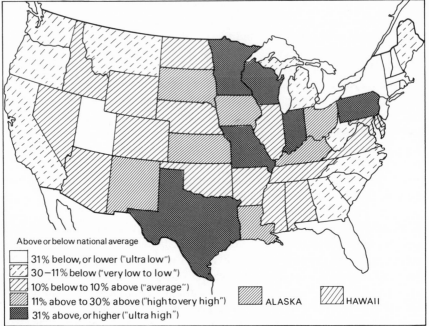

(b) Retention index for German (national average 0.41 percent)

Figure 12.4. Mother-tongue retention index for French and German, by state. The national average retention index is the number of natives of natives who claim the language as their mother tongue, divided by total number of mother-tongue claimants; a separate index is computed for each state and this is compared with the national average.
Source: United States Census 1970

For French, the figures are 127,000 U.S. residents born in France and 100,000 usual speakers of French, yielding a seemingly much higher retention rate of 78.7 percent. This high retention turns out to be an illusion, however, since the figure of 100,000 French speakers includes many from French Canada and Haiti; the foreign-born figure of 127,000, on the other hand, consists only of persons from France.

In July, 1975, an estimated 1.3 million persons lived in non-English-speaking households. Three-quarters of this group were in Spanish-speaking households. Especially portentous for the future is the fact that children (aged 4–18) in Spanish-speaking households constituted 85 percent of all children in non-English-speaking households. The 96.5 percent Spanish enrollment in 1973–74 Title VII programs is thus seen to be quite appropriate.

There is every indication that these trends will be intensified in the future. Aside from the French-speaking (creole) Haitians, the likelihood of a renewed, large-scale immigration from French Canada, France, or Germany is remote. Also, the birth rate of such immigrants tends to be relatively low and they assimilate rapidly.

By contrast, the number of illegal immigrants from Mexico is growing to huge proportions. According to a report in the *Wall Street Journal,* September 19, 1977 (Lancaster 1977), the present 3.5 percent Mexican annual population growth and substantial disparity of wealth between the two countries are the prime factors in inducing Mexicans to cross the border into the United States. The number of illegal migrants for 1976 alone is officially estimated at 1,562,000, but agents in the field put it as high as 4 million or more. This forecasts a wholesale shift from English monolingualism to Spanish/English bilingualism in vast areas of the country. The overwhelming majority of bilingual/bicultural programs in the future will, of necessity, involve Spanish.

In their function as ethnic languages of large numbers of native-born Americans, we have seen that French and German have played an important role in the nation's past. While France has been a kind of godfather to the United States, one could well say that a good part of Germany *is* the United States.

The future of French and German lies almost entirely in their function as foreign languages, not as first or second languages. Educators, politicians, and language planners will have to decide what role they will play as objects of study by American students with English or Spanish mother tongue. If German language study could be abolished overnight in the World War I period, it could presumably be reinstated tomorrow as a part of the curriculum at all levels of the educational system, if the USA came to see maintenance of linguistic ties to our roots in continental Europe as a goal which federal action should promote (see Chapter 23).

FURTHER READING

The books on French settlers in what is now the United States make interesting reading for the glories of the colonial past, but contribute little to our understanding of the real importance of France and the French in the launching and development of the United States. Tisch 1959 makes lively reading. McDermott 1965, 1969 gives a detailed and vivid account of French colonial life in Upper Louisiana (present-day Missouri and Illinois). For linguistic studies of Cajun French and Louisiana Créole, see Further reading in Chapter 4.

Books on the Germans are much greater in quantity, a few of them being historical works as good as any yet written about the United States. Faust 1927 is a masterpiece, and Hawgood 1940 is not far behind. Kloss 1974 provides clear geographic evidence of the magnitude of the German ethnic heritage sector of the American population. Several studies of the German language in the United States are available, such as Gilbert 1971, 1972.

The speech and writing of Jews*

DAVID L. GOLD

For over three thousand years of recorded history, Jewish communities have had distinctive patterns of language use; they have been exposed to a myriad of non-Jewish languages and have created about two dozen Jewish languages of their own. Time after time, a Jewish community has shifted from one language to another, but even though LANGUAGE SHIFT is almost by definition an instance of acculturation, it has not necessarily signaled weakened communal cohesiveness or deculturation. Despite losses from assimilation, exogamy, and conversion, the cohesiveness of Jewish communities has generally remained high. The newly adopted language has been Judaized – made over into an expression of Jewish culture, reflecting the activities, values, and history of its speakers – turned into a Jewish sentiment as well as an instrument.

For example, around the turn of the millennium, Jews from France and Italy settling in the Rhineland began abandoning Zarphatic and Italkian (the Jewish correlates of French and Italian, respectively) and at the same time began acquiring the language of their new non-Jewish neighbors. First used only as a tool for communication with non-Jews, what was later to be known as Yiddish had by the twentieth century become a totally Jewish language, an integral component as well as faithful reflection of Ashkenazic culture. The language shift had signaled a degree of acculturation, but no loss of communality.

Jewish communities have characteristically used more than one language, each for different communicative functions. One of them has always been Hebrew, which has a special place in Jewish history as *leshon hakodesh* 'the language of sanctity.' In every traditional Jewish community, the Jewish script has also been used, not only for writing Hebrew, but also for any language Jews have used natively.

The three Jewish languages of greatest importance in the United States have been Yiddish, Hebrew, and Dzhudezmo. Hebrew is a Semitic language, related to Arabic and Aramaic. It was the MOTHER TONGUE of the Jewish people in ancient times and has been the vehicle of most sacred Jewish writings. Hebrew ceased to be anyone's native language around A.D. 200, but has continued in specific

* This paper was written thanks to a grant from the Merkaz Leklita Bamada. I am also grateful to Joshua A. Fishman, George Jochnowitz, Mordkhe Schaechter, Donna Schlar, Lois C. Schlar, and Werner Weinberg for comments on an earlier version.

functions in Jewish communities to the present time. At the end of the nineteenth
century, a movement began to extend its use to other domains and this eventually
led to the renewed use of Hebrew as a native language and its present role as the
chief language of the state of Israel.

Dzhudezmo is superficially most like Spanish, but very different from it when
looked at closely. It was once the chief language of Sefardic Jews (Jews of the
Iberian Peninsula and their descendants), but is now habitually used by only a
handful of older people. Like all Jewish languages, it was traditionally written in
the Hebrew alphabet, but today it is almost always printed in the roman alphabet.

Yiddish is superficially most like German, but, like Dzhudezmo and Spanish,
very different from it when seen at close range. It was the native tongue of all
Ashkenazic Jews (most Jews of Central and Eastern Europe and their descendants) until the end of the eighteenth century. Despite shifts to other languages
and barbarous acts of genocide perpetrated against its speakers, Yiddish is still
the Jewish language with the largest number of native speakers. It has almost
always been written in the Jewish script.

Aside from these separate Jewish languages and several other less important
ones used in the United States, the varieties of English used by Jews are in many
instances sufficiently distinctive to be collectively called Jewish English. The
story of Jewish speech and writing in the United States is a history of waves of
immigration from different parts of the Jewish world, the immigrants' contact
with English and other languages they met here, and their struggle to maintain or
to abandon the languages they brought with them.

Jewish immigration

Jewish settlement in the United States may be divided into three main periods.
The first of these was the Sefardic period, which lasted from the second half of
the seventeenth century until the second or third decade of the nineteenth, and
during which communal leaders were Sefaradim, i.e. Iberian Jews and their
descendants (often called "Spanish" and/or "Portuguese Jews"). This was
followed by the Western Ashkenazic period, during which hegemony passed
from the Sefaradim to the Ashkenazim, i.e. Yiddish speakers and their descendants. During this period, which lasted until the 1870s or 1880s, most of the
Jewish immigrants and communal leaders were Western Ashkenazim: Yiddish
speakers or their descendants from Germany, Holland, Alsace, Bohemia,
Switzerland, and western Hungary (often called "German Jews" or, in early
nineteenth-century American English, "Dutch Jews"). The most recent period
has been the Eastern Ashkenazic one, from the 1870s to the present, when
leadership largely passed from the Western Ashkenazim to the majority of new
settlers and their descendants, Eastern Ashkenazim, i.e. Yiddish speakers from
the Russian and Austro-Hungarian empires, their successor states, and Rumania
(often called "Polish," "Russian," or "Russian Polish Jews").

This breakdown into three periods is of course a simplification, for at no time
has Jewish immigration been homogeneous. Thus, for example, during the
period of Sefardic communal leadership, the majority of settlers were actually

Ashkenazim, so numerous in fact that the oldest synagog in New York City, Shearit Yisrael (commonly known as "the Spanish and Portuguese Synagog" to this day), was founded by both Ashkenazim and Sefaradim, and has had a majority of Ashkenazic members since at least 1729 (Glanz 1956–7: 9). Also, beginning around 1890 and continuing until 1924, i.e. during the Eastern Ashkenazic period, thousands of Sefardic Jews from the Ottoman empire and its successor states settled in the United States; and during the 1930s and 1940s, thousands of Western Ashkenazim, mainly from Germany, found refuge there. Finally, in the 1960s and 1970s, thousands of Hebrew speakers have emigrated from Israel to the United States.

Religiously, culturally, and linguistically, we find a multitude of Jewish groups in the United States. They range, for example, from the least to the most Americanized, from the ultra-Orthodox to the atheistic, and from the exclusively Yiddish-speaking to those whose speech and writing hardly differ from those of non-Jewish English speakers.

Little is known about the early linguistic history of Jews in the United States (communal and other records, combed time and again for historical, economic, and social data, have rarely been utilized for linguistic research). For example, the twenty-three Jews who unexpectedly landed in New Amsterdam in September 1654, after fleeing Recife, Brazil, when it was wrested from the Dutch by the Portuguese, may have used any of a number of languages: Dzhudezmo, Portuguesic (the Jewish correlate of Portuguese), Dutch, or perhaps Papiamentu (a language now used in the Netherlands Antilles). At least some of these could certainly communicate in Dutch (for they had been living in a Dutch colony), but we cannot be sure what language or languages they used among themselves.

Today's student of Jewish languages must be careful when he reads in the secondary literature that Sefaradim spoke or wrote "Spanish" or "Portuguese." The language names used even in primary documents (including those written by Sefaradim themselves) must be approached with caution. In the last quarter of the eighteenth century, for example, Shearit Yisrael's school taught "Hebrew, Spanish, English, writing and Arithmetick" according to a contemporary document (Davis 1963: 27), yet there is good reason to believe that students were not instructed in Spanish, but reading of the Ladino translation of the Jewish Scriptures. Ladino is a literary variety of Dzhudezmo, used, for instance, in translating sacred Jewish writings. Similarly, most Jews now living in the United States would report their primary language simply as "English"; this is true in a rough way, yet it would be more accurate to speak, in most cases, of a number of varieties of *Jewish* English.

The settlers of the first period left no trace whatsoever on non-Jewish varieties of English, and it is highly doubtful that even their few Jewish descendants have retained any Jewish linguistic characteristics from that period. By the time of the tercentenary of American Jewry in 1954, Jewish leaders were embarrassed to find that few descendants of those who had come during the first period still considered themselves Jews. As in many countries, each wave of immigration had been followed by a period of settling-in and then assimilation; had it not been for succeeding waves of fresh newcomers, total disappearance of the

Jewish community could hardly have been averted. Indeed, most people in the United States who now consider themselves Jews are the children or grand-children (at most the great-grandchildren) of immigrants.

The Western Ashkenazim of the second period came at a time of language shift in the old country. The shift took place first in Germany and then in Holland and elsewhere during the second half of the eighteenth century and has continued to the present day. At different times, in different places, and in different ways, Yiddish, the traditional language of Ashkenazic Jewry, was being replaced by (more or less Yiddish-influenced varieties of) German, Dutch, Czech, Hungarian, French, and other languages. The immigrant generations of Western Ashkenazim, like the Sefaradim, were therefore linguistically heter-ogeneous. Their speech, whether German, one of the other European languages, or American English, was heavily colored by the influence of the Yiddish lan-guage and the Jewish cultural experience in the United States. Both Jews and non-Jews noticed the characteristic Jewishness of speech and made fun of it. As late as 1888 an editorial in the *American Hebrew* called for the publication of English texts for Jewish youth in a language that would not "move them to mirth" (*American Hebrew* 35, May 11, 1888).

As time went on, the linguistic characteristics of the Western Ashkenazic period tended to disappear, and nowadays it is doubtful that even their Jewish descendants retain any of them, apart from a few Western Yiddishisms which have also entered non-Jewish English, such as *kosher* 'ritually pure; approved, acceptable,' *shlemil* 'a fool, a loser,' *nebish* 'a nonentity, a loser.'

Contemporary American Jewry began to take shape in the 1870s, and like Israel, the other main demographic and cultural center of world Jewry today, it rests on the foundations of Central and Eastern European Jewry, the most pop-ulous and culturally the most vibrant branch of the Jewish people for the last three hundred years or so, until the twelve-year Nazi war on the Jews (1933–45) almost completely destroyed it. As we will see below, the major determinant of American Jewish English is therefore, not surprisingly, Eastern Yiddish. Before dealing with the third period in greater detail, we must look at the linguistic situation of the immigrants before they came to the United States. Afterwards we will take up Dzhudezmo and Hebrew in this country, and finally Yiddish and Jewish English.

Before immigration

In the traditional Ashkenazic communities of Central and Eastern Europe, two Jewish languages were used, Yiddish and Hebrew. Yiddish was the language used by Jews for communicating with one another in all normal circumstances; Hebrew was the language of most set prayers (though a few set prayers were in Yiddish), of Jewish scholarly writings (though sacred and semi-sacred Jewish texts were always orally discussed in Yiddish), of communal records (though here a mixed Hebrew–Yiddish scribal language emerged), and a subject of instruction in Jewish schools (though the medium of instruction was always Yiddish).

Religious works for the less learned (whether men or women) were in Yiddish, those for the more learned in Hebrew. Yiddish translations of the Jewish Scriptures and of prayerbooks were available for students or the less learned. The Talmud, however, was generally not translated from *leshon hakodesh* into Yiddish, since it was studied only by the learned, who were assumed to be able to read it in the original. Collected tales about saintly Jews (like stories about *Der Besht,* the founder of the Chasidic movement) and those who had acquired a measure of sanctity might appear in Hebrew (as these stories did), but they were orally told in Yiddish.

The distribution of functions for Yiddish and Hebrew described above is more complicated than sketched here. In any case, one must avoid the oversimplifications and errors found in the less reliable secondary literature, such as "Yiddish was spoken and Hebrew was written," "Yiddish books appeared only for women," or "Hebrew was spoken in the schools and by the learned."

For communicating with non-Jews, Ashkenazim used the appropriate non-Jewish language, such as German, Polish, or Ukrainian, though in a number of cases, non-Jews (mostly people employed by Jews or who frequently had contact with them) acquired some knowledge of spoken Yiddish. Ashkenazim had few contacts with other Jews. Even in cities with both Ashkenazic and Sefardic communities, as in Germany, Holland, and England, there was not much contact; when there was, the local non-Jewish language was probably used, though learned Jews might have used Hebrew in intercommunal contact. If an Ashkenazi and non-Ashkenazi had no common VERNACULAR, they would also resort to a simplified form of spoken Hebrew if both knew it.

What we see here, then, is lasting but imbalanced multilingualism. Lasting, because it continued for well nigh a thousand years; imbalanced, because the languages had different functions and no Jew had equal competence in all of them. The two Jewish languages served an integrative function as ethnic boundary markers (binding the members of the community together), whereas the non-Jewish ones served instrumental purposes only (playing a merely utilitarian role). Yiddish and *leshon hakodesh* were thus both instruments and sentiments; the non-Jewish languages were instruments only.

The situation was similar in traditional Sefardic communities in the Ottoman empire: Dzhudezmo and Hebrew were the two Jewish languages employed (along much the same lines as Yiddish and Hebrew for Ashkenazim) and, according to time and place, Turkish, Greek, Arabic, and other languages were the non-Jewish ones.

Beginning at the end of the eighteenth century (among Western Ashkenazim) and the second half of the nineteenth century (among Sefaradim in the Ottoman empire and among Eastern Ashkenazim), varying numbers of Jews abandoned, to varying degrees, Yiddish and Dzhudezmo, replacing them by non-Jewish languages. And as we will see below, a number of Western Ashkenazim also abandoned Hebrew, to varying degrees, as a liturgical language or vehicle of Jewish scholarly writing.

The shift from use of Polish or Turkish, for example, as an instrumental language to an integrative one required greater skill in its employment; whereas before Jews could generally not read or write these non-Jewish languages (having no need or desire to) and were far less competent in speaking them than they were in Yiddish or Dzhudezmo, increased acculturation brought with it (and even required) greater oral fluency and written competence.

For many, oral BILINGUALISM or multilingualism was no longer imbalanced, but increasingly balanced, indicative of weak identification with either speech community. The balanced bilingual usually had a low level of allegiance to both groups, feeling as much (or as little) at home or accepted in one as in the other. Problems of group identity thus arose, and people with double loyalties often sought appropriate names for themselves. Whereas traditional Jews were simply *yidn* or *dzhidyos* 'Jews,' some nontraditionalists called themselves *deutsche Staatbürger jüdischen Glaubens* 'German citizens of the Jewish faith' (in Germany) or *Turcs de confession israélite* 'Turks of the Jewish faith' (in Turkey). This language change, unlike earlier ones, signaled much more than a mere wish to be able to communicate better with the non-Jewish communities. In most cases, it was to result in deculturation and total or near total integration into the non-Jewish world. Some of those who had participated in the language shift felt, in fact, that the two groups, Jewish and non-Jewish, constituted mutually exclusive worlds and that one of them must, therefore, be abandoned entirely.

These conflicts of values and allegiances were most acute for Western Ashkenazim. Sefaradim and Eastern Ashkenazim were affected much less. Old World linguistic, religious, and cultural tensions were eventually brought to the New World, and the availability of English and of American culture was to constitute yet another factor in the modern American Jew's struggle to cope with new conditions.

Dzhudezmo

Most Jews who came to the United States from the Ottoman empire and its successor states (mainly from the 1890s to 1924) were native and primary speakers of Dzhudezmo. At the time of their emigration, much of the centuries-old traditional Sefardic culture was already disappearing, being replaced in part by aspects of Turkish, Greek, French or other non-Jewish cultures. However, Dzhudezmo had hardly begun to be replaced as the native language of Sefaradim, as it was to be in these communities in the following decades. These immigrants were therefore still representative of the traditional functional distribution for Jewish and non-Jewish languages outlined above.

In the United States, these Sefaradim continued to use Dzhudezmo among themselves, but without making any special efforts to foster its continued use by their descendants. Transmission, in any meaningful sense, of Dzhudezmo and of Sefardic culture to the generation born in the United States has therefore been almost nil. Most American-born children of Dzhudezmo-speaking immigrants can understand and speak a rudimentary form of the language, but they are much stronger in English. Reading and writing Dzhudezmo in the traditional

Jewish script is unknown among the American-born, and knowledge of most aspects of traditional culture is virtually absent. Knowledge of other languages used in the old country (Turkish, Greek, or French) was not passed on to the American-born generation. By the third generation, even passive knowledge of simple spoken Dzhudezmo has practically disappeared. Constituting a minority within a minority, Sefaradim are becoming increasingly absorbed into the Ashkenazic community: although the immigrant generation usually married among themselves, the second generation married Ashkenazim as often as other Sefaradim, and the third generation almost always marries non-Sefaradim. In most cases, what remains by the third generation is often only a surname and other vestigial remembrances of an ethnicity long passed.

By the time some Sefaradim realized that the tide of massive self-willed deculturation should be stemmed, it was too late. There were no Dzhudezmo periodicals, publishers, theaters, radio programs, schools, cultural groups, or research organizations to rally around. The organizational capacity for collective action was also weak, being limited to about a dozen synagogs and a few small benevolent and fraternal societies. One cannot now speak of a Dzhudezmo-speaking community at the national, regional, or even local level, since Dzhudezmo speakers have no communications media (the last newspaper closed over thirty years ago), and communication networks function only among family, friends, business associates, or at the Sefardic old-age home in New York City. Dzhudezmo-speaking neighborhoods have disappeared and the synagogs and societies have either been anglicized or dissolved.

Hebrew

Leshon hakodesh as a liturgical language and as the written language of traditional Jewish scholarship is common to all traditional Jewish communities. Hebrew as a normally spoken language in modern times is characteristic primarily of the Jewish community in the Land of Israel, beginning in the twentieth century.

Leshon hakodesh as the vehicle of traditional Jewish scholarship was rare in colonial or independent America during the first and second periods of Jewish immigration. Aside from Bibles and prayerbooks, only one original Hebrew book had been published there until the end of the 1860s (when Eastern Ashkenazim started coming in large numbers): *Avne Yehoshua* (New York, 1860), a commentary on the Ethics of the Fathers by the Warsaw-born rabbi, Yehoshua Falk.

In the mid- and late-nineteenth century, a controversy emerged over the use of Hebrew as a liturgical language (similar to that begun in Germany at the end of the eighteenth century). Traditionalists wished to retain Hebrew and argued that Hebrew was *leshon hakodesh* 'the language of sanctity.' Innovators countered that few worshipers could understand it and that, rather than recite prayers by rote, they should switch to a language they could understand. Orthodox Jewry, the most conservative branch, has remained steadfast in its full retention of Hebrew in the liturgy; however, the sermon and other nonliturgical parts of the service, formerly in a Jewish language such as Yiddish or Dzhudezmo, are now in the vernacular of the majority of worshipers: still Yiddish in ultra-Orthodox synagogs and some form of (Jewish) English in the others. Conservative Jewry, the intermediate branch, has introduced a few prayers in English; sermons and announcements are always in (Jewish) English. Reform Jewry, the most innovative branch, began replacing Hebrew by German in the nineteenth century, and then, as German became less and less known to American Jews, by English. In recent years, however, the more conservative Reform congregations have been re-emphasizing *leshon hakodesh* at the expense of English. The almost all-English service, once found in some highly innovative Reform congregations, has probably disappeared by now.

The pronunciation of *leshon hakodesh* became controversial several decades after a standard for Modern Spoken Hebrew began emerging, in the first decade of the twentieth century, in the Land of Israel. This standard is different from *all* earlier and contemporary pronunciations. Popular belief notwithstanding, it is not identical with "the Sefardic pronunciation of Hebrew" (there are actually *many* Sefardic pronunciations), but is an Ashkenazified version of what early Hebrew language-planners thought Biblical Hebrew sounded like.

Synagogs in the United States have had to decide whether or not to modify their pronunciations of *leshon hakodesh* in accordance with the new standard. Orthodox congregations have generally continued to use a traditional pronunciation (i.e. not the current Israeli standard) although, especially among the American-born, their traditional pronunciation has usually been modified in certain ways, not infrequently under English influence. Some Conservative synagogs and Reform temples have adopted the Israeli standard, though probably not the majority. American-born Conservative and Reform Jews are also influenced by English in their pronunciation of Hebrew. Because this new standard is not identical with any Sefardic pronunciation, the few Sefardic synagogs in the United States (all Orthodox or Conservative) have had to take a stand on this issue too. They tend to adopt the Israeli standard for three reasons: (a) the widespread myth equating it with "the Sefardi pronunciation" makes the shift palatable; (b) because of the scarcity of Sefardic rabbis and cantors, several Sefardic synagogs in the United States have Ashkenazic rabbis or cantors, who are much better acquainted with the Israeli pronunciation than with any Sefardic one; and (c) as the number of foreign-born Sefaradim decreases, so too does knowledge of the traditional Sefardic pronunciations. In all the Jewish congregations, these tendencies are most noticeable among the American-born; the immigrant generation usually adheres to the pronunciation learned in the old country.

With regard to secular Hebrew culture, most Jews who came to the USA during the first and second periods were traditional Jews and thus uninterested in it. It was not until the 1870s that Eastern Ashkenazic immigrants provided adequate support for a true movement toward secular Hebrew culture. A few non-Ashkenazim took part in this movement, notably the Italian Jew, Sabato

Morais, and the Sefaradi, Henry Pereira Mendes. Sefaradim who arrived in the third period had no interest in (or little knowledge of) secular Hebrew culture, and neither did most of the Western Ashkenazim who came in the 1930s and 1940s.

The years from 1914 to 1960 were the heyday of secular Hebrew culture in the United States. Hebrew poets, prose writers, playwrights, and journalists, most of them Eastern European-born Jews with Yiddish as their native language, published in both languages and made a lasting contribution to Jewish culture. However, despite the millions of hours spent in teaching the language, a native Hebrew-speaking community, which could provide an on-going audience as well as a source of new talent, was never established. Few native or even primary speakers of Hebrew have been American-born, and as the European-born Hebrew activists have died, Hebrew letters in the United States have declined. Expository writing (educational journalism, the essay, literary criticism, and scholarly research) continues to lead a precarious existence in the weekly *Hadoar,* the monthly *Bitsaron,* and a few other publications.

Thousands of Hebrew speakers from Israel began settling in the United States in the 1960s and 1970s (and smaller numbers had come earlier). Some estimates put the number of Israelis in the United States and Canada at over 335,000. Like their counterparts in other post-traditional, secularized, and technological societies, the younger immigrants usually have little or no interest in "highbrow" culture (whether a traditional Jewish culture, secular Hebrew culture, or secular Yiddish culture). Most of them concentrate on acquiring the material comforts of American living and the ABCs of pop culture rather than keeping up with the "heavy stuff" in *Hadoar* or *Bitsaron.* A former librarian at the Jewish Education Committee of New York City recalls how Israeli-born Hebrew teachers would ask for *Hadoar* only if they had to consult the want-ads for a job (Falkov 1977: 9). In December, 1976, a Hebrew daily, mostly with news about Israel, began appearing in New York City, reached a circulation of about 4,000, but closed after two months.

Because Jewish emigration from Israel is regarded with disdain by the Jewish community in both Israel and the USA, these settlers try to keep a low profile as a group and do not as a rule organize as other immigrant collectives usually do. There is an Israeli Students' Organization for the United States and Canada (whose members are supposed to be temporary residents only). A few cafés, restaurants, and night clubs serve as points of congregation for habitués of such places. In October, 1977, an Israeli Social Club opened in New York City. There is a special Sabbath edition of *Haarets* (an Israeli daily) prepared for Israelis abroad, and in 1977, approximately six hours a week of popular Hebrew songs and news about Israel (in Hebrew) were broadcast on a New York City radio station. This radio program was aimed exclusively at Jewish immigrants from Israel, not students of Hebrew or adherents of the Hebrew culture movement. By 1977, there were so many immigrants from Israel in New York City (humorously called the fourth largest Israeli city) who were viewed as potential or actual United States citizens that a mayoral candidate broadcast

campaign messages in Hebrew on this station. The radio also carried calls for
Israelis and ex-Israelis to join the Zionist Organization of America or the Cherut
wing of the Zionist movement.

These Hebrew speakers do not organize schools, synagogs, or cultural groups
and hardly participate in (or even support) the Hebrew culture movement in the
United States. Hebrew will continue to be spoken natively here only if there are
fresh immigrants from Israel, with no appreciable effect, whatever their numbers,
on the Hebrew culture movement.

Hebrew as used in the United States has generally not influenced Jewish or
non-Jewish varieties of English, though Zionist publications show a much higher
percentage of lexical Hebraisms than other Jewish English publications: for
example, *chaver* 'comrade, member,' *beseder* 'OK.' Hebraisms in general English are either old loans which first appeared in Bible translations (*cherub,
behemoth* and *leviathan*) or recent borrowings from Israeli Hebrew (*Keneset*
'Israeli parliament', *kibuts* '[kind of] collective settlement' and *moshaw* '[kind
of] communal settlement'). A few culinary terms (*falafel, chumus, tchina,* and
pita), also from Israeli Hebrew, are now being popularized by Israeli restau-
rateurs in the United States.

Yiddish

Yiddish in the USA has had a brighter history than other immigrant Jewish
languages, thanks to the large numbers of native speakers who immigrated, and
to the vibrancy of Yiddish culture in the old country – vibrancy which was felt
in the USA, at least as long as there were immigrant Yiddish speakers. The few
Yiddish speakers who arrived during the first and second periods made no
appreciable contribution to Yiddish culture, but those of the third period, much
more numerous and better organized, have left a rich legacy in every imagin-
able field: literature, journalism, theater, film, radio, music, religious scholarship, pedagogy, linguistics, historiography, and folkloristics. Yiddish-lan-
guage fraternal organizations, service organizations, philanthropic groups,
cultural clubs, labor unions, religious groups, schools, and research organizations have been no less important. In order to understand the position of
Yiddish language and culture in the United States, we must backtrack and look
at conditions in Central and Eastern Europe.

As long as Yiddish was the undisputed language of Ashkenazic Jewry (with
the special functions reserved for *leshon hakodesh*), there was no articulated
Yiddishist movement nor was there a need for one – the very speaking and
writing of Yiddish was in itself a tacit Ashkenazic language ideology. In the
sixteenth and seventeenth centuries, however, Yiddish speakers in Italy shifted
to Italkian (the Jewish correlate of Italian) and at the end of the eighteenth
century, a shift to other languages began in Western Ashkenazic communities.
Starting at the end of the last century, many middle and most upper class Jews
in the large cities of the Russian and Austro-Hungarian empires, their successor
states, and Rumania also abandoned Yiddish to greater and lesser degrees,

some of them completely. There was also a small Hebraist movement, which gained some momentum with the rise of Zionism. However, all these losses were not substantial, for even up to the Nazi war on the Jews, most Ashkenazim knew Yiddish. It is estimated that about 5 million of the 6 million who were murdered in the Holocaust were speakers of Yiddish.

In reaction to Hebraism and to the shift to other languages, an expressly formulated Yiddishist language ideology began emerging in the 1890s. It was a language ideology, but not a national ideology. Political independence or even autonomy in Europe was not sought; at most, cultural autonomy was fought for in some countries and actually attained in some places after World War I. The Yiddishist movement was concerned with both external and internal aspects of the language: it sought to secure as many speakers and as many functions for Yiddish as possible within the Ashkenazic community (external planning), and it sought to regulate the linguistic behavior of Yiddish users by standardizing and enriching the language (internal planning).

The Eastern Ashkenazic Jews who emigrated to the United States during the third period (mostly between 1881 and 1924) were almost all native and primary speakers of Yiddish. Between 1880 and 1910, for example, 1.5 million Jews emigrated, 70 percent of them from the Russian empire; only a handful of the latter were not Yiddish speakers.

Yiddish was thus virtually universal as a means of communication among Eastern Ashkenazim in the United States. However, articulated Yiddishism was uncommon, because the movement began gaining ground in Europe only in the 1920s and (especially) the 1930s, by which time most of the immigrants were already in the USA and no longer directly, if at all, touched by new winds blowing in the old country.

Yiddish language and culture have flourished in the USA only as long as there have been fresh immigrants to fill the ranks vacated by those who were turning to Jewish English. This shift was not the result of direct pressure from without; i.e. there have been no government restrictions on language use. Rather, America, with its unparalleled freedoms, its seemingly limitless opportunities for advancement – a New World in the fullest sense – provided Ashkenazic (and other) Jews with a relatively congenial atmosphere such as they had generally not known for centuries. America became a model, and, to the extent that features of American life did not conflict with each Jewish immigrant's or his child's model of himself, he tried to adopt them or imitate them as best he could. The attractiveness of the non-Jewish world, on the one hand, and the desire on the part of many to cast off verbal and nonverbal behavioral patterns reminiscent of the old country and its troubles, on the other, have led to a massive language shift, usually within the space of a single generation.

Efforts to stem the erosion of Yiddish language and culture in the United States were weak before the Holocaust. Most of the immigrants were unacquainted with secular Yiddishism (which did not really develop in Europe until after most immigrants had already left for the United States), and few of its leaders made their way here. Orthodox Jews maintained the language better than others, but the fact that their leaders felt a need to call for its continued use as early as the 1890s shows that a language shift was in progress none the less.

That Yiddish language and culture were vibrant here only as long as new immigrants continued to arrive does not mean that some knowledge of the language was not acquired by the first native-born generation. In rare cases, it was consciously handed down from parents to children. More often, children acquired it because it was their parents' primary language, in which the parents expressed themselves with least effort and spoke to each other and to others of their generation. The fact is that a majority of first-generation children were bilingual in (usually only spoken) Yiddish and (both spoken and written) English.

Many acquired Yiddish first or both Yiddish and English at the same time, but as they grew older, attended public schools, and made their way in the American world, their knowledge of the two languages became less and less commensurate, so that by adolescence they were usually stronger in (Jewish) English, and almost always literate only in that language. The next generation grew up hearing only Jewish English from their parents, generally acquiring at most passive knowledge of spoken Yiddish if they heard it often enough from grandparents, or if the neighborhood still had an immigrant flavor.

The period of greatest vigor for Yiddish language and culture in the United States extended from the 1890s to the 1950s, peaking in the 1920s or 1930s. It is no coincidence that secular Hebrew culture had its heyday from around 1914 to 1960, for it was sustained almost exclusively by those same immigrant generations who were the producers and consumers of secular Yiddish culture.

As Yiddish has declined, it has generally become a ludic language, i.e. one used for language play, for many of its speakers' children and grandchildren. Unacquainted with the treasures of Yiddish culture created during a thousand years of Jewish life in the old country, or with the rich heritage left by the immigrant generations in the United States, many of the American-born have thought Yiddish suitable only for low comedy and vulgar humor. One of the characteristics of declining languages or varieties is their restriction to special purposes, such as comedy; in the case of Yiddish this seems to have been extreme, so much so that many American-born Jews simply cannot believe anyone uses the language for other purposes. For them, Yiddish is intrinsically humorous and regarded only with a condescending tolerance. The special status acquired by Yiddish among these people is highlighted by the considerable number of vulgarisms and jocularisms of Yiddish origin in American Jewish English (e.g. *shmok* 'dope, jerk, S.O.B.'). All Jewish languages (except Hebrew) have traditionally been stigmatized in the United States by most of their speakers' descendants and ironically even by a number of those who themselves are speakers of these languages.

By the end of the 1960s, the outlook seemed bleak to secular Yiddishists (whose numbers had increased somewhat after many Holocaust survivors found refuge in the USA). However, toward the end of that decade and especially in the 1970s, a new trend became evident: whereas earlier those universities which offered Jewish studies programs were concerned almost exclusively with Jewish religion and history and with Hebrew language and culture, the college generation of the 1970s (by now mostly the grandchildren of immigrants) "discovered" Yiddish and Yiddish culture (though not yet other Jewish languages and cultures). What the immigrant and his children were often eager to shed has become a source of interest and pride for the third generation.

Yiddishist leaders, previously concerned with maintaining existing immigrant generation organizations, looked in the 1970s to students as their only remaining hope. The less realistic saw elementary Yiddish courses as "chairs of Yiddish studies," announced a "revival" of Yiddish, and at one conference, the poet Yankev Glatshteyn proclaimed it "an eternal language."

But it was too late. However, before we can see why this new interest in Yiddish will probably be only transitory, we must describe the different kinds of Yiddish users in the USA.

Yiddish-speaking Jewry in the United States is split along several lines. The major division is between secularists and Orthodox Jews. The latter are divided into Chasidic and non-Chasidic groups; Chasidic Jews are further split into sects each of which is headed by a *rebe*.

Most of the present-day Orthodox Yiddish users are Eastern European-born Jews or their children. It is too early to tell how the language will fare among their American-born descendants, but if Yiddish does survive in the USA as a normally spoken and written language, it will be among these Orthodox Yiddish users. The latter have no interest in establishing ties with secular Yiddishists, because they fear "contamination" from "worldly" Jews and because a secularist Yiddishist ideology is alien to them. Ironically, secular Yiddishists have an articulated Yiddishist ideology, but dwindling numbers of actual speakers and now only the most tenuous of communication networks. Yiddish-speaking Orthodox Jews, on the other hand, are much more numerous (and on the average much younger), but have no articulated Yiddishist policy, since the language is taken as a given in a much broader, all-encompassing Jewish way of life in which it has traditionally not been given special emphasis.

Secular Yiddishism in the United States has been only a language ideology; cultural autonomy did not even have to be requested, for the free air of America provides it. The teaching of Yiddish in public high schools, provision of Yiddish-English bilingual programs, and Yiddish versions of certain government publications have all been requested in New York City in the 1960s and 1970s and generally granted.

Yiddish language ideologues try to stress the merits of Yiddish in a number of ways: its value as an instrument, as a link with the millennial culture of Ashkenazic Jewry, and its symbolic value as an ethnic boundary marker. However, cogent argument is one thing and turning interested students or others into members of a language community is another. For one thing, because (Jewish) English is now so omnipresent among secular Jews, what most of the non-native new Yiddishists are really speaking is English with Yiddish words, and even in the few secularist families in which the American-born have heard

Yiddish since infancy, their use of it is far different from that of their parents or grandparents. For another, though most Yiddish cultural activists and community leaders are elated at the growing interest of students and others, their common response has usually not been a concerted one. Secular Yiddishists are divided into so many small or minuscule organizations that a joint effort at making the most of the new interest in Yiddish is hampered.

There has ensued a spate of conferences, committees, clubs, proclamations, resolutions, slogans, buttons, T-shirts, festivals, celebrations, and minor periodicals, but all of these may be more symptomatic of the splintered character of Yiddish-speaking Jewry than of the strength of Yiddish as a living language in America. In earlier days, for example, there may have been a Yiddish daily, serving the needs of its readers without fanfare (as in Philadelphia or Montreal); today, a "Yiddish committee" irregularly issues a small bulletin full of promotional material on Yiddish. Celebrations like the "Hundredth Anniversary of the Yiddish Press in America" (1970) or the "Eightieth Anniversary of the *Jewish Daily Forward*" (1977) create a false sense of continuity and security: at most two generations of the same family have been Yiddish-reading, and a handful of periodicals have survived only because fresh settlers came to replace those who had shifted to English.

Those secular Yiddish organizations which have been able to overcome problems of declining membership have succeeded in doing so only by gradually shifting to English, with less natural use of Yiddish, and by showcasing the language for descendants of its speakers. Thus, the Workmen's Circle and the YIVO Institute for Jewish Research, formerly all-Yiddish-speaking groups with almost all-Yiddish publications, have become mostly English-speaking and English-publishing. At the YIVO few staff members now remain with a good command of either the spoken or written language, and at the Workmen's Circle only the dwindling number of branches with immigrant memberships still function in Yiddish. Groups such as the Yidisher Arbeter-Bund, Yidisher Sotsyalistisher Farband, and Yidisher Kultur-Kongres (the first two labor organizations, the third a cultural organization), on the other hand, are still all Yiddish-speaking and -publishing, but their activities have been reduced considerably because of shrinking membership.

From the 1940s to the 1960s, the United States was the world center for Yiddish linguistic studies. As the master builders of modern Yiddish linguistics have died, few have come forward to replenish their ranks.

Only two productive linguists remain, Mordkhe Schaechter (standardization and enrichment; see Schaechter 1969, 1975, 1977) and Joshua Fishman (sociology of language; see, e.g., Fishman 1965b). The plethora of beginners' courses, even those taught as graduate courses, will apparently be to no avail.

Jewish English

The best cover term for varieties of English used by Jews is "Jewish English." It has sometimes been called "Yinglish," a blend of *Yiddish* and *English*, but this is a jocular and often pejorative term that is best avoided. It is ambiguous in that it could refer to Yiddish-influenced English or to English-influenced Yiddish, and as a name for all Jewish varieties of English, it would be a misnomer for those created by non-Ashkenazim, such as Sefardic Jewish English.

There are several reasons why specifically Jewish varieties of English develop. First, adults more often than not learn a second language imperfectly, and their use of this language shows the influence of other languages they know. For example, a native speaker of Yiddish who learns English as an adult, may speak English which shows Yiddish INTERFERENCE. This language variety is passed onto succeeding generations and becomes fused, i.e. a permanent or potentially permanent feature of the variety. Yiddishisms are thus found in the English of many American Jews who do not know Yiddish, even those several generations removed from it or those, such as Sefaradim or other non-Ashkenazim, whose ancestors did not speak it at all. A second factor in the development of Jewish varieties of English is a result of the modification of English to reflect Jewish culture and the cohesion of the Jewish community. Marriages, residential and occupational preferences, social contacts, and communications networks are usually denser between Jews than between Jews and non-Jews. Thus, a pervading sense of community fosters the preservation of specifically Jewish linguistic features.

There are varieties of Jewish English, and these varieties are determined by the same factors which contribute to the development of other varieties of English (see Chapter 3). For example, in the regional variety, British Jewish English *particular* 'devout' = American Jewish English *religious* or *observant,* as in "They're very particular" (for American English "They're very religious/observant"). Varieties peculiar to a specific time period also exist, for example, *killer* was used in formal American Jewish English in colonial times, but now only *ritual slaughterer* is found. Stylistic varieties range from formal to informal, for example, formal *ritual slaughterer* = usual *shoykhet* in current American Jewish English. There are other distinctions according to such parameters as religious community, age, sex, and all may be as narrowly or broadly defined as need be. For example, one can distinguish Western and Eastern Ashkenazic Jewish English: Jews who came here from Germany in the 1930s and 1940s say *to omer* 'to count the forty-nine days between Passover and the Feast of Weeks' (e.g. "Have you omered yet?"), whereas Eastern Ashkenazim say *to count sfire* or *to tseyl sfire.*

Speakers and writers of Jewish English can usually CODE-SWITCH between this and a non-Jewish variety. For example, in addressing a co-speaker, one might say (in current American Eastern Ashkenazic Jewish English), "In what shul does your zeydi daven on shabes?" which in non-Jewish English becomes, "At what synagog does your grandfather worship on the Sabbath?" The *normal* variety used by Jews in addressing other Jews is Jewish English. If they code-switch to non-Jewish English, one or more of these factors is present: (a) the addressee is not Jewish; (b) the addressee is Jewish, but does not understand the speaker's variety of Jewish English; (c) the addressee understands Jewish English, but the speaker wants a hearer who does not to understand him also. Conversely, Jewish English, especially those varieties most different from non-Jewish ones, may occasionally be used to *prevent* hearers from understanding; this cryptic use of language is well-known in many societies.

People are successful at code-switching to the extent that they perceive the differences between the two varieties and know the appropriate forms in the variety being switched to. For example, many speakers of American Jewish English know that *shul* 'synagog' is not normally used in non-Jewish varieties, and they would therefore replace it when switching. Few, however, realize that the expression, *I need it like a hole in the head* is originally Jewish English, translated directly from the Yiddish expression, *Kh'darf es vi a likh in kop*. In fact, many non-Jewish speakers use this expression without being aware of its Jewish origin. It is easiest to replace vocabulary items, harder to switch to non-Jewish SYNTAX and style, and hardest to switch off subtle PHONOLOGICAL characteristics of Jewish English such as INTONATION or details of pronunciation.

Jewish English is an identity marker, all the more effective to the extent that it differs from non-Jewish varieties. Not all Jews have felt the need for such markers. In 1888, Marcus Jastrow, a founder of Conservative Judaism (fluent in Yiddish, Hebrew, and Aramaic!) wrote: "Our religious institutions, our Sabbaths and festivals, our ceremonies and customs, our domestic life, our worship, our sacred language, all that distinguishes us from others, these are the tools, the armaments, wherewith we have yet to work [to fulfill Israel's vision]" (Davis 1963: 462–3), but not one word, apparently, about a distinctive vernacular and ordinary written language. Bernard Drachman, another founder, was even more specific fourteen years later: "[Jewish] teachers should be . . . masters of a pure English" (Davis 1963: 248). This attitude was in full accord with the tenets of the Enlightenment movement, founded by Moses Mendelssohn in Germany during the second half of the eighteenth century, namely that in speech and writing Jews should be no different from others. However, since verbal culture both reflects and is shaped by nonverbal culture, Jewish life could not go on without some kind of at least minimally different communolect. The staid English or German prose of nineteenth-century nontraditionalists contained religious terminology borrowed from Christian varieties or created from purely non-Jewish elements (e.g. "to return the Scrolls of the Law to the Holy Ark," "a Jewish minister, the Reverend A.P. Mendes"), yet even here Jewish elements were incorporated – elements from Yiddish, Hebrew, and other Jewish langauges, which must have been more frequent in less formal varieties.

A public call for the cultivation of Jewish English, on the other hand, has been made only once to my knowledge:

The class vocabulary should include words standard in normal Jewish conversation and their use is to be encouraged. Although students should know how to refer to these items in English, the norm should be *motse-shabes* – not *Saturday night*, *davn* – not *pray*, *bentshn* – not *recite Grace After Meals*, *yon-tef* – not *holiday* . . . Respect should be accorded to the ideal of *sheym shomayim shogur beficho* 'the name of G-d habitually on your lips' . . . Compositions and reports . . . can include specific Jewish topics as well as general topics, and in such cases writing with the interpolation of Hebrew words would be encouraged . . . These and a host of other similar innovations and applications can do much to make the entire day spent in yeshiva of one fabric – Jewish in thought, speech, and deed. (Breslauer 1973: 13–14)

Unlike older Jewish languages, which have traditionally been written iń the Hebrew alphabet, Jewish English is almost always written in the roman alphabet, because most of its users have had training in written non-Jewish English. In earlier times, when Jews underwent less acculturation than now, most of them could not read or write other scripts and anything they wrote was naturally in the Jewish script. However, Jewish English (or even non-Jewish English) texts are occasionally found in the Jewish script in private correspondence for cryptic purposes, or if the reader or writer or both do not know the roman alphabet. Even in otherwise all-Latin-letter printed texts some Hebrew or Yiddish words, phrases, proverbs, or quotations may appear in the Jewish script (see Baron 1950: 119, 128 for examples in Jewish English and German).

Jewish English is still taking shape and we cannot yet write comprehensive phonological, grammatical, LEXICAL, or stylistic descriptions of it. There are varieties which are very different from non-Jewish English ("From this the rebi learns out the din that on shabes and yon-tef it's not permitted to . . ." – with Yiddish intonation) and others which are not. Some varieties are disappearing, including all those whose main determinant is not Eastern Yiddish. In addition, even some features of Eastern Yiddish-based Jewish English are tending to disappear – for example, *peyntner* 'painter,' *karpintner* 'carpenter,' *v* for *w*, and *oy* for *er*, as in *soykl* 'circle.'

What is only incidental individual interference and what has become integrated into Jewish English would have to be determined for each of its many varieties. In any case, probably no one who identifies himself as a Jew speaks and writes English without at least a few Jewish characteristics, and even rarer are those Jews who do not at least understand some Jewish English. Geographically, Jewish English is most distinctive in New York City. With its large Jewish population, it is easy for Jews to maintain dense communications networks among themselves (and even advance considerably up the social, economic, and cultural ladders), without too much contact with non-Jews – much easier, say, than in New Orleans or Honolulu.

Several rules have become firmly established in all varieties whose main determinant is Eastern Yiddish. Phonology: The *-e* at the end of Yiddish words (pronounced like the *-a* of *sofa*) is changed to an *i* (pronounced like the *y* of *city*) in Jewish English, for example, *rebe* 'Chasidic leader' and *khale* 'Sabbath bread' become *rebi*, *khali* or *hali* (pronounced like *holly*). Grammar: Yiddish verbs are integrated into Jewish English by dropping the *-(e)n* of the Yiddish infinitive – to *bentsh* 'to recite the Grace after Meals,' *davn* 'to pray,' *kvetsh* 'to complain,' *shlep* 'to drag,' etc. are from *bentshn, davenen, kvetshn, shlepn*. Lexicon: Among Jews whose celebrations of the Feast of Lights has been Americanized, many English collocations in which *Christmas* (or occasionally *Thanksgiving*) appears have Jewish English equivalents with *Khanike* (usually spelled *Chanuka*): *Chanuka greetings* (e.g. "Sincerest Chanuka Greetings," "May the Chanuka Festival Bring Abundant Blessings of Health and Happiness to All People of Good Will"), *the Chanuka season, Chanuka party, Chanuka card, Chanuka decorations, Chanuka bush* (cf. *Christmas tree*), *Chanuka present, gift-wrapped for Chanuka, traditional Chanuka latkes with all the trimmings* (cf. *Thanksgiving turkey with all the trimmings*).

Of all the many varieties of American Jewish English, only those spoken by Eastern Ashkenazim during the third period have influenced some varieties of non-Jewish English. We have already noted the exceptional *kosher, nebish, shlemil,* adopted during the second period from the speech of Western Ashkenazim, the preponderant group at the time. Since these words have had a century or more to diffuse into American English, it is not surprising that they are generally better known to non-Jews than most of the more recent loans, like *tumler* 'a male entertainer, as formerly employed by Jewish resorts in the Catskill Mountains, who combined the duties of a comedian, activities director, and master of ceremonies to keep the guests amused throughout the day; any lively, prankish, or mischievous man.'

Most of the loans from Jewish into non-Jewish English are vocabulary items, including productive morphemes like *-nik* and *-shm-*, as in *beatnik, fancy-shmancy.* Some are syntactical patterns with attendant intonation, as in *Great art it isn't* or *This is coffee!?,* and, especially in New York City, some intonation patterns for identical Jewish and non-Jewish syntactical patterns (e.g. *We found books, pictures, furniture, clothes* with a Jewish English enumerative intonation). Grammatical and lexical influence can be exerted through written media, but intonation patterns can be borrowed only by hearing them; hence their higher frequency in New York City.

It must not be overlooked that influence on non-Jewish English is coming from Eastern Ashkenazic Jewish English as spoken by American-born Jews rather than directly from Eastern Yiddish or the Eastern Ashkenazic Jewish English of the immigrant generation. The foreign-born, most of whom remained strongest in Yiddish, were certainly not imitated by non-Jewish Americans, and it was not until their children and grandchildren, stronger in Jewish English than in Yiddish, began making their way in the non-Jewish world that non-Jewish English was affected to any extent. This can be proven linguistically also. To take one example: English *khutspe* means both 'impudence' and 'guts'; in Yiddish it means only 'impudence' and the two English meanings can be explained only by assuming that speakers of Jewish English modeled their use of *khutspe* on English *nerve,* which has both meanings.

Jewish English has not necessarily been developing or declining in successive intergenerational deviations from or approximations to non-Jewish English. Developments in either direction are possible: either a constantly widening gap between Jewish and non-Jewish English or a constantly narrowing gap. The former would be likely only where non-Jewish English is absent as a corrective, i.e. where contact with non-Jews is minimal or nonexistent (as for many of the ultra-Orthodox). If there is continuous contact, it is unlikely that non-Jewish

English would not serve to correct the grosser features of Jewish English, especially when contact increases or if the features can be easily controlled by the speaker. Another factor to be considered is nonverbal culture: the highly Americanized Jew evidently has little need for Jewish vocabulary, whereas the actively Jewish person does.

Future trends

Several trends of language use in Jewish communities in the United States have already been mentioned, and they may be expected to continue, although it is difficult to predict whether new trends may set in. The use of Dzhudezmo as a spoken and written language in the United States seems likely to disappear, leaving little or no trace on the speech of American Jews. Yiddish shows signs of a steady decline as a normal spoken and written language among secular Jews, but as we have noted, there is new interest in Yiddish language and culture, and Eastern Yiddish, through Eastern Ashkenazic Jewish English, is continuing to be a major determinant of American Jewish English. At the present time the most vital use of Yiddish seems to be in the ultra-Orthodox communities who lead the most distinctively Jewish life of all American Jews and have the least contact with non-Jews.

Hebrew continues to have its special place in American Jewish life as in other Jewish communities. Most Jews study some Hebrew at some time in their lives, and Hebrew seems likely to continue in use as a liturgical language, the language of much of Orthodox religious scholarly writings, and the vernacular of Israelis coming to the United States.

Most research about the speech and writing of Jews in the USA has concerned Yiddish: How has the language changed here, who uses Yiddish, when, and what attitudes do people have towards it? (See Further Reading.) Let us hope that Jewish linguistic and sociolinguistic studies will expand and deepen to reach all facets of language: the same questions being asked about Yiddish need to be asked about Dzhudezmo, Hebrew, Jewish English, and other Jewish languages. By far, the most interesting questions concern Jewish English: Has its influence on American English peaked or is it continuing? Will Jews and non-Jews become increasingly aware of it, as they have of Black English? Will it be cultivated consciously (as Breslauer advocates) or will Jews try to approximate non-Jewish English as best they can?

FURTHER READING

The best introduction to Jewish languages is Birnbaum 1971; for more on specific Jewish languages see *For Max Weinreich On His Seventieth Birthday: Studies in Jewish Languages, Literature, and Society* and the review-essay on it by Gold 1974.

An excellent summary of the main features of Yiddish is Uriel Weinreich 1971. Max Weinreich's monumental four-volume *History of Yiddish* (1979) is in fact the most important book ever published about any Jewish language. Fishman 1965b deals with the history and use of Yiddish in the United States and includes a small section on Hebrew in the USA. Certain aspects of Yiddish in the USA are treated in Gold 1972, 1977a.

For brief introductions to Dzhudezmo see Gold 1977b, in press b. On the emergence of Modern Hebrew see Gold, in press a.

14

Slavic languages in the new environment*

VĚRA M. HENZL

Although some 5 million people in the United States today are MOTHER-TONGUE speakers of Slavic languages, most Americans know very little about either the languages or their speakers. People may confuse Slovak and Slovenian or think that Yugoslav is a language. Even Polish, which ranks along with Spanish, German, Italian, and French as one of the "big five" immigrant languages, is not known to the general public except by jokes and stereotypes, and the Polish Americans do not have a recognized minority ethnic status comparable to the Hispanic community. The purpose of this chapter is to fill this gap in public knowledge by presenting a brief overview of the Slavic languages in use in the United States and placing them in the historical and linguistic perspective of their development. Case studies of American Polish and American Czech are further included in order to demonstrate the role of ethnic organizations, as well as the influence of active LANGUAGE CULTIVATION in the maintenance of these languages in the USA.

Slavic immigration to the USA

Many Americans hold the stereotype of the Slavs as poorly educated, though in 1451 Eneas Silvius, later Pope Pius II, described housewives from the Czech town Tábor as more literate in the Bible than some Italian bishops. Slavs are also thought of as clad in their colorful folk costumes and toiling in their postage-stamp sized fields, yet today Slavic scientists are developing technologies to put man into space. Ignorance and misconceptions about the coming of Slavs to the American continent are equally widespread. It is customary to call the Slavs a "new immigration," even though the evidence suggests that Slavic settlers were already on the shore of America when the *Mayflower* was approaching the coast. The earliest Slavic migrants to America were among the explorers of the new continent. Most of them arrived as sailors aboard European vessels, such as the Pole, Jan of Kolno, who came with a Danish expedition to Labrador in 1476 (Haiman 1974: 5), the Serbs from Dubrovnik who accompanied Columbus sixteen years later, or the Croats, swept away from their wrecked ship off the

---

* I wish to thank David V. Henzl for the collating and graphic interpretation of the statistics in Tables 14.1–2 and Figures 14.1–14.3.

coast of North Carolina in the sixteenth century and later assimilated into the indigenous population of what are still called Croatan Indians (Albin and Alexander 1972: 1). The only fully fledged colonizers were of course the Russians who, after the discovery of Alaska in 1741, kept steadily moving along the Pacific coast down toward San Francisco, erecting their Fort Ross nearby.

Quite early during colonial times, a number of adventurous and wealthy families of diverse Slavic backgrounds settled along the East coast. There are sources documenting the activities of a few of the Czechs, such as the Thirty Years' War émigré, surveyor Augustin Heřman who arrived in New Amsterdam in 1633, drew the map of Virginia and Maryland, and founded a large estate. Others were the colorful merchant prince Bedřich Filip and especially a female relative of his, known for being seriously courted by George Washington, and the co-signer of the Declaration of Independence, Vilém Paca (Čapek 1970: 9). The early Polish settlers included the famed Generals Kosciuszko and Pułaski, who fought along with Lafayette in the Revolutionary War, and the poet Julian Niemcewicz, Washington's esteemed friend and biographer (Haiman 1974: 29).

Before the eighteenth century, religious reasons were among the major incentives for the migration of the Slavs to America. On the one hand, religious immigration consisted of travelers who wanted to do missionary work in the newly discovered land, and, on the other, of refugees who were exposed to political persecution in Europe because of their religious beliefs. Under the first rubric fall some of the few recorded Czech, Croatian, and Slovenian Jesuits whose missions brought them mainly to the southern parts of the American continent. One of them, Ferdinand Konščak, a Croat, also known as Padre Consago, is remembered for his draft of the first map of Lower California (Albin and Alexander 1972: 3). Among the early religious exiles taking refuge in America, there was an appreciable number of the members of *Jednota českobratrská* (the church of the Czech Brethren, also called the Moravian Brethren), which was ordered to be dissolved in 1627 as a consequence of the defeat of Protestantism in the Bohemian phase of the Thirty Years' War. As most of them were traveling via Poland and Saxony, they frequently entered the American continent as part of a German immigrant group. With a steadily increasing stream of newcomers still in the eighteenth century, the Brethren were able to engage in extensive religious and educational activities in American missions, which they organized first in Georgia and shortly thereafter also in Pennsylvania and North Carolina (Čapek 1970: 19).

In the period between 1848 and World War I, economic factors played the strongest role in the emigration of the greatest masses of Slavs from Europe. At first, immigration to the USA was stimulated by the opportunity of acquiring cheap land, as well as by the outbreak of the Californian gold craze, both of which attracted thousands of European peasants, workers, and craftsmen whose chances for making a living were being seriously threatened by the growing industrial revolution. With the exception of the Czech immigrants, who, as a rule, were the most educated and well-to-do, many of these Slavs, equipped with few professional skills and minimal financial means, were a source of cheap labor. They poured into large industrial cities of the American East and Midwest to make fast money there. As indicated by the escalated immigration figures from 1899–1908, an exodus of some 1.5 million Slavs (including 83,698 Czechs, 320,047 Slovaks, 738,012 Poles, 102,036 Ruthenians and Ukrainians, and 53,454 Russians, besides an undisclosed number of South Slavs) occurred just before the outbreak of World War I, when the poor economic and social conditions in Europe were worsened by political persecution of Slavic populations. During this decade, some of the originally very small Slavic enclaves grew into large ethnic settlements within the rising industrial centers, such as Chicago, Detroit, Pittsburgh, Cleveland, Buffalo, and New York, still the strongest bastions of the Slavic element in the USA (Balch 1969: 248).

Certain waves of the Slavic immigration had a predominantly political character. In contrast to other immigration patterns, these groups included people of extremely diverse socio-economic backgrounds. For example, among the masses of the Polish peasants who arrived during the course of the last century, there was a strong representation of the politically disenchanted intelligentsia fleeing Poland after the unsuccessful attempts of 1848, 1863, and 1870 to restore independence from the Germans and Russians. The trend of seeking political exile in the USA has continued throughout the twentieth century when the rise of Nazism and Communism posed new threats to the political sovereignty of the Slavic nations and to the civil rights of their peoples. The coming of Hitler to power in the 1930s and the rise of Communism from the outbreak of the Bolshevik Revolution in Russia to the 1968 Russian invasion of Czechoslovakia have forced thousands of Slavs, including especially many Slavic Jews, to leave Europe.

Slavs of the professional classes are the most recent immigrants to the USA. This group consists of people who are highly skilled and fit into the American "brain drain" immigration pattern of the last decades. Although Slavic scientists, educators, and artists were frequent visitors to America during the colonial and early republic days, only rarely were they motivated to taking permanent residency on American soil. The high position of the professionals on the socio-economic ladder has given them much freedom to influence their integration into the American society, so that both the assimilated Slavic American, as Vladimir Nabokov was, and the exiled Slav of Alexander Solzhenitsyn's stature have continued to live creatively in their new environment.

Scarcity of documents about the composition of the American population during the colonial period, as well as inconsistencies in the reporting of the ethnic origin of Americans in the U.S. census records, fluctuating from "nationality" to "country of origin" and "mother tongue," pose difficulties in estimating the exact size of an immigrant group through time. Furthermore, the native land of a Slavic people may have been part of different political entities during the course of the last centuries, and immigrants of identical ethnic background were registered in different categories at different census periods. For example, the speakers of Slovak were classed either as Slovaks, Czechoslovaks, Hungarians, or even Austrians, depending on which political power ruled over Slovakia at the moment of the claimants' emigration. In the early 1900s, religious affiliation was

Table 14.1. *Summary of U.S. census data on Slavic Americans, 1910–1970*

Ethnic group	1910 G1–G2	1920 G1–G2	1930 G1	1940 G1–G3	1960 G1	1970 G1–G3 Total no.	1970 G1–G3 Percentage of Total U.S. population	1970 G1–G3 Percentage of Source population[a]
Polish	1,707,640	2,436,895	965,899	2,416,320	581,936	2,437,938	1.2	7.4
Czech	539,392	622,796	201,138	520,440	91,711	452,812	0.2	4.8
Slovak	284,444	619,866	240,196	484,360	125,000	510,366	0.3	11.3
Serbo-Croatian	129,254	200,421	109,923	153,080	88,004	239,455	0.1	2.0
Slovenian	183,431	208,552	77,671	178,640	32,108	82,321	0.04	4.1
Russian	95,137	731,949	315,721	585,080	276,834	334,615	0.2	0.3
Ukrainian	35,359	95,458	58,685	83,600	106,974	249,351	0.1	0.6
"Other Balto-Slavs"	—	—	—	—	—	19,745	0.01	—
Total	2,974,657	4,915,937	1,969,133	4,421,520	1,302,657	4,326,603	2.1	1.7
Percentage of U.S. population	3.2	4.7	1.6	3.4	.7	2.1		

Note: G1, G2, and G3 indicate the immigrant generations covered in the census.

G1 = First generation, i.e. foreign-born Slavic Americans.

G2 = Second generation, i.e. native-born of foreign parentage.

G3 = Third generation, i.e. native-born of native parentage.

[a] Speakers in principal nation of origin, pp. 302–3.

Table 14.2. *Distribution of Slavic ethnic groups for states and metropolitan areas of 250,000 or more*

Rank State	Population		Rank Metropolitan area	Population
All Slavic Americans by mother tongue.				
1 New York	620,209	(3.4%)[a]	1 Chicago, IL	486,677
2 Pennsylvania	591,404	(5.0%)	2 New York, NY	317,694
3 Illinois	526,017	(4.7%)	3 Detroit, MI	262,187
4 Michigan	370,086	(4.2%)	4 Pittsburgh, PA	203,521
5 New Jersey	352,324	(4.9%)	5 Cleveland, OH	186,323
6 Ohio	344,222	(3.2%)	6 Philadelphia, PA	148,364
7 California	231,577	(1.2%)	7 Buffalo, NY	132,545
8 Wisconsin	172,639	(4.0%)	8 Los Angeles, CA	105,894
9 Connecticut	163,254	(5.4%)	9 Milwaukee, WI	88,516
10 Massachusetts	157,317	(2.8%)	10 Newark, NJ	84,393
Czech Americans by mother tongue				
1 Illinois	65,553		1 Chicago, IL	61,021
2 Texas	64,938		2 New York, NY	26,242
3 Nebraska	33,806		3 Cleveland, OH	21,599
4 New York	33,500		4 Houston, TX	14,478
5 Ohio	30,049		5 Los Angeles, CA	11,648
6 California	28,338		6 Minneapolis, MN	8,896
7 Minnesota	25,531		7 Omaha, NE	8,704
8 Wisconsin	24,934		8 Pittsburgh, PA	6,264
9 Iowa	18,288		9 Dallas, TX	6,151
10 Michigan	15,492		10 Detroit, MI	5,570
Slovak Americans by mother tongue				
1 Pennsylvania	164,141		1 Pittsburgh, PA	69,593
2 Ohio	89,197		2 Cleveland, OH	43,645
3 New Jersey	49,953		3 Chicago, IL	27,631
4 New York	41,659		4 New York, NY	22,987
5 Illinois	33,610		5 Youngstown, OH	19,016
6 Michigan	21,267		6 Wilkes, PA	15,020
7 Connecticut	19,373		7 Philadelphia, PA	13,732
8 California	18,153		8 Detroit, MI	13,702
9 Indiana	13,674		9 Johnstown, PA	12,360
10 Wisconsin	8,558		10 Newark, NJ	11,672

298

VERA M. HENZL

Table 14.2. (*contd.*)

Rank State	Population	Rank Metropolitan area	Population
Polish Americans by mother tongue			
1 New York	390,706	1 Chicago, IL	326,801
2 Illinois	346,148	2 Detroit, MI	203,913
3 Michigan	280,543	3 New York, NY	160,088
4 Pennsylvania	273,094	4 Buffalo, NY	119,508
5 New Jersey	214,684	5 Philadelphia, PA	94,092
6 Massachusetts	134,055	6 Pittsburgh, PA	72,432
7 Ohio	132,023	7 Cleveland, OH	66,855
8 Wisconsin	118,642	8 Milwaukee, WI	65,992
9 Connecticut	114,180	9 Newark, NJ	50,636
10 California	82,641	10 Paterson, NJ	44,533
Russian Americans by mother tongue			
1 New York	76,218	1 New York, NY	61,614
2 California	51,631	2 Los Angels, CA	24,562
3 Pennsylvania	43,117	3 Chicago, IL	15,638
4 New Jersey	32,672	4 San Francisco, CA	14,336
5 Illinois	16,976	5 Philadelphia, PA	13,740
6 Ohio	14,012	6 Pittsburgh, PA	11,643
7 Connecticut	13,142	7 Detroit, MI	9,742
8 Michigan	12,982	8 Paterson, NJ	9,157
9 Massachusetts	11,758	9 Cleveland, OH	7,306
10 Florida	10,494	10 Boston, MA	7,155
Ukrainian Americans by mother tongue			
1 New York	52,069	1 New York, NY	27,591
2 Pennsylvania	49,398	2 Philadelphia, PA	21,055
3 New Jersey	33,117	3 Chicago, IL	18,790
4 Illinois	19,773	4 Detroit, MI	15,158
5 Ohio	18,632	5 Pittsburgh, PA	11,668
6 Michigan	11,050	6 Cleveland, OH	10,664
7 California	9,655	7 Newark, NJ	10,506
8 Connecticut	4,884	8 Rochester, NY	5,702
9 Minnesota	4,343	9 Paterson, NJ	5,506
10 Massachusetts	3,311	10 Los Angeles, CA	4,919

Table 14.2. (*contd.*)

Rank State	Population	Rank Metropolitan area	Population
Serbo-Croatian Americans by mother tongue			
1 Ohio	27,331	1 Cleveland, OH	22,384
2 Pennsylvania	10,203	2 Chicago, IL	7,030
3 Illinois	8,247	3 Pittsburgh, PA	5,979
4 California	5,681	4 Duluth, MN	3,911
5 Wisconsin	5,434	5 Milwaukee, WI	3,584
6 Minnesota	5,072	6 New York, NY	1,991
7 New York	3,427	7 Los Angeles, CA	1,934
8 Michigan	2,876	8 Detroit, MI	1,600
9 Colorado	2,290	9 San Francisco, CA	1,382
10 Indiana	1,431	10 Akron, OH	1,233
Bulgarian Americans by country of origin			
1 Pennsylvania	37,785	1 Chicago, IL	28,810
2 Illinois	33,673	2 Pittsburgh, PA	25,842
3 Ohio	31,218	3 New York, NY	15,562
4 California	30,557	4 Los Angeles, CA	14,335
5 New York	19,888	5 Cleveland, OH	13,696
6 Michigan	17,047	6 Detroit, MI	12,127
7 Indiana	11,155	7 Milwaukee, WI	6,669
8 Wisconsin	9,493	8 San Francisco, CA	4,983
9 New Jersey	7,061	9 St. Louis, MO	4,681
10 Minnesota	5,196	10 Akron, OH	4,014
Slovenian Americans by mother tongue			
1 California	3,506	1 New York, NY	1,619
2 New York	2,742	2 Los Angeles, CA	1,172
3 Illinois	2,037	3 Chicago, IL	956
4 Ohio	1,754	4 Detroit, MI	375
5 Michigan	1,662	5 Toledo, OH	357
6 New Jersey	889	6 San Francisco, CA	202
7 Pennsylvania	752	7 Cleveland, OH	194
8 Indiana	690	8 Buffalo, NY	121
9 Massachusetts	597	9 Seattle, WA	110
10 Florida	573	10 Milwaukee, WI	109
		11 Gary, IN	103

[a] Percentage of the total population.
Source: Based on data from the 1970 U.S. census. (In this census, statistics based on the immigrants' mother tongues are available only for speakers of Polish, Czech, Slovak, Serbo-Croatian, Slovenian, Russian, and Ukrainian. The numbers quoted for Bulgarian refer to immigrants whose country of origin is Bulgaria. No reliable sources of statistics have been established for the American speakers of Sorbian, Ruthenian, Belorussian, and Macedonian.)

often used as a convenient device for the ethnic classification of the Slav, for example, immigrants from Galicia may have been registered as Poles, rather than Ukrainians, Ruthenians, or Russians, if they declared themselves Catholic.

Even the 1900 U.S. census, reporting that among Americans, 687,671 were natives of Poland, 685,176 of Russia, 434,617 of Austria (probably including South Slavs), 356,830 of Bohemia (most probably all Czechs), and 216,391 of Hungary (including most probably Slovaks), offers no precise information on the ethnic background of these immigrants. Yet it does suggest that at the turn of the century, when the total U.S. population was a third of its present size, a number close to 2,380,000 Americans might have been of Slavic parentage. The breakdown of this number by states indicates that a large number of the Slavic Americans were settled in the North Atlantic and Midwest states, mainly Pennsylvania (595,116), New York (292,443), Illinois (194,898), New Jersey (114,093), Ohio (107,119), followed by Massachusetts, Connecticut, Michigan, Wisconsin, Missouri, Minnesota, Maryland, West Virginia, Indiana, Texas, and California, in that order (Balch 1969: 253).

Later U.S. census reports, which capture more accurately the ethnic characteristics of the Slavic contingent in the USA, reflect both historical developments in Europe and changes in American immigration policies. Economic crises, political uprooting in revolutions, world wars, governmental coups, and the continuous racial discrimination of many European nations, were strong incentives for extensive migration of the Slavs. Though, as the census figures indicate, there have been periods, such as the World War II years, when the figures are low because emigration was not possible. At the same time, variation in the census figures has also been related to fluctuation in the popular appreciation of various ethnic groups among the Americans. Since the collection of the U.S. census data is based on voluntary self-report of the sample population, it is also likely that at different census periods immigrants were differently motivated to claim their non-English heritage. The Bureau of the Census has collected data on the Slavic ethnic groups in the USA at the end of each decade of the twentieth century except the 1950s, as shown in Table 14.1. Since the generations covered were different and the elicitation of the census information for each decade was influenced by a different set of factors, leveling of the data that would allow a trend analysis is difficult and lies beyond the scope of this chapter.

The present distribution of the individual Slavic ethnic groups by states and metropolitan areas of 250,000 or more inhabitants, based on the 1970 U.S. census data, is shown in Table 14.2. In general, these statistics reflect the original immigration trends of each of these groups, although California, as the most rapidly growing state, has been increasing the concentration of the Slavs in its population. Nonetheless, the high density of Slavic Americans in Illinois and New York has been preserved in all the Slavic groups, with Chicago containing the largest groups of the Polish, Czech, and Serbo-Croatian Americans, and New York City containing the largest groups of the Russian, Ukrainian, and Bulgarian Americans. Most Slovak Americans live in Pittsburgh, and Slovenian Americans in Cleveland. For the geographic distribution of the 1970 concentration of the Slavic, Polish, and Czech Americans by states see Figures 14.1–14.3.

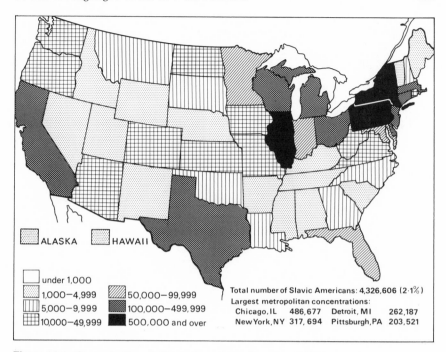

Figure 14.1. Concentration of Slavic Americans, by states (1970)

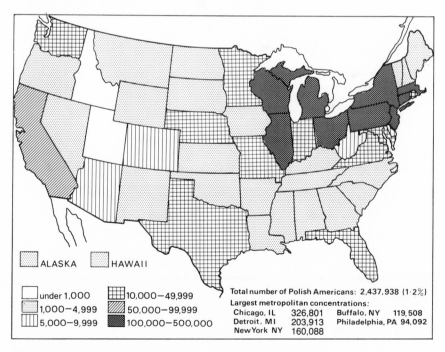

Figure 14.2. Concentration of Polish Americans, by states (1970)

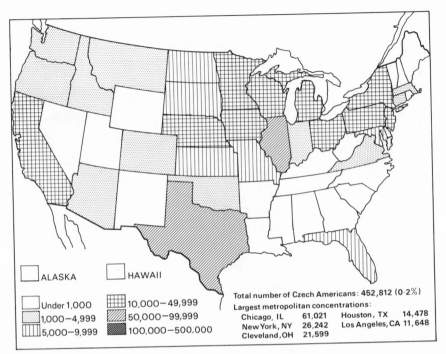

Figure 14.3. Concentration of Czech Americans by states (1970)

The Slavic languages and their standardization

The Slavic languages are a branch of the Indo-European LANGUAGE FAMILY; they are spoken by some 250 million people in Europe and Asia, in addition to the many Slavic emigrants dispersed throughout the world, including the American continent.

The original homeland of the early Common Slavic speakers is believed to have been in Eastern Europe, in an area north of the Carpathian mountains. During the period between the fifth and the ninth centuries, as the early Slavs began to expand to a larger territory of Europe, the previously homogeneous language started to develop DIALECTAL differentiation, eventually yielding three linguistically and geographically defined language groups. Today the most extensive by far is the East Slavic group, including some 125 million speakers of Russian, 45 million speakers of Ukrainian with some 300,000 speakers of Ruthenian, and 10 million speakers of Belorussian, all within the Soviet Union. The West Slavic group includes over 9 million speakers of Czech and 4 million speakers of Slovak, the two official languages of Czechoslovakia, 33 million speakers of Polish, and some 50,000 speakers of Sorbian (also referred to as Wendish), a minority language spoken in East Germany. To the South Slavic group belong the languages of Yugoslavia and Bulgaria. The languages of Yugoslavia include Slovenian, spoken by 2 million people, Serbo-Croatian, spoken by 6 million Croats and more than 6 million Serbs, and Macedonian, spoken by over 1 million people; Bulgarian (together with Macedonian also called the Balkan Slavic languages) comprises some 8 million speakers. Linguistically also belonging to the South Slavic group is Church Slavic (or Old Church Slavonic), which is the liturgical language of the Orthodox and some Catholic Slavs of all three of the major Slavic language groups.

The Slavic languages, in spite of their immense geographical spread, are linguistically closer to each other than the languages in some other branches of the Indo-European family. They are closer to one another, for example, than English and German, two sister languages of the Germanic branch.

Most of the Slavic languages have retained their original INFLECTIONAL SYSTEM in nouns, pronouns, adjectives, and verbs, and along with this complex system they share great variability and functional utilization of word order in the sentence. To illustrate this point, consider the Russian equivalent of an English sentence, for example, *The student didn't see the professor.* In the Slavic languages the object *professor* would be marked by a suffix, and therefore the sentence translates into Russian in a variety of possible arrangements, rather than only the "subject-verb-object" pattern which is obligatory in English. Typically, a Russian would place in final position the word which conveys the most important information for the listener; for instance (examples are transliterated into the Latin alphabet):

(1) Student nevidel *professora* [answering the question, "Whom didn't the student see?"]

(2) Professora nevidel *student* [answering the question, "Who didn't see the professor?"]

(3) Student professora *nevidel* [answering the question, "The student didn't do what?"]

The Slavic verb, in contrast to English, includes a large amount of grammatical information within a single word. By means of inflection, it can not only express the agent and the time of an action, for example, in Czech $zpív + á + m$ 'I sing' versus $zpív + á + š$ 'you (intimate) sing,' but can also distinguish between various kinds of completed and ongoing actions, a concept called ASPECT by the grammarians, as in Czech $zpív + a + ly$ 'they (fem.) sang (for an undisclosed period of time)' versus $za + zpív + a + ly$ 'they (fem.) sang (once),' $do + zpív + a + ly$ 'they (fem.) sang (and completed it).'

A typical characteristic of the sound system of the Slavic languages is the richness of the PALATAL and PALATALIZED consonants which are pronounced with a kind of "sticky" *y* quality. The name of the former Russian prime minister *N*i*k*ita *S*e*rg*eevi*ch* Khru*shch*ev (palatal and palatalized consonants italicized) would be a good example of this phenomenon. In all but the Bulgarian and Macedonian languages, a number of consonants, such as *d, t, n, l, r, z, s,* occur in "hard/soft" doublets, and the meaning of a word can change by a mere change in this palatalization feature, e.g. Czech /jdete/ 'you go' versus /jḍete/ 'go' (imperative); /ti/ 'you' versus /ṭi/ 'these'; Russian /tikaṭ/ 'to address informally' versus /ṭikaṭ/ 'to tick'; /nanka/ 'napkin' versus /ṇaṇka/ 'nurse,' etc.

Another common feature of the Slavic phonologies, apparent in loans and surnames of Slavic origin, such as *borshch, Brzezinski,* and the like, is consonant clustering. Although the average frequency of vowel occurrences in the Slavic languages is close to 50 percent (only 38 percent in English), paradoxically enough, examples of words including sequences of as many as seven consonants, or lacking vowels altogether, can easily be drawn from any of the Slavic languages, for example, Bulgarian /zvezda/ 'star,' Polish /gżmot/ 'thunder,' Slovak /slnko/ 'sun,' Serbo-Croatian /prst/ 'finger,' Czech /scvrkls/ 'you shrank,' /kfspři:mene: / 'to the erected.'

The vocalic system of the Slavic languages, in contrast to the eleven-vowel system of English, is relatively simple, consisting of the five basic vowels /i, e, a, o, u/. The East and the Balkan Slavic languages further reduce their vocalic systems in unstressed syllables; for instance, both Russian and Belorussian operate with only a three-vowel system of /i, a, u/ under these conditions. Standard Polish, on the other hand, in addition to the common stock has two nasal vowels, /ę/ and /ǫ/, although these are disappearing in the everyday language. Czech and Slovak, as well as Serbo-Croatian and Slovenian, differentiate between short and long vowels, for example, Czech /bili/ 'they beat' versus /bi:li: / 'white,' Serbo-Croatian /žena/ 'woman' versus /že:na/ 'women' (genitive). Slovak and Serbo-Croatian also admit long /r:/, as in, for example, Serbo-Croatian /grk/ 'Greek' versus /gr:k/ 'bitter'; Slovak additionally can also have a long /l:/, as in /stl:p/ 'pole.'

Stress always falls on the first syllable of words in Czech and Slovak and on the next to the last syllable in Polish: compare Smétana, the Czech composer, and Paderéwski, the Polish musician and statesman. The East and South Slavic languages, on the other hand, have a free accent, which means that stress occurs, as in English, on any syllable of the word, for example, in Russian /ádres/ 'address,' /adresát/ 'addressee,' etc., and it can move from one syllable to another when the word is inflected, for example, Russian /adresováṭ/ 'to address' versus /adresúju/ 'I address.'

Although the composition of the LEXICON reflects most tangibly the differences between the individual Slavic languages, there are still some two thousand basic words that are shared by all the members of the Slavic language family. For instance, the root /misl/ 'think' appears with little differentiation in all the equivalent Slavic words, i.e. Czech *myslit,* Slovak *mysliet',* Sorbian *myslić,* Polish *myśleć,* Ukrainian мислити, Belorussian мысліць, Russian мыслить, Slovenian and Serbo-Croatian *misliti,* and Macedonian and Bulgarian мисли. Formation of new words is typically executed in all the Slavic languages by derivational processes, mainly consisting in addition of prefixes and suffixes to the basic words. Prefixation for verbal aspect and suffixation for the formation of nouns are enormously productive processes, and it is not uncommon to find whole sequences of affixes within one word, for example, in Czech *ne + pro + na + jím + a + tel + ný* 'not for rent.' New words are also produced by compounding of independent roots, for example, Croatian *more + plov + ac* 'sailor' ('sea-fare-r'), and lately also by compounding of abbreviations, which is a rather prolific pattern of Russian much imitated by other Slavic languages, for example, *kom* + *so* + *mol* + *ec* 'member of the Communist Youth Union' in which each of the first three syllables is the first syllable of a word in the original expression.

The course of the standardization processes of the Slavic languages, in which they developed from one unwritten VERNACULAR to a number of standard literary, national, or official state languages, has been closely connected with the diverse circumstances in the history of the Slavic ethnic groups. As the social and political organization of the Slavs became differentiated through time, the languages took their independent paths of development, acquiring new forms and assuming new functions serving the various new needs of the speakers.

The tribal vernacular was first written in the ninth century. This first written Slavic language, the Church Slavic, was used predominantly for liturgical and literary purposes of all the Slavic groups, as well as the non-Slavic Rumanians. Within a short time, however, the Western Slavs, whose cultural orientation kept them in close contacts with Western Europe, adopted Latin as the medium of writing, and later as the model for GRAPHIZATION of the vernacular languages. This transition, while opening new avenues to the learned world, which used Latin as a LINGUA FRANCA well through the dawn of the modern age, initiated a historical break in the unity of the Slavic language family, the consequences of which still affect communication among Slavs today. Two alphabets resulted, the first, Cyrillic, to be used for some Slavic languages, and the Latin alphabet for others. In spite of similarity among the spoken Slavic languages, the two different alphabets, as well as the different writing conventions (how specific sounds are represented graphically) keep them apart. Those using Latin letters are Czech, Slovak, Sorbian, Polish, Slovenian, and Croatian, and those using Cyrillic letters are Russian, Belorussian, Ukrainian, Ruthenian, Serbian, Macedonian, and Bulgarian, as well as Church Slavic.

Romanization, or use of the Latin alphabet, by the Western Slavic languages during the middle ages, developed in a rather scientific fashion, thanks to the analytical approach of a young avant-garde professor of Prague University, Jan Hus (1369–1415), whose radical orthographic reform in many ways foreshadowed modern language planning practices. Hus' introduction of a diacritic script in Czech, using the DIACRITIC MARKS ´ *čarka* for vocalic length and · *nabodeníčko* (later changed to ˇ *háček*) for consonantal palatalization, made it possible to write each meaningful sound unit of speech by one and the same graphic symbol (e.g. *š* for /š/), which largely contributed to the consolidation and simplification of the process of writing and reading, as well as to the unification of orthoepy (correct pronunciation). With the exception of Polish, which uses a digraphic script (in which one sound is often represented by two Latin letters, e.g. *sz* for /š/), the remaining languages of this group, i.e. Slovak, Sorbian, Slovenian, and Croatian, have largely adopted the writing conventions of Czech.

The Cyrillic alphabet is derived from the Glagolitic script constructed in the ninth century in Moravia (today's Czechoslovakia) by the Byzantine missionaries Cyril and Methodius, who produced the first Slavic translation of the Bible.

CROATIAN	SERBIAN
Gradovi Jugoslavije	Градови Југославије

1. Najveći grad Jugoslavije
   je Beograd, koji je glavni
   grad Srbije, a istodobno i
   glavni grad Jugoslavije.

1. Највећи град Југославије је
   Београд, који је главни град
   Србије, а истовремено и
   главни град Југославије.

2. Beograd ima otprilike jedan
   milijun stanovnika.

2. Београд има отприлике један
   милион становника.

3. Nalazeći se na brijegu, gdje
   se sastaju Dunav i Sava,
   Beograd je danas, kao i u
   prošlosti, važna spona
   između Zapada i Istoka.

3. Налазећи се на брегу, где се
   састају Дунав и Сава,
   Београд је данас, као и у
   прошлости, важна спона
   између Запада и Истока.

4. Povijest kaže da su Kelti u
   četvrtom stoljeću prije
   Krista na tom mjestu sa-
   zidali grad (Singidunum).

4. Историја каже да су Келти у
   четвртом веку пре Христа
   на том месту сазидали град
   (Сингидунум).

5. Kasnije su došli Rimljani,
   koji su tu, u Beogradu
   (Singidunum), držali vojni
   garnizon.

5. Доцније су дошли Римљани,
   који су ту, у Београду
   (Сингидунум), држали војни
   гарнизон.

6. Hunski vođa Atila razorio je
   grad u petom stoljeću
   poslije Krista.

6. Хунски вођа Атила разорио је
   град у петом веку после
   Христа.

7. Slavenski narodi naselili su
   se ovdje u početku
   devetog stoljeća.

7. Словенски народи су се овде
   населили у почетку деветог
   века.

8. Za one koji vole povijest,
   Beograd je jedan od naj-
   zanimljivijih gradova
   Evrope.

8. За оне који воле историју,
   Београд је један од најинте-
   ресантнијих градова Европе.

Figure 14.4. Sample of the Latin and the Cyrillic scripts of Serbo-Croatian (reprinted from Magner 1972: 175)

Because of the Byzantine origin of these two priests, the Glagolitic, and subsequently also the Cyrillic script are in fact variants of the Greek alphabet which have been adapted to the Slavic sounds. Although the regions where Church Slavic stayed in use developed national versions in the course of time, the prestigious Russian version influenced directly the later standardization of the individual languages of the whole group. The Cyrillic script of Russia, particularly its "westernized" stylistic revision codified during the rule of Peter the Great, served as the model in the graphization of the remaining East Slavic and Balkan vernaculars. Although the Russian script is phonetic in essence, the manner of marking palatalization does not follow the conventional one-to-one fit between the sound and the graph; pairs of palatalized and nonpalatalized consonants are in fact not represented by different sets of consonantal letters, rather, palatalization is indicated by the form of the vowel letter following the consonant. The script possesses sets of parallel vowel letters, namely а, э, ы, о, у and я, е, и, ё, ю both of which represent the sounds of /a, e, i, o, u/, but the latter set, in addition, marks palatalization of the preceding consonant.

Graphization in the East and South Slavic languages is still strongly influenced by the religious traditions which originated the historical split in the graphic unity of the Slavic languages. An interesting example is the case of Serbo-Croatian, the South Slavic language which is written both in the Latin script by the predominantly Roman Catholic Croats and in the Cyrillic script by the Orthodox Serbs (see Figure 14.4). Similarly, in Belorussian and Ruthenian, the Uniate Catholic speakers prefer to use the Latin alphabet for writing. In the American environment, where, because of English, the Latin alphabet is predominant, the tendency to replace the Cyrillic script of the immigrant languages by the Latin equivalent is very strong.

Slavic languages in contact

The languages of the Slavs developed in contact with other languages and have been influenced by them. From the time of their earliest contact with the languages of writing, Church Slavic and Latin, the Slavic languages have absorbed elements, chiefly in the area of abstract vocabulary, from these two powerful sources. Thus, the languages of the Eastern Slavs and the Balkan Slavs became laden with admixtures of Church Slavic, while in the West Slavic group, LOANWORDS were furnished by Latin. Just as we have in English pairs of synonym words, one of which is of domestic Anglo-Saxon origin (e.g. *make up*), and the other borrowed from Latin (e.g. *constitute*), lexical doublets such as Czech *hlava* (originally Czech) 'head, chapter' and *kapitola* (Latin loan) 'chapter,' or Russian голова (originally Russian) 'head' and глава (Church Slavic loan) 'chapter head,' occur in the Slavic languages. As in English, the borrowed words are typically used in technical or formal language styles and REGISTERS while the domestic ones occur in casual speech.

Since geographically the Slavic languages, except Sorbian, form an uninterrupted continuum, much interference has also taken place between adjacent Slavic languages, and actually in many of the borderline zones, fuzzy interdialectal varieties appear. The variety of Czech spoken along the Slovak border is a typical example of this phenomenon; while officially classed as a dialect of Czech, it could equally well be considered a dialect of Slovak. The more highly standardized Slavic languages were influential in their spread over larger neighboring areas whenever favorable historical opportunities arose. For example, Czech, because of its early history of cultivation, enjoyed a high prestige in

Poland, Slovakia, Sorbia, and Slovenia from the time of the late middle ages, and became the model for standardization of the vernaculars spoken in these countries. Polish, in turn, penetrated further to the east, carrying many of the western linguistic phenomena into Ukrainian and Belorussian, and in an indirect manner, to Russian as well.

However, linguistic interference in the Slavic languages has not been restricted to a mutual influence among the members of the Slavic group. A glance at the map reveals that each of the Slavic peoples is also in direct contact with a non-Slavic nation. Since at times, the closeness of these contacts has been even more intense than it is today, every Slavic language bears some vestige of interference which can be traced to a language belonging to other Indo-European branches, for example, German, Italian, Albanian, Greek, Romanian, Lithuanian, or Latvian, or to a language which is not of Indo-European origin at all, such as Hungarian, Estonian, Turkish, or any of the large number of languages in contact with Russian in Asia. The most pervasive phenomenon has been the transfer of lexical material, which can be documented by examples from virtually any of the Slavic languages, for example, Serbo-Croatian *tepih* 'carpet' < German *Teppich*, Slovak *bosorka* 'witch' < Hungarian *boszorkány*, Slovak *cap* 'buck' < Romanian *ţap*, Polish *talerz* 'plate' < German *Teller*. Some of the borrowing has taken an intricate path of development disguising the foreign origin of the word by translating its parts into the Slavic language, for example, Czech *pod + pis* 'signature' < German *Unter + schrift*, Polish *czaso + pismo* 'journal' < German *Zeit + schrift*, Bulgarian *vlak* 'train' < German *Zug* (< French *train*). Consequences of a deeper interference of the non-Slavic languages on the structure of a Slavic vernacular can be illustrated particularly in the case of Bulgarian and Macedonian. For an extensive period of time, these South Slavic languages have been exposed to Greek and Turkish, which not only are spoken in the neighboring territories, but for a time had an official language status on the Balkan Peninsula. Subsequently, the vernaculars adopted from them some characteristics that are otherwise not found in the Slavic languages. Even some of the features which are fundamental for the typological characterization of the Slavic language group, such as the case system, have gradually been eliminated from Bulgarian and Macedonian.

It should be also noted that the lexicons of the Slavic languages possess words which were borrowed from English, though none of the Slavic languages (except Russian during its role in Alaska and Czech during its shortlived contacts with the American army in 1945) has ever come into direct touch with English speakers. Nonetheless, as elsewhere in the modern world, English is the most popular foreign language among the Slavs. Particularly in the area of technical and scientific terminologies, English words become much assimilated into the native lexicons, for example, Czech *tým* 'team,' *dispečér* 'dispatcher,' etc., but cases of fashionable Americanization of Slavic lexicons in recent years have occurred also for social and psychological reasons.

The American environment with its exuberant variety of immigrant languages provides a natural language laboratory in which it is possible to examine language development in diverse contact situations. The Slavic languages used by speakers residing in the United States, being no exception to the common fate of the immigrant languages, have gradually become deviant from those used in the original countries. The reason for this course of development is twofold. First, according to the varying degrees and types of social and linguistic contact of the immigrants with the speakers of the dominant language of the American host country, the Slavic immigrant languages have become modified by a progressive interference of American English. Second, relative to the time span which has elapsed since the immigrants left their homeland, the Slavic languages in the USA have been used and also learned by successive generations under social conditions which have been increasingly different from those which had existed and have developed in the original home countries.

A description of the languages of the American Slavs depends in large part on knowledge about why some immigrants passed them on almost intact from father to son, and others lost them within a single generation. This information tells us the ways in which English has influenced American Slavic languages and the social conditions in which the TRANSPLANTED LANGUAGES have survived. Since all these languages have registered changes which can be ascribed to coexistence with American English and American social institutions, each would lend itself to study of the new patterns which evolved in the language attitudes and practices as well as in the languages themselves. Here, an analysis of American Polish and American Czech will suffice to demonstrate the character of some of these changes and to discuss some mechanisms which have helped Slavic immigrants maintain their mother tongue amidst the pressures of the American melting pot.

Characteristics of Slavic American languages

The development of a gap between an original Slavic language and its immigrant variety is inevitable, as much as some immigrants wish to deny it. Naturally, the extent and nature of the deviance can vary from speaker to speaker, and can be manifested either by structural changes, or by changes in its use. In the former case, the immigrant speaker uses words, grammatical patterns, or sounds which do not belong to the Slavic language, but are in fact borrowed from English. In the latter case, the immigrant speaker possesses a different set of styles and registers, most often due to the fact that in the American environment certain language functions are exclusively served by English. The misuse of the archaic peasant style instead of the formal variety of Polish appropriate for official state speeches, by an interpreter during the visit of President Carter to Warsaw, is a typical illustration of such a gap. The following examples of deviations from the norm of Standard Polish (P) and Standard Czech (C) can be attributed to the influence of American English in a prolonged contact situation. They are actual citations drawn from studies of American Polish (AmP) by Doroszewski (1938) and Lyra (1962), and American Czech (AmC) by Henzl (1975).

Lexicon. To be short of words is one of the most common signs of an incipient language loss. Whenever an immigrant cannot remember a Slavic word, he may substitute its English equivalent, translating it eventually back into Slavic.

American Slavic	Standard Slavic	American English
AmP: starajcie się o permit	P: starajcie się o pozwolenie	worry about the permit
AmP: przy pomocy X-ray	P: przy pomocy rentgena	by X-ray
AmC: dopis na January third	C: dopis z třetího ledna	the letter on January 3rd
AmC: a potom von shouts, křičí	C: a potom křičí	and then he shouts

By and large, switches into English occur with vocabulary that is connected with the immigrant's American environment, although it may often include names of the months, numbers, and other common words as well. The investigation of a large corpus of immigrant speech has revealed progressive phonological and morphological integration of English loanwords into the Slavic lexicon, as in:

American Slavic	Standard Slavic	American English
AmP: drokstor	P: drogeria	drugstore
AmP: gemblerka	P: graczka	gambler (fem.)
AmP: sfiksuj	P: naprawuj	fix (imp.)
AmC: štór	C: obchod	store
AmC: popíček	C: štěňátko	puppy (dim.)
AmC: zrentovali	C: pronajali	they have rented

Often without recognizing the English influence, Slavic Americans use LOANSHIFTS, i. e. etymologically Slavic words the use of which is extended according to a similarity in sound, meaning, or both with an English word.

American Slavic	Standard Slavic	American English
AmP: teatr (P 'opera house')	P: kino	(movie) theater
AmP: ma karu (P 'he has a cart')	P: ma auto	he has a car
AmC: dostal zvonek (C 'he got a bell')	C: telefonovali mu	he got a ring (phone call)
AmC: má káru (C 'he has a cart')	C: má vuz	he has a car

Another type of subconscious lexical interference of English in the ethnic tongues of the Slavic Americans are CALQUES or translations of English phrases.

American Slavic	Standard Slavic	American English
AmP: dobre czasy	P: używanie życia	good time
AmC: poslední jméno	C: příjmení	last name

Grammar. As with the lexicon, both the process of forgetting Slavic grammatical rules and interference of American English take place in grammatical patterning. In the use of the case system, for instance, Slavic Americans often choose the wrong suffix, or attempt to simplify the morphology by applying the case ending in only one member of a phrase, or by dropping it altogether, particularly when the case can be indicated by a preposition (as in English).

American Slavic	Standard Slavic	American English
AmC: jména vašich spolubydlící	C: jména vašich spolubydlících	the names of your roommates
AmC: okolo to dítě	C: okolo toho dítěte	around the child

A common error which causes misunderstanding is the use of prepositions according to the range of meanings they possess in American English, such as:

American Slavic	Standard Slavic	American English
AmP: *od* dnia *do* dnia	P: *z* dnia *na* dzień	*from* day *to* day
AmC: *na* autobuse	C: *v* autobuse	*on* the bus

Simplification of morphophonemic alternations is another common process in immigrant Slavic languages. For example, in the verbal paradigm, the American speakers often overextend one form of the stem to all forms of the verb.

American Slavic	Standard Slavic	American English
AmP: um*i*ą-umieć	P: umieją-umieć	they can-to be able to
AmC: pla*ká*-plakat [or] pláče-plá*č*et	C: pláče-plakat	he cries-to cry

Since the Slavic languages do not have the sequence of tenses rule which a speaker of English automatically applies in converting a direct quotation, for example, "He ask*ed*, 'What *is* her name?'," into indirect discourse, as "He ask*ed* what her name *was*," its transfer into an immigrant Slavic language may result in a substantial deviation in meaning.

American Slavic	Standard Slavic	American English
AmC: Ptal se [past], co *bylo* [past] její jméno	C: Ptal se [past], co *je* [present] její jméno	He asked what her name was

Here the American Czech would mean in Standard Czech "He asked what her name had been." The English passive is often imitated by Slavic Americans, though it is rarely used in Slavic languages, except in formal written registers.

American Slavic	Standard Slavic	American English
AmP: siostry byli rodzeni [passive] w Polsce	P: siostry urodziły się [active reflexive]	The sisters were born in Poland

The use of infinitives in place of a subordinate clause, not admissible by the syntactic rules of Slavic languages, is another common interference of English.

American Slavic	Standard Slavic	American English
AmC: Byli jsme rádi *dostat* dopis	C: Byli jsme rádi, *že jsme dostali* dopis	We were glad to receive the letter

The Slavic languages do not possess an article and thus do not distinguish definiteness in noun. While the omitting of articles is a characteristic of English spoken by the Slavs, late generation Slavic Americans, on the other hand, tend to supply it in the Slavic languages by using demonstrative pronouns in the position of the English definite article, as in for example:

American Slavic	Standard Slavic	American English
AmP: *ta* dobra gazolina	P: dobra gazolina	the good gas

Contrary to English but like many other European languages, Slavic languages differentiate between an informal and a formal address form in pronouns and second person verb forms. The general use of the informal pattern in the speech of Americans of Slavic background can be attributed not only to the influence of English, but also to the fact that the immigrants typically use the Slavic languages only in the informal speech registers, i. e. with family, friends, etc., where the intimate address constructions are appropriate. In communication with Slavic speakers who do not share the American background, however, a failure to pay respect to the conventional formality rules can bring ridicule to the speaker and embarrass the listener.

Phonology. The long coexistence of the Slavic languages with American English has marked the speech of many of the late generation Slavic Americans with some American pronunciation features. The speakers themselves, by and large, are quite unaware of a deviance in their phonology, except for a few sounds, such as the Czech *ř*, which are not part of the sound inventory of American English and are difficult to produce. Often, however, the manner in which the Slavic languages are pronounced in the USA is a reflection of English.

One of the areas of serious pronunciation interference from English, for example, is in the manipulation of INTONATION and stress. A Slavic American, who in his speech is accustomed to the English rhythmic patterns which easily move stress to various positions, as in, for example, *telegráphic* versus *telégraphy*, undoubtedly finds it difficult to switch to a regular syllabic stress distribution especially in Slavic cognates and to produce, e.g. /'tele͵graficki:/ in Czech where the first syllable is always stressed, or /͵telegra'fični/ in Polish which accentuates the second syllable from the end of the word. It is therefore not surprising to find that the transfer of English stress habits into the Slavic languages is a common source of a "foreign accent" in the speech of American immigrants.

Another noticeable deviance in pronunciation is the ASPIRATION of VOICELESS STOPS in the Slavic languages. English /p, t, k/ are strongly aspirated, especially in word-initial position. In Slavic languages the /p, t, k/ are not aspirated at all, and Slavic Americans tend to substitute the English pronunciation. Also, VOICED consonants at the end of words in Slavic languages are usually devoiced to their voiceless counterparts (e.g. -*b* is pronounced like -*p*). Slavic Americans often pronounce the consonants with full voicing according to the spelling. Thus, a Czech American may say /od/ instead of /ot/ for Czech *od* 'from.' However subtle, aspiration and voicing are among the most persistent types of English interference in the speech of Slavic Americans.

The five basic vowels of the Slavic languages are not diphthongized, but many Slavic Americans tend to add an off-glide or extra length to vowels in open syllables as is done in English; this is a habit that is very difficult to unlearn.

Loss of palatalization is a common phenomenon in American Slavic languages and the frequency of its occurrence often increases in proportion to the articulatory complexity of the particular sound, such as the Czech *ř*. Most often, sounds which do not exist in English, such as the palatal consonants, the *ch* sound, etc., are replaced by their most similar English counterparts.

American Slavic	*Standard Slavic*	*American English*
AmC: [nema:]	C: [ŋema:]	deaf
	C: [nema:]	he has not
AmC: [dobrže]	C: [dobře]	well
[dobže]		
[dobje]		
[dopše]		
AmP: [proše]	P: [prośe]	pig
	P: [proše]	please
AmP: [hoč]	P: [xoć]	although

Slavic Americans often ease the pronunication of a consonantal cluster by dropping some of its consonants, rearranging it to match a sequence familiar in English, or simply by inserting a vowel, such as:

American Slavic	*Standard Slavic*	*American English*
AmP: [zom]	P: [zomp]	tooth
AmC: [nedlik]	C: [knedli:k]	dumpling
[klednik]		
AmC: [bratər]	C: [bratr]	brother

The ethnic community in the maintenance of Polish

During the history of Polish immigration to the United States, the ethnic community has most favorably influenced the chances of its members to retain competence in their mother tongue in an environment in which English possessed all the social privileges of an official language (see Chapter 1). Polish ethnic communities, often collectively referred to as Polonia, provided cohesive social units familiar in pre-emigration life, and a buffer to the new and foreign American world. The community served particularly well for Polish immigrants arriving during the peak immigration period, who, like many of their fellow Slavs, were from the strata of Polish society whose lifeways had been connected to the social structure of village life.

The Polish rural immigrants who first came to America were for the most part little interested in assimilation to the larger American society. It was not, as is often erroneously assumed, their inadequate level of literacy, general education, and professional skills, which set limitations on their early integration into the American society. Rather, the explanation can be found in the fact that most of the early immigrants came with no serious intention to settle, but only to raise money with which they could upgrade their social position in their native village by buying more land or by regaining their indebted property. For the same reason, these immigrants, who were by and large farmers, did not take advantage of their skills in agriculture, but sought the fast money of factories and coal mines instead. The novelty of work demands and living conditions required major adjustments from urban Polish settlers. Speaking a common language and sharing common traditions, these settlers developed spatially and ethnically segregated Polish neighborhoods within the cities, such as Milwaukee (1862), Chicago (1864), and Buffalo (1870).

The second type of immigrants, substantially less numerous than the previous group, consisted of Polish peasants attracted to America by the easy opportunity to acquire land. These immigrants came to establish a permanent home in their rural farming communities centered around a church, and continued many traditions from the old country. Quite frequently, transition to life here was in the hands of the local parish priests. In Poland, the priest often acted as chief organizer of the emigrant group, and in America, the erection of the church was the first symbolic mark of the foundation of an ethnic community. The very first Polish ethnic community and parish, Panna Maria ('Virgin Mary') in Texas, was founded in 1854 by a young Polish Catholic priest, Leopold Moczygęba who, together with his four brothers, brought a group of a hundred families from his poverty-stricken village in Prussian-occupied Silesia to Galveston in Texas, which was still a young pioneer state of the Union. Shortly after their arrival, the priest corresponded with parishioners back home urging them to join him in the new land. His persuasion met with enthusiastic response; some 1,300 Poles arrived in Texas within two years. Foundations of similar Polish ethnic communities were established during the same period in Polonia, Wisconsin (1885), Parisville, Michigan (1857), and other Midwestern states.

For two generations of Polish Americans, the ethnic community served as the source for perpetuation of their linguistic heritage. The Polish American community was a continuation of the original Polish village, which provided immigrants with an opportunity to carry on their traditional, social, spiritual, cultural, and welfare activities. Among the institutions of the ethnic community, the church and its parish organization was the most prominent unifying force. The ethnic church parish priests helped organize the parochial schools, and establish the ethnic press and social organizations, promoting the perpetuation of the Polish language along the way. At the turn of the century, the network of parochial schools in which instruction was given in the Polish language was approximately 500 with an enrollment of about 70,000 students and staff of some 1,000 teaching nuns and secular teachers. Although the structure of the Polish communities began to change when the third generation students spread beyond its boundaries, there were as late as the 1940s, 585 elementary schools, 72 high schools, and 58 colleges which belonged to the Polish Americans (Lopata 1976: 51).

Similarly, the Polish immigrant press has had a long history of involvement in both ethnic and religious matters of Polish communities in America. The first Polish immigrant newspaper, *Echo z Polski* 'Echo from Poland' (New York, 1863–5) was atypical in the sense that its primary concern was with politics in Poland. However, the second, *Orzeł Polski* 'The Polish Eagle' (founded in 1870 in Washington, Missouri, by a Jesuit priest, Alexander Matuszek), and its off-shoot papers, *Pielgrzym* 'The Pilgrim' and *Gazeta Polska Katolicka* 'The Polish Catholic Gazette,' dealt with news of Polonia. During the years, much of the Polish immigrant press became secularized, but its interest and influence in the ethnic communities was maintained. Out of the several hundreds of periodicals, to which the World War I period alone contributed more than a hundred new titles, many were phased out after a relatively short publishing span, and the present records still show a declining trend, listing three dailies (Chicago, Detroit, and Jersey City), nine weeklies, seven biweeklies, and five monthlies (Ayer 1977: 1059).

Ethnic social organizations are another institution of the ethnic community which substantially eased immigrants' adjustment to the American environment, and also helped preserve the Polish ethnic heritage and language in the USA. The largest of these have been the Polish Roman Catholic Union, organized in 1873, and the currently influential Polish National Alliance (1880). Although they have primarily focused on the spiritual needs of the immigrants (establishing churches, schools, press, radio, libraries, etc.), they have also provided financial support to members in case of illness or death, promoted local business and professional services, and organized recreational facilities.

In accordance with the changes in the evolution of the immigrant life in the United States, the Polish ethnic community has been changing its structure and social functions. Though it is very likely that its role in promoting the Polish language may decline in the future, it remains undisputable that its historical role in the maintenance of the Polish language in the USA during the building up of Polonia has been most significant.

Language cultivation in the maintenance of Czech

The case of Czech and its use by American speakers offers an excellent example for study of the maintenance of an immigrant language in relation to the cultivation of its prestigious variety. For several reasons, Czech is particularly suited for a systematic investigation of this question. The structure of the language itself is unique among the Slavic languages in that Standard Czech displays a variability of a DIGLOSSIC nature, ranging across two functionally defined norms: Literary Czech, the medium of writing and formal speaking (especially in lectures, politics, church, mass media, education, theater, etc.), and Colloquial Czech, the medium of informal, predominantly spoken, communication. While most of the vocabulary and grammatical structures are shared by both codes, there are features in which Literary Czech is formally distinct in phonology, morphology, as well as syntax and lexicon, from all other varieties of Czech. The origin of this diglossia is bound to the historical formation of the code of Literary Czech, in the language of classical Czech literature, representing a historically older stratum of the currently spoken language. Subsequently, Literary Czech, obsolete for casual conversational use, gave way to regional supradialectal varieties of Czech, and one of them, originally spoken in Prague, acquired the function of an all-national colloquial language. Most other European languages have a clear-cut dichotomy of standard language versus folk speech. In the Czech context, a three-member system exists: a native regional dialect (and/or a supradialect) used in the "home" situation, a colloquial variety used in "outside" informal situations, and the Literary Czech used for formal speeches and writing. Interestingly enough, no direct correlation between the educational and socio-economic status of the speakers and the preference for the literary variety in speech has ever been established.

The rules for the use of Literary Czech in writing are almost absolute, since in most instances, nonadherence to the literary forms in written communication carries degrading social implications, signaling the writer's inability to use the language properly. In spoken communication, however, there are fewer conditions in which the use of Literary Czech is obligatory. Because of its dependence on situational formality, it is the only appropriate variant for use when a speaker represents a public institution, such as the state, a national organization, church, etc. It is also the exclusive code used within social institutions, such as education and the mass media, which are either directly or indirectly responsible for maintenance of the literary language in the society. Apart from these clearly formal situations, there are those in which the speaker behaves as a private person, i.e. ordinary conversation. In the circumstances of common everyday communication, the concept of social formality is often rather fluid. There are several independent aspects of every particular situation in which communication takes place, such as the nature of the physical setting where people meet, the topic discussed, the psychological disposition of the speaker, and the roles and relationship between interlocutors, which have bearing on the speaker's choice of language.

Language cultivation is a concept of language planning that has played a vital role in the development of Czech. Its role as a preventive measure against language loss in adverse circumstances was already stressed by the linguists of the Linguistic Circle of Prague in the period between the world wars. Members of this group claimed that the only reason Czech resisted the pressures of Germanization in the eighteenth century was that Middle Czech had been exposed to an extensive cultivation treatment: otherwise, it would have followed the pattern of Old English which became heavily Gallicized in the middle ages (Mathesius 1947: 441). Attention to language and its refinement has had a long tradition among Czech linguists, dating from the time of the Reformation to the modern era of the Czechoslovak Academy, and a sophisticated use of the language has been viewed as an important part of the constituents that make up the national culture. Although the authors of the original language cultivation theses (Havránek and Weingart 1932) conceived cultivation (particularly in respect to the codification of the language norm) primarily as a linguistic question, they also recognized the role of education and literary figures in changes both in the language form and in attitudes toward language.

Originally, the norm of Literary Czech was looked for in the language of literature. Later, however, as the focus of language study moved away from the "elite" group of the society to the "average" language user, the concept of the norm was broadened to include good literary and technical writing, as well as speech and the linguistic intuitions of the intelligentsia. The theoretical analysis of the properties of the literary language helps reveal the norm and leads to the promulgation of the norm in codification by means of official grammars, dictionaries, and spelling and pronunciation manuals issued by the Academy.

The final objective of the codification is to establish unification and flexible stability of the norm among the users of the literary variant. The experience of the nineteenth-century purism showed that the expressive means of the language may become seriously reduced in the effort to secure the stability of the norm. Now, students of language cultivation recognize that one of the foremost tasks of language planning is the resolution of the tension between the need for stabilization and the need for functional differentiation. To that end, the code is subjected to continuous revision and critique by the theoretical analysis of the natural development of the norm, so that the role of the linguists in the process of codification consists in setting the framework for the future evolution of the literary norm.

Language planners have also paid considerable attention to the manner in which linguistic cultivation has been implemented, though rarely have they themselves participated in it. Traditionally, the popularization of the code of Literary Czech has been carried out by the literary works of the national writers, and the mass media have brought the ideal form to the language users. Additionally, the media have established special "language corners" which discuss innovations of the code and offer solutions to particular linguistic problems. The most efficient means for the dissemination of the literary language, however, has always been instruction in school, particularly because schools deal with language users whose psychological condition is still responsive to an alteration of speech habits.

Lastly, it should be noted that an indispensable factor influencing the outcome of language cultivation through time, has been the positive attitude of Czech speakers and the high esteem in which they have held their literary language. Though the magnitude of that favorable linguistic attitude may vary in time and with each individual, an average speaker would nonetheless regard his literary language as an expression of his patriotic and national pride, as well as an expression of his belonging to the Czech national culture.

Promotion of good usage of Literary Czech is differently realized in the American environment for all three crucial components of the cultivation process: the language planners responsible for the norm, the writers producing the resources from which the norm is derived, and the media of education and mass information serving as channels for the implementation of the norm.

The role of the language specialist in the immigrant context differs strikingly from that of the language planner in the original country, simply because there is no authoritative power responsible for making effective decisions about the immigrant language and its use. American linguists, according to their credo "Leave your language alone," have been little interested in analyzing or controlling variability in English, and they have no language academy or equivalent organization whose responsibility it would be to cultivate the language in the Prague sense.

While there is a body of good literary works written by Czech Americans (such as those who have published with the American house, Nakladatelství 68 or the Swiss house, Konfrontace), the production is small in comparison to publications available to the reader in Czechoslovakia. Nonetheless, it has represented an excellent source of the modern variety of Literary Czech and, with some limitations, an example of its use in the American environment.

The channels of implementation of the good usage of Literary Czech in the United States, though limited in comparison to those available in Czechoslovakia, have still been the most powerful source for maintenance of this variety by American speakers. The Czech settlers stood very early in the forefront of ethnic educational efforts in America, opening Czech schools in Racine, Wisconsin (1850), Wesley, Texas (1859), Milwaukee, Wisconsin (1862), Chicago, Illinois (1864), and New York, NY (1865). Estimates pertaining to the number of Czech ethnic schools and student enrollment vary through time. At the turn of the century, Čapek (1920) talked of 8,000 students in sixty-nine Czech schools; by 1946, Rouček (1968) claimed that the USA had 104 parochial elementary and high schools which were all-day schools and taught Czech as an obligatory subject, and eighty-eight free-thinker schools whose curriculum was designed to teach Czech grammar, spelling, reading, and writing in special afternoon or weekend classes. The only Czech college still existing in America, St. Procopius College, was opened in 1887 in Chicago and in 1901 was moved to the new campus in Lisle, Illinois; two other colleges, both founded by the Benedictines, went out of existence in the early twentieth century. The teaching of Czech as a foreign language in public schools has been sporadic; currently a few high schools in the Chicago area and in Texas offer Czech. In institutions of higher education, courses in Czech were first introduced in 1890, in Oberlin College. The number of departments offering Czech as part of their curriculum has slowly but steadily increased; in the late 1970s, twenty-nine colleges and universities offered instruction in Czech.

Ethnic radio broadcasting has grown to be a convenient medium for reaching a wide circle of individuals in the immigrant community. Czech broadcasting in the USA is now available in those major metropolitan areas which include a significant Czech minority, and ranges from a once-a-month schedule in cities such as San Francisco to a daily program (subsidized by the Czech community) in Chicago. Journalism, however, has traditionally been the most widely used agency of cultural and linguistic contacts within ethnic communities. For Czech immigrants, it is also a mass medium with which they were thoroughly acquainted in their pre-emigration life. The first American Czech weekly paper was printed in Racine, Wisc. in 1860. With occasional fluctuation in the number of new periodicals emerging and others disappearing, Czech journalistic activity in America reached its peak in the 1930s and has since been slowly declining. At present it amounts to one daily, nine weeklies, eleven monthlies, and one quarterly. The most popular periodicals are the daily *Hlasatel* 'The Herald' and the weekly *Hlas Národa* 'Voice of the Nation,' both published in Chicago, and the New York weekly *Americké Listy* 'American Papers.'

A medium of language cultivation which is uniquely suitable for the immigrant milieu is communication with the original homeland: making visits to the country or meeting visitors and newly arrived immigrants from the homeland.

Access to the modern variety of the language can also be obtained through contemporary film, theater, and records, especially of popular songs, which often touch on current social and political events, and can reveal many interesting aspects of the latest language innovations. Written resources, books and periodicals published in Czechoslovakia, are the most easily accessible medium for an immigrant interested in keeping abreast with the modern literary language. Active use of Literary Czech in writing, although commonly confined to personal letters, may be the best type of practice, particularly when done under the supervision of an experienced language user.

The selection of types of contact with the current language, as well as the intensity and frequency of contact, influence the maintenance of the literary language by the immigrant. However, effectiveness of language cultivation is also dependent on his interest in the affairs of the contemporary generation of his original compatriots and his tolerance of current events in the old country. Absorbing changes in both language and other facets of life which may have occurred by a natural course of development after his emigration depends on a receptive attitude. Thus, the consequences of personal communication with speakers of the contemporary variety of the literary language can differ from one immigrant to another. For example, the opportunity to converse with native speakers can be ineffective in upgrading the speech of immigrants who maintain a negative attitude toward the contemporary generation because of political or other biases.

The role of the various means of language cultivation in the maintenance of Literary Czech by American speakers was examined in an experimental sociolinguistic analysis of the speech of eighty-four adult Czech Americans of first to fourth generation. The objectives were to assess information on the knowledge and actual use of Literary Czech by the immigrants, who had a diverse background in language cultivation, and to investigate whether a positive correlation between the factors of cultivation and the degree of language maintenance could be established (Henzl 1975). Statistical analyses of the data demonstrated that the maintenance of literary elements in the speech of the immigrants was significantly related to the cultivation of their Czech in formal schooling, their active use of Literary Czech, their contact with Czechoslovakia, and their overall attitude to the maintenance of Literary Czech in the USA.

The level of language maintenance had a significantly different realization in the various generational categories of the immigrants, which further reflected their different responsiveness to the social formality of the speech events. As a rule, Czechoslovakia-born speakers, who have evidently had the greatest exposure to the various means of cultivation, as well as the most natural opportunity for practice with the different varieties of the language, showed a wider distinction between the formal speech (90.8 percent use of Literary Czech) and the informal speech (30.4 percent use of Literary Czech) than the late generation speakers whose use of Literary Czech in equivalent situations ranged from 41.6 percent to 10.8 percent.

With respect to the nature of English interference in the speech of the immigrants, for all the generational categories in the study, a significantly high negative correlation was found between the use of the Literary Czech and English elements in their Czech. Active cultivation of the immigrant language, then, can be viewed not only as a vehicle for minimizing the growing gap between the immigrant language and the language currently used in the original country, but also as a mechanism by which interference of the dominant language in the immigrant language is inhibited.

Outlook for the future

Both of these historically significant patterns in the maintenance of the Slavic immigrant languages, interaction in the ethnic community and active language cultivation, have begun to assume new forms during recent years. At the early period of their immigration history, all Slavic groups had formed more or less self-contained ethnic islands, the boundaries of which were largely based on language. For the first two immigrant generations, then, language was the primary indicator of ethnicity. However, once the immigrants acquired a good knowledge of English and learned the skills provided by American education, the cohesiveness of the ethnic communities came to be disrupted and their members dispersed into wider environments. Many of them have continued to be loosely connected with the social organizations of their ethnic community, introducing English into their activities. Ethnic organizations have become bilingual and have opened their doors also to English monolingual membership. Under these conditions, maintenance of the Slavic immigrant languages has been gradually shifting to the more sophisticated phase of conscious cultivation of the ancestral languages in American educational facilities, or by contacts with Slavic speakers of the original countries. In both of these approaches, interest in the ethnic language has become part of a broader concept of ethnicity, often accompanied by study of Slavic history, arts, literature, economics, etc., and thus placed on a more solid basis for the future.

FURTHER READING

The literature on Slavic languages in the USA is very uneven, and mention of the state of the languages themselves is usually incidental to more general studies of the Slavs in America. The well-known book by Balch 1969 (first published in 1910) is certainly still worth reading for general coverage. Dvornik 1962 treats the historical background outside the USA; it is a regular textbook in courses on Slavic cultures. The most convenient reference work on the structure of the Slavic languages is De Bray 1980.

The best works on Slavic languages in the USA are unpublished doctoral dissertations which may be obtained from University Microfilms, such as Lyra 1962 for Polish, Henzl 1975 for Czech, Meyerstein 1959 for Slovak. Several collections of papers are, however, valuable; notably Gilbert 1970, which contains articles on West Slavic languages in the USA, and *General Linguistics* 16.2–3, which is devoted to studies of South Slavic languages.

Since Polish Americans constitute the largest group of Slavic Americans, they are more fully covered than the others. The *Polish Review* contains articles on the Poles and their language in the USA. The report by Sanders and Morawska 1975 reviews all the existing literature on Polish Americans, including a section on language.

Finally, some of the numerous works of the political sociologist Joseph Rouček treat the Slavic minorities in America (e. g. Brown and Rouček 1952; Rouček 1968).

15

The Filipinos: a special case*

JAMES and MARIA BEEBE

The "special relationship" between the United States and the Philippines has greatly affected Philippine history and the lives of its people – both those in the Philippines and those who immigrated to the United States. A series of political events and changing socio-economic conditions in the early part of the twentieth century triggered an intermittent but dramatic growth of Filipino immigration to the United States. Both the special relationship and the continuing large-scale immigration of Filipinos date from 1898, when a mock battle in Manila Bay marked the end of 300 years of Spanish colonial domination and the beginning of American colonial domination. The United States succumbed to what Mark Twain called the "Philippine Temptation," and for the next forty-six years the Philippines was a colonial possession of the United States. During this period, the official attitude of the U.S. government toward its possession reflected a statement attributed to President McKinley that it was the duty of America "to educate the Filipinos and uplift and civilize and Christianize them and to fit the people for the duties of citizenship." Such a mission seemed to call for a shift in the language habits of the Filipino people.

Language in the Philippines

A multilingual society with over eighty indigenous tongues, the Philippines presented a considerable challenge to the representatives of the U.S. govern-ment charged with establishing English as the common medium of communica-tion. Though Spanish had been the official language before the American occupation, various study commissions sent to the Philippines between 1898 and 1902 determined that the great majority of Filipinos used not Spanish, but one or more of the numerous indigenous languages. The Commission of 1902 further determined that none of these languages could be used in public instruc-tion since there were few books and other instructional materials available. It also reasoned that if the government made the local languages the media of school, only a limited number of wealthy and urban people would learn English

* This article was prepared prior to employment with the Agency for International Development and the opinions and views expressed are those of the authors and are not necessarily those of the Agency for International Development.

322

and the maintenance of power by a handful of individuals would thus be perpetuated. The Commission assumed that many Filipinos would maintain their native language "in the intimate relations of life" and learn English as a "literary language in the commercial and public affairs" of the nation (Report of the Philippine Commission 1902: 880–1; cited in Forbes 1928: I, 439–40).

Unlike Puerto Rico, another U.S. territory acquired in 1898 (see Chapter 10), the Philippines under the first decades of U.S. domination had a consistent language policy pushing English as the major language. Numerous commissions and outspoken individuals intermittently pointed out the failures of the educational system to spread English to a wide sector of the population, but the official position continued to promote English as the common means of communication. In 1919, English, in addition to being the medium of school instruction, became the official language for use in local government and the legal system. However, the forces arguing for a NATIONAL LANGUAGE had by the 1930s gathered considerable support, and there were numerous debates on which of the indigenous tongues should be the choice. Though there were more than eighty languages spoken in the Philippines, eight were spoken by the greatest percentages of the population. These eight were: Cebu-Visayan (Cebuano), Tagalog, Ilokano, Hiligaynon (West Visayan), Bikol, Samar-Leyte, Pampango, and Pangasinan. All these languages belong to the Austronesian LANGUAGE FAMILY which extends from Hawaii to Madagascar and from Formosa to Easter Island west of Chile and includes Tonga and Samoa, as well as Borneo, Celebes, Java, Sumatra, the Malay Peninsula, and the Philippines. Tagalog was in many ways the choice most frequently and prominently mentioned for a national language, and in the decade of the 1930s, innumerable studies, linguistic and sociological, reported the merits of Tagalog.

In 1937, the President of the Philippines issued a proclamation making Tagalog the basis for the national language. Beginning in 1939, the official public policy for education was to permit the use of local languages as auxiliary media of instruction. The teaching of the national language based on Tagalog began in 1940. In 1957, the Board of National Education implemented a plan to use the indigenous language of the local geographic area as the medium of instruction in grades 1 and 2. The national language could be used as a means of instruction at all levels, and English was to be taught as a subject. Upper-level grades and colleges were expected to continue English as the medium of instruction. In 1959 *Pilipino* became the official name for the national language, which was essentially the same as Tagalog.

The 1957 decision to use the local language for educating the child in the first two grades was, at least in theory, based on Aguilar's (1948–57) Iloilo Language Experiment One. This experiment suggested that initial instruction in the local language contributed to the subsequent learning of the curriculum in English. The adoption of the policy may have been a premature decision considering the methodological problems of the research, the unavailability of instructional materials in the local languages, and the inadequacy of teacher preparation. Only in 1967–8 were books in twelve Philippine languages (the

Table 15.1. *Percentage of Filipinos whose mother tongue is one of the eight major languages*

Language	1960	1970
Cebu-Visayan/Cebuano	24.12	24.2
Tagalog	21	24.5
Ilokano	11.7	11.3
Hiligaynon/West Visayan	10.4	10.2
Bikol	7.8	6.8
Samar-Leyte	5.5	4.8
Pampango	3.2	3.3
Pangasinan	2.5	2.3

Table 15.2. *Percentage of population able to speak Pilipino, English, and Spanish*

Year	Pilipino	English	Spanish
1939	23.4	26.6	2.6
1948	37.1	37.2	1.8
1960	44.4	39.5	2.1
1970	55.2	44.7	3.6

eight major languages plus four others – Cebu-Visayan, Tagalog, Ilokano, Hiligaynon, Bikol, Samar-Leyte, Pampango, Pangasinan, Magindanaw, Tausog, Ibanag, and Samal, listed in descending order by number of speakers) printed for use in the schools. By about the time the books in these languages reached the classrooms, official language policy in the Philippines was shifting again. New experiments seemed to show that instruction in any language could be effective (English, Pilipino, or vernacular) if good teachers and good instructional materials were available. Also, forces were moving toward greater use of Pilipino in the nation. After a succession of proposals, surveys, and commission reports, a language policy of bilingual education was enunciated in 1974 which called for the use of Pilipino as the medium of instruction in social studies, character education, work education, health, and physical education, and the use of English in the other courses. As this new policy was being implemented, the Philippines undertook massive programs of teacher training and the production and dissemination of textbooks.

Shifts in national language policy since 1900 have been instrumental in bringing about the present language situation in the Philippines. There has been an expansion in the use of both English and Tagalog/Pilipino. The number of people identified as being able to speak English increased from close to zero in 1900 to 26.6 percent in 1939, and 44.7 percent in 1970. Pilipino is spoken as a MOTHER TONGUE in Metro Manila, the Philippines' major city and in the nearby provinces. In 1970 only about 25 percent of the population spoke Pilipino as a mother tongue (see Table 15.1), but approximately 55 percent were able to speak Pilipino for some communicative functions (see Table 15.2). The number of people identified as being able to speak Pilipino increased from 23.4 percent in 1939 to 55.2 percent in 1970.

The choice of which language or languages one speaks depends on many factors, including the participants, settings, and purposes of communication. Those who speak Pilipino as a mother tongue use it in home and community settings and supplement it with English in school. Those who use a mixture of Pilipino and English in peer relationships generally use the latter with those above their status, and the former with those below. Individuals of high socioeconomic status use more English than Pilipino across all situations, whether they are speaking, reading, or writing. Pilipino is used to show intimacy, solidarity, and nationalism, but it lacks the status of English.

The Philippines is like many other newly independent Asian nations in being highly multilingual and in having the language of a former colonial power unifying its government, educational system, and professional classes. It is unlike most Asian nations, however, in having an indigenous national language written in the roman alphabet. Filipinos also have a relatively high rate of literacy and widespread ability to use English in some communicative functions. These characteristics of language use and literacy in the Philippines had a strong influence on the nature of language maintenance and adjustment to employment opportunities which characterized Filipino immigration to the United States.

Filipino immigration

The Filipinos had fought and defeated the Spanish before the Americans arrived in Manila Bay; they wanted independence, not the exchange of one colonial power for another. Only after a bloody pacification program were the Americans able to move ahead with their educational "mission." Education required schools, and even before all armed resistance to the Americans had ended, decisions were made to establish a public school system, to use English as the medium of instruction, and to import American teachers to staff the schools while training Filipinos as teachers. American language and culture were to be imported into the Philippines, and, as early as 1903, government scholarships were available for Filipinos who wanted to study in the United States. Many of the earliest Filipino immigrants were scholars who chose to remain in the United States.

While the rhetoric used to describe the relationship between the United States and the Philippines emphasized what the United States did for the Philippines, the actual basis of the relationship was what the Philippines could do for the United States. The traditional economic relationship between colonial power and colony defines the colony as a market for the finished goods of, and a source of raw materials for, the colonizing power. In addition, the Philippines provided labor for jobs Americans would or could not fill. At about the same time the

United States acquired the Philippines, it also annexed Hawaii. The expansion of the sugar industry in Hawaii required cheap labor which China and Japan initially supplied. The Chinese Exclusion Law of 1900 and the Gentlemen's Agreement of 1907 disrupted these traditional sources of labor for Hawaii at about the same time the Philippines came under American control. The USA saw the Philippines as an ideal source of cheap labor, because, under American occupation, it would be "free from the danger of being abruptly closed by restrictive immigration legislation" (Rabaya 1971: 189). While only about 160 Filipinos were actively recruited, word of the opportunities for wealth and adventure spread rapidly. By 1919 there were 25,000 Filipinos in Hawaii, and the 1920 census identified 5,603 Filipinos residing in the United States mainland, many of whom were government scholars (Racelis and Pecson 1959). Another contributing factor to the early immigration of Filipinos to the United States was their recruitment as messboys for the United States Navy in World War I. After the war, many of these Filipinos stayed on in the United States, particularly on the West Coast (McWilliams 1973).

The 1920s were a period of rapid economic expansion on the West Coast. Filipinos found numerous low-status jobs available: busboys and janitors in the hotels and restaurants, fruit pickers, rice harvesters and cannery workers in the growing agricultural industry. Filipinos needed only a health card and credit for the passage across the Pacific to secure U.S. jobs. The Immigration Act of 1924, restricting opportunities for other groups, did not affect Filipinos, because they were considered neither aliens nor citizens but nationals who traveled with American passports.

In 1923, 2,426 Filipinos arrived in California and approximately 2,000 Filipinos came to the USA each year between 1923 and 1929. Among those who came to California, males outnumbered females fourteen to one, 84 percent were under 30 years of age and 77 percent were single. Those who worked in hotels, restaurants and private homes were usually paid about $67.00 a month plus room and board; those who found jobs in the agricultural industries received an average of $3.00 a day. Some employers preferred Filipino workers to White and Mexican workers, because the former were considered steadier, more tractable, and more willing to put up with longer hours, poorer board, and worse lodging facilities.

During the Depression, Whites viewed the Filipinos as an economic threat, and the same jobs which Whites had been unwilling to accept during the 1920s were suddenly being fought for. The youth, maleness, and freedom from family ties of Filipino workers increased both their impact on the job market and their visibility. Their age and sex imbalance in proportion to the rest of the population brought them into conflict with the dominant White majority, especially when they had contact with White females. Anti-Filipino race riots occurred in Exeter, California in late 1929 and in Watsonville, California in January, 1930. The Exeter incident occurred when Whites threw "missiles" at Filipinos who were in the company of White women. In Watsonville, the immediate cause of a riot which led to the death of a Filipino was the employment of White female entertainers by the Palm Beach Filipino Club (Bloch 1930).

In the aftermath of these riots and the publicity caused by them, the California legislature passed a resolution petitioning Congress to restrict Filipino immigration. The intention of the restriction was to limit the number of Filipinos available to American labor and thus increase opportunities for other groups of U.S. workers. Filipino immigrants of the 1920s and 1930s were the victims not only of general economic conditions, but also of general anti-Oriental discrimination. Hotels and restaurants often barred Filipinos. When housing could be found, a dozen or so often had to share a single room or apartment. Competition in the labor market and the age and sex imbalance of the Filipino community combined with the appearance of questionable life styles to increase the negative views society at large held about Filipinos. There were few opportunities for them to learn acceptable grammatical rules and styles of English usage. Success in the English dominant world of work required use of English, be it ever so poor, but social interaction usually was with other Filipinos, and native languages predominated. Filipinos had brought with them a certain innocence about American life coupled with high expectations of what America could offer.

Western people are brought up to regard Orientals or colored people as inferior . . . Filipinos are taught to regard Americans as equals . . . The terrible truth in America shatters the Filipino dream of fraternity . . . If I had not . . . studied about American institutions and racial equality in the Philippines, I should never have minded so much the horrible impact of American chauvinism. (Carlos Bulosan, quoted in Melendy 1972: 141)

Neither were there laws for government authorities to protect Filipinos against the shattering of their American dream.

The Philippine Independence Act of 1935 granted independence in 1946 to the Philippines. The Act also established an immigration quota of fifty Filipinos a year and it seemed as though Filipino immigration had ended. Not only was new immigration halted, but the Repatriation Act of 1935 offered Filipinos in the United States free transportation back to the Philippines on the condition that they could not re-enter the United States. However, economic conditions in the Philippines were worse than those in the USA, and by 1935 many Filipinos had been in the USA for more than a decade. Only about 2,000 of the more than 100,000 Filipinos then in the United States chose to return to the Philippines under the Repatriation Act.

World War II began a new chapter in immigration from the Philippines to the United States. The invasion of the Philippines by the Japanese, and the heroic but ultimately futile defense of Bataan and Corregidor by Filipino and American troops, increased American consciousness about the Philippines. During and immediately after the war, some of the discriminatory bans against Filipinos were lifted. Many Filipinos in the United States were able to get better paying jobs in shipyards and other defense facilities. Most eligible Filipinos enlisted in the U.S. army or navy, providing themselves a basis for citizenship.

Table 15.3. *Shifts in the top five users of immigrant visas 1967–75*

1967		1969		1971		1973		1975	
Mexico	42,371	Mexico	44,623	Mexico	50,103	Mexico	70,141	Mexico	62,552
Cuba	33,321	Italy	23,617	Phil.	28,471	Phil.	30,799	Phil.	31,323
Italy	26,565	Phil.	20,744	Italy	22,137	Cuba	24,147	Cuba	28,100
Britain	24,965	Canada	18,582	Cuba	21,611	Korea	22,930	Korea	25,611
Canada	23,442	Jamaica	16,947	Greece	15,939	Italy	22,151	India	14,336

Until the Immigration and Nationality Act of 1952 established an Asian Pacific quota of 100 per country, immigration was very limited and the few Filipinos who immigrated were generally either in the United States military or close relatives of Filipinos who had become U.S. citizens. Within the quota of 100, preferences were given to skilled workers, parents of American citizens, and spouses and children of permanent resident aliens.

The Immigration and Naturalization Act of 1965 (effective in 1968) increased the annual allotment of visas to 20,000 per country, and continued to give preference to skilled workers, especially professional, and relatives of permanent residents, while excluding from the numerical limitation parents, spouses, and the unmarried children of American citizens. This triggered the second wave of Filipino immigration to the USA, one which continues to this day. The impact of the new immigration law is evident in Table 15.3. In 1967, Filipinos were not even among the top five users of immigration visas, but they jumped to third place in 1969 and have remained second to Mexico since 1971. Since certain close relatives of U.S. citizens are not affected by the annual numerical limitation of 20,000, there is likely to be an increase in immigrants from the Philippines, as the number of Filipinos becoming U.S. citizens increases. Between 1960 and 1970, foreign-born claimants of Filipino languages as their mother tongue more than doubled. In 1975, the total number of mother-tongue claimants of Filipino languages was 311,000 (see Chapter 22).

The 1965 Act made it explicit that preference was given to employment categories in short supply in the United States, such as doctors and nurses. Once again, the Philippines became an exporter of labor to the United States, and a direct contributor to America's economic and social well-being. And once again Filipino immigrants, like their predecessors, found little truth in the American dream. Skilled professionals, trained in medical and technical fields, discovered their opportunities limited by more subtle, but still powerful, forms of discrimination: their foreign credentials were not recognized, their foreign accents unacceptable. Consequently, in the 1970s the urban Filipino community suffered from underemployment. Many trained workers, unacceptable to their U.S. professional colleagues, had to take low-skill jobs in order to support themselves (Melendy 1976). When Filipinos did find employment in their fields, they were often paid lower wages than were White professionals (Rabaya 1971). As a result, in a study of income levels in Chicago, New York, San Francisco, and Los Angeles (Cabezas 1977), with median White income taken as 1.0, median Filipino income registered as 0.6.

Meanwhile, Filipinos in California agriculture continued to organize against oppressive working conditions and pay. The formation of the Agricultural Workers Organizing Committee (AWOC) in 1959 furthered a history of resistance and strikes dating back to the 1930s (Melendy 1976). The union, led by Larry Itliong, merged with Cesar Chavez's National Farmworkers Association (NFWA) in 1966, and together the Chicanos and the Filipinos forced California agribusiness to accept unionization (Vera Cruz 1971). Yet general economic conditions for the Filipino community at large have continued to show widespread economic discrimination.

The 1970 U.S. census provides the only nationwide profile of Filipinos in America, but because of continued immigration since 1970 and a normal fertility rate, the 1970 population of Filipinos probably represents only about 53 percent of the present population. The 1970 U.S. census enumerated 350,082 persons of foreign stock whose country of origin was the Philippines. Of these 184,842 were listed as foreign-born and 165,240 as natives of foreign or mixed parentage. Since the census was completed, immigration has increased the size of the Filipino community by at least 240,000. Assuming a very consistent natural growth rate of at least 2 percent for both Filipinos already present in 1969 and for those who have immigrated since then, natural growth rate would have increased the community by another 72,000. The Filipino community in the United States could have been expected to exceed three quarters of a million people by 1980.

Despite the limitations imposed by the passage of time and the growth of the community as a result of immigration, the 1970 census is illustrative for what it says of the situation of Filipinos in the United States at the time of the census. Personal mean income of employed persons for the total U.S. population in 1969 was $5,817, some 13 percent greater than the $5,149 mean income of employed Filipinos. Only 12 percent of employed Filipinos earned more than $10,000 compared to 25 percent of the total U.S. population. The unemployment rate for Filipinos in 1969 was 4.4 percent as compared to a 3.9 percent rate for the total U.S. population. Although 49 percent of all Filipino men had completed high school (a rate 5 percent lower than men in the total U.S. population) and 64 percent of all Filipino women had completed high school, only 28 percent of all Filipino men and 23 percent of all Filipina women had attended college as compared to rates of 37 percent for men and 27 percent for women in the total U.S. population. The overall picture that emerges from the 1970 census suggests that Filipinos in the United States are (or were in 1970) somewhat more likely to earn less, to be unemployed, and to have less education than the average U.S. citizen.

A Filipino community profile

Additional insights about the Filipinos in the United States are provided by preliminary results from a 1978 census-type socio-economic study of 1629 (of an estimated 1800) Filipinos living in Mountain View, California, a town approximately half way between San Francisco and San José (Beebe 1978). While there is no evidence to suggest that Filipinos in Mountain View are typical of all Filipinos in the United States there is also no evidence to suggest they are atypical of Filipino Americans in other communities. Filipinos have been present in Mountain View since the 1920s, and at present comprise about 3 percent of the population.

Results from the Mountain View study suggest there is great variability within the Filipino community. About 80 percent of the resident Filipinos are immigrants, of whom 60 percent have immigrated since 1970. While some immigrants find employment in jobs for which they are qualified, other immigrants work at lower-level jobs than those for which they have been trained; 60 percent of all employed Filipinos with any post-secondary education are working outside the field for which they were trained. Of the Filipinos born in this country, and no longer full-time students, only 12 percent have earned a four-year college degree. Of the Filipinos born in the Philippines who were students immediately before immigrating and are no longer students, approximately 35 percent had not finished high school when they came to this country. Of these, only 58 percent finished high school after arriving in the U.S., and only 10 percent finished a four-year college course. Among other things, these results suggest that many Filipinos may be underemployed and that the failure to complete school may be a major problem with serious implications for future employment. The average annual income for employed Filipinos in Mountain View is $9,500, with 30 percent earning less than $7,000 and 6 percent earning more than $16,000. Employed individuals account for almost 50 percent of the total population. Students enrolled in schools account for 30 percent of the population and children too young to go to school comprise another 9 percent of the population. The average age is 28, with 40 percent of the population under the age of 20. More than 60 percent of those over the age of 15 are married; 89 percent of the Filipinos in Mountain View are Catholic.

Questions about language use by Filipinos in the United States involve three related issues: What languages do they know how to speak, what factors influence the choice of a language for a given situation when options are available, and what factors influence the acquisition of Filipino languages by Filipinos born in the United States? There are no nationwide studies on any of these issues and only limited and sometimes speculative information on the first two from the census-type socio-economic study of Filipinos in Mountain View.

The Mountain View study asked about the languages individuals used when growing up, the language currently used most often at home, and the languages spoken outside the home. Of the respondents in the Mountain View study, 33 percent grew up speaking Ilokano. Ilokanos (the same name applies to both language and ethnic group) originally occupied a narrow band of land between the mountains and the South China Sea on the upper western coast of the island of Luzon. Over a century ago, population pressures and limited land resulted in the large-scale migration of Ilokanos to other parts of the Philippines. Ilokanos were among the first Filipinos to immigrate to the United States, and even though they comprise only about 11 percent of the Philippine population, their presence in large numbers in the United States is compatible with their image in the Philippines as "hard working adventurers." The second most common language used while growing up was English (27 percent); the third most common Tagalog (24 percent). The remaining 16 percent was split among thirteen other languages. English was the language reported as currently used for conversation at home by the largest group (42 percent), followed by Ilokano (25 percent), and Tagalog (24 percent). The remaining 8 percent spoke one of seven different Filipino languages at home.

The great majority of individuals (95 percent) were able to speak English with some degree of competency; 64 percent spoke Tagalog, and 40 percent Ilokano. While speakers of Cebu-Visayan have traditionally been the largest language group in the Philippines, only 5 percent of the Filipinos in Mountain View spoke this language. Although more people have grown up speaking Ilokano than Tagalog, only slightly more currently used Ilokano at home than used Tagalog, and almost 50 percent more people could speak Tagalog than could speak Ilokano. Though English was the language spoken by only 27 percent while growing up, 42 percent currently used the language at home.

The Mountain View study provided two indicators of language choice in situations where options are present. One respondent from each household was interviewed and data were collected from the respondent concerning other members of the household. The only limit on the choice of respondent was that he or she had to be at least 16 years old. The interviewers introduced themselves in Tagalog and presented the respondent with a letter written in both English and Tagalog. Respondents were informed that identical questionnaires in English and Tagalog were available and were asked which one they preferred. Sixty percent chose to conduct the interview in Tagalog. This contrasts sharply with a study on fertility attitudes among Filipinos in the San Francisco Bay Area, in which a Filipino interviewer asked respondents in English which language they preferred for the interview; 95 percent chose English (Card 1978). In both studies, a few of the respondents who chose English were reported as having trouble either understanding or answering some questions.

A second aspect of language use revealed by the Mountain View study is that 44 percent of all individuals watched a local Filipino television program every Sunday afternoon, and another 25 percent watched it one or more times a month. While much CODE-SWITCHING between English and Tagalog occurred on this variety-type program, about 60–80 percent of the language used was Tagalog. It was primarily when a guest on the program did not speak Tagalog that English was used, and then only for conversing with that guest, with some introductory remarks to the studio audience in either Tagalog or a mixture of Tagalog and English. While Tagalog dominated the broadcast media directed at Filipinos living in the Bay Area, English was used almost exclusively in the several Filipino newspapers in the USA. However, only 15 percent of the Filipino households in Mountain View had subscriptions to Filipino newspapers.

Tagalog in U.S. bilingual education

There is strong indication that Filipinos will continue to immigrate to the United States in sizeable numbers and will continue to concentrate in certain geographical areas. The growing Filipino population strongly suggests that BILINGUAL EDUCATION for Filipinos is likely to increase. The experience Filipinos bring with them to this country has definite implications for the design of bilingual education for Filipino immigrants.

One issue that must be resolved is the choice of language. In the Philippines, the choice of Tagalog–Pilipino was a political decision based on a rationale of national unification. In the United States, the choice of which Philippine language to use is also a political decision on the community level.

Filipinos, just as other non-native English speakers in bilingual education programs in the USA, are greatly affected by the underlying philosophy and goal of bilingual education. If it is TRANSITIONAL, it is designed to facilitate the mastery of English; if it is MAINTENANCE-ORIENTED, it is designed to help speakers maintain and develop communicative competence in their native language; if it is enrichment-oriented, it is directed not only toward a specific minority group, but also to other interested populations (see chapters 21 and 23). If bilingual education is a transitional step, there is some justification for use of Philippine languages other than Tagalog. However, it should be noted that this approach failed to succeed in the Philippines, because of the lack of curriculum materials in the various languages, a problem in the United States also. The choice of Tagalog as the language for bilingual instruction is compatible with maintenance and enrichment orientations, since the chances for maintenance of any Philippine language would seem to be enhanced by concentration on one particular language. It is probably unrealistic for schools to try to maintain immigrant languages which have limited spoken use and minimal written materials. In contrast to other Philippine languages, Pilipino/Tagalog has a fairly extensive written literature, some curriculum materials, and some linguistic analyses. Most important for the immigrant community, Pilipino has become a LINGUA FRANCA and is the language used in television and radio broadcasts in the United States and in movies imported from the Philippines. Also, with the extensive new national project for the preparation and distribution of textbooks in Pilipino (Sibayan 1979), excellent instructional material should become available at all levels.

The similarities of structure and shared vocabulary of the Filipino languages have traditionally made it easy for Filipinos to acquire communicative competence in other Philippine languages. Though Tagalog differs radically from English in sounds, methods of word formation, and in sentence construction, it is similar in many ways to the other major languages of the Philippines though it is not mutually intelligible with these languages. An excellent discussion of Tagalog structure is found in Ramos (1971), and much of the discussion that follows is based on her analysis. The Pilipino sound system is based on five vowels: low central *a,* mid central *e,* high front *i,* mid back *o,* high back *u;* and the consonant PHONEMES *p, t, k, b, d, g,* ʔ (glottal stop), *m, n, ŋ, y, l, r, s, w, h.*

Pilipino word formation is very different from English. Most Pilipino words are made up of *roots* which are substantive, verbal, and adjectival in meaning, and *affixes* which indicate aspect, focus, and mode, among other things. The particular combination of root and affixes determines the specific meaning of a word. For example, some of the possible combinations of affixes with the root word *aral* 'study' are the verbs *magaral* 'to study,' *mangaral* 'to preach,' *makaaral* 'to be able to study,' *makiaral* 'to join someone in studying,' the nouns *pagaaral* 'studies' and *aralan* 'place for studying,' and the adjective *palaaral* 'studious.' The use of affixes also makes it possible to turn almost any Pilipino word into a verb. For example, the adjective *malaki* 'big, tall' can become the verb *magmalaki* 'to be proud'; the noun *bato* 'stone' can become *mambato* 'to throw stones'; the adverb *bigla* 'suddenly' can become *mabigla* 'to be surprised.' Reduplication is another method used in word formation and can be used to indicate, among other things, intensity and plurality, for example, *maganda* 'pretty': *magandang maganda* 'very pretty'; *Magaganda ang mga babae* 'The women are pretty.'

Pilipino sentences are usually formed by a verbal or a nonverbal comment (predicate) followed by a topic (subject) as in:

	Comment		*Topic*	
Verbal comment	*sumayaw*	*ang bata*	'The child danced'
Nonverbal comment			
adjective	*maganda*	*ang bata*	'The child is pretty'
adverb	*bukas*	*ang prosisyon*	'The procession is tomorrow,
preposition	*sa barrio*	*ang sabong*	'The cockfight will be in the barrio,
nominal	*guro*	*ang babae*	'The woman is a teacher'

There is no equivalent to the English verb *to be*.

A very important feature of Pilipino is called *focus,* defined as the grammatical relationship between the verb and the topic. Focus may be viewed roughly as referring to English voice: active indicating that the actor is the subject of the sentence, and passive indicating that the object or goal of the action is the subject. In actor focus, the topic is the actor of the action and in goal focus the topic is the object of the action. The correspondence ends here since in addition to actor and object focuses, Tagalog focuses include locative, benefactive, and instrumental.

The child bought bread from the store for his mother
    with his father's money

can be expressed in Pilipino as (topic italicized):

Bumili *ang bata* ng tinapay sa tindahan para
    sa nanay niya sa pamamagitan ng pera ng tatay
    niya [actor focus]
Binili ng bata *ang tinapay* sa tindahan para
    sa nanay niya sa pamamagitan ng pera ng
    tatay niya [goal focus]

Binilhan ng bata ng tinapay *ang tindahan* para
   sa nanay niya sa pamamagitan ng pera ng
   tatay niya [locative focus]

Ibinili ng bata ng tinapay sa tindahan *ang*
   nanay niya sa pamamagitan ng pera ng tatay niya [benefactive focus]

Ipinangbili ng bata ng tinapay sa tindahan para
   sa nanay niya *ang pera* ng tatay niya [instrumental focus]

In the Philippines, there has been a tendency for the development of regional dialects of Pilipino, and apparently the varieties of second language Pilipino developing in various regions are more like one another than are the older dialect varieties of Pilipino used in the provinces surrounding Manila. Standardization of Pilipino has been encouraged by the growth of mass media such as radio and movies and more recently television. Almost all of the media have been produced in Metro Manila, and the producers usually have attempted to use varieties of Tagalog that can not be identified with specific subregions. The introduction of Pilipino as a subject in school and the subsequent use of Pilipino as a medium of instruction has also encouraged standardization. The Institute of National Language in Manila has the primary function of standardization of Pilipino, but has been beset by conflict between the purists and the anti-purists. The purists have argued for a Pilipino language stripped of Western influences, for example, using *salumpuwit* for 'chair' instead of *silya* (borrowed from Spanish) and *aklat* for 'book' instead of *libro* (borrowed from Spanish). For the anti-purists, these suggestions have represented a "refusal to grow into the modern world" (Yabes 1967: 130). For loanwords, the anti-purists have preferred "to spell the word as it is spelled in the lending language" (Sibayan 1974: 236). In order to spell foreign names and certain loanwords, the twenty-letter *abakada*, the Philippine alphabet consisting of the vowels *a, e, i, o, u* and the consonants *b, k, d, g, h, l, m, n, ng, p, r, s, t, w, y*, was officially expanded in 1971 to include the following foreign letters *c, f, j, n, q, v, x, z, ch, ll*, and *rr*.

Extensive contact between Pilipino and English has resulted in code-switching, the alternating use of Pilipino and English on the word, phrase, clause, or sentence level. Consider the following examples:

(1)   Send me *pala* fancy earrings
      'By the way, send me fancy earrings'
(2)   When did we ever ran out of food, *kailan pa?*
      'When did we ever ran out of food, when?'
(3)   Bubut just delivered a baby boy. *Pogi*
      'Bubut just delivered a baby boy, a handsome baby boy'
(4)   *Ang laki ng* table directly proportional *sa ranggo*
      'The size of a table is directly proportional to rank'

In these examples, code-switching is used as a verbal strategy, to convey social information (size of table as an indicator of rank), to emphasize, to add color to

an utterance. Pilipino–English code-switching is rule-governed, that is, SYNTAC-
TIC constraints operate on code-switching on the word, phrase, and clause
levels. In and around Metro Manila, English–Pilipino code-switching appears
to be gaining both social acceptance and social prestige. Radio programs, comic
books, advertisements, and even poetry employ code-switching. This seems to
be true also among Filipinos in this country.

Contact between Philippine languages and English has also brought structural
changes in the English used by Filipinos. Some scholars argue that there is now
a Standard Filipino English which educated Filipinos speak and which is
acceptable in educated Filipino circles. This Standard Filipino English differs
from Standard American English in its sound system and in its use of English
expressions which are neither American nor British, but are similar to expressions in Pilipino. For example, when a Filipino wants to get off the bus, he
says *I will go down the bus*. Llamzon (1969) has proposed that instead of
Standard American English, Filipino English should be standardized and considered as the norm in Philippine language teaching.

Another variety of English recognized in the Philippines is *carabao* or 'water
buffalo' English; it is generally regarded as poor English. Some Filipinos, when
asked if they speak English, say *A little only, carabao English*. Some of its
features include a simplified PHONOLOGY, as in the use of *b* for *v*, and a simplified
grammar. For example, the past is expressed by the base form of the verb: *I
plant many tree (yesterday)*; subject verb agreement for the third person singular is reduced to the simple form: *The man wash, The child go, The father eat;*
negation is expressed as *She no eat, He no more hair, They not sleeping*. Some
kinds of past actions are expressed as *wen* (< *went*) + verb, as in *wen eat,
wen go*. In effect, this is a kind of pidginized English heard not only in the
Philippines, but also among some less educated newly arrived Filipino immigrants in the United States.

The varieties of Pilipino in the Philippines and the questions they have raised
regarding choice of a standard variety and use in public schooling present
similar problems for bilingual programs for Filipinos in the United States.
Which variety of Pilipino/Tagalog should be used in bilingual education? The
choice of "pure" Pilipino would seem to be dysfunctional because the Pilipino
spoken by many immigrants and used in the mass media available in the United
States is the street variety of the language. For the English component of a
bilingual program, one must also consider that although many Filipinos speak
English, the English they speak is not the same as Standard American English.
If one assumes that many Filipinos speak Standard Filipino English, then instructional strategies can be adopted that concentrate on those elements of
Standard Filipino English incompatible with Standard American English. Important areas of divergence between the two varieties include the phonology and
nuances of uses of the language. For some Filipinos who speak a variant form
of Filipino English, greater emphasis should also be placed on grammatical
structure. Unfortunately, there is, at present, no test instrument that the schools

can use to ascertain the extent to which the English the Filipino brings to the classroom is a Filipino variety.

In many ways, other Asian minorities have been much more visible and their existence more widely known than that of the Filipinos. The Filipinos are, indeed, a special case, similar in some respects to the Chinese and Japanese, yet different, because of the relations between the USA and the Philippines. In terms of types of jobs entered, they share many experiences with Mexican Americans of the twentieth century. Puerto Ricans and Filipinos have the shared experience of U.S. English language policies in their territories. It is indeed difficult to lay out the precise differences in language use between Filipino communities and other language groups. Far more data from socio-linguistic studies of language use in homes and communities are needed before a comprehensive view of the special case of Filipinos in the U.S. is possible.

FURTHER READING

One should begin research on the language situation in the Philippines by reading a general history of the area. Forbes 1928 and Agoncillo 1969 are classics, but Lightfoot 1973 may be a better choice for a brief yet fairly comprehensive introduction. Critical for understanding the origins of the special relationship between the Philippines and the United States is Wolf 1968.

The historical background of language decisions in the Philippines during the Spanish era is given in Phelan 1959. The Spanish friars wrote grammars of the indigenous languages and fostered their use to the extent that Spanish did not become a lingua franca during the Hispanic domination of the Philippines. A series of articles on "The histori-cal development of the Philippine national language" (e.g. Lopez 1930; Frei 1949) in the *Philippine Social Sciences and Humanities Review* (known as *Philippine Social Science Review* 1929–41) are excellent primary sources for the debates regarding Tagalog as the choice for a national language. These sources also reveal the integral role both language scholars and educators played in this debate. In no other territory or state of the USA has language research played so great a part in affecting governmental decisions as in the Philippines. At particular points of decision making in the 1950s and 1960s, major governmental bodies delayed policy making until the results of experiments or language surveys could be reported. Despite references to language research in the formulation of policy, basic decisions on language choice for education and use in government have been political decisions, and results of studies inconsistent with new policies have been sometimes ignored.

The role of language in education in the Philippines is the subject of many articles and monographs. Prator's report of 1950, an influential monograph, is still worth reading although it is difficult to obtain. Of the score of publications by Bonifacio Sibayan, the most informative and accessible are Sibayan 1975, which treats the methods and out-comes of the language survey of 1968–9, and Sibayan 1979, which brings language education policies up to date and gives an extensive bibliography. Pascasio 1977 is a collection of papers on bilingualism and bilingual education in the Philippines, most of them written by people active in research or implementation of bilingual education policies. The volume of papers *Literature and Society* (Bresnahan 1977) is not directly on this topic, but it gives valuable background on national and regional literatures in the Philippines and the special functions of literature in a "developing" society. Saito's 1973 ethnographic bibliography, in addition to references to general materials concerning Philippine linguistics, contains numerous references to all of the major language groups and to most of the minor languages. The most comprehensive bibliography of Philippine linguistics remains J. Ward 1971. Gonzales 1973 and Gonzales, Llamzon, and Otanes 1973 contain valuable material on Philippine linguistics. A comprehensive treatment of Tagalog structure, including syntax, is found in Ramos 1971 and Schachter and Otanes 1972.

Any study of the Filipino immigrant in the USA must be placed in the context of an understanding of other Asian American immigrant experiences. The most comprehensive Asian American sourcebooks are Tachiki, Wong, and Odo 1971, and Gee 1976; the former is sometimes dated in its rhetoric, but it touches on concerns still relevant in the 1980s. Nee 1974 is a series of oral histories, as is a collection compiled by Asian Americans for Community Involvement 1978.

For the history of the two waves of Filipino immigration (1920 to early 1930s and 1965 to the present), there are relatively few sources. Bibliographies of materials concerning Filipinos in this country are Norell 1976 and Saito 1977. UCLA's Asian American Studies Center has published a sensitive and insightful reader on Filipinos in the USA (1976), while Vallangca 1977 presents a highly personalized "history" of the experiences of the first wave of immigrants. Bloch 1930 presents facts about Filipino immigration into California from 1920 to 1930.

Bulosan 1973 (first published 1932) is a very readable autobiographical account of the experiences of an immigrant during the 1930s. The sociologist Bogardus was the first American social scientist to study the Filipino immigrant, and there are no subsequent studies similar to those he completed for the first wave of immigrants (1927–8, 1931–2, 1936). The Filipinos in Hawaii during this early period are treated in a study by Cariaga 1974 (first published 1936).

Muñoz 1971 provides a personalized account of the characteristics of different waves of Filipino immigrants, and Melendy 1977: Part 1 offers a brief, but objective, account of Filipinos in the USA throughout the twentieth century. Beebe 1978 provides detailed demographic information on education, employment, immigration, and language use and, until results from more general samples of Filipinos in America become available, provides the only source of this type of information on the lives of Filipino immigrants during the 1970s. Since this chapter was written additional data have become available on language use of persons of Filipino origin, as of spring 1976 (National Center for Education Statistics 1979). No other immigrant group of equal size has been so neglected by social scientists and linguists as have the Filipinos; perhaps the need for data on which to make decisons related to bilingual education will promote more research in Filipino American communities.

16

Profile of a state: Montana

ANTHONY F. BELTRAMO

The Treasure State, an inspiring and unpredictable land, belongs to two distinct regions of the USA, parted by the Continental Divide. The eastern two-thirds of the state belongs to the Great Plains: treeless, level, and semiarid. The western side, cloven into high and rugged mountains, is part of the Pacific Northwest. In surface area, Montana ranks fourth in the Union, and in the 1980s these 146,000 square miles house slightly over three-quarters of a million people – five inhabitants per square mile.

It is a common view from the outside that Montana's population is an extension of the upper Midwest: conservative, rural, and Protestant. In fact, however, there is an impressive diversity of cultural backgrounds represented in the state. In his book *Inside U.S.A.*, John Gunther reported finding in Montana,

a big and varied blanketing of foreign born. More than forty-five percent of all Montanans are foreign born or of foreign or mixed parentage. Moreover they are not predominantly of one racial group, like the Mexicans in Los Angeles or Scandinavians in Washington. Montana has Canadians, Swedes, Poles, Italians, Cornishmen, Jugoslavs, Finns, and vast quantities of Irish; in the mines of Butte not less than forty different foreign stocks are represented (1947: 157).

That was in 1947. Heavy foreign immigration has ceased, but many communities have managed to maintain the ways of the original settlers after half a century or more of residence in the state. Language, the most distinctive marking of these clustered peoples, is at times vaunted as a prized possession. The situations of Montana's most popular languages, with something of their backgrounds, will be sketched in the following pages.

The populating of Montana can be separated into nine or ten successive waves. The first was the arrival of present-day Montana's American Indians, which was surprisingly recent; only one of the current tribes lived in the region at the dawn of European exploration. The next group was a small stream of French-speaking trappers and English, Scottish, and American fur traders. They sought quick wealth and, for the most part, did not settle. Ownership of the region changed from French to American, but the French still came. Placer miners came next, from the West, the South, and the Mississippi Valley. These settlements too were ephemeral; boom towns came and went.

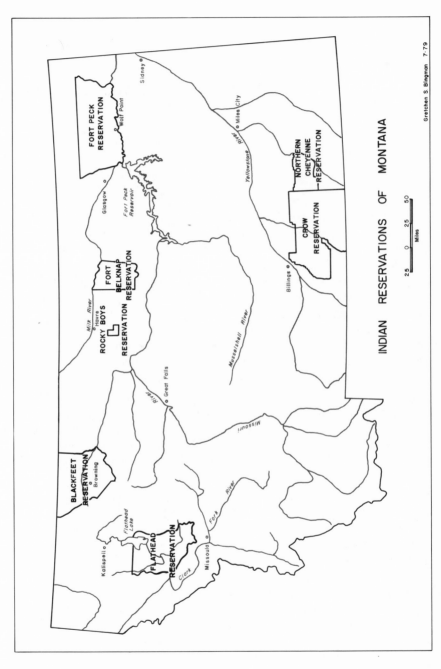

INDIAN RESERVATIONS OF MONTANA

Gretchen S. Bingman 7-79

Figure 16.1. Indian reservations in Montana

Cattle and sheep herders came in large numbers from the 1870s on. The next great influx was brought by the railroad, between 1880 and 1890. Occupations such as deep mining, lumber, and farming require stable settlement, and the railroad provided some security. Later, between 1900 and 1920, dry-land farmers came to Eastern Montana, coaxed in by the railroads themselves. Many of them were driven away after a few years by an agonizing drought. The procession continued with oil and natural gas workers arriving in the 1920s; Mexican American migrant laborers in the sugar-beet fields, before and since the Depression of the 1930s; and, most recently, refugees from the war in Southeast Asia.

American Indian languages

American Indians in Montana number about 42,000; most of these, some 35,000, live on or near reservations, 5,000 in larger cities throughout the state (in particular, Great Falls, Butte, and Helena), and the rest in other areas. Thus, about 6 percent of the state's residents are Native Americans. Since 1920, their numbers have tripled, and they continue to increase at this rate. Except for the Landless Indians, most Montana Native Americans live on or near seven reservations. There is a striking variation among these grant areas in size, land use, and population. Here we will quickly locate them, from the most populous to the least.

The Blackfeet Reservation, which is home for more than 11,000 Indians, extends south of the Canadian border, eastward from Glacier National Park, toward the Great Plains. Its headquarters is at Browning, gateway to the Park. Fort Peck Reservation occupies over two million acres of rolling range land in northeastern Montana, with the Missouri River as its southern boundary. Most of its 7,500 Indians live in the southern part. The Crow Indian Reservation lies in south-central Montana, mostly in Big Horn County, and its Indian population is about 6,500. The reservation contains the site of the defeat of U.S. army General George A. Custer, in June, 1876, by a gigantic Sioux–Cheyenne command under Chief Sitting Bull. Had Custer listened to his Crow scouts, who knew what lay ahead, things might have turned out differently.

Perhaps the most scenic of Montana's Indian grant lands is the Flathead Indian Reservation, in the state's northwest, with Flathead Lake at the north and awesome mountains to the east, west, and south. There are about 3,000 Indians in the area. Adjacent to the Crow Reservation but most isolated with regard to non-Indian civilization is the Northern Cheyenne Reservation, in the south-central state. Its population is about 3,000. Two thousand Indians reside on the Fort Belknap Reservation in north-central Montana. Its northern boundary is the Milk River, within 50 miles of the Canadian border. Less than 50 miles west of Fort Belknap is the Rocky Boys Reservation, in the Bear Paw Mountains. "Rocky Boys" is the name of the reservation only, not a tribal name. It is the smallest of the seven reservations, lowest in population (about 1,500), and the most recently established – by executive order (as was the Northern Cheyenne Reservation), not by treaty.

In overall living conditions and prosperity, the Flathead Reservation at present exceeds others in the state. Employment is generated by recreation and operation of resorts on Flathead Lake. Timber, Christmas trees, and rental rights on Kerr Dam bring profits. For the other reservations, in general, the existing means of nonfederal support are incapable of keeping up with population growth. For the Crows, coal resources and development of small industries may brighten the future. But, on the whole, reservation life is one of poverty.

The languages represented on Montana's reservations fall into a number of major families. As mentioned above, their presence in Montana does not go back very far in time. Several important developments from outside the area exerted pressure to affect the language configuration considerably in the two centuries before white men arrived. One was the Europeans' settlement of the East Coast, many years before the fur trade even attracted Whites to explore further west. Indian tribes of the East, disrupted and displaced by the colonizing Whites, pushed westward in migrating waves into Montana regions. A second movement was the invasion from the south by the belligerent Shoshoni, arriving on horses acquired from the Utes, and originally from the Spaniards. Third, the powerful Blackfeet entered from the northeast, also before 1700. In sum, by the time white men explored Montana's land, none of the tribes they encountered east of the Continental Divide had lived there before 1600. And on the western side, the only old-timers were the Flatheads.

The major language stocks represented on these reservations are *Algonquian*, *Siouan*, *Salishan* and *Kutenai* (see Chapter 6). Except for Kutenai, these are the names of large, inclusive family groupings. Although their languages are brought into proximity in Montana now, these linguistic families differ from each other more than do the Germanic, Romance, Slavic, and Greek languages.

The Algonquian languages claim the greatest numbers of people. Cree and Chippewa (Ojibwa) are heard on Rocky Boys Reservation, where the two tribes have become so merged through intermarriage that the group is now referred to as the Chippewa-Cree Tribe. The speech of the two tribes, when they were still landless in the early part of this century, did not differ much more than, for example, British English compared with that of the Southern United States. On Fort Peck Reservation, there are also quite a few Cree and Chippewa families (Turtle Mountain Chippewa, of North Dakota). At Fort Belknap, the language of the Gros Ventres (or the "Falls People") is Atsina. (This group should not be confused with the Hidatsa-speaking Gros Ventres of North Dakota, whose language is Siouan, not Algonquian). The use of Atsina is in sharp decline. The future holds much more for Northern Cheyenne, used on the Northern Cheyenne Reservation, whose citizens also call themselves the "Morning Star People." Finally, the language of the Blackfeet Reservation is Blackfoot, which in reality is a merging of three mutually intelligible forms: Piegan (the true Montana Blackfeet), Kainah (or Blood), and Siksika (Northern Blackfeet). The Piegan Blackfeet, classic plains warriors, are favorite subjects in the paintings of Montana artist Charlie Russell.

The Siouan languages in Montana are Crow, Teton (Western Dakota or Lakota, usually referred to as "Sioux"), and Assiniboine. The three are about as closely related as Italian, Spanish, and Portuguese. Crow, spoken on the Crow Reservation, enjoys the fullest use of them all; Absaroke or "Crow" is what the group calls itself – "Bird People." This group represents one of the earliest migrations into Montana from the East, where its ancestors broke away centuries ago from the Sioux Nation. At Fort Peck, Teton-Sioux and Assiniboine are the main Indian languages. These two are about as similar to each other as Spanish and Portuguese – perhaps a bit closer. The Assiniboine Indians are also enrolled at Fort Belknap, along with the Gros Ventres (Atsina), bringing together languages of two distinct families.

The Salishan languages make up the most widespread of the North American Pacific Coast families, the eastern or Interior Salishan branch extending into western Montana. Of this group, the languages of the Flathead and Pend d'Oreille (or Kalispel) Indians are very closely related. These two tribes share a common history of dread of the Blackfeet. They have intermingled since the 1700s, and today there are probably no "full-blood" Pend d'Oreille Indians. By 1800, the two groups had allied with the Kutenai Indians, whose ancestry is uncertain.

The Kutenai language, a one-member family of its own, has not been related to any other. The Flathead Reservation is now occupied by both Salishan and Kutenai people. Their tribes are merged politically as the Confederated Salish and Kootenai Tribes, endorsing a contact of languages as distinct from each other as English and Turkish.

Late in the nineteenth century, vagrant bands of Indians came into Montana from North Dakota, and others came from Canada, exiled after a Cree rebellion led by Louis Riel against the Canadian government. These were the last American Indians Montana received from outside in significant numbers. They included the "half-breeds" or Métis. Until the federal government provided for the establishment of Rocky Boys Reservation in 1916, these groups of "Landless Indians" moved about the state, quite unattached. In 1951, Montana's remaining Landless Indians were granted a State Corporate Charter, which allows organization as a nonprofit corporation, and authority equal to that of other Indian councils. Unattached groups from various tribal origins, mostly Chippewa and Cree, but others as well, were served in this way.

In his fascinating book *Strange Empire,* which is concerned with the Riel rebellion, Montana historian Joseph Kinsey Howard says the following about the language of the Métis:

The youngsters . . . could rarely be collected in one place long enough for an integrated course of instruction. As a result few Métis could read or write . . . Most of them spoke at least two languages, French and Cree, and many quickly added other Indian tongues and English. Some even learned German while they were in contact with Selkirk's De-Meuron veterans. Their own patois, still spoken by them throughout the West, is a mixture of French and Cree or Chippewa with some English words. The base is an

344   ANTHONY F. BELTRAMO

obsolete French of a type said to be still heard in Normandy and Picardy, and a large
vocabulary of terms applying to the prairie has been added. Words French in origin have
been given new meanings.

French was the "official" language, used in letters and documents. It was also
favored over English for spoken intercourse with whites and is still preferred by the elder
Métis and widely used by them in Canada and the United States. As used in their own
homes, the patois is more Cree than French (1952: 42–3).

But their PATOIS, a French-based CREOLE, is not understood by the Cree (see
Chapter 8). Métis is the name given to this speech variety as well as the people,
and to everyone it is "some kind of French." There are perhaps 2,000 still
speaking this creole in Montana.

About 4 percent of the place names in Montana are explained by Indian
presence. Some are Indian words with an approximate English transcription:
Peritsa 'crow,' Ekalaka 'swift one,' Nashua 'meeting of two streams,' Yaak
'arrow.' Others are translations directly into English: Big Sandy, Bitterroot; or
secondhand, from French translations: Blackfoot, Hellgate. The names of
chiefs are also found on the map, transcribed or translated: Charlo, Arlee,
Saltese, Moiese, Lame Deer. Finally, the names of whole tribes have been
used: Bannack, Kalispell, Absarokee, Fort Assiniboine, Sioux Pass, and Pon-
dera (a rendering of Pend d'Oreille).

What are the prospects for survival of Montana's Native languages? In some
cases, the language will likely disappear with the death of their current speakers, or at best, after another generation. For a few languages, on the other hand,
there are signs indicating that they will not disappear so quickly. Four of these
signs are: the diversity of the repertoire of languages in the community; vitality
of outside contacts in the language; the perceived difficulty of the language; and
the popular value given to the language as a mark of cultural heritage. These
points will be considered now in more detail.

Diversity in language repertoires. Where there is a one-tribe, one-reservation
state of affairs, the tribal language is more intact, because speakers of different
Indian languages on the same reservation turn often now to English in conversation. Overlooking the role of English for the moment, certain favorings between
tribal languages are apparent. At Fort Peck, Assiniboine yields more often to
Sioux; but on the Fort Belknap Reservation, Assiniboine apparently takes the
lead over Gros Ventre. Flathead and Pend d'Oreille, mutually intelligible dialects, are essentially one and the same on the Flathead Reservation. What it
comes down to is that some speakers of Flathead (or "Salish") say they are
descendants of the Pend d'Oreille. As for the speakers of Kutenai, it was always
they who learned Salish, not the other way around, partly because they were
outnumbered during active settlement by perhaps two to one. Kutenai has
practically disappeared. At Rocky Boys, although Chippewa is still spoken,
Cree is dominant. In effect, Cree is the reservation language. However, for all
those settings where there is more than one Indian language, English is being
increasingly used.

Native LANGUAGE MAINTENANCE is better on the Crow, Northern Cheyenne, and Blackfeet Reservations, each of which is associated with a single Indian tongue. All three languages are in active use; all three, but especially Crow and Cheyenne, still claim monolinguals; many children enter school with no knowledge of English. The effort to promote BILINGUAL EDUCATION is found on all reservations, but it has been most successful in Crow. Indian literacy is greater in Crow, even though Blackfoot and Cheyenne (and Cree) have a practical ORTHOGRAPHY (see Chapter 7).

Outside contacts. Same-language contact with speakers beyond reservation boundaries may help to sustain language usage. The Northern Cheyenne are in touch with Southern Cheyenne; Blackfoot extends into Canada; and the Dakotas augment the resources for Montana's Sioux, which may help explain its prevalence over Assiniboine.

Perceived difficulty. Native speakers themselves promote or discourage retention (or new study) of languages by hastening to show that they are inherently simple or difficult. Cree is supposedly a simple language to learn, but Cheyenne is believed to be very difficult. Also, the relative difficulty of Kutenai is given as the reason Salishan has prevailed.

Cultural heritage. Montana's new Constitution, approved in June 1972, declares:

The state recognizes the distinct and unique cultural heritage of the American Indian and is committed in its educational goals to preservation of their cultural integrity. (Art. X, Section 1, Par. 2)

In 1975, a state Indian Studies Project, after an interpretation of Article X, recommended that the State Board of Regents "urge teacher-training institutions to establish bilingual–bicultural educational programs to insure that elementary and high school teachers understand the Indian students' cultural frames of reference." Recommendation XI also states: "For the nation's children for whom English is a second language, the passivity, the emphasis on the printed word and the major cultural organization of the conventional classroom too often result in language deficiency and increasingly negative self-concepts." From Recommendation XIV: "Language is learning and using language–which means the classroom must be a place where experiences that are the basis for mastery of skills are needed to increase the involvement of children with language." These excerpts illustrate that in those contexts in which Native language education might be defended, it is often carefully avoided. "Language," for most educators, will surely be read as "English."

Nevertheless, at the reservation level, some progress is evident toward providing for the non-English-speaking learner. This is especially true on the one-tribe reservations. With the help of federal funds, texts and workbooks have been developed in the language, story books written to capture folklore, workshops offered, and linguists hired to help define the standard (see Chapter

6). To many Indians, the vigor of their language is symbolized in the existence of a revised dictionary, or in the promise of one.

In the 1970s, there were new signs of concern for language survival on mixed reservations. In the summer of 1977, a meeting was held at Fort Belknap to involve scholars in developing a Gros Ventre program for this gravely endangered language. From the conference came the following suggestions for both institutions of language maintenance and revival of opportunities for use of the language: establishment by the Gros Ventres of a language association, school classes and cultural activities taught in the language, regular meetings of native speakers, and adult classes for the middle generations of Gros Ventres, a majority of whom have no knowledge of the language. (See Chapters 6 and 7 for larger perspectives on American Indian languages and their maintenance.)

French

The use of French in Montana comes from several sources. From the days of French Canadian fur trappers, French made its way into northern Montana from Canada. French came too in the era of heavy European emigration at the end of the nineteenth century: as the language of new wives of American fighting men, arriving from France at the end of World War I; as the second language of Basque sheep herders in northeastern Montana; and, most recently, as one of the languages of Asian refugees.

During the 1600s the founders of New France, centered at Montreal and Quebec, counted on rich profits from fur trapping and trading in the West. French *coureurs de bois* 'forest runners' and *voyageurs* 'explorers' pushed their search for untapped fur areas persistently westward. Another lure was the dream of finding the "Northwest Passage," an imagined waterway which might provide a direct trade route to Asia. One who took this quest very seriously was the trader–explorer Sieur de La Verendrye. In 1743, his sons, Louis-Joseph and François, probably became the first white men to enter Montana.

Even with France's surrender of all American possessions by the Treaty of Paris (1763), its influence in the Northwest and its trading competition with the English did not stop. In the early 1800s, the French brought expert Iroquois trappers from the East into western Montana, hoping the Iroquois would teach their skills to the local Flatheads. Through these contacts, the Flatheads also learned about Christianity, and they soon clamored for a "Black Robe" who would share with them the "white man's Book of Heaven." So, through the French, Roman Catholicism was introduced in the Bitterroot Valley in the 1840s.

The unfolding drama of early French activity in the State places its main characters widely over space and time, and leaves today's Montana with a sense of a French cultural substrate. Part of the old French legacy is the place names, fossil reminders of fur trading days; for example, Choteau, Robare (from French *Robert*), Dupuyer. Another part of this legacy is the family names of mixed-blood Indians, descendants of the offspring of the transient French.

omesteading land in America, and the lumber industry, attracted
ers from France in the past, especially from Alsace-Lorraine. A few
er French people in Kalispell and Billings still use French to some ex-
ny of the French speakers there, and some in Frenchtown as well, are
ides.''

or a majority of Montanans, *Frenchman* means French Canadian. It is
ily the shared border with Canada, where French is an enduring colonial
age, that has supplied Montana with its French speakers. They are mostly
nced in life, since their migration has not been continued. Some older resi-
ts in Frenchtown (near Missoula), Butte (and nearby Anaconda and Oppor-
ity), Bonner, Milltown, Columbus, Jordan, St. Ignatius, Great Falls, Glen-
ve, and numerous towns in eastern Montana still speak the language with each
her. Some listen to French Canadian radio. Frenchtown, established in the
860s, was named for its earliest inhabitants by French Canadians. Until recent
years, St. John's Day (June 24) was observed there in a noisy celebration hon-
oring the patron saint of the parish.

In reduced numbers, Basques and Southeast Asians have brought French to
Montana from societies where it is the second or third language. Basques, who
generally got their footing elsewhere in the West before entering Montana's
sheep country, are more often of French descent than Spanish. Vietnamese and
''Laotians'' (e.g. Vietnamese formerly residing in Laos, and the Laotian
Hmong – ethnically there are very few Lao in Montana) know French because it
was a school language for them. They speak, read, and write it, and could use it
amongst themselves, but find no occasion for it. Their LINGUA FRANCA is Lao.

English

Most of what is now Montana lay within French territory at the dawn of the
nineteenth century. In 1803, Napoleon scrapped his dream of a new French
empire in the western hemisphere, and his sale of the Louisiana Territory in the
same year meant the transfer to the United States of an immense area between
the Mississippi River and the Continental Divide – fifteen future states. American Federalists, who had objected to the purchase, questioned the acquisition
of areas differing in culture and nationality from the original United States. But
President Jefferson assured the nation that this would be resolved through
American expansion and settlement. From that time on, Anglification of the
new regions was endorsed and viewed as quite natural. For a full century, English-speaking people were the most prominent settlers with the exception of
the Germans (see Chapter 12). The managers of the fur-trading companies were
usually English or Scottish. The gold rush, which began in 1862, brought mostly Whites from the Eastern and Midwestern United States.

In the migrations out of the Southeast following the Civil War, a small number of Blacks made their way as far west as Montana. Work in the industrial
mining towns later in the century attracted Blacks in greater numbers.

Today most of Montana's Blacks live in cities in the middle part of the state:
Butte, Helena, Great Falls, Lewistown, and Billings; the greatest numbers are

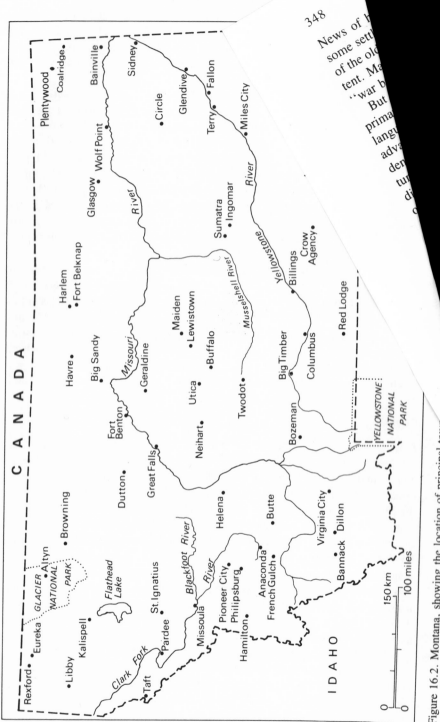

Figure 16.2. Montana, showing the location of principal towns

News of
some sett
of the ol
tent. M
"war b
But
prima
langu
adv
de
tu
d

in Billings, where between 500 and 700 families live. In the last century, Blacks first found employment in the mines, hotels, and gambling houses of Butte and Helena, and as cowboys. In the decade 1880–90, the number of Blacks in Montana increased from fewer than 400 to around 1,500. The African Methodist Episcopal Church has been their main denomination. A newspaper, *The Colored Citizen,* was owned and managed by Helena Blacks in the 1890s. The early 1900's saw two more Black papers: *The Montana Plaindealer* (Helena) and *The New Age* (Butte). Various Black organizations, previously quite active, have disbanded in recent years with the fading of racial tensions. The tensions have not disappeared, but, in striking contrast to the 1930s, Blacks can now be found in all levels of society.

For English-speaking Whites of other parts of the United States as well as the British Isles, the potential in the late nineteenth century for the cattle and sheep industry was very important. The confinement of Indians to reserve lands, removal of the buffalo, a rising worldwide demand for beef, and improved access by railroad, all cleared the way for Montana's livestock boom of the 1880s. Many large cattle herds had been owned by Germans, but after the first big droves (mid-1800s) stockmen were predominantly English and Scottish. Sheepmen arrived later than cattlemen; the sheep business was not big until after 1870. Again, most of the herders were English and Scottish, but the Scots were predominant. Important investors from outside the state were also English-speaking; big cattle companies from Nebraska, New Hampshire, Nevada, and Texas came.

The bringing of big money into Montana had other profound effects on the population's ethnic composition. Butte, which quickly grew as a gold mining town in the 1860s, first dwindled, then revived again with silver mining in the 1870s. But it was Butte's endowment of copper that guided its future. Marcus Daly, an Irishman who had emigrated to America in the 1850s, was a hard-rock-mining expert who arrived in Butte in 1876 to assess potential investments for powerful out-of-state capitalists. His target was the Anaconda Mine, which was producing silver, but soon laid bare the richest source of copper yet found. Daly's financial backing enabled him to purchase new properties and rapidly expand the mine. A huge reduction works and smelter were constructed 26 miles west of Butte, and around these grew the company town of Anaconda. With his partners, Daly invested in other industries. The subsequent growth of the Anaconda Company and its subsidiaries was to reach many areas of Montana life.

To provide labor for all phases of his mining operation, Daly imported thousands of workers from out of state. Many were Irishmen, coming from other parts of the mining west, or directly from Ireland. Later in the 1880s, Welsh and Cornishmen came, then more Englishmen, along with a score of other nationalities. By then, Butte and Anaconda's core settlement and cultural bent were vigorously Irish American. The Irish brought along strong labor union and Democratic loyalties and were to have a powerful role in shaping Montana politics. These facts generally worked to the advantage of other nationality groups as miners. But on occasion, religious and cultural differences, the lack of a "language barrier" for the Irishmen, a love of politics, and a resentment of newcomers made things difficult for others.

Spurred on by the needs of the expanding railroads, coal mining activities developed near Great Falls and Billings in the 1880s and 1890s. The coal in Carbon County, in south-central Montana, brought miners from many nations, but particularly from the British Isles, to the town of Red Lodge. In 1910, Red Lodge had a population of 5,000, and was one of the most colorful and polyglot areas in the state.

Thus the language of American English monolinguals came to coexist with that of other English-speaking ethnic groups. Though modified by different groups in different regions in accordance with the varying conditions of language contact, English took root as the dominant language of the new state. For most speakers of other languages, American Indian or immigrant accommodation to English became the rule.

Since the mid-1900s, the production of wood, oil, and gas has employed workers in less distinct nationality patterns than did industries in the late nineteenth century and early twentieth. However, many of the ethnic communities established in the earlier times have maintained their ways to some extent. A latter-day advantage is that improved travel and communications allow related groups separated by distance to fraternize more easily.

Today, through the Caledonian Society, the Scots are, across the state, the best organized socially of the native-English-speaking groups. "Gatherings of the Clans" attract hundreds, especially in the eastern towns, such as Miles City. One can learn traditional dancing, piping, and be introduced to ageing speakers of Gaelic, the language which opened the festivities at the 1977 Red Lodge annual Festival of Nations.

In Butte, where the Irish once filled ten Catholic churches, the "Irish wake" is still observed, but the separate boarding houses, which served miners of different counties of Ireland, are a memory. The excellent musical choruses and bands of the Cornish "Cousin Jacks" are long gone, too. But everyone there knows about these things, and there is still the Ancient Order of Hibernia, St. George's Day, and St. Patrick's Day.

The immigrant languages

The Montana Language Survey.   The sections that follow are the result of a survey, carried out during 1976–7 concerning Montana's immigrant languages, the ones brought in by settlers after domination by English was established. The basic purpose of the survey was to answer certain questions raised by the language teaching profession, and it was sponsored in its early stages by the Montana Association of Language Teachers. What they desired was an account of the linguistic resources present in the state that were not due to formal language instruction. More specifically, the survey attempted to: (a) describe the linguistic diversity created by immigration into the state; (b) classify the languages and characterize broadly the sociolinguistic setting of the major ones; and (c) sketch the historical background behind the major linguistic communities. The survey was intended to raise further questions and to stimulate interest in this largely neglected area of Montana life.

Interviews with persons native or close to each immigrant group would have been the ideal data-gathering method; with limited resources, however, it was decided instead to turn to a postal questionnaire. Initial respondents recommended others, and since return postage was provided, the overall response was good: around 60 percent of the mailings were returned.

The questionnaire itself, designed by this writer, was divided into two Parts. Questions in the first pertained to historical and social settings and to factors in the situation favoring the use of the language: Did the original settlers come from generally the same regions of the old country? When did most of them arrive? What attracted them? Were there other places in Montana where members of this culture lived? – and so on. Answers to questions such as these followed personal data on the respondent, including his generational distance from the foreign-born speakers, and information on whether or not he still used the language. Questions on traditions and customs, correspondence with the old country, travel and visiting, ethnic organizations and their language use, knowledge of English, and the degree of community concern for maintaining the culture, traditions, and language were also included. If the language referred to was no longer used in a respondent's community, the respondent did not continue to Part Two, which only dealt with language variety and function. In this Part, the respondent listed situations in which the language was either used or not used. Topics such as the age, dialects, and attitudes of speakers were dealt with also.

The questionnaire was three pages in length, and a cover letter was attached, explaining the general purpose of the project. The respondent was assured he would remain anonymous. The questionnaire, richest single supply of information on language in Montana, could be further supplemented by a variety of other resources:

1. *Library research.* Special Montana collections, the Montana Historical Society, Masters' theses housed at Montana universities (and sometimes outside the state), clipping files in newspaper offices and libraries, and local histories (recently, for example, resulting from the work of regional U.S. Bicentennial Commissions)
2. *Direct consultation with informants.* Ministers, bilingual and migrant education experts, language teachers, the state coordinator for foreign language education
3. *Recorded materials* from oral history projects
4. *Participant-observation* at regional and local cultural events
5. *Census data*

In the present study, most of the above were used at some time to supplement the basic sociolinguistic survey. What follows is a broad sketch of Montana's immigrant language situation possible from these sources. Unless otherwise noted, quotations in the pages which follow are taken from responses to the questionnaire. Such a survey answers relatively few questions about language forms and functions; in fact, a summary of survey data may often give an impression of superficiality. However, surveys are the necessary first step to the deeper linguistic and ethnographic research on specific languages which can provide insight into the dynamics of American society and serve as a basis for language policy decisions in education and elsewhere.

Some didn't stay. The special circumstances of settlement soon after 1900 deserve a note here and should be kept in mind, for disruptive events with definite language outcomes were to set back the newcomers' dreams. In effect these can be summed up as two processes: depopulation and de-ethnicization. Some minority groups experience these processes over generations, but for Montana's foreign-born in the first quarter of this century, they were sudden and traumatic.

Natural as well as man-made events were to reduce the ranks of those who planned to stay. Drought was the greatest evictor. After the 1880s, railroad agents extended to Europe their advertising campaigns for new settlers. Later they were joined by land dealers and merchants, eager for profits. Around 1910, homestead laws were liberalized, and there was the added lure of exaggerated promises for new dry-land farming methods. The propagandizing worked. Thousands poured into eastern and central Montana from out of state and overseas. The seven years from 1910 to 1916 provided rain, bountiful harvests, and easy credit. But the next seven brought drought, wind-fed fires, and grasshoppers. Only a forth of the homesteaders stayed to see it through.

Another ugly instrument of depopulation was World War I. The vote and military service were ways for a new citizen to display his Americanism. Most foreign-born Montanans were as eager to enlist as anyone else. By 1917, the nature of migration into Montana had created a "young men's state," with a disproportionate number of men of military age. And they volunteered heavily, even before conscription. After Selective Service quotas were set up, Montana's quota was based on a population estimate nearly twice what it should have been – a blunder unexplained to this day. As a result, the war put nearly 10 percent of Montana's people in uniform and killed or disabled 10 percent of these. Moreover, a great many veterans (at least 25 percent above the national average) decided not to march home again to raise families in Montana. Montana ceased being a young men's state.

A heavy blow to ethnicity came with the cancerous anti-German sentiment attending the world war. This attitude was well-articulated in Montana through "Councils of Defense," legalized at the state level in 1918 and promptly organized into county and local units. One of the Councils' specific orders, directed at purging the state of "unpatriotic" and "ungrateful" people, forbade the use of German under any circumstances (see Chapter 1). The pleas of ministers to be allowed to conduct church services in German were routinely rejected. The Councils also instructed libraries to destroy books; banned were such titles as *German Song Book* and *First German Reader*. It was time to submerge all signs of German-ness, and the German community never recovered (see Chapter 12). To some extent, anti-German attitudes became generalized as anti-foreign; immigrants of other backgrounds recall situations where there was fear that any non-English speech might mark one as pro-German. In those super-patriotic times, ethnicity suffered all around. These, then, were mechanisms which operated only briefly but created lasting obstacles to the promotion of diverse languages and cultures in Montana.

German and Scandinavian languages. In Montana, French and English are the only languages surviving from European colonial origin. The German language has noncolonial immigrant status. Until the last two decades of the nineteenth century, most German-speaking Montanans originated in Germany. Beginning in the 1880s, in addition to natives of Germany, sizeable groups came from Switzerland, Austria-Hungary, and parts of Russia.

Most German-speaking people came to Montana as grain farmers. But placer mining brought them in, too. In fact, the first currents of immigration came around the time of the gold rush. Mine workers arrived directly from Germany or through other mining regions of the West, following the news of Montana's buried treasures. A site named German Gulch yielded gold southwest of Butte in the 1860s. Germans were important in the early development of the state's mineral resources. Samuel T. Hauser, for example, built the state's first smelter (near Bannack), and also served as governor of the Territory. Another German immigrant and mining genius was F. Augustus Heinze, a "copper king." Heinze's financial and political confrontations with the Amalgamated Copper Company (later renamed the Anaconda) amounted to Amalgamated's only real obstacle to eventual control of Butte's mining district.

Norwegians and other Scandinavians arrived about the same time as Germans, in smaller numbers, to mine in the ravines. "Norwegian Gulch" was developed southeast of Butte, from 1864 to 1874. In the western counties, the lumber industry also brought large numbers. Anton Holter came from Norway and set up the first sawmill in Montana, at Virginia City (1863). The lumber industry enrolled more Scandinavians than Germans. As late as 1925, half of the men employed in manufacturing and distribution of lumber were still Scandinavians. The Bonner Sawmill, largest in the state, employed mostly Scandinavians and Finns.

There were around 1,600 Germans and Scandinavians in the state in 1870, and 2,400 by 1880. Both years, nearly half of their group was employed in the mines. Many were helping to build the central branch of the Great Northern Railway. By 1890, according to Grimsby,

a great number of Swedes and Norwegians, who had been employed in railroad construction work, remained. Some of them took up homesteads around Great Falls, and were instrumental in building up that city, or they went to work in the silver mines at Neihart, 65 miles south of Great Falls; others were employed in the coal mines at Sand Coulee. The Great Falls territory had a large Scandinavian population in 1890. When the smelters were built, a number of expert Norwegian smelter men came to Great Falls from Haugesund, Norway, to work in the smelters. The majority of these stayed and are still residents of the city and the surrounding countryside. After working the smelter, they took up land and became prosperous farmers and stock men. As early as 1890,

Cascade County, of which Great Falls is the county seat, had a large Scandinavian population. (Grimsby 1926: 77–8)

Thus, Germans and Scandinavians arrived in significant numbers earlier than most other immigrants from Europe. Twenty years before becoming a state, Montana began direct advertising campaigns overseas as one means of bringing Europeans in, and Germany and Scandinavia were its first targets. Minnesota had been attracting some settlers from these countries in the 1860s; consequently, territorial governor J. M. Ashley thought Montana would benefit as well. In 1869 he set up two agencies, one to distribute state pamphlets in Scandinavia and Germany, and another to contact immigrants as they landed in New York. Europe was soon to hear about Montana through other channels as well. Newspapers in the larger cities printed immigration pamphlets; the Montana Immigration Society was created in 1872; and in the 1880s, railroad representatives started going to Scandinavian countries to drum up interest.

The growth of Lutheranism in the West was, of course, the deciding factor for many who came, for this has been the national faith of Denmark, Norway, and Sweden, as well as Finland, since the Lutheran Reformation in Germany. In 1885, a pastor of the Norwegian Lutheran Church organized Montana's first Lutheran congregation, at Sweetgrass, the largest rural Norwegian settlement in the state at that time. The main religious services were given in Norwegian. Early on, it became the custom to hold afternoon services in English at the request of the congregation, which was a mixture of other Scandinavians, Scots, Indians, halfbreeds, and French Canadians. An itinerant German Lutheran pastor was stationed at Helena in 1886. It was 1895 before the Swedish Augustana Synod was able to provide Montana with a minister.

During the years of heaviest migration (i.e. until 1920), the number of Germans in Montana at any given time was about equal to all Scandinavians together. Within the Scandinavian group, viewing the state as a whole, Norwegians have generally outnumbered Swedes and Danes: Swedes by three to two, Danes by three to one. Scandinavians have contributed notably to twentieth-century Montana's cultural and political life, with examples in John Erickson (Governor 1925–33), J. Hugo Aronson (Governor 1953–61, "The Galloping Swede"), Forrest Anderson (Governor 1969–73), and Danish-born artist Olaf Carl Seltzer.

The German Language.   Through the displacement of three major groups – Germans from Russia, from Germany, and from Central Europe – and sectarian groups such as Mennonites and Hutterites, the German language came to Montana. Immigrants from colonies in Russia have been important carriers of German to Montana. The majority are in the Laurel–Billings area, and they have also established themselves in the vicinities of Hardin, Miles City, Glendive, and Wolf Point. There are thousands throughout eastern Montana. The religious affiliation of those coming from northern regions of Russia (Volga River area) is about half Protestant, half Catholic. Most of their ancestors were Hessians.

From southern Russia came Protestants, whose dialect was predominantly Swabian. Most of the Protestants were Congregationalists by the time of their arrival in America. A few Jews were among the Russian Germans; they continued to assimilate into the German group after emigration (see Chapter 13).

It is common wisdom in eastern Montana that Germans from Russia have assimilated more slowly than Germans from Germany. This is perhaps due in part to their experience as a minority group in another non-German country. It should also be noted that the Germans who had settled in Russia brought a higher level of literacy and general education than that of their Russian neighbors. Several generations in these circumstances must have provided some "training" for resistance to assimilation in the American setting.

Before long, the use of German was limited to home and church, and few people born since 1950 speak it. But it is still buoyed up by a strong ethnic feeling among the Russian Germans. Although the language was generally abandoned in the church by mid-century, a Congregational church in Billings regularly holds a German service today. In January, 1978, the Yellowstone Valley Chapter of the American Historical Society of Germans from Russia was organized in Billing. The Society publishes a newsletter and a journal, promotes genealogical research and maintains co-ethnic ties with groups elsewhere (e.g. in South America). The Herbstfest, an annual harvest festival held in Laurel since 1973, was inaugurated by the Germans from Russia. Now, its program admits all Germans, and even other ethnic groups locally present such as Hispanos and Yugoslavs. This is a symbolic reminder that the former insularity of the Russian German community has been broken. Intermarriage is common. Through the encouragement of active participation in the wider society, the decline in use of German has been hastened.

Most of the Mennonites coming into Montana were Germans from Russia. Shortly after 1900, for example, a group of about twenty-five families settled in Bloomfield (eastern state), near Glendive. Some came through secondary migration, having spent a quarter century in central North Dakota, and now seeking more spacious farmland. Their sect had grown out of the Anabaptist movement, a religious revival that accompanied the Reformation in the early sixteenth century. Exemption from the draft was one of the privileges they sought in their centuries-long quest for religious freedom.

In 1917, with patriotism and anti-German sentiment reaching hysterical levels at times, the threats by Councils of Defense led to a mass exodus of Mennonites into Canada. Perhaps a thousand families left. Times were harsh for those who stayed. The Mennonite minister in Glendive was nearly lynched for his pacifist views and use of German. When it was revealed in court that no members of the church board were pro-German, things quieted down. But wartime punishment for speaking their native tongue was an especially severe blow to the Russian German Mennonites, who believed that the preservation of German was necessary for the survival of their church. To them, religious schooling meant instruction in the Bible and in the German language; the two were nearly inseparable. Interestingly, the Swiss Mennonites (few as they are in

Montana) report no early objections to English in the churches. Again, it may be the Russian Germans' experience over several generations of using a minority language elsewhere that binds their language more tightly to religion.

An account of the variety of dialects brought to Montana from Germany and Austria would require that each locale be examined separately, an impossibility here. One can expect to find any dialect imported at one time or another. Concerning the religious affiliation of Germans, Lutherans predominated prior to World War II, but since the late 1940s, the emigration from West Germany has brought about as many Catholics as Protestants. There is no historical kinship felt between these people and the Germans from Russia.

German communities enjoyed a certain amount of renewed immigration, especially around 1950, and there are small tracts where German language and customs are quite alive. Fallon is a village located in eastern Montana between Miles City and Glendive. Its population of around three hundred is almost exclusively German. The original settlers did not come directly from Germany but from central North Dakota, as many Russian Germans have done. However, an additional group of around thirty arrived from Germany after World War II, intermarried and settled there, a stimulus to maintenance of German ways. Two German American churches help bind the community: Evangelical Congregational and Missouri Synod Lutheran. Ministers find it natural to incorporate some German in the singing and funeral services. Half the Fallon adults use German regularly at home and informally outside the home. Some of their children reach school age as bilinguals. A handful of the recent arrivals are nearly monolingual.

The Germans' desire for periodicals resulted in Montana's most active ethnic press ever, a miniature picture of the brilliant German press in more populous states. From the late 1800s until the world war, papers came and went. There were weeklies and semi-weeklies. During the 1880s, there were the *Montana Argus* and *Montana Freie Presse* (both from Helena), and the *Butte City Freie Presse*. The 1890s saw *Familienblatt* and *Montana Herald* (Great Falls), and *Montana Journal* (Butte); in the early 1900s, *Montana State Journal* (Butte), *Plevna Herald,* and two organization monthlies, *Der Hermanns-Söhne in Montana* and *Der Lutherische Wächter* (both from Helena). These were short-lived, and none had a circulation over a thousand. German Montana's biggest newspaper in endurance and readership was the twelve-page Helena weekly *Die Montana Staats-Zeitung* which ran, some years as a bi- and tri-weekly, from 1886 to 1917. Serving Idaho also, its circulation in 1905 reached 2,200. In format it fits the description of any capital-city paper, with a Sunday supplement and special sections for news from Germany and German American enclaves. From 1914 on, front-page events in Europe prompted reflective editorial-page essays on the issues of being German in the United States. One of the issues was language. After years of consensus on the view that only through use of the native language could German culture be preserved in the United States, in November, 1914, the paper stated:

It was to be expected that some of our good, old Germans would take offense at the English in the *Montana Staats-Zeitung*. But it was necessary. Times have changed . . . Had we recognized this gradually advancing change years ago, and accommodated ourselves to it, the German communities in the U.S. would be better off today. But we decided not to have anything to do with those who didn't speak German. The national language is English . . . If we want to incorporate our good characteristics into the formation of the national character, then it can only happen through the English language.

Before the swirl of suspicion and high costs forced its closure three years later, the paper carried a bilingual title and articles in English.

Prior to World War I, German Americans throughout the United States expressed their kinship in the formation of numerous organizations, or *Vereine*, of which Montana had its share. Perhaps the most influential was the Order of the Sons of Hermann (Hermanns-Söhne), a fraternal lodge named for "that great deliverer of our forefathers from the domination of the Romans." There were many others around the state – singing clubs, veterans' organizations, money raising clubs, patriotic, drama and gymnastics clubs. State and regional gatherings, such as choral festivals, brought Germans together on an annual basis. Today, Kalispell and Great Falls have German Clubs; there is an Edelweiss Club in Billings. What is visible of Montana's immigrant German today is the tip of a melting, once gigantic iceberg.

The most recent German-speaking arrivals, quite independent of the groups already discussed, are the Hutterite Brethren, who live a life of austerity in small, isolated colonies in the central and northern part of the state. Like the Mennonites, Hutterites mark their beginnings in the Anabaptist movement. They also adhere strictly to the precepts of common ownership of property and community of goods.

Coming first to Dakota Territory in the 1870s, the Hutterites enjoyed certain advantages for survival on the Plains frontier. For most homesteaders, life in vast, unpopulated areas meant isolation. Women, especially, recall the loneliness and the fear of distance from doctors. But for the Hutterites, the colony answered religious needs, and the extra space allowed room for communal expansion. In drought years, the failure of the average settler's single crop was a disaster, but Hutterites had quickly diversified and could survive more easily. In good years, the average Plains farmer worried about supply of workers, while the Hutterite found a ready labor reserve on the commune. Most other newcomers sought to improve their social and economic status. Not Hutterites; they came to preserve, at most to renew, what was already for them a desirable way of life. What will drive them away is a climate of intolerance, a demand that they give up traditional ways and integrate into the larger society. Faced with such an ultimatum, Hutterites do not resist, but move on to a friendlier frontier. In this strategy, they have had centuries of experience.

Slightly more than 2,000 Hutterites now live in Montana, about the same number as in the Dakotas. A given colony belongs to one of three "leuts" or peoples, named for their early leaders in America: Schmiedeleut, Dariusleut, and Lehrerleut. Some differences in dialect, belief, and dress distinguish them. All three are found in Canada, where there are about twice as many Hutterites as in the USA. In the Dakotas there are only Schmiedeleut, and those who came to Montana are Dariusleut (now in eight colonies) and Lehrerleut (in twenty-three). Montana's thirty-one settlements are located near towns. The population of a colony is kept to between sixty and one hundred or so, by splitting and thus creating a new settlement.

Hutterite youngsters receive a double-track education in Montana, one in German, one in English. In accordance with state law the colonies hire licensed teachers for their English schooling. Along with this, the children must attend "German school" from age 5 to 15, where study of the Bible and German progress together. Hutterites do not encourage their children to pursue education beyond age 16, the minimum age required by law.

The special lives of these people support three forms of language: High German, the Hutterite dialect of Low German, and English. Standard or High German, called simply "German," is the language children first learn to read and write; it is used primarily for religious matters. "The principles of our belief, taken from the New Testament, have been written in the German language. Therefore we are anxious to keep up in the language," wrote one colonist. Hutterite German or *Hutterisch,* which has no written tradition, is the common language at home and of all daily interaction in the colony, except with the teacher at the "English school," who generally does not know German. LOANWORDS recall the coexistence with surrounding languages over the years; their number from English is increasing. English is used at school and in dealings outside the colony. All Hutterites speak English, but men, because of commercial transactions outside the colony, are more at home with it than women or children through the mid-teens.

The idealized Hutterite colony is one that has succeeded in isolating itself from the outside world to preserve a centuries-old lifestyle. How closely does the real colony conform to this? In 1976 an "English school" teacher-observer, writing admiringly from a Montana colony, was compelled to note that the demand for luxuries which make life more enjoyable was increasing (Leiby 1976). Articles such as phonographs and radios were forbidden, but most families now owned these things and kept them in locked cabinets. More youngsters were seeking a high school education through correspondence courses. Compromises were being made in the discipline of those boys who succumbed to outside ways. The elders hoped that by relaxing some of the rules, they could keep the boys in the colony. As long as such compromises do not upset their program of language maintenance, the Hutterites will continue to foster in Montana a type of German whose speakers are actually increasing, not declining.

Norwegian.   Leading all Scandinavian languages in Montana for its momentum and numbers, Norwegian can also claim a striking new surge of interest.

More than any other ethnic group in Montana today, Norwegians are viewing their old language as an object to be reclaimed. For perhaps 20,000 adults, which include recent immigrants, the language was only placed "on hold" anyway, never lost.

In 1978, the Governor declared May 17 as Norwegian Constitution Day in Montana. His proclamation acknowledged the many Montanans who are of Norwegian descent (especially residents of Yellowstone County). This public notice also acclaimed the success of Eastern Montana College's Scandinavian Studies program in its first year, enriched by a gift of books from the Norwegian government; and praised foreign language study as an aid to understanding one's own language and culture. In fact, Norwegian is the single language in Montana whose academic programs attract mostly students of native descent. New courses at the college level and library books give added respectability and boost pride; the Norwegian knows that fine works are within reach. There are serious new students of literature and folklore. But what the majority want is an active, speaking command – not for church, not for political unity, but for simple fellowship and good times. Along with know-how about cooking and the folk arts, a knowledge of Norwegian is for maintaining ties with friends and family, including those in Norway.

Attracted to northern, central, and eastern Montana in the early days by good farm land, to western Montana by the lumber industry, and to the mining towns and railroads, Norwegians are everywhere. As to regional origin, the migration history is so complex and protracted that no part of Norway is excluded. The survey indicated, however, that a majority of Norwegians in Montana came from western Norway and the southwest coast. Many Norwegians also came into Montana after residence in Minnesota and North Dakota. There is one Montana Norwegian newspaper on record. It was *Indlandsposten*, published at Great Falls from 1915 to 1917.

Norwegian Montanans are on the whole indifferent to the ongoing controversy which still divides Norway itself – between proponents of *Landsmål* ('country language,' an elevating of more conservative, more "Norwegian" language to standard use) and those favoring *Riksmål* (closer to Danish). In her engaging book *Birchland: a journey home to Norway*, Joran Birkeland, born of immigrant Norwegian parents, says that she only understood the language question after traveling to the old country herself. She had grown up in Montana with Norwegian cultural items, whose traditions she had not appreciated until making the trip to Norway as an adult.

> But it was not the Bergen dialect that the man on the gangplank used as he, a representative of the Government, began his welcoming address. It startled me when I heard it for – shades of Montana! – in every accent it was the dialect I had heard in the barn and the hay corral at home on the ranch. It was the dialect of the newcomers from Norway whom Father brought from town to help with the haying or the shearing, the dialect I remembered Father defending as the true Norwegian, but which I recalled Mother rejecting in silence. It all came back to me now. I had paid little attention to the dispute at the time. As children, we were only dimly aware of the differences between Father and Mother. (Birkeland 1939: 19)

That Norwegians in Montana have little patience for the question is clear from the sociolinguistic survey. What Einar Haugen concluded about Norwegians in other areas of the United States applies as well in Montana today: "It appears to be a general rule that the immigrant resents changes in his old homeland which deviate from the pattern which he carried away at his departure" (Haugen 1969: 177)

Social and cultural bonds are strengthened by the Lutheran Church and Sons of Norway Lodge (Butte has a Daughters of Norway, too), and these organizations offer conversation courses in the language, on demand, in many towns. Constitution Day, Leif Erickson Day, Scandinavian Day, and all-Norwegian (annual) church services are some of the events planned by Norwegians around the state.

With this kind of support, what vitality does Norwegian show in the state today? The possibility of keeping it going is exciting to Montana's Norwegians. Older native speakers, however, still say that they have little opportunity to use it. Reports of its use in the Sons of Norway Lodge are "some," "none," "10 percent," "for singing," and so on. As for the interest expressed in reviving the language, everyone agrees that it is increasing, a very recent movement. Classes in Norwegian are populated both by native speakers who want to keep up, and by members of the third and fourth generations, for whom it is a foreign language. Beginning classes fill a room, intermediate classes (except at the college level) run to only half a dozen. Certainly, though, it is these groups that will provide the force behind the serious language-revival efforts now in germination.

Danish.   Danes, who make up the smallest Scandinavian group, are now spread across the state, but still favor the extreme northeast corner where they came to homestead at the dawn of the twentieth century. There they found fairly level land and small lakes, reminiscent of parts of Denmark. From Sidney to the Canadian border numerous settlements developed at Andes, McCabe, Dagmar (named for Denmark's queen), and Westby (*-by* 'town') – now Montana's most eastern town, once North Dakota's most western; and nearby places. The Danes brought farming skills and crafts. The Lutheran Church served as the hub of Danish spiritual and social life, as it still does in many of these places. Other groups went to Circle and Big Sandy. Somewhat earlier (from the 1880s), Danes were drawn to Great Falls and Butte. Montana's Danes were from all parts of Denmark; a substantial number in Butte came from Kolding.

The little farming communities were sometimes called "Danish colonies." As other Scandinavians did, the Danish began right away to organize through cooperative enterprises: a fire insurance company, a coal mine, and so on. They took a lively interest in local affairs, in American laws and parliamentary procedure, and by the 1920s Danes were serving as representatives at the state level. The Danish Brotherhood was organized in 1910. Some of its early purposes were to help members obtain citizenship and generally make their way.

Ignorance of English could not be tolerated long; Danish was unnecessary baggage, if not a barrier. One woman who spoke only Danish until starting school remembered her first teacher, who taught both Sunday School and the grade school. At the church, this teacher used Danish with the children. But in regular school, she "did not understand Danish." Everyone knew the teacher was doing "the right thing," because the children soon learned English.

Today, the Danish Brotherhood Lodge still makes nominal use of the language. An annual Fall Fest, a three-day program of Danish cultural activities including lectures by invited speakers, also features one all-Danish church service. About 200 of Sidney's people of Danish background still understand the language. In these rural areas, as well as in Butte, older people still receive some letters and papers from the old country. This is the extent of Danish found in Montana.

Swedish. Swedes, especially the earliest to come, mostly took up farming in the central and northern part of the state, and logging in the west. However, urban centers attracted more Swedes than Danes, and the greatest concentration of Swedes was in Butte, where there is still a chapter of the Vasa Brotherhood. They are still strongly represented in Great Falls. Urban and rural Swedes are probably in balance now. The concentrations of Sweden's population seem proportionately represented, that is, southern regions of origin predominate. From Minnesota, the most "Swedish" state, immigrant settlements thin out westward into North Dakota and Montana. Most of Montana's early Swedes came directly from Europe, but an increasing proportion coming after 1900 report having lived first in Minnesota and North Dakota.

Today Swedes enjoy celebrating their heritage, and join Scandinavian clubs in a few of the larger towns. They take part in Scandinavian Day each August at Red Lodge. The decline in the use of Swedish, however, has been uninterrupted. Montana Swedes recall Sunday School and church services being given in Swedish until around 1920. In step with Swedish American church practice across the USA, services shifted into English in the mid-1920s. Swedish is no longer the language for conducting meetings, but it is a conversational language among Swedes and between Finns and Swedes at Scandinavian social affairs. It is used informally when older people visit or in letters to relatives.

Finnish. Finns belong socially with Scandinavians in Montana, even though linguistically they do not. There are various reasons for the connection. Montana's advertising to potential settlers reached Finland about the same time as the Nordic Scandinavian countries. Due to the special position of Swedish in Finland, most Finns brought Swedish-Finnish bilingualism, which facilitated their contact with Swedes as immigrants. The welcome extended to other Scandinavians by Scandinavian groups has included the Finns. Today, Finns benefit along with the other Scandinavians in the group fare for charter flights to their ancestral countries.

Finns are scattered around the state. They began arriving in the 1890s and early 1900s, going to mines and farms. Migration was reduced to a trickle after 1920; some Finns have continued moving into Montana from states to the east, especially Minnesota. The largest clusterings that have formed are reported from around lumber mill, mining and smelter towns: Milltown (near Missoula), once named Finntown, Red Lodge, Butte–Anaconda, Great Falls, and Billings. After a period in Billings, some left and took up homesteading. Smaller towns repeatedly named are in the Billings area and east of Great Falls.

As for those regions of Finland from which Finns in Montana originated, only vague patterns emerge. In Billings, most are from northern Finland. Dialects are Pohjanmaan, Hamelainen, and Uudenmaan. Red Lodge claims north-central and west-central areas (Vaasa Province), but also the south and east. Karelian is heard there. Great Falls represents all parts of Finland but the northern area. There are a few Estonians there, too. Estonians also live in Liberty County, in the far northern part of the state.

In polyglot Butte, the Finnish miners crowded into their own districts, with Slavs, Italians, and Irish as neighbors. An old miner remembers the first two English words he learned: *job*, then *raise*. The Finns created a town within a town. They ran big public sauna baths, boarding houses, many bars, barber shops, and stores. Now, for a quarter of a century, Butte has watched its old neighborhoods literally crumble away. The underground mining of copper has given way to open pit mining, turning the city into a giant crater and scattering its old residents. The Helsinki Bar is all that is left of a once colorful Finntown. The Finns who left chose destinations all over the USA.

But many have stayed. In Butte, Billings, and Red Lodge, those who know Finnish number in the hundreds. The second generation language has developed into "Finglish," containing many English words adapted grammatically, but still Finnish. It is recognized as not as "correct" as the older peoples' language. Finnish is used with family and friends. It is gone from the church. Virtually all Finnish speakers know English now. Butte and Billings report that about 5 percent, all senior citizens, know little or no English. Red Lodge has a Kalevala Society, and the Festival of Nations also brings Finnish speakers together.

Dutch. Memories of Dutch have outlived use of the language itself in several spots in Montana, notably the Belgian Colony near Valier (north-central state). In 1912 and 1913, Father Victor Day of Helena made trips to Belgium, bringing back about a dozen families to farm the rich land and establish a Catholic church. All spoke "the Belgian," which they were anxious to shed for English in their adopted land. In special night classes, exhausted farmers struggled with English and citizenship lessons. No efforts were made to associate with Dutch speakers in other parts of the state. The Belgian Colony is still there but the original families are greatly dispersed. Many descendants live in Valier.

Most speakers of Dutch coming to the state were Protestants from the Netherlands. Settlers in rural Conrad (near Valier) dedicated a Dutch Reformed church in 1909. Some points in its language history were:

1910 – The congregation issued a call for a regular pastor, stipulating that services were to be in Dutch
1918 – The congregation voted to hold services in the "American Language" every other Sunday
1919 – The word "Dutch" was dropped from the church name.
1925 – Services in Dutch were discontinued

The Montanans noted for still speaking Dutch (and Frisian, too) are Hollanders living in rural areas around Bozeman. In the mid-1890s, some twenty families came to Gallatin County from the Netherlands to make their homes. All spoke Standard Holland Dutch, but their home languages varied. Those who came from Groningen and Gelderland used the Dutch dialects of these provinces. Others came from Friesland and spoke Frisian, a separate language, at home. A few were from Zeeland. Remarkably, descendants of these settlers are still in Gallatin County. They form the communities of Churchill and Amsterdam and number about 300 families today. The Christian Reformed Church, distinctly American, has always been the focus of community life. There are two congregations to accommodate the 240 families who belong. Children attend the private Manhattan Christian School. Dutch survives here because of the cohesion maintained by this group over four generations. Yet, a close look reveals that hardly anyone under age 50 now speaks Dutch. Without regret, the Hollanders marked its demise as the church language during World War I. English has thus been the language in most homes for half a century.

In the late 1940s, Dutch enjoyed a kind of revival when about eighteen families, mostly relatives of the established Hollanders, arrived from the Netherlands and settled permanently. For ten years, Holland Dutch was again featured in church services. But now, the only daily reminder of the old language is a "Dutch brogue" in the English of a few. Some parents talk of introducing Dutch as a foreign language in the elementary school. And older people look forward to the annual Dutch hymn sing held in Bozeman each fall.

The Slavic languages.   Most Montanans of Slavic background mark their origins in northwestern and southern regions of Eastern Europe; a few are Russian. From northwestern areas come Polish, and from what is now Czechoslovakia, Slovak and Czech. Southern Slavs brought Bulgarian and the languages of modern Yugoslavia: Slovenian, Croatian, and Serbian (see Chapter 14).

Slavic people were arriving as early as the gold rush (1860s), and came later in the nineteenth century to help build railroads. But the major movements began around 1900, when they arrived to work in the industrial mines and smelters. Slavs worked alongside Italians, Greeks, and the more firmly rooted Scandinavians and Irish. Many took jobs in the coal mines near Great Falls and Red Lodge, and worked on road construction crews in those areas. A few came to farm in the east.

Professor H. G. Merriam, writing in 1943, claimed that "seven hundred Serbs, Bulgars, Albanians, Montenegrins, Ukrainians, Russians, and Jugoslavs celebrate Christmas in Butte on January 7'' (Merriam 1943: 162). Merriam also noted that in 1921, fifty-two nationalities had been found in that city alone. To chronicle the fate of each of these would demand much time and space. The next few paragraphs on Eastern Europeans will only outline the stories of some very representative language groups, whose experiences show much in common with those who came from other areas.

Polish. The Poles in Montana numbered around 5,000 by 1910, most of them clustering in Butte, Great Falls, and near the coal mines. In Stockett, a coal town, 1,000 miners worked at the peak of mining operations. Only about a hundred spoke English; the rest spoke Polish, other Slavic languages, and Italian. On a small scale, these settlements echoed the Polish populations of many thousands taking shape during this era in mining and industrial districts elsewhere in the USA.

Esteem for their language and home culture is highly apparent in Polish Montanans. So is their belief in and support of general American education, probably more so than among other Slavic groups. In line with Polish Americans elsewhere, the great majority belong to the Roman Catholic Church, a church shared by many nationalities. Partly for these reasons, while the urban Polish have improved their lot in America, their ancestral language has suffered in use. Customs connected with Easter and Christmas are still observed, and Polish cooking is important. Except in Butte, however, it cannot be said that Polish families remain in tightly compacted neighborhoods, as they do in cities of the eastern United States. In Butte, first and second generation members use Polish in homes and when Polish families meet. Younger members know old sayings and songs.

There have been some Polish farming communities in Montana. Far to the north in Liberty County, where there were many Polish and Russian settlers, a town called Warsaw was founded in 1912, near Chester. Silesia, near Billings, was named for Silesia Springs by an immigrant who built a brewery there. St. Phillip's, a town near the eastern border, was settled around 1910 when several Polish families migrated from Minnesota. In 1911 they built St. Phillip's Catholic church; a school followed, as did stores and more homes, and for years the village remained mostly Polish. Farmers, when they retired, moved into the village nearer each other. Meanwhile, through their interest in citizenship, voting, and greater involvement in society, newer generations were acculturated. By the time the church burned down in the 1950s, hardly any of the original settlers were left and many descendants had moved away, many to Miles City. However, despite great discontinuities in the functioning of Polish in their lives, Polish Montanans continue to express strong pride in their language and in having spoken it.

Czech and Slovak. The coal mines near Tracy and Great Falls received laborers from eastern Slovakia, between 1910 and 1925. To the other mining and smelter towns (primarily Red Lodge, Butte–Anaconda, and East Helena) went emigrants of western Slovakia, and northern and western Bohemia, regions of modern Czechoslovakia.

Some Czechs and Slovaks also settled in agricultural areas. The greatest concentration of Czechs is to be found in Lewistown, and in communities surrounding it within a 40-mile radius. West of Lewistown is Kolin, established in 1913 and named after a city in Bohemia. Czechs were also successful ranchers in the Square Butte area, northwest of Kolin. There are several hundred Czechs and Slovaks in the state who still use their first language. Czech is spoken daily in homes and at reunions, and in some church services (especially for Christmas).

Serbo-Croatian. For the South Slavs generally, it was not the "pull" of good fortune in the American West that drove them there as much as the "push" of bad fortune at home. From the labor standpoint, they found work in the mines and quarries alien to their accustomed ways. But during five centuries of oppressive rule under Austrians, Hungarians, Turks, and others, they had nurtured the ideals of freedom and self-determination. In the intolerable years prior to World War I, the possibility of realizing these elsewhere looked better than ever. Those who came were often well educated. Some pioneers remember schooling in both their Slavic language and German. After the world war, hundreds decided to stay in Montana.

Serbians came to Montana as early as the 1880s. Before 1900, the town of Belgrade, near Bozeman, was named by a Serbian immigrant. But the largest groups were to be located in Butte, Billings, and Anaconda. Red Lodge and Black Eagle also have many, and Serbians are outnumbered there by Croatians. At one time there were seven Serbian lodges in the state, and Butte Serbs produced three newspapers. But the most enduring foundation has been the Serbian Orthodox church founded in Butte in 1904. Slavs travel from all over Montana to hear services, especially at Easter and Christmas. The priest of this church reported that Church Slavonic is used in services, and that the choir much prefer this language to English for singing, finding it more melodious. Serbs and Croats alike feel that modern Serbian is more archaic than other Slavic varieties, closer to the language of the church, and that it has been a cohesive force for the Serbian community. Indeed, Serbs report for their language a higher proportion of second and third generation usage than other Slavic language groups, and estimate that between 50 and 80 percent of those speaking Serbian also read and write it. Many younger Serbs have married "outside" or moved away, but at a slower rate than other groups. Moreover, in the third and fourth generations, there has been a definite renewal of interest in Serbian heritage and traditions. Fewer are moving away than in the 1960s. Even those who are "one-fourth Serbian" are getting more in touch with their ancestry. A loose affiliation is felt with Serbian groups elsewhere: Black Eagle, Billings, and Calgary (Canada). It was not difficult to plan a United States Bicentennial program of Serbian songs and dances, though the planning was, admittedly, done in English.

The Croatians have substantial groups in Black Eagle, Lewistown, East Helena, Red Lodge, and all places already mentioned for Serbian. That American Slavic groups tended to grow through chain migration is demonstrated in Black Eagle, where at least 75 percent of the pioneer settlers came from Bribir, Croatia (northern Yugoslavia). Stone masons, also from Bribir, brought their skills to Lewistown. Practically unknown in that town in 1900, they numbered about 400 by 1910. Like other Slavic groups, Croatians had taught each other that dependence on the mines and smelters was a transitional stage, and they should seek education and jobs elsewhere. Unlike the Serbians, who attended Eastern Orthodox church services in their own language, these and many other Slavs have followed Roman Catholicism. So the church further aided the Croatians' entry into the American mainstream, bringing them into contact with many nationalities. Intermarriage was frequent. As a consequence, it is primarily the first generation pioneers, now in their seventies, eighties, and nineties, who speak Croatian.

Other groups.   Bulgarians and Ukrainians, prodded by steamship advertising at the turn of the century, also came to mine and build railroads, as well as to farm. East of Miles City, the town of Plevna was named by Bulgarian railroad workers. In 1910, Russians named the town of Kremlin, near Havre. About the same time, farmers from Odessa settled in the community of Seventynine, north of Billings, and observed the customs of South Russia for many years. Miles City and Circle have also had Russian communities. Apparently, native-brought Russian has all but disappeared in Montana, but the situation needs more study.

Montana's Slavs have enjoyed meeting in lodges and clubs, fanned into existence by the American fraternal movement, and they maintain active organizations through which the language is preserved or at least encouraged. In Red Lodge there is the Slovenian National Benefit Society and the Croatian Fraternal Union; the latter also has branches in Great Falls, Butte, and Anaconda. Butte and Billings have a Serbian National Federation Lodge.

On a less elegant note, some of the most common epithets used on immigrants were applied first to Slavic people, and might be mentioned here. This Irish verse from Butte reflects the resentment held for newcomers around the turn of the century:

> O Paddy dear and did you hear the news that's goin' round?
> They're firin' all the Irish that are workin' underground.
> Oh, I've rustled at the Belmont and I've rustled at the Con,
> And everywhere I've rustled they're puttin' Bohunks on.

Coming into the Northwest, some words applied to foreigners in the East came to be used indiscriminately, extending beyond Slavic groups. Whereas in eastern U.S. cities, *Bohunk, Polack,* and *Hunyak* referred to Slavic types, these were not synonymous. In Montana things were simpler. The only criterion was that an English speaker defame a non-English speaker: a Swede could be called a *Polack*. The term *Honyocker* adapted from *Hunyak* referred disparagingly to immigrant homesteaders of any background, who came to Montana between 1910 and 1920. *Hunyak* possibly originated in Czech *huñác* 'shaggy fellow'; cf. Serbo-Croatian *gûnj* 'peasant jacket,' figuratively 'peasant.' In Montana, *Honyocker* replaced the earlier cowboy term *pilgrim*.

Hungarian. Simultaneously with other groups attracted from central Europe, most Hungarians arrived in Montana between 1890 and 1920. A few have entered since the 1950s. There are a dozen or so families with Hungarian names in Butte, and a few in Billings, Red Lodge, and Missoula. In Butte there is a street named after Louis Kossuth, a mid-nineteenth-century revolutionary leader and orator. Perhaps there are two hundred people who can speak Hungarian in the whole state. But there have not been, apparently, any self-reinforcing settlements sending for additional kin, and no single dominant region of Hungary provided immigrants to Montana. Hungarian Montanans appear to be quite cut off from their old country and from each other as well. The only interest in promoting the language comes from native speakers at professional levels, who have recently suggested starting a newsletter or a library-based resource center.

Greek. Greeks have entered Montana more recently and steadily than other Europeans. The arrival of Greek speakers falls more or less naturally into two periods, an early one from around the turn of the century until 1920, and a later one, from the 1920s to the present.

In the early decades, most Greeks who came to Montana were young males who did not plan to stay. They hoped to earn and save money, then return to Greece. Propaganda by steamship companies and Greek press reports of job opportunities lured hundreds to the mines of Butte, the smelter at Great Falls, and railroad work. In western Montana, they were to find a topography and climate which reminded them of their homeland.

By 1910 there were well over 1,000 Greeks in Montana. They maintained a strong pride in being Greek, in using their language, and lived in tightly knit neighborhoods. During this time they (and other groups) endured great prejudice, which can only have been aggravated by their abiding loyalty to Greece. However, during and following World War I, Americanization came to be more attractive to the Greek immigrants, and many decided to stay. In this way, settlement and employment were facilitated for later arrivals. Around 1920, the end of the initial period of immigration, a further encouragement to settlement came when Greek Orthodox churches were established in Great Falls and Missoula.

It was during the 1920s that Greeks began arriving in families. Some still came with plans of returning after saving money, but this was less common than before. Those who did stay for good were not generally happy with mining or railroad jobs, and the main settlements were to be formed in Missoula, Havre, and Billings, besides Great Falls and Butte. There are now also Greeks in Philipsburg, Helena, Miles City, Kalispell, and Bozeman. Some have stayed in their original occupations but many established small businesses: tailors, florists, confectioners and pastry shop owners, shoe repairers, and restaurant owners.

Greek immigration to Montana has actually leveled out, instead of falling off as it did for many nationality groups, and has continued to add new first generation members. Relatives are brought in a pattern of "chain migration." In Havre, most Greeks have come in the last twenty years, some as recently as the early 1970s. Missoula also has a very new group. As a result, in Havre, Butte, and Missoula at least, estimates of monolinguals among Greeks are given as between 10 and 20 percent.

Residential patterns have come to be less tightly clustered. Since the 1920s, Greek families are found scattered throughout the cities. But important over-riding organizations, especially the Greek Orthodox Church, hold them together culturally and psychologically. Greeks often point out that they do not participate much in the church aside from paying their membership and attending weddings, funerals, and baptisms. But this is simply to say that alongside Lutherans and Methodists, they are not frequent churchgoers. In fact, the Greek Orthodox Church remains a powerful magnet to the community, serving both as ethical and national unifier, for it is the national church of Greece. Montana Greeks continue to identify with it. Another organizing body is the American Hellenic Educational Progressive Association (AHEPA), a secular fraternal organization founded in the 1920s. There are branches in at least three cities: Missoula, Great Falls, and Butte.

Still other organizations are Daughters of Penelope and the Greek Ladies of Philoptochos Society. These appear to arise from the special social needs of this ethnic group, and not as transitional or "training" clubs for participation in analogous American organizations.

In most Montana towns, Greeks say their language comes from "all over Greece," but in Missoula the strongest dialect is Kalavritini (from Peloponnesus). Areas of western Greece and Macedonia are also cited by immigrants as their home region. In Bozeman many Greeks came from the village of Malakasion.

As is traditionally the case around the USA, Greeks in Montana, with some notable exceptions, have not been active in local politics, labor, or civic activities. Some explain this through the preoccupation in early years with saving enough money to return to Greece or to bring more relatives to the state. In recent years, aloofness from local affairs has softened, while the Greek community continues to draw newcomers from the old country, and it would be difficult to find a more patriotic American group.

Social gatherings of these people are thoroughly Greek, and hospitality runs high. But it seldom occurs to them to invite non-Greeks because Greek is spoken much of the time. The larger community is welcome, not shut out. When Greeks come together socially, they become indifferent to social status within the group, and to individual shortcomings as well, which are a family matter.

The traits of open-door clannishness and equal respect on social occasions, plus those of thrift and self-help in daily affairs, combine in a way of life that sustains the Greek language. Most Montana Greeks give a high rating to the importance of keeping their language. It is used in the home, in liturgy, informally at family and community gatherings, and by special agreement in social club meetings. Papers and letters arrive regularly from Greece. Old World and American Greeks exchange visits. There is a small but hearty reference group of monolinguals, replenished by continuing immigration. These factors favorable to language retention in defined functions have similarly converged for other languages, but in an earlier, less hospitable Montana. The "delay" has provided for Greek a more permissive atmosphere than that which prevailed before 1930. And historically, the presence over many decades of a significant group intending to return to Greece must have aided resistance to assimilation in language. It is reported that members of all ages speak it regularly. It is a good bet that some young Montanans will welcome the twenty-first century in Greek.

Italian. Italian found its way into Montana through two patterns of settlement, a thin one driven by religion and a thick one driven by economics. Throughout the 1830s, Indians of western Montana made repeated requests to the Jesuits at St. Louis College for a permanent mission. At last, Father Pierre Jean De Smet, a Belgian, made the trip into Flathead country, then went back to Missouri to recruit more priests for the work. Italy was a traditional source of Jesuit missionaries. The outcome of De Smet's early work in the Bitterroot Valley was the founding of St. Mary's Mission (1841), the first church in Montana and, for many, the very genesis of their state's history.

In numbers, the impact of Italian Catholic missionaries, counting priests and laity together, was not great. Only a few dozen came between 1840 and 1900; their objective was not that of bringing Italian settlers; Italian Jesuits worked side by side with Belgians, Austrians, French, and Germans; and obligations elsewhere did not always allow long-term, undivided attention for a Montana mission. Even so, when we consider that they generally brought a high level of training, leading just as naturally to brilliant careers in Europe, and that they accomplished much in an unfamiliar and sometimes hostile environment, it is no wonder that local respect and appreciation are still strong for these Italian pioneers.

Linguistically, it was Montana's Indian languages, not Italian, that were promoted by the work of these missionaries. Gregorio Mengarini, the first to be left in charge of St. Mary's Mission, eventually published *Grammatica Linguae Selicae: a Selish or Flat-Head Grammar* (1861) and *A Dictionary of the Kalispel or Flat-Head Indian Language* (1877). Mengarini was assisted with his *Dictionary* by Giuseppi Giorda, who delivered sermons in six languages (including Nez Percé, Flathead and Blackfoot). Alexander Diomedi wrote a three-volume Kalispel *Dictionary,* printed between 1876 and 1879. *A Kootenai Grammar* was written in 1894 by Philip Canestrelli, in Latin, for use by missionaries. Still another example is Anthony Morvillo's *A Dictionary of the Nez Percé Language* (1895).

Later arrivals from Italy did not come to follow Jesuit precedents, but to find work. The first generation ancestors of today's Montanans of Italian descent probably never exceeded 10,000. Even so, their roles in mining and city building were important. Despite heavy advertising campaigns by the railroads, few Italians seem to have been attracted to farming in eastern Montana. There were some. For example, a group of Piedmontese came to settle near Glendive, beginning in the 1890s. One immigrant pioneer had heard through advertising about farming in Montana. He arrived and soon found a job herding sheep. Others of his native village followed him, and eventually about a dozen families were homesteading at Intake. Besides success in farming, the Italians' paramount concerns became American citizenship and participation in the wider community. The prohibition of speaking Italian in schools was accepted as logical and just. Since the Catholic church at Glendive was nearly 20 miles away, they pooled efforts with several other Christian denominations in building what is now a Congregational church. Thus, despite the similarity in background of these settlers, their use of Italian was lost quite early.

Railroad work explains the presence of some Italian Montanans, for example in Missoula and Helena. Often, those of the second generation can speak the language and on social occasions, do so "just for fun." Dialectal backgrounds are scattered (see Chapter 11). Mixed marriage is the reason given for letting the language slip. In order to hear Italian today, one goes to the smelter and mining towns. Black Eagle, a suburb of Great Falls and site of the Anaconda smelter, has since the 1890s been the home of hundreds of Italians. Today, the nationality groups most frequently associated with development of the smelter are Italian, Slavic, and Greek. Big Italian weddings, the *bocce* ball court, and Italian dinners at the Catholic church were once cohesive functions; the Christopher Columbus Lodge still is. In Anaconda, several hundred can still speak Italian. Most first generation speakers say they are from places between Rome and Naples – Campobasso, for example. St. Ann's Day (July 26) brings Italians together, as does the St. Ann's Society.

Butte's Italian community is the largest of all. Mine workers arrived in greatest numbers between 1880 and 1910. Meaderville, the mining camp where most Italians clustered, could boast forty-three *bocce* ball courts by 1890. In St. Helena's Parish, services were held only in Italian. Northern Italy and the Swiss border are the places of origin most often mentioned. Traditional and religious celebrations bring the people together. Fluency in the language belongs mostly to the elders. But there are many third and fourth generation Italians and half-Italians joining their parents in keeping ties with the old country.

Red Lodge, which brought Italians to the coal mines, maintains the language perhaps best of all. About a hundred still actively use it, enough for it to be used in meetings when Italians gather. Most say they are from Piemonte and other parts of northern Italy, but in meetings it is Standard Italian that is used. Providing some help in the retention of Italian are the annual Festival of Nations, and such organizations as Druidesse, the Italian Girls' Victory Club (a charity club) and Unione Fratellanza. There is some evidence that here, more than in other towns, younger generations are making efforts to retain the language. There has never been an Italian press for Montanans. Some now subscribe to *L'Eco d'Italia,* published in San Francisco.

Spanish. In the early 1800s, numerous Spanish speakers came from Louisiana and the province of New Mexico (see Chapter 9) into what is now Montana, to hunt and trap. Some married Indians. If the Spanish as residents assigned any place names to Montana's map, none of these has survived. Schoolbook writers are wont to include the naming of Montana as an example of Spanish legacy in the American West. In fact, the idea of the name originated with U.S. Congressman James M. Ashley of Ohio, who chaired the House Committee on Territories in the 1860s. Ashley had picked the name up somewhere; he did not know Spanish. Before President Lincoln signed the bill creating Montana Territory (May, 1864), the name competed with other proposals in both the House and Senate. Whether a Spanish origin was ever mentioned or not is debatable, but it was the fact that the form was found in Latin that saved "Montana" in the last stages of the Senate discussion:

MR. HOWARD: I was equally puzzled when I saw the name in the bill. . . I was obliged to turn to my old Latin dictionary. . . It is a very classical word, pure Latin. It means a mountainous region, a mountainous country.
MR. WADE: Then the name is well adapted to the Territory.
MR. HOWARD: You will find that it is used by Livy and some of the other Latin historians, which is no small praise.
MR. WADE: I do not care anything about the name. If there was none in Latin or in Indian I suppose we have a right to make a name; certainly just as good a right to make it as anybody else. It is a good name enough.

Similarly, Montana's state motto, *Oro y Plata* ('Gold and Silver') was not bestowed by Spanish speakers but by Anglos using dictionaries. The most important Spanish place name in Montana is that of Montana's first trading post, Fort Manuel Lisa, named for its founder who left Louisiana in 1807 to set up a fur trading business on the Yellowstone at the mouth of the Big Horn River. Don Manuel gained profits and the respect of Indians, but eventually had to abandon the fort amid growing unrest by the Blackfeet during the War of 1812. No trace of the fort remains.

Much later in the century, railroad jobs brought in laborers from various parts of Spanish America, and some stayed. The early 1900s saw an increase in seasonal workers, but the people who stayed grouped themselves mostly in urban centers. More recently, a number of Cubans and Puerto Ricans (see Chapter 10) have made their homes across Montana, notably in Flathead County, where they are in occasional contact with the Spanish of Mexican migrant workers. Differences in the dialects are met with some derision, some laughter, on all sides. A Latin American Festival is held there each spring.

In Butte, Spanish is used in homes and at church; St. Joseph's Parish gathers Spanish speakers of varying origins, especially Coahuila (northern Mexico), which is close enough to visit. On December 12, a special celebration is held to honor Our Lady of Guadalupe, the patron saint of Mexico. Other Latin American countries are represented too. A kind of promotion for Spanish can be shown in the working arrangements between the Anaconda Company and Latin America, where (in Mexico and Chile) the Company made dazzling purchases of mine properties in the 1920s. In the days before Anaconda's mines in Chile were nationalized (1971), Montanans employed by the Company could, for example, take a three-year assignment with a Chilean operation. As returnees, several of these people have taken part in and encouraged Hispanic events around Butte.

For some idea of the volume of Spanish presently heard in Montana, we must refer not only to maps but to calendars – the ones kept by county extension offices and the Montana Migrant Council. Clearly, despite the increased mechanization in farming methods, Montana farms and orchards will continue for a long time to draw non-English-speaking workers on a seasonal basis. Over 90 percent of these are Spanish-speaking. Two regions of the state attract these transient workers in the late spring and summer. In the northwestern part, on the shores of Flathead Lake, cherries must be hand picked for fresh packing. In the southeast, sugar beets are harvested mechanically but thinned and hoed by hand. Until the 1960s, sugar beets were grown on a larger scale in western Montana as well, and a scattering of Spanish speakers can be found from those days. In much smaller numbers, migrant sheep shearers spend part of their spring in northeastern Montana.

For the few hundred *mexicanos* who are placed in the cherry orchards, the Montana encampment is short: from mid-July to mid-August. Their migrating stream has followed fruit crops from California, through Oregon, Washington, Idaho and into western Montana, returning to Washington in the fall.

In the eastern and southern part of the state each May, hundreds of families fan out into the Yellowstone and Missouri River valleys to work for beet growers. Most are Mexican and Texas Mexican laborers, riding a migratory route different from the fruit-crop circuit. The migrants' route originates in southwestern U.S. border areas, provides the beet farm labor through July, moves eastward to help with crops in other parts of the Midwest, and then back home. Some people remain in Montana until September to hoe and weed for later crops. Adult members of these families are frequently monolingual in Spanish, or very nearly so. A temporary residence, group isolation from the larger society, and simplified daily engagement with the dominant society make learning English a less urgent matter than it was for the immigrant settler.

The human needs attendant on the transients' cyclical coming and going are very basic ones: sufficient work, attention to health, and daytime care for small children. Migrant schools and social service centers exist along the Yellow-stone Valley, and the migrant laborer can at least perpetuate his accustomed lifestyle. To improve his lot, more is available to him. Even while working, he is entitled to special vocational, literacy, and consumer education. In the Bill-ings area, nearly a dozen programs, sponsored federally and locally, are set up to serve these needs. But their life is one of "eat-and-run"; the great majority of workers from the borderlands continue to make the seasonal rounds and are gone by the end of the summer.

However, each year a few decide to stay, partly as the result of migrant agencies' efforts to provide vocational training into anchored jobs, and to "relocate" these families. In combination with work opportunities, the new-comer often finds that regional or family ties can be maintained to some extent in sympathetic neighborhoods. Strength and visibility of Mexican cultural elements certainly add to the desirability of putting down roots. This is not to say that the new neighbors find districts that are uniformly Mexican; they cluster in places where Hispanos of varied provenience have been at home for many decades. Increasingly, however, the Spanish of Montana is Northern Mexican. Spanish-speaking Anglos often refer to it as "Tex-Mex," or an "Indian dialect" of Spanish.

In this region, numerous Hispanic Montanans are counted in Sidney, Glendive, Miles City, and smaller towns along the Yellowstone: Fairview, Forsyth, Hysham, Ballantine, Worden. But if Mexican Montana had to name a capital, it would be Billings, the home of some 3,000–4,000 Spanish speakers (5 to 6 percent of the population). Important for sugar refineries and oil, and the site of two colleges, Billings has many Hispanos who trace their Montana settlement (or their parents') to the 1920s and before. It is these second and third generation members who most actively support service and social clubs: the Concilio Mexicano and the Latino Club, the Foreign Language Club, and the college foreign language honorary society, which invites the public to functions. Natives of several American countries – Argentina, Paraguay, Venezuela, Chile – live here and participate. A few are working temporarily for refineries in Montana. Spain is also represented. Our Lady of Guadalupe church (Mexico's patron is honored here on December 12, as in Butte) is the center for religious celebrations through the year. These functions attract Hispanos throughout eastern Montana, and so do patriotic Mexican festivals held in public on May 5 and September 16. To further strengthen an Hispanic awareness, the Concilio Mexicano sponsors a Spanish radio program each Sunday.

What about bilingual education? The wealth of teaching materials available as never before from around the Spanish-speaking world, together with the human resources in good supply, could resolve the question of mechanics. A third crucial ingredient – something resembling an educators' commitment to biculturalism as a trait to be nurtured continually, with the involvement of schools – will be sought in vain. Neither the summer nor school-year curriculum incorporates such an "innovation," despite the fact that schools serve bilingual learners and employ bilingual staff. To establish literacy in English is, apparently, the best favor the school can do; prevocational and consumer education come next.

Reviewing now the composite picture of Spanish in Montana, we can tentatively identify two basic groups who speak it. One is residentially stable, literate, confidently bilingual, and dialectally heterogeneous while publicly desirous of overlooking (even denying) dialectal differences to favor Spanish as a means to social unity. The other is highly mobile, nonliterate, more nearly monolingual, linguistically homogeneous, and self-conscious of the way their knowledge of Spanish sets speakers apart from Anglos and established Hispanos alike.

Basque. In the mid-nineteenth century, the rise of the sheep industry in western states introduced herding traditions associated with various nationalities, and most uniquely, the ways of the Basques.

A sheep herder could turn flock owner in a short time. Typically, he would accept a good share of his pay in ewes; after a year's increase he combined with another new owner. Developers of herds commonly joined with men of their own nationality – the French, Basques, and Portuguese more exclusively, perhaps, than others. The competition for feed and display of know-how frequently saw the Basques emerging most successful. By the 1890s, for example, membership in California's state wool growers association was two-thirds Basque.

In Montana, sheepmen trailed flocks in great numbers into the eastern part of the state from the late 1870s onward. Shortly before the turn of the century, drought conditions forced many Basques out of the Southwest, northward into the mountain states, some of them settling in Montana sheep country. The biggest concentrations settled around Glasgow and Miles City. Several prominent Basque families entered these areas between 1900 and 1910, bringing names like Etchegare, Oronos, and Etchart. They enjoyed high success privately and lent leadership statewide to the wool growers. Through the first third of the century, the lure of good grazing land continued to attract Basques. The steady decline in sheep raising since the 1930s reduced the Basque population but many Basque-/English-speaking families are still to be counted in Sidney, Miles City, Plentywood, Malta, Glasgow, and nearby towns.

Judging from personal communications, there are some Spanish Navarrese Basques in the region, but most descend from Frenchmen. For Spanish and French alike, it is the use of Euskara (the Basque language) that has given solidarity to the group, although this is enjoyed mostly by adults and elders now. Some maintain contacts with relatives in the Pyrenees, by letter and travel. There is no Montana Basque press but the newspaper *Voice of the Basques* from Boise, Idaho reaches quite a few. In the Sidney area, the Catholic church draws Basques together. Each August a French Basque priest is welcomed and entertained.

Hebrew and Yiddish. According to the *American Jewish Yearbook,* Montana's Jews numbered 545 in 1973, and only the state of Wyoming listed fewer. But while in Wyoming they cluster in Cheyenne, in Montana they are more scattered; Billings is the only town with as many as a hundred Jews. Kelson (1950) noted that the modern decline in numbers draws attention from the Jews' earlier importance to the state. For example, it was likely that the number of Jews who have helped govern Montana was, in proportion to the Jewish population, greater than that of any other state. He lamented the tendency of Jews to leave the smaller cities and towns of Montana to live in New York and California.

At the present time, Billings' Temple Beth Aaron has the largest Jewish congregation, numbering about a hundred. Rabbi Horowitz is the only rabbi in the state and in immense areas of surrounding states. Volunteer members teach Hebrew in Sabbath School. A few youngsters choose to continue with Hebrew lessons beyond bar mitzvah. Most Jews came to Billings from eastern states, the Dakotas and Minnesota. Yiddish, the Jewish language closely related to German and written using the Hebrew alphabet (see Chapter 13) served an important function in the pioneer days, but is now spoken by only two or three people.

The membership in Butte is sixty people strong, primarily second generation members of Butte's last substantial influx of Jews, occurring in the 1880s and 1890s. Thus, the congregation is old and getting older; younger members tend to intermarry and move out. The majority of the Jews in the last big group were from overseas: more than half from Russia, a quarter from Germany, the remainder mostly from Poland. Yiddish was the common language that bound them together. Today, forty of the sixty understand Yiddish; half a dozen find occasion to use it. Hebrew is used in the prayer service, including hymns. The people prefer hearing it sung. The remainder of Montana's Jews are located primarily in Great Falls, Helena, and Missoula. Apparently none of these groups now possesses the numbers and cohesion to develop what might be called a Jewish community.

Arabic.   Arabic is still used to some extent in the homes of 150 or so Lebanese whose fathers and grandfathers came to the industrial towns soon after 1900. Most of these pioneers were merchants and traders, and preferred not to work permanently in the mines. The largest assembly of Lebanese is in Butte, where they have formed the American Lebanese Peace Society. The Lebanese enjoy socializing together and use the language in their planned functions. The varieties of Lebanese mentioned are Hadchite (the most frequent), Zahle, and Beirut. Other Montana towns, which have smaller groups, are Missoula, Billings, Helena, Great Falls, and Hamilton.

Asian languages.   *Chinese.*   The Chinese, who never settled in rural areas, first came in the 1860s with the railroads. Many of them came directly from China to join Montana's crews. They also came with placer miners, following the inland-moving mining frontier from California. In 1870, they were Montana's largest foreign population, numbering 2,000.

True sojourners, holding on to thoughts of returning to China, they joined frontier society to run the "service industries." In Butte, for example, they would serve meals and fill lunch pails for miners, for Japanese laborers employed by the railroads, and later for Koreans engaged in beet farming. The Chinese provided tailor shops, laundries, and herb doctors. The Chinese population swelled slightly until around 1900, then steadily declined as other groups poured in. By the 1930s, most had left for the Pacific Coast or returned to China.

Their actual mining activity consisted in scavenging placer claims for tailings after other miners had left. The Chinese accumulated in towns associated with

Alder Gulch (southeastern state): Adobetown, Junction City, and Virginia City, where there was a Buddhist temple; in settlements in the Nine Mile Valley, near Missoula; and Helena and Butte, which had extensive Chinatowns by the 1880s. Butte had a Chinese Baptist Mission during the 1890s.

The record of prejudice against the Chinese on the frontier, though probably no worse than in other parts of the country then, is a melancholy one. It tells of job discrimination, special laws against their owning mines, picket and boycott tactics, and physical attack. Only Blacks and Indians endured as much discrimination.

Those who reached Montana had left many parts of China. The majority spoke Cantonese in its various subdialects. Over the years, newspapers have been available from San Francisco and Seattle. Now, with the old Montana Chinatowns reduced to a handful of families each, Chinese has virtually disappeared.

Japanese. Japanese speakers in Montana belong to families of former railroad workers, there are a few "war brides" all around the state, and recent arrivals from Hawaii. To this day, the fashionable comparison between the Chinese and Japanese who came to work finds the latter less content to remain in inferior positions, or to accept menial work or live in segregated districts. In Whitefish, Japanese were brought in soon after 1900 to work on the railroad. Those that eventually settled, bringing their families, came to earn praise for their success in business or their efficiency in truck farming. Marriages between first generation Issei and Whites were accepted, even when interracial marriage was illegal in Montana.

Recently, a public panel was formed in that area as one of a series of meetings on local ethnic heritage. The Japanese declined to participate, no longer considering themselves a distinct "ethnic group." Even where Japanese has survived as a home language, there is practically no interest in having the younger generation maintain the language.

Korean. A number of Koreans came to Montana early in this century as political refugees, when Korea came under Japanese occupation. A few remain, for example, around Butte, as vegetable farmers. More recent arrivals, numbering a dozen or so in each place, live in Polson, Arlee, Lolo, Great Falls, Missoula, Helena, Plentywood, Kalispell, Whitehall, and Havre. A large proportion are the wives of United States service men. They speak Korean when they get together, but not daily at home. Some receive magazines from Korea. One celebration they observe is the Korean Thanksgiving in the fall.

Southeast Asian languages. Appearing first in 1976 and presently numbering some 300 in the state (200 of these in the Bitterroot Valley and the city of Missoula), a group of Laotian refugees is cautiously feeling its way onto Montana's scene. They are Hmong, members of an adaptable but highly independent "hill tribe" of Southeast Asia. In this phase between their old world and technological society, Hmong families are currently living in farm dwellings or trailers in town getting what jobs they can, driving themselves hard when they find work, and attending job training and English classes, mainly at the technical center in Missoula.

The Montana Hmong call Laos their home, but trace their geographic origins to southern China (Kweichow province, within known history). Centuries of bullying by southward-moving Chinese colonists, beginning in earnest in the fourteenth century A.D. (Ming Dynasty), forced this ethnic group into other provinces and into North Vietnam, much of Laos, and Thailand. Their homeland was scattered, high mountain communities, until around 1960, when there were nearly 350,000 Hmong in the world. The recent war in Southeast Asia was devastating to the Hmong. Fully a tenth died; the rest are scattered – thousands resettled in Thailand, hundreds in France and Australia, and there are several thousand in the USA.

As determined by political loyalties and clan divisions solidified during French colonial days, which ended in 1953, the war saw Hmong fighting on both sides. Over two-thirds of them sided with the pro-Western Royal Lao government, the remaining 100,000 joined the Communists. The Hmong came to Montana through the resettling efforts of General Vang Pao, a Laotian Hmong leader whose troops had fought, with some success, in the losing battle against the Communist-led Pathet Lao. The Lutheran Church and various agencies acted as Montana sponsors in the resettling process. Vang Pao selected the Bitterroot Valley for his people because ''it looks like home and makes my heart feel glad.''

The name Miao is the one linguists and ethnographers use to refer to this group and its language. Many of the terms generally used to describe the Hmong, their ethnic divisions, dialects, and dress, were first applied by the Chinese. According to some Hmong, Chinese officials ordered them to dress in distinct ways in order to exaggerate cultural differences, and thus prevent concerted revolt as well. The major varieties considered are, in translation: Black, Flowery, White, Green, Striped (a subgroup of White, according to Montana Hmong), Red, and Blue Hmong. How closely these correspond to dialect boundaries is difficult to know. There are apparently no Black Hmong in Montana. It is reported that White and Green Hmong, the groups best represented in Montana (overwhelmingly White), did not intermarry before the war and had problems understanding each other's speech. Life in refugee camps changed things. They learned to adjust to differences in pronunciation and to communicate well across dialects. In fact, the majority of these newcomers prefer to overlook group names and the divisions suggested by them, to emphasize the unity of the Hmong in Montana. As a whole, the Hmong dislike the term Miao, because they see it as Chinese, meaning 'rice sprout.' Some Hmong say it is a neutral label, recalling rice-growing ancestors, but for others it is ''not a polite word,'' in effect like 'hayseed' or 'hick.' The term Hmong, on the other hand, means for some 'free men,' for others 'men on top.'

Together with Yao, Miao forms a branch whose linguistic affiliation is in dispute. Greenberg (1953) has hypothesized that the Miao–Yao languages form a separate branch of Sino-Tibetan; they have also been classified as Mon-Khmer, Tai, and Sinitic. Miao is a tonal language, monosyllabic, containing many words borrowed from Chinese, French, and Lao.

Among the speakers of Miao, whose social scheme is highly patriarchal, most older men know some Chinese. Montana Hmong generally speak Lao. Thus, the languages commonly in command on arrival in Montana are the home language, Hmong (Miao); Lao, the national language; French (especially for men); and perhaps Chinese, as determined by circumstances.

It is through oral tradition that the system of beliefs is transmitted among speakers of Miao. Hmong religious practice shows elements adopted through prolonged contact with the Chinese, Tibeto-Burmans, and Tai. Animistic beliefs, ancestor worship, offerings to local and household deities, exorcism, and animal sacrifice, are maintained or are within recent memory.

In Hmong life, natural objects are often given spiritual qualities. To some degree, this seems to extend to the graphic representation of language. Some Hmong tell of an ancient kingdom whose laws were written in old script, and the books containing them were condemned and burned by the Chinese. But the old inscriptions, they say, were preserved when clever Hmong women worked them into the embellishment on their skirts. The Hmong can no longer ''read'' them; designs which are said to have originated this way are more like charms. And today, in Montana, Hmong women embroider designs which symbolize the English words they have learned.

The literary forms that are found – stories, songs, parts of heroic cycles – are also brought orally to Montana. Accuracy is most important in each retelling. It is explained that learned leaders who could read and write were the first to be captured in the Chinese persecution of the Hmong; thus, written versions were lost.

Scholars generally agree that there was no writing system indigenous to Miao. Several romanized alphabets have now been devised for the language. Before 1961, Hmong who were in school were learning to read and write in both Lao and Miao. The Hmong in Montana, however, are not much at ease with these writing conventions, and in fact show little interest in having their home language in print. They are not enthusiastic about the idea of writing a Hmong–English dictionary either; after all, one already exists for Lao and English, they say. Meanwhile, the compulsion to attend English classes is growing stronger. Reading and writing practice is done in English, along with drill in speaking.

Over many centuries of resettlement, the Hmong have shown a remarkable ability to accommodate while resisting absorption by host cultures. The next few years will see the outcome of this ability in the USA.

The Vietnamese in Montana are fewer in number than the Hmong, but are spread more widely, in groups, around the state. There are handfuls in Billings, Polson, Columbia Falls, Baker, Dillon, and Red Lodge; about ten families each in Helena and Missoula, and fifty families or so in Great Falls. Some came directly from South Vietnam, others after various lengths of time in Laos. There are young adults who were born and raised in Laos. Most are Buddhist or Catholic. Protestant churches (Lutheran, Seventh Day Adventist) are assisting in the settlement of the Vietnamese. In their transition to American life, the relationship to a sponsor is very significant, and usually a dependent one at first.

These refugees are rapidly learning English, but speak Vietnamese ("the standard kind") among themselves. Their readiness to acculturate is very high. At the same time, naturally, they are hungry for news about their homeland, and some Communist papers do reach them, as well as publications from the U.S. government in Vietnamese. They have a better command of French than the Hmong, and use it sporadically with Americans, but speak Lao, not French, with other Asians.

Conclusion

These, then, turn out to be the most populous languages that have been brought into Montana. The survey technique of sending questionnaires to individuals knowledgeable about subgroups proved to be valuable in the preliminary work toward understanding the linguistic situation of the state. The returns often provided information in areas not previously envisioned by the researcher. For example, immigrant letters sent to the old country which many families have apparently saved over the years, can give important insights into changes in culture and language. Some Montanans have collected ballads and songs which relate immigrant experiences. The fact that so much information still resides with older, first generation members gives a certain amount of urgency to further work and promises scholars interested in both linguistic and social history research invaluable primary data.

FURTHER READING

This chapter is about two different things: the business of doing language surveys and the state of Montana. To find out more about language surveys, the best place to start is probably Ohannessian, Ferguson, and Polomé 1975. It is a collection of papers on the methods and results of language surveys together with reports on particular surveys. None of these is on the USA, but many of the principles are applicable wherever surveys are done. Surveys of American states comparable to the Montana survey are rare, but see Voegelin, Voegelin, and Schutz 1967 for an interesting description of the language situation in Arizona, emphasizing American Indian groups. Several chapters in Fishman et. al. 1966 give data from surveys organized by language, religion, or other parameters and show the kinds of information which can be obtained from sociolinguistically oriented surveys. Several chapters in the present volume report on community surveys of various types (e.g. Chapters 10, 11, and 15). Recently, in the wake of legislation and court decisions about language in education, a number of school districts around the nation have undertaken surveys of language use in their communities, but such surveys are often hastily done and the results are only rarely published.

Background information on Montana's history and population can be found in a standard history of the state such as Malone and Roeder 1976 (see especially pp.

265–73) but this has nothing to say about language. One historical article, Merriam 1943, gives an account of the ethnic groups in the state, but it is out of date and it does not discuss American Indians. For Montana's Indian languages, the dictionaries and other language texts produced by nineteenth-century Jesuit missionaries are maintained in the Indian Language Collection by the Society of Jesus (Oregon Province 1976). This material is available on microfilm. From time to time, *Montana, The Magazine of Western History*, has a relevant article, most often on an Indian group but sometimes a biographical sketch of a Jewish merchant or a Norwegian pastor, or the like, which refers to language. Several specialized studies on particular groups have appeared as unpublished M.A. theses and the like, but they are generally old and inaccessible. For example, Grimsby 1926 discusses the Scandinavians in Montana, and Lee 1947 ably describes the Chinese groups, but Haugen's classic book, *The Norwegian Language in America* 1969, is more informative and available, although not so localized. Kelson's 1950 M.A. thesis on the Jews of Montana is likewise old and inaccessible; Fishman 1965b is of more general value but does not mention Montana.

Part IV

Language in use

Introduction

The first step in describing the language situation in a nation is to provide an inventory of the languages spoken there – where they came from, where they are spoken, their basic structure, and the linguistic relations among them. The first three Parts of this volume have done this for the USA, at least for the major languages and a number of special cases. The language inventory is, however, only the first step. Next comes an account of how the languages are used.

This means not only the fundamental question of the sociologist of language, "Who speaks what language to whom and when?" (Fishman 1965), but how the languages change as they are used for different purposes, and how the people of the nation make use of their language resources as they engage in the manifold patterns of communication in the life of the nation. These questions are meaningful whether the nation is overwhelmingly monolingual like Greece, richly multilingual like India, or somewhere in between, like the USA and most other countries. What kind of language is used in law courts, doctors' offices, classrooms, places of worship? What are the basic communication networks in the nation and what strategies of language use appear at critical points in the networks? In everyday conversations, how do people manage their interactions of buying and selling, making friends, telling stories, arguing, getting themselves out of trouble, and all the hundreds of daily tasks in which the use of language is central? When and how do people write – from grocery lists and application forms to advertising copy and historical novels? The questions are endless, since the use of language is all-pervasive, and the variations in the forms and functions of language are the indicators and indeed part of the substance of social patterning and social change.

It is not only that the possible questions about language use are endless; the approaches that can be followed in looking for answers are many and varied. Some scholars work with questionnaires and surveys and analyze their data with accepted statistical techniques (e.g. Cohen 1975: Ch. 9), and some keep constantly observing the language used around them and present their insights in witty and compelling prose (e.g. Goffman 1971). Some investigators make extensive recordings of verbal exchanges and use their texts to classify and describe the kind of language behavior in which they are interested (e.g. Rosenberg 1970 on Black sermons; Mehan 1979 on classroom talk), while some take short transcripts of speech and subject them to minute investigation and analysis (e.g. Schegloff 1968 on the openings of telephone conversations; Labov and Fanshel 1977 on the language of a psychotherapeutic interview). Some students of language in use set up experimental situations to elicit particular kinds of language behavior, and by comparing the outcomes of different values of selected variables, reveal significant patterns and regularities (e.g. Snow 1972 on mothers' talk to young children). And there are many other approaches. The specialists go by many names: DISCOURSE analysts, psycholinguists, ethnographers of communication, pragmaticists, conversational analysts, communication specialists, speech scientists, sociolinguists . . .

The rapidly growing supply of published papers on language use in the USA doubtless includes both trivia and profound discussions, but at this stage of our knowledge, it may not be easy to tell the one from the other. Some things are evident, however. First, the coverage is unsystematic and spotty, determined by the current interests of the investigators rather than by the possible importance or general public interest of the results. The language specialists do not operate in terms of overall plans or general research strategies, even of the most tentative or sketchy kind.

Second, the results of the scientific study are hardly ever communicated to the general public or to people who are coping with language problems in the society. Occasionally, an item attains a momentary bit of journalistic attention, for example a study of male–female differences in speech. Generally, however, popular authors, writers of editorials, and political and educational leaders keep repeating the conventional wisdom of our society: the quality of English is declining, individual BILINGUALISM is a handicap, societal bilingualism is divisive, DIALECT variation is being eradicated by the mass media.

Third, the study of language in use is almost entirely local, synchronic, and contemporary, without serious attention being paid to trends from the past, or possible future directions, or comparison with other nations. Patterns of language use in the past have changed, present patterns are changing, and we can expect changes in the future. In other fields, it may be accepted that some kind of baseline data are necessary so that future studies can be measured against them, but in the study of English and the other languages of the USA, we seem condemned to talk about trends across time or possible outcomes of policy changes always without reliable comparable data which could be used for reasonable projections.

The papers selected for Part IV of this volume are, as might be expected, varied in choice of questions asked and research approaches followed, but they share some essential characteristics. Each is in an area in which there is some popular recognition of language problems, and each offers some facts and interpretations which are somehow relevant to the problems it touches on. It has often been noted that legal language is difficult for the layman to understand or use, and Chapter 17 gives us some perspective on this issue, based on the author's own research and that of others on the actual use of language in legal contexts. Similarly, doctors and patients have long complained about the difficulties of communication between them, and Chapter 18 introduces us to some of the research on the use of language in medical contexts. This chapter, unlike the others, includes an extended example of the use of Spanish and English in the same interaction, thus giving an indication of possible cross-language problems in other areas. Chapter 19 on interethnic communication problems focuses on what the authors call "communicative style," which includes nonverbal signals and such nonlinguistic phenomena as the quality of voice. Differences in communicative style often cause more serious problems in intergroup communication than differences in the structure of the language itself. Chapters 20 and 21 respond directly to current concerns of "back to basics" and BILINGUAL EDUCATION, and they do so in the context of present-day research and some historical–comparative perspective. Chapter 22 differs from the others in that the problem it copes with is the need for numbers in making policy decisions on language use; it provides the best statistics currently available. Finally, Chapter 23 presents Fishman's own strong views on American language values and language policies, but his presentation grows out of some of the richest research experience on the American language scene, as in his *Language Loyalty in the United State* (1966) and *Bilingualism in the Barrio* (Fishman, Cooper, Ma et al. 1971).

This Part of the volume gives just a tantalizing taste of what could be said about language use in the USA, but it gives an indication of what is being learned about many aspects of the language situation. We hope it serves a further aim: to convince the reader of the value of language research and the need to have more and still better research on language in the USA.

17

The language of the law*

WILLIAM M. O'BARR

Within the United States, there is considerable receptivity to the notion that the needs and problems of non-English speakers should be given greater attention than they have received in the past. In 1974 in the LAU v. NICHOLS case, the Supreme Court required school boards to provide education in languages other than English in order to guarantee state-supported education to non-English speakers (see Chapter 21).[1] Lawyers and the courts have also begun to consider new ways to take into account the problems of non-English speakers. This concern stems in part from the case of Negrón v. New York[2] in which a Spanish-speaking defendant was provided a summary, rather than a full translation, of the evidence given against him in criminal proceedings. Judicial reasoning in this case was predicated on *constitutional rights* – in this instance the right of a criminal defendant to confront his accuser(s) face to face in a court of law as guaranteed under the sixth amendment. Not speaking the language of the court, it was argued, erects a barrier between the defendant and the court. It is as though he were enclosed in a glass booth, seeing but not hearing the court proceedings.

Both the Lau and Negrón cases are much more than isolated court decisions involving language rights in U.S. schools and courts – they are a part of a greater trend toward concern with civil rights and egalitarian participation in governmental and public institutions. This trend, as Leibowitz (1976) has shown, is a significant alteration in public attitude and official policy which began after World War II and includes such landmark court decisions as Brown v. Board of Education[3] and the two cases referred to above. Of special interest from a legal perspective are the hearings held by the U.S. Congress between

* This chapter is a revised research report of the Law and Language Project of Duke University. The background research on which this paper is based was conducted during 1974–6 under Grant GS-42742 from the Law and Social Science Program of the National Science Foundation. The author wishes to thank Marion Parker for her bibliographic assistance.

1. In 1974, the U.S. Supreme Court in Lau v. Nichols (414 U.S. 563) used the 1964 Civil Rights Act to invalidate de facto exclusion of non-English-speaking students from federally assisted schools.
2. In 1968, the U.S. Supreme Court of Appeals for the Second Circuit in U.S. ex rel Negrón v. New York (434 F. 2d 386) held that the sixth amendment to the U.S. Constitution requires that a non-English-speaking defendant be provided with a complete translation of the proceedings.
3. Brown v. Board of Education, 347 U.S. 483 (1954). For an analysis of the impact of this decision during the succeeding two decades, see Kluger (1975).

1974 and 1978 on the problems faced by non-English speakers in courts. After a lengthy legislative process extending over three congresses, the "Court Interpreters Act" was signed into law in 1978, establishing for the first time regular procedures and standards for court interpreters in place of the highly variable treatment which non-English speakers had previously received in federal courts (Pousada 1980).[4] The degree of this concern over the rights of non-English speakers is indeed a significant departure from the past and marks a genuine change of attitude toward those who do not speak English. Pressures brought to bear by ethnic associations no doubt expedited the process, but equally important is the fact that such changes and sensitivities are a part of the ethos and political attitudes of contemporary America. The "melting pot" notion has given way to a greater tolerance of ethnic and linguistic diversity (see Glazer and Moynihan 1970).

What all this means for the legal rights of non-English-speaking litigants is that significant efforts are being made to increase the comprehension of trial participants about the content of the proceedings. These changes should help to provide quality interpretive services for those who cannot understand court proceedings. However, almost no efforts have been made to change the language of the courtroom, i.e. to operate the court in languages other than English or to simplify the language of courtroom proceedings. Either of these changes would alter the oral language of the court so as to be more in line with that of the litigants. Except in a few very limited situations, no such changes have taken place. This is in contrast with reforms which have taken place in some Canadian courts (for example, those of New Brunswick) where English-speaking judges have been given intensive courses in French in order to enable them to conduct proceedings in the language of the litigants. But considerations of bringing the court language in line with that of the people have not characterized American attitudes toward legal reform. The recent emphasis on providing interpretive services for non-English speakers has been the only major move to alter traditional patterns of communication in the courtroom.

We shall have more to say shortly about pressures for maintaining the language of the law as it presently exists, but consider first some further implications of the kinds of changes which are and are not taking place in American reform movements. Attention is being focused on non-English speakers, rather than on those who do not speak the language of the court. Without minimizing in any way the significant and serious difficulties which non-English speakers have in American courts, greater attention should be paid to those who must go to court, but who, because of their own linguistic abilities and of the peculiar forms of language used in court, do not comprehend the language in which the

4. Legislation dealing with court interpretation for both bilingual proceedings and persons with hearing impairments was first introduced in the 93rd Congress (1974). Neither the original bill (Senate Bill 1724 in the 93rd Congress) nor a slightly revised version (Senate Bill 565 in the 94th Congress) was approved by the full Congress prior to adjournment. In 1978, a further revised bill entitled "Court Interpreters Act," was approved by the full Congress and signed into law. See U.S. House of Representatives Report 95–1687; U.S. Senate Report 95–569; and Public Law 95-539 (approved October 28, 1978). The law provides for consecutive interpretation of bilingual proceedings and of proceedings involving hearing impaired persons in federal courts.

court operates. Even well-educated speakers of American English often find it difficult to understand the language used in court. Their lawyers serve the role of interpreter, explaining throughout the "meaning" of what is transpiring. This interpretation is necessary because the language of the courtroom is anything but ordinary English. Its lexicon and syntax are alien to twentieth-century American English; it is as distinctive as the archaic forms of the King James English Bible. Its similarities to contemporary English deceive the ear; it sounds as though it should be understandable to speakers of English; but the assumption that it is comprehensible is indeed largely just that – an assumption rather than a demonstrated fact. Both the oral and the written forms of the language of the law are alien to the styles of speaking and writing used by most Americans. The concerns for language reform in American courts, while important and significant with regard to the non-English speaker, have hardly touched the problems of comprehension faced by English speakers in understanding legal language.

The nature of legal language

An anthropologist, Charles Frake, writing about a Philippine people whom he studied, noted:

The Yakan legal system is manifest almost exclusively by one kind of behavior: talk. Consequently, the ethnographer's record of observations of litigation is largely a linguistic record, and the legal system is a code for talking, a linguistic code. (Frake 1969: 109)

A lawyer, David Mellinkoff, assessing the language used by legal professionals in contemporary America, described law as a "profession of words" (Mellinkoff 1963: vi). Similarly, a philologist, Frederick Philbrick, analyzing forensic style among English-speaking lawyers, observed:

Lawyers are students of language by profession . . . They exercise their power in court by manipulating the thoughts and opinions of others, whether by making speeches or questioning witnesses. In these arts the most successful lawyers reveal (to those who can appreciate their performance) a highly developed skill . . . (Philbrick 1949: vi)

All these observers are pointing out the pre-eminence of language in legal processes, both in this culture and in others. Yet, despite the close connection of and importance of language to law, neither social scientists, linguists, nor lawyers have paid much attention to it.

Studies of legal language by lawyers

Most studies of legal language by lawyers have focused on written rather than spoken forms. The most systematic and extensive treatment of the nature and origins of legal language by a lawyer is David Mellinkoff's *The Language of the Law* (1963) which carefully traces modern American legal usages from their roots in Anglo-Saxon, Latin, French, and pre-modern English. In introducing his study, Mellinkoff observed:

In a vast literature the portion devoted to the language of the law is a single grain of sand at the bottom of a great sea. The profession is properly more concerned with rights, obligations, and wrongs, and the incidental procedures . . . At this writing, the subject of "language" is absent from most law indexes and only in capsule form in the rest. It is certainly not too early, nor is it too late, to commence a systematic examination of the language lawyers use. (Mellinkoff 1963: vi)

Since most of Mellinkoff's materials are drawn from the legal literature, and only incidentally from his own observations in courtrooms, distinctions between the spoken language of the courtroom and the written language of legal documents, motions, opinions, and the like receive little attention. Nonetheless, his observations are astute. The following list of thirteen characteristics of the language of the law is abstracted from his work (1963: 11–29). While all these attributes occur to some degree in ordinary, everyday English, it is their greater frequencies and co-occurrences which characterize legal language. It should also be noted that many of these attributes are overlapping; that is, a given expression may illustrate several of these characteristics.

1. *Common words with specialized legal meanings*
   action 'law suit,' *instrument* 'legal document,' *presents* 'this legal document,' *serve* 'deliver legal papers,' etc.
2. *Rare words from Old and Middle English*
   aforesaid, forthwith, witnesseth, and various words built on the roots of *here, there,* and *where* (such as *hereafter, herein, thereon, therewith, whereas, whereby*), etc.
3. *Latin words and phrases*
   corpus delicti, mens rea, nolo contendere, nulla bona, res judicata, venire, etc.
4. *French words not in the general vocabulary*
   chose in action, demurrer, fee simple, esquire, voir dire, etc., plus others which are more common, but are used in legal contexts: *assault, battery, counsel, felony, heir, plaintiff, tort, suit, reprieve,* etc.
5. *Terms of art*
   contributory negligence, eminent domain, garnishment, judicial notice, injunction, negotiable instrument, prayer, stare decisis, etc.
6. *Professional jargon*
   inferior court, issue of fact, issue of law, order to show cause, pursuant to stipulation, reversed and remanded, without prejudice, etc.
7. *Formal expressions*
   approach the bench, the deceased, arrested in flagrante delicto, comes now the plaintiff, Your Honor, may it please the court, know all men by these presents, etc.
8. *Words with flexible meanings*
   adequate, approximately, clean and neat condition, extreme cruelty, obscene, promptly, satisfy, undue interference, worthless, etc.
9. *Attempts at extreme precision*
   absolutes such as *all, none, irrevocable, never;* restrictions such as *and*

no more, and no other purpose, shall not constitute a waiver; unlimit-
ing phrases such as *including but not limited to, shall not be deemed to
limit, nothing contained herein shall;* etc.

10. *Wordiness*
    annul and set aside 'annul,' *entirely and completely remove* 'remove,'
    totally null and void 'void,' *written document* 'document,' etc.

11. *Lack of clarity*
    In one way or another jurors must be told: "If Mrs. Smith's injury was
    caused partly by Mr. Jones's negligence and partly by her own negli-
    gence, she cannot recover." Here is a typical way of saying this in a
    form jury instruction:

You are instructed that contributory negligence in its legal significance is such an act or
omission on the part of the plaintiff amounting to a want of ordinary care and prudence
as occurring or co-operating with some negligent act of the defendant, was the proximate
cause of the collision which resulted in the injuries or damages complained of. It may be
described as such negligence on the part of the plaintiff, if found to exist, as helped to
produce the injury or the damages complained of, and if you find from a preponderance
of all the evidence in either of these cases that plaintiff in such case was guilty of any
negligence that helped proximately to bring about or produce the injuries of which
plaintiff complains, then and in such place the plaintiff cannot recover. (Mellinkoff
1963: 26)

12. *Pomposity*
    use of words evoking respect such as *solemn, supreme, wisdom,* etc.;
    characterizations of contrary opinion and evidence as *absurd, mere,
    unconscionable,* etc.; self-righteous expressions as *can be no question,
    clearly pointed out, dispose of the argument, excluded in unmistakable
    language, true and controlling principles,* etc.

13. *Dullness*

It is sometimes assumed that an important subject deserves ponderous treatment, and
this dread of inappropriate levity has saddled the law with a weight of equally inappropriate dullness . . . The fundamental and still litigated distinction between inten-
tional and negligent wrongs has been expressed by Holmes in eleven lively words: " . . .
even a dog distinguishes between being stumbled over and being kicked." (Mellinkoff
1963: 29)

Mellinkoff stresses the origins of contemporary American legal language
which help explain many of its more peculiar characteristics. "The truth, the
whole truth, and nothing but the truth" – poetic and rhythmical to be sure – is
related to the ancient oaths of Old English. The influence of Anglo-Saxon,
Latin, French, and older forms of English are reflected throughout contemporary usage in legal language. The use of many words when fewer would suffice
(see characteristic *10* above) is related to the multilingual origins of English
law. *Acknowledge* (Old English) is often coupled with *confess* (Old French); *act*
(French or Latin) with *deed* (Old English); *breaking* (Old English) with *entering*
(French); and so on. The habit of using synonyms also includes terms originat-

ing from the same language, as in *by and with, each and every, have and hold* (all from Old English) and in *aid and abet, cease and desist, null and void* (from French or French–Latin).[5] Lengthy sentences and sparse punctuation – hallmarks of legal writing – owe their origins, at least in part, to the lack of faithfulness in copy-making prior to the advent of printing; in part to the influence of printers who, because of the nature of their craft, could not slough over squiggles and dots but had to make decisions about what, if any, forms of punctuation to use; and in part to the weight of tradition, once the precedent of lengthy, sparsely punctuated sentences had been established.

Studying the etymology of the language of the law gives one some sense of justification for its peculiar forms and usages. But the fact of the matter is that neither lawyers nor laymen, for the most part, are either schooled in philology or interested enough in it to develop much appreciation for the origins of twentieth-century American legal language. Rather, lawyers are engaged in practising the law, not studying it; and laymen – be they litigants, witnesses, or jurors – tend to be interested in the instrumental aspects of language, not in its history.

From time to time, the suggestion is made that simplification of legal language would improve its utility for both legal professionals and laymen. Such suggestions are usually countered quickly by those who defend legal language as more precise, actually shorter, and more durable and intelligible than ordinary English (Mellinkoff 1963). The call for change and popularization of legal language, however, is not merely a twentieth-century phenomenon. Mellinkoff reports a variety of such efforts since French was first introduced into England following the Norman Conquest. The populist versus elitist arguments are remarkably similar over the centuries. A set of articles published in 1959 and 1960 serve to illustrate the nature of such arguments.

The anti-conventional position was made well by John W. Hager in his article "Let's Simplify Legal Language" (1959). Hager summed the situation up this way:

When a man gives you an orange, he simply says: "Have an orange." But when the transaction is entrusted to a lawyer, he adopts this form: "I hereby give and convey to you, all and singular, my estate and interest, right, title, claim and advantages of and in said orange, together with its rind, skin, juice, pulp, and pips and all rights and advantages therein and full power to bite, suck, or otherwise eat the same or give the same away with or without the rind, skin, juice, pulp and pips, anything hereinbefore or hereinafter or in any other means of whatever nature or kind whatsoever to the contrary in anywise notwithstanding." (Hager 1959: 74–5, quoting from *The Tulsa Tribune*, October 6, 1959)

5. In a study of language in religious contexts, Ferguson (1976: 105) notes the high frequency of word pairing in the English of the Book of Common Prayer used in the Anglican Church. He finds the same two types of pairing as described for written legal language, namely, the combination of Romance loanwords with Anglo-Saxon glosses as well as the use of two synonymous words or phrases originating from the same language. In addition to occurring in at least two registers of English (religious as well as legal language), the practice of pairing is quite common in many languages. See, for instance, the study of pairing in Rotinese by Fox (1974) and in Zinacantan by Bricker (1974). Their evidence suggests that pairing in other languages may also be due to borrowing, specific stylistic traditions of particular languages, or, as with English, both reasons.

Hager, admittedly overstating his case at times in order to point out the seriousness of the problem as he sees it, noted that complicated legal language (or legalese) is found in legislative enactments, jury instructions, documents prepared for clients' use, pleadings, and in materials used in law schools. Lawyers, judges, and law professors are the ones responsible for perpetuating these forms. Arguing that most complicated legal pronouncements have far simpler and more easily understood equivalents in everyday English, Hager believed that changes in such a direction would serve both lawyers and law students as well as laymen. The place to begin introducing such changes was, in his opinion, the law school.

Hager found four main problem areas which he argued were in need of change: (a) using archaic, obsolete forms which have passed out of ordinary usage; (b) using Latin and French words and phrases when English terms could be used instead; (c) assigning unusual legal meanings to ordinary English terms; and (d) writing unusually long sentences which often have little or no punctuation and contain many exceptions and qualifications. Learning to use this kind of language is an arduous task for law students. It results in obscuring simple, everyday ideas and puts understanding them beyond the reach of "most people."

Hager's essay contains some specific suggestions for transforming legal language into a form more like that of everyday English.

Most language used in law can be simplified so that it needs no official interpreters. Its meaning could be made clear to almost everyone. There is nothing heretical or antiliterary in this idea . . . Law is one device for social control. It should be written in plain, ordinary English so that the average layman understands it. Nor is this argument that legal language should be simplified a new one. As early as 1776, Jeremy Bentham demanded that laws be codified in such clear language that the ordinary man could understand his legal rights. (Hager 1959: 85)

Hager's objectives amount to making legal usage more intelligible to laymen, who are, after all, the consumers of the work of lawyers. He contends that the suggested reforms would also benefit lawyers, who are unnecessarily burdened by the complexity of the language they use. Why then, if there is any validity to these claims, has legal language persisted? What purpose does it serve?

Hager himself suggested at least one reason for its persistence. In discussing jury instructions, he noted that most "would seem to be prepared with an eye toward an eventual appeal. Instructions would seem to be phrased to gain approval by an appellate court and not written to be understood by the jurors for whose guidance they, theoretically, at least, are given" (1959: 80). This orientation of linguistic usage within the law toward legal institutions rather than toward the public at large is one of the most basic reasons why its special form appears to have been preserved. The goal is legal accuracy and consistency, not popular understanding and ease of comprehension.

Hager's article was followed in the same journal a few months later by an article entitled, "Let's Not Oversimplify Legal Language" (Aiken 1960). In his defense of legal usages, Aiken argued that "it will not do to re-tailor the legal lexicon to fit the transient tempos of each succeeding popular age" (p. 363). Aiken cited "such terms as *res, ipsa loquitur, caveat emptor,* proximate cause, indenture, bequeath, devise, and hereof, whereof, whence, hence, foregoing, said, etc., as entirely appropriate and acceptable modes of expression, properly used. Properly used, they are often the decided superior of ordinary words which have no associated specialization of meaning" (p. 362). He, like Hager, found "a rampant and progressing decline of legal literacy, characterized by redundancy, obscurity of meaning, poor grammar, and practical abandonment of every classical virtue of the compositional art" (p. 363). His recommendations and solutions carry none of Hager's populist tones. Instead, he suggested: (a) elevating the standard of ordinary English by improving the primary and secondary educational processes to the point where the average word-vocabulary is at least quadrupled; (b) placing a heavy emphasis on multilingual proficiency, so as to permit frequent usage of more precise and meaningful foreign words and phrases than are contained in English; (c) requiring both legal and unabridged English dictionaries as texts in law schools; (d) requiring a demonstration of superior competence in English composition skills as a prerequisite for taking bar examinations; and other similar measures.

This exchange between Hager and Aiken is typical of the positions taken by lawyers in assessing the state of legal language. Similar exchanges have occurred at other times in the legal literature (cf. Beardsley 1941; Morton 1941; Gerhart 1954; Bowman 1975; Younger 1976). Often witty and amusing in themselves, the two sides tend to make the same basic arguments each time. The reformers suggest that legal language is unnecessarily complex and should be simplified in order to make it more intelligible to the public at large and of less burden to legal professionals themselves. They argue that the same ideas, for all intents, can be uttered in everyday English with greater clarity and no loss of meaning. The traditionalists argue that the importance of consistency in interpretation by the courts of particular words, terms, and even entire legal forms outweighs the advantages of popularizing and simplifying legal usage. Those who wish to preserve the form of legal language point out the serious legal difficulties which could arise by departing from conventions as a result of unpredicted and unexpected interpretations being given by the court to any new usage.

Those who argue for the preservation of the nonordinary form of legal language are more concerned with how other legal professionals will interpret the language of the law than they are with laymen comprehending it. Much of courtroom dialogue is addressed "to the record" (i.e. couched with the potential of an appeals court in mind). Legal documents are prepared according to standard form books – not because these are tried and tested for lay comprehension – but because they ensure a greater predictability of how the courts will interpret such documents.

Finally, the self-serving interests of lawyers are also involved to some degree. In commenting on the reluctance of lawyers in the British Isles to purge the English courts of French, Mellinkoff had this to say about the interests of lawyers in the thirteenth century: "What better way of preserving a professional monopoly than by locking up your trade secrets in the safe of an unknown tongue?" (Mellinkoff 1963: 101). The political scientist, Murray Edelman, commenting on twentieth-century American legal language has made essentially the same observation: "It is precisely its ambiguity that gives lawyers, judges, and administrators a political and social function, for unambiguous rules would, by definition, call neither for interpretation nor for argument as to their meaning" (Edelman 1964: 139). The language of the law is viewed as protecting both the law and the lawyer.

Studies by linguists and other social scientists

A variety of efforts by linguists, psychologists, sociologists, and anthropologists have touched in one fashion or another on the nature and functions of legal language. Several different approaches characterize the concerns of linguists. Some focus on the written language, others on both oral and written uses, still others on speech in use in specific legal situations. Thirty years ago, Frederick A. Philbrick, a semanticist and philologist, wrote *Language and the Law: the semantics of forensic English* (1949). His illuminating analysis is based almost entirely upon written records of trial courts, speeches by lawyers, and judicial opinions. The spoken language of the courtroom, except insofar as it is represented in legal writings, does not enter into his concern.

Scholars with a more general interest in the nature and uses of the English language have typically not pondered the language used in the legal contexts. Quirk, for instance, in his book on *The Uses of English* (1962), notes the distinctiveness of legal language but does not analyze it in any detail. Crystal and Davy's *Investigating English Style* (1969) stands in marked contrast. In their efforts to understand English stylistics, Crystal and Davy not only argue strongly for the importance of studying the English used in legal contexts but also distinguish between written and spoken legal language. But like most others before them, they give unequal treatment to the two. While an entire chapter is devoted to the language of legal documents, only a few pages in a final chapter on suggestions for further analysis are devoted to spoken legal language. Nonetheless, Crystal and Davy offer a number of astute observations about the nature of written legal language, among them:

It is essentially visual language, meant to be scrutinised in silence: it is, in fact, largely unspeakable at first sight, and anyone who tries to produce a spoken version is likely to have to go through a process of repeated and careful scanning in order to sort out the grammatical relationships which give the necessary clues to adequate phrasing. (1969: 194)

whoever composes a legal document must take the greatest pains to ensure that it says exactly what he wants it to say and at the same time gives no opportunities for misinterpretation. The word "say" is important in this context, because when a document is under scrutiny in a court of law, attention will be paid only to what . . . it appears to declare: any *intentions* of the composer which fail to emerge clearly are not usually considered in arriving at what the document means. . . (1969: 193)

A concern to understand how the intentions of speakers were understood in the courtroom led some linguists to focus on *spoken* as opposed to *written* legal language. This research distinguishes the efforts of many linguists and other social scientists working in the 1970s from those working earlier, as well as from most legal scholars who continue to devote their attention almost exclusively to written legal language. Until recently, the contention that legal language is largely incomprehensible by laymen has gone untested. It does not take a social scientist to point out the difficulty which the ordinary layman has in interpreting the language of a lease or purchase agreement; and the form of jury instructions is so inherently complex that assertions that jurors have difficulty in comprehending them typically pass unchallenged.

Two separate teams of American researchers – each including lawyers and psycholinguists – have recently begun to investigate the bases for difficulties in comprehending legal language in specific contexts, for example, in jury instructions. Although their work is not yet completed, their research hypotheses are worthy of attention. Both teams are attempting to show that the form of language used in jury instructions, particularly its SYNTAX, is the basis of the incomprehensibility of typical jury instructions. The reasons lie, they hypothesize, in certain neurological aspects of language processing and in the particular way in which jury instructions are formulated. Most English sentences, for example, tend to be right-branching (i.e. the verb comes early in the sentence and complex constructions follow it). An examination of uniform jury instructions as used in many jurisdictions reveals a high frequency of left-branching sentences (i.e. ones in which complex constructions precede the verb). Such sentences are more difficult for English speakers to process. The combination of abstruse vocabulary and complex syntactic forms makes the language of jury instructions especially difficult to understand. Both research teams have demonstrated that standard jury instructions are poorly understood by most jurors and that alteration of some of the more troublesome linguistic features significantly increases comprehension (Sales, Elwork, and Alfini 1977; Elwork, Sales, and Alfini 1977; Charrow and Charrow 1979, 1980). These studies are being conducted by Bruce Sales (psycholinguist, University of Nebraska) and James Alfini (lawyer, American Judicature Society); and by Robert Charrow (lawyer, Howard University) and Veda Charrow (psycholinguist, American Institutes for Research).

Although sociolinguists are concerned with relating language to the social context in which it exists, few have devoted any real concern to the courts and other legal processes as a context for studying socially patterned language variation. Only two sociolinguistically oriented research teams – one directed by William O'Barr at Duke University and the other directed by Brenda Danet at Boston University – have been active in this field.

The Duke project began formally in 1974, and had two major goals: studying major forms of language variation in the trial courtroom ethnographically, and using the findings from this phase of the work to formulate and test experimentally hypotheses about the effects of language variation on the critical courtroom audience – the jury. Attempting to describe the major forms of stylistic variation in the trial courtroom, O'Barr, Conley, and Lind (1976) identify four varieties of language used in the trial courtroom which they studied.

Formal spoken legal language: the variety of spoken language used in the courtroom which most closely parallels written legal language; used by the judge in instructing the jury, passing judgment, and "speaking to the record"; used by lawyers when addressing the court, making motions and requests, etc.; linguistically characterized by lengthy sentences containing much professional jargon and employing a complex syntax.

Standard English: the variety of spoken language typically used in the courtroom by lawyers and most witnesses; generally labeled "correct" English and closely paralleling that taught as the standard in American classrooms; characterized by a somewhat more formal LEXICON than that used in everyday speech.

Colloquial English: a variety spoken by some witnesses and a few lawyers in lieu of Standard English; closer to everyday, ordinary English in lexicon and syntax; tends to lack many of the attributes of formality which characterize Standard English; used by a few lawyers as their particular style or brand of courtroom demeanor.

Subcultural varieties: varieties spoken by segments of the society which differ in speech style and mannerisms from the larger community; in the case of the particular courts studied in North Carolina, these varieties include Black English and the dialect of English spoken by poorly educated Whites.

These varieties of spoken language in the courtroom constitute all REGISTERS (Ellis and Ure 1969) of court talk actually observed. No speaker was ever found who used all four registers, but most speakers were noted to shift among possibilities within their own repertoire in response to situational changes. Divisions among the varieties are not clear-cut, and the varieties may for any individual form a continuum or may be mixed in actual usage. A lawyer, for example, is likely to address prospective jurors during *voir dire* in a casual colloquial style, as though seeking solidarity with jurors. He may joke frequently during this aspect of the trial and adopt a speech style "like ordinary folks." When questioning witnesses, he is likely to distance himself from hostile witnesses – by attempting to make colloquial or subcultural varieties appear "stupid" and unlike him, or by attempting to suggest that expert witnesses for the opposition are using "big words to obscure relatively simple matters." Degree of formality and other variations in presentational style in the courtroom have been described ethnographically by the Duke team and shown to be related to significant differences in the credibility, trustworthiness, competence, etc. of both witnesses and lawyers in simulations of the courtroom

(Conley, O'Barr, and Lind 1978; Lind and O'Barr 1979; O'Barr and Lind in press).

Danet's project, which began in 1975, aims to follow the "fitting of words to deeds" through the various stages of the legal process from first contacts between lawyer and prospective client through the public trial. Danet reports a case studied by her research team in which an aborted fetus is referred to variously as *subject, baby, child, product of conception,* and *fetus*. She argues (1980a) that these differences in terms of reference reflect successive transformations of "reality" in the evolution of court cases. This perspective is illustrated by Danet's earlier work (1976) with some of the language used in the Watergate hearings.

At least one political scientist, Murray Edelman (1964), has addressed himself to the forms and meanings of legal language in America. Edelman views legal language as a tool of social control and as a means of preserving the interests of the privileged, wealthy, and educated. His analysis, although brief and not based on detailed observation of actual speech forms used in courtroom contexts, is suggestive of the perspective which has been taken by many of the psycho- and sociolinguists who have actually done empirical work on language variation in legal contexts.

Anthropologists, who have traditionally had a greater interest in language than many of the other social scientists, have done relatively little when it comes to studying language and legal processes. Reviewing the anthropological study of law in 1965, Laura Nader pointed out that there has been very little attention paid to the relations between law and other aspects of social life such as economics, language, ecology, or stratification and rank systems (1965: 17). Over a decade later, the situation is scarcely different. Although the literature of legal anthropology has grown considerably, there have been only a few studies which have given legal language more than passing attention.

The exceptions fall into two major groups. First are studies focusing on systems of legal categorization and conceptualization in particular cultures. Working within the framework of cognitive anthropology, Frake (1969) studies Yakan concepts of litigation and shows how this Philippine people distinguish between talk that constitutes legal DISCOURSE and that which characterizes other behavior. Another paper, by Black and Metzger (1965), offers a method for eliciting native categories for use in studying law ethnographically. From the perspective of social anthropology, Fallers (1969) explores how the Soga of East Africa conceptualize actual events in terms of rule infractions which the court will consider. Although Bohannan (1969) and Gluckman (1969) approach the problem of understanding and interpreting native legal categories quite differently, their discussions reflect the great concern which British social anthropologists have, as a rule, devoted to systems of categorization in the cross-cultural study of law. All these studies, despite some differences in approach, aim toward the study of systems of categorization or conceptualization in the law of particular societies. Their emphasis on concepts is of course

closely related to language and thought, and efforts are made in these studies to
show how the organization of the law and legal processes is reflected in the
structure of language used in legal contexts.

A second concern of anthropologists working on language and legal processes is exemplified by a collection of essays edited by Maurice Bloch, *Political Lanugage and Oratory in Traditional Society* (1975). Unlike those anthropologists who focus on systems of legal categories, the efforts of Bloch and
his collaborators are devoted toward considering how people talk about politics
and law. Bloch argues that most of what anthropologists know about politics
and law in traditional societies has been learned, not through direct study, but
through listening to how people talk about these topics. Yet as listeners, anthropologists have devoted so much concern to the attempt to cull out the essence of
politics in action via the indirect route of asking questions of informants that
they have, for the most part, failed to listen to how people talk about politics,
and hence have missed one of the richest and most revealing sources of data of
all – the language of politics. His argument, while more focused on politics than
law, applies equally well to the study of the language of the law.

Similar concerns lay behind a symposium entitled "Fighting With Words"
organized by Don Brenneis and Andrew Arno for the 1973 Annual Meeting of
the American Anthropological Association. Arno considered how the sociolinguistic rules of etiquette in a Fijian village actually function to manage
interpersonal conflicts while Brenneis concentrated on rhetorical strategy, also
in Fiji. Laura Lein focused on verbal settlements of disputes among Black
American children. And Jan Rus reported on his study of dual legal systems in
bilingual–bicultural Mexican communities and the opportunities which alternative legal systems provide. Most of these papers have now been published.
Taken together, they illustrate the richness of ethnographic data available to
social scientists interested in the political and legal uses of language (Arno
1976a, b; Brenneis 1978; Lein and Brenneis 1978; Rus 1973).

In addition, the book *Language and Politics* (O'Barr and O'Barr 1976)
examines the relation of language to the operation of formal institutions of
government (particularly courts, councils, and legislatures) in developing countries, including such topics as: how multilingualism complicates the operation of
formal institutions, how language is used to control or restrict access to political
participation and to courts, and how interpreters may bias court proceedings in
instances where they must be used.

*Political Language and Oratory in Traditional Society, Language and Poli-
tics,* and the "Fighting With Words" Symposium all focus attention on ways in
which language factors enter into and shape political and legal processes. They
thus represent a second major approach among anthropologists to the study of the
language of the law. In all instances, however, their concern tends to be almost
exclusively focused on spoken language, not upon the written language of the
law.

This interest in spoken language among anthropologists is due no doubt to the
traditional concerns of anthropologists with societies in which writing was either

absent or played a relatively minor role. Psycho- and sociolinguistic concerns with spoken language reflect the contemporary interest among linguists in language in context, in language as it is actually used. But whatever the specific reasons behind this greater emphasis among social scientists on spoken language in legal contexts, its effect in part is to offer a major complementary approach to the greater concern shown by legal scholars and some linguists with written legal language.

How little concern lawyers tend to place on spoken language is amply demonstrated by a quick perusal of the major textbook dealing with language and its relation to the law, Bishin and Stone's *Law, Language, and Ethics* (1972). Great effort is devoted to understanding – or attempting to understand – such topics as reasoning processes, the structure of language, the meaning of words, and the nature of ambiguity in language. Almost nothing is said in several hundred pages about spoken language, and hence the language of the courtroom. Attention is directed here, as elsewhere within the law, to opinions, documents, and treatises – not to the courtroom or the lawyer–client interaction as a domain where the role and influence of language needs consideration. Clinical aspects of law school curricula, including especially trial practice, tend to account for only a small proportion of the course offerings. Some trial practice courses are beginning to include sections dealing with linguistic and PARALINGUISTIC aspects of interaction, but the overall proportion of concern devoted to spoken language in or outside the courtroom within the law is indeed small. The assumption that spoken language in legal contexts is merely the actualization of the written model is clearly outdated. Old ideas sometimes die slowly, but the beginnings of a serious interest among some lawyers at least in spoken legal language can be noted in the gradual incorporation of communication into law school curricula and in the interest shown by lawyers in the potential contributions of social science research findings to the art of trial practice.[6]

The language of the law – vehicle or obstacle?

After deliberating for several hours, a jury foreman rang for the bailiff, who announced in turn to the judge that the jury had a question to ask of the judge – would he please explain again the meaning of ''approximate cause'' since the jury was unclear about its meaning. The judge, taken aback somewhat by the request, proceeded to read once again from his book of pattern jury instructions the standardized explanation given in his state for the legal concept *proximate cause*. His only preceptible alterations in this second reading of the instructions were greater attention to precision in enunciation and a slower tempo. Not one word of the original instruction was altered. Although obviously concerned by the misunderstanding the jurors had possibly effected by the transfor-

---

6. Some trial practice instructors now include materials drawn from such sources as Schelfen (1964), Eisenberg and Smith (1971), and Fast (1971). However, these materials focus on paralinguistic aspects of comunication. The inclusion of linguistic topics in a more strict sense is not common. In response to press reports about a paper giving some results from my own research project presented at the 1975 American Anthropological Association Meeting, I have received more than 400 letters and inquiries from practising attorneys and judges requesting further information about my research.

mation of the word *proximate* into *approximate*, he bowed to convention and did not offer his own paraphrase of the meaning of *proximate cause* for the jurors – for everything he said was methodically recorded by the court reporter and might later be scrutinized by an appeals court. Sticking by the standard explanation would not constitute a basis for an appeal of the case should the defense lose. Introducing his own interpretation, no matter how genuinely the effort to be faithful to the accepted legal meaning of the term, might provide the basis for an appeal of the case. The jurors, stonefaced as before, shuffled once again out of the courtroom to resume their deliberation.

A commercial for an insurance company frequently aired on the national television networks in 1976 advertises policies written in "ordinary, everyday English" and promises that their policies – unlike those of their competitors – do not require law degrees to interpret.

Both of these situations from my own experience demonstrate in practical contexts the issue to which we have been addressing ourselves in a variety of ways: the questions of for whom the language of the law is intended and whose interests are facilitated by the particular usages found in conventional legal language. The problem is one to which no simple solution can be offered. On the one hand is the problem of consistency in interpretation of legal language by the courts – a matter of no small importance when drawing up a contract, a will, or any sort of legal document. On the other hand lies the problem of the ability of the consumers of the law to understand what the law says – whether this be in their contracts, in their role as jurors in a court of law, or in some other aspect of the law. The issues at law and before the court, after all, are not those of lawyers – but of their clients. The most cynical critics of legal language argue that the clients must pay their lawyers to draw up contracts which are always written in unintelligible legalese and then pay them once again to interpret (usually at a later date) what the contract means. They ask why this intermediary role – of first complicating and later attempting to interpret – is really necessary. The standard rebuttal is of course that the use of accepted legal conventions, particularly the language of legal documents, ensures a consistent and highly predictable interpretation by the courts. Thus, dependent upon which perspective one takes, the language of the law is seen as either a vehicle or an obstacle.

Wherever one looks – whether it be the courtroom, an office conference between a lawyer and his client, or a written document – these two interests seem at odds with one another and result in the maintenance of the gap between legal convention and popular understanding of what transpires. When confronted with the choice, most clients seem to be swayed rather easily by the argument for consistency. Hence, the service they buy from lawyers is a kind of insurance policy against unpredictable interpretations. And because legal systems relying heavily upon precedent tend to operate in this fashion, it creates a firm, safe, and critical role for lawyers. Legal professionals are deeply concerned themselves about radical alterations of accepted (and hence predictable) conventions. The attitude of the trial judge in the episode involving the request for an explanation of the term *proximate cause* is typical of the reaction of most American lawyers to alterations of form. And more than one lawyer has hastened to point out the potential danger inherent in the insurance policies which claim to be written in "ordinary English" – for it is not yet known, they point out, how the courts will interpret such language.

Given the importance of preserving modes of expression in systems based upon precedent, one of the most significant roles which a lawyer thus provides for his client is that of interpreter. He is the channel of access to the law; he is the "bilingual" who can act as interpreter between the language of his client and the language of the law and the courts. Viewed from this perspective, one of the most important qualities of a lawyer is his ability as an interpreter. When the role of the lawyer is looked at as that of an interpreter, it is of interest to note that most emphasis is placed in the education of lawyers on their abilities to interpret in one direction only – from the ordinary, everyday code into the legal code. This is what happens, in effect, when a client approaches a lawyer. They begin talking about the problem which has brought them together; the next step in the legal process is for the lawyer to translate the problem originally expressed in the everyday code into legal concepts. Most lawyers also attempt to explain along the way – to interpret what is happening to their clients. The training which they receive in law school is almost entirely devoted to the process of interpreting from the everyday into the legal code and for operating within the legal code. Training lawyers to interpret the law to laymen receives no serious consideration in law school. Successful lawyers work out ways of dealing with this, and those who may be liked and preferred by clients may be especially good in the interpretation of the law code into everyday language. But this is not an aspect of the role of lawyers which receives any serious attention in the legal education process, while it could be said that the other aspects of their interpretive role (e.g. from everyday into legal codes, and functioning within legal codes) are given considerable concern during the three years of formal legal education which most lawyers undergo.

Increasing access to the law

There are at least two sorts of people who do not speak or understand legal language. First, there are those who, in a society like the United States which uses only English for most public purposes, are non-English-speaking or at least do not speak English well enough to use it in legal contexts. Secondly, there are those who speak English, but do not command the language of the law. While a relatively small percentage of the American population falls into the first category, most others belong, to some degree, to the second.

As noted earlier, there has been an increasing concern within the last few years in American society about improving the access of non-English speakers to the law. After four years of hearings, the U.S. Congress was able to pass a law designed to ameliorate some of the problems faced by non-English speakers in dealing with the courts and the law. And at least one state, California, has commissioned a study of the language needs of non-English-speaking persons in relation to the state's justice system.[7] Up to now, the treatment of non-English speakers in various federal, state, and local jurisdictions has been highly variable. In some instances, well qualified interpreters have been available, while in others the interpretation role has been limited to only some aspects of the legal process (in court, for example, but interpreters are not systematically provided in lawyer–client conferences). Who pays, who interprets, and who checks on the accuracy, quality, and form of interpretations are still subject to much variation within the American legal system since the 1978 legislation applies to federal courts only. However, the problem is being recognized as one in need of some concern, and those who worked in support of the federal law hope that many states will enact similar legislation to deal with these issues in state courts.

The other issue, that of the needs of the English speaker who does not understand the language of the law, has unfortunately not received equivalent concern. The courts tend to make a number of assumptions about language abilities which are clearly untested and at least in some instances probably unfounded. These assumptions include such notions as: (a) anyone who speaks English does not require interpretation of court talk; (b) in any instance where English court talk requires interpretation, such interpretation is the responsibility of legal counsel, not of the court; (c) jurors can and do hear all evidence (although usually instructed to call problems of hearing due to noise, volume, etc. to the court's attention, jurors in actuality tend to be reluctant to call conditions which keep them from hearing to the attention of the court); (d) jurors understand the testimony of the court (although they are not usually allowed to ask any questions of witnesses, especially to clarify something a witness or lawyer says); (e) "English-speaking" jurors understand "English-speaking" witnesses (regardless of cultural background and differences in dialect); (f) "English-speaking" witnesses understand "English-speaking" lawyers (regardless of cultural background or differences in dialect); (g) pattern jury instructions – which have been carefully scrutinized for their legal accuracy – are understandable to jurors; (h) variations in presentational style, on the part of witnesses and lawyers, while possibly important are not matters with which the law should concern itself since these are not questions of fact, but of idiosyncratic, stylistic variation.

While many legal professionals realize that these assumptions are unwarranted and may produce great difficulties in the law, they, and the institutions of the law, continue to operate as though these are valid assumptions. These are not the only assumptions which the law and the courts make about the nature of the language and the communication system in which the law operates, but these suffice to point out the extent to which they do not fit empirical reality. Several current social science studies further illustrate this divergence.

7. See "A Report to the Judicial Council on the Needs of Non-English Speaking Persons in Relation to the State's Justice System," prepared for the Judicial Council of California by Arthur Young and Company, Sacramento (January, 1976).

The assumption that presentational style is not as important as the facts has been challenged by the findings of several recent studies. Loftus and Palmer (1974) conducted an experiment in which the subjects viewed films of automobile accidents and later answered questions about events occurring in the films. The question "About how fast were the cars going when they *smashed* into each other?" elicited higher estimates of speed than questions using the verbs *collided, bumped, contacted,* or *hit* in place of *smashed.* Questions of the form "Did you see *the* broken headlight?" as opposed to "Did you see *a* broken headlight?" encouraged experimental subjects to say "yes" more frequently.

The Duke University team has conducted several experimental studies aimed at testing the general proposition that the way in which a witness gives testimony may indeed affect the way it is received. A multidisciplinary research team – consisting of anthropologists, sociolinguists, social psychologists, and lawyers – conducted the research in three phases. First, the team collected more than 150 hours of audio tape recordings in a trial courtroom, making it possible to base the experiments on actual court talk. Second, these recordings were analyzed to reveal actual patterns of sociolinguistic variation in the courtroom. Third, these empirical studies formed the basis for experimental studies of the effects of such variations as difference in male and female language use, sequencing phenomena (hesitations, interruptions, etc.), length of answers to questions, etc. The experimental studies reveal that forms of variations such as these – typically ignored as unimportant by the court – have significant effects on evaluation of testimony, witness credibility, effectiveness of legal counsel, and more generally, attitudes toward the legal process itself (O'Barr and Conley 1976; O'Barr et al. 1976; Conley et al. 1978; Erickson, Lind, Johnson, and O'Barr 1978; Lind, Erickson, Conley, and O'Barr 1978; Lind and O'Barr 1979; O'Barr and Lind in press).

The studies of jury instructions by research teams mentioned earlier have related goals. They too have shown that the assumptions courts make about the comprehensibility of jury instructions are unfounded and that reforms taking into account some of the psycholinguistic communication problems related to comprehensibility should be considered in rewriting pattern instructions.

All of these studies, whether about witness behavior or juror comprehension, can contribute information about the validity of assumptions which the courts now make about the degree to which effective communication actually occurs through the language currently used in trial courtrooms. Demonstrating the degree to which legal assumptions about communication are indeed valid is a first step toward eventually reforming the legal process to make it more comprehensible to those who use it. It is not inconceivable that reforms are possible which attempt to maximize both consistency in interpretation (the most potent argument for maintenance of standard forms) and comprehension of laypersons (the argument insisting that the law should be intelligible to those who use it). Clearly this is not a matter best handled through more polemics such as the exchange between Hager and Aiken reported earlier. What is needed instead is a greater understanding, through empirical social science research, of the degree to which assumptions that courts make about the communication and linguistic systems in which they are imbedded are indeed supported by empirical evidence. As such evidence comes in, the possibility of reforms which increase access of the populace to the law in realistic and needed ways will be possible.

Implications for the training of lawyers

There are many implications to be drawn from this review of the nature of legal language in the American legal system. Some are specifically applicable to the state of affairs with regard to language in the American legal system, but many of the lessons are generalizable to other national legal systems which may be predicated on different legal principles and assumptions or may operate in different kinds of linguistic environments.

The most basic dilemma lies in the necessity of choosing between consistency of interpretation and wide popular access to the law, especially through reforms in the direction of using language easily comprehensible to laypersons. That these goals are often at odds with one another is the most perplexing problem with regard to any program of changes in the language used in the American legal system. Few would dispute that both are worthy goals; but many would contest the relative emphasis placed upon the two. Consistency of interpretation is a fundamental ingredient in a system of law based heavily upon precedent, and equality of access to the law is a basic and fundamental American value. Solutions which help achieve one of these goals while frustrating the realization of the other are not desirable. Thus, the suggestions made below are predicated on the assumption that both consistency and access are equally desirable goals for the American legal system.

Perhaps the most serious implications have to do with the nature of legal education, and the degree to which it prepares lawyers for the roles which they must play in the society of which they will be a part. Recalling the suggestion that the lawyer's role can be likened to that of an interpreter, there are serious discrepancies between what a lawyer is taught to do and what he is actually required to do in the practice of law. Law school curricula tend to be oriented not toward the training of trial lawyers, but toward teaching for the practice of law in other contexts. Clinical programs are typically small, at least in the more prestigious law schools, and few of the courses are directed toward trial practice. First-year law students are often told by their teachers something to the effect: "We are not here to teach you to be a courtroom lawyer, but how to think." Although the specific language may vary, the message is the same: the law is comprised of a set of ideals; the practice of law is something which can be picked up once legal thinking is mastered; and trial practice is low in prestige. Little wonder then that the discrepancy between elitist and populist orientations toward the law should emerge.

A first step in effecting any serious change would be a greater incorporation into the law school curriculum of the methods of trial practice. Although the last several years have seen a substantial increase in the number of trial practice courses offered within law school curricula as well as a growing emphasis on continuing education for practising legal professionals, the Chief Justice of the United States has publicly questioned the professional competence of many lawyers. Even with increased emphasis during the 1970s, the degree of clinical education which a law student receives does not begin to compare with the clinical experience considered necessary in the education of physicians. If greater attention were paid to teaching how to practice law, with special reference to the roles which the trial lawyer must necessarily play, a typical law school curriculum would include not just instruction in how to translate problems which emerge in everyday life into legal concepts, and how to argue within the conventions of the law, but also some instruction in the interpretive processes which lawyers must perform in explaining the law and legal processes to their clients. If done well, such training might include such subjects as socio- and psycholinguistics.

But the successful incorporation of such courses into the curricula of law schools may depend heavily upon the degree to which social scientists are able through current and future research programs to demonstrate that current assumptions about communication held within the law and by the courts are unwarranted. If we are to expect lawyers to do much teaching about the relations between language and the law, we must – through a variety of basic and applied research efforts – demonstrate the nature of this relationship.

Other important areas into which a concern with increasing the sensitivity of lawyers to language and its significance in legal processes might extend include studies of BILINGUALISM (how it operates at both individual and societal levels, how it is a matter of degree and situation rather than an all-or-none proposition, how DIALECTAL and subcultural variation within language communities is similar to bilingualism, etc.); translation (the nature of translation and interpretation as processes, how spoken versus written translation or interpretation processes differ, different forms of interpretation, the kinds of biases which are introduced by variation in interpretive processes, etc.); language and persuasion (the importance of differences in presentational style, including not only verbal but paralinguistic aspects as well, biases which are introduced through variations in question form, choice of words, etc.); and so on.

The single and most important point which needs to be recognized is that law school curricula pay little or no specific attention to the nature of language and its relations to legal processes. While changing and modernizing the legal language is indeed a goal worthy of consideration, the far more important issue is making lawyers more aware of the nature of the medium in which they operate. If sensitivity to language could be increased, then many of the problems associated with the particular forms used in contemporary American legal language would be greatly reduced in significance. For even radical reforms of legal language bringing it much closer in line with contemporary usage could be only a temporary solution at best unless those who make, interpret, and administer the law – i.e. the legal professionals – have some understanding themselves of the roles of language in structuring thought, influencing attitudes, providing or denying access, and so on. To quote David Mellinkoff once again: "It is certainly not too early, nor is it too late, to commence a systematic examination of the language lawyers use" (1963: vi). While Mellinkoff wrote these words with his legal audience in mind, they carry as much weight for social scientists – for without helping to provide information about how language operates in specifically legal contexts, it is foolhardy to expect much about language to be incorporated into the education of lawyers. The fault lies not just with law schools in not teaching about language, but also with those who study language in not providing assistance first through basic research about language and law topics and secondly through materials specifically oriented toward the demonstration of principles about language in specifically legal contexts.

FURTHER READING

While a large number of passing references to the language of the law can be found in legal and social science writings, few articles or books deal with the subject directly or in much detail. The more substantial sources for further reading are mentioned in the text of the chapter.

To read further on the subject of *written legal language*, virtually the only work of any substance is Mellinkoff 1963, recently issued in paperback. The book deals with the etymology and characteristics of legal language and contains an extensive bibliography. Beyond this, readers are encouraged to consult Crystal and Davy 1969 whose treatment, although brief, raises many interesting questions, and Edelman 1964: Ch. 7, which discusses written legal language as one of the many varieties of political language in the USA.

Current research on *spoken legal language* considers the comprehensibility of jury instructions and the language used in legal (primarily courtroom) contexts. For further reading on the language of jury instructions, readers are encouraged to follow the work of the Charrows (see Charrow and Charrow 1979, 1980 for a comprehensive report on their findings) and the work of the Elwork–Sales–Alfini research group who are currently preparing a book tentatively entitled *Jury Deliberations*. For reports on the work conducted by O'Barr and his colleagues at Duke, see O'Barr and Conley 1976 (an early, but suggestive paper on the legal implications of variations in responses of mock jurors to different speech styles used by lawyers and witnesses); Lind and O'Barr 1979 (a general review of the experimental studies with special attention devoted to a consideration of the underlying psychological processes which appear to be involved); O'Barr and Lind, in press (a consideration of the value of multidisciplinary, collaborative efforts involving ethnography and experimentation); and Conley et al. 1979 (a comprehensive review of the research program written especially for persons with legal training and/or a special concern for the legal implications of the research findings). Danet's project is reviewed in her unpublished paper presented at the 1978 World Congress of Sociology (Danet 1978). A revised version of this paper is included in a comprehensive review of studies of language in the legal process (Danet 1980b).

18

Language and medicine

AARON V. CICOUREL

The way that doctors and patients talk to each other is a major concern to everyone, particularly in health-conscious North America. This chapter will explore some of the communicational strategies used by doctors and patients. By examining communicational strategies in the organizational context of a private physician's office, clinic, or hospital, I hope to give the reader some idea of the way language can influence medical care delivery.

The plan of the chapter is first to review some recent literature on doctor–patient interaction to indicate how language plays a central role in the communication and transfer of information in medical settings. The review of the literature will also touch upon a problem that we know very little about: Do doctors address patients of different social class, ethnic, and educational background differently? Actual transcripts of doctor–patient communication will then be examined to indicate the way in which particular styles of language are used, and the effects of the style and content of the messages used on each participant's understanding of what happened. Excerpts from actual medical history reports will be used to indicate the way the physician orients his professional report to other doctors. This professional orientation can mean that the patient's problem as seen by the patient may not appear in the report, and/or that the communication problems that emerged during the interview are never reported. The chapter will close with a general discussion of doctor–patient interviews and the kind of language and reasoning used by physicians in the delivery of health care. The summary and conclusions will raise the question of the ways in which changes in communication between doctor and patient can be brought about.

Different views of doctor–patient communication

One major view of doctor–patient communication (Korsch, Gozzi, and Francis 1968; Francis, Korsch, and Morris 1969; Korsch and Negrete 1972) is that poor communication has been the result of the doctors' using technical and turgid language which confuses patients. These authors note that the physician's inability or failure to establish an appropriate "bedside manner" or personal rapport or empathy is a serious drawback to adequate communication. The

407

patient's need for emotional reassurance is viewed as a key factor in medical communication with patients. Korsch and Negrete (1972) provide an example they insist is typical, in which a mother sees a doctor in a hospital clinic about her infant son's persistent and ominous cough. The physician is said to pursue his interests in the patient by asking a few perfunctory questions, while failing to greet the mother and engage in the common use of names. The essential upshot of the encounter is that the doctor discovers the cause of the cough but does not explain his findings to the mother, yet proceeds to prescribe several remedies and the suggestion of an additional examination after a few days. The mother becomes upset when the doctor ignores her concern about the baby, and because she cannot understand the reasoning behind the remedies prescribed, simply buys cough medicine and does not go back for the additional examination. The physician is viewed as seeing the mother as uncooperative because she did not come back for the follow-up examination.

The studies by Korsch and her associates note the importance of doctor–patient communication in the practice of medicine in the USA, where "getting the message across" is crucial in fields like general practice, pediatrics, and internal medicine (and, we should add, obstetrics and gynecology). In these areas considerable time should be spent on psychological factors, and the necessity of good communication as well as technical knowledge becomes imperative. The authors studied 800 visits by 800 different patients in the emergency clinic of the Los Angeles Children's Hospital. Each interview (except for 300 used for control purposes) was audio-taped and the mother of the child was interviewed immediately afterwards. A follow-up of each case occurred within fourteen days to find out if the mother had complied with the doctor's instructions.

The research of Korsch and her associates involved primarily young doctors with one to three years of pediatric experience. The authors note, therefore, that the responses of the mothers might have been different if the pediatrician had been someone long associated with the family. The effects of the particular types of communication observed were nevertheless felt to be relevant for any medical setting, despite expected differences because of the specific nature of the emergency room. The utterances of the doctor to the patient and the patient to the doctor were analyzed according to a coding scheme devised by Bales (1950) in which categories are used to interpret the interviews (see Table 18.1).

The research team found that 76 percent of the mothers were more or less satisfied with the way in which the doctor handled the medical interview. But about one-fifth of the mothers felt the physician had not given them an adequate description of what was wrong with their child. Half of the mothers, after leaving the doctor's office, felt that they were still not sure what factors had led to their baby's illness. Korsch and Negrete (1972) note that this last finding is bothersome because mothers often blame themselves for the illness of their young infant and need reassurance on this score. The study also found that 42 percent of the mothers heeded the doctor's instructions, while 38 percent had managed to follow part of the physician's advice, and 11 percent had simply

Table 18.1. *Coding categories of Korsch and her associates*

1. *Negative affect*	2. *Positive affect*
Shows antagonism	Simple attention
Shows tension	Strong agreement
Disagrees	Tension release
	Friendliness
3. *Neutral questions*	4. *Neutral statements*
Seeking instructions	Introductory phrases
Seeking opinion	Gives information
Seeking information	Gives opinion
	Gives instruction

Source: Korsch and Negrete 1972.

ignored the doctor. In 8 percent of the cases the physician had not given a prescription or advice to the mother. The authors state that the mothers who were most satisfied with the doctor's advice tended to follow the instructions given. Those mothers who did not always follow the physician's advice, yet were satisfied with the information given, were felt to be ambivalent about the seriousness of the illness. These mothers were not clear on the physician's remarks about treatment, and other practical problems.

The results of coding each utterance for content and tone of voice for affect revealed that the doctors often used language that was too technical for the mother. As a result of the technical language, many mothers misinterpreted the terms used by the physician. The term "lumbar puncture" was taken to mean that the lungs would be drained by an operation instead of the use of a needle or syringe for extracting spinal fluid. Another mother did not understand that to be "admitted for a work-up" meant that the child would have to be hospitalized. Even though the use of medical jargon impressed some mothers, it did not provide them with helpful information. An interesting finding reported by the authors is that higher education did not result in mothers being more satisfied with the physician's communication.

Mothers also reported that little effort was made by the doctor to be personal or friendly during the interview. Many mothers reported that the physician seemed to ignore completely their remarks about what was bothering them about the baby's illness, including details that were felt to be important in understanding what was wrong with the child. What was perhaps especially interesting about the communication between mother and doctor was that 26 percent reported that they had not told the physician what was bothering them the most about their child, because they either did not have a chance to do so or did not receive any encouragement from the doctor. This often meant that mothers were unable to focus on what the doctor was in fact telling them. But of the 625 mothers who felt that the physician had been able to understand the issues with which they were concerned, 83 percent reported they were satisfied.

The article by Korsch et al. (1968) indicated that few mothers questioned the doctor's professional competence, and many of the interviews seemed to conform well with some notion of good communication and patient satisfaction. But less than half of the mothers felt that the doctor had been friendly and interested in her remarks. The authors suggest that a few open-ended questions by the doctor at the beginning of the interview would greatly improve communication. Such questions would allow the patients to express their problem in their own words. The study showed that the physician did more talking than the mother, and the doctors seldom showed positive or negative affect by voicing their approval or disapproval of something. What seemed to be of greatest concern to the mother was the doctor's "attitude" toward her during the interview. Specific aspects of the doctor's talk obviously contribute to this notion of "attitude," but we need more detailed studies to pinpoint what this intuitively appealing idea means in actual encounters between people.

Another view of language and medicine which overlaps somewhat with the work by Korsch and her associates, can be found in the recent literature. It derives from studies directed by Waitzkin (Waitzkin and Stoeckle 1972; Waitzkin and Waterman 1974; Waitzkin and Stoeckle 1976) which addressed such issues as the way in which the doctor told patients about their diagnosis and prognosis, especially in cases of serious illness, and the way in which the transfer of information between doctor and patient reflected expert or professional communication with clients or patients. Waitzkin is concerned with the more general problem of whether the control of information in doctor–patient communication is the basis for the exercise of power in maintaining a stratified relationship.

A specific issue of the research of Waitzkin and associates is the set of conditions the physician thinks about when deciding how much information to give the patient about his diagnosis and prognosis, even when the patient is an adult and the head of the family. How much should be told can depend on the patient's family's wishes, the circumstances of his life at the time, perhaps religious background or beliefs, and the nature of the illness.

In a preliminary study the authors found the communication process to be similar to what has been stated above by Korsch and her co-workers. The average time spent by the doctor telling the patient about his illness during an average twenty-minute interview was less than one minute, yet the doctors thought they had spent most of their time telling the patient about the illness. Waitzkin and associates found that in the pilot study they conducted with ten patients, less than 10 percent of the doctor's remarks could be called "scientific" in nature, and the physician seemed to avoid giving the patients direct responses about their problem.

In a larger study, the authors became concerned with the characteristics of doctors, patients, and the organizational context in which actual contacts occurred. Specifically, the research addressed the criteria used by physicians to decide the information they will tell the patient about the illness. The question became one of deciding the way in which characteristics of the physician, the patient, and the situation influenced the information transmitted to the patient. This study, however, is still being analyzed and actual findings are not available. The research reported by Waitzkin and Stoeckle (1976) consists of three small samples from different settings. One sample was obtained from a group of ten internal medicine specialists practising in a hospital in Massachusetts. The doctors' interaction with 10 consecutive patients was recorded for a total of 100 patients interviewed. The second sample came from three outpatient departments in three hospitals in northern California and 30 physicians who worked in these outpatient departments and in private practice. Each doctor's interviews with five consecutive patients in the hospital setting and in private practice were recorded for a total of 300 patients. The third sample involved longitudinal observations of doctor–patient interaction between 6 internists and 36 patients over a nine-month period in a second hospital in Massachusetts.

Waitzkin and Stoeckle (1976) provide some illustrations of one type of data used in their ongoing research on doctor–patient interaction. An example follows:

(1) P: How am I, doc?
(2) Dr: You're fine. Everything's going to be all right.
(3) P: What are my chances?
(4) Dr: Your chances are good. Can't predict – everyone's different.
(5) P: Is my heart okay? How's my blood pressure?
(6) Dr: There's something the matter with your arm. Your vessels to the brain are clear as a whistle. Blood pressure is okay.
(7) P: But before you said the pain was nothing. Why are you going to do tests? Can I do anything to make my blood pressure go down?
(8) Dr.: Often the swelling of the vein leaves a tag that protrudes. It's like scar tissue, nothing to worry about. Yes, blood pressure like that may just be a sign of age, but since the change was sudden, we're gonna check out other possibilities.

(Waitzkin and Stoeckle 1976: 267–8; the interview continues for only a few more lines)

The authors use this doctor–patient interview to explain their coding procedure. The least to most technical remarks are scored by judges on a scale from 1 to 6. The same scale is used to decide the "globality or specificity" of the patient's questions and the doctor's responses, and whether a referent (e.g. *blood pressure* or some part of the body) or a label (e.g. the name of a disease or test) is used. Additional judgments are made about the causal or noncausal nature of the explanation, and its probabilistic or nonprobabilistic nature. These assignments are not easy to make because an utterance can have more than one meaning at any of the three levels of criteria just cited. It is also difficult to know if the assignments reveal anything about what each participant understands about the other's remarks.

The research by Waitzkin and associates includes considerable questionnaire and interview data about the doctor's professional attitudes and political ideology, as well as a host of other factors such as professional experience, type of practice, and just about everything else that a standard survey and demographic study might ask about the doctor, the patient, and the organizational setting and relationship between the physician and patient.

The ongoing research of Waitzkin and his associates promises to tell us a great deal about the sociological factors associated with medicine as a profession. We should also learn about the clinical settings and relationships that doctors have with patients, and general characteristics about doctors and patients. The results of this broad and detailed study should do much to improve our knowledge of medical communication. Most studies have been more restrictive in scope and more modest in design. They include research showing that patients seem to follow the doctor's advice more often when they receive more information from the doctor about what is wrong with them (Davis 1968, 1971; Francis, Korsch, and Morris 1969; Haggerty and Roghmann 1972), while also suggesting that giving the patient his or her own medical record improves the patient's response to treatment (Shenkin 1973).

A study in Germany by Siegrist (1977) shows many of the same characteristics that are discussed by Korsch and her associates. Interviews of 200 doctors and their patients were tape recorded at three hospitals in West Germany. The doctors were found to disregard the patients' demands for information, especially if the patients were from low status settings such as prisons and state mental hospitals. The physician would simply keep talking without paying attention to the patient or give the patient PARALINGUISTIC signals that suggested that the patient's questions were trivial or irrelevant to the interview. There were sudden shifts of topics to avoid difficult or sensitive issues or situations, and an avoidance by the doctor of giving delicate information. When no clinical results were available to report to the patient, the doctor would use communicational tactics to avoid the issue. The patients were left with considerable uncertainty.

The general issues that emerge in studies of doctor–patient communication are those of language and culture. The doctor's cultural setting is described as "middle class" or "upper middle class." The life style, ways of thinking, and dialect of the physician are seen as different and troublesome for most patients (Kimball 1971). When the patient's cultural background is ignored or not understood, then specific problems of miscommunication emerge in the medical interview. For example, reactions to pain can vary by ethnic group (Zborowski 1952), with some (Jewish and Italian Americans) responding more emotionally than others (Irish Americans). Some ethnic groups are said to be more emotional about the presentation of symptoms than others, producing a selective process in choosing symptoms to bring to the doctor's attention (Zola 1966). In addition to interviews with the patients and or families about the patients' complaints, Zola also used checklists, forced-choice questions, attitude questions, demographic background, medical records, and a series of ratings by each patient's examining physician, to pursue the relationship between culture and symptom. The Irish Americans in Zola's study seemed to hedge their replies when asked about pain, but spoke of their chief problem in terms of specific dysfunction. The Italian Americans spoke about their problem in more diffuse terms, often failing to identify a specific malfunctioning as their main concern. The Irish Americans seemed to limit and understate their difficulties, while the Italian Americans seemed to spread and generalize their problems.

Several studies (Bart 1968; Mechanic 1972) suggest that patients who can use a vocabulary of physical and psychological stress that the physician understands may perhaps be viewed as hypochondriacs. Patients more commonly use a vocabulary for describing distress which differs from that of the doctor, and this group poses most of the problems for the physician because they come from uneducated or cultural groups whose modes of expressing emotional distress differ from those of the middle class. Or, some patients are inhibited from expressing their distress because of the middle class norms, leading, in many cases, to more emphasis on their bodily complaints (Mechanic 1972).

A study by Shuy (1976) focuses on such issues as the extent to which patients come to feel they must talk to physicians with a vocabulary that is peculiar to the doctor. Shuy is also interested in situations where the doctors reveal a desire to talk in terms that will be easily understood by their patients. He proposes a continuum, at either end of which physicians and patients use and fully understand only their own language, and with intermediate points where the doctor or patient uses his language but understands the other's, and where each speaks and understands the other's language. Using a questionnaire administered to 105 patients at the Georgetown University Hospital, Shuy found that 45 percent of the patients felt that the physician did understand patients' problems. Thirty-eight percent of the respondents felt that the medical personnel used words that were hard to follow, while 45 percent felt patients often found it difficult to tell the doctor their problems. Many of the patients (70 percent) felt the doctor withheld information the respondents felt should be known to them.

Shuy and his associates also tape recorded over 100 interviews, and found that most of the exchanges were conducted in "doctor language," with the patients trying to simulate this language whenever possible. Serious breakdowns occurred when the patients could (or would) not speak to the physician on the latter's terms, and when doctors could (or would) not understand the patient's vocabulary. The paper by Shuy contains many useful examples of how confusions arise and the way problems may be resolved or left ambiguous.

But there are other, though more modest, ways in which we can examine the issue of language and medicine. One of these is to study actual language use as it reflects or correlates with the social status of speakers. A second approach is one in which language use and the doctor's reasoning are the focus of our attention.

Language as a reflection of status differences

The idea that language use between persons in everyday life and organizational settings reveals status and power differences is a familiar theme but one that is

difficult to document empirically. Instead of focusing on the control of information and its relation to the exercise of power in social interaction among professionals and their clients or patients, a broader view of this problem of language
in society can be obtained by examining socialization settings. The way language is used with children in most societies reflects notions of status differences very similar to those found in professional settings.

Recent work in developmental psycholinguistics suggests that the mother's
speech is adjusted in a way that takes the child's competence and the child's
needs as a language learner into account (Shipley, Smith, and Gleitman 1969;
Remick 1971; Snow 1972; Phillips 1973; Newport 1976; and Newport, Gleitman, and Gleitman 1977). The mother's speech to the child as recorded in these
studies can be used as an index of status and power differences based on the
mother's superior control of information and speech, and the child's narrow
preconceptions about the world and his restrictive information processing
strategies. The mother's preorganization of data to be communicated to the
child not only reveals clear status and power differences, but also facilitates, by
the use of particular speech styles, the child's ability to participate in specific
forms of communication.

A related way that studies of language and cognitive development in the child
can tell us something about status and power differences in communication can
be found in the way children and adults will alter the quality of their speech in
moving from one conversation to another. This observation can be inferred
from work by Shatz and Gelman (1973) and Gelman and Shatz (n.d.). These
authors indicate that the content of speech can remain pretty much the same, but
the actual words used, the focus, and the number of repetitions used by the
speakers, among other conditions, will vary by the type of listener that a
speaker addresses. By looking at the data presented by Gelman and Shatz
sociologically, we can suggest that speakers have and utilize general and specific notions about the structure of social relations that pertain to status and
power differences when they speak to each other. In another study, Blount
(1972) has noted the way that the social and conversational status of speakers
and listeners can influence the frequency of use of particular sentence types in
conversation. What seems to be clear about the studies of language and conversational development in children is that adults or parents routinely expose their
children to norms or rules about how and with whom to speak, and this exposure goes beyond the child's limited linguistic and sociocultural environment
(Cicourel 1977a,b). Children role-play family situations and many others, including how to take the role of doctor and patient (Corsaro n.d.; Andersen
1977).

The developmental studies cited above have used a somewhat different type
of coding procedure for revealing the significance of communicational differences that can reflect status and power. Instead of using a coding scheme like
that of Bales or the system followed by Waitzkin, in which some general
categories are used that are assumed to reflect status and power differences in
social interaction, the psycholinguistic and sociolinguistic approaches derive

their categories from the structure of language and philosophy of language studies that deal with SPEECH ACTS. The traditional sociological procedure is based on familiar coding practices in psychology and sociology where rating scales are used by different judges. The linguistic orientation depends on the way language structure marks how questions are asked, the forms used for requesting information in a language, and the way that language structure limits the speaker to particular SYNTACTIC forms and SEMANTIC devices that may or must include nonverbal information such as voice INTONATION, facial features, and body posturing and movement. The general point is to reveal the ways in which status and power are reflected in the specific language used for directing the interaction, talking about mental states, asserting something, clarifying a remark, requesting information, using imperative and declarative utterances, while also revealing the ambiguities of language that can lead to unclear inferences about the social meaning of an utterance.

A number of conditions are associated with communicational strategies and these need to be understood if we are to develop coding procedures that are closely linked to the structure and processing of language in studies of language and medicine. Specifically, we need to know the ways in which speech reveals cooperation between speakers and listeners (Lakoff 1973b, Grice 1975), what a speaker means and intends by different utterances (Searle 1969), and the way in which the speech act is understood by a listener. Earlier attempts to code social interaction and reveal status and power differences that would inform us about doctor–patient communication overlap with the linguistic orientation proposed in this chapter. The former strategy relies on general social categories that did not recognize the important roles that perceptual, syntactic, semantic, and PRAGMATIC information play in passing judgments on what people do in conversational exchanges.

The methodological digression of this section was necessary to give the reader some idea of how judgments are made about doctor–patient communication. What is perhaps most important about the differences between the two approaches outlined above is that current linguistic orientations stress the examination of language in its social context. The focus, therefore, is on a restricted number of cases that are examined carefully, instead of a large sample of cases that by the very conditions of the study preclude a careful examination of the speech acts in their pragmatic context. The designation of an utterance as being a question, a declarative statement, or an imperative, requires a coding procedure that examines immediately prior utterances as well as utterances that follow the target remark.

How do doctors talk to patients?

In most interview situations one person asks a question and the other person tries to give a reply. In medical interviewing a similar format is followed, but some questions can come in clusters to see if a pattern begins to emerge that can be related to one of several theories about the central nervous system, endocrine balance, enzyme deficiencies, vascular problems, etc. The physician is often unclear about the patient's medical problems when the interview starts, but at the outset the doctor will often begin to make guesses about some possible trouble spots. Each possible trouble spot can trigger off one or more smaller trouble spots that may require considerable detail from the patient's memory as well as the physician's memory about certain characteristics associated with a disease. The question–answer sequences can change their direction and content many times; sometimes this can happen rather abruptly (Heath 1980a).

A physician's specialty can influence what he knows about medicine and the types of cases that tend to get seen frequently. We might suggest a useful analogy here between an expert or master chess player and a weak player (Cicourel 1974). The expert seems to recognize "good" and "bad" moves more easily, and the strong player also seems to be able to reconstruct a chess position more accurately after only five seconds of looking at the board (Simon and Barenfeld 1969; Chase and Simon 1973). For our doctor–patient situation this means that the reasoning used by a specialist when asking questions and receiving answers can be different from that of a general practitioner or a different specialist. The way in which this expertise can be followed in the actual interview may never be shown by the medical history report. Consequently, doctors using another physician's report would not always be able to reconstruct the specialist's thinking or the way the information was obtained from the patient.

We can begin to illustrate some of the points described above by providing the reader with some materials from two interviews. The first is a private practice case of hypertension that included a highly trained specialist in internal medicine and an articulate patient with higher than average education (three years of college). The second is an epilepsy case that comes from a university teaching hospital clinic and involves a low-income family that divides its time between Tijuana, Mexico, and parts of Southern California. The physician in this case is a third-year resident in neurology.

The material is presented in the way developed by Cicourel (1974, 1975): the actual dialogue between doctor and patient is given in transcript form, and then the doctor's written report of the interview is given as it appeared in an initial part of the medical history. This method of presentation will give the reader an opportunity to see the differences in the way the physician talks to the patient and the way he writes for his colleagues professionally and legally.

The opening lines of the hypertension interview began (Table 18.2) with the doctor telling the patient the reason for tape recording the exchange. The patient in (4) simply responds with "All right." The physician continues his explanation in (5) but the patient again agrees to the taping. What is not evident from the transcript is that I had spent about one-half hour with the patient prior to the doctor and had already indicated that we wanted to tape the interview while explaining the nature of the research project. The setting was a comfortable private office that consisted of a suite of rooms. The general setting could be

Table 18.2. *Hypertension case – Dialogue, 1st part*

(1) I: (unclear) How are you?
(2) P: Fine, thank you.
(3) I: I'm Dr. Huntley (as door is closed) and uh thanks for (slight laugh) undergoing your first interview. (Sounds as if the patient may have mumbled a low-keyed acknowledgement.) (p.) Aas you know, uh and we're going ta re (s.p.) record this one because we're trying to get better ways of getting medical facts from patients (p.) in order to (s.p.) maybe get a more systematized approach to medical interviews.
(4) P: All right.
(5) I: So we get more information and consequently help you and other patients, better (P: low mumble like 'mmh') and also we're teaching medical students how to talk to (s.p.) patients, so this is helpful too. That okay with you?
(6) P: Yes, that's fine (in low voice that sounds quite "agreeable")
(7) I: Good (s.p.) great. (p.) Now let me have the history form ⌐ you filled out.
(8) P: ⌊ I haven't'
(9) I: That's all right, I'll go through it with you.
(10) P: And, yah, because some of them, you know, I put a question mark beside them, 'cause I'm (I: 'yah') you know (p.)
(11) I: Why don't you sit over there, I can talk to you ⌐ better
(12) P: ⌊ You like this one better (patient mumbling something here).
(13) I: Get a big pillow (p. movement of objects heard) get out of the sun. Now just tell me your (s.p.) primary (s.p.) problem that you want us to focus on. What is bothering you at the moment?
(14) P: Well, Dr. B said I had high blood pressure. (p.)

I = interviewer (physician)   p. = pause
P = patient   ⌐ = simultaneous speech
s. p. = slight pause
Source: Cicourel 1974.

described as upper middle income to high income. This is the first visit for the patient and she did not know before arriving for her appointment that she would be asked for permission to tape record the interview.

While the patient was waiting for the doctor, she was given a medical history form to fill out. A reference to this form is made in (7) and the patient indicates in (8) that she has not done something. In (9) the physician assumes the patient has not filled out the form, but in (10) it appears that the patient may simply have meant that she did not answer all the questions. In (11) the medical history form is forgotten as the doctor attends to making the patient comfortable and to ensuring that he is in a position to speak with her without any problems. Further remarks by the doctor about the patient's comfort begin (13), and it ends with two questions.

Table 18.3. *Hypertension case – Doctor's report*

---

(1) This is the first office visit for this 34-year-old officer's wife referred by Dr. Y for evaluation of hypertension.
(2) IMMEDIATE PROBLEM: The patient was first told of modest blood pressure elevation at age 31 when she consulted an American physician in Germany for palpitations and chest discomfort.
(3) Apparently the palpitations were related to emotional stress.
(4) An EKG was negative.
(5) Phenobarbital was prescribed.
(6) The physician noted that her blood pressure was "up a little."

Source: Cicourel 1974.

The opening lines of this hypertension case reveal a polite exchange that shows the doctor being concerned about the patient's comfort and his own interest in having her in an optimal position for the interview. Specific questions direct the patient's attention to "your primary problem" and "what is bothering you at the moment?" The patient responds to the "primary problem" question.

The dialogue material that corresponds to the medical summary information in Table 18.3 (3)–(6) is given in Table 18.4. Before this table is discussed, however, the reader should note that several technical terms (*hypertension, modest blood pressure elevation, palpitations, chest disorder, emotional stress*) are used in Table 18.3. The terms *modest blood pressure elevation, chest disorder,* and *emotional stress* are somewhat ambiguous. They each depend on additional information and hence more context that has to do with age, other possible illnesses, pregnancy, and environmental conditions prior to and at the time of the patient's examination in Germany. The possible source of the "emotional stress" is not discussed in the interview. But later stages of the interview do reveal a past psychiatric experience some seven to eight years earlier, after the patient had given birth to her first child. The incident in Germany when the blood pressure was noted as "up a little" occurred four to five years after the patient had given birth to her first child. At the time of the initial questions on the high blood pressure in Germany, there were no remarks about the psychiatric experience.

In the first lines of Table 18.4 the doctor asks the patient to wait before telling him about the present condition of her blood pressure so that he can first get at

Table 18.4. *Hypertension case – Dialogue, 2nd part*

---

(1) I: Okay, now in terms of your blood pressure, uh, before you get back to that again, uh were you at any time in the past aware that your blood pressure was modestly elevated? Did any doctor tell you

Table 18.4. (*contd.*)

(2)	P:	⌈(cut off by patient) ⌊Just that (s.p.) ⌈fellow in Germany and he didn't seem ⌈to
(3)	I:	⌊during an exam?
(4)	I:	⌊when was that, who was that fellow in Germany?
(5)	P:	Dr. G. (Patient and interviewer laugh.)
(6)	I:	Your husband is in the military I gather.
(7)	P:	Yes, you know why (I: Yeah) I uh, I, I thought you already asked me that because I
(8)	I:	Right (laughs slightly)
(9)	P:	because (?) the girl in the other room asked me the same thing; I don't know his name (laughing) either.
(10)	I:	When were you, how old were you uh (p.) when you were in Germany? When you were in Germany at that time?
(11)	P:	(mumbling and unclear initially) I'd say three years ago.
(12)	I:	Okay, so you were about 31, and uh did you go on a routine (s.p.) check? But you don't go to doctors routinely.
(13)	P:	No.
(14)	I:	You must have had a complaint then. Why ⌈did you see Dr. G?
(15)	P:	⌊I did, I went in one Sunday afternoon, because I felt like I was having pains in, and uh, and you know heart, you know (s.p.) was acting funny, so I had my husband take me in.
(16)	I:	Your heart was beating fast ⌈and you had some chest discomfort.
(17)	P:	⌊Yeah, and so they did one of those (s.p.) those, things
(18)	I:	Electrocardiograms
(19)	P:	I believe (s.p.) with a little (p.) (unclear term) things like this.
(20)	I:	Right, and what did the doctor say?
(21)	P:	He said it looked all right.
(22)	I:	It looked okay.
(23)	P:	But he put me on uh (p.) phenobarbital; told me to come back the next day to see (p.) somebody else, (I: Right) general fellow and I went in and everything looked fine, so I said great forget it, you know (s.p.) and then I went in (s.p.) finally decided I'd better have (p.) (I: Yeah) (laughing here and unintelligible) and Dr. G. said it was up a little bit. (I: The uh (cut off)) But he didn't say (hesitating here) that was all (p.) it was up a little bit.
(24)	I:	So once, twice when you saw Dr. G he found it to be (hesitation) up a little bit (P: No) is that correct? or just the second time?
(25)	P:	The first time I didn't see, yeah, I didn't see G the first time, (I: Okay) I saw, just (s.p.) whoever was there, you know. Well, have you ever been in the Army?

I = interviewer (physician)	p. = pause
P = patient	⌈ = simultaneous speech
s.p. = slight pause	(?) = unintelligible speech

Source: Cicourel 1974.

the details about her past history of blood pressure problems. In (1) and (2) the physician begins to probe the patient's memory about being aware or being told about her blood pressure being "modestly elevated." Note that the doctor uses the term "modestly elevated," which also appears in the written medical summary. The patient can be assumed to have understood the doctor because she cuts him off in (3) before the physician can finish the sentence that ends with "during an exam?" She seems to have understood what he wanted to hear because the patient casually mentions "that fellow in Germany." But the patient does not finish her remark because the physician interrupts in (4) to ask, using the patient's language and not a professional title, about "that fellow." The patient, in (5), provides the doctor's name and title. There is some confusion about "that fellow in Germany" to which I shall return below.

Lines (6)–(9) are not clear because in (6) the doctor seems to be asking a simple question that could be coded under the schemes reportedly used in the literature cited above as "asking for information." In (7) the patient seems to be saying that she assumed the physician had already asked her about her husband's occupation. The doctor's "Yeah" in (7) and "Right" in (8) could be coded as "shows support," but we can also identify these remarks as fairly standard aspects of cooperative, polite conversation. The dialogue becomes confusing because in (9) the patient implies that the receptionist also asked about her husband's occupation; at least this is what the first part of her utterance suggests. If we place a period at the end of "thing" in (9), it doesn't help matters because the second part of (9) would not make sense as stating that she did not know her husband's name, but it does make sense to say that she is referring to the doctor in Germany, who she apparently stated was "Dr. G" in line (5). The dialogue does not provide additional clarification at this point because the physician shifts the topic in (10) to how old the patient was in Germany and also asks when she was in Germany. This type of compound question can be coded as asking for information, but it does not pose a single unequivocal question, but two questions that are related. The patient in (11) responds to the second question instead of stating her age directly. The doctor, therefore, establishes the age of the patient indirectly because a few minutes earlier he has asked the patient her age and she has responded with "34." Notice that prior information again figures in the physician's remarks when in (12) he not only establishes the patient's age, but goes on to infer that she could not have gone to see the doctor for a routine check of her health because earlier she had told him that she was "the opposite of other people" because she didn't "like to see doctors. *Really.*" The doctor interrupted at this point to say "Now don't scare me now." The patient continued with "I don't, just don't like your profession."

Let me digress further. The patient's voice when saying she did not like doctors could be called "light," as if she were trying to soften what she was saying. The doctor seems to have taken it the same way; that is, both recognized that each was serious and each cooperated, or so it seems, to avoid any kind of impasse or confrontation. The doctor went on to say that "People should stay away from doctors (laugh) (slight pause) unless it's absolutely essential. I couldn't agree with you more.'' The dialogue can be coded as ''shows agreement,'' but this would miss the point. For in lines subsequent to these just quoted, the patient indicates how she becomes nervous about going in for pap smears and tries to avoid them. It is the connected discourse and not abstract coding that reveals how the patient and doctor continue to establish a relationship during the interview, using various devices to get their points of view across in ways that would not damage the purpose of the exchange. The doctor states that her nervousness is common with doctors as well and then quickly shifts the topic that was being discussed before the digression about disliking doctors. The remarks by the patient could be coded as ''shows antagonism'' several times, but the tone of the voice sounds like that of someone who is expressing some delicate convictions very diplomatically, despite the directness of the actual words used. Coding the transcript in terms of the meanings of singular utterances is difficult even when looking at the remarks immediately preceding and following the utterance being coded, yet they can lead to interesting and important frequency counts of different kinds of remarks. This kind of coding can also lead to misinterpretations of the extended dialogue because of the fact that both patient and doctor remember earlier remarks and use them to initiate and comment on later remarks.

In (14) the doctor again asks two related questions, but the patient chooses to respond to the first question. The term ''complaint'' seems to have been responsible for the patient giving her response in terms of specific complaints like saying she ''was having pains'' and that her heart ''was acting funny.'' If the doctor had only asked the second question, the patient may not have responded in the same way. The physician's response translates the patient's remarks into somewhat more formal language without being technical. The patient's ''having pains'' seems to have become ''chest discomfort,'' while the reference to the heart ''acting funny'' seems to have been changed to the heart ''beating fast'' in (16). The medical summary used the terms ''palpitations'' for ''beating fast'' or the heart ''acting funny,'' while the term ''chest discomfort'' was retained in the doctor's notes and subsequently dictated summary. The doctor continues to interpret the patient's remarks by labeling ''one of those . . . things'' (17) as ''electrocardiograms'' (18).

In (22) the physician repeats the last part of the patient's remark in (21) that the EKG ''looked all right.'' This is a familiar device for getting someone to continue talking but also, hopefully, now clarifying the last remark that is repeated. The reference to phenobarbital is included in the doctor's summary statement. But in (23) we can observe the apparent confusion noted above in (4)–(9) when a Dr. G was mentioned and it was also stated that the patient did not know someone's name. Lines (24)–(25) indicate that the patient saw a general practitioner, perhaps, the first time (the ''general fellow'' and ''fellow'' of (23) and (2)), and then Dr. G when she went ''finally'' in for an apparent checkup that revealed that her blood pressure ''was up a little bit'' (23). The ''up a little'' is what the physician recorded in his notes and final medical

422 AARON V. CICOUREL

summary. The doctor did not ask about what was bothering the patient in Germany, yet the medical summary reveals that it was apparently due to "emotional stress." The summary statement does not show that two doctors were consulted in Germany, and that the first one, seen on an emergency basis, did not view the patient's blood pressure as unusual. But for some reason this was not clarified in the interview; the patient decided she had better have another doctor examine her, and this resulted in her blood pressure being called "up a little."

The second interview, the epilepsy case, will be discussed briefly to indicate how complicated the medical interview can be in a different setting, that of a teaching hospital clinic. As in the hypertension case, we will discuss the opening lines of the interview, a portion of the dialogue between doctor and patient (or patient's family) which followed, and the write-up of an initial part of the medical history. The reader is asked to compare the two cases throughout. For example, the reader will notice that in the opening lines of the dialogue in the epilepsy case (Table 18.5), the doctor makes no remarks about the patient being "comfortable." The doctor's opening remark was not recorded because permission to obtain the tape recorded interview was being asked as the physician asked the patient's uncle why the boy was at the hospital clinic. The entire interview is conducted in a small examining room that contained the doctor, the uncle, the mother, the patient, and the translator–researcher. The medical history and examination lasted approximately twenty minutes in contrast to the hour or more for the hypertension case.

The initial part of the medical history written by the doctor is in Table 18.6. The dialogue for the epilepsy case we wish to examine is in Table 18.7 and involves a family that divides its time between Tijuana, Mexico and a border city on the American side of the frontier. The mother and patient do not speak English, but the uncle manages fairly well. In the medical report, nothing is said about the difficulties of conducting the interview and deciding on the accuracy of the information obtained. I will focus on the second statement of the doctor's medical summary. The DISCOURSE in Table 18.7 shows how the topic of the mother's pregnancy was discussed. The doctor in (1) asks the uncle if the patient had ever had "a convulsion with a high fever" when he was a baby. This use of the term "convulsion" in this context probably confused the uncle despite having heard it a few minutes earlier. At that time the term was used interchangeably with "epileptic" by the doctor, and the uncle seemed to follow this because this term was used by him in his opening remarks to the physician. The uncle's question to the mother in Spanish asked if the patient had experienced "something like this" as a child where we must presume that "this" meant an epileptic attack. The mother's response included "nothing" and an unintelligible remark. The doctor persists in (6) by asking the mother in Spanish if the patient had a fever as a child, and the mother again says "nothing." The uncle then tells the mother in (8) that she had told him something about an incident or condition that is referenced in the dialogue. The mother begins to tell about her pregnancy with the patient and the fact that she had been

Table 18.5. *Epilepsy case – Dialogue, 1st part*

(1)	(There were very few opening remarks and the doctor asked why the patient, his mother, and his uncle were at the walk-in clinic. The uncle responds.)
(2) U:	(inaudible) uh, huh, sorry not heart attack, epileptic attack, looks like that.
(3) I:	Okay.
(4) U:	You know, and we got doctors in Tijuana (p.) and he says maybe they play or the touch some special thing over here maybe this would be happening. Cause they don't put too much attention, he says as long as he don't play (p.) and we forget it. But he go to Mexico City in vacations and (p.) in 6 August he got the second one.
(5) I:	Ah-ha.
(6) M:	(Continual incomprehensible remarks in Spanish.)
(7) U:	And he got like a chicken pox between that time, he got a Dr. T in Mexico City. and Dr. T sent him to us because he knows he go back over here.
(8) I:	Okay, did he have the chicken pox before or after the attack or what?
(9) U:	No, between August (p.) between tw . . .
(10) M:	(Mother interrupts and directs remarks in Spanish to the uncle, but the remarks are unclear.)
(11) U:	. . . seis de agosto? [sixth of August?]
(12) M:	(inaudible) pero no le dió muy fuerte ┌ (inaudible) [but it didn't hit him very hard]
(13) U:	└ Is he got the chicken pox between the 6 August (p.) to 23.
(14) I:	Okay.

I = interviewer (physician) M = mother
U = uncle p. = pause
Source: Cicourel 1975.

Table 18.6. *Epilepsy case – Doctor's report*

(1) The patient is a 15-year-old, right-handed, Mexican male.
(2) The mother's pregnancy was uneventful, except that she had rubeola in her sixth month.
(3) The baby was a full term pregnancy.
(4) The birth weight was not obtained.
(5) Cephalic presentation delivered vaginally.
(6) There were no difficulties in the newborn period.
(7) Infancy, childhood and early adolescence had been normal with no history of meningitis, serious head trauma, staring spells, febrile seizures or other major illnesses.

Source: Cicourel 1975.

Table 18.7. *The epilepsy case – Dialogue, 2nd part*

---

(1) I: Never had. But when he was a baby, did he ever have a convulsion with a high fever?

(2) M: (inaudible)

(3) U: ¿Que si estuvo (?) (hesitates)cuando estuvo niño algo así?
       [That if he was   when he was a child did he have something like this?]

(4) M: Nada (?)
       [Nothing]

(5) U: No, but with (cut off by I)

(6) I: (?) la fiebre?
           [fever]

(7) M: Nada (?)
       [Nothing]

(8) U: Pero pero tú dijiste que, dijiste tú (cut off by mother)
       –But but you said that, you said]

(9) M: ah cuando (p.) estaba yo en estado, tenía yo sarampion (p.) U: whe . . .)
       [ah when   I was pregnant,   I had the measles
       tenía yo como seis meses.
       I was about six months along.]

(10) U: When she got six months (?) uh (p.) pregnant she got like (looks to translator–researcher) uh chicken pox is sarampion?

(11) T: Sí.
       [Yes.]

(12) U: Chicken pox.

(13) M: Estaba en estado.
       [I was pregnant.]

(14) I: Uh huh, okay, but he never had a ⌈ convulsion (cut off)
(15) T: ⌊ Oh, perdón, es measles.
                                          [Oh, pardon me, it's measles.]

(16) U: Measles.

(17) T: Es measles, she had measles, right.

(18) I: Was it the three-day or ten-day measles?

(19) U: ¿No te acuerdas cuánto te duró?   ¿Tres dias o diez dias?
       [Don't you remember how long it lasted?   Three days or ten days?]

(20) M: ¿Qué?
       [What?]

(21) U: Lo que te dió a ti cuando estabas en estado.
       [What hit you when you were pregnant.]

(22) M: ¿El sarampion? Pues cuánto dura el sarampion?
       [The measles? Gosh how long does measles last?]

(23) U: Pues hay de tres o diez dias.
       [Well, there's three or ten days.]

(24) M: De tres dias y pienso (p.) yo creo que sí.
       [Three days and I think   I believe that's right.]

(25) U: ¿De cuánto? ¿diez o tres?
       [How long?   ten or three?]

Table 18.7 (*cont.*)

---

(26) M: No (p.) pues me dió muy fuerte la calentura.
      [No   well the fever hit me very hard.]
(27) U: ¿Duró mucho tiempo?
      [Did it last a long time?]
(28) M: Y dijo el doctor que si no (p.) me quitaba la fiebra me moría yo y (U: uh huh)
      [And the doctor said that if I couldn't get rid of the fever I would die and]
      Que me vi mal (a?) con el sarampion.
      [That I (saw myself?) was (really) sick with the measles.]
(29) U: Sí pero (p.) she feel (p.) sick through that time.
(30) I: Yah, but did it last (laughs) three days?
(31) U: Oh, did it last three days (everyone begins to speak simultaneously here. The
      mother mentions her fever again. The uncle's Spanish to the mother is not clear
      as the doctor breaks in.)
(31) I: Three day measles or the ten day measles? (laughs) Does she remember? (There
      is a pause here as the uncle looks to the patient and the doctor points to the
      mother.) No, her. Her.
(33) M: Ah no, ¿donde me salió? Pues nada más me salió aquí, aquí.
      [Ah no, where did it come out (on me)? Well nothing more came out (but) here
      and here.]
(34) T: ¿Pero cuántos dias duró?
      (But how many days did it last?]
(35) M: A, hijos, no acuerdo. Estaban todos enfermos (p.) los otros.   (I: Okay, uh)
      [Oh my gosh, I don't remember.   Everyone was sick   the others
      a todos les dió y a mi también (p.)   a los otros ⌐ muchachos.
      it hit everyone and me too   and the other | boys.]
(36) I: ⌐ Okay, okay (p.) So he
      never had a seizure when he was a baby. Has he ever been seriously ill in his
      life?

I = interviewer (physician)   p. = pause
U = uncle   [= simultaneous speech
M = mother   (?) = unintelligible speech
T = translator-researcher

Source: Cicourel 1975.

ill with the measles. The extended discussion in (14)–(35) is rather confusing
for the doctor who was trying to see if the patient had had a convulsion at some
time before those that had occurred in the past few months. But the duration of
the measles is never clearly established. Some of the communication gets a little
garbled in the translation. The mother treats the episode as obvious; it happened, but it was not something someone would remember precisely, because
from her point of view the very fact that she and everyone else were sick was
more than enough grounds for not remembering much of anything. So the topic

of childhood fevers and seizures was never discussed in a satisfactory manner. What happened instead was an extended discussion of the mother's measles during her sixth month of pregnancy with the patient. The physician gives up and in (36) concludes that the patient "never had a seizure when he was a baby." The technical language may never have been understood here because the discussion shifted from the patient having any history of convulsions and fever as a baby to the mother's experiences during her sixth month of pregnancy.

Throughout the interview given in Table 18.7, the same remarks are made in different ways. Coding each remark separately would not reveal the general confusions and misunderstandings that occurred frequently throughout the interview. In this epilepsy case it is difficult to know if the patient or his mother ever found out much about the epilepsy problem and its prognosis. There are many episodes that could be described as "hilarious," but the fact is that the patient and his mother and uncle learned very little from the experience. Moreover, there are increasing numbers of cases reported in the media in which children do not receive needed medical attention because of communication barriers (e.g. "Hospital and parents couldn't talk, so baby dies," *San Francisco Examiner*, December 29, 1979).

In spite of his knowledge of the uncle's difficulties with American English, the doctor found it difficult to alter the language he used. He attempted to explain some of the terms he employed, but although these explanations were not technical in a medical sense, they were often technical to the uncle, given his limited American English vocabulary.

Summary and conclusions

Doctor–patient communication shows that professionals are not always thinking about their clients when there is direct, face-to-face contact, despite the fact that the exchange is taking place because the patient requests the help of the physician. The doctor's training and background orient him to observations and questions that are designed to help the patient with certain medical problems. But this may lead to confusions or miscommunication because of differences in social status, cultural background, language problems, and a lack of awareness of the way persons experiencing anxiety, because of suspected illness, cannot remember details or a sequence of prior events. Despite these problems created by the patient's speech, the doctor's knowledge of different areas of medicine creates evidence for deciding what can be inferred from the answers received. The physician engages in a kind of selective listening that often means simulating an interest in what the patient is saying, while trying to figure out what else to ask that would clarify some guesses being developed about what is wrong with the patient.

We can describe various rules about how polite conversation is to occur, including the use of proper turns at talking and introducing topics, and the use of appropriate speech acts that reveal the apparent intent of a question and the apparent meaning given to it by a response. But these rules do not provide us with enough information to grasp many obvious and subtle features of the doctor–patient exchange. The physician, for his part, can become aware of the general appearance of the patient and infer various kinds of information from what is being said. But the doctor remembers more than he can write down, and more than is ever told to the patient. The doctor can notice various features of the patient's skin color, perspiration, facial expressions, all or some of which may trigger questions that the patient does not understand.

It has been difficult to study the conditions of doctor–patient communication in a larger context of what information is considered appropriate for such exchanges besides the expected ones of symptoms and medical, social, psychological, and family background. The issues of fees, insurance and payment plans, and expensive operations require extensive observation if first-hand information is sought. My observations of these conditions (and they do not arise frequently on the many occasions I have participated in medical settings) suggest that the physician will attempt to have the patient discuss the matter with someone else. On some occasions, the physician will seek out colleagues known to be doing research on a particular medical problem in the hope that the patient's case might interest them in performing certain tests or operations that could reduce the patient's medical expenses. I am not aware of any careful studies on this topic.

I will close the chapter by discussing briefly some possible ways in which many of the issues described earlier might be changed in the future. First of all, changes are occurring because of new directions in medical education. These changes take considerable time, however. More medical schools are offering courses that address the doctor–patient relationship directly. More written material is becoming available for medical students and physicians. But there remains considerable resistance both on the part of medical faculties and medical students, while many physicians in private practice are convinced that special training in doctor–patient communication is not necessary. In the United States little or nothing is done about making patients more aware of how to talk with their physicians, what questions to ask, how to insist on explanations that can be understood, or on receiving literature that can explain a problem in terms the patient can understand. Some pharmaceutical firms and companies that produce equipment for doctors often publish pamphlets or small books about illness, treatments, preventive medicine, and the like. The U.S. government has published such materials for many years, but few persons are aware of them or how to obtain them. Some European countries have apparently started programs on giving patients more information about medical services and what can be expected from their doctors. In the USA, changes are being proposed and partially implemented that will create more stringent procedures for monitoring patient care, for the prescription of particular tests and drugs, and for the justification for operations considered "necessary." But such changes come very slowly, and the issues described in this chapter undoubtedly will be with us for many years.

FURTHER READING

Within this chapter, there is an extensive review of the literature on doctors and their responses to and uses of language. Other studies not referred to in the chapter deal with these same issues, although generally in a different way, with less concern for explicit models of analysis. Several provide summary overviews or collections of papers on the topic. Cassell, Skopek, and Fraser 1976 and Cassell and Skopek 1977 offer summaries especially useful to linguists. An entire section of the *Journal of Communication* 25. 3 (Summer 1975) is devoted to communication problems in medical contexts. A unique contribution is the linguistic work done by D. J. G. Bain, a medical doctor who has done several research projects on doctor–patient communication in Great Britain (1976, 1977). Bennett 1976 gives a summary of similar kinds of research.

Of particular importance in medical education is communication across cultures. Candlin, Bruton, and Leather 1974 is a set of working papers and Candlin, Bruton, Leather, and Woods 1977 a teachers' guide to English language skills for medical personnel whose first language is not English and for whom a majority of patients are English monolinguals. Other sources on intercultural communication include Edgerton and Karus 1971, Dixon 1974, Shuy 1974, Carp and Kataoka 1976, and Fernandez-Caballero et al. 1977. The literature from the nursing profession reflects a keen awareness of communication problems and interpersonal skills, for example, Scarlett 1976 and Farrell, Haley, and Magnasco 1977.

A much neglected area of medical communication is that between pharmacists and patients/customers. Therefore, an overview (based on the research of Hoar and Hoar, a pharmacist–linguist team) is given here. Growing professionalism in the practice of pharmacy has resulted in more patient-orientation and less product-orientation. An increasing number of pharmacists now describe their role as that of drug and health counselor/educator (e.g. Hoar 1972; Francke 1976). Pharmacists practising in hospitals have developed this potential more rapidly than have pharmacists in community practice, and studies have shown their work resulted in improved patient attitudes and greater knowledge of and compliance with medication regimens (Madden 1973). Studies of pharmacist interactions in these new roles have highlighted the importance of a private relaxed situation (Malahy 1966; Beardsley, Johnson, and Wise 1977) for allowing patients to ask questions of their pharmacist and to retain information.

Pharmacists in the role of counselor/educator in community settings have shown less success than their counterparts in hospitals; Knapp, Knapp, and Engel 1966 point out that pharmacists did not often volunteer information and patients did not often seek it; moreover, patients often considered the information pharmacists did provide inadequate or irrelevant (Wertheimer, Shafter, and Cooper 1973; Gambrell and Jackson 1978). Linn and Lawrence 1978 point out that a patient's ethnic background is likely to influence the amount of information sought; non-English-speaking Spanish and Asian minorities were more likely to seek advice than were Caucasians and Blacks who spoke fluent English (perhaps a reflection of the higher status accorded pharmacists in nations other than the USA).

As pharmacists shift their role, the liability of pharmacists for warning patients of serious side effects of drugs and obtaining their informed consent becomes a major issue. Campbell and Grisafe 1975 found that pharmacists had difficulty following regulations that required them to explain to patients (or their agents) the necessary information for proper use of prescribed drugs. One way of altering this situation is to improve the teaching of communicative skills in pharmacy education (Grissinger, Wolfe, and

Cohen 1973; Love, Wiese, and Parker 1978). Another solution may involve combining oral and written information for patients. Fox 1969 found a combination of both superior to verbal communication alone, but Clinite and Kabat 1976 found written communication without verbal reinforcement inferior to no communication at all. The problems of devising written information for patients who do not read English or any language at all were examined by Liberman and Swartz 1972. Relevant to this issue is the preparation of patient package inserts (PPIs), a proposed source of printed information for patients about various drugs. Ligouri 1977 provides an overview of the purpose, content, and dispensing of PPIs by pharmacists. The language contained in these PPIs is now being studied by linguists of the American Institutes for Research. Ligouri 1978 has used the Flesch test to examine comparative readability. Hoar and Hoar, in press, discuss the absence of psycholinguistic precision in such readability metrics.

19

Ethnic differences in communicative style*

JOHN J. GUMPERZ and JENNY COOK-GUMPERZ

The USA has always been known as a land of ethnic diversity, where settlers from all parts of the world have found a home and live and work side by side. But the nature of this diversity and its function in American society have changed greatly in recent times. Throughout the nineteenth and part of the present century, agricultural regions were dotted with colonies of European settlers who had preserved their own language and aspects of their old cultural institutions. Inner-city metropolitan districts tended to take the form of aggregates of distinct neighborhoods where immigrants from the same Old World localities could congregate.

Wherever they lived, and whatever they did to earn a living, the new settlers had in some way managed to recreate their own ethnic environment. In their daily lives, they surrounded themselves with their own religious and voluntary organizations and service industries. These institutions provided a safe world for the newcomer. They both protected and to some extent continued the life style of the home from one generation to the next, while at the same time buffering the assimilation into the new society.

Yet in their contact with society at large, these settlers took over the values and political aspirations of the majority group. English was unquestioningly accepted as the sole medium for official communication and the standard for evaluation of ability and occupational achievement, while their native languages remained confined to home use.

With the increasing pace of social change of the last decade, the industrialization of agriculture, the absorption of local regions into the market economy, the centralization of education and the growing influence of state and national government, the pace of assimilation has increased enormously. The children and grandchildren of the earlier colonists have moved into suburbs where they have formed new friendship and kinship ties. They have all but given up their parents' and grandparents' life style and language, so that few signs of the old ethnic islands remain. Other immigrants from Latin America, the Caribbean Islands, Asia, and from the rural American South have moved into the inner cities. These newcomers

* Work on this paper was supported by NIMH grant MH-26831. Our analysis of the example on pages 439–41 draws on the work of Mark Hansell and Cheryl Seabrook. We are grateful for their assistance.

have taken up their predecessors' positions within the economic system, but because of the changed socioeconomic climate, they have had little opportunity to organize their own community base.

New speech events for old communities

Given the strength of pressures for assimilation and the rapidity – when compared to multilingual situations elsewhere – with which the home languages are being given up, one might assume that consciousness of ethnic distinctness is also disappearing. In the period immediately after World War II, this did indeed seem to be the case. Yet during the last two decades, in the United States, as well as elsewhere in Europe and throughout the Third World there has been an apparently unexpected rise in ethnic consciousness. A new generation of ethnic associations has arisen which has adopted the organizational forms and techniques of modern political pressure groups to challenge long established practices of the society at large. Minority DIALECTS and languages, formerly used only in local groups, are now demanding public acceptance. For example, previously stigmatized forms of Black English can regularly be heard on public media. Pocho, the street Spanish of the Californian Barrio has come to be adopted as an important literary medium by the younger group of Chicano writers. There has, moreover, been a sudden rise in awareness of the potential linguistic biases which underlie existing methods of evaluating ability and occupational achievement, and demands are being made for greater tolerance and acceptance of diversity in education, employment, and the judicial system. A paradoxical situation has thus been created by which, on the one hand, local languages are rapidly giving way to English, while on the other hand, assumptions about the need for a uniform standard language and for conformance to accepted communication styles are being challenged.

How do we explain this paradox? How do we account for the sudden concern with reviving symbols of ethnic identity, which on the surface at least seem to have little communicative import? One possible explanation could be that, because of the lack of hard data on language usage, the real extent of linguistic diversity has been underestimated, and that there are unsuspected grammatical difficulties which stand in the way of minority speakers' efforts to gain access to public resources and participate as equals in public affairs. Recent sociolinguistic research concerned with such questions has indeed revealed a great deal of new information on the everyday speech of hitherto little known groups. Convincing evidence has been accumulated to show that all human speech is governed by systematic rules of grammar, so that we cannot account for the colloquialisms of minority groups by assuming that they reflect the decay from a known literary standard. Even the most deviant dialect forms can be explained as resulting from universally valid laws of linguistic change. Language variation in modern urban populations of differing ethnic origins is thus both systematic and rooted in speakers' history and cultural background.

However, when it comes to using linguistic analysis to measure the differences among such ethnically based speech varieties and to explain how speech varieties function as social symbols and affect the individuals' ability to carry on their everyday affairs, difficulties arise. Much attention has been devoted to the statistics which show that speakers of minority dialects and languages do badly in school, have difficulty in passing occupational tests and in obtaining managerial positions requiring ability to communicate in formal English.

It is not at all clear that the difficulties involved here are attributable solely to what we may call language distance: the PHONOLOGICAL and grammatical distinctions that separate the speech varieties in question. The educational problems of ethnic minorities have become acute only during the last few decades. The earlier ethnic islands were not noted for educational difficulties, even though children often entered school speaking little or no English. Of the current generation of bilinguals, moreover, non-English-speaking children of recent immigrants from Latin America and Africa tend to do as well as or better than average, while bilinguals who grew up in the United States, and already speak the street English current in their neighborhoods, perform below the norm. Similarly, BILINGUAL EDUCATION among American Indians seems most effective with relatively isolated and largely monolingual groups and least effective where children already speak pidginized varieties of English. Adult Asians and Africans, moreover, whose English, when taken sentence by sentence is quite grammatical, often have difficulty in getting their point across, while others of European background who make many more purely grammatical errors do not encounter major communication difficulties.

To the extent that communication difficulties in modern urban settings are associated with language, therefore, they seem to have to do with differences among conversational styles of English rather than with grammar as such. To understand how these differences function, we must go beyond grammar to look at conversational conventions and how they relate to the total social and communicative setting in which language is used.

Examination of the communicative import of the change in function of ethnicity in modern technological societies suggests some explanations. We have pointed out that key factors in the recent changes are the disintegration of local neighborhoods and the increasingly direct role governmental agencies have in family affairs. As long as the old ethnic islands were intact, communication with monolingual English-speaking outsiders, while perhaps frequent in terms of mere quantity of contacts, could nevertheless remain quite limited in scope. The most meaningful relations in an individual's life, relations involving uninhibited casual talk, intensive discussions, and requiring strategies of verbal persuasion, were those with kin, neighbors, and others of similar background. A group of personal intermediaries, lawyers, political leaders, doctors, and businessmen could be called on to "speak for" the minority group member, that is to mediate contact with others and to help in such tasks as job placement, securing public assistance, and access to community services.

Advanced technological societies, as Habermas (1971, 1979) has pointed out, require increasingly complex ways of management and greater reliance on bureaucratic conventions. In such societies, individuals must deal directly with a host of public officials. To be effective a person must be able to read and interpret complex written instructions, fill out questionnaires, or present an oral argument to some-one who may have little first-hand acquaintance with the values and concerns that motivate the argument.

Such contacts between lay individuals and officials or professionals have in fact given rise to a new set of characteristically urban speech events, such as inter-views, counseling sessions, committee meetings, interrogations. The ability to be effective in such gate-keeping events is crucial to economic success in modern societies. Yet such effectiveness requires familiarity with norms of behavior, styles of argumentation, and modes of reasoning which are quite different from those of the local face-to-face communities. Note, for example, that while in these public encounters lay client and official interact as social equals, what is said is interpreted in relation to written sets of statutes and criteria of evaluation to which the official has privileged access. All participants must abide by, and must justify decisions in terms of the rules, but it is the official who translates the client's words into relevant categories which serve as the standards by which outcomes are judged. In doing so, the official may rely on unstated conventions and cultural assumptions which are significantly different from those of the uninitiated lay person.

In his book on juvenile justice, Cicourel (1968) vividly describes the semantic problems that arise in one such speech event when a probation officer is forced to resort to official categories of aggression to evaluate the behavior of a teenage parolee who, against his own inclination, has found himself compelled to inter-vene in a fight to support a friend in need of help. While problems of communica-tion involved in such public encounters are general and affect everyone, it can easily be seen that in situations of ethnic diversity, where conversational styles differ, these stylistic differences may create additional difficulties. In this chapter, we will analyze several instances of public encounters to show how ethnic background can affect interpretation of intent and evaluation of performance.

Conversational cues

Before going into the discussion of actual examples, we need to give some background information on the nature of conversational signaling processes and on the ways they differ with ethnic background. Recent work in INTERACTIONAL COMPETENCE and nonverbal communication provides some initial insights into what is involved. Human interaction of all kinds is always accompanied by gestural and postural signals. The most noticeable and most frequently discussed of these consist of conventionalized signals or emblems such as handshakes, head nods, and bows, which function somewhat like words in that they are for the most part consciously employed and have meanings that can be described in the abstract, apart from the actual interaction. There are however many other move-ments which play an even more important role in the conduct of interaction (Ekman and Friesen 1969; Birdwhistell 1970). These cues, which include eye blinking, gaze direction, facial orientation of interactants, head, limb and torso movements, as well as postural orientation of interactants, are emitted without conscious planning and take place out of awareness, yet they play a key role in enabling participants to create and maintain conversational involvement. Micro-analysis of filmed or videotaped exchanges reveals that signaling at this level is interactively produced (Condon and Ogsten 1969). Speakers' messages are met by listeners' acknowledgments and speaker and listenership cues are synchronized in ways which recall the ensemble playing in music or ballroom dancing. When speakers, for some reason, are unable to establish such synchrony, exchanges are likely to be brief, and significant communication becomes more difficult to achieve.

Unlike words or emblems, the cues involved in conversational synchrony have no meaning by themselves, but within the context of a particular speech situation, they provide important information regarding the interaction. An outsider who knows the relevant signaling conventions can look at a group of interactants, and by observing their postural orientation and body movements, can learn a great deal about what they are doing and what their interpersonal relationships are. Partici-pants themselves rely on these signs in judging where the talk is going, in following the often subtle shifts in mood and focus, and planning their own contributions. We refer to the reciprocal signaling involved here as *contextualization*, since it serves to frame the interaction and to associate what is done with one or another of a range of culturally sanctioned activities (Cook-Gumperz and Gumperz 1976; Gumperz 1976b).

Along with body movements, auditory cues also play an important role in the contextualization process. Listeners employ verbal back-channel signals (Yngve 1970) such as *uh hum, right,* and *yes,* which are coordinated or alternate with nonverbal cues. Speech rhythm, voice quality, intonation, and stress placement are similarly synchronized. Everyday speech, furthermore, contains a whole host of formulaic expressions, greetings, conversational openers and closings which serve to identify and channel the interaction.

Studies of conversation from this perspective demonstrate that by giving infor-mation about the activity and interactants, contextualization also plays a key role in enabling participants to go beyond the literal meaning of what is said to interpret what is intended, what it is that motivates a particular utterance, what is ultimately wanted. Consider the following brief exchange recorded in a university office. The speakers are a student who has just been employed as a research assistant and a secretary who takes care of the personnel work:

(1)   A: Good morning.
(2)   B: Hi John.
(3)   A: Howdy.
(4)   B: How ya doin?
(5)   A: Fine ah . . . do you know . . . did you get anything
(6)   back on those forms you had me fill out?
(7)   B: Like what?
(8)   A: I wonder if they sent you a receipt or a copy of . . .
(9)   B: You mean on your employment form?
(10) A: Yeah.

Note the seemingly anomalous double exchange of greetings in the beginning. Schegloff and Sacks (1973) have pointed out that the second part of such redundant sequences serves to indicate readiness to talk. But more is involved. B acknowledges A's relatively formal "Good morning" with "Hi," which A then accepts with his own colloquial reply in (3). In this way the two interactants jointly negotiate an informal, friendly tone for what is essentially a business encounter. At (5), A initiates his request with "Fine ah . . .," employing a hesitation signal to hold the floor. The actual request is then preceded by a false start and another hesitation pause. The exchange then proceeds smoothly, but, when at (8), A hesitates once more, B interrupts him to supply the necessary information.

One might argue that A is relatively evasive or unsure of what he wants. Why didn't he make his request directly? Given the informal tone of the encounter, however, his indirectness can also be seen as a form of politeness. He certainly does manage to induce B to guess what he wants. No matter what our interpretation of the event, the two interactants clearly communicate and they do so by virtue of the fact that they share a set of contextualization conventions. They both know, for example, (a) that "Good morning," "Hi," and "Howdy" can be interpreted as greetings varying in degree of informality; (b) that potentially they could all be used in this setting; and (c) that selection among them can determine the quality of the following action. They furthermore agree how to use prosody to signal hesitations, false starts, and distinctions between new and old information as well as on when to yield the floor.

Although the basic prosodic mechanisms involved in contextualization are in large part universal, their use in particular contexts and their association with particular sets of words and sentence structure is a matter of cultural convention. Hall (1959) and his students have pointed to significant cross-cultural differences in the communicative use of body distance, gaze direction, and torso and limb movements. Recent studies by Erickson and his students (Erickson 1975; Erickson and Schultz 1981) reveal similar differences among residents of a single large Midwestern metropolitan area.

Erickson filmed and tape recorded a series of student-counselor advising sessions in which ethnic backgrounds of both counselors and students varied. Interaction in such sessions is usually seen as expressively neutral or instrumental, directed toward the goal of helping the student in planning course work or discovering academic strengths and weaknesses. Counselors can hardly be said to be prejudiced, as defined by the usual attitude measures. Yet Erickson's highly detailed and subtle indices showed significant, if complex, relationships between the amount of useful information that the student obtained and the ethnicity of participants.

The interviews were analyzed at three levels or channels of communication: (a) nonverbal signals, such as gaze direction, proxemic distance, KINESIC rhythm or timing of body motion and gestures; (b) PARALINGUISTIC signals – voice, pitch, and rhythm; (c) implicit semantic content of messages. A series of indices was constructed which served to isolate instances of interactional a-synchrony, or "uncomfortable moments" in the interview. Identification of such passages was found to be highly reliable when checked both across coders and against the evaluations of original participants who were shown the film.

The results reveal a direct relationship between these *indices of a-synchrony* and the amount of *usable information* that the student derived from the interview. The greater the synchrony was, the greater was the amount of practical information obtained. A-synchrony, in turn, was related (a) to similarity of ethnic background of participants and (b) to ability to find some common base of experience on which to build the interaction.

What seems to happen is that, at the beginning of each conversation, there is an introductory phase when, as in our example above, interpersonal relationships are negotiated and participants probe for common experiences or some evidence of shared perception. If this maneuver is successful, the subsequent interaction is more likely to take the form of an interrelated series of moves in which speakers cooperate to produce a well-coordinated sequence of exchanges. The ability to establish a common rhythm is a function, among other factors, of similarity in ethnic background. Thus, in spite of the socially neutral nature of the interviews, it seems that in American cities Poles, for example, communicate most efficiently with other Poles, less easily with Italians, even less easily with Jews, and least easily with Puerto Ricans and Blacks. It is important to note that, while participants can learn to identify moments of uncomfortableness when viewing their own tapes, their interpretations of what happened and why often differ greatly. Furthermore, Black counselors seem somewhat less affected by ethnically different advisees than their White counterparts. Perhaps the communication difficulties they experience in their own everyday lives make them more tolerant of ethnically based differences in communication styles. In any case, the phenomena involved are automatic, not readily amenable to conscious control.

Blacks and Whites

How do dialect and language differences in modern American communities relate to contextualization conventions? Consider the problem of Black English. Although linguists concerned with this topic have concentrated largely on phonology and sentence grammar and have found only minor differences between Vernacular Black English and Standard American English at this level, there is a rich and growing literature in the area of folklore and folk literature which points to far-reaching differences in lexicon and discourse rules (Abrahams 1972; Kochman 1972). Among the most commonly discussed LEXICAL terms are those in the realm of sports, popular music, and drug and street culture, many of which have passed into the general vocabulary. But more interesting for our discussion are the many formulaic expressions including proverbs, greetings, and leave-taking formulas. There are also many terms used to describe culturally specific speech activities such as "sounding," "marking," and "signifying" (Mitchell-Kernan 1971), and "boasting" and "bragging" (Kochman 1979; Chapter 5, this volume). The first three words are peculiar to Black English. In the second case, common English words carry ethnically specific meanings. However, such terms are more than mere idiomatic expressions with culturally specific meanings; they serve as metaphoric statements of what is intended in a particular stretch of discourse. Consider the following conversation reproduced in Mitchell-Kernan (1971: 95–9). The participants are the researcher (R), her informant (B), and B's friend (M). The episode begins as R is about to leave.

B: What are you going to do Saturday? Will you be over here?
R: I don't know.
B: Well, if you're not going to be doing anything, come by. I'm going to cook some chit'lins. (rather jokingly) Or are you one of those Negroes who don't eat chit'lins?
M: (interjecting indignantly) That's all I hear lately – soul food, soul food. If you say you don't eat it you get accused of being saditty [= affected, considering oneself superior]. (matter of factly) Well, I ate enough black-eyed peas and neckbones during the depression that I can't get too excited over it. I eat prime rib and T-bone because I like to, not because I'm trying to be White. (sincerely) Negroes are constantly trying to find some way to discriminate against each other. If they could once get it in their heads that we are all in this together, maybe we could get somewhere in this battle against the man.
(M leaves)
B: Well, I wasn't signifying at her, but like I always say, if the shoe fits, wear it.

Kernan comments that while the manifest topic of B's question was food, M was suggesting that B had indirectly accused her and R of being assimilationists. She goes on to say:

An outsider or non-member (perhaps not at this date) might find it difficult to grasp the significance of eating chit'lins or not eating chit'lins. B's 'one of those Negroes that' places the hearer in a category of persons which, in turn, suggests that the members of that category may share other features, in this case, negatively evaluated ones, and indicates that there is something here of greater significance than mere dietary preference.

Chit'lins are considered a delicacy by many Black people and eating chit'lins is often viewed as a traditional dietary habit of Black people. Changes in such habits may be viewed as gratuitous aping of Whites, thus implying derogation of these customs. The same sort of sentiment often attaches to other behavior such as changes in church affiliation of upwardly mobile Blacks. Thus, not eating or liking chit'lins may be indicative of assimilationist attitudes, which in turn imply a rejection of one's Black brothers and sisters . . .

It is not clear at the outset to whom the accusation of being an assimilationist was aimed. Ostensibly, B addressed her remarks to R. Yet M seems to indicate that she felt herself to be the real addressee in this instance. The signifier may employ the tactic of obscuring his addressee as part of his strategy . . .

The technique is fairly straightforward, the speaker simply selects a topic which is selectively relevant to his audience. A speaker who has a captive audience, such as a minister, may be accused of *signifying* by virtue of his text being too timely and selectively *a propos* to segments of his audience . . .

Although M never explicitly accuses B of signifying, her response seems tantamount to such an accusation, as is evidenced by B's denial.

Kernan here provides a clear illustration of how culture and ethnic background can affect interpretation of talk. In the course of a group's history, certain ways of speaking become associated with certain types of speech activities and come to signal the communicative goals associated with these activities. In this way, when used in the appropriate situation, they can be understood as indirect means of conveying communicative intent, of suggesting how what has been said should be interpreted. That is, whether it should be interpreted as an evaluation, an explanation, a humorous remark, part of a narrative, a criticism, or as a mere statement.

By using these indirect strategies, speakers can imply something without putting themselves on record as having said it and risk being called impolite. Messages, in these cases, are inherently vague. The signaling load is carried as much by context as by LEXICON and grammar. But in deciding what the context is, listeners rely both on extralinguistic information about participants and settings, and on verbal and nonverbal features of the utterances themselves. How something is articulated and how it is pronounced is crucial for determining what is said. Claude Brown implies this in his description of White Americans' difficulties in using and understanding what he calls 'the language of soul.'

The White folks invariably fail to perceive the soul sound in soulful terms. They get hung up in diction and grammar, and when they vocalize the expression it's no longer a soulful thing. In fact, it can be asserted that "Spoken Soul" is more a sound than a language. It generally possesses a pronounced lyrical quality which is frequently incompatible to any music other than that ceaseless and relentlessly driving rhythm that flows from poignantly spent lives. Spoken soul has a way of coming out metered without the intention of the speaker to invoke it. There are specific phonetic traits. To the soulless ear the vast majority of these sounds are dismissed as incorrect usage of the English language and, not infrequently, as speech impediments. To those so blessed as to have had bestowed upon them at birth the lifetime gift of soul, these are the most communicative and meaningful sounds ever to fall upon human ears: the familiar "mah" instead of "my", "gonna" for "going to", "yo" for "your." "Ain't" is pronounced "ain"; "bread" and "bed", "bray-ud" and "bay-ud"; "baby" is never "bay-bee" but "bay-buh"; Sammy Davis, Jr., is not "Sammee" but a kind of "Sam-eh"; the same goes for "Ed-deh" Jefferson. No matter how many "man's" you put into your talk, it isn't soulful unless the word has the proper plaintive, nasal "maee-yun". (Brown 1972: 136)

Reliance on contextualization to convey intent indirectly is an efficient mode of communication, highly economical of effort, since it enables one to convey a great deal of information in just a few words. Interaction in small face-to-face groups such as prevail in ethnic islands, where background assumptions and relevant signaling systems are shared, favors the development of such strategies, and speakers who have grown up in these situations often have difficulty in shifting to more highly lexicalized strategies. But in public urban settings, such sharedness cannot be assumed, even when, on the surface at least, participants seem to have similar background. One important function of ethnically specific greeting and conversational openers is to test for shared background and values. The following example, taken from an oral report by a graduate student interviewer in a survey of a low income Black neighborhood illustrates this.

The contact for the interview had been made through the survey office. The student arrives, rings the bell, and is met by the husband, who opens the door, smiles, and steps toward him saying:

Husband: So y're gonna check out ma ol lady, hah?
Interviewer: Ah, no. I only came to get some information. They called from the office.
(Husband, dropping his smile, disappears without a word and calls his wife)

The student reports that the interview was stiff and quite unsatisfactory in that only perfunctory answers were given and little information was volunteered. Being Black himself, he knew that he had "blown it" by failing to recognize the significance of the husband's speech style in this particular case. The style is that of a verbal game, used to "check out" strangers, to see whether or not they can respond with the appropriate idiom. Intent on applying the interviewing techniques he had learned in the university, the interviewer failed to notice the husband's stylistic cues. Reflecting on the incident, he himself states that, to show that he was onto the husband's game, he should have replied with a Black dialect phrase like *Yea, I'ma git some info* ("I'm going to get some information") to prove his familiarity with and approval of local verbal etiquette and culture. Instead, his Standard English reply was taken by the husband as an indication that the interviewer was not "one of us" and, perhaps, not to be trusted.

Difficulties in decoding intent increase when signaling systems are not shared. The following is an extract from an ethnographic group interview recorded in 1969 by one of the authors and analyzed by Hansell and Seabrook (1978). The interviewees were teenage Black students in an urban alternative high school, who formed a discussion group to talk about problems of adjustment. The researcher had asked to attend a meeting to tape informal Black English speech. In explaining his research, he had mentioned the then-current views of educators who tended to attribute school failure among Blacks to lack of verbal skills. He had said that his goal was to collect data with which to disprove such stereotypes.

Active participants in the interview are the researcher (G), his research assistant (M) and two Black teenagers (W) and (B). Several other Black teenagers are listening. "What do we talk about?" marks the beginning of the interview proper.

(1)   G: What do we talk about?
(2)   W: Oh, you guys pick a subject, any old subject, you know.
(3)   G: Any old subject?
(4)   B: Any ol θæŋ [= thing]
(5)   W: Are yòu oppòsed to . . . to the wàr?
(6)   M: Yeah.
(7)   W: Are yòu (Black teenagers laugh) oppòsed to the dràft?
(8)   G: Yeah. Well I can afford to be opposed.
(9)   W: Tell me about your wàr lìfe, was it ìnteresting?
        I mean yo mìlitary sèrvice lìfe. Was it ìnteresting?
(10)   G: Oh, it wasn't very interesting. No.
(11)   W: Tell me, what part of the sèrvice you go into, the àrmy?
(12)   G: I was in the army
(13)   W: (interrupting) Well, what wàr was you in?

(14)   G: Second World War.
(15)   W: Second . . . did you . . . how you . . . you . . ., whère did you gò?
(16)   G: I was in Europe.
(17)   W: That's the ònly plàce?
(18)   G: That's the only place.
(19)   W: Uh hum.
(20)   G: England, France and Germany.
(21)   W: Oh, well.
(22)   G: In those days, well . . .
(23)   W: I mean was you reàlly in àction?
(24)   G: Oh, once or twice.
(25)   W: Did you kìll ànybody?
(26)   G: I don't know, I shot a couple of times.
(27)   W: You bùsy shoòtin huh?

After a few minutes the talk shifts to the coming presidential elections.

(28)   W: Did you agrèe with the elèctions?
            (group laughter)
            Did you agrèe with the elèctions? You first.
(29)   M: Me first. No. Next question.
(30)   W: Why dò yòu nòt agrèe?
(31)   M: Why do I like what?
(32)   W: Why dòn't yòu agrèe the elèctions?
(33)   M: Oh.
            (group laughter)
(34)   M: Thought it was a joke.
(35)   G: Huh?
(36)   M: Thought it was a joke, joke. A joke, you know.
(37)   W: Oh, it was a joke.
(38)   M: Yeah.
(39)   W: Oh, oh the whole thing was a joke to you.
(40)   M: Right.
(41)   W: I hear you.
(42)   G: Who'd you vote for?
(43)   W: I, oh well, if I just hàd to?
(44)   G: Yeah, if you just had to.
(45)   M: Next time you have to.
(46)   W: Òh (falsetto).
(47)   G: Next time around, you have to vote.
(48)   W: Well like ah, I ain't hàd to règister from the (tense vowel) gìt go.
(49)   G: Um?
(50)   W: I ain't hàd to règister to vote from the begìnning.
(51)   G: You didn't?
(52)   W: I mean . . . I mean don't . . . don't I have that choice?
(53)   G: That's right.

(54) W: Well then . . .
(55) G: So you're not gonna vote, huh?
(56) W: No, for what (loudly)?
(57) G: (inaudible)
(58) W: (loudly) For what? Now either one of them git ùp there, you know what they gònna do?
(59) B: Right on
(60) W: The dogs gonna gìt the ìn, you know they gon just put us lower in the ghetto and throw a little
       (sung)
       Black man on TV and make you θæŋk [= think] they doin somethin for you.
       (group laughter)

W and B's speech in these examples reveals many of the linguistic variables characteristic of Black English. Note the vowel [æ] in "thing" (4) and "think" (60), the loss of [r] in "your" (9), the lack of agreement in "was you" (23), the "I ain't had to" and the "from the git go" (48). As is common with speakers of Black English, these variables alternate with more "standard" variables, such as the [ɪ] in "thing" (39), the [ŋ] in "interesting" (9). But use of these Black variables is more than simply a marker of ethnic identity. It serves clear communicative ends and the researcher's failure to perceive this significantly affects the success of the interview.

The researcher's goal was to initiate a relatively informal discussion, a free exchange of personal opinions about a subject of sufficient interest to induce participants to display their persuasive skills. To that end, he was willing to allow the group to choose a topic of their own. The actual interview, however, takes a quite different form. Beginning with (4), it is the interviewees who take control and begin to question the interviewer. Their questions have a formulaic, game-like character, which serves to constrain rather than encourage free expression of opinion. On a number of occasions, such as in (8), and again in (10), (16), and (22), the interviewer attempts to develop themes of his own, but his moves are cut off by new lines of questioning. It seems as if the teenagers are more concerned with the questioning process as such than with the actual content of the answers.

A closer examination of the phonetic and prosodic characteristics of the teenagers' talk and of the response they receive from other teenage peers gives an insight into their communicative intent. The initial clue comes from B's "θæŋ" in (4). While a casual observer might regard this as a normal feature of the speaker's style, examination of B's talk elsewhere, shows that this is not the case. Apart from minor features of accent, his speech is quite close to Standard California English. Given what occurs elsewhere in these tapes, his pronunciation can be seen as a signal, a way of overcommunicating Blackness, as if to say, 'if you want to hear Black talk, I'll give you some.' B's remark is immediately followed by W's question "Are you opposed to the war," which is spoken in slow, peculiarly contoured style (marked by accent marks in the transcript). This question is then repeated verbatim with exactly the same intonation to address the second researcher, and questions with similar prosody recur throughout the two passages whenever the teenager attempts to take over or maintain topical control.

What the teenagers seem to be doing is playing a game, a television interview game, which perhaps they have played before, and for which they have developed signaling conventions which are not understood by the researchers. Note M's failure to understand W's "Why do you not agree?" Black variables are being used as part of that game, partly as a way of alluding to general Black values, of dissociating the individual from what is said and of labeling certain aspects of the message as political statements. Note the way phrases like "military service life," "was you really in action," "what war was you in," and "you busy shootin huh" are picked out from the rest of the talk. The major political statement comes at the end, beginning with (48). The style here is quite Black and several idiomatic expressions occur which are not understood by researchers.

While the explanation of what is "really meant" by these stylistic strategies will always be controversial, it is clear that throughout these two passages, the researchers are unable to decode the teenagers' communicative intent. They cannot, for example, distinguish personal opinion from game talk. They persist in trying to elicit opinions when the teenagers have no intention of being serious. Even though they sense their own lack of control, they fail to catch on even in the second passage when the teenagers once more fall into their game-like questioning strategy. Different signaling systems are at work and, as a result, communication breaks down.

Code-switching as a contextualization strategy

Our discussion so far has concentrated on stylistic differences among speakers of English. There is evidence to show that even with bilinguals who continue to speak their own language at home, certain conversational conventions arise which distinguish urban minority groups both from their monolingual compatriots at home and from the majority group members among whom they live. A typical example of such conversational strategies is conversational CODE-SWITCHING, the juxtaposition of passages of speech belonging to two different grammatical systems, within the same exchange (Gumperz 1980).

Consider the following examples:

1. *Spanish-English*
   A. Well, I'm glad I met you.
   B. *Ándale pues.*
      [O.K., swell.]
2. *German-English*
   A. Where is my coat?
   B. Over there *in dem Schrank da.*
      [in the closet there.]

Such examples are frequent in the speech of many urban bilinguals, yet linguists concerned with the study of grammatical systems as such tend to neglect the phenomena as transitional, an instance of language change in progress which cannot be studied systematically. Code-switching is one of the chief characteristics of the variety of California Chicano Spanish called Pocho, which until recently was held in low regard. Pejorative stereotypes about code-switching prevail even among students of folk culture. Barbara Kirschenblatt-Gimblet, in an article on narrative performances among Jews in Canada (1974), analyzes several instances of dialect humor in which the juxtapositions of Yiddish and English phrases serves to create humorous effect. Yet she notes that many folklorists refuse to recognize this type of material as a legitimate form of Yiddish. Nathan Ausubel, author of the well-known *A Treasury of Jewish Folklore* (1948), refers to the large body of Jewish dialect jokes which are not Jewish at all but which are ''the confections of anti-Semites who delight in ridiculing the Jews.''

The following examples taken from Chicano speech will illustrate some of the communicative uses of code-switching. The first comes from a story told in the course of an informal discussion involving two Chicanos. The speaker is reporting on what her father said about her children.

A: To this day he says that . . . uh . . . it's a shame that they don't speak Spanish. *Están como burros.*   *Les habla uno y*   ''What he
[They are like donkeys.] [Someone talks to them and]
say, what's he saying?''

The switch to Spanish here marks the sentence as a personal comment on the preceding one. English for this speaker as for many other bilinguals is associated with the outgroup while Spanish is associated with ingroup talk. This contrast is built upon in this passage to suggest the distinction between generalized statements and personal opinion.

In the following passage, a speaker talks about her experience with trying to give up smoking.

A: . . . they tell me ''How did you quit Mary?'' I didn't quit I . . . I just stopped. I mean it wasn't an effort that I made *que voy a dejar de*
[that I'm going to stop
fumar porque me hace dano o this or that uh-huh. It's just that I used to
smoking because its harmful to me or]
pull butts out of the waste paper basket yeah. I used to go look in the . . .
se me acababan los cigarros en la noche I'd get desperate *y ahi*
[would run out on me the cigarettes at night]   [and there
voy al basurero a buscar a sacar.
I go to the wastebasket to look for some.]

Note how the contrast between the ''we'' code Spanish and the ''they'' code English symbolizes varying degrees of speaker involvement in the message. Spanish statements are personalized while English reflects more distance. The speaker seems to alternate between talking about her problem in English and acting out her problem through Spanish.

Code-switching in these examples is used as a conversational strategy in ways which recall the use of Black variables in the earlier ethnographic interview. The meaning in each case is different, however, because of the difference in context.

In contrast to the English conversational strategies which affect conversation in public settings, code-switching by its very nature is used only in ingroup situations. The fact that it occurs as a common practice in most urban settings, however, has some important consequences for educational policy in bilingual schools.

The examples we have analyzed should be sufficient to illustrate the fact that even though some minority languages are disappearing, along with other overt markers of ethnicity, other conversational conventions arise which significantly affect interethnic communication. Misunderstandings now tend to take the form of misreading of intent, rather than of problems in decoding factual statements; yet they nevertheless have linguistic basis. Research in this area is still in the beginning stage (Gumperz 1978), but it seems clear that there continue to be significant communication difficulties which stand in the way of full participation of minority persons in public affairs and affect the education they receive.

FURTHER READING

Any suggestion of a ''problem'' in communication across ethnic groups was, for the most part, avoided in serious scholarly work until the past two decades. Jokes, short stories, and novels often portrayed ethnic groups at odds in their understanding of each other, perpetuating stereotypic characterizations of the language habits of minorities. By the 1960s, however, students of language in the USA began openly to discuss communication patterns of members of different ethnic groups, and certain behaviors, such as body gestures, eye gaze, and space usage were identified (E. T. Hall 1959, 1966). In effect, social scientists attempted to break through the seeming invisibility of problems in interethnic communication, ''in which communication becomes virtually impossible among people who not only operate from different codes and are unaware of how these differences may interfere with effective communication, but, even worse, are often unaware that there are even different codes in operation'' (Kochman 1971:3). Some studies focused on the differences between the communicative patterns of ethnic groups and seemed to emphasize that the ''problem'' of miscommunication was created by those who differed from the mainstream (e.g. Smith 1966, Smith 1973; Rich 1974; Condon and Yousef 1975).

More recently, social scientists, especially linguists and anthropologists, have begun to study the communicative patterns – prosodic, proxemic, kinesic, and linguistic – of *all* the communicants in conversational interactions. Careful analysis of the communicative strategies of members of both majority and minority members in interethnic communication situations shows areas of both congruence and conflict. Gumperz 1976a, 1977, 1978, 1980 emphasizes the prosodic differences in communicative strategies and the differences in definitions and interpretations of speech events on the part of members of different ethnic groups. Erickson 1975, Erickson and Shultz 1981 stresses the importance of body movements and speech rhythm of members of different ethnic groups in an intense communicative situation such as a counseling interview. Tannen 1979 discusses the role of expectations and past experiences on the part of Greek Americans interpreting a film. Duran 1981 provides numerous examples of the discourse strategies of Hispanics in the United States and emphasizes the implications of these for classroom practices. Valdés Fallis 1976, 1978b, 1980 offers examples of code-switching communicative strategies used by Chicanos in interethnic communication. Hall 1977 discusses some basic assumptions about information and sources of information which he feels affects communication across ethnic groups.

Following the Civil Rights movements of the late 1960s, much of the work on interethnic communication focused on Black – White interactions. Kochman 1971, 1972, 1979, Labov 1972a, Mitchell-Kernan 1972a,b, Wolfram and Fasold 1974, and Mitchell-Kernan and Kernan 1975, 1977 emphasize differences in styles of speaking and types of communicative events in which members of Black communities gain expertise. Ways of gaining this communicative competence as children are illustrated in Mitchell-Kernan and Kernan 1977 and Whatley, in press.

20

Language in education:
standardization versus cultural pluralism*

COURTNEY B. CAZDEN and DAVID K. DICKINSON

Education has never only taken place in regular school and college classrooms. In the United States today, it is taking place in increasingly varied settings. In 1976, Congress passed the Mondale Lifelong Learning Act, which recognized that people of all ages are turning to informal as well as formal educational institutions for skills for new jobs and careers, cultural enrichment, and personal growth; and that opportunities for learning should be available throughout life – perhaps by means of educational vouchers redeemable at any time from birth to death. While this Act was at least partly motivated by the self-interest of educators who see decreasing numbers of Americans in the traditional student age groups, it also recognized as a fact to be considered in public policy what is obvious in any community.

In Boston, for example, the *Peoples' Yellow Pages* lists pages of new educational opportunities outside traditional institutions of higher education. They include:

a school for learning the skills of community organization;
free programs in basic reading, English as a Second Language, and preparation for the High School Equivalency Diploma, held in public schools, a hospital, and a church;
an automobile repair training school, and tutors in advanced electronics;
a free university with courses in medical ethics and the politics of food;
a learning partnership for intergenerational study and action around questions of aging, meeting in apartment buildings and a settlement house;
health education and laboratory assistant training in a medical technical institute in the Black and Hispanic community;
a center for paralegal training and educational programs for prisoners.

Even the tradition-bound Harvard University Faculty of Arts and Sciences has established a Center for Continuing Education with noncredit programs open to the public on topics as diverse as family genealogy, the history and tasting of wine, the stock market, and stress.

* We are grateful to Holly O'Donnell of the National Council of Teachers of English and James Squire of Ginn & Co. for help in obtaining information for this chapter.

We know nothing about language in any of these educational settings: what language skills they demand, what ways of speaking or writing they encourage or suppress; what effects they have on the COMMUNICATIVE COMPETENCE of the participants. To ask such questions is to raise anew the important issue of how much a person's communicative competence can change and grow in adulthood.

But as long as the years from 6 to 16 are years of compulsory education, they assume special importance. In those ten to eleven years, every child in this country must spend 1,000 hours a year (5+ hours per day for 180 days) in formal classrooms, where sanctioning particular kinds of language use is a universally accepted objective. What language is sanctioned – valued or suppressed – will bring both benefits and costs. It will affect the achievement of particular academic goals, the development of particular verbal abilities, and the view the child builds of others and of self.

It is easiest to document the effects of education on the size of a person's vocabulary. Children are prodigious word learners. Estimates of the numbers of words understood by the average 6-year-old at the beginning of school range from 6,000 to 8,000. If we suppose that word learning begins at about 1 year, then preschool children must be learning new words at the rate of three or four per day, or roughly one for every three waking hours. The rate of vocabulary growth slows down, but it continues throughout life, and it is powerfully influenced by education.

A clear picture of this growth comes from a study of mature speakers of French in Montreal, but the results almost certainly apply to mature speakers of English in the USA as well. Hour-long interviews about everyday life were taped with a carefully selected sample of speakers – from 15 to 85 years of age, varying in income, residential area, occupation, and present or past educational attainment. With the aid of computers, the number of different words in each subject's interview was counted, and that number then related to age and socio-economic variables. In the Montreal population represented by this sample,

each person incorporates new words into his productive vocabulary at a slowly decreasing rate over time, but this rate can be magnified up to five times through intensive education . . . any contribution to richness of vocabulary from such socioeconomic factors as residential milieu or occupational status of parent are completely accounted for by the effects of these factors on education attainment. (Sankoff and Lessard 1975: 689)

Vocabulary richness is only the most obvious residue of the thousand hours per year of compulsory education and post-secondary education to which they may lead. Other aspects of language knowledge and ways of speaking will also affect a child's educational progress and be affected by it as well.

Language education

Language education in public schools in the USA means education in the use of English. Some elementary children attend bilingual schools (see Chapter 21); some secondary school children study one or more foreign languages; but all children are taught and evaluated in English.

The development of each student's language abilities is the special responsibility of the Language Arts program in elementary school and the English program in high school. Elementary school teachers typically report devoting 50 percent of their instructional time each day to some aspect of Language Arts in kindergarten through grade 3, and somewhat less in grades 4 – 6. In high schools, students have one daily period for English, usually one-sixth or one-seventh of the school day.

One would expect, simply by definition, that language education should include time for developing competencies in expressing ideas (productive language) as well as understanding the ideas of others (receptive language) and in both oral and written modes. But in actual practice, children's time is spent overwhelmingly in listening and reading.

Language	Oral	Written
Productive	Speaking	Writing
Receptive	Listening	Reading

One reason for this weighting toward receptive language is a matter of the sheer number of students and the limited time that teachers have for teaching them. School classrooms are one of the most crowded human environments; few adults are confined for five or more hours per day in so few square feet per person. Thirty children per classroom can listen simultaneously – mostly to the teacher. But creating a classroom organization in which more than one person can talk at a time takes a courageous teacher and a supportive principal, no matter how common that conversational structure is in adult life – in buses and restaurants, for example.

With the availability of inexpensive audio cassette recorders, many classrooms now have "listening centers." It is important to note how this new technology is being used in traditional ways; the quiet of the classroom need not be broken while the child hears a story via earphones. More productive use – for recording children's stories, or discussions, or their practice in reading aloud – occurs only in exceptional classrooms.

Even though only one person talks at a time, thirty children can write simultaneously. But then teachers need time to read and grade their compositions. According to one study carried out for the California Council of Teachers of English, high school teachers reading a 250-word composition (less than one double-spaced typed page) need an average of 3.5 minutes just to assign a grade, and 8.6 minutes to write comments substantive enough to teach writing and thinking. With a teaching load of at least 125 students (5 classes a day of 25 students each) and one short assigned composition per week, a high school English teacher would need 18 hours of out-of-class time just to react to student papers (Applebee 1978). Another reason for the weighting toward receptive skills is that testing them is so much easier. We return to the influence of tests on language education below.

The particular receptive language abilities stressed in Language Arts programs are learning to read, and learning discrete aspects of language use: handwriting, punctuation, spelling, and knowledge of Standard English grammar. Some instructional time is spent on vocabulary development, but the limitations on opportunities to speak and write mean that productive use in school of newly learned words and meanings is largely confined to workbooks and duplicated worksheets. In high school English classes, the emphasis shifts to literature. A national study of high school English in the late 1960s found that time devoted to literature in grade 10 was approximately twice that of language and composition, and by grade 12 that emphasis increased to almost 3 to 1.

One published Language Arts and English program, Houghton Mifflin's *Interaction* program, is unusual for its integration of speaking, listening, reading, and writing. Conceived in the 1960s on the basis of the best research on language development and language use, and translated into a set of imaginative materials for all grades by the mid-1970s, the program has received widespread professional acclaim but disappointingly low sales.

Social influences

Language education – like all aspects of education in any society – is influenced by larger social forces which impinge on the schools. Of particular importance has been the steady movement toward centralization during the past century. This movement has manifested itself in several ways: a decrease in the number of school districts from 200,000 in 1870 to 17,000 in 1970, and a concomitant increase in the sizes of both districts and individual schools (Pittenger 1977); the mass marketing of standardized tests and of texts produced for a national market; and a concentration of decision making about instructional materials and the allocation of instructional time at higher and higher administrative levels that are farther and farther removed from the classroom.

Children experience these aspects of centralization most directly in the selection of the texts they are assigned to read. Forty-five percent of children go to school in the twenty-two states where public funds can be spent only for books that have been approved, or "adopted," by a single statewide committee. Now that Public Law 94-142 guarantees the rights of all children with special needs to an appropriate education within the public school system, it seems likely that the same requirements for "adoption" and the same pressures for standardization will begin to affect preschool education as well.

But these pressures toward standardization are not the whole story. Over the past two decades, social forces opposing these centralizing and homogenizing influences have also been at work. The Civil Rights movement and its successors such as the Black Power movement have helped to sensitize educators to the importance of language as a medium for cultural self-expression and individual self-concept. Linguistic research in the same period has affirmed the structural integrity of all dialects of English. And in many communities there have been organized expressions of the traditional American belief in the local control of schools.

In this chapter we examine topics about language and education that have been important to the general public, to educators, or to language scholars in the recent past – considered roughly the years from the mid-1960s to the late 1970s. We begin by discussing the Back-to-Basics movement along with standardized testing upon which it leans so heavily. We then examine three conflicts between standardization and cultural pluralism: in the status of nonstandard varieties of English in the classroom; in patterns of classroom interaction; and in controversies about the language and related values in Language Arts texts.

Back-to-Basics and standardized tests

One particular aspect of language in education – the Back-to-Basics movement – dominated the news in 1977; and both its propaganda and its evidence tells as much about American society as it does about what children do or don't learn in school.

The propaganda message is clear. In one week in June, 1977, commencement time around the country, Columbia Broadcasting System (CBS) evening news produced a five-part series called "Trouble in the Classroom." The first "trouble" is the decline in standardized test scores around the country. In the opening words of the CBS newscaster on June 6:

High school graduation day. Proud parents. Relieved students. They've made it at last. But, for the spring class of 1977, does the ceremony symbolize much of anything at all? Increasingly, parents, students and the depressing and irrefutable test scores say no . . . Declining test scores have made headlines all over the country. In New York, since 1966, among ninth graders, reading and math scores declined significantly in both the cities and suburbs. In California, in 1969, in the 12th grade reading test, over half the answers were correct, but, by 1976, substantially more than half the answers were wrong. In Iowa, the combined reading and math scores for 12th grade remained constant from 1965 to 1967, but then they began a decline, which continued through 1976. Everywhere there is outrage.

The overall message is that schools are not doing as well as in some idealized past. And, to make these facts even more alarming, the second "trouble" reported in the series – juxtaposed to create a subliminal sense of a close relationship – is violence.

Apart from such propaganda, evidence on changing language skills over the years is much less clear. In an historical analysis, Daniel and Lauren Resnick compare the literacy standards of seventeenth- to nineteenth- century Europe to the United States today. Whereas reading instruction in past centuries aimed at either a low level of literacy for a large number of people or a high level of literacy for an elite, today our goal is the ability to read new material and glean new information from that material in the population at large. This high and universal criterion is only about three generations old, and according to the Resnicks:

> unless we intend to relinquish the criterion of comprehension as the goal of reading instruction, there is little to go *back* to in terms of pedagogical method, curriculum, or school organization. The old tried-and-true approaches, which nostalgia prompts us to believe might solve current problems, were designed neither to achieve the literacy standard sought today nor to assure successful literacy for everyone. Whatever the rhetoric of the common school, early dropping out and selective promotion were in fact used to escape problems that must now be addressed through a pedagogy adequate to today's aspirations. While we may be able to borrow important ideas and practices from earlier periods, there is no simple past to which we can return. (1977: 385)

But of course, to any parent, change over much shorter periods of time becomes important. According to the media, at least, certain language skills have declined over the past decade. What is the evidence here?

The two largest testing programs are the Scholastic Aptitude Tests (SAT) administered by the College Entrance Examination Board (CEEB), and the National Assessment of Educational Progress (NAEP). The SAT is taken by adolescents heading for college. Verbal questions are of four types: vocabulary items about antonyms and analogies, and reading tests of sentence completion and reading comprehension. Here are practice questions for both types of vocabulary items:

Antonyms (opposites)
BABBLE: (A) irrigation (B) pollution (C) meaningful speech (D) useful object (E) weakness of intellect
Analogies
CHOIR: SINGERS: (A) victory: soldiers (B) class: teacher (C) crowd: protestors (D) challenge: duelists (E) orchestra: musicians

(CEEB 1977)

Across the country, it is true, scores on these SAT verbal subtests declined from an average of 478 in 1963 to 429 in 1977 on a scale of 200-800 points. In other words, only about one-third of the 1977 test-takers did as well as half of their counterparts did fourteen years before (CEEB 1977).

It is easy to dismiss these results as unimportant because the multiple-choice format necessary for machine scoring so restricts the kind of language use being tested; and we have no information about other language skills that may be more stable or even increasing in power and distribution among the same age group. As Rexford Brown, Director of NAEP, said about the SAT numbers at a conference sponsored by the National Institute of Education in the same month as the CBS news special, "The most we can say about the verbal test score declines is that language use is changing (which is not surprising) away from a standard implicit in existing multiple choice tests" (Brown 1981). The CEEB says its tests have not been made harder. But the sample of words included in the tests may not be as representative of what young people know today as it was in the past. Young people may know as many words as they did, but their knowledge may be less adequately sampled. Since we lack information about changing frequencies of word use in speech and writing, there is no way to check the representative validity of the CEEB word sample.

It is harder to dismiss the data from the NAEP's own periodic testing, both because the population from which their sample is drawn is all Americans of a particular age – out of school as well as in; and because their test of writing requires actual compositions. In 1969 and again in 1973, a national sample of 9-, 13- and 17-year-olds was asked to write for a wide variety of demands such as a thank-you note, ordering a kite through the mails, a job application, a response to music, an imaginative role-play, or an organized report. When essays written in 1969 were mixed with those in 1973 on the same topic, experienced English teachers judged the 1969 essays of the 13- and 17-year-olds to be superior. Subsequent analyses of discrete features of the compositions showed that what had changed in the four years was not compliance with the conventions of usage, spelling, or punctuation, but qualities of coherence that transcend those details (Brown 1980).

The most ambitious attempt to understand what may be causing these test score declines is the report of the Advisory Panel on the Scholastic Aptitude Test Score decline, *On Further Examination* (CEEB 1977). Especially interesting are the research studies commissioned by the Panel. Their report can be interpreted not just as possible causes of a shift in one particular kind of language indicator (the declining scores), but more broadly as glimpses of changing patterns of language use in some domains of American life.

According to the CEEB analyses, the drop in scores in the first half of these fourteen years, from 1963 to 1970, can be explained by an expansion of the test-taking group to more students from low income families and ethnic minorities who have always scored below average on such tests. While cultural bias in particular test items may explain part of these subgroup differences, it cannot be the whole story. As long as ability to answer these kinds of verbal questions predicts success in college, we need to understand why such skills are unequally distributed among certain subgroups of young people, and what can be done to change that distribution. Denying all importance to the test results can only aid those already at the top.

Expansion of the test-taking group stopped in 1970, and the CEEB sought explanations of the continuing decline through the 1970s in more pervasive factors influencing these particular language skills in school and society. One school influence is the level of difficulty, or "challenge," of school textbooks. It is reasonable that both the readability levels (SYNTACTIC complexity and vocabulary difficulty) of the texts, and the cognitive complexity of workbook questions, would influence the development of particular linguistic skills tested by the SAT. In one study commissioned by the CEEB, Jeanne Chall obtained 1st, 6th, and 11th grade texts published over the thirty-year period 1947–1977, and analyzed trends on the readability measures. She found compelling evidence of a positive relationship between the level of challenge of textbooks used by pupils and the scores they achieved on the SAT verbal tests. Pupils from the low score years had read easier books. The relationship was strongest for the early elementary books, presumably because older students read more widely in books of their own choice. Chall also noted a particularly low level of challenge in writing. Textbook assignments call for underlining, circling, and filling in single words. Few assignments ask students to write a paragraph, story, letter, or theme (CEEB 1977).

A pervasive influence outside of school is television. In a review commissioned for CEEB, Wilbur Schramm concluded that in the fourteen years before children take the SATs, they spend an average of three hours a day watching television, more time than is spent on any other activity except sleep. According to research that Schramm reviewed, children who watch more television go to bed later, are less likely to be read to by their mothers before they learn to read, and spend less time reading themselves once they have learned to read; although television may contribute some vocabulary knowledge and specific information, especially in the elementary years, higher-than-average amount of television watching is associated with lower-than-average school performance. Unfortunately, it is hard to evaluate the importance of such statements, because we know so little about the language children hear from the television set, or how family conversation is affected when the set is turned on.

Not all studies of changes in children's reading skills over the years report a decline. A study of the 1976 reading achievement of 8,000 6th graders and 8,000 10th graders in Indiana found that they did as well as their counterparts had done on exactly the same test in 1944. Because the dropout rate is less now than it was thirty-four years ago, the 1944–45 sophomores included proportionately fewer who might have scored poorly on the test, and therefore the record of the 10th graders in 1976 actually showed an improvement (*New York Times,* April 17, 1978).

However one evaluates this evidence on trends in the reading and writing skills of school-age Americans, we must be concerned about the rush to testing as a solution to educational problems, and concerned as well about what the testing frenzy says about our society. The latest manifestation of this frenzy is the competency testing movement. As of February, 1978, forty of forty-six states responding to a survey were doing something about competency tests for high school graduation – either already giving them, constructing them, or planning to do so (Chall 1978). A national competency examination for high school graduation has even been proposed, but such a departure from the traditional American control of education at state and local levels was "overwhelmingly rejected" at an invitational conference sponsored by the U.S. Department of Health, Education, and Welfare in March, 1978 (*New York Times*, 5 March 1978).

Not only the students are being tested. In at least one city, Dallas (the nation's eighth largest urban school district), all 535 first-year teachers had to take a mental ability examination, and half of them "failed": "After the Dallas Times Herald obtained a copy of the scores, which showed that administrators who took the test did even worse than the teachers and that both groups did worse than a sample of high school students at a private school in affluent North Dallas, the district released the results" (*New York Times*, 23 March, 1978).

Some of the pressures for more and more tests undoubtedly come from real dissatisfactions with the results of the schools and from sincere desires to find some way to make them more accountable for preparing people with the literacy skills needed in adult life. But while tests can point to the existence of educational problems, they cannot solve them. As Chall asks, "Is it possible that these new competency tests can accomplish what the years of standardized achievement testing have not?" (CEEB 1977).

Even more worrisome is the danger that the pressures exerted by the tests and the media propaganda about them will make schools less effective rather than more. The pressures will almost certainly reinforce the view that language can be developed as a set of discrete, measurable subskills ready for assembly and integration at some later time. They will almost certainly aggravate the already serious imbalance between means and ends – an imbalance between too much attention to drill on the component skills of language and literacy and too little attention to their significant use.

As an example of this imbalance, here are the findings of an independent review committee of the K-12 English and Language Arts program in a suburban school system in Massachusetts, finished and presented to the community in March, 1977. The following summary is one of the committee's major observations:

Although the guidelines for language arts stress developing basic communication skills through regular and meaningful use, isolated and extensive practice in discrete "basic skills" currently pervades the schools from the first grade to the last. Responding to real or imagined community pressures, able and conscientious teachers are providing abundant practice in aspects of grammar, spelling, punctuation and capitalization, and the conventions of language usage. To a considerable extent, these are dead-end assignments, leading nowhere. The tools are taught, but in an isolated and fragmented manner. Handwriting, spelling and composition are taught in separate, relatively brief time blocks and these tools are too rarely used particularly in the content areas of math, science, and social studies. Observers did report an occasional exception; for example, a stimulating fifth grade classroom where children were reading and responding to literature, writing observations from science, and composing imaginary travel accounts, and skills were taught in the context of applied use.

Our strong impression – from our own recent teaching experience in California and Pennsylvania, and from reports of teachers and parents around the country – is that the review committee's report on that one school system in Massachusetts applies to most of the elementary schools in the USA today. (One parent in Minnesota actually kept and counted the duplicated worksheets done by his child in first grade in 1977–8: 865, or five per day.) Responding to real or imagined community pressures, able and conscientious teachers all over the country are providing abundant practice in discrete measurable basic skills; while classrooms where children are integrating those skills in the service of exciting speaking, listening, reading, and writing activities are rare exceptions.

Such a fragmented approach to teaching is to be expected when teachers must work in an environment where children's learning and their own competence in teaching is judged by performance on standardized tests. Though teachers are increasingly being made aware of the complexities of language and cognitive development, they cannot afford the time to teach language in an integrated manner for fear of being accused of ignoring the subskills if test scores are low. In the teaching of reading, this dilemma is aptly captured in a comment by Lillian Weber, a veteran educational innovator in the New York City public schools:

New York is in the grip of a kind of schizophrenia. While we find an increase in understanding about the multi-stranded way in which children enter into reading, we find an equal increase in pressure for the sort of extremely segmented, detailed program that gives some sort of safety in a sequential approach to learning. (reported in Kohn 1978:19)

Writing is a particularly acute example of the contradictions between ends and means. The Back-to-Basics propaganda blames the schools because "Johnny can't write," but education supply companies report that sales to schools of lined composition paper are down, while sales of duplicating paper used for short answers continue to rise. Moreover, if writing is an "endangered species," in Donald Graves' words, it is endangered outside of school as well as in. Americans are writing fewer personal letters and the U.S. Postal service estimates an even lower volume in the years ahead (Graves 1978b).

In recognition that the content of standardized tests does exert an influence back on the curriculum, the CEEB decided in 1977 to include a twenty-minute essay in college entrance achievement tests. The essay had been included from 1963 through 1971, then eliminated because it cost $500,000 to score and contributed little to the predictive value of the overall test scores. Now it is being reinstituted as a way of validating, to teachers and the public alike, the importance of writing in our society – at least in school.

If tests have become the most important symbolic validation of the expenditure of instructional time, it is tempting to suggest that oral language be included in

Table 20.1

Competency	Application Examples		
	Occupational	Citizenship	Maintenance
Listen effectively to oral English	Understand directions given by job supervisor	Understand directions to a jury from a judge	Understand a doctor's directions for taking prescribed medication
Perform social rituals appropriately	Greet customers appropriately	Request an appointment with a public official	Introduce strangers to one another

evaluation programs; maybe that would exert pressure for more attention to productive language skills. The difficulties with such an assessment are many and severe, but some attempts are being made. In California, since 1975, schools receiving state money for early childhood programs must include an oral language component along with reading and mathematics, and must evaluate growth in oral language as well.

Two California school districts provide contrasting examples of how this is being done. District A has a "language continuum" on which each classroom teacher checks the appropriate skills observed in the classroom performance of each student. The continuum has twenty-one *receptive items* (from "Points in the direction of the source of a sound" through "Interprets material through dramatic play, role playing, or pantomime") and fifty *productive items* (from "Expresses needs and wants verbally" through "Gives oral reports"). District B focuses on "speaking relevantly." Each teacher conducts an activity such as a class meeting or creative dramatics while the aide observes and records. During the first ten minutes, all of each child's reponses are rated as relevant, irrelevant, nonparticipant, or goofing off.

Nationally, as part of the current movement to specify minimum competencies that all students should possess upon graduation from high school, the Educational Policies Board of the Speech Communication Association established a Task Force in 1977 to redress the neglect of oral language and formulate a list of minimal speaking and listening competencies for high school graduates (Bassett, Whittington, and Staton-Spicer n.d.). From a comprehensive search through published literature and curriculum guides from all fifty states, they arrived at a list of twenty competencies. According to the Task Force, each is "functional" – actually needed in adult life; "educational" – appropriate for school instruction; "general" – needed by persons in all subcultures in the nation; and important in occupational, citizenship, and personal ("maintenance") life. All twenty competencies "are basic to two-person interactions (face to face or via telephone), small group discussions, as well as public speaking situations. In addition, the listening skills also are applicable to messages from radio, television and motion pictures.'' The first and last of the twenty competencies, with ''application examples'' for each, are given in Table 20.1. Realistic and important as such competencies are, we wonder how they could ever be evaluated on a mass scale. If ways were found to assess them, it would be unfair to do so unless they were actually taught in the schools. This seems unlikely. As Roger Shuy points out, students get little chance to practice even a competency so basic to the acquisition of knowledge as ''seeking clarification'':

> It has been often lamented that children are so busy answering questions that they do not get adequate opportunity to ask them. This is particularly strange in the context of learning, where the learner might be thought to be the seeker after knowledge, the one who has unanswered questions which desperately need answers . . .
>
> The traditional education framework calls more for teachers seeking clarification about what students know than for students to seek clarification about what they, themselves, are trying to learn. (Shuy 1978)

The full implication of the narrowly technical Back-to-Basics movement is apparent when we realize that it is the only significant precollege curriculum movement in any subject area in the USA today. When Elizabeth C. Wilson looks back on twenty years as Director of Curriculum for the suburban school system of Montgomery County, Maryland, she writes:

> At present writing, there is no question that the educational management experts and the cult of efficiency are again in the ascendance. Accountability, management by objectives, action plans, performance objectives and evaluation of students, teachers and administrators are today's watchwords. So, also, is the development and delivery of computer managed instruction in, first, the basic skills, and then, all other subjects . . . As a society, we have lost a vision about what education ought to be. (quoted in Kohn 1977: 19)

As with the problem of violence to which CBS news linked the declining test scores, we are asked to accept law-and-order solutions. Societal factors influence not only the conditions which education is supposed to correct, but also the particular forms that educational solutions take. In a society such as the USA today, with no viable plans for eliminating either inequality or unemployment, it is tragic but not surprising that subcultural differences in language skills important in education continue to exist, and that more effort is put into tests for selecting those who have those skills than into finding ways to teach those who don't.

Standard English versus dialect differences

In 1974, an exhibit of Native American children's art was shown around the country. Among the strikingly beautiful drawings and paintings, a few pieces of writing were also displayed. One of those writings, by an Apache child in Arizona, can speak for many children:

Have you ever hurt
   about baskets?
I have, seeing my grandmother weaving
   for a long time.
Have you ever hurt about work?
I have, because my father works too hard
   and he tells how he works.
Have you ever hurt about cattle?
I have, because my grandfather has been working
   on the cattle for a long time.
Have you ever hurt about school?
I have, because I learned a lot of words
   from school,
And they are not my words.

As we have seen, students of all ages do learn words in school. But all too often, this happens in situations where their own ways of speaking are denigrated and put down.

No language is spoken in exactly the same way by all its speakers. One controversy over the principles by which language varieties – or DIALECTS – are admitted or excluded in school is whether books written in nonstandard English should be used for beginning reading instruction. Arguments for the use of such materials are moral, scientific, and instrumental. Morally, there is the right of any people to use of their particular language variety in school. Scientifically, the descriptive linguistic research by William Labov, Roger Shuy, Walt Wolfram, and others has documented in great detail the rule-governed nature of all varieties of English; and no one has found a shred of evidence for any intrinsic relationship between dialect differences in language forms and the roles of language in learning and thinking. Instrumentally, starting where the children are, in this case with their own speech patterns, may be the most effective starting place for leading them where the schools want them to go.

Because Black children are the largest group of speakers of a particular dialect of English, research on dialect differences has concentrated on this group and is only now extending to others (e.g. Wolfram and Christian (1976) on speech patterns in Appalachia). Because there is a more complete story to tell, we concentrate on this group here too.

In the recent past, the first books for children in Black English were produced during the summer of 1965 by one of the first Head Start programs in the country, the Child Development Group of Mississippi (CDGM). The books were transcriptions of stories told by preschool children in the Head Start centers. For example:

Pond

If a toad hop up on you and wet on you
It make a big blister on your feet.

(from Mt. Peel, Mississippi)

Today

We supposed to take a nap but we reading instead.
My Daddy he helping make a kitchen in the schoolhouse.

(from Holly Springs, Mississippi)

During the prolonged and bitter fight for federal refunding of CDGM the following year, Senators Eastland and Stennis attacked it on the Senate Floor. In the account of that fight, the *New York Times* reported:

The attack was broadened to include the qualifications of the group's school teachers and its educational materials. One book, designed to teach children to read by retelling their own stories in their own language, was criticized because it included a line that read, "My dog eat meat." (March 7, 1977)

When the omission of a verb ending in a sentence of a 4-year-old child in rural Mississippi reaches the halls of Congress, we realize how controversy over an intellectually innocuous difference in language forms reflects, while it masks, conflicts over social power.

Three years later, during 1969, two sets of elementary school readers written in nonstandard dialect became more widely available – one produced by the Education Study Center in Washington DC, and the other by the Chicago Board of Education. Attitudes toward such materials, and toward Black dialect itself, have been mixed, especially within the Black community.

These different attitudes were expressed in interviews that two Black colleagues, Betty Bryant and Melissa Tillman, conducted with community leaders, preschool teachers, and parents in the Black community in Boston in 1969. The community leaders were the most positive in their attitudes toward Black English, and the most resentful that it is always Black people who have to change: "survival" means not only economic survival in White-dominated society, but also psychological survival as a people; language for intragroup solidarity, for "going home," is as important as language for "making it." And the myth that language education is the way out was not only questioned but rejected: control over one's life is critical; language programs without that control are at best false hopes, and at worst another kind of racism.

The teachers expressed more conflict about language: maybe it's an illusion that survival in the White community requires Standard English, maybe we should be paying more attention to language for thinking and for creativity.

The parents' views were clear: whether they rejected Black English because it originated in the slave experience or appreciated it for its power of expression, they felt it had no place in school. They acknowledged that "most of us have two faces," but since children will learn to speak Black English at home anyway, it is the job of the school to teach in, and to teach, Standard English (Cazden, Bryant, and Tillman 1972).

A more recent and more systematic study of the attitudes of Black parents toward Black English in East Palo Alto and Oakland, California confirms the Boston picture. The California parents valued Black English for purposes of group solidarity and the preservation of Black culture. But especially those parents who did not themselves speak Standard English depended on the schools to help their children learn it, and rejected, as inappropriate for school use, books such as *I be scared of the dark* in Chicago's Psycholinguistic Reading Series. Mary Hoover, who conducted the study, concluded that these parents are not suffering from linguistic "self-hatred," as some observers have claimed, but rather that they express accurate sociolinguistic knowledge of relationships between particular language forms and the situation – oral and written – in which they are appropriate (Hoover 1978).

Where feelings among Black parents are this firm, it is not surprising that attempts to use texts written in dialect have encountered opposition, for instance in Philadelphia where the Educational Study Center readers were introduced. And when research failed to show that such materials help Black children achieve the goal of literacy in Standard English, it became even harder to convince parents of the value of their use.

The concept of what can be called "transitional bidialectal education" has not disappeared. In 1977, Houghton Mifflin published a set of readers called *Bridge: a cross-culture reading program* for junior and senior high school students. Written by three Black educators, Gary and Charlesetta Simpkins and Grace Holt, it contains stories in three versions. Here are the opening sentences of one story, "A Friend in Need," in each version:

Black Vernacular

No matter what neighborhood you be in – Black, White, or whatever – young dudes gonna be having they wheels . . . You know how Brothers be with they wheels. They definitely be keeping them looking clean, clean, clean.

Transition form

No matter what neighborhood you look at – Black, White, rich or poor – if you find teenagers, you find old cars . . . They love they cars. They spend most of their time taking care of them.

Standard English

Young guys, Black or White, love their cars. They must have a car, no matter how old it is. James Russell . . . spent a great deal of time keeping his car clean. He was always washing and waxing it.

Even the directions for workbook exercises are written in dialect: "Go for what you know about the story . . . Check out each sentence down below. There ain't but one right answer to each question, so don't be picking out two." Interviewed in the *Boston Globe,* Gary Simpkins explained that "We try to provide kids with a code-switching ability" by starting with language familiar to them. It is too early to know how these readers for older students will be accepted, or how effective they will be.

The implications of dialect differences for education are not limited to questions about the language of texts for beginning readers. Linguists participated in the formulation of a language policy for the television reading show for children aged 7 to 10 years, *The Electric Company*, which went on the air in the fall of 1971. One decision faced by Children's Television Workshop (CTW) in planning that show was which varieties of English should be used on the air, and its decision became important because of the national visibility and audibility of the results.

Should nonstandard English ever be heard or appear in writing? If so, how should it be spelled? No issue aroused more debate in CTW planning meetings and no aspect of the show stimulated more mail once *The Electric Company* went on the air. Samuel Gibbon, producer of the show, explained:

When we speak of dialect, it's important to distinguish between accented speech and real dialectal differences in syntax. As far as accents are concerned, we want children who speak with various regional or ethnic accents to understand that the correspondence of printed symbol to speech sound holds true equally well for their pronunciation as for so-called ''standard network English'' pronunciation. We will, therefore, include in the program segments in which a single word is pronounced with a variety of accents.

The more difficult question is how to deal with the syntactic differences between standard English and the non-standard dialect variants, such as what some linguists have come to call Black English. ''The Electric Company'' curriculum is based on the premise that printed language is simply an encoding into a graphic form of the spoken language system the child has already mastered . . . Our advisors have recommended that it would be useful to the non-standard-English-speaking child to reinforce his confidence in the printed code by occasionally showing him that his own speech patterns can be encoded in print.

In showing non-standard English in print on the program, we will observe several guidelines. First, we will never misspell words in English in order to reflect accent. Only correctly spelled English words will appear. Second, presentation of dialect speech in print will be limited to dramatic situations in which that speech is appropriate.

On *The Electric Company*, written language is read out loud in a wide range of accents; colloquial (or ''hip'') vocabulary is often seen in print, for instance ''Dig my sharp, shiny shoes'' in a segment on *sh*; and non-standard syntax is heard, for instance in the spoken punch line to one segment on silent *e*, ''I have known me a lot of dudes who was duds.''

The goal of the show is to help children read Standard English. The position on varieties of speech patterns was taken in order to make the show as relevant as possible to the children its producers hoped to help. It was also taken to avoid penalizing children for nonstandard pronunciation in oral reading, which teachers often misinterpret as lack of comprehension.

The most serious implication of dialect differences for education is the danger that teachers, who have themselves grown up in a racially segregated and stratified society, will interpret differences in speech patterns as differences in underlying intelligence and educability. Evidence has accumulated (e.g. Shuy and Fasold 1973) that the education of Black children is affected indirectly but powerfully by the effects of their nonstandard speech on the expectations about their intellectual capabilities that teachers build up. Efforts to counter these impressions have been widespread – in courses on language for prospective teachers and speech therapists, and through in-service workshops on language variation in many school systems, especially those such as Louisville, Kentucky which are in the process of desegregation.

We don't know what the effects of these efforts have been. At least on the surface, progress has been made. It would be unthinkable today to find in the *New York Times* a full-page advertisment such as appeared in December, 1968 (for the *National Observer*): a primary-age Black girl seated at a school desk, hand raised to say "De chirren trawl to de scream ta see de frinly snail." And at the bottom of the page: "Translation: 'The children crawled down to the stream to see the friendly snail.' An example of the speech problems that make learning difficult for rural school children."

Roger Shuy, a linguist who has conducted many workshops for teachers through the Center for Applied Linguistics in Washington, DC, finds hopeful signs of more subtle changes as well. In an article on "The study of vernacular Black English as a factor in educational change" (1973), he suggests that greater sensitivity to language differences has led to more natural language in reading books for children, more widespread understanding that a child's translation of a reading book into dialect does not represent a reading problem, and some realization that learning to speak Standard English is not necessary for learning to read. In his view, one other important role of dialect studies is that:

Social dialect has provided a physical, observable focus for an issue which might otherwise be too abstract to be observed. It has been difficult, for example, to identify aspects of Black culture which are agreed upon by authorities and are clearly distinguishable from non-Black culture. Since Vernacular Black English has both qualitative and quantitative differences from other varieties, it provides a more physical focus. With such a focus, many questions of group identity, cultural pluralism and style can be clearly addressed in the classroom. (1973: 303–4)

Patterns of classroom interaction

Language is not only the direct object of curriculum goals in Language Arts and English. It is also the medium through which children learn all other subjects in the school curriculum, and through which teachers evaluate their learning. In this sense, there is not only language education, but language *in* education. But these two relationships between languages and education seem more separate in the classroom than in their effects. To use vocabulary as an example once more, it is likely that the effect of school on vocabulary growth is far more an indirect result of the reading, writing, talking, and listening that students do across the curriculum than of whatever vocabulary is taught explicitly in a block of time labeled Language Arts or English.

In the other direction, it is likely that the demands for particular language competencies will affect children's educational achievement as much in social studies or science as in Language Arts or English itself. It is important, therefore, to look at what the patterns of language use in classrooms actually are. The picture that follows of distinctive features of classroom talk is put together from historical surveys, reviews of research, and a detailed description of life in one classroom.

Talk in school, like talk in families, takes many forms. But there is usually one speech event which is considered by participants as the "heart" of the life of the institution. In many families, the heart would be the gathering at meals, in dining room or kitchen. In most American public school classrooms, the heart is what is variously called a "recitation" or a "lesson." These lessons have been described by many observers over the past fifty years, and the descriptions are remarkably similar: the teacher leads and controls the talk on a particular topic with an entire class of twenty-five to thirty students or some subgroup of the class; the students are usually seated at their desks in rows, though more informal arrangements of chairs in a circle, or of primary grade children on the floor at the teacher's feet, can be found. Teachers talk about two thirds of the total time, primarily asking and evaluating questions that require factual answers from individual students. The questions are predominantly "test" questions to which the teacher already knows the answer:

Ordinary conversation
Speaker 1: Can you tell me the time?
Speaker 2: Half-past ten.
Speaker 1: Thanks.

Lesson talk
Teacher: Can you tell me the time?
Student: Half-past ten.
Teacher: Right!

Only a brief time is allowed for a student to answer; and students are rarely encouraged, or even allowed, to comment on another student's talk.

Because this lesson structure is familiar to many of us from our own past experience, it may not be obvious that it is not the only structure possible. Children could answer the teacher's questions in chorus rather than individually; their responses could consist of memorized passages rather than statements of remembered facts; children could leave their seats and be questioned individually and privately at the teacher's desk rather than publicly in a group of their peers. There must be situational as well as historical reasons why this lesson structure has been so stable in this country over the past half-century (Hoetker and Ahlbrand, Jr. 1969). In some respects, this lesson structure is different from all children's conversational experience outside of school; in other respects, it poses aggravated problems for children from particular cultural backgrounds.

For all children, the rules for taking turns, for "getting the floor," are different from family talk, partly just because of the size of the group. Children have to learn not only what to say in school but how and when to say it. INTERACTIONAL COMPETENCE, as well as substantive knowledge, is necessary for school success. Hugh Mehan (1979) has done a detailed analysis of the turn-allocation procedures in one inner-city primary-grade classroom. While they may differ in details from procedures in other classrooms, his analysis shows the kinds of interactional skills that all children have to learn.

In this classroom, students were selected to answer the teacher's questions in one of three ways, which he calls INDIVIDUAL NOMINATION, INVITATION TO BID, and INVITATION TO REPLY:

Individual nomination

T. Patricia, does jelly begin like Sabrina or like Jerome?

The next turn to talk is allocated only to Patricia no matter how many other children know the test question answer.

Invitation to bid

T. Raise your hand if you know where Leola's house would go on this map.

Students must raise their hands and wait for an individual nomination.

Invitation to reply

T. I called the tractor a mmm . . .

More than one student at a time can reply, without being named or getting the floor by bidding.

It is obvious from this description that getting the floor and avoiding reprimands for talking "out of turn" is much more complicated than remembering "not to interrupt," or remembering to "raise your hands." But only the latter rules are taught to the children explicitly; the more complicated system that is actually in operation they have to pick up for themselves.

"Test" questions are one feature of classroom lessons with which some children have more out-of-school experience than others. In some families, they are common. Imagine a typical story-reading scene: young child on mother's lap or next to her on the sofa, with mother making conversation by asking many questions such as "What animal is this? And what color is he?" etc., etc. To the participants, it doesn't seem like interrogation; children and parents alike get pleasure from demonstrations of what the child has learned. But because of differential experience with such question-and-answer sequences, children come to school differentially prepared to participate in classroom lessons.

The competitive and public performance required in these lessons also poses a problem for children from some cultural backgrounds. Susan Philips (1972) was the first to document this source of interference for Native American children on the Warm Springs reservation in Oregon. She found that in social gatherings at home on the reservation, each individual decides the form and time of participation for himself, and there is no leader who has the right to compel the participation of one person in the presence of others. When they fail to "speak up" in Anglo-style classrooms, the Native American children are termed "silent" or "shy." The same problem has since been observed in schools for other Native American children in Canada and Alaska by Frederick Erickson and his students.

There is less descriptive research on Hispanic interactional styles, but a 1972 report of the U.S. Commission on Civil Rights Mexican American study suggests that a conflict between their ways of speaking and the school's may exist for members of that ethnic minority as well. They reported observations of teacher-student interaction in nearly 500 English-speaking elementary and secondary classrooms in Southwestern United States. In these classrooms, teachers praised or encouraged Anglos 35 percent more than they did Chicanos, accepted or used Anglos' ideas 40 percent more than they did those of Chicanos, and directed 21 percent more questions to Anglos than to Chicanos. And this in classrooms which had been selected from only those schools with no previous record of civil rights violations or investigations, and in which teachers were aware that an observer from a federal civil rights agency was present. It is easy to conclude that the teachers were discriminatory in their distribution of questions, or that the Chicano students knew fewer of the answers. More likely, the problem lies with neither group alone, but with cultural differences in interactional styles.

These differences have not yet received the attention from researchers or teachers that dialect differences have received. In the fall of 1965, just after the first summer of Head Start when the booklets in Black English were produced by the Child Development Group of Mississippi, a group of scholars – anthropologists, linguists and psychologists – was assembled by the U.S. Office of Education to discuss priorities in research on children's language and its relationship to school success. Although Chomsky's transformational grammar was then in the ascendancy, and research on language was almost exclusively focused on language structure, these scholars looked beyond structural features of language and dialect to questions about how children use language in particular social settings. They believed that school problems could be better explained by problems in language use than in language structure, and called for such research, particularly in classrooms and communities of children from low income families and ethnic minority communities. But Philips' study on the Warm Springs reservation is still one of the few home-school comparisons, and official recognition that more than language is involved in establishing conditions for equality of educational opportunity has come only recently, through the movement for BILINGUAL/bicultural EDUCATION.

In 1975, the Office of Civil Rights of the U.S. Department of Health, Education, and Welfare (HEW) published the document known as the "Lau Guidelines," specifying how school systems could comply with the Supreme Court decision in LAU v. NICHOLS in San Francisco. The second guideline states that "the determination of which teaching style(s) are to be used . . . should include an assessment of the responsiveness of students to different types of cognitive learning styles and incentive motivational styles." The goal is education that is responsive to cultural as well as linguistic differences among children. And these cultural differences are acknowledged to include differences in the interactional contexts in which people prefer to learn and to demonstrate what they have learned in some kind of performance. Even for the objective of helping minority students to learn the ways of speaking of the dominant culture, it seems likely that some transitional but more culturally responsive forms of classroom organization would help.

Pressures for decentralization and local control of schools have brought some schools at least partially under indigenous control, most often in the schools on Indian reservations run by a tribe under contract with the Bureau of Indian Affairs. In some instances, Native American teachers have organized their classrooms in more culturally appropriate ways, so that their questions and especially their evaluations are directed to children only in private. But forces pressing toward standardization, such as the training and professionalization of teachers, may militate against nonstandard interaction patterns even there.

Controversies over multicultural texts

The goals of Language Arts and English education have always included the humanizing influence of the intensifications of experience provided by literature. This humanizing effect can be accomplished most effectively for all children if the literary selections include writings by and about diverse peoples.

Progress toward such diversity has been slow. One recent study found that the Black characters in children's trade books more than doubled between 1965 and 1976, but 86 percent of these books still depict an all White world (Chall, Radwin, French, and Hall 1979). We know of no comparable comparison of textbooks, but pressures against racism and sexism have been stronger on textbook publishers, and newer texts do include a greater diversity of characters, cultures, and language varieties. The availability of paperback books has further increased the diversity of reading material available in classrooms.

But such changes toward a more pluralistic view of American life sometimes erupt into controversy. A nationally publicized controversy occurred in 1974 in Kanawha County, West Virginia, over the selection of Language Arts texts. But this was not an isolated incident. In two states where we regularly read local newspapers, Massachusetts and Maine, protests over the content of books assigned in school took place in 1977. Because the West Virginia story is the best documented, it raises the most important questions, and we therefore briefly report the New England incidents first.

In Chelsea, Massachusetts, a working class city of 30,000 northeast of Boston, the focus of controversy was a seventy-seven word poem by a 15-year-old New York girl that was included in a paperback anthology. "The city to a young girl" expresses in explicit street terms the anger the author felt toward men who treat women as sexual objects. When the Chelsea School Committee banned the poem as obscene, a Right to Read Committee of librarians, teachers, students, and parents plus the Massachusetts Library Association filed a class-action suit. In an editorial critical of the School Committee's action, *The Boston Globe* (August 2, 1977) pointed out the irony of banning a poem that was itself a complaint against oppressive patterns of language use.

In Maine, protests in at least eight towns attacked numerous books assigned in high school English classes. The books objected to are on what the American Library Association calls its "Titles Now Troublesome" list – books as new as *One Flew Over the Cuckoo's Nest* and as old as *The Grapes of Wrath*. Parents objected to explicit descriptions of sexual activity and the use of four-letter words, but the *Maine Times* (July 15, 1977) commented that "the offending books are only symbols of what some parents perceive as the abdication by schools of their role in upholding traditional moral standards." And Father St. Pierre from Lisbon Falls, Maine, is quoted as saying that the controversy is really not about books but about control – between those who feel they have some control over their lives and those who don't.

Kanawha County, West Virginia, includes the state capital, Charleston, but is otherwise largely rural Appalachian in culture. In 1974, the school board, the curriculum advisory council they appointed, and the top professional educators all represented the more educated, middle class urban population. And a county-wide consolidation of schools in which more than fifty schools had been closed in the ten years between 1964 and 1974 produced increasingly centralized bureaucratic control. In the face of overwhelming control of educational policies beyond the local community, the rural people fought for what they saw as a threat to their children and their communities in a battle over words in books.

In the spring of 1974, English Language Arts texts were selected by a committee of professional educators, in accordance with state curriculum guidelines requiring the selection of books "which depict and illustrate the intercultural character of our pluralistic society." A year-long protest ensued over two of the series selected: *Communicating* (grades 1–6) published by D.C. Heath, and *Interaction* (grades 4–12) published by Houghton Mifflin. The protest was both about the parents' right to participate in textbook selection and about particular writings in the books the professionals had chosen. Objections were made to writings by Eldridge Cleaver, Langston Hughes, and Malcolm X, among others; to the inclusion of Bible stories as "myths"; and to suggested assignments that would bring personal experience and home lives into the classroom. At the opening of school in September, 1974, a school boycott was organized and 4,500 coal miners in Kanawha and neighboring counties walked out of the mines in sympathy. Violence broke out, and disruptions in the schools and communities continued throughout the 1974–75 school year. In the final resolution, the disputed texts were removed from the classrooms, and the goals of Language Arts and English were narrowed to an emphasis on skills (Candor 1976).

While national right-wing groups entered Kanawha County in support of the protesters, the local movement had other roots. And while it ended up reinforcing a Back-to-Basics curriculum, different motivations sent it there. Protests against literature selections in New England and West Virginia are related to the Back-to-Basics movement in two quite different ways. Both the Back-to-Basics movement and the would-be censors seek a solution to social problems in a return to an idealized past. Perceptions of inadequate linguistic skills, of loss of control over school curriculum, and of a disintegration of shared values are social facts. Reactions to these fears build an educational policy on a sense of loss of a better past that can somehow be recaptured. But in another way, the protests converge with the Back-to-Basics movement not in ends but in means. In seeking to conserve the values of small, rural communities from what is seen as the contamination of urban wickedness, the protesters ask the schools to stick to basic skills and leave their values alone.

The protests relate to the issues of cultural differences in language forms and interactional styles in another respect. All involve a conflict between an increasingly standardized institution and more local, indigenous norms and values. Ironically, Kanawha County has its own radical labor history. But those local roots of social criticism are not represented in the nationally compiled texts. For example, there is no mention in these books of "Mother" Mary Jones – a woman born in Ireland in 1830 who became a charismatic labor organizer in West Virginia's bituminous coal fields.

We do not know whether giving an honored place to Mother Jones in Appalachian schools would make the words of other people's leaders like Eldridge Cleaver or Malcolm X more understandable. But these controversies force us to realize that true cultural pluralism cannot be standardized and legislated from the top down. It must be grounded in the self-respect accorded to very particular ways of speaking and relating. From that base, it might be possible to build bridges of understanding and respect for the particular ways of other communities, far as well as near.

FURTHER READING

The literature on language in education is so large that these suggestions are extremely selective and, even together, do not constitute a comprehensive view.

Of texts for teachers on Language Arts and English, Moffett and Wagner 1976 is well supported by language acquisition research. Shaughnessy 1977 presents a sympathetic analysis of the "basic writing" problems of the first years of open admission students at the City University of New York. Graves 1978a provides an assessment of the effect of Back-to-Basics on writing. Houts 1977 contains articles on standardized achievement and IQ tests that were originally published in *The National Elementary Principal*.

Burling 1973 is a good entry to the literature on nonstandard dialects of English. Mehan 1979 is a detailed case study of the lessons in one inner-city primary school, and Cazden, John, and Hymes 1972 includes descriptions of cultural differences in the communicative competencies students bring and the demands teachers make. For further discussion of the Kanawha County textbook controversy, see Hillocks 1978 and the reply by Dawkins 1978, an author of one of the controversial series. Nelkin 1977 and Fitz-Gerald 1979 give more general discussions of textbooks, and decisions about them, as issues of educational policy.

Although this chapter is about language in education in the USA, we have much to learn from the British experience. *A Language for Life* (1975) is the report of an official governmental committee of inquiry into all aspects of language in education. Stubbs 1976 is a broad and readable introduction to sociolinguistic perspectives on classroom language. Mathieson 1975 is an excellent historical and sociological study of "English and its teachers," which unfortunately still has no parallel in the USA.

21

Bilingualism and education

CHRISTINA BRATT PAULSTON

BILINGUALISM is a very old and common phenomenon in the world. Our neighbors in Canada and in Mexico have always been aware that theirs are bi/ multilingual nations, and indeed the writings from the time of the very early Spanish explorers comment on the many languages they found in Mexico and on some of the resultant problems. But it seems that it is only recently that we in the United States have become aware at the national level that we are also a multilingual nation. It was particularly federal legislation instituting BILINGUAL EDUCATION (BE) which brought about this awareness.

Many children across the country now go to school in two languages, usually in their MOTHER TONGUE and in English. On this large scale, BE is a new direction in the history of U.S. education. Parents, teachers, principals, and schoolboards have a lot of questions, as do judges who have to rule on cases of BE, journalists who have to write about it, and professors who have to train the teachers. Congress wants to know if BE is worth it; there are policies to be made and money to be spent. Parents and principals worry that the children might not learn English well if they study in their mother tongue. They also worry about finding teachers who speak Navajo or Cantonese or Spanish as well as English, and finding textbooks and curricula for the children. The schoolboards want to know where the money is going to come from and why these children can't learn English the way their grandparents did, in an English monolingual school. Judges ask whether it is true that BE is a more efficient way of teaching English and the three Rs to non- or limited English-speaking children so that the schools through BE will provide all children with an equal opportunity of learning. Some journalists worry that BE might be divisive. Noel Epstein asks in the *Washington Post* "The question is whether the potential benefits outweigh the potential costs. Would the result be more harmony or more discord in American society?" (1977a: C4).

Professors would like to know the answer to all those questions, but they also have more practical questions. Should children learn to read in the mother tongue first and then in English or should they not waste time and instead learn to read in both languages at the same time? In which language should the children do mathematics? The teachers have even more questions of this kind, and there certainly are many problems which have to be dealt with in BE. But we also need to realize that much of the present interest surrounding bilingualism and bilingual

education, both in the United States and Canada, is the result of the practical
problems educators are facing in schooling children in a second language (L₂),
one they have difficulty understanding.

Also, the point needs to be mentioned that the social meaning of two languages in bilingual situations is not necessarily different from the social meaning
of DIALECTAL variation in monolingual settings. That is, the social meaning that
speaking Navajo and being Indian, or speaking Spanish and being Chicano,
implies to some people of being from "the wrong side of the tracks" is not very
different from the social meaning of speaking some nonstandard dialect of English such as Black English or Appalachian English. People do at times, and not
very politely either, use language to put others down and to gain an advantage.
Such behavior is more obvious with the use of two separate languages than with
two dialects, one standard and the other nonstandard, but it is the same sort of
behavior nevertheless. The use of two different languages serves to underscore,
to set into relief, the functions of language in society and in man's relationship to
man.

This chapter will seek to examine some aspects of group bilingualism, the
connection between bilingualism and education, and to explore the development
of BE in the United States as a result of existent group bilingualism.

Group bilingualism

We first need to consider what is meant by bilingualism. Most definitions
involve the competence of the individual in a second language, and range from
having native-like ability in both languages to simply minimal use, such as
tourist phrases. But most people probably agree that bilingualism is more something in the middle, not an all-or-none property but "an individual characteristic that may exist to degrees varying from minimal competency to complete mastery of more than one language" (Hornby 1977: 3). The definition one
wants to use really depends on the questions one asks. If we consider bilingual
simultaneous interpreters, obviously the definition of minimal competence
won't do. For example, most bilingual interpreters (in contrast with translators
who work with written documents) grew up as children with the use of two
languages; however, one of these languages is considered their stronger, and
they usually translate from their weaker language into their stronger. So even
someone who seems completely bilingual will tend to favor one language, and
complete bilingualism is a rare phenomenon.

Much more common is the bilingual individual who uses two languages
alternatively, each having a separate realm of functions. A common pattern is
the use of one language at home and another at work. If the second language is
learned before puberty, the individual's L₂ pronunciation and grammar may be
native-like, but he will probably not know all the vocabulary which goes with
the realm of the first language. It is a rare parent who has more than one diaper
language. Conversely, the parent is not likely to know in the mother tongue all
the vocabulary belonging to the child's eventual occupation. For example,

professionals who have done all their advanced studies in a second language may not feel satisfied using their mother tongue to discuss professional matters. I often feel quite foolish discussing linguistics with my Swedish colleagues because my native Swedish is constantly interrupted by English phrases and words. Don't worry, say my colleagues, we do it too. We call it Swenglish. CODE-SWITCHING, changing from one language to another, is common among bilinguals and often depends on the topic or realm for which one or another language is appropriate (see Chapters 9 and 10).

If the second language is learned after puberty, the individual will usually have – for reasons we understand as yet imperfectly – what is called a "foreign accent" for the rest of his life, although his vocabulary and grammar may be equal to those of the most educated speaker. The former Secretary of State Henry Kissinger is a good example. Without the continued use of his original mother tongue, the individual may, as did many immigrants to the United States, virtually forget his first language of which only his accent in English and a few words remain.

Bilingualism is a very complex phenomenon which must be analyzed in a number of its component parts: competence in the sound system, vocabulary, and grammar of a language; the realm of its functions, which may involve space or topic or channel (like oral or written use); and the time and manner of acquisition. But all of these definitions and illustrations have in common a basic concern with the individual's use of two languages.

Another concern in the study of bilingualism is group bilingualism, which may be unofficial as in the United States or official and institutional as in Canada. Institutional bilingualism recognizes that "each citizen has the right to use the official language of his or her choice in dealing with the federal government and as a medium for working within the federal administration" (Spicer 1974: 5). Institutional bilingualism does not mean that all individuals are bilingual but often the opposite with only a small group serving as brokers between the two groups. For example, Lieberson's Canadian data (1970) show 67.4 percent of the population as monolingual in English, 19.1 as monolingual in French and only 12.2 percent classified as bilingual. Rather, institutional bilingualism is a matter of political policy about which decisions are made primarily on political and economic grounds and reflect the values and opinions of those in power. But since the issues discussed about institutional bilingualism are always overtly those of language, there is often considerable confusion whether these issues are in fact matters of political, economic, religious, cultural, or linguistic concern. The present language problems in Canada basically do not concern language, but rather the power relationship between Francophone and Anglophone Canadians in which the Francophones have chosen to mobilize along the line of language boundaries. Institutional bilingualism need not lead to strife and breakdown of internal cohesion; the most frequently cited example is peaceful Switzerland with institutional quadrilingualism: German, French, Italian, and Romansh. Institutional bilingualism is a very interesting topic of study, but it lies outside the scope of this chapter which deals with group bilingualism in the United States which does not have institutional, official bilingualism.

In the United States, it was the massive school failure of children of limited or non-English-speaking ability which finally forced the authorities to acknowledge the existence of bi/multilingualism, and eventually to legislate into effect BE programs. Gaarder (n.d.) makes the crucial distinction between elitist bilingualism and folk bilingualism. Elitist bilingualism is the hallmark of the intellectuals and the learned in most societies, and, one might add, of the upper class in many societies such as those in Western Europe. It is a matter of choice. Not so with folk bilingualism which is the result of ethnic groups in contact and competition with a single state, where "one of the peoples becomes bilingual involuntarily in order to survive." Elitist education has never been a problem, and upper and middle class children do perfectly well whether they are schooled in the mother tongue or in the L_2, although we really do not know why; this chapter is primarily concerned with BE as a result of ethnic groups in contact and competition, as a result of folk bilingualism.

It is helpful to look at Schermerhorn's (1970) work on *Comparative Ethnic Relations* in an attempt to analyze the consequences of BE in North America, the direct result of ethnic groups in contact. Schermerhorn points out that the "probability is overwhelming that when two groups with different cultural histories establish contacts that are regular rather than occasional or intermittent, one of the two groups will typically assume dominance over the other" (1970: 68), and he says elsewhere that it is the nature of this dominance which is the major factor in ethnic relations (1972: 379ff). The central question then in comparative research in ethnic relations (immediate causal factor of a group's bilingual status) is "what are the conditions that foster or prevent the integration of ethnic groups into their environing societies?" (1970: 14). The percentage of members of a group who become bilingual can be seen as a concomitant condition of the degree of integration. Schermerhorn sees three major causal factors as determining the nature of the relationship between ethnic groups and the process of integration into the environing society. The first refers to the origin of the contact situation between "the subordinate ethnic and dominant groups, such as annexation, migration, and colonization," the second to "the degree of enclosure (institutional separation or segmentation) of the subordinate group or groups from the society-wide network of institutions and associations," and the third to "the degree of control exercised by dominant groups over access to scarce resources by subordinate groups in a given society" (1970: 15).

Lieberson, Dalto, and Johnston (1975) point out the failure of developmental factors, such as urbanization, to account for cross-national changes in language diversity. They consider the very rapid LANGUAGE SHIFT in the United States: "For the descendants of literally tens of millions of immigrants, English became the mother tongue in a matter of a few generations (Lieberson and Curry 1971). It is reasonable to ask how it came about that the shift was so rapid in the United States compared with that in the vast majority of nations" (1975: 53).

They conclude, like Schermerhorn, that one must consider the origin of the contact situation. The development of race and ethnic relations will be different in settings where the subordinate group is indigenous from those where the subordinate group consists of a migrant population. Superordinate groups are not as likely to shift languages as are subordinate groups. A group with political power and economic dominance is in a strong position to maintain its language. Such a group may become bilingual but this is not the same as mother-tongue shift; if mother-tongue shift occurs, it is likely to be very slow (Lieberson et al. 1975: 53). The role of Swedish in Finland illustrates that point, and gives us an example of an ethnic group in demographic and political decline which uses its native tongue to maintain its boundaries for ethnic survival, but its continued role in Finland is best explained by the former superordinate status of its mother-tongue speakers.

Subordinate groups who are indigenous at the time of contact, either through colonization as in the case of the American Indians or through annexation as in the case of the Chicanos in the U.S. Southwest, are unlikely to change rapidly. Immigrant subordinate groups are the only groups likely to show rapid rates of mother-tongue shift, and in the United States, as Lieberson et al. show, the immigrant experience was one of extraordinarily rapid shift. In contrast, within the same nation and often with access to education through public schooling, the indigenous subordinate groups (like the Chicanos, Louisiana French, and Indians) have changed at a much slower rate. In 1940, 20 percent of the Whites in Louisiana still reported French as their mother tongue although the state had been purchased from France in 1803, almost 150 years before. In New Mexico, conquered in 1846, nearly 45 percent of the native parentage population (third or later generation) reported Spanish as their mother tongue in 1940. Since a fair proportion of this population was not of Spanish origin, much more than half of the Spanish-speaking population had not shifted (Lieberson et al. 1975). In contrast to Louisiana, the Southwest has a steady trickle of new immigrants, legal and illegal, from Mexico, and no one really knows the exact rate of language shift, but Thompson (1974) calculates that in Texas, Spanish has remained the mother tongue for 80 percent of the third generation.

The Indian population probably has been the slowest to become bilingual. Lieberson et al. cite census data which show that as recently as 1900 slightly more than 40 percent of the Indian population could not speak English (see Chapter 6). Many of those who did speak English also maintained their Indian mother tongue, and Lieberson et al. conclude that "it is clear that mother-tongue shift was far slower than for the subordinate immigrant groups" (1975: 56).

These findings on language shift through a bilingual generation and LANGUAGE MAINTENANCE with or without concomitant bilingualism raise some issues which are important for a more accurate understanding of the nature of bilingualism. They also illustrate the importance of a comparative approach in this field of study. The questions which come to mind are: Why would the immigrant experience result in such rapid language shift with no apparent educational problems when the indigenous groups encountered such difficulties? Why have the latter maintained their mother tongue? What is the mechanism of language maintenance? It is clear, I think, that the mechanism of language shift in the United States has been bilingualism:

Immigrant languages disappear because they do not transfer from one generation to the next. Typically in the United States the first generation prefers to speak the non-English tongue, the second generation is bilingual, and the third claims English as its mother tongue, learning the immigrant language mainly through contact with the grandparents. (Thompson 1974: 7)

What is not clear are the factors which resulted in the language maintenance or slow rate of shift of the indigenous populations. Just what is the role of mother-tongue language in the ethnic minority groups and why do these groups insist on maintenance bilingual programs rather than accept transitional assimilation goals? (MAINTENANCE BILINGUAL EDUCATIONAL PROGRAMS seek to maintain the mother tongue in addition to English; TRANSITIONAL BILINGUAL EDUCATION PROGRAMS attempt a rapid shift to English only.)

Language shift can be seen as an indicator of integration into the environing society; thus we can rephrase the first question slightly; Why did the immigrants to the United States integrate into the larger society more rapidly and completely than did the indigenous groups? As Lieberson et al. (1975) point out, one reason was that the indigenous groups already had a set of social and cultural institutions *in situ* through which they attempted to pursue their preconquest activities. Another reason was that they tended to be spatially isolated.

These two reasons are both subsumed under Schermerhorn's variable of degree of enclosure. The less the two groups share sociocultural institutions, i.e. the same churches, the same schools, the same jobs, the higher the degree of enclosure within that society. In plural societies, "institutions of kinship, religion, the economy, education, recreation and the like are parallel but different in structure and norms. Ordinarily this is compounded by differences in language and sometimes by race as well" (1970: 124).

The degree of control by the Anglo dominant group over access to goods and services also influenced the situation. The contact situations within the same nation between the Anglo-Americans and the Chicanos, the Puerto Ricans, the Amerindians, were all the result of military conquest. The Chicanos were segregated to one part of town and given access only to menial type jobs. The Indians were isolated on reservations where no opportunity for jobs existed. The immigrants, on the other hand, were given access to jobs. Brudner's thesis (1972) that jobs select language learning strategies remains highly predictive. When jobs were available which required a knowledge of English, the ethnic minority members became bilingual. Without access to rewards, English was and is not salient.

Schermerhorn also posits intervening or contextual variables which modify the effect of the independent variables. The most important is the agreement or disagreement between dominant and subordinate groups on collective goals for the latter, such as assimilation or pluralism. Schermerhorn sets up a paradigm of which one purpose is to "specify the social contexts that can serve as intervening variables in answer to the scientific query, 'under what conditions' " (1970: 85). He bases his discussion on a typology of the different policies adopted by minority groups in response to their unprivileged position: assimilation, pluralism, secession, and militancy. Schermerhorn points out that assimilation and pluralism really refer to cultural aspects while secession and militancy refer to structural. To clarify the problem, he insists on the analytic distinction between culture and social structure. Culture refers to behavior learned through socialization, based on norms and values. It encompasses such obvious features as language, dress, cuisine, but also values and beliefs. Social structure, on the other hand, refers to the systematic social relationships of members which place them in groups and which relate them to the major institutions of a society, such as economic and occupational life, religion, family, education, law, government, and recreation. In order to deal with the difficulty of applying cultural features to conditions which involve social features, he suggests the paired concepts of centripetal and centrifugal trends in social life. "Centripetal tendencies refer both to cultural trends such as acceptance of common values, styles of life, etc., as well as structural features like increased participation in a common set of groups, associations, and institutions" (1970: 81). To keep the two aspects distinct, he calls the first assimilation, the latter incorporation. Centrifugal tendencies among subordinate groups refer to trends that serve to foster separation from the dominant group, whether in cultural or social features. This frequently means retention of the group's distinctive traditions in spheres such as language, religion, recreation, etc., as well as demands for endogamy, separate association, and the like.

Schermerhorn's major point is that integration, which involves the satisfaction of the ethnic group's modal-tendency, whether it be centripetal or centrifugal, depends on the agreement or congruence of views by the dominant and subordinate groups on the goals of the latter.

The immigrants' goals were clearly those of assimilation; they had voluntarily left "the old country" with its frequently unsatisfactory conditions behind. The indigenous groups, in contrast, did not seek contact with the dominant Anglos but found it imposed on them; their groups in their entirety were brought into the environing society with their culture intact. Today many subordinate ethnic groups in the United States do not want to abandon their cultural distinctiveness; rather they want access to goods and services, to the institutional privileges held by the English-speaking middle class, i.e. economic incorporation but not assimilation. One important aspect of resisting assimilation is the maintenance of the mother tongue, in the same way as language shift is an important aspect of assimilation.

The goals for all non-English-speaking groups as seen by the dominant group have always been assimilation, acceptance of "the American creed," and socialization into American ways and values. Since this was also the goal of the immigrants, they willingly acquiesced to the assimilation process, and the

476   CHRISTINA BRATT PAULSTON

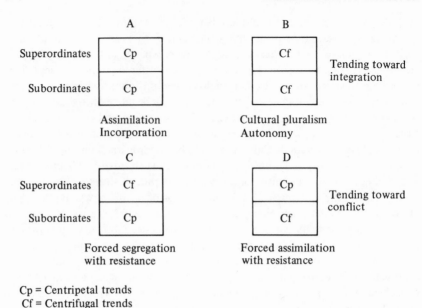

Cp = Centripetal trends
Cf = Centrifugal trends

Figure 21.1. Congruent and incongruent orientations toward centripetal and centrifugal trends of subordinates as viewed by themselves and superordinates (reprinted from Schermerhorn 1970: 83 by permission of The University of Chicago Press. Copyright © 1970 by The University of Chicago Press)

relationship between the dominant group and the immigrants is best characterized by Cell A (Figure 20.1), a situation tending toward integration. Anything less became considered unpatriotic; for example, I have been told more than once when I criticized some feature of American life "If you don't like it here, why don't you go back to where you came from?"

The indigenous groups, on the other hand, tended to resist assimilation, and their situation is symbolized by Cell D. In this situation, characterized by conflict, indigenous groups resisted assimilation at the same time they were denied access to goods and services and were separated institutionally from the English-speaking group. Members of indigenous groups did not shift to English to the same degree and at the same rate as the immigrant group. The degree to which the indigenous groups became bilingual probably depended mostly on access to jobs which required a knowledge of English; the degree to which they maintained the mother tongue probably depended most on the resistance against assimilation. One should recognize that educational institutions have limited power in dealing with language acquisition or the lack thereof, a learning process which is primarily the result of social factors. Still, the role of the school in situations of language shift or language maintenance cannot be ignored; it was the single most important institution in facilitating the rapid language shift of the European immigrants in the United States. Yet schools for indigenous groups were not a force strong enough to cause massive language shifts. The degree of group enclosure and the kinds of jobs of each group ultimately determine the role of schools in language shift.

The connection between group bilingualism and education

The schools which form part of the formal educational system of a nation typically act in the interest of the dominant group's perceived goals for minorities. R. G. Paulston's case study of the Swedish Same or Lapps (1976) illustrates a typical intolerance of cultural pluralism by the larger society except when it sees its own purposes furthered. Consistently, when the national economy favored reindeer herding, the collective goals for the Lapps as seen by Swedish officials included the use of Lappish and support of Same culture; otherwise the goals were Swedish and assimilation. It also illustrates the typical attempts by the dominant group to use schooling as the primary means of controlling the language use of minority groups. This control of language use has in most cases one of two objectives: language maintenance or language shift.

Education and language maintenance. The concern about mother-tongue maintenance and the too rapid shift to the other tongue is a concern usually held by ethnic group members rather than government officials, and consequently the European immigrant groups in the United States frequently resorted to various forms of private BE, often in connection with a local parish. Fishman et al. in *Language Loyalty in the United States* (1966), document the attempts by various ethnic groups to maintain the traditional mother tongue in addition to English:

Now the question no longer is: how shall we learn English so that we may take part in the social life of America and partake of her benefits; the big question is: how can we preserve the language of our ancestors here, in a strange environment, and pass on to our descendants the treasure which it contains? (Bothne in Fishman 1966: 7)

These attempts of mother-tongue maintenance through private schooling among the European groups have not been successful, at least not when the attempts were motivated by language loyalty *per se,* i.e. simply by love and appreciation of the original language.

But ethnic groups may wish to use language for purposes other than an appreciation of their cultural heritage. Mother-tongue maintenance is an efficient means of maintaining ethnic boundaries (Barth 1969). The trilingual Old Order Amish is an example of a group who use language for the maintenance of group boundaries both to keep their members in and outsiders out. The Amish originally emigrated to the United States for reasons of religious freedom, and the Pennyslvania Old Order Amish is a Protestant religious group characterized by

horse and buggies for transportation, no electricity in their homes, farm animals for farming, the occupation most engaged in; education only to the eighth grade; plain dress;

refusal to accept government benefits such as social security; and the use of Pennsylvania Dutch, a German dialect from the speech of German Rhenish Palatinate; German;
and English. (Yoder 1976: 2–3)

German is used for sermons, prayers, and bible reading from the Luther Bible,
the 1534 translation. Since Pennsylvania law requires school attendance until
15 and the Amish do not permit education past the eighth grade, many Old
Order Amish spend an additional year after eighth grade in a special intensive
program learning German, thus fulfilling the legal requirement while serving
their own purpose. English is learned in school and is used in any exchange
with "English" or "gay" persons (a term used to refer to nonmembers).
English is also used for nonreligious reading. Pennsylvania Dutch is the mother
tongue and is spoken in the home, always at church-related social activities, and
often to other church members even in the "English" world, such as in the
grocery store (Yoder 1976). Members have a strong feeling that

German is the better form of the language, richer, deeper, more capable of expressing
deep thoughts than either Pennsylvania Dutch or English. The deep thoughts in one's life
are those relating to God. So take away German, and one has taken away that aspect of
his life. (Yoder 1976: 10).

For the deeply religious Amish, it is clear that the functional distribution of
language use contributes to the motivation for staying within the church and for
resisting the obvious temptations to join one of the less conservative churches,
like that of the Mennonites, who do not have the same extreme restrictions on
daily life. Nor do the Mennonites make similar use of language and indeed their
present-day high school generation is monolingual in English. It is also clear
that the continued maintenance of both Pennsylvania Dutch and German is not
due to language loyalty but to religious loyalty which utilizes languages for the
maintenance of group boundaries.

   The affluent Amish illustrate the point that groups become bilingual when
they have access to goods and services which require a knowledge of English.
Their business dealings with the "gay" world necessitate a knowledge of
English which they learn primarily in the public schools. The Amish also
illustrate the point that mother-tongue maintenance depends on a resistance
against assimilation. Not only do they maintain the mother tongue, but they also
add Standard German, learned through formal or informal instruction, as an
additional language, crucial to the transmission of the group's basic values.

   Schools also serve to further language learning as a function of boundary
maintenance in maintaining elite or social status. The private upper class French,
German, or English schools in Latin America are an example. So are the
English public schools (schools which are in fact private and elite) where the
students master RECEIVED PRONUNCIATION (the linguist's label for the Queen's
English) which will indelibly mark them as members of the upper class. Another example is the present rage for IMMERSION PROGRAMS in Canada.

   The present language situation in the province of Québec is a result of a
power struggle between the economically dominant Anglo-Canadians and the

politically dominant Franco-Canadians. Through legal measures, the French have been able to enforce a knowledge of French as a requisite for access to a number of jobs. As a result, about 50 percent of the English-speaking children in Montreal enter kindergarten in French immersion programs (in which French is used as a medium of instruction), with the hope by their parents that they will learn sufficient French in school to be able to qualify for future positions. Language is used by the French as a mechanism for maintaining ethnic boundaries in order to deny English-speaking Canadians access to scarce jobs, and Anglo-Canadians resort to the schools in order to learn French so that they can maintain their socio-economic status quo.

All of these attempts at language maintenance or group boundary maintenance through language have been initiated voluntarily by the group itself as an attempt to control language use through schooling.

Maintenance of a language or, more correctly, attempts at maintenance of a language through national educational policy may also be enforced on an ethnic group from the outside, by the dominant group. The situation of the *Gastarbeiter* (guest workers for a limited duration) in Germany and other European countries are a case in point. Willke estimates that "the number of children directly affected by migration movements within Europe is about six million" (1975: 359), a number which education officials find impossible to ignore. In the case of temporary migrants, mother-tongue maintenance by the children takes on extreme importance as the basis for successful reintegration into their country of origin, and national educational policy reflects this fact.

In the Federal Republic of Germany the policy of temporary or permanent immigration varies, and as Abadan-Unat illustrates in his discussion of the schooling problem of Turkish migrant children in Bavaria, this policy becomes reflected in the educational policy:

It should be noted that while Bavaria from the beginning stood firm on the provisional nature of foreign labour employment and insisted on keeping the rotation principle, the Lander with larger industrial concentration fought for complete integration and recruitment without restrictions. Thus it becomes clear that the shaping of education policies was determined, until the out-break of the energy crisis, by the degree of industrial absorption of foreign labour rather than pedagogical or humanistic considerations. (1975: 316)

In Europe, in other words, the economic situation tends to dictate actual educational policies as regards mother-tongue maintenance of the migrant children. With the present economic trend, enforced mother-tongue maintenance through schooling is likely to be remembered as the long ignored policy recommended by the Standing Conference of European Ministers of Education in November of 1974:

Migrants' children should be assured of a good knowledge of their mother tongue and indigenous culture, for the mother tongue is one of the foundations of their development and is likely to facilitate the learning of other languages. (Council of 1974, cited in Willke 1975: 364)

Education and language shift.   This last point is indicative of the major
concern of educational officials in regard to migrant and ethnic minority children alike throughout the world. One concern is mother-tongue maintenance;
the other, and usually considered by far the graver, is the concern that the
children are not properly learning the second language (L_2), the official language of the nation. In contradistinction to language maintenance, the learning
of the L_2 is a concern which is shared by everyone, educational officials,
community leaders, parents, and the children themselves. It becomes a shared
concern because the inevitable result of an inadequate knowledge of the L_2 is
massive school failure and the denied possibility of social mobility. And that
becomes a political question.

The end of the 1960s saw a revival of ethnic minority identity, at both a
cultural and a political level (see Chapter 19). The successful experience of the
Blacks when they showed a united front and the persuasive power of the bus
strikes and the marches of the Civil Rights movement were not lost on other
ethnic minorities. The melting pot came to be regarded as a myth, and the new
slogan was – and is – "from melting pot to salad bowl." Schermerhorn (1970)
points out that ethnic groups that come into contact through annexation or
colonialization most often differ in goal orientation from groups who come into
contact through voluntary migration. The Anglo superordinate group maintained its goal as assimilation for all, but the annexed Chicanos and the colonized Indians refused. They prefer to maintain their cultural identity, of which
language is an integral part, and their goal is cultural pluralism with structural
incorporation, i.e. access to goods and services and to social institutions like
education and justice. In short, they want to retain their values and ways of
being without being denied their fair share. This conflict is also mirrored in the
educational sector. Many controversial issues of BE in the United States can
best be understood if seen as part of a larger political movement which pits the
subordinate ethnic minorities, rebelling against economic exploitation, in a
power struggle with the dominant majority.

The actual situation is far more complicated than Schermerhorn's elegant
framework allows for. It is a moot point how voluntary migration is, if the
alternative is a bloody revolution as in the case of the escaped middle and upper
class Cubans or semi-starvation as in the case of the illegal immigrants from
Mexico. The Puerto Ricans migrate to New York and Chicago, but there is also
considerable back-migration to Spanish-speaking Puerto Rico. Consequently
many of the children know neither English nor Spanish well and feel ill at ease
in both cultures. Puerto Ricans, unlike Mexican immigrants, are legal citizens
of the United States. The major official language of Puerto Rico is Spanish, and
many Puerto Ricans resent the situation in which as U.S. citizens they are
denied the use of their official mother tongue on the continent (see Chapter 10).
They also resent the transitional assimilationist goals of bilingual education
because, unlike nineteenth-century parish-directed and private-sector-sponsored
bilingual education programs for mother-tongue maintenance, current programs
in the United States are seen by the government officials as an efficient way of

teaching the national language where the goal is language shift through bilingualism.

TEFL, TESL, and TESOL

The earliest manner of dealing with the problem of instructing children in English which they did not understand was simply to ignore the problem. Children were put into regular classrooms with other English-speaking children in a "sink-or-swim" situation; such classes are today sometimes referred to as "submersion" classes to distinguish them from the Canadian immersion programs.

The first advance in methodology and curriculum came from the field of TEFL, the teaching of English as a foreign language. Structural linguists throughout the world had been asked to contribute their expertise in the teaching of English as a foreign language, as a LANGUAGE OF WIDER COMMUNICATION (LWC), and professional TEFL came to have a strong linguistic component. The major impetus and contribution to the field in the USA is often attributed to Charles Carpenter Fries, who in the early 1940s established the English Language Institute at the University of Michigan. Fries' methods, intended for adult foreign students, were later adopted by TESL, the teaching of English as a second language.

The distinction between a foreign and a second language, apparently made first by British specialists (see Chapter 2), may be more important theoretically than practically as the two share many of the same methods and techniques. A second language is the non-home but critically important public language of a nation which *must* be learned by its citizens for full social, economic, and political participation in the life of that nation. It is the relationship between the super- and subordinate groups which give second language learning its significant characteristics, and which distinguish it from learning a foreign language where attitudes are fairly neutral.

It is probably fair to say that TESL has never been given a fair chance in our public schools. The development of Fries' aural/oral method, intended for adults, came to contain primarily mechanical type drills which the students could parrot without ever understanding a word, though this was never Fries' intention. These pattern drills were then used with schoolchildren instead of the modified Language Arts program they needed. Not surprisingly, the result was discouraging. What is surprising is that the term TESL (or often simply ESL) became identified in parts of the country with this particular method of teaching English as a second language, and TESL today is often rejected out of hand by educators who feel its methods are artificial. This is indeed unfortunate because TESL has made large theoretical and methodological advances during the last fifteen years, and a well-run TESL classroom bears little resemblance to the once predominant pattern drill classes. Another reason why TESL has not been given a fair chance is the insufficient number of teachers who are trained in methods of teaching English to non-English-speaking children; very few states require or recognize TESL teacher certification.

TEFL and TESL became united in TESOL, teaching English to speakers of other languages, which stands both for the field and for the national professional organization which was founded in 1966. The range of special interest groups within the organization testifies to the diversification of special needs within the field: (a) teaching English abroad; (b) ESL in English-speaking countries; (c) ESL in elementary schools; (d) ESL in secondary schools; (e) ESL in higher education; (f) ESL in bilingual education; (g) ESL in adult education; (h) teaching Standard English as a second dialect; and (i) applied linguistics.

The present criticism of ESL by BE proponents is unfortunate for a number of reasons. ESL remains the only feasible alternative in schools who have students from a large number of different language backgrounds; BE is just not possible in such situations. Also, the consistent criticism of ESL as a pedagogical methodology (albeit for primarily political reasons) may serve to discredit the entire field of ESL; and it must be remembered that a major component of a BE curriculum is precisely ESL. Without further advances in ESL methodology at the elementary level, BE may itself become discredited in the eyes of those who set national policy. The worst possible outcome anyone could envisage in TESOL is a return to the submersion classes.

The recent development of bilingual education in the United States

The so-called BILINGUAL EDUCATION ACT was approved in 1968. It was the Title VII amendment to the 1965 Elementary and Secondary Education Act, and it provided the first federal funds for BE in legislation:

designed to meet the needs of children of limited English-speaking ability from low income families, so that these children will gain sufficient proficiency in English to keep up with their monolingual English-speaking peers in the educational system. Although the Title VII amendment is often referred to as ''The Bilingual Education Act,'' this is rather misleading, since the long range goal is not bilingualism but proficiency in English. (National Institute of Education 1975: 6)

From the legislators' viewpoint, the programs are compensatory in nature, and their objective is a more rapid and efficient acquisition of English; such programs have become known as the transitional model.

The landmark case in BE was LAU v. NICHOLS in which a Chinese parent took the school board of San Francisco to court. ''The plaintiffs claimed that the absence of programs designed to meet the linguistic needs of such [non-English-speaking] children violated both Title VI and the Equal Protection Clause of the Fourteenth Amendment to the Constitution'' (Teitelbaum and Hiller 1977a:142). In 1974 the Supreme Court unanimously ruled in favor of Lau, avoiding the Constitutional issue and relying solely on Title VI of the Civil Rights Act of 1964: ''for students who do not understand English are effectively foreclosed from any meaningful education'' (Geffert, Harper, Sarmiento, and

Schember 1975). In other words, equal treatment does not constitute equal opportunity.

Subsequently, the Office of Civil Rights of the Department of Health, Education, and Welfare (HEW) appointed a task force which worked out a set of guidelines for implementing the Lau decision, the so-called Lau "remedies," which caused a considerable furor. The constant excuse given by school administrators who did not want to implement bilingual education programs in their schools was that the children did not need it because they already had an ESL program. So, the Lau "remedies" state again and again that an ESL program is not acceptable in a BE program. Some people involved in ESL have mistakenly taken this to mean that the children are not to be taught English. The "remedies" do end with a footnote which states that an ESL component is an integral part of a bilingual education program, and most certainly the task force never meant that the children were not to learn and be taught English. The Lau "remedies" can best be understood as a political document: it is the understandable though unfortunate reaction of minority group members who have seen that the only real advances to their people come through political action.

The Lau "remedies" are implemented by the Lau Centers which serve under HEW. The federal government does have indirect control over the states through the allocation of federal funding (total HEW expenditures on BE and/or ESL projects for fiscal year 1979 amounted to nearly $150 million), and school districts which are judged out of compliance with the Lau decision risk losing all their federal funding. This is a powerful argument for the implementation of BE and one which even the most conservative school board is not willing to fight. And so, slowly, through Lau violation rulings, litigation, and also through voluntary action at the state level, BE programs are being implemented across the United States. Massachusetts was the first state legislature to pass statutes mandating BE, and its Massachusetts Transitional Bilingual Education Law of 1971 has served as a prototype for other states. However, instilling the notion of BE in the minds of citizens, educators, and administrators is clearly a legal–political process rather than the pragmatic–educational policy that Congress presumably intended with its transitional Bilingual Education Act of 1968.

The U.S. programs may legally be transitional in nature, but the major proponents for them, especially those members of the ethnic groups involved in implementing the new directives, invariably refer to the programs as bilingual/bicultural and see the objectives as stable bilingualism with maintenance of the home culture as well as the home language. So far, as the National Institute of Education report points out, "the Guidelines for the Title VII programs have been interpreted loosely enough" (1975: 6) to allow for maintenance programs as well as for transitional programs. In general, it is considered a crucial point in maintenance programs to have teachers who are members of the same ethnic group as the children, an ideological rather than a pedagogical consideration. The consequence of such policies on the children's English language acquisition may well be an issue for future consideration.

Bilingual education changes the requirements of teacher competencies, and many programs are accompanied by chronic teacher strife as tenured Anglo teachers get fired in a job market without jobs in order to make room for bilingual teachers. It is understandable that principals grumble, but the typical rejoinder is "the shoe is on the other foot now," meaning the ethnic minorities have long known what it is to be denied access to jobs, and now it is the Anglos' turn. It is very much a confrontation of interest groups in competition for scarce jobs, and from this viewpoint it is comprehensible that the discussion about pedagogical methodology sometimes takes the form of BE *contra* ESL.

In actual fact, as long as one considers BE apart from its policy, it is immediately apparent that teaching English to minority children (inevitably ESL) is held by everyone to be an important function of BE programs. The standard and generally acceped U.S. Office of Education definition of BE makes this point clearly:

Bilingual education is the use of two languages, one of which is English, as mediums of instruction for the same pupil population in a well organized program which encompasses part or all of the curriculum and includes the study of the history and culture associated with the mother tongue.

The forms which BE programs actually take in classrooms vary considerably. Some classes have bilingual teachers who divide the school day between the L_1 and the L_2 in clearly separate units; others have bilingual teachers who use the so-called "concurrent translation" approach in which they alternate languages sentence by sentence. The latter approach may well be detrimental to learning, yet the method is widespead. Other classes function with an English-speaking teacher and an aide who is a native speaker of the children's L_1. Such arrangements have been much criticized in that it is held that the children internalize the lower status the aide holds *vis à vis* the teacher. As always the truth is not absolute: it is true that many teachers misuse their aides for clerical services (like endless photocopying), but it is also true that some aides are as good or better than the regular teacher, and students realize this. The practice of using aides had its origin in expediency; there were no bilingual teachers available. With continued implementation of BE, the teacher/aide arrangement is likely to be phased out; at present many aides are pursuing some form of teacher certification.

Other classes have only a monolingual English teacher in a regular program but are visited during the week by an ESL-trained teacher who works specifically on English language acquisition with some children in so-called "pull-out" classes. Obviously, such programs do not deserve to be called *bilingual*, and they tend to be vehemently criticized by regular teachers, ESL teachers, and BE teachers alike. The regular teachers tend to dislike the commotion, the ESL teacher wants more time with the children, and the BE teacher wants the children taught in the mother tongue. Still, in the not uncommon situation of some fifteen children from ten different language backgrounds at five different grade levels, it is understandable that the practice is sometimes necessary. And if we listen to the children, it may not be totally reprehensible. At a recent conference in Toronto, eight tenth graders, who had immigrated to Canada four years earlier, insisted in the face of determined questioning that the most helpful experience at first had been their pull-out ESL classes.

The fact of the matter is that there is very little systematic knowledge of techniques and procedures for teaching children a second language at the elementary level which is coherently anchored in a theory of language acquisition. The elaboration of such a body of knowledge is an important priority for the future development of BE, because without it there could be disillusionment with the entire approach of BE. That would be a great pity because we do know that it is easier for non-English-speaking children to begin their schooling in BE programs.

The United States has always been a multilingual nation and indeed was characterized by multilingualism long before it became a nation. This fact has long been ignored officially, and only recently has official policy in the educational sector of the federal government faced the problems which attend the schooling in English of children from other mother-tongue groups. Bilingual education in the United States today is a matter of federal law; the process of implementation reflects the sociopolitical situation. Slowly the children are coming to have an education which is an affirmation of their language and culture, an enormous task in a country as large and as diverse as the United States. But one that seems likely to be fullfilled. And finally, the children themselves should have the last word on bilingual education: "Uno tiene mas opportunidad de aprender inglés sin necesidad de avergonzarse ['One has a better opportunity to learn English and without having to feel ashamed and make a fool of oneself']" (Velasquez 1973: 151, my translation).

FURTHER READING

There exists a rapidly increasing literature on bilingual education in the United States, and it is difficult to know where the reader should begin. A good place is with the historical development of language policy in the United States. Heath's 1976a article on colonial language status is excellent, and Fishman et al.'s *Language Loyalty in the United States* (1966) gives a clear picture of the later immigrant experience. A more up-to-date account can be found in Lourie and Conklin 1978.

Andersson and Boyer 1978 is a broad and readable descriptive study. The Center for Applied Linguistics' multidisciplinary series *Bilingual Education: current perspectives* (1977–8) has a more scholarly and academic approach. The proceedings from the Georgetown University Round Table on Languages and Linguistics 1978 (Alatis 1978) is also a good source.

For those interested in the pedagogical aspects of bilingual education, there are a number of good sources. The most specific and practical is Saville-Troike 1976, which is written for the classroom teacher. Rather more general are Abrahams and Troike 1972 and Spolsky 1972, but both give a very good picture of the educational problems minority children face in the United States.

Finally, for the reader who wants to consider bilingualism and education in other countries, there is Spolsky and Cooper 1978.

22

Statistics on language use*

DOROTHY WAGGONER

Efforts to obtain data on language characteristics of persons in the United States began with questions on the ability of those aged 20 and older to read and write in any language in the decennial censuses of 1840, 1850, and 1860. Statistics on literacy were obtained for the first time for the population 10 years of age and older in 1870. This effort was continued thereafter in the decennial censuses through 1930 and in sample surveys in 1947, 1952, 1959, and 1969. Information on speaking ability in English was sought for the native- and foreign-born White population aged 10 and older beginning in 1890. In that year, enumerators were instructed to record persons who were unable to speak English "so as to be understood in ordinary conversation." They were instructed to record the name of the non-English language or DIALECT spoken. Unfortunately for the student of non-English language usage in the United States, the non-English language responses were not tabulated. In 1900, when this information was compiled for the foreign White stock (foreign-born White persons and native-born White persons of foreign or mixed parentage), enumerators were only expected to record whether or not the persons being counted could speak English. As with the literacy question, a question on English-speaking ability was asked in the successive decennial censuses through 1930. In 1930, when the statistics were compiled only for the foreign born, data for foreign-born White persons 10 years of age and older were tabulated for the first time by country of birth and by literacy, but not by MOTHER TONGUE.

Questions on ability to speak English and literacy in English were asked separately for Native Americans in the decennial censuses of 1880, 1890, and 1950. In 1880 it was assumed that they spoke their tribal languages, and data were gathered on how many spoke other languages such as English, Spanish, or French. In 1890, the schedule for Native Americans requested information on the native languages spoken and whether the individuals were literate in them, as well as whether they could write and speak English. The same questions asked of the general population on literacy and ability to speak English were asked for Native Americans in the censuses from 1910 to 1930. In the 1950

* This chapter was written by Dorothy Waggoner in her private capacity. No official support or endorsement by the National Center for Education Statistics is intended or should be inferred.

supplementary schedule, Native Americans were asked whether or not they were literate in English or spoke English and whether or not they were literate in or spoke any other language.

The mother-tongue question was first asked in a decennial census in 1910. In that year and in 1920, enumerators gathered data for the foreign White stock. In 1930, the question was asked of all persons of foreign birth but data were tabulated only for White persons. Not until 1940 was the question asked for a sample of the entire population, including native-born children of native-born parents. At that time, three out of five of the non-English mother-tongue claimants among the White population for whom data were published were born in the United States. In 1960, the mother-tongue question was again asked only for the foreign born.

In all the censuses through 1960, except that of 1940 – and that of 1950 when the question was not asked – the mother-tongue question referred to the language of customary speech in the homes of immigrants prior to their immigration to the United States. When data were gathered on their children – in 1910 and 1920 – the mother tongue meant the usual language of their parents' homes in the old country. However, when the question was asked of a sample of the total population in 1940, the mother tongue was defined as the language spoken in earliest childhood. This was interpreted as the language spoken by the enumerated individual himself. The "marked increase" in the reporting of English as the mother tongue of the second generation of European immigrants between the censuses of 1920 and 1940 is attributed by the Bureau of the Census to this change (U.S. Bureau of the Census (hereafter Census) 1943: 3).

It will be noted that, except for 1940, the concern was with the mother tongues of the European immigrant populations and their children. When data were collected on persons from other parts of the world, as in 1930 and 1940, they were tabulated only for White Europeans, "since most persons of the other races speak one characteristic language – English for the Negroes, Chinese for the Chinese, Japanese for the Japanese, etc." (Census 1943: 1). The 1960 tabulations of the mother tongues of the foreign born were the first to show all languages, including Asian, African, and those of the few Native Americans who were born outside the United States. None of these censuses, except that of 1940, provided any data on the native-born speakers of the European languages whose parents were also born in the United States.

In 1970, the mother-tongue question was asked of a sample of the entire population and data were published for all languages. The question – "What language, other than English, was spoken in this person's home when he was a child?" – was meant to be self-explanatory. However, because of the possible different interpretations, the Bureau of the Census reinterviewed a sample of 11,102 persons who had responded to the question. Of these, 14.9 percent had responded that a language other than English was spoken in their childhood homes. In 73.5 percent of the cases, the individuals reported in the reinterviews that they themselves spoke the language (Census 1974:10). It was also learned that 12.1 percent of the persons who reported in the reinterview that they spoke a non-English language in their homes as children had responded to the question in the census that only English was spoken in their childhood homes. For the group who reported in the reinterview that other family members, but not they themselves, spoke a non-English language in their childhood homes, 47.8 percent had responded to the census question that only English was spoken. These cases amounted to a quarter of the persons reporting a non-English mother tongue in the reinterview sample.

By the late 1960s, changes were taking place in the United States to increase the need for more comprehensive statistics on minorities, including statistics on language minorities. Ethnic minorities had begun to make their special needs known. Considerable social legislation was enacted, designed to correct inequities. Administration of this legislation required objective information about the size of the various minority groups and their educational and economic status in the society. As the second largest ethnic minority in the United States after Blacks, persons of Hispanic origin were seeking their fair share. To meet the need for better data on Hispanics, the Bureau of the Census piloted a new question asking individuals to identify themselves by origin or descent in the Current Population Survey (CPS) of November 1969. This question was then used in a 5 percent sample of the population in the 1970 decennial census. The November 1969 CPS also included, as additional identifiers of the Spanish origin group, questions which were designed to elicit the numbers of persons of Spanish language background. It included the mother-tongue question which would be used in 1970 – "What language, other than English, was spoken in . . .'s home *when he was a child?*" In addition, for the first time, this CPS included a question on current language – "What language, other than English, is *now* usually spoken in . . .'s home?" Language-specific information on literacy was also requested for the first time of the whole population. The CPS had questions about whether individuals could read and write English and whether they could read and write the current household language if it was other than English. If a non-English mother tongue different from the current household language was reported, information was obtained on whether individuals could read and write the mother tongue now and, if not, whether they could speak and understand it.

While apparently not influencing the November 1969 CPS or the 1970 census, the questions and procedures for which were already largely determined, another event took place at this time which made the collection of better language statistics even more important. As a part of the Education Amendments of 1968, Congress passed the BILINGUAL EDUCATION ACT (Title VII of the Elementary and Secondary Education Act of 1965, as amended by P.L. 90-247). This Act enabled the U.S. Office of Education to provide funds to school districts for programs employing the home language, as well as English, in the instruction of limited-English-speaking children from homes in which languages other than English are dominant. To establish the need for these programs, neither the limited current language information provided by the November 1969 CPS and, for Hispanics, in the March 1972 CPS, nor the mother-tongue data from the 1970 census were adequate. The former did not provide information about all the language minorities for which data were needed. The latter provided ample coverage of languages but no indication of the extent to which the mother tongues were spoken in the homes of the children of school age. Neither source provided any direct indication of the English language proficiency of children from non-English language backgrounds. English language proficiency became a crucial issue for public policy especially after the 1974 Supreme Court decision in LAU *v.* NICHOLS, which ruled that failure of school districts to provide non-English-speaking children with special assistance constituted a denial of equal educational opportunity under the Civil Rights Act of 1964 (see Chapter 21).

When the Bilingual Education Act came up for renewal in 1974, Congress included a provision addressing the lack of appropriate data. It wrote into the Act a mandate to the National Center for Education Statistics (NCES) to conduct a survey to determine the number of persons from non-English language backgrounds with "difficulty speaking and understanding instruction in the English language," which would provide a statistical basis for this and other programs serving the needs of language minorities. Efforts to accomplish this task are still underway as this chapter is written. However, data on non-English language usage in the United States are now available in greater detail than ever before from a pilot survey which NCES developed in 1975. This was the Survey of Language Supplement to the Current Population Survey. It was conducted by the Bureau of the Census for NCES in July 1975.

This chapter brings together non-English mother-tongue data from the 1970 decennial census with data on the non-English language background and current language usage of the U.S. population in July 1975 available from the Survey of Languages. Data on recent immigration from the U.S. Immigration and Naturalization Service are also cited to supplement the findings from the census and the Survey of Languages.

Readers should keep in mind the differences between censuses and sample surveys. Although the decennial censuses are, by definition, enumerations of everyone in the country, in fact, in recent years, certain information has been gathered only for samples of the entire population. Thus, the mother-tongue information was gathered for a sample of 5 percent of the population in 1940, for the foreign born in a sample of 25 percent of the population in 1960, and for a sample of 15 percent of the population in 1970. This means that approximately 30.5 million persons were asked the mother-tongue question in 1970. Since the mother tongue data from the 1970 census used in this chapter come from the 1-in-1,000 public use sample, the estimates here are based upon approximately 30,500 individual records. Data therefore differ somewhat from the published figures based upon the entire 15 percent sample.[1]

---

1. The Bureau of the Census published tables of standard errors for the estimates from the 1970 census (cf. Census 1972).

The Current Population Surveys are monthly sample surveys conducted by the Bureau of the Census primarily to supply information on the labor force status of the population for the Bureau of Labor Statistics. Unlike the recent decennial censuses in which data were largely collected by mail, the CPS employs interviewers to make personal contact with approximately 47,000 households per month in a nationally representative sample of the fifty states and the District of Columbia. In July 1975, the language questions were completed for approximately 42,000 households.[2] Data from the U.S. Immigration and Naturalization Service represent complete counts.

Non-English language backgrounds

In the absence of official data relating to the language backgrounds of the U.S. population, it is not possible to document statistically the extent to which languages other than English were spoken in the United States prior to the great waves of European immigration in the late nineteenth and early twentieth centuries. It is not possible to document the extent to which the native-born population retained non-English languages at least in their homes prior to 1940. Data on the non-English language backgrounds of the U.S. population – as opposed to data on the languages of immigrants and their children – begin with the decennial census of 1940. In that year, for the first time, individuals were asked about their mother tongues regardless of their place of birth or that of their parents, and data were published for the entire White population. In 1940:

Nearly 22 million White persons reported mother tongues other than English; they constituted 18.6 percent of the White population of the United States
Three out of five claimants of mother tongues other than English were native born
Nearly half of the claimants were of foreign or mixed foreign and native parentage; they were "second generation" Americans
Nearly 5 million persons reported that their mother tongue was German; persons of German language background were nearly a quarter of all White persons claiming non-English mother tongues; Italian and Polish were the second and third largest groups; Spanish claimants were fourth; Yiddish and French also had more than 1 million claimants each

In 1970, when the mother-tongue question was asked for the entire population and data were published for all persons regardless of race:

More than 33 million persons, or 16.3 percent of the entire population, reported non-English mother tongues
Three out of four non-English mother-tongue claimants were born in the United States

2. Tables of standard errors provided by the Bureau of the Census for the language questions in the Survey of Languages are available in Waggoner, n.d.

Two claimants in five were "second generation" Americans

More than a third of the non-English mother-tongue claimants were born in this country of parents also born in this country

Nearly 8 million persons reported Spanish as their mother tongue; Spanish mother-tongue claimants constituted nearly one in four of all claimants of non-English mother tongues in the United States; German was second in number of claimants followed by Italian and French; Polish and Yiddish also had more than 1 million claimants each

A million and a half persons reported Asian or Near Eastern languages; one person in twenty with a non-English mother tongue claimed one of these languages

The Survey of Languages Supplement to the July 1975 Current Population Survey asked the mother-tongue question of persons aged 14 and older. In 1975:

Nearly 28 million persons claimed mother tongues other than English in the population aged 14 and older; they constituted 17.8 percent of the 14 and older persons in the United States

Comparative data are available for 1970 and 1975 for persons aged 15 and older. They indicate that:

The numbers of persons aged 15 and older in the United States with non-English mother tongues remained virtually constant between 1970 and 1975; however, the proportion of this group in the total population fell from 19.8 percent in 1970 to 17.8 percent in 1975

Non-English mother-tongue claimants were somewhat less likely to be native born in 1975 than in 1970; in 1970 three out of four non-English mother-tongue claimants aged 15 and older were native born; in 1975 only seven out of ten were native born

In 1970 German still had the most claimants in the 15-plus age group; by 1975 Spanish had taken its place; German claimants fell from 20 percent of the total to 15 percent; Spanish claimants rose from 18 percent to 22 percent of the total non-English mother-tongue claimants

The Chinese, Filipino, Japanese, and Korean proportion of the 15 and older non-English mother-tongue claimants in 1970 was less than 3 percent; in 1975 these four language groups accounted for 5 percent of the total

Table 22.1 provides comparative data on non-English mother-tongue claimants aged 15 and older in 1970 and 1975 for the languages studied in the Survey of Languages.[3] It will be noted from this figure that, while the total numbers remained virtually the same, there were shifts in estimates for the different language groups. There was almost certainly an increase in claimants for two of

---

3. Although there were a number of languages with a larger number of claimants in the 1970 census, Greek and Portuguese were selected for study in the Survey of Languages because there were children from these groups in need of bilingual education programs.

Table 22.1. *Estimated numbers of claimants of non-English mother tongues aged 15 and older, 1970 and 1975 (000s)*

	Data from the 1970 Census	Data from the July 1975 Survey of Languages
Total persons	28,565	27,664
Selected European languages		
German	5,776	4,218
Spanish	5,057	5,974
Italian	3,809	3,846
French	2,200	2,214
Greek	387	429
Portuguese	290	361
Selected Asian languages		
Japanese	320	447
Chinese languages	293	478
Filipino languages	172	307
Korean	46	151
Other languages	10,216	9,239

Note: Detail may not add to total shown because of rounding.
Sources: U.S. Census of Population, 1970, 1-in-1,000 public use sample; National Center for Education Statistics, Survey of Languages Supplement to the July 1975 Current Population Survey of the U.S. Bureau of the Census Waggoner n.d. Table 3.

the languages studied – Spanish and Korean. German appeared to lose claimants (see Chapter 12).

Tables 22.2 and 22.3 display the 1970 and 1975 data by language, selected age group, and nativity. In 1970 fewer than one in five of the non-English mother-tongue claimants was a school-age or younger child; 35.7 percent were aged 25 to 49, and 37.8 percent were 50 or older. However, Spanish mother-tongue claimants were notably younger than the average for all the languages. Nearly 44 percent of Spanish claimants were 18 or younger and only 13.4 percent were 50 or older. Spanish claimants constituted less than a quarter of all claimants of non-English mother tongues. They constituted more than half of the school-age or younger group. Among other language groups with a million or more claimants in 1970, French also exceeded the average proportion of school-age or younger children. Nearly 22 percent of French claimants were 18 or younger. In contrast to these relatively young populations, the claimants of Yiddish, German, Polish, and Italian, among the groups with a million or more claimants in 1970, were proportionately older. Three out of five claimants of Yiddish and more than half of the German mother-tongue claimants were aged 50 and older.

Table 22.2. *Estimated U.S. population with mother tongues other than English, by language, selected age group, and nativity: 1970 (000s)*

Mother tongue	Total	Under 5	5–14	15–18	19–24	25–49	50 and older
			All persons with non-English mother tongues				
Total	33,659	1,593	3,501	1,368	2,481	12,009	12,707
Selected European							
Spanish	7,889	946	1,886	621	873	2,508	1,055
German	6,188	112	300	135	292	2,134	3,215
Italian	4,052	59	184	105	246	1,747	1,711
French	2,650	128	322	125	231	965	879
Polish	2,347	*	88	62	126	937	1,108
Yiddish	1,526	*	*	31	89	452	917
Norwegian	642	*	*	*	*	207	395
Swedish	632	*	*	*	*	159	425
Slovak	540	*	*	*	*	216	278
Hungarian	495	*	*	*	*	177	257
Greek	493	39	67	*	39	204	123
Czech	439	*	*	*	*	153	246
Dutch	352	*	*	*	*	128	155
Portuguese	334	*	32	*	*	142	107
Russian	285	*	*	*	*	73	180
Lithuanian and Latvian	260	*	*	*	*	90	136
Ukrainian	250	*	*	*	*	79	129
Serbo-Croatian	246	*	*	*	*	103	97
Finnish	237	*	*	*	*	80	128
Danish	193	*	*	*	*	55	125
Armenian	81	*	*	*	*	37	*
Irish and Scots Gaelic	76	*	*	*	*	*	43
Flemish	74	*	*	*	*	*	45
Rumanian	71	*	*	*	*	*	30
Slovenian	56	*	*	*	*	*	*
Selected Near Eastern and Asian							
Japanese	405	*	66	*	*	193	89
Chinese	397	*	76	*	61	140	64
Filipino languages	209	*	*	*	*	91	50
Arabic	201	*	*	*	*	101	52
Hebrew	110	*	*	*	*	30	46
Korean	70	*	*	*	*	*	*

Table 22.2. *Estimated U.S. population with mother tongues other than English, by language, selected age group, and nativity: 1970 (000s)—continued*

		Age group					
Mother tongue	Total	Under 5	5–14	15–18	19–24	2549	50 and older
Native American	243	*	56	*	31	71	34
Other non-English	1,616	93	178	62	149	610	524
		U.S.-born persons with non-English mother tongues					
Total	25,085	1,457	2,951	1,065	1,849	9,192	8,571
Selected European							
Spanish	5,967	889	1,648	492	656	1,703	579
German	4,838	100	241	97	225	1,671	2,504
Italian	3,021	53	159	81	196	1,511	1,021
French	2,147	114	282	108	196	779	668
Polish	1,940	*	77	54	108	854	821
Yiddish	1,085	*	*	30	76	402	546
Norwegian	558	*	*	*	*	186	334
Swedish	483	*	*	*	*	138	308
Slovak	457	*	*	*	*	202	211
Hungarian	332	*	*	*	*	134	150
Greek	298	33	47	*	*	130	44
Czech	357	*	*	*	*	135	187
Dutch	204	*	*	*	*	69	104
Portuguese	200	*	*	*	*	99	60
Russian	148	*	*	*	*	58	63
Lithuanian and Latvian	187	*	*	*	*	64	92
Ukrainian	156	*	*	*	*	48	74
Serbo-Croatian	148	*	*	*	*	68	52
Finnish	199	*	*	*	*	75	96
Danish	137	*	*	*	*	37	92
Armenian	53	*	*	*	*	*	*
Irish and Scots Gaelic	30	*	*	*	*	*	*
Flemish	42	*	*	*	*	*	*
Rumanian	48	*	*	*	*	*	*
Slovenian	50	*	*	*	*	*	*
Selected Near Eastern and Asian							
Japanese	249	*	49	*	*	116	54
Chinese	144	*	47	*	*	30	*
Filipino languages	45	*	*	*	*	*	*
Arabic	128	*	*	*	*	66	30
Hebrew	74	*	*	*	*	*	32
Korean	*	*	*	*	*	*	*

Table 22.2. *Estimated U.S. population with mother tongues other than English, by language, selected age group, and nativity: 1970 (000s)—continued*

Mother tongue	Total	Under 5	5–14	15–18	19–24	25–49	50 and older
Native American	231	*	56	*	*	66	33
Other non-English	1,105	87	151	45	91	409	322
Foreign-born persons with non-English mother tongues							
Total	7,912	98	400	237	533	2,641	4,003
Selected European							
Spanish	1,727	43	184	101	191	755	453
German	1,233	*	*	*	43	446	688
Italian	989	*	*	*	40	218	682
French	415	*	*	*	*	166	186
Polish	393	*	*	*	*	75	285
Yiddish	433	*	*	*	*	47	386
Norwegian	80	*	*	*	*	*	59
Swedish	143	*	*	*	*	*	114
Slovak	81	*	*	*	*	*	67
Hungarian	162	*	*	*	*	42	107
Greek	184	*	*	*	*	72	78
Czech	75	*	*	*	*	*	56
Dutch	143	*	*	*	*	57	49
Portuguese	124	*	*	*	*	42	45
Russian	136	*	*	*	*	*	117
Lithuanian and Latvian	70	*	*	*	*	*	44
Ukrainian	94	*	*	*	*	31	55
Serbo-Croatian	96	*	*	*	*	35	44
Finnish	37	*	*	*	*	*	31
Danish	56	*	*	*	*	*	33
Armenian	*	*	*	*	*	*	*
Irish and Scots Gaelic	44	*	*	*	*	*	*
Flemish	32	*	*	*	*	*	*
Rumanian	*	*	*	*	*	*	*
Slovenian	*	*	*	*	*	*	*
Selected Near Eastern and Asian							
Japanese	128	*	*	*	*	74	35
Chinese	241	*	*	*	38	104	50
Filipino languages	157	*	*	*	*	71	48
Arabic	70	*	*	*	*	33	*
Hebrew	36	*	*	*	*	*	*
Korean	45	*	*	*	*	*	*
Native American	*	*	*	*	*	*	*
Other non-English	424	*	*	*	49	169	176

Table 22.2. (*contd.*)

		Age group				
Mother tongue	Total	Under 5	5–14	15–18	19–24	25–49	50 and older
Persons with non-English mother tongues whose place of birth was not reported							
Total	662	38	150	66	99	176	133

* Less than an estimated 30,000 persons.
Source: U.S. Census of Population, 1970, 1-in-1,000 public use sample, unpublished data.

Table 22.3. *Estimated U.S. population aged 15 and older with mother tongues other than English, by language, selected age group, and nativity: July 1975 (000s)*

		Age group			
Mother tongue	Total	15–18	19–24	25–49	50 and older
All persons with non-English mother tongues					
Total	27,664	1,335	2,463	11,517	12,348
Selected European					
Spanish	5,974	663	953	3,113	1,244
German	4,218	85	203	1,418	2,512
Italian	3,846	109	269	1,555	1,914
French	2,214	117	236	896	965
Greek	429	*	*	202	159
Portuguese	361	*	*	181	127
Selected Asian					
Chinese	478	*	60	256	127
Japanese	447	*	62	232	136
Filipino	307	*	*	166	78
Korean	151	*	*	100	*
Other non-English	9,239	211	565	3,400	5,063
U.S.-born persons with non-English mother tongues					
Total	19,682	986	1,779	8,090	8,827
Selected European					
Spanish	3,842	515	675	1,964	688
German	3,272	67	151	1,075	1,979
Italian	2,931	82	235	1,301	1,313
French	1,802	96	184	735	787
Greek	231	*	*	118	63
Portuguese	204	*	*	98	79

Table 22.3. (*contd.*)

Mother tongue	Total	15–18	19–24	25–49	50 and older
			Age group		
Selected Asian					
Chinese	155	*	*	91	*
Japanese	267	*	*	122	92
Filipino	57	*	*	122	92
Korean	*	*	*	*	*
Other non-English	6,901	160	411	2,539	3,791
	Foreign-born persons with non-English mother tongues				
Total	7,859	341	678	3,381	3,460
Selected European					
Spanish	2,116	145	278	1,138	555
German	931	*	51	338	525
Italian	911	*	*	253	596
French	408	*	52	157	178
Greek	191	*	*	81	94
Portuguese	157	*	*	83	*
Selected Asian					
Chinese	321	*	*	165	103
Japanese	178	*	*	110	*
Filipino	251	*	*	134	69
Korean	127	*	*	82	*
Other non-English	2,266	*	152	839	1,229
	Persons with non-English mother tongues whose place of birth was not reported				
Total	122	*	*	*	61

* Less than an estimated 50,000 persons.

Note: Detail may not add to total shown because of rounding.
Source: National Center for Education Statistics, Survey of Languages Supplement to the July 1975 Current Population Survey of the U.S. Bureau of the Census, unpublished data.

Comparing the non-English mother-tongue claimants in 1970 and 1975, it may be noted that the overall proportions among the age groups aged 15 and older remained relatively the same. The proportion of Spanish claimants aged 15 to 18 was more than twice the proportion for all language groups together. French claimants in this age group were also proportionately more than the average for all the languages. The proportion of German claimants in the oldest age group,

DOROTHY WAGGONER

Table 22.4 . *Estimated numbers of selected European non-English mother-tongue claimants, by language, nativity, and parentage: United States, 1940 and 1970 (000s)*

					Native born			
	Total		Foreign born		Foreign and mixed parentage		Native-born parentage	
Mother tongue	1940[a]	1970[b]	1940[a]	1970	1940[a]	1970	1940[a]	1970
Total	21,778	30,332	8,242	6,759	10,623	12,577	2,915	10,478
German	4,950	6,188	1,589	1,233	2,436	2,341	925	2,497
Italian	3,767	4,052	1,561	989	2,080	2,398	125	623
Polish	2,416	2,347	802	393	1,429	1,273	186	667
Spanish	1,861	7,889	428	1,727	714	1,854	719	4,113
Yiddish	1,751	1,526	924	433	773	938	53	147
French	1,412	2,650	360	415	534	760	519	1,387
Swedish	831	632	432	143	374	390	34	93
Norwegian	658	642	233	80	344	325	81	233
Russian	585	285	357	136	214	126	14	*
Czech	520	439	160	75	279	220	82	137
Slovak	484	540	172	81	284	359	29	98
Hungarian	453	495	241	162	199	272	13	60
Greek	274	493	165	184	102	231	6	67
Lithuanian	273	260[c]	123	70[c]	141	147[c]	9	40[c]
Dutch	267	352	103	143	103	114	61	90
Finnish	230	237	97	37	118	144	15	55
Danish	227	193	122	56	95	117	9	*
Portuguese	216	334	84	124	121	143	12	57
Slovenian	178	56	76	*	97	45	6	*
Serbo-Croatian	153	246	71	96	77	126	5	*
Ukrainian	84	250	36	94	45	141	3	*
Armenian	68	81	40	*	26	40	2	*
Rumanian	66	71	43	*	20	36	2	*
Flemish	54	74	32	32	18	37	5	*

* Less than an estimated 30,000 persons.
[a] White population only.
[b] Includes 518,000 persons for whom nativity and parentage were not reported.
[c] Includes Latvian.

Note: Detail may not add to total shown because of rounding.
Sources: U.S. Census of Population, 1940; U.S. Census of Population, 1970, 1-in-1,000 public use sample, unpublished data.

those 50 and older, was 10 percent higher than the overall average in 1970 and grew to 15 percent higher in 1975. The proportion of older Italians also appeared to be growing between 1970 and 1975.

Birthplace and parentage of the non-English background population. The 1940 census data provided official evidence for the first time that there are substantial numbers of native-born persons, many of them the children of native-born parents, who maintain languages other than English at least in their homes. These data refute the common misconception that most persons with non-English language backgrounds in the United States are foreign born. Table 22.4 indicates that in 1940, three out of five White non-English mother-tongue claimants in the United States were born here. By 1970, the proportion of native-born to foreign-born persons with non-English mother tongues of all races was better than three out of four. Of the group 15 years of age and older who were asked the question in the July 1975 Survey of Languages, the proportion of native-born to foreign-born persons with non-English mother tongues was somewhat lower. Compared with 74 percent of non-English mother-tongue claimants 15 years of age and older who were native born in 1970, 71.6 percent of the 15 and older group in 1975 were born here. The exceptions to these statistics are the Chinese, Filipino, and Korean groups, the large majority of whose claimants were born abroad.

Comparisons of non-English mother-tongue claimants by nativity of parents are not possible for 1975. Place of birth of parents was not asked in the Survey of Languages. However, 1940 and 1970 data for the claimants of twenty-four European languages by nativity and parentage are shown in Table 22.4. From this table, it will be noted that nearly half of the claimants of these languages were "second generation" Americans in 1940. Native-born claimants of these languages whose parents were also native born constituted 13.4 percent of the total group. Fewer than two out of five claimants of these languages were foreign born. Foreign-born claimants were the majority of claimants of only nine of the languages. In 1970, "second generation" claimants of these languages were two in five, and more than a third of all claimants were native born of native parentage. Fewer than a quarter were foreign born. There were no languages among these twenty-four with a majority of claimants who were foreign born in 1970. The native-of-native parentage claimants of four languages – French, Spanish, German, and Norwegian – exceeded the average for all twenty-four languages for this group in 1970. Native-of-native claimants of French and Spanish were more than half of all claimants for those languages. Those two languages and German accounted for more than three-quarters of the native-of-native parentage claimants for these twenty-four mother tongues in 1970.

Because the questions were worded and interpreted differently in 1940 and 1970, it is not possible to assess the meaning of the disproportionate increase in the native-of-native parentage group between 1940 and 1970. However, it is surely not amiss to speculate that one of the factors has to do with a change in

Table 22.5. *Estimated numbers of selected Asian and Near Eastern mother-tongue claimants, by language, nativity, and parentage: United States, 1960 and 1970 (000s)*

Mother tongue	1960 Foreign-born only	Total[a]	1970 Foreign-born	Native born Foreign or mixed parentage	Native-born parentage
Total	397	1,534	770	566	136
Japanese	95	405	128	185	64
Chinese languages	90	397	241	128	*
Filipino languages[b]	74	209	157	36	*
Arabic	50	201	70	108	*
Hebrew	38	110	36	59	*
Korean	9	70	45	*	*
Other Asian and Near Eastern languages	41	142	93	33	*

* Less than an estimated 30,000 persons.
[a] Includes 62,000 persons for whom nativity and parentage were not reported.
[b] Published figure for Tagalog for 1960; 1970 figure includes various Filipino languages.
Sources: U.S. Census of Population, 1960 (Census 1966); U.S. Census of Population, 1970, 1-in-1,000 public use sample, unpublished data.

attitudes toward linguistic and cultural differences, and that there were many more persons willing to acknowledge non-English mother tongues in 1970 than were willing to do so in war-clouded 1940.

Asian language backgrounds. It has been pointed out that the 1940 data were the first available on the non-English language backgrounds of the U.S. population regardless of place of birth of individuals or their parents. However, because the 1940 data were published only for the White population, the 1970 census provides the first comprehensive information on language backgrounds other than European in the United States. Five Asian and Near Eastern languages had 100,000 or more claimants in 1970. Since no data were tabulated on these languages previously, except for Arabic, it is impossible to know to what extent these languages were the mother tongues of U.S.-born persons prior to 1970. Nevertheless, with the 1960 data for comparison with the 1970 data for the foreign born, the first effects of the 1965 repeal of the restrictive immigration quotas on groups claiming Asian mother tongues can be seen. These data are displayed in Table 22.5.

Koreans are one of the more recent Asian groups to immigrate to the United States. In the decade 1960–70, foreign-born claimants of Korean increased five-fold. In 1970 this group constituted more than two thirds of the claimants of Korean. Foreign-born claimants of Chinese and Filipino languages also increased substantially – more than two and a half times for the Chinese languages and more than twice for the Filipino languages. Foreign-born claimants of Chinese languages constituted nearly two-thirds of their group in 1970, and foreign-born claimants of Filipino languages three-quarters. Foreign-born claimants of Japanese increased only a third in the decade of the 1960s and constituted less than a third of the total Japanese mother-tongue group. Among Asian and Near Eastern languages with more than 100,000 claimants in 1970, Japanese, with 64,000 native-born claimants whose parents were also native born, was alone with a substantial "third generation." One person in six who reported Japanese as their mother tongue in 1970 was in this group.

The proportion of foreign-born claimants among all claimants aged 15 and older of the four Asian language groups studied in the Survey of Languages increased from 1970 to 1975, reflecting the continuing immigration. Japanese was still the exception, however. Only Japanese claimants were more likely to be native born than foreign born. Three out of five persons with a Japanese mother-tongue were born in this country in 1975. More than 80 percent of Korean and Filipino mother-tongue claimants in 1975 were foreign born and 67 percent of persons with Chinese mother tongues were born outside the United States. More than two in five of the mother-tongue claimants for the four Asian language groups were adults in the age range of 25–49.

Immigration and non-English language backgrounds. As shown by the census figures for 1940 and 1970 and the Survey of Languages, immigration has not accounted for most persons with non-English language backgrounds in the United States, at least since before World War II. In 1940, and to a greater extent in 1970, most persons with non-English language backgrounds were born in this country. By 1970, more than a third of them were native-born children of parents who were also born here. The proportion of foreign-born persons in the population generally has been decreasing with each decennial census. In 1940, 8.8 percent of the total population were born abroad. By 1970, only 4.7 percent of the population were born abroad. However, after reaching its lowest point in a hundred years in the decade of the 1930s, immigration to the United States has been rising again. As the great waves of European immigration did in the last decades of the nineteenth century and the early years of the twentieth, recent immigration has been bringing new language groups to the United States and new strength to some of the old-established language groups in this country. This process has been accelerated with the repeal of the restrictive Asian immigration quotas in 1965. Growth in foreign-born claimants of Asian mother tongues has already been noted.

During the decade of greatest immigration, 1901–10, more than nine out of ten immigrants came from Europe. During the decade 1931–40, when, for the

Table 22.6. *Immigrants admitted to the United States, by selected country of birth and year of admission: years ending June 30, 1971–June 30, 1975*

Country of origin	Total	Year admitted				
		1971	1972	1973	1974	1975
Total	1,936,281	370,478	384,685	400,063	394,861	386,194
Spanish-speaking	638,356	113,133	121,561	136,168	135,494	132,000
Mexico	318,075	50,103	64,040	70,141	71,586	62,205
Cuba	110,687	21,611	20,045	24,147	18,929	25,955
Dominican Republic	67,051	12,624	10,760	13,921	15,680	14,066
Colombia	29,114	6,440	5,173	5,230	5,837	6,434
Ecuador	22,979	4,981	4,337	4,139	4,795	4,727
Spain	18,584	4,125	4,386	4,134	3,390	2,549
El Salvador	10,513	1,776	2,001	2,042	2,278	2,416
Argentina	10,149	1,992	1,819	2,034	2,077	2,227
Guatemala	9,090	2,194	1,640	1,759	1,638	1,859
Peru	8,440	1,086	1,443	1,713	1,942	2,256
Panama	7,934	1,457	1,507	1,612	1,664	1,694
Honduras	6,186	1,146	964	1,329	1,390	1,357
Chile	5,348	956	857	1,139	1,285	1,111
Other Spanish-speaking countries[a]	14,206	2,642	2,589	2,828	3,003	3,144
English-speaking	184,895	39,348	37,897	35,453	37,144	35,053
Jamaica	61,445	14,571	13,427	9,963	12,408	11,076
United Kingdom	53,020	10,787	10,078	10,638	10,710	10,807
Trinidad and Tobago	33,278	7,130	6,615	7,035	6,516	5,982
Guyana	14,320	2,115	2,826	2,969	3,241	3,169
Ireland	8,251	1,614	1,780	2,000	1,572	1,285
Barbados	7,878	1,731	1,620	1,448	1,461	1,618
Australia	6,703	1,400	1,551	1,400	1,236	1,116
European (except Spain, U.K. and Ireland)	354,722	79,980	73,749	76,098	65,540	59,355
Italy	93,151	22,137	21,427	22,151	15,884	11,552
Greece	58,519	15,939	11,021	10,751	10,824	9,984
Portugal	55,933	11,692	10,343	10,751	11,302	11,845
Austria and Germany	35,016	8,147	7,449	7,128	6,736	5,556

Table 22.6. *Immigrants admitted to the United States, by selected country of birth and year of admission: years ending June 30, 1971–June 30, 1975–continued*

Country of origin	Total	Year admitted				
		1971	1972	1973	1974	1975
Total	1,936,281	370,478	384,685	400,063	394,861	386,194
Yugoslavia	28,908	6,063	5,922	7,582	5,817	3,524
Poland	20,555	2,883	4,784	4,914	4,033	3,941
U.S.S.R.	9,147	718	902	1,248	1,161	5,118
France	8,810	2,001	1,966	1,845	1,634	1,364
Romania	7,308	1,643	1,329	1,623	1,552	1,161
Hungary	7,041	1,549	1,698	1,624	1,288	882
Czechoslavakia	6,342	1,799	1,783	1,552	683	525
Netherlands	5,007	1,163	988	1,016	1,024	816
Other European countries[b]	18,985	4,246	4,137	3,913	3,602	3,087
Asian and Near Eastern (except Jordan, Lebanon, Iraq and Syria)	574,064	96,824	113,815	117,566	122,061	123,798
Philippines	153,254	28,471	29,376	30,799	32,857	31,751
Korea	112,493	14,297	18,876	22,930	28,028	28,362
China, Taiwan and Hong Kong	107,120	17,622	21,730	21,656	22,685	23,427
India	72,912	14,310	16,926	13,124	12,779	15,773
Japan and the Ryukyus	25,910	5,326	5,770	5,645	4,887	4,282
Thailand	21,131	2,915	4,102	4,941	4,956	4,217
Vietnam	16,250	2,038	3,412	4,569	3,192	3,039
Iran	13,413	2,411	3,059	2,998	2,608	2,337
Israel	9,878	1,739	2,099	1,917	1,998	2,125
Turkey	9,092	1,748	1,986	1,899	1,867	1,592
Other Asian and Near Eastern countries[c]	32,611	5,947	6,479	7,088	6,204	6,893

504   DOROTHY WAGGONER

Table 22.6 *Immigrants admitted to the United States, by selected country of birth and year of admission: years ending June 30, 1971–June 30, 1975—continued*

Country of origin	Total	Year admitted				
		1971	1972	1973	1974	1975
Total	1,936,281	370,478	384,685	400,063	394,861	386,194
Arabic-speaking	49,713	10,280	9,755	8,868	10,432	10,378
Jordan	13,210	2,588	2,756	2,450	2,838	2,578
Egypt	11,967	3,643	2,512	2,274	1,831	1,707
Lebanon	10,303	1,867	1,984	1,977	2,400	2,075
Iraq	8,838	1,231	1,491	1,039	2,281	2,796
Syria	5,395	951	1,012	1,128	1,082	1,222
Other Western Hemisphere countries	104,381	26,259	22,071	19,674	18,021	18,356
Canada	47,817	13,128	10,776	8,951	7,654	7,308
Haiti	27,130	7,444	5,809	4,786	3,946	5,145
Brazil	5,899	1,413	1,089	1,213	1,114	1,070
Other countries not identified	23,535	4,274	4,397	4,724	5,307	4,833
Other areas	30,150	4,654	5,837	6,236	6,169	7,254
Africa (except Egypt)	20,983	3,129	4,100	4,381	4,351	5,022
Oceania (except Australia)	9,160	1,523	1,735	1,855	1,816	2,231
Other countries not identified	7	2	2	0	2	1

[a] Costa Rica, Nicaragua, Uruguay, and Venezuela.
[b] Denmark, Sweden, Switzerland, and other European countries not identified.
[c] Indonesia and other Near Eastern and Asian countries not identified.
Source: U.S. Immigration and Naturalization Service 1975: 65, Table 14.

first time since 1840 immigration fell below 1 million, two-thirds of immigrants still came from Europe. By 1961–70 the number of immigrants had risen again to over 3 million, but only one-third were from Europe. Nearly two out of five were from Mexico, Central and South America, and the West Indies, and an eighth were from Asia. During the five years from 1971 to 1975, nearly 2 million immigrants were admitted to the United States. Forty-one percent were from Mexico, Central and South America, and the West Indies, nearly a third were from Asia, and only a fifth were from Europe (U.S. Immigration and Naturalization Service 1975: 63–64). Table 22.6 shows the number of immigrants for the years 1971–5 by selected country of birth arranged to the extent possible by national language. From these data it will be noted that the largest number of immigrants from a single country of birth, more than 300,000, were from Mexico. The Philippines, Korea, and Cuba provided more than 100,000 immigrants each. Only Italy, among the European countries of birth, contributed close to 100,000. Greece and Portugal were below India and Jamaica as countries of birth of between 55,000 and 100,000 immigrants admitted to the United States between 1971 and 1975. Spanish-speaking countries combined contributed a third of all immigrants to the United States between 1971 and 1975. Nearly 640,000 persons were admitted from Mexico, Spain, and Spanish-speaking countries of the Caribbean, Central, and South America in those years.

Current language use

The mother-tongue data and – indirectly – the statistics on immigration provide insights into the language backgrounds of the U.S. population prior to 1975. However, with the Survey of Languages Supplement to the July 1975 Current Population Survey, it is possible to estimate for the first time the extent to which non-English languages in general, and ten languages in particular, are currently spoken in the United States among persons 4 years of age and older. The ten languages are Spanish, German, Italian, French, Greek, and Portuguese, among the European languages, and the Chinese languages, the Filipino languages, and Japanese and Korean, among Asian languages. At least one of these ten languages is spoken in the households of more than three out of four persons in households in which languages other than English are in current use.

According to the Survey of Languages:

One person in eight aged 4 or older in the United States lives in a household in which a language other than English is spoken; there are 25.3 million such persons

Nineteen million persons who speak languages other than English reside in households in which languages other than English are currently spoken; one person in ten aged 4 or older in the United States speaks a language other than English in a household with a non-English language

More than one-third of the persons who speak languages other than English speak those languages as their usual languages

Of persons aged 4 or older, 1,600,000 do not speak English at all

Current language and mother tongue. Data from the Survey of Languages reveal for the first time the relationship of mother tongue to current usage. Of the persons 14 years of age and older reporting non-English mother tongues in the Survey of Languages, only 54 percent reside in households in which non-English languages are currently spoken. Fewer than two out of five speak non-English languages as their usual languages. However, language groups

506   DOROTHY WAGGONER

differ widely in their current language environment. A large majority of
Spanish, Chinese, Filipino, and Korean mother-tongue claimants live in
households in which these languages are currently spoken. More than half of
the Spanish mother-tongue claimants and nearly half of Chinese and Korean
claimants speak their mother tongues as their usual languages. In contrast,
fewer than one in three German mother-tongue claimants has any present home
contact with German. These data are shown in Tables 22.7a and 22.7b

Households using a language other than English. Tables 22.8 and 22.9
provide information on the 25.3 million persons aged 4 and older who reside in
households in which languages other than English are spoken by language
background and selected age group and by usual household language and
bilinguality. English is the usual language in the households of nearly
two-thirds of these persons. In those of another quarter, English is spoken, but
the non-English language is the usual household language. In the households of
5 percent of these persons, English is not spoken at all.

Nearly two out of five persons in households with non-English languages are
in Spanish-speaking households (see Chapters 9 and 10). Eleven percent are in
Italian-speaking households (see Chapter 11), and 9 percent each are in French-
and German-speaking households (see Chapter 12). The Asian languages
together account for 6.6 percent of the persons in households in which
languages other than English are spoken.

There are 7.7 million school-age children in households in which languages
other than English are spoken; 3.3 million of them – nearly half – are in
Spanish-speaking households. Persons in Spanish-speaking households account
for more than three out of five of the persons in households in which a
non-English language is the usual or the only household language.

In the Survey of Languages, information was not obtained on the languages
spoken by individuals in households in which the only household language
reported was English. However, individual language data were obtained for the
25.3 million persons aged 4 and older in households reporting the use of
non-English languages either as usual or second languages. Approximately a
quarter of the persons in these households speak only English. Data on the other
18.7 million persons who speak languages other than English in households
with non-English languages are displayed in Table 22.10 and 22.11. As shown
in Table 22.10, more than a third of these persons – 6.5 million – speak the
non-English language as their usual language; 1.6 million persons do not speak
English at all.

The speakers of Spanish account for 44 percent of the total persons speaking
languages other than English in households with non-English languages.
Another 10 percent are speakers of Italian. French and German speakers
account for between 7 and 8 percent each, as do the four Asian language groups
together. There are 4.2 million school-age children speaking languages other
than English. More than two-thirds of them are Spanish-speaking. Spanish

Table 22.7a. *Estimated number of claimants of non-English mother tongues aged 14 and older, by current language environment and mother tongue: United States, July 1975 (000s)*

Non-English mother tongue	Total mother-tongue claimants	In households where only English is spoken	In non-English language households				
			Total	With English usual individual language	With non-English usual individual language	Individual language not ascertained	Household language not ascertained
Total	27,966	12,774	15,144	9,584	5,407	127	75
Selected European							
Spanish	6,144	600	5,541	2,386	3,130	*	*
German	4,228	3,015	1,205	1,078	106	*	*
Italian	3,864	1,971	1,873	1,426	430	*	*
French	2,240	1,105	1,121	855	258	*	*
Greek	432	102	329	217	108	*	*
Portuguese	369	126	242	144	97	*	*
Selected Asian							
Chinese languages	486	87	399	159	238	*	*
Japanese	453	140	308	214	95	*	*
Filipino languages	311	50	261	148	114	*	*
Korean	153	*	129	56	73	*	*
Other[a]	9,286	5,554	3,706	2,901	758	*	*

* Less than an estimated 50,000 persons.

[a] Includes persons who reported a mother tongue other than English but not the specific language.

Note: Detail may not add to total shown because of rounding.

Source: National Center for Education Statistics, Survey of Languages Supplement to the July 1975 Current Population Survey of the U.S. Bureau of the Census = Waggoner n.d.: Table 4.

Table 22.7b. *Current language environment of selected non-English mother-tongue claimants aged 14 and older: United States, July 1975*

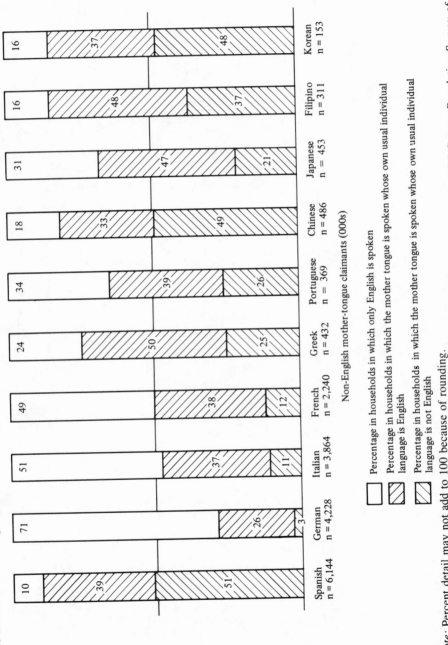

Non-English mother-tongue claimants (000s)

	Percentage in households in which only English is spoken
	Percentage in households in which the mother tongue is spoken whose own usual individual language is English
	Percentage in households in which the mother tongue is spoken whose own usual individual language is not English

Note: Percent detail may not add to 100 because of rounding.
Source: National Center for Education Statistics, Survey of Languages Supplement to the July 1975 Current Population Survey of the U.S.

Table 22.8. *Estimated numbers of persons aged 4 and older in households in which languages other than English are spoken, by usual household language, bilinguality of household, and non-English household language background: United States, July 1975 (000s)*

Non-English household language background	Total persons in households in which languages other than English are spoken	Persons in bilingual households		Persons in households in which English is not spoken
		English the usual language	The non-English language the usual language	
Total	25,344	17,573	6,491	1,256
Selected European				
Spanish	9,904	5,085	3,883	937
Italian	2,836	2,303	442	81
German	2,269	2,112	138	*
French	2,259	1,974	274	*
Greek	488	324	148	*
Portuguese	349	206	130	*
Selected Asian				
Chinese languages	534	181	323	*
Japanese	524	415	95	*
Filipino languages	377	255	114	*
Korean	246	117	119	*
Other	5,559	4,602	826	124

* Less than an estimated 50,000 persons.
Notes: In a limited number of cases, persons were reported in households in which non-English languages are spoken but it was not ascertained whether English is also spoken. Detail may not add to total shown because of rounding.
Source: National Center for Education Statistics, Survey of Languages Supplement to the July 1975 Current Population Survey of the U.S. Bureau of the Census = Waggoner n.d.: Table 9.

speakers account for 61.8 percent of the persons whose usual or only language is not English.

Language groups vary in their proportions of persons who speak the non-English languages as their usual or only languages, as shown in Table 22.12a. Three out of five Chinese-speaking persons are dominant in Chinese. Almost half of the Spanish speakers are dominant in Spanish. In contrast, nine out of ten German speakers usually speak English.

Table 22.9. *Estimated numbers of persons aged 4 and older in households in which languages other than English are spoken, by selected age group and non-English household language background: United States, July 1975 (000s)*

Non-English household language background	Total	Age group				
		4–5	6–18	19–25	26–50	50 and older
Total	25,344	928	6,739	2,972	8,093	6,611
Selected European						
Spanish	9,904	524	3,279	1,357	3,427	1,316
Italian	2,836	68	599	285	765	1,120
German	2,269	60	527	205	703	771
French	2,259	*	623	303	678	614
Greek	488	*	124	52	173	123
Portuguese	349	*	87	*	128	105
Selected Asian						
Chinese languages	534	*	120	76	208	108
Japanese	524	*	129	63	196	115
Filipino languages	377	*	133	*	141	61
Korean	246	*	73	*	113	*
Other	5,559	135	1,044	566	1,562	2,251

* Less than an estimated 50,000 persons.

Note: Detail may not add to total shown because of rounding.
Source: National Center for Education Statistics, Survey of Languages Supplement to the July 1975 Current Population Survey of the U.S. Bureau of the Census, adapted from Waggoner n.d.: Table 6.

Non-English language dominance and place of birth.   It was noted earlier that the majority of persons with non-English language backgrounds in the United States were born in this country. For the 1975 non-English mother-tongue claimants aged 15 and older, nearly three-quarters were native born. Among persons whose usual current language is a language other than English, however, 57.4 percent were born in foreign countries. As shown in Table 22.12b the proportions of foreign born to native born vary by language group. Fewer than two out of five French speakers were born abroad. Only 45 percent of the Spanish speakers were born abroad. In contrast, there is a very high correlation between speaking the Filipino languages (see Chapter 15), Korean, Portuguese, Italian, and Greek as usual languages and foreign place of birth.

Statistics on language use.   The effort to document the language characteristics of the entire U.S. population is a new endeavor. Official statistics, until

Table 22.10. *Estimated numbers of persons aged 4 and older who speak languages other than English in households where such languages are spoken, by usual language, bilinguality, and non-English language: United States, July 1975 (000s)*

Non-English language	Total persons who speak languages other than English in households with non-English languages	Bilingual persons Whose usual language is English	Whose usual language is not English	Persons who do not speak English
Total	18,719	12,189	4,888	1,632
Selected European				
Spanish	8,243	4,212	2,934	1,093
Italian	1,879	1,432	299	148
French	1,452	1,182	233	*
German	1,389	1,257	101	*
Greek	384	260	113	*
Portuguese	279	169	78	*
Selected Asian				
Chinese languages	475	195	224	56
Japanese	372	261	90	*
Filipino languages	317	205	99	*
Korean	182	92	75	*
Other	3,748	2,925	642	175

* Less than an estimated 50,000 persons.

Notes: In a limited number of cases, persons were reported as speaking languages other than English, but it was not ascertained whether they also speak English. Detail may not add to total shown because of rounding.
Source: National Center for Education Statistics, Survey of Languages Supplement to the July 1975 Current Population Survey of the U.S. Bureau of the Census = Waggoner n.d.: Table 13.

relatively recently, have served to obscure rather than to illuminate the degree to which languages other than English have been maintained by the population. With the increasing recognition of Hispanic ethnics in U.S. society has come an awareness that there are substantial numbers of Spanish and other language minorities in the country and that members of these groups have problems of access to public services, the courts, voting rights, and education related to their proficiency in English. The Congressional mandate of 1974 was a response to the need for better language statistics. The Survey of Languages

Table 22.11. *Estimated numbers of persons aged 4 and older who speak languages other than English as their usual or second languages in households where such languages are spoken, by selected age group and non-English language: United States, July 1975 (000s)*

Non-English language	Total	Age group				
		4–5	6–18	19–25	26–50	50 and older
Total	18,719	508	3,701	2,031	6,639	5,842
Selected European						
Spanish	8,243	372	2,529	1,139	3,010	1,192
Italian	1,879	*	138	115	574	1,037
French	1,452	*	196	213	515	525
German	1,389	*	127	93	512	646
Greek	384	*	71	*	153	114
Portuguese	279	*	53	*	114	91
Selected Asian						
Chinese languages	475	*	88	67	192	106
Japanese	372	*	*	*	172	108
Filipino languages	317	*	93	*	128	63
Korean	182	*	*	*	94	*
Other	3,748	*	312	274	1,177	1,939

* Less than an estimated 50,000 persons.

Note: Detail may not add to total shown because of rounding.
Source: National Center for Education Statistics, Survey of Languages Supplement to the July 1975 Current Population Survey of the U.S. Bureau of the Census = Waggoner n.d.: Table 15.

Supplement to the Current Population Survey of July 1975, cited in this chapter, was the pilot study undertaken to fulfill the mandate. The principal response was the Survey of Income and Education which was conducted by the Bureau of the Census in Spring 1976 with assistance from the National Center for Education Statistics which added the language questions. The 1980 census continued the effort to document current usage and to estimate the size of the population with limited-English proficiency related to a non-English language background.

Table 22.12a. *Language dominance of persons aged 4 and older speaking languages other than English in households where such languages are spoken: United States, July 1975*

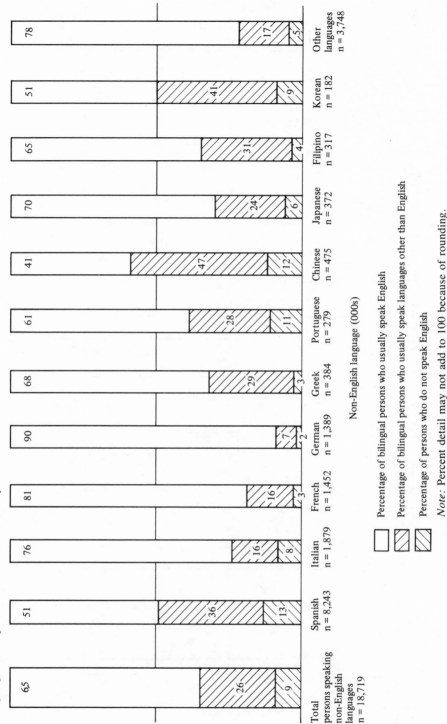

Non-English language (000s)

□ Percentage of bilingual persons who usually speak English

▨ Percentage of bilingual persons who usually speak languages other than English

▨ Percentage of persons who do not speak English

Note: Percent detail may not add to 100 because of rounding.
Source: Waggoner n.d.: Chart 5.

Table 22.12b. *Percentage of non-English-dominant persons aged 4 and older in households in which languages other than English are spoken who are foreign born: United States, July 1975*

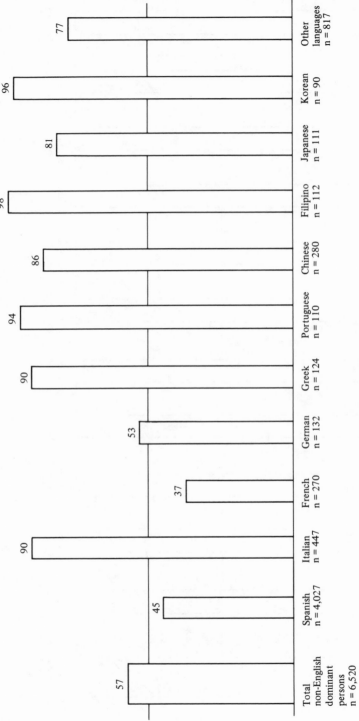

Non-English usual language (000s)

Source: Waggoner n.d.: Chart 7.

FURTHER READING

The basic analysis of the census mother-tongue data in relation to language maintenance in the United States through 1960 is contained in the chapter "Mother tongue and nativity in the American population" in Fishman et al. 1966. Census figures constitute one of the principal sources of statistical information on language use in the USA as well as other countries, but they often pose problems of interpretation. Lieberson 1966 gives an informative statement of the values and problems in the use of census data on language.

The wording of questions relating to language in the decennial censuses is contained in U.S. Bureau of the Census (hereafter Census) 1973. However, the form reproduced for 1910 does not contain the mother-tongue question which was added for foreign-born persons or their foreign-born parents by an amendment to the census legislation. The mother-tongue data from the 1970 census were published in Census 1973a, b. Only national totals by nativity and parentage were published for all languages. State totals and totals for standard metropolitan statistical areas and cities of 250,000 population or more were published for twenty-six languages, including American Indian languages as a group and Japanese, Chinese, and Arabic, of the non-European languages. Totals for counties and smaller cities were published for French, German, Polish, Russian, Yiddish, Italian, and Spanish.

The fullest data on American Indian languages were published in Census 1973c. Data on Spanish mother-tongue claimants are available for states and cities in standard metropolitan statistical areas in which there are at least 5,000 Spanish language, Spanish origin, or birthplace persons in Census 1973e. Problems of counting the Spanish language background population in the 1970 census are discussed in U.S. Commission on Civil Rights 1974.

Language data from the November 1969 and the March 1972 Current Population Surveys are found in Census 1971a, b, 1973f. Additional data from the Survey of Languages Supplement to the July 1975 Current Population Survey are contained in Waggoner n.d.

The U.S. Immigration and Naturalization Service publishes an annual report on immigration which includes a summary of immigration to the United States dating back to the first records in 1820.

Data on non-English language background persons and other information from the Survey of Income and Education, analyzed too late for use in this chapter, are included in four bulletins issued by the National Center for Education Statistics: 1978a, b, c, 1979, and in Waggoner 1978.

23

Language policy:
past, present, and future

JOSHUA A. FISHMAN

Relative to the early 1960s, when I was at work on *Language Loyalty in the United States* (Fishman et al. 1966), the total picture of language life in our country may be characterized by the adage *plus ça change, plus c'est la même chose*. On the surface a great deal has changed, but in my most pessimistic moments I wonder whether the change isn't mostly in our intellectual sophistication, sociolinguistic at its core, to discuss, analyze, and prescribe with respect to language in society. Basically ours is still a society whose peculiar genius is not along the lines of linguistic sophistication, sensitivity, or concern. Technology, productivity, standard of living, consumerism, populism, democracy, these and many other descriptions apply, but a concern for language is not generally among them. Neither language as an exquisite human gift, nor even English as an instrument or as a symbol, are part of the man-in-the-street's patrimony, his concept of what the United States is, what it stands for, what he or it is proud of, what he or it is stirred by, inspired by, committed to.

Even the exasperated know-nothingism of "this is, after all, an English-speaking country" is cognizant only of two purported rewards resulting therefrom: political unity and communicational ease. English for our masses is a LINGUA FRANCA rather than a thing of beauty, elegance, precision, purity, or greatness. "It works"; it is an instrumentality; but as such, it is not an object of love, affection, devotion, emotion. For good or for evil, we have developed a civilization that is not sentimental about language, languages, or even about its own language. If our college youth is not heart-broken that the WHORFIAN HYPOTHESIS has, in its strong version, become decreasingly supportable (Fishman and Spolsky 1977), neither is it thrilled by the worldwide spread of English. English is for them what it is for all but a small number of English teachers and "professional Englishmen" in the USA: a modern Aramaic which all of mankind would adopt because of the material benefits to which it is an open sesame, rather than because of any internal spirit that animates it (Fishman 1977a; Fishman, Cooper, and Conrad 1977). We are the ultimate GESELLSCHAFT, never having had much collective GEMEINSCHAFT to begin with. We are the ultimate modern society. The mysteries for which words are crucially needed, which language creates and which only language can solve – religion, philosophy, literature, ideology – are not the mysteries we dwell upon most.

516

We glory in the least humanistic mysteries and there is precious little language and little language preciousness to be found among them. The state of language policy in the United States cannot but be a reflection of the above state of linguistic astigmatism that characterizes our national life more generally.

Language shift policy

The greatest American linguistic investment by far has been in the Anglification of its millions of immigrant and indigenous speakers of other languages. Without either constitutional or subsequent legal declaration or requirement that English is the OFFICIAL (let alone the NATIONAL) LANGUAGE, a complex web of customs, institutions, and programs has long fostered well-nigh exclusive reliance upon English in public life. The result of two centuries of the foregoing is that literally hundreds of millions of Americans have been led, cajoled, persuaded, embarrassed into, and forced to forget, forego and even deny languages that were either their MOTHER TONGUES, their COMMUNAL LANGUAGES, or their personal or communal additional tongues. The Soviet Union has attained universal Russification within sixty years, thus denying us the world's speed record with respect to LANGUAGE SHIFT. However, the Soviet Union, as the inheritor *par excellence* of both Marx and Herder, has at least, thus far, only attained universal *familiarity* with Russian as a second language. Only a very minor proportion of the total ethnically non-Russian population has given up its own mother tongue for Russian (Lewis 1972; Silver 1974), even though just that shift is very noticeable among smaller nationalities, particularly those most urbanized and those most impacted by "planned" (forced) migration into or out of their own areas. Thus language shift in the USSR, with its nationality republics, nationality regions, and nationality districts (all of them purportedly "autonomous"), is primarily language displacement rather than language replacement. Language shift in the USA is quintessentially replacive. English as a second language has become English as a first language and the latter, in turn, has become English as an only language. No Herderian, Jeffersonian, or even ordinary "little culture" protective institutions have been available to stem the tide. Certainly the cultivation of such has not usually been deemed a public responsibility, in the public good, to be paid for out of public funds.

Nevertheless, this picture is not exactly as it was in the early 1960s, the major difference being the BILINGUAL EDUCATION ACT (Fishman 1976). First funded in 1967–8, refunded in 1973–4, and again in 1979–80, the Act was primarily an act for the Anglification of non-English speakers and not an act for BILINGUAL-ISM. Ironically, "Bilingualism" has become a newspeak euphemism for "non-English mother tongue." "Bilinguals" are thus non-English mother-tongue speakers; "bilingual teachers" are those who teach them; "bilingual programs" are those that Anglify them. This usage is uniquely American and barely disguises the negative semantic field to which it pertains. Under the aegis of the Bilingual Education Act, funds have been provided to state education departments, universities, and local school districts for experimental/demonstration programs that temporarily employ non-English mother tongues as co-media of instruction until (hopefully within three years or less), the pupil's English is good enough to become the sole medium of instruction. Thus, the act is basically not an act *for* bilingualism, but, rather, an act *against* bilingualism. It may contribute not merely to displacing non-English mother tongues from the instructional process, but to replacing them entirely (Kjolseth 1973; Fishman 1977b; Gaarder 1977).

The Act provides for teaching the culture as well as the language of non-English-speaking students to students of "limited English-speaking ability." Guidelines of the Act also permit a small proportion of English-dominant students to participate in classes funded under the Act; however, realities of urban demography being what they are, such magnanimity does not go much beyond the co-presence of Blacks and Hispanics. Evaluation has invariably been in terms of English test–retest gains among the "bilinguals" or non-English mother-tongue students. Quite predictably these gains have generally (i.e. on a nationwide scale) not proven themselves to be significantly higher than those of bilinguals not receiving BILINGUAL EDUCATION (American Institutes for Research (hereafter AIR) 1977). A simplistic approach to "evaluating" bilingual education – whatever unknown mixture that may represent of teacher preparations, teaching methods, curricular materials, etc. – ignores the possibility of gains in other cognitive areas as well as in various noncognitive areas (including that of cultural security) for the bilingual child (not to mention the possibility of gains for participating Anglo children as well). Many careful local studies *have* revealed significant gains for "bilinguals" receiving bilingual education (see e.g. Cohen 1975, and various studies mentioned in Fishman 1976). Contrasts between these studies and those which purport to show national trends underscore the peculiar double-bind of American public bilingual education in the late 1970s. It is damned if it does and damned if it doesn't. If it *does* bring about a rapid transition to English then it will no longer be needed. If it does *not*, it will also no longer be needed. This is hardly a context conducive to the development of educational expertise, stability, and achievement.

While TRANSITIONAL BILINGUAL EDUCATION has been increasingly faulted as insufficiently transitional (U.S. General Accounting Office (hereafter GAO) 1976; AIR 1977; Epstein 1977 a, b), other developments have tended to reinforce it. The U.S. Supreme Court's LAU v. NICHOLS decision (1974) has led to bilingual education in many school systems that might otherwise have done nothing in particular for their students of "limited English-speaking ability," or would have been content merely to offer them help in the acquisition of English *per se*. The Court's insistence that learning English and getting an equitable education were not the same thing, and that due process was denied when the latter was not forthcoming (even if the former was being pursued), has fostered bilingual education, frequently under threat of being found in noncompliance of federal law, as the remedy of choice. This remedy itself, however, has, at times, been called into question because of desegregation considerations (Teitelbaum 1977a, b) and bilingual education therefore finds itself confronted by a four-front war: (a) negative evaluatory evidence, (b) civil rights (desegregation) concerns; (c) union members fearful of losing jobs to "bilingual" teachers; and (d) ethnic divisiveness sometimes headlined by the press (Epstein 1977a; *New York Times* editorial "Bilingual Danger," November 22, 1976).

Language maintenance policy

Ethnic shift into the mainstream Anglophone middle class phenotype is the most common American minority experience. It epitomizes simultaneous social mobility, social integration, mass participation in the symbolic political institutions, and the setting aside of prior affect and intimacy. For these various reasons, the widespread re-ethnification or heightened ethnicity experiences of the past decade have been deeply worrisome to many, both at the grass-roots and the pseudo-intellectual levels, at the very same time that they have been espoused by an unprecedented number of others. A number of policy considerations have heightened the resulting tension and, as is usual in connection with ethnicity, language dimensions have quickly come to the fore, both for advocates and for opponents.

Sociological and sociolinguistic theory are both still too immature (with respect to what ethnicity is and how or why it is linked to language) to explain why it is that supposedly subdued and suppressed ethnicity sentiments blossomed forth all over the world in the late 1960s and early 1970s. The common American cocktail party variety of expertise blames it all on the Blacks (i.e. on contagion spread by the advocates of Black is Beautiful, Black pride, Black soul), but this is not only an ineffectual response to the worldwide nature of the phenomenon but it does nothing to explain even its American manifestations. Neither such notions as "the bent twig" (a metaphor of Isaiah Berlin 1972), whereby repressed ethnicity must ultimately "snap back," nor the assumption of purely opportunistic alternation between purportedly "rational class struggle" (Gellner 1964; Glazer and Moynihan 1975; Patterson 1975) and "irrational ethnicity" (Devereaux 1975; Isaacs 1975) are more than metaphor or bias in the face of the distribution of the ethnicity phenomenon historically, geographically, economically, and sociopsychologically. Three thousand years of Euro-Mediterranean social theory with respect to the nature of ethnicity, its recurring link to language, its developmental relationship to sociocultural change, its mutability and modernization, have been lost and are only now being retrieved (Fishman 1977c, d). Modern capitalist, Marxist, and neutralist social theory with respect to ethnicity uniformly viewed it as a vanishing, irrelevant, or undesirable aberration in market-dominated Gesellschaft, and, in the processes of this self-serving astigmatism, lost sight of language in society as well. Little wonder then that the reappearance of both ethnicity and language in American public life has elicited the opposition of intellectuals who had predicted its doom and of journalists, union leaders, and ordinary folk who were themselves byproducts of the surrender and denial of the very attributes which others were now acclaiming.

Bilingual education has stumbled into the troubled waters of language and ethnicity, much to its own surprise. What began as a major effort to Anglify "the last unfortunates" has come to be criticized as building a political and/or economic power base for ethnic proto-elites who purportedly refuse to let their clienteles integrate into the mainstream. Economic self-interest is presumably acceptable if pursued by the oil lobby, by the teachers' unions, and by our most reputable universities, but is considered meanly divisive if pursued by Hispanics, Native Americans, or other ethnics (Novak 1972; Jaipaul 1973). Political organizations and modern mass media channels of public influence are acceptable if adopted by mainstream Anglophones, but are disruptive if adopted by "bilinguals." Party politicians have a useful relationship and responsibility to the masses, but are merely self-seeking and power-hungry if they foster an ethnic base and seek to maintain its viability. Bilingual education is said to contribute to such a power base as is the general rebirth of ethnicity. Monolingual education is, on the other hand, seen as nonpartisan, and is equated with "the public good" rather than with its own political power or self-interest.

It is hard to say what the ethnicity stress has contributed to non-English LANGUAGE MAINTENANCE in the United States. A new "language loyalty" study would be needed to arrive at integrated empirical and theoretical understanding of this question. The few data-connected straws in the wind are hard to confirm and even harder to interpret. Obviously, many more people claimed non-English tongues in 1970 than did so in 1960, even in the absence of massive (non-Hispanic) immigration and contrary to all trends since 1930 (see Chapter 22). Obviously ethnic studies programs at American colleges and universities have led to a mushrooming of language courses. Languages are now taught which were hardly represented (or entirely unrepresented) in university teaching a decade ago (Scanpresence 1977). However, neither claiming a mother tongue nor enrolling in ethnic studies is extremely relevant to actual language use or language knowledge. It is most probably true that an attitudinal improvement (even halo-ization) has taken place, that mother tongues which were neither claimed nor studied before are now claimed and studied – but it also seems likely that such increased positiveness can be maintained and fostered for quite some time without any corresponding impact on either language knowledge or language use. Indeed, it is possible for language attitudes to improve in compensatory fashion as both use and knowledge decrease (Committee on Irish Language Attitudes Research 1975). This may well be what is occurring for most non-English tongues in the USA. It is not at all clear, particularly in the absence of further immigration from their respective home countries, what improved institutional bases they might reasonably hope for that would reintroduce and maintain them in families, neighborhoods, churches, organizations, and mass media. All of these have been already overwhelmingly Anglified quite a while back (Fishman et al. 1966).

For Spanish, Native American languages, and for Vietnamese (the last merely representing a recent and non-recurring immigration), this situation is different. It is particularly so for the Spanish population which is numerically large, indigenized, and still growing as the result of legal and illegal immigration and a predictable birthrate. People who claim Spanish as their mother tongue constitute a huge proportion of all those in the USA who claim a mother tongue other than English. What is more, they use their language more than other groups, i.e. they contribute an even larger proportion of all those who primarily speak a language other than English. Understandably, Spanish bilingual education programs also account for the bulk of bilingual programs throughout the USA, although, all in all, sixty-eight languages were involved in 1976–7 and over seventy in 1977–8. Spanish, at the very least, seems destined to a lengthy – if not vigorous – life in the USA.

Interestingly enough, while journalists, teachers' union representatives, and perhaps a good portion of U.S. citizens are concerned that bilingual education may "build in" non-English enclaves into American political and social life, experienced students of American *hispanidad* fear just the opposite: that bilingual education will dissipate forces urging Spanish language maintenance in the USA (Kjolseth 1973; Gaarder 1977). No doubt, both arguments give too much credit to education as an independent causal factor in language shift and ethnic shift (see Chapter 21). As a distinctly secondary status system, education prepares an individual for participation in one or another primary status system whose impact on language maintenance is likely to be much more decisive than that of education *per se*. In modern Gesellschaft-like societies, the most powerful status system is that of the work-sphere. Thus, were our economy to be a rapidly expanding one, it would reward the participation of Hispanics and initially do so – as it did with the immigrant masses of the 1880–1920 period – even prior to their acquisition of English facility. The cycle thereupon established between higher economic reward and English fluency can continue to spiral upward at slightly below the rate at which the economy expands. In the absence of such expansion, prior knowledge of English may be individually facilitative, but can hardly have massive social mobility significance at a time when unemployment among monolingual English speakers is itself so widespread. The school simply cannot compensate for absence of economic opportunity in the society at large. It cannot "prime the pump." Schools most commonly require societal support in order to succeed, and this is certainly as true of bilingual education as it is of monolingual education. Moreover, schools are rarely independent causal forces with respect to the economy or society at large.

If the schools have probably not fostered non-English language maintenance in the USA – not even in their bilingual education guise – other factors have been equally inconsequential. Neither "old country" sponsored efforts (tourism, visiting scholars and lecturers, subsidies for local cultural institutions, etc.), nor federally sponsored programs (e.g. the fiscally anemic and politically governed Ethnic Heritage Act, and the meager ethnic components of the National Endowment for the Humanities and the National Endowment for the Arts, etc.) seem to have had much impact on language maintenance in the USA. In both cases the scale is too small and stance taken is too conflicted for any major positive consequences to obtain (Fishman, 1980).

A number of court decisions may ultimately be more crucial, being both more forceful and more massive in their reach. Just as law has given a major impetus to regular (rather than demonstration) bilingual education programs, so several suits currently working their way through the courts may do for all government welfare programs what the Voting Rights Act has done for various non-English languages on the ballot. Just as such languages (usually Spanish and Native American languages, but also, here and there, Tagalog, Ilocano, Japanese, and others) are required to be on the ballot wherever more than 5 percent of the population in any election district is not literate in English, so these still pending suits may ultimately tend to require that all government services and programs be in the languages of those whom they serve. In the absence of such accommodation by government to the language of the populace, a *prima facie* case for inequity in delivery of government services is a distinct possibility. Given the Supreme Court's repeated unwillingness to declare English to be the obligatory language of public services, given the official status of Spanish in Puerto Rico (not to mention the co-official status of French in Louisiana and of Spanish in New Mexico), and given the continued growth of the Hispanic and Native American proportions of our population (as well as their continued spread into all urban areas), the likelihood that there will be increasing legal accommodation to their rights and needs is very great. Additional local statutes (such as that in effect in New York City requiring that the language of contracts and warranties/guarantees be the same as the language in which sales or agreements have been orally effected) will almost certainly add to the overall equity foundation for language maintenance in the United States. However, equity is a general principle rather than a language-focused policy in any substantive sense.

Language maintenance in the USA is not part of public policy because it is rarely recognized as being in the public interest. Until it can be so considered, it must be freed from the suspicion of divisiveness and incompatibility with progress, modernity, and efficiency. Languages must be viewed as a precious natural resource, rather than as a sword of Damocles. Like all resources, it can be squandered, put to reprehensible uses, or husbanded and developed for the greater general good. However, it may be impossible to arrive at this point of view and to formulate policies for such purposes in connection with languages other than English when the latter itself is so far from our consciousness and from our notion of the natural resources that we seek to protect and to cultivate. Too much of a spotlight on English may be contraproductive in this connection, but too little is also a handicap. Meanwhile I sense a striving and longing among most Hispanic graduate students and bilingual educators, as well as among many of their Native American counterparts, on behalf of language maintenance – a striving much more articulated, unembarrassed, and moving than any that I came across in the early 1960s – but an even more pained and poignant inability with respect to how this goal can be attained.

The ethnicity movement may have freed many Hispanics and other ethnics from earlier complexes and fears, but it has not yet led them to effective new solutions or programs. It has resulted in the legitimization of smaller-scale bonds, interests, loyalties, and sentiments, and in the open verbalization of disenchantment with large-scale standardization (in government, industry, ideology, education, entertainment, dress, and diet) that was previously so admired as the wave of the future. For many, ethnicity interests, together with "do it yourself," environment and resource protection, urban neighborhood maintenance, and decentralization of government, represent a return to personal, direct, unique participatory involvement. The big establishments and even the big counter-establishments have failed to provide either peace, plenty, or participation. But ethnicity is not the only smaller-scale force in modern life, and it is definitely not the only one seeking governmental support and recognition. However, alone among all of the other contenders, ethnicity is the only factor with a well-established negative semantic field associated with it, among both intellectuals and along America's "Main Street." When language and ethnicity maintenance are presented in their own right, as a natural right, they evoke images of Quebecization and Balkanization. What is for some "a thing of beauty and a joy for ever" is for others regressive, explosive, and deceptive. There is no doubt in my mind that language and ethnicity in America can *not* make it on their own, in terms of public policy and at public expense, both because they are too weak (although stronger than in the early 1960s) and also because the opposition to them is ready-made and, therefore, ever ready. Ethnicity and bilingualism need to be retooled so that their "image" will appear to be as much in line with the public good as is the image of other recognized self-interest groupings in American life.

Language enrichment policy

Both language shift policy and language maintenance policy are polar reactions to the language and ethnicity nexus. What the one seeks to overcome the other seeks to preserve. Although polar opposites, they are essentially engaged in a discourse that employs similar terms and reacts to similar concerns. It is the level of integration to be sought in society that separates them more than anything else. What is at stake is the validity of lower-order bonds and the desirability or possibility of higher-order ones that coexist with lower-order ones. The disagreement in this respect is nearly 2,000 years old. It springs from the Judeo-Greek (and Eastern Orthodox Church as well as early Islamic) rejection of the Western empire and the Western church view that universality was God's will and that lower-order bonds naturally fell away as mankind inevitably evolved toward one, higher, all-inclusive language and ethnicity. Not until the nineteenth century did this debate transfer to a different metaphor. Johann Gottfried Herder finally set aside the old debate (in which he too had engaged as champion of the suppressed Germans against the then imperial French) by adopting the view that the entire world needs to share and foster as many languages as possible.

LANGUAGES OF WIDER COMMUNICATION (LWC) were of no interest to Herder for they were merely soulless lingua francas, pragmatic conduits for instrumental purposes (Fishman 1978). The world always had and always would acquire these for the unavoidable mundane functions that they fulfilled. However, human dignity, ingenuity, love and kindness, idealism, altruism, sensitivity, hope and perseverance, and triumphs over travail – all of these reflections of what was most nobly and creatively and tenderly human – were preserved and fostered only by the variety of the languages that characterized all the peoples of the world. Herder raised the banner not so much of maintenance as of diversity. Diverse talents are needed to save the world from emptiness and mechanization and inhumanity, and these talents are the spontaneous gifts of various peoples, each animated by the spirit of its mother tongue. But languages can be shared. They can function not one at the expense of the other but one in addition to the other. A world made safe for little languages, through which people will feel deeply and think creatively, would be a better, more humane, more accepting and more innovative world for one and all. Herder's final years were spent advocating a world of many languages and, therefore, a world of many solutions to be shared across their original boundaries. A little over a century later, the American Benjamin Lee Whorf traveled pretty much the same path, beginning with the view that each truly different language sparked a truly different reality and world view among its speakers. By the end of his life, however, he had begun to argue that all of mankind and even natural science itself would benefit from the relative linguistic determinism that structurally diverse languages brought about. Different solutions require different inputs, and language is the ultimate input in all that is distinctly human about us.

What is it that Herder and Whorf can contribute to American language policy discussions and deliberations? They are spotlights of faith in language and languages amid the darkness of technology and mankind mechanized and in-sensitized. Languages must be shared as a common good but before they can be shared, they must be saved, loved, treasured. National policy toward this end finally lifts languages off of the ethnicity versus anti-ethnicity (lower ethnicity versus higher ethnicity) treadmill and sets them into a new universal orbit in which uniqueness serves not itself but the general good. Perhaps such a view could inform American language policy in the future. Congressman Paul Simon of Illinois seems to have this in mind when he suggests that languages need to be put back into the American economy rather than merely retired from active service. Recognizing the tremendous waste involved in eroding languages in homes and communities while trying to implant them anew via schools and colleges, he advocates federal support, including enrichment bilingual education, for their increased cultivation, study and instruction. Significantly, he views all of this not in terms of assistance to the poor, to the non-English-speaking or to the ethnics, but very distinctly as a contribution to the general diplomatic, commercial, intellectual, and aesthetic welfare of the country at large. We all need "all those languages" in order to enrich our lives, our country, and our world (Simon 1977).

It is too early to tell what will come of this very recent and largely unprecedented policy viewpoint (note its predecessor view in Fishman et al. 1966: Chapters 1 and 5). It has its counterpart in the new Louisiana educational provision that while every non-Anglo child has a right to a state-funded education, partially via his mother tongue, every Anglo child has a corresponding right (a cultural right) to receive part of his education via another language in order to attain his maximal personal enrichment. If both types of children can ultimately wind up in the same classroom, one motivated by transitional and maintenance considerations and the other by enrichment considerations, an optimal *modus vivendi* will have been attained. A secret long known to elites all over the world, that the education of their children provides them with greater opportunity, greater insight, deeper appreciations, greater sensitivity, additional aesthetic and cultural dimensions when it is conducted via more than one language of instruction (Lewis 1976), is slowly being revealed to the public at large and is beginning to compete for public funds. As such it could become an alternative type of public education, available to the fortunate and gifted (fostering a new popular definition of "bilinguals" and bilingualism in the American context), an approach that would do for American bilingual education what immersion did for the Canadian: yield outstanding results because those involved were self-selected to succeed (see Chapter 21). The experience of the Florida Dade County schools and of a multitude of bilingual private and parochial schools under the most diverse auspices all point to the success potential of enrichment bilingual education.

However, if enrichment language policy is limited or restricted to the schools alone, it will fail as surely as either transitional or maintenance policy when similarly restricted. What is needed is an enrichment policy that views the multilingualization of American urban life as a contribution to the very quality of life itself. Michael Novak has been calling for the creative preservation of our urban diversity (Novak 1972) as has Monsignor Baroni (*New York Times,* April 20, 1977: B1). This cannot succeed without a language component but this component must have broader outreach as well. Neighborhoods live a life of their own in terms of most family, face-to-face experiences. However, neighborhood fairs can be shared, as can neighborhood pageants and parades. On the other hand a policy of support for non-English films, plays, television and radio, opera and song, press and poetry would stimulate generally shared enrichment experiences, but these would also trickle down to particular significance in particular neighborhoods.

Language policy involves a vision of America. A multilingual enrichment policy envisages a multilingual America as being in the public good. We support a multiparty system. We support a multilateral productive machine, i.e. one that operates both in the consumer and in the industrial capacity markets. Our anti-trust laws aim to diversify the economic market place. We can similarly diversify the cultural market place. Other countries do it. Ireland does it less successfully and Wales more successfully. Norway does it vis-à-vis two "kinds" of Norwegian. Holland has begun to do it vis-à-vis Dutch and Frisian. Switzerland has long done so – not through bilingual education but through multilingual services of various kinds (McRae 1964). Peaceful multilingual polities – where multilingualism is a public trust and a public good – are far from rare (Mackey and Verdoodt 1975; Savard and Vigneault 1975). We still have the possibility of opting for such a policy, particularly in conjunction with our Spanish language treasures. No fear of dissension is needed in order to frighten us into it. There is a vision of American magnanimity involved, but more than that, a vision of American possibilities, opportunities, appreciations, sensitivities, that we all should savour. "Brotherhood" does not mean uniformity. A shared diversity can be the true meaning of the American promise: "to crown thy good with brotherhood from sea to shining sea."

FURTHER READING

Serious, well-informed discussions of American language policy are rare, and most of those which exist focus only on limited aspects of policy. One of the finest and most influential, Parker 1961a, was devoted almost completely to foreign language instruction in formal educational contexts, mentioning neither the teacher of English (except as a foreign language) nor the existence of ethnic minority languages in the USA. A parallel volume, 1961b, did not mention languages other than English or deal with English as a foreign language. Both could easily be regarded as special pleading by the foreign language and English language teaching professions. A somewhat more inclusive viewpoint appeared in the late 1960s and early 1970s in the foreign language profession (e.g. Grittner 1971; Brod 1979), as educators began to react to notions of cultural pluralism and bilingual education.

The steps leading to the appointment of a Presidential Commission on Foreign Language and International Studies in 1978 stimulated a number of papers on American language policy with special reference to foreign language research and teaching, including the papers for the conference sponsored by the Modern Language Association and Georgetown University on "Language in American Life" (Gerli, Alatis, and Brod 1978; see especially papers by Allen, Ferguson, Thompson). The most focused recent statement is Grant 1978, which explores the legal status of English and other languages in a variety of contexts, federal and state, and concludes with specific recommendations for a national language policy. This article, though full of information, does not mention the teaching of English as a school subject or the existence of variant forms of English.

Both legal and historical approaches to language policy have been taken by a number of scholars, who have sought to support the ideological bases of the Bilingual Education Act of 1968. Kloss 1977 is the most comprehensive treatment; Leibowitz 1969, 1971, 1976 show the development of legal approaches to language policy in education, voting, and employment; Heath 1977, 1978 examine the ideological underpinnings of language policies related to raising literacy standards or imposing "minimal competency" tests for high school diplomas, simplifying the language of public regulation, and providing for bilingual education; García 1978 treats the issue of testing; Hernández-Chavez 1978 discusses the various philosophies of bilingualism supported by various groups in the United States; Milán 1978 argues for a comprehensive language policy in a desegregated school system. Macias 1980 surveys the history of the language policies of the USA with respect to protection of human rights.

Glossary

ACROLECT The standard or variety of highest prestige in a speech community which has great variability in social dialects. Cf. BASILECT.

APICO-ALVEOLAR A speech sound made by the tip (apex) of the tongue approaching or touching the gum ridge (alveoli) just behind the front teeth.

ASPECT A grammatical category of verbs which indicates the nature or manner of the action (e. g. perfective, durative), as opposed to tense, which indicates the time of the action.

ASPIRATION The *h*-sound which may follow a stop consonant, as in the usual pronunciation of the *p* in *pin* in English.

AUXILIARY LANGUAGE A language used for communication between people who do not understand one another's mother tongues. Cf. LINGUA FRANCA; PIDGIN.

BASILECT The variety of lowest prestige or most deviant from the standard in a speech community which has great variability in social dialects. Cf. ACROLECT.

BILINGUAL EDUCATION (BE) An educational program in which two languages are used in the instruction. Cf. MAINTENANCE BILINGUAL EDUCATION; TRANSITIONAL BILINGUAL EDUCATION.

BILINGUAL EDUCATION ACT The federal statute passed in 1968 as Title VII of the Elementary and Secondary Education Act; it provided for federal support of bilingual education programs.

BILINGUALISM The use of two languages by the same person (individual bilingualism) *or* by the same social group (group, institutional, or societal bilingualism).

BROKEN LANGUAGE An imperfect variety of language used by people who are in the process of acquiring the language.

CALQUE A borrowing from another language in which the specific meaning of a word or parts of a word in the source language is imitated by the borrowing language. Cf. LOANSHIFT, LOANWORD.

CODE-MIXING The transferral of linguistic units from one language to another, usually to extend the style or register range of a language; it includes extended borrowing of not only single lexical items, but also clauses, collocations, idioms, e.g. inserting *respeto* in an English sentence. Sometimes used to refer to the indiscriminate mixing of two languages by an individual learning a second language. Cf. INTERFERENCE.

CODE-SWITCHING Changing from one language or language variety to another in the course of using a language; usually determined by the particular function, participants, or setting and the identity the speaker wishes to project. E.g. switching from English to Spanish in a conversation.

COLLOCATION A particular combination of words; usually refers to a highly frequent combination or an especially striking one.

COMMUNAL LANGUAGE A language the use of which is especially characteristic of a particular religious group or similar division of society.

COMMUNICATIVE COMPETENCE Knowledge of the language skills and related behavior required to communicate in a given society; distinguished from linguistic competence, which refers only to knowledge of the structure of a language.

CONSONANT CLUSTER A sequence of two or more consonant sounds; sometimes called a consonant blend.

COPULA The linguistic form which connects the subject with its predicate complement, such as the verb *to be* in English, as in "Jane *is* a doctor."

CREOLE/CREOLE LANGUAGE A language derived from a pidgin which is the mother tongue of a speech community. Cf. PIDGIN; PIDGINIZATION.

CREOLIZATION The process of elaboration in vocabulary, grammar, and register variation by which a pidgin becomes a creole.

CYRILLIC An alphabet, derived from the Greek alphabet, which is used to write Russian, some other Slavic languages, and a number of non-Slavic languages spoken in the Soviet Union.

DECREOLIZATION The process in which a creole language gradually merges again with the base language from which it was originally pidginized; occurs when a creole comes into close contact with the base language as a model in the same speech community.

DESCRIPTION The setting down, in systematic fashion, of the linguistic characteristics of a language variety as actually used, as opposed to prescription, in which ideal or desired characteristics are set down.

DIACRITIC MARKS Modifying marks, such as accents (e. g. ´`) and subscripts (e. g. ˌ), which indicate a modification of the sound represented by the letters they are placed on.

DIALECT A regional or social variety of a language which is distinguished by features of pronunciation, grammar, or vocabulary from other varieties.

DIALECTAL Pertaining to dialects or dialect variation. Dialectal variation in a language depends on where the speaker comes from in the society (geographically or socially); registral variation depends on the occasions of use (e. g. status of addressee, situational context).

DIALECT ATLAS A collection of maps or map-like representations showing where particular features of pronunciation, grammar, or vocabulary are used in a speech community; it may include maps which show major dialect boundaries.

DIALECT GEOGRAPHY/DIALECTOLOGY The study of dialect variation in languages, often with reference to the historical processes which result in the variation; also called linguistic geography.

DIALECT LEVELING The process by which a set of dialects lose their distinctive traits and become more like one another.

DIALECTOLOGIST A specialist in dialectology or dialect geography.

DIGLOSSIA A language situation in which two very different varieties of a language are functionally complementary, one (H, the "high" variety) being used for written and formal spoken purposes, the other (L, the "low" variety) for ordinary conversation. Adjective: DIGLOSSIC.

DIMINUTIVE Special form (usually of a noun) which is used to indicate small size, affectionate regard, or use by children (e. g. English *doggie* for *dog*).

DISCOURSE Connected speech (or writing) which extends beyond a single sentence and may be analyzed in terms of larger units.

DISSIMILATION The change of a speech sound to become different from a neighboring sound and thus presumably easier to pronounce, as when one of two successive *r*s is changed to *l*.

FRICATIVE A consonant sound produced by making a constriction somewhere in the vocal tract which creates friction noise (e. g. English *f, v, s, z*).

GEMEINSCHAFT A society characterized by strong mutual bonds of feeling and kinship, as opposed to Gesellschaft.

GENERAL AMERICAN ENGLISH The relatively uniform kind of English spoken throughout most of the United States, excluding the East Coast and the South.

GESELLSCHAFT A society characterized by relatively impersonal, institutional bonds rather than close personal ties. Cf. GEMEINSCHAFT.

GLOTTAL STOP The speech sound made by complete closure of the glottis; it is heard in English in such expressions as *oh-oh*, exclamation of surprise, or the negative *uh-uh*.

GRADIENT STRATIFICATION Stratification (of sociolinguistic variables) which moves gradually along a social dimension such as age or class without sharp jumps; as opposed to sharp stratification.

GRAPHIZATION The process of "reducing a language to writing," i.e. the creation and adoption of a writing system for a previously unwritten language.

H FORM *or* H variety *or* H language. See DIGLOSSIA.

HORTATORY Including both addressee(s) and speaker in an order or exhortation to do something; said of a verb form such as an imperative or subjunctive (e. g. English *let's*).

IDEOGRAPHIC Representing words or morphemes of a language rather than its sounds (said of writing systems). Cf. SYLLABARY.

IMMERSION PROGRAM Educational program for language acquisition in which the pupils are instructed completely through the medium of the language to be acquired and their mother tongue is taught only as a subject.

IMMIGRANT LANGUAGES Languages in a nation which are used primarily by immigrants to the nation or their descendants, as opposed to colonial languages and indigenous or autochthonous languages.

IMPLICATIONAL RELATION In sociolinguistics, the relation between two linguistic features such that one is present only if the other is; often this is asserted for a whole series of features, as in a decreolization situation.

INFLECTIONAL SYSTEM/INFLECTIONS The system of prefixes or suffixes which mark grammatical categories such as number and case in nouns or person and tense in verbs.

INTERACTIONAL COMPETENCE The knowledge of how to carry on verbal interactions in a given speech community, involving such issues as politeness, turn-taking, or bringing a conversation to a close.

INTERFERENCE The effects which knowledge of one language has upon the learner or user of another language, such as a foreign accent or misuse of words.

INTONATION The pattern of rise and fall in the fundamental pitch of clause or sentence which indicates such different values as question versus statement, surprise, or emphasis.

INVITATION TO BID The act of requesting the members of a class to volunteer to answer a question or undertake a project, as distinct from other verbal acts of the teacher such as nomination or questioning.

INVITATION TO REPLY The act of requesting the members of a class to volunteer to answer a question.

ISOGLOSS A line on a map which shows the boundary of one or more dialect features in a language; also refers to the feature itself or the imaginary line on the earth corresponding to the isogloss on the map.

ISOGLOSS BUNDLE A number of isoglosses which coincide or fall very close to one another; held to mark a more important boundary than an isolated isogloss.

JARGON A variety of language characteristic of specialists or workers in the same occupation or members of a particular clique or social group. Also, a pidginized, hybrid form of speech in which the speakers use mostly simplified items from their own languages with little stable structure to the jargon itself.

KINESIC Pertaining to body movements considered as a communicative system functioning in addition to human language. Kinesics: the study of kinesic communication.

KOINÉ A dialect-leveled variety of a language which spreads as a common form of the language for interdialect communication. Named from the ancient Greek koiné which spread as a lingua franca around the Mediterranean in the Hellenistic period.

L FORM or L variety or L language See DIGLOSSIA.

LANGUAGE CULTIVATION Language planning which is intended to preserve and improve a language.

LANGUAGE FAMILY A group of related languages which can be shown to be continuations of a single language at an earlier point in time.

LANGUAGE MAINTENANCE Preservation of the use of a language by a speech community, under conditions where there is a possibility of shift to another language.

LANGUAGE OF WIDER COMMUNICATION (LWC) A language which is widely (often internationally) used as an additional language by people of different mother tongues; often applied to former colonial languages such as English and French.

LANGUAGE SHIFT The change in regular use or mother-tongue status of one language to another in a speech community, as when members of an immigrant community shift from their original mother tongue to the language of their new country. Cf. LANGUAGE MAINTENANCE.

LANGUAGE UNIVERSALS Characteristics held to be true of all human languages, or at least true unless a conflicting universal tendency interferes.

LAU v. NICHOLS A decision of the U.S. Supreme Court in 1974 which found that the Board of Education of San Francisco failed to provide equal access to education by requiring Chinese-speaking pupils to attend instruction in English only. It has been the basis for legislation, regulations, and policy decisions on bilingual education.

LEVELED COLONIAL LANGUAGE A language in which substantial dialect leveling has taken place because of the mixing of populations from different regions and the new functions of the language in the colonial situation.

LEXICAL Pertaining to words or to the vocabulary of a language, as opposed to sounds or grammar.

LEXICON The vocabulary of a language or of an individual speaker, i.e. the total stock of words, word formatives, and idioms; as opposed to the sound system and the grammar.

LINGUA FRANCA A language used for communication between speakers of different mother tongues. Cf. AUXILIARY LANGUAGE; PIDGIN.

LINGUISTIC INSECURITY A sociolinguistic attribute measured by the number of cases (out of a prepared list) in which a speaker reports that his own pronunciation differs from what he regards as the correct pronunciation.

LOANBLEND A word of which part is taken from another language and part is from the language to which the word belongs.

LOANSHIFT A word which has changed its meaning under the influence of a word in another language.

LOANWORD A word taken from another language; such a word is said to be "borrowed" from the source language.

MAINTENANCE BILINGUAL EDUCATION Bilingual education which is intended to maintain the language skills of a language minority along with skills in the mainstream majority language. Cf. TRANSITIONAL BILINGUAL EDUCATION.

MONOGENETIC Having a single origin; applied to a theory of the origin of pidgins and creoles.

MORPHOLOGY The study of the structure of words or word formation; also used to mean the system of word structure or word formation of a given language. Adjective: MORPHOLOGICAL.

MOTHER TONGUE The language acquired naturally in one's childhood. Variously defined in different census surveys as the first language acquired or the language primarily used in one's family as a child.

NATIONAL LANGUAGE A term used in several senses, including: (a) a language indigenous to a particular nation, as opposed to a language brought in from outside; (b) a language recognized by a nation as its own distinctive language; (c) a standard language.

NATURAL LANGUAGE A language that is or could be the mother tongue of a human speech community, as opposed to such symbolic systems as artificial languages or computer languages.

NOMINATION The act of calling upon a student in class to recite, as distinct from other communicative acts such as a question, an evaluation, or a request for a response in unison.

OFFICIAL LANGUAGE A language which is legally prescribed as the language of governmental operations of a given nation.

ORTHOGRAPHY The writing system or spelling accepted as the norm for a particular language.

PALATAL Pertaining to the palate, specifically a consonant or semivowel which is produced by placing the blade of the tongue near or touching the palate (e.g. English *y*, *sh*, *ch*).

PALATALIZED Said of a speech sound, usually a consonant: modified by having a simultaneous or immediately following *y*-quality, made by placing the front of the tongue near the palate, (e. g. Russian *ny* in *nyet* 'no').

PALATAL LATERAL A palatal consonant of *l*-quality, as the sound spelled *gl* in Italian.

PARALINGUISTIC Pertaining to vocal sounds or sound qualities functioning as a communicative system supplementary to language proper; includes such phenomena as whisper, voice quality, chuckling.

PATOIS A nonstandard, local variety of a language; often used in a somewhat derogatory way, a "mere" patois.

PHILOLOGY The scholarly study of language and literature, especially linguistic and cultural interpretation of texts. Adjective: PHILOLOGICAL.

PHONEMIC Pertaining to distinctive sound differences in a language or to the phonemes, the minimum units of speech sound which manifest these differences. For example, a phonemic transcription (enclosed in slant lines / . . . /) is a transcription in which every symbol represents a phoneme. Cf. PHONETIC; PHONOLOGICAL.

PHONETIC Pertaining to speech sounds. For example a phonetic transcription is one enclosed in square brackets [. . .], which represents the pronunciation.

PHONOLOGY The study of the organization of speech sounds into the sound systems of human languages; also used to mean the sound system of a given language. Adjective: PHONOLOGICAL.

PICTOGRAPH A pictorial representation of an object or event which serves as part of a communication system; pictographs may be forerunners of a fullfledged writing system for a language.

PIDGIN A form of language, reduced in vocabulary, simplified in grammar, and typically containing elements from several languages, which arises for restricted communication functions between speakers of different mother tongues; it is no one's mother tongue.

PIDGINIZATION The process of (usually rapid) simplification in grammar and vocabulary which characterizes the formation of a pidgin.

POLYGENETIC Of multiple origin; often applied to theories of pidgins and creoles which assert that they have arisen independently many times. Cf. MONOGENETIC.

PRAGMATIC Pertaining to those aspects of language use or the nonlinguistic context which contribute to the meaning of utterances in a language. Pragmatics: the study of pragmatic aspects of meaning.

RECEIVED PRONUNCIATION (RP) The kind of British pronunciation characteristic of English public schools, the universities of Oxford and Cambridge, and many educated speakers of English; described in detail by the phonetician Daniel Jones in textbooks and dictionaries.

REGISTER A variety of a language characterized by features of vocabulary, grammar, and pronunciation which is used in special settings or for special purposes, such as legal talk, classroom register, baby talk. Cf. DIALECT.

SCHWA An indistinct, typically unstressed vowel such as the sound of the *a* in *about,* which is represented by the symbol "ə." Named from a vowel of this type in Hebrew.

SEMANTIC Pertaining to meaning in language. Semantics: the study of semantic aspects of language.

SHARP STRATIFICATION Sociolinguistic stratification in which there are striking jumps in the linguistic variable being measured, depending on differences in age, class, or the like. Cf. GRADIENT STRATIFICATION.

SOCIAL INDICATOR A linguistic feature which indicates, by its presence or frequency of occurrence, membership in a particular social group such as a class, age, or ethnic group. Differs from a social marker in that it does not regularly indicate stylistic differentiation.

SPEECH ACT A minimum functional unit of speech activity, such as asking a question, making a promise, or giving a greeting; the form and use of such acts are interpreted in terms of the shared rules of a speech community.

SPEECH COMMUNITY A population which shares patterns of language use setting it apart from other communities; the normal focus or framework of sociolinguistic research.

SPIRANT See FRICATIVE.

STOP A consonant sound made by complete closure of the vocal tract at some point (e.g. *p, b, d, k*).

SYLLABARY A writing system which consists of a set of symbols each of which tends to represent a syllable. Differs from an alphabet, in which each symbol tends to represent a phoneme.

SYNTAX The part of grammar which concerns the arrangement of words in sentences, the constructions in which the words occur, and the systematic structural relations between sentences. Adjective: SYNTACTIC, SYNTACTICAL. Cf. LEXICON; MORPHOLOGY; PHONOLOGY.

TEFL The teaching of English as a foreign language, regarded as a profession or field of study.

TESL The teaching of English as a second language, in the special sense of a language which has an important role in the country, typically as the medium of education and the language of government, as in former British colonies.

TESOL The teaching of English to speakers of other languages regarded as a profession or field of study; includes TEFL and TESL. Also the name of the principal American professional organization in this field.

TOPONYMY The study of place names. Also used to mean the set of place names used in a certain area.

TRANSITIONAL BILINGUAL EDUCATION Bilingual education which is intended to facilitate the entry of a language minority into the mainstream monolingual educational program. Cf. MAINTENANCE BILINGUAL EDUCATION.

TRANSPLANTED LANGUAGE A language spoken by a community which is the result of migration from the homeland of the language.

UNIVERSAL LANGUAGE A language proposed or intended to serve as a means of communication throughout the world in addition to or replacing the multiplicity of current languages; also used to mean an ideal language which could express all possible meanings more effectively than natural languages.

VELAR Pertaining to the soft palate (velum), specifically a consonant which is produced by raising the back of the tongue near or touching the soft palate (e.g. English *k*, German *ch* in *Bach*).

VERNACULAR The ordinary spoken language of a community, as opposed to a superposed standard, a Classical language, or a dominant national language which is not the local vernacular.

VOICED Produced with vibration of the vocal cords, such as the consonant sounds of *z*, *m*, or *d* in English. Cf. VOICELESS.

VOICELESS Produced without vibration of the vocal cords, as in the consonant sounds of *p* or *sh* in English. Cf. VOICED.

WHORFIAN HYPOTHESIS The hypothesis, formulated by the American linguist Benjamin Whorf, that the grammatical structure of a language significantly affects the thought processes of its speakers.

Bibliography

A Language for Life. 1975. Report of the Committee of Inquiry appointed by the Secretary of State for Education and Science under the Chairmanship of Sir Alan Bullock FBA. London: Her Majesty's Stationery Office.

Abadan-Unat, N. 1975. Educational problems of Turkish migrants' children. *International Review of Education* 21: 309–22.

Abbott, Grace. 1917. *The Immigrant and the Community*. New York: Century.

Abernethy, Thomas Perkins. 1961. The South in the new nation, 1789–1819. In *A History of the South*, Vol. IV. H. Stephenson and E. Merton Coulter, eds. Baton Rouge, LA: Louisiana State University Press and the Littlefield Fund for Southern History of the University of Texas.

Abrahams, Roger D. 1970. *Deep Down in the Jungle*. Rev. edn. Chicago: Aldine Publishing Company.

   1972. *Toward a Black Rhetoric: being a survey of Afro-American communication styles and role relationships*. Texas Working Papers in Sociolinguistics 15. Austin, TX: University of Texas.

Abrahams, R. and R. Troike. 1972. *Language and Culture Diversity in American Education*. Englewood Cliffs, NJ: Prentice-Hall.

Achebe, Chinua. 1973. English and the African writer. In *The Political Sociology of the English Language: an African perspective*. The Hague: Mouton. First published in translation, Kampala, 1965.

Acosta-Belén, Edna. 1975. *Spanglish: a case of languages in contact*. New Directions in Second Language Learning, Teaching, and Bilingual Education. Washington, DC: TESOL.

Adams, John. 1856. *Life and Works of John Adams*. 10 vols. Boston: Little, Brown.

Adams, Ramon F. 1968. *Western Words: a dictionary of the American West*. Norman, OK: University of Oklahoma Press.

Agoncillo, Teodoro. 1969. *Short History of the Philippines*. New York: The New American Library.

Aiken, Ray J. 1960. Let's not oversimplify legal language. *Rocky Mountain Law Review* 32: 358–64.

Alatis, James E., ed. 1978. *International Dimensions of Bilingual Education. Georgetown University Round Table on Languages and Linguistics 1978*. Washington, DC: Georgetown University Press.

Albin, Alexander and Ronelle Alexander. 1972. *The Speech of Yugoslav Immigrants in San Pedro, California*. The Hague: Vijhoff.

Alexander, D. A., J. D. E. Knox, and A. T. Morrison. 1977. Medical students talking to patients. *Medical Education* 11: 390–3.

Alford, Thomas Wildcat [Ganwrpiahsikv].1929. *The Four Gospels of Our Lord Jesus Christ in Shawnee Indian Language*. Xenia: W.A. Galloway.

Algeo, John. 1974. Review of *Black English*, by J. L. Dillard. *American Speech* 49: 142–6.

Allen, Harold B. 1973–6. *Linguistic Atlas of the Upper Midwest*. 3 vols. Minneapolis: University of Minnesota Press.

Allsopp, Richard. 1972. *Why a Dictionary of Caribbean English Usage?* Circular "A" of the Caribbean Lexicography Project. Barbados: The University of West Indies.

Alonso, Manuel Antonio. 1949. *El Jíbaro*. Río Piedras, PR: Colegio Hostos. First published 1849.

Alvarez Nazario, Manuel. 1961. *El elemento afronegroide en el español de Puerto Rico*. San Juan: Instituto de Cultura Puertorriqueña.

1977. *El influjo indígena en el Español de Puerto Rico*. San Juan, Universidad de Puerto Rico: Editorial Universitaria.

1979. Evolución histórica y realidad hablada del dialecto Jíbaro Puertorriqueño. Paper delivered at 4 Simposio de Dialectología del Caribe Hispánico. Universidad Interamericana, San Germán, Puerto Rico.

American Institutes for Research (AIR). 1977. *Interim Report, Evaluation of the Impact of ESEA Title VII Spanish/English Bilingual Education Programs*. Palo Alto, CA: AIR.

American Italian Historical Association (AIHA). *Newsletter*. Department of History, University of Florida, Gainesville, FL 32611.

American Italian Historical Association, Western Regional Chapter. 1977. *Newsletter* 4.1.

Andersen, Elaine. 1977. Learning to Speak with Style: a study of the sociolinguistic skills of children. Ph.D. dissertation, Stanford University.

Andersson, Theodore. 1969. *Foreign Languages in the Elementary School: a struggle against mediocrity*. Austin, TX: University of Texas Press.

Andersson, Theodore and Mildred Boyer, eds. 1970. *Bilingual Schooling in the United States*. 2 vols. Washington, DC: U.S. Government Printing Office.

1978. *Bilingual Schooling in the United States*. 2nd edn. Austin, TX: National Educational Laboratory Publishers.

Anisman, Paul H. 1975. Some aspects of code switching in New York Puerto Rican English. *Bilingual Review* 2: 56–85.

Applebee, Arthur N. 1978. *A Survey of Conditions in the Teaching of English, 1977*. Urbana, IL: ERIC Clearinghouse on Reading and Communication Skills and National Council of Teachers of English.

Arno, Andrew. 1976a. Joking, avoidance and authority: verbal performance as an object of exchange in Fiji. *Journal of Pacific Studies* 85: 71–86.

1976b. Ritual reconciliation and village conflict management in Fiji. *Oceania* 47: 49–65.

Asian Americans For Community Involvement (AACI). 1978. *Why America?* Palo Alto, CA: AACI.

Aspira. 1976. *Social Factors and Educational Attainment among Puerto Ricans in U.S. Metropolitan Areas, 1970*. New York: Aspira of America.

1977. *Aspira versus the Board of Education of the City of New York: a history*. New York: Aspira of America.

Atwood, E. Bagby. 1953. *A Survey of Verb Forms in the Eastern United States*. Ann

Arbor: University of Michigan Press.

Ausubel, Nathan, ed. 1948. *Treasury of Jewish Folklore*. New York: Crown.

Avis, Walter S., ed. 1967. *A Dictionary of Canadianisms on Historical Principles*. Toronto: W. J. Gage.

Ayer Directory of Publications. 1977. Philadelphia: Ayer Press.

Babcock, C. Merton, ed. 1961. *The Ordeal of American English*. Cambridge, MA: Riverside Press.

Bailey, R. W. and J. L. Robinson, eds. 1973. *Varieties of Present-day English*. New York: Macmillan.

Bain, D. J. G. 1976. Doctor–patient communication in general practice consultations. *Medical Education* 10: 125–31.

1977. Patient knowledge and the content of the consultation in general practice. *Medical Education* 11: 347–50.

Baker, S. J. 1966. *The Australian Language*. 2nd edn. Sydney: Currawong.

Balch, Emily G. 1969. *Our Slavic Fellow Citizens*. New York: Arno Press. First published 1910.

Bales, R. F. 1950. *Interaction Process Analysis: a method for the study of small groups*. Reading, MA: Addison-Wesley.

Bamgbose, Ayo. 1971. The English language in Nigeria. In *The English Language in West Africa*. J. Spencer, ed. London: Longmans.

Bannon, John Francis. 1970. *The Spanish Borderlands Frontier 1513–1821*. New York: Holt, Rinehart, and Winston.

Baratz, Joan and Roger Shuy, eds. 1969. *Teaching Black Children to Read*. Washington, DC: Center for Applied Linguistics.

Barker, George C. 1930. *Pachuco: an American–Spanish argot and its social function in Tucson, Arizona*. University of Arizona Social Science Bulletin 18. Reprinted 1970.

Barnes, William C. 1960. *Arizona Place Names*. 2nd edn. Revised by Byrd H. Granger. Tucson: University of Arizona Press.

Barnett, Lincoln. 1964. *The Treasure of our Tongue: the story of English from its obscure beginnings to its present eminence as the most widely spoken language*. New York: Alfred A. Knopf.

Baron, Salo W. 1950. Moritz Steinschneider's contribution to Jewish historiography. In *Alexander Marx Jubilee Volume*. Saul Lieberman, ed. English Section. New York.

Bart, P. B. 1968. Social structure and vocabularies of discomfort: What happened to female hysteria? *Journal of Health and Social Behavior* 9: 188–93.

Barth, F., ed. 1969. *Ethnic Groups and Boundaries*. Boston: Little, Brown.

Bartlett, John R. 1848. *Dictionary of Americanisms*. New York: Bartlett and Welford.

Barzini, Luigi, Jr. 1930. *New York Italiana*. New York and Milan: G. Agnelli.

Basile Green, Rose. 1974. *The Italian-American Novel: a document of the interaction of two cultures*. Rutherford, NJ: Farleigh Dickinson University Press.

Bassett, R. E., N. Whittington, and A. Staton-Spicer. n.d. The Basics in Speaking and Listening for High School Graduates: What should be assessed? Unpublished MS. Department of Speech Communication, University of Texas, Austin, TX.

Basso, K. H. and N. Anderson. 1973. A Western Apache writing system: the symbols of Silas John. *Science* 180: 1013–22. Reprinted in *Advances in the Creation and Revision of Writing Systems*. J. A. Fishman, ed. The Hague: Mouton. 1977.

Baugh, Albert Croll. 1935. *A History of the English Language*. New York: D.

Appleton-Century. Rev. edn. with Thomas Cable. Englewood Cliffs, NJ: Prentice-Hall 1978.

Beardsley, Charles A. 1941. Beware of, eschew, and avoid pompous prolixity and platitudinous epistles. *Journal of the State Bar of California* 16: 65–9.

Beardsley, R. S., C. A. Johnson, and G. Wise. 1977. Privacy as a factor in patient counseling. *Journal of the American Pharmaceutical Association* 17.6: 366–8.

Beck, Theodoric Romeyn. 1830. Notes on Mr. Pickering's "Vocabulary of Words and Phrases, which have been supposed to be peculiar to the United States." In *The Beginnings of American English: essays and comments.* M. M. Mathews, ed. Chicago: University of Chicago Press.

Beebe, James. 1978. *The Filipinos in Mountain View, California: a census-type socioeconomic survey.* Mountain View, CA: Filipino Association of Mountain View. Available as ERIC Document No. ED 161995.

Beltramo, Anthony F. 1972. Lexical and Morphological Aspects of Linguistic Acculturation by Mexican Americans of San José, California. Ph.D. dissertation, Stanford University.

Bennett, A. E., ed. 1976. *Communication Between Doctors and Patients.* Nuffield Publications Series London and New York: Oxford University Press.

Bentley, Harold W. 1932. *A Dictionary of Spanish Terms in English with Special Reference to the American Southwest.* Columbia University Studies in English and Comparative Literature. New York: Columbia University Press.

Berkhofer, Robert F., Jr. 1972. *Salvation and the Savage: an analysis of Protestant missions and American Indian response, 1787–1862.* New York: Atheneum.

Berlin, Isaiah. 1972. The bent twig: a note on nationalism. *Foreign Affairs* 51.

Beverley, Robert. 1947. *The History and Present State of Virginia.* Louis Wright, ed. Chapel Hill, NC: University of North Carolina Press. First published 1722.

Bickerton, Derek and Carol Odo. 1976. *Change and Variation in Hawaiian English.* Final Report, National Science Foundation Grant No. GS-39748. Vol. I: *General Phonology and Pidgin Syntax.*

Bilingual Review. 1974. Landmark decision. 1.7.

Billigmeier, Robert Henry. 1974. *Americans from Germany: a study in cultural diversity.* Belmont, CA: Wadsworth.

Biondi, Lawrence S. J. 1975. *The Italian-American Child: his sociolinguistic acculturation.* Washington, DC: Georgetown University Press.

Birdwhistell, Ray. 1970. *Kinesics and Context: essays on body motion communication.* Philadelphia: University of Pennsylvania Press.

Birkeland, Joran. 1939. *Birchland: a journey home to Norway.* New York: Dutton.

Birnbaum, S. A. 1971. Jewish languages. In *Encyclopaedia Judaica.* Jerusalem: Macmillan Co.

Bishin, William R. and Christopher D. Stone. 1972. *Law, Language, and Ethics: an introduction to law and legal method.* Mineola, NY: The Foundation Press.

Black, Mary and Duane Metzger. 1965. Ethnographic description and the study of the law. *American Anthropologist* 67: 141–65.

Blackbird, Andrew J. [Mack-aw-de-be-nessy]. 1897. *Complete Both Early and Late History of Ottawa and Chippewa Indians of Michigan: a grammar of their language personal and family history of author.* Harbor Springs: Babcock and Darling.

Blanco, Antonio. 1971. *La lengua española en la historia de California.* Madrid: Cultura Hispánica.

Bloch, Louis. 1930. *Facts about Filipino Immigration into California*. Special Bulletin No. 3. San Francisco: Department of Industrial Relations.

Bloch, Maurice, ed. 1975. *Political Language and Oratory in Traditional Society*. London and New York: Academic Press.

Blount, B. G. 1972. Parental speech and language acquisition: some Luo and Samoan examples. *Anthropological Linguistics* 14: 119–30.

Boas, Franz. 1911. Introduction. *Handbook of American Indian Languages*. Bulletin 40, Part 1. Bureau of American Ethnology, Washington, DC: Government Printing Office.

    1932. Notes on some recent changes in the Kwakiutl language. *International Journal of American Linguistics* 7: 90–3.

Bogardus, E. S. 1927–8. Filipino immigrant problems. *Sociology and Social Research* 13: 472–9.

    1931–2. What race are Filipinos? *Sociology and Social Research* 16: 274.

    1936. Filipino repatriation movement in the U.S. *Sociology and Social Research* 21: 67.

Bohannan, Paul. 1969. Ethnography and comparison in legal anthropology. In *Law in Culture and Society*. L. Nader, ed. Chicago: Aldine.

Bolton, Herbert Eugene. 1917. The mission as a frontier institution in the Spanish-American colonies. *American Historical Review* 23: 42–61.

    1921. *The Spanish Borderlands: a chronicle of Old Florida and the Southwest*. New Haven, CT: Yale University Press.

Bolton, Herbert E. and Thomas M. Marshall. 1920. *The Colonization of North America 1492–1783*. New York: Macmillan.

Bowen, J. Donald. 1952. The Spanish of San Antonito, New Mexico. Ph.D. dissertation, University of New Mexico.

    1976. Structural analysis of the verb system in New Mexican Spanish. In *Studies in Southwest Spanish*. J. D. Bowen and J. Ornstein, eds. Rowley, MA: Newbury House.

Bowman, Byrne A. 1975. Who says lawyers are lousy writers! *Barrister* 2: 47–9.

Bradley, N. Ruth. 1976. Bilingual education and language maintenance in Acadian Louisiana. In *Identité culturelle et francophonie dans les Amériques*. E. Snyder and A. Valdman, eds. Québec: Les Presses de l'Université Laval.

Brandt, Elizabeth Anne. 1970. On the origins of linguistic stratification: the Sandian case. *Anthropological Linguistics* 12: 46–50.

    1975. Linguistic diversity in Southwestern Indian languages. In *Southwestern Indian Languages and Linguistics in Educational Perspective*. M. F. Heiser and G. C. Harvey, eds. San Diego: Institute for Cultural Pluralism.

Brasch, Ila W. and Walter M. Brasch. 1974. *A Comprehensive Annotated Bibliography of American Black English*. Baton Rouge, LA: Louisiana State University Press.

Brenneis, Donald. 1978. The matter of talk: political performance in Bhatgaon. *Language in Society* 7: 159–70.

Breslauer, S. M. 1973. Yeshiva education: reclaiming the secular departments. *The Jewish Observer* 8: 13–19.

Bresnahan, Roger J., ed. 1977. *Literature and Society: cross-cultural perspectives*. Manila: United States Information Service.

Brewer, Jeutonne and Paul Dickerson Brandes, eds. 1976. *Dialect Clash in America: issues and answers*. Metuchen, NJ: Scarecrow Press.

Bricker, Victoria A. 1974. The ethnographic context of some traditional Mayan speech genres. In *Explorations in the Ethnography of Speaking*. R. Bauman and J. Sherzer, eds. Cambridge, England and New York: Cambridge University Press.

Bright, Elizabeth. 1971. *A Word Geography of California and Nevada*. Berkeley and Los Angeles: University of California Press.

Bristed, Charles Astor. 1855. The English language in America. In *Cambridge Essays*. London: Parker.

The Britannica Review of Foreign Language Education. 1968. Chicago: Encyclopedia Britannica, Inc. Vol. I.

Brod, Richard I. 1979. Options and Opportunities: new directions in foreign language curricula. *ADFL Bulletin* 10.4: 13–18.

Broussard, James F. 1942. *Louisiana Creole Dialect*. Baton Rouge, LA: Louisiana State University Press.

Brown, Claude. 1972. The language of soul. In *Rappin' and Stylin' Out* T. Kochman, ed. Urbana, IL: University of Illinois Press.

Brown, Francis J. and Joseph S. Rouček, eds. 1952. *One America: the history, contributions, and present problems of our racial and national minorities*. New York: Prentice-Hall.

Brown, Rexford. 1981. Levels of writing ability in America. In *Writing Process, Development and Communication*. C. H. Frederiksen and J. F. Dominic, eds. Baltimore, MD: Erlbaum.

Brudner, Lilyan. 1972. The maintenance of bilingualism in southern Austria. *Ethnology* 11: 39–54.

Bulosan, Carlos. 1973. *America is in the Heart*. Seattle, WA: University of Washington Press. First published 1932.

Burling, Robbins. 1973. *English in Black and White*. New York: Holt, Rinehart, and Winston.

Burnaby, Barbara J. and Robert J. Anthony. 1979. Orthography choice for Cree language in education. Ontario Institute for Studies in Education, Toronto. *Working Papers on Bilingualism* 17: 108–34.

Cabezas, Amado Y. 1977. A view of poor linkages between education, occupation, and earnings for Asian Americans. Paper presented at the Third National Forum on Education and Work, San Francisco.

Calvet, Louis-Jean. 1974. *Linguistique et colonialisme: petit traité de glottophagie*. Série Bibliothèque Scientifique. Paris: Payot.

Campbell, R. K. and J. A. Grisafe. 1975. Compliance with the Washington State Patient Information Regulation. *Journal of the American Pharmaceutical Association* NS 15.9: 494–5, 528.

Campisi, Paul J. 1948. Ethnic family patterns: the Italian family in the U.S. *The American Journal of Sociology* 53: 443–9.

Candlin, Christopher N., Clive J. Bruton, and Jonathan H. Leather. 1974. *Four Working Papers. Doctor–patient Communication Skills (DOPACS) Materials*. Lancaster, England: University of Lancaster.

Candlin, Christopher N., Clive J. Bruton, Jonathan H. Leather, and Edward G. Woods. 1977. *Teachers' Book. Doctor–Patient Communication Skills (DOPACS) Materials*. Lancaster, England: University of Lancaster.

Candor, C. 1976. A History of the Kanawha County Textbook Controversy, April 1974–April 1975. Ph.D. dissertation, Virginia Polytechnic Institute and State University.

Canestrelli, Philip. 1894. A Kootenai grammar. In *Indian Language Collection: the*

Pacific Northwest tribes. Oregon Province of the Society of Jesus. Microfilm edition. Spokane: Gonzaga University. Reprinted in *International Journal of American Linguistics* 4: 1–84. 1926.

Čapek, Thomas. 1970. *The Čechs (Bohemians) in America*. Westport, CT: Greenwood Press. First published 1920.

Card, Josefina J. 1978. *Antecedents and Consequences of the Motivation for Fertility Control: a cross-cultural study of Filipino migrants and Caucasian controls*. Palo Alto, CA: American Institutes for Research.

Cariaga, Roman R. 1974. *The Filipinos in Hawaii*. Honolulu: University of Hawaii. First published 1936.

Carp, Frances M. and Eunice Kataoka. 1976. Health care problems of the elderly of San Francisco's Chinatown. *The Gerontologist* 19: 30–38.

Carr, John Foster. 1912. *Guide to the United States for the Jewish Immigrant:* New York. Connecticut Daughters of the American Revolution.

Casiano Montañez, Lucrecia. 1975. *La pronunciación de los Puertorriqueños en Nueva York*. Columbia: Ediciónes Tercer Mundo.

Cassell, Eric J. and Lucienne Skopek. 1977. Language as a tool in medicine: methodology and theoretical framework. *Journal of Medical Education* 52: 197–203.

Cassell, Eric J., Lucienne Skopek, and Bruce Fraser. 1976. A preliminary model for the examination of doctor–patient communication. *Language Sciences* 43: 10–13.

Cassidy, Frederick G., ed. Forthcoming. *Dictionary of American Regional English*. Cambridge, MA: Belknap Press.

Castañeda Shular, Antonia, Tomas Ybarra-Frausto, and Joseph Sommers. 1972. *Literatura Chicana: Texto y Contexto*. Englewood Cliffs, NJ: Prentice-Hall.

Cazden, C. B., B. H. Bryant, and M. A. Tillman. 1972. Making it and going home: the attitudes of Black people toward language education. In *Language in Early Childhood Education*. C. B. Cazden, ed. Washington, DC: National Association for the Education of Young Children.

Cazden, C. B., V. P. John, and D. Hymes, eds. 1972. *Functions of Language in the Classroom*. New York: Teachers College Press.

Cedergren, Henrietta. 1973. The Interplay of Social and Linguistic Factors in Panama. Ph.D. dissertation, Cornell University.

Center for Applied Linguistics. 1977–8. *Bilingual Education: current perspectives*. 5 vols. Arlington, VA: Center for Applied Linguistics.

Centro de Estudios Puertorriqueños. 1976. An Initial Study of the Language Use of Five Puerto Rican Children in a Bilingual Classroom. Unpublished MS. Language Policy Task Force.

Chall, J. 1978. *Minimum Competency Testing*. Harvard Graduate School of Education Association Bulletin 22.

Chall, J., E. Radwin, V. W. French, and C. Hall. 1979. Blacks in the world of children's books (1973–5). *Reading Teacher* 32: 527–33.

Charrow, Robert P. and Veda R. Charrow, 1979. Making legal language understandable: a psycholinguistic study of jury instructions. *Columbia Law Review* 79: 1306–74.

Charrow, Veda R. and Robert P. Charrow. 1979. Characteristics of the language of jury instructions. In *Georgetown University Round Table on Languages and Linguistics 1979*. J. E. Alatis and G. R. Tucker, eds. Washington, DC: Georgetown University Press.

Chase, W. G. and H. A. Simon. 1973. Perception in chess. *Cognitive Psychology* 4: 55–81.

Childers, Wesley. 1959–61. Foreign language offerings and enrollments in public secondary schools, Fall 1959. In *Reports of Surveys and Studies in the Teaching of Modern Foreign Languages*. New York: Modern Language Association of America.

Cicourel, A. V. 1968. *The Social Organization of Juvenile Justice*. New York: Wiley.

1974. Interviewing and memory. In *Pragmatic Aspects of Human Communication*. C. Cherry, ed. Dordrecht: D. Reidel.

1975. Discourse and text: cognitive and linguistic processes in studies of social structure. *Versus: Quaderni di Studi Semiotici* 12.2: 33–83.

1977a. Interpretation and summarization: issues in the child's acquisition of social structure. In *Studies in Social and Cognitive Development*. J. Glick and A. Clarke-Stewart, eds. New York: Gardner Press.

1977b. Discourse, autonomous grammars, and contextualized processing of information. In the *Proceedings of the Conference on the Analysis of Discourse*. Institut für Kommunikationsforschung und Phonetik, University of Bonn, Germany.

Clark, William Philo. 1885. *Indian Sign Language*. Philadelphia: L. R. Hammersly.

Claudel, Calvin. 1955. Louisiana folktales and their background. *Louisiana Historical Quarterly* 38: 35–6.

Clinite, J. C. and H. F. Kabat. 1976. Improving patient compliance. *Journal of the American Pharmaceutical Association* 16.2: 74–6, 85.

Clyne, Michael G. 1967. *Transference and Triggering*. The Hague: Mouton.

Cohen, Andrew D. 1975. *A Sociolinguistic Approach to Bilingual Education: experiments in the American Southwest*. Rowley, MA: Newbury House.

Colcock, Erroll Hay and Patti Lee Hay Colcock. 1942. *Duskyland: Gullah poems and sketches of Carolina low country*. Clinton, SC: Jacobs Press.

College Entrance Examination Board (CEEB). 1977. *On Further Examination: report of the Advisory Panel on the Scholastic Aptitude Test Score Decline*. Princeton, NJ: CEEB.

Coltharp, Lurline H. 1965. *The Tongue of the Tirilones: a linguistic study of a criminal argot*. Alabama Linguistic and Philological Series 7. University, AL: University of Alabama Press.

Committee on Irish Language Attitudes Research (CILAR). 1975. *Report*. Dublin: CILAR.

Condon, W. and W. D. Ogsten. 1969. Speech and body motion. In *Perception of Language*. P. Kjeldegaard, ed. Columbus, OH: Charles Merrill.

Condor, John C. and Fathi Yousef. 1975. *An Introduction to Intercultural Communication*. New York: Bobbs-Merrill.

Conley, J. M., W. M. O'Barr, and E. A. Lind. 1978. The power of language: presentational style in the courtroom. *Duke Law Journal* 78.6: 1375-99.

Conwell, Marilyn J. and Alphonse Juilland. 1963. *Louisiana French Grammar*, Vol. I: *Phonology, Morphology, Syntax*. Janua Linguarum Series Practica 1. The Hague.

Cook-Gumperz, Jenny and John J. Gumperz. 1976. Context in children's speech. In *Papers on Language and Context*. J. Cook-Gumperz and J. J. Gumperz, eds. Language Behavior Research Laboratory. Working Paper 46. University of California, Berkeley.

Cordasco, Francesco. 1974. *The Italian-American Experience: an annotated and classified bibliographical guide*. New York: Burt Franklin.

1975. *The Italian Community and its Language in the U.S.* Totowa, NJ: Rowman and Littlefield.

Cordasco, Francesco and La Gumina Salvatore. 1972. *Italians in the U.S.: a bibliography*. New York: Oriole Editions.

Correa-Zoli, Yole. 1970. Lexical and Morphological Aspects of American Italian in San

Francisco. Ph.D. dissertation, Stanford University.

1973. Assignment of gender in American Italian. *Glossa* 7.2: 123–8.

1974. Language contact in San Francisco: lexical interference in American Italian. *Italica* 51.2: 177–92.

1977. Trinidad, Colorado Area: language survey. Unpublished MS. Department of Foreign Languages and Literatures, California State University, Hayward.

1978. San Francisco: language survey. Unpublished MS. Department of Foreign Languages and Literature, California State University, Hayward.

Corsaro, W. A. n.d. Social-ecological Constraints on Children's Communicative Strategies. Unpublished MS. University of Indiana.

Coues, Elliot, ed. 1897. *New Light on the History of the Greater Northwest. The Manuscript Journals of Alexander Henry and of David Thompson, 1799–1814. Exploration and Adventure Among the Indians on the Red, Saskatchawan, Missouri, and Columbia Rivers.* New York: Harper.

ed. 1965. *History of the Expedition under the Command of Lewis and Clark.* New York: Dover Publications. Republication of the 1893 edn.

Craddock, Jerry R. 1973. Spanish in North America. In *Current Trends in Linguistics,* Vol. X. T. A. Sebeok, ed, The Hague: Mouton.

Crawford, James M. 1978. *The Mobilian Trade Language.* Knoxville, TN: University of Tennessee Press.

Crewe, W. J., ed. 1977. *The English Language in Singapore.* Singapore: Eastern Universities Press.

Critchfield, Richard. 1977. They still come home to Huecorio. *The Christian Science Monitor* 69.196: 14–15 (August 31).

Croft, Sir Herbert. 1797. *A Letter, from Germany to the Princess Royal of England: on the English and German Languages.* Hamburgh, Fauche.

Crystal, David and Derek Davy. 1969. *Investigating English Style.* Bloomington, IN: Indiana University Press.

Cuneo, Ernest. 1975. *Bilingual Teaching is a Grave Error.* Long Island Press (June 19).

Cunningham, Irma A. E. 1970. A Syntactic Analysis of Sea Island Creole (Gullah). Ph.D. dissertation, University of Michigan.

Dalby, David. 1969. Black through White: patterns of communication in Africa and the New World. Hans Wolff Memorial Lecture, Bloomington, IN.

1972. The African element in Black American English. In *Rappin' and Stylin' Out.* Thomas Kochman, ed. Urbana, IL: University of Illinois Press.

Danet, Brenda. 1976. Speaking of Watergate: language and moral accountability. *Centrum. Working Papers of the Minnesota Center for Advanced Study in Language, Style, and Literary Theory* 4: 105–38.

1978. Language in the legal process: an overview. Paper presented at the 9th World Congress of Sociology, Uppsala, Sweden.

1980a. "Baby" or "fetus"? Language and the construction of reality in a manslaughter trial. *Semiotica.*

1980b. Language in the legal process. *Law and Society Review.* Special issue.

Davis, Irvine. 1964. The language of Santa Ana Pueblo. *Anthropological Papers* 69: 53–190. In Bulletin 191 of the Bureau of American Ethnology.

Davis, M. S. 1968. Variations in patients' compliance with doctors' advice: an empirical analysis of patterns of communication. *American Journal of Public Health* 58: 274–88.

1971. Variation in patients' compliance with doctors' orders: Medical practice and doctor–patient interaction. *Psychiatric Medicine* 2: 31–54.

Davis, Moshe. 1963. *The Emergence of Conservative Judaism: the Historical School in 19th century America.* New York: Burning Bush Press.

Davis, Philip. 1920. *Immigration and Americanization: selected readings.* Boston: Ginn.

Dawkins, J. 1978. Textbook author comments on Hillocks. *School Review* 87: 124–6.

Day, Richard R. 1972a. Patterns of Variation in Copula and Tense in the Hawaiian Post-creole Continuum. Ph.D. dissertation. University of Hawaii.

 1972b. *The Teaching of English to Hawaiian Creole-speaking Children.* ERIC Report ED 076 973.

 1980. *Issues in English Creoles: papers from the 1975 Hawaii conference.* Heidelberg: J. Verlag. Groos.

Dearholt, D. W. and Valdés-Fallis, G. 1978. Toward a probabilistic model of some aspects of code-switching. *Language in Society* 7: 411–19.

De Bray, R. G. A. 1980. *Guide to the Slavonic Languages.* 3rd rev. edn. 3 vols. Columbus, OH: Slavica Publishers.

De Stefano, Johanna S. 1973. *Language, Society, and Education: a profile of Black English.* Worthington, OH: Charles A. Jones.

Devereaux, George. 1975. Ethnic identity: its logical foundations and its dysfunctions. In *Ethnic Identity: cultural continuities and change.* G. de Vos and L. Romanucci-Ross, eds. Palo Alto, CA: Mayfield.

Dillard, J. L. 1972. *Black English: its history and usage in the United States.* New York: Random House.

 1975. *All American English: a history of the English language in America.* New York: Random House.

 1976a. *American Talk: where our words came from.* New York: Random House.

 1976b. *Black Names.* The Hague: Mouton.

Diomedi, Alexander. 1879. Kalispel Dictionary. Unpublished MS. St. Mary's Mission, Montana.

Di Pietro, Robert. 1976a. *Language as a Marker of Italian Ethnicity.* Rome: Studi di Emigrazione.

 1976b. The verbal magic of Italian in the New World. In *Proceedings of the Third Annual LACUS Forum.* Columbia, SC: Hornbeam Press.

 1977. The need for a language component in the study of Italian Americans. In *Perspectives in Italian Immigration and Ethnicity.* S. M. Tomasi, ed. Staten Island, NY: Center for Migration Studies.

Dixon, Mim Harris. 1974. Comparison of Communications Patterns Relating to Fertility Control in Four Health Care Systems in Interior Alaska. Ph.D. dissertation, Northwestern University.

Dockstader, Frederick J. 1955. Spanish loanwords in Hopi: a preliminary checklist. *International Journal of American Linguistics* 21: 157–9.

Dodge, Richard Irving. 1959. *Our Wild Indians, or Thirty-three years' personal experience among the Red men of the Great West. A Popular Account of their social life, religion, habits, traits, exploits, etc., with thrilling adventures and experiences on the Great Plains and in the mountains of our wide frontier. With an Introduction by General Sherman.* New York: Archer House.

Dohan, Mary Helen. 1974. *Our Own Words.* New York: Knopf.

Doroszewski, Witold. 1938. *Jezyk Polski w Stanach Zjednoczonych A. P.* Warsaw: Prace Towarzystwa Naukowego Warszawskiego.

Dozier, Edward P. 1951. Resistance to acculturation and assimilation in an Indian Pueblo. *American Anthropologist* 53: 56–66.

 1956. Two examples of linguistic acculturation. *Language* 32: 146–57. Reprinted in

Language in Culture and Society. D. H. Hymes, ed. New York: Harper and Row. 1964.

Drechsel, Emanuel J. 1976. "Ha, Now me Stomany That!" A summary of pidginization and creolization of North American Indian languages. *International Journal of the Sociology of Language* 7: 63–81.

Drucker, Philip. 1939. Rank, wealth, and kinship in Northwest Coast society. *American Anthropologist* 41: 55–64.

Duran, Richard. 1981. *Latino Language and Communicative Behavior.* Norwood, NJ: Ablex.

Dvornik, Francis. 1962. *The Slavs in European History and Civilization.* New Brunswick, NJ: Rutgers University Press.

Edelman, Murray. 1964. *The Symbolic Uses of Politics.* Urbana, IL: University of Illinois Press.

Edgerton, Robert B. and Marvin Karus.1971.Mexican American bilingualism and the perception of mental illness. *Archives of General Psychiatry* 24: 286–90.

Edwards, Jonathan. 1788. *Observations on the Language of the Muhhekaneew Indians.* New Haven, CT: J. Meigs.

Ehrenfried, Joseph. 1834. *Colloquial Phrases and Dialogues in German and English.* Philadelphia: J. A. Speel.

Eisenberg, A. M. and R. R. Smith, Jr. 1971. *Nonverbal Communication.* Indianapolis: Bobbs-Merrill.

Ekman, Paul and Wallace Friesen. 1969. The repertoire of non-verbal behavior: origins, usage, coding, and categories. *Semiotica* 1.1.

Elías-Olivares, L. 1976. Ways of Speaking in a Chicano Speech Community: a sociolinguistic approach. Ph.D. dissertation, University of Texas, Austin.

Ellis, J. and J. N. Ure. 1969. Language varieties: register. In *Encyclopedia of Linguistics, Information, and Control.* London: Pergamon.

Elwork, A., B. D. Sales, and J. J. Alfini. 1977. Juridic decisions. In ignorance of the law or in light of it. *Law and Human Behavior* 1: 163–90.

In press. *Jury Deliberations.* New York: Plenum.

Epstein, Erwin H., ed. 1970. *Politics and Education in Puerto Rico.* Metuchen, NJ: The Scarecrow Press.

Epstein, N. 1977a. The bilingual battle: should Washington finance ethnic identities? *The Washington Post,* June 5, C1.

1977b. *Language, Ethnicity, and the Schools: policy alternatives for bilingual–bicultural education.* Washington, DC: Institute for Educational Leadership, George Washington University.

Erickson, Bonnie, E. Allan Lind, Bruce C. Johnson, and William M. O'Barr. 1978. Speech style and impression formation in a court setting: the effects of "powerful" and "powerless" speech. *Journal of Experimental Social Psychology* 14: 266–79.

Erickson, Frederick. 1975. Gatekeeping and the melting pot: interaction in counseling encounters. *Harvard Educational Review* 45.1: 44–70.

Erickson, Frederick and Jeffrey J. Schultz. 1981. *Talking to "The Man": social and cultural organization of communication in counseling interviews.* New York: Academic Press.

Espinosa, Aurelio M., Jr. 1909–13. Studies in New Mexican Spanish. *Revue de Dialectologie romane* 1: 157–239, 269–300; 3: 251–86; 4: 241–56; 5: 142–72.

1930–46 *Estudios sobre el español de Nuevo Méjico.* 2 vols. Biblioteca de Dialectología Hispáno-americana 1, 2. Translation of Espinosa 1909–13 by Alonso and Rosenblat. Buenos Aires: Universidad de Buenos Aires.

Espinosa, Gilberto, trans. 1933. *History of New Mexico by Gaspar Perez de Villagra*. Los Angeles: The Quivira Society.

Evans, G. Edward, Karin Abbey, and Dennis Reed. 1977. *Bibliography of Language Arts Materials for Native North Americans*. Los Angeles: UCLA American Indian Studies Center.

Fairchild, Henry Pratt. 1926. *The Melting-Pot Mistake*. Boston: Little, Brown.

Falk, Yehoshua. 1860. *Avne Yehoshua*. New York.

Falkov, Ilya [Elye Shulman]. 1977. A daily Hebrew newspaper in New York. *Der Veker* 61: 9–10.

Fallers, Lloyd A. 1969. *Law Without Precedent: legal ideas in action in the courts of colonial Busoga*. Chicago: University of Chicago Press.

Farber, M. 1973. Letter to the editor. *The Jewish Observer* 8: 28.

Farr, William E. and K. Ross Toole. 1978. *Montana: images of the past*. Boulder, CO: Pruett Publishing Co.

Farrell, M., M. Hally, and J. Magnasco. 1977. Teaching interpersonal skills. *Nursing Outlook* 25: 322–5.

Fasold, Ralph. 1969. Tense and the form "be" in Black English. *Language* 45: 763–76.

Fasold, Ralph and Roger Shuy, eds. 1970. *Teaching Standard English in the Inner City*. Washington, DC: Center for Applied Linguistics.

Fast, Julius. 1971. *Body Language*. Philadelphia: Lippincott.

Faust, Albert Bernhardt. 1927. *The German Element in the United States*. 2nd edn. 2 vols in 1. New York: The Steuben Society of America.

Feeling, Durbin. 1975. *Cherokee–English Dictionary*. William Pulte, ed. Tahlequah: Cherokee Nation of Oklahoma.

Ferguson, Charles A. 1976. The Collect as a form of discourse. In *Language in Religious Practice*. W. J. Samarin, ed. Rowley, MA: Newbury House.

Ferguson, Charles A. and Charles B. Debose. 1977. Simplified registers, broken language, and pidginization. In *Pidgin and Creole Linguistics: present state and current trends*. A. Valdman, ed. Bloomington, IN: Indiana University Press.

Fernández, Micho. 1972. A glossary of Spanglish terms. *New York Magazine*, August, 7: 46.

Fernández, Roberto G. 1973. The Lexical and Syntactical Impact of English on the Cuban Spanish Spoken in Southeastern Florida. M.A. thesis, Florida Atlantic University, Boca Raton.

Fernández-Caballero, Carlos, S. A. Otterbein, and Teresa L. Romano. 1978. The Spanish-speaking patient and the emergency medical services system. *Emergency Medical Services* 7.4: 57–9, 91.

Fernández Flórez, Dario. 1965. *The Spanish Heritage in the United States*. Madrid: Publicaciones Españolas.

Fernández Méndez, Eugenio. 1970. *Historia cultural de Puerto Rico (1493–1968)*. San Juan: Ediciones "El Cemi."

Fernández-Shaw, Carlos M. 1972. *Presencia española en los Estados Unidos*. Madrid: Ediciones Cultura Hispánica.

Figueroa, Loida. 1972a. La cuestión del idioma en Puerto Rico: una baralla inconclusa. In *Tres puntos claves*. San Juan: Editorial Edil.

1972b. *History of Puerto Rico*. New York: Anaya Book Co.

Finegan, Edward. 1980. *Attitudes toward English Usage: the history of a war of words*. New York: Teachers College Press.

Firth, John R. 1930. *Speech*. London: Ernest Benn. Reprinted London and New York: Oxford University Press. 1966.

Fishman, Joshua A. 1965a. Who speaks what language to whom and when? *Linguistique* 2: 67–88.

— 1965b. *Yiddish in America: Sociolinguistic description and analysis.* Bloomington: Indiana University.

— 1966. Italian language maintenance efforts in the U. S. and the teacher of Italian in American high schools and colleges. *The Florida Foreign Language Reporter* 4: 3, 4, 26.

— 1972. Review of J. L. Rayfield, *The Languages of a Bilingual Community. Language* 48: 969–75.

— ed. 1976. *Bilingual Education: an international sociological perspective.* Rowley, MA: Newbury House.

— ed. 1977a. *Advances in the Creation and Revision of Writing Systems.* The Hague: Mouton.

— 1977b. *Bilingual Education: current perspectives, social science.* Arlington, VA: Center for Applied Linguistics.

— 1977c. Ethnicity and language. In *Language, Ethnicity, and Intergroup Relations.* H. Giles, ed. New York and London: Academic Press.

— 1977d. Knowing, using, and liking English as an additional language. *TESOL Quarterly* 11.

— 1977e. Language, ethnicity, and racism. In *Georgetown University Round Table on Languages and Linguistics 1977.* Muriel Saville-Troike, ed. Washington, DC: Georgetown University Press.

— 1977f. *Language and Nationalism.* Rowley, MA: Newbury House.

— 1978. Positive bilingualism: some overlooked rationales and forefathers. In *Georgetown University Round Table on Languages and Linguistics 1978.* J. E. Alatis, ed. Washington, DC: Georgetown University Press.

— 1980. Ethnicity and language maintenance. In *Harvard Encyclopedia of American Ethnic Groups.* S. Thernstrom, ed. Cambridge: Harvard University Press.

Fishman, Joshua A. and John E. Hofman. 1966. Mother tongue and nativity in the American population. In *Language Loyalty in the United States.* J. A. Fishman, ed. The Hague: Mouton.

Fishman, Joshua A. and Bernard Spolsky. 1977. The Whorfian hypothesis in 1975: a sociolinguistic appreciation. In *Language and Logic in Personality and Society.* H. Fisher and R. Diaz-Guerrero, eds. New York: Academic Press.

Fishman, Joshua A. et al. 1966. *Language Loyalty in the United States.* The Hague: Mouton.

Fishman, Joshua A., Robert L. Cooper, Roxana Ma et al. 1971. *Bilingualism in the Barrio.* Bloomington: Indiana University Press.

Fishman, Joshua A., Robert L. Cooper, and Andrew W. Conrad. 1977. *The Spread of English: the sociology of English as an additional Language.* Rowley, MA: Newbury House.

FitzGerald,F. 1979. Onward and upward with the Arts: rewriting American history. *New Yorker,* March 5 and 12.

Fitzpatrick, Joseph P. 1971. *Puerto Rican Americans: the meaning of migration to the mainland.* Englewood Cliffs, NJ: Prentice-Hall.

Flannery, Regina. 1937. Men's and women's speech in Gros Ventre. *International Journal of American Linguistics* 12: 133–5.

Fletcher, Alice C. 1890a. A phonetic alphabet used by the Winnebago tribe of Indians. *Journal of American Folklore* 3: 299–301.

— 1890b. The phonetic alphabet of the Winnebago Indians. In *Proceedings of the Ameri-*

can Association for the Advancement of Science, 38th Meeting, August, 1889, Toronto.

Flexner, Stuart Berg. 1976. *I Hear America Talking: an illustrated treasury of American words and phrases*. New York: Van Nostrand.

Forbes, W. C. 1928. *The Philippine Islands*. 2 vols. Boston: Houghton-Mifflin.

Foreign Language Annals. 1976. *Modern Foreign Language Registration Figures, Institutions of Higher Education, 1972 and 1974*, Vol. IX.

1977. *Modern Foreign Language Enrollment Figures, Public Secondary Schools, 1970–1974*, Vol. X.

Foreman, Grant. 1938. *Sequoyah*. Norman, OK: University of Oklahoma Press.

Fortier, Alcee. 1884–5. The French language in Louisiana and the Negro–French dialect. *Publications of the Modern Language Association* 1: 96–111.

1894. *Louisiana Studies: literature, customs, dialects, history, and education*. New Orleans: F. F. Hansell.

1904. *History of Louisiana*. 4 vols. New York: Joynt.

Foster, Brian. 1956. Recent American influence on Standard English. *Anglia* 73: 328–60.

1976. *The Changing English Language*. Harmondsworth, Middlesex, England: Penguin Books. First published Macmillan. 1968.

Fox, James J. 1974. ''Our ancestors spoke in pairs'': Rotinese views of language dialect and code. In *Explorations in the Ethnography of Speaking*. R. Bauman and J. Sherzer, eds. Cambridge, England, and New York: Cambridge University Press.

Fox, L. A. 1969. Written reinforcement of auxiliary directions for prescription medications. *American Journal of Hospital Pharmacy* 26: 334–41.

Fraenkel, Gerd. 1959. Yaqui phonemics. *Anthropological Linguistics* 1: 7–18.

Frake, Charles O. 1969. ''Struck by speech'': the Yakan concept of litigation. In *Law in Culture and Society*. L. Nader, ed. Chicago: Aldine.

Francis, V., B. M. Korsch, and M. J. Morris. 1969. Gaps in doctor–patient communication: patient response to medical advice. *New England Journal of Medicine* 280: 535–40.

Francis, W. Nelson. 1958. *The Structure of American English*. New York: The Ronald Press Co.

Francke, D. E. 1976. Roles for pharmacy practice. *Drug Intelligence and Clinical Pharmacy* 10: 593–5.

Franklin, Benjamin. 1959. *Papers of . . .* 21 vols. Leonard W. Labaree, ed. New Haven, CT: Yale University Press.

Frei, Ernest J. 1949. The historical development of the Philippine national language. *Philippine Social Sciences and Humanities Review* 14: 367–400.

Fuchs, Estelle and Robert J. Havighurst. 1973. *To Live on This Earth: American Indian education*. New York: Doubleday.

Fucilla, Joseph G. 1949. *Our Italian Surnames*. Evanston, IL: Chandler's.

1975. An historical commentary on the Italian Teachers Association subsequent to recent publication of its Annual Reports. *Italian Americana* 2.1: 101–7.

Gaarder, B. n. d. Political Perspectives on Bilingual Education. Unpublished MS.

1977. *Bilingual Schooling and the Survival of Spanish in the United States*. Rowley, MA: Newbury House.

Gage, William W. and S. Ohannessian. 1974. ESOL enrollments throughout the world. *Linguistic Reporter* 16.9: 13–16.

Galván, Roberto A. and Richard V. Teschner. 1975. *El diccionario español de Tejas. The Dictionary of the Spanish of Texas (Spanish–English)*. Silver Springs, MD: Institute of Modern Languages.

Gambino, Richard. 1974. *Blood of My Blood: the dilemma of the Italian-Americans*. Garden City, NY: Doubleday.

Gambrell, J. E. and R. A. Jackson. 1978. The community pharmacist as a source of information for the patient. *The Apothecary* 90: 10–12, 56–9.

Gamio, Manuel. 1930. *Mexican Immigration to the United States*. Chicago: University of Chicago Press. Reprinted New York: Arno. 1969. Paperback reprinting New York: Dover. 1971.

Gans, Herbert J. 1967. Some comments on the history of Italian migration and on the nature of historical research. *International Migration Review* 1: 5–9.

García, Gilbert Narro. 1978. Test encounters of the third kind. In *Georgetown University Round Table on Languages and Linguistic 1978*. James E. Alatis, ed. Washington, DC: Georgetown University Press.

Gayarré, Charles. 1903. *History of Louisiana*. 4 vols. 4th ed. New Orleans: Hansell.

Gee, Emma, ed. 1976. Counterpoint: perspectives on Asian America. Los Angeles: UCLA Asian American Studies Center.

Geffert, H. N., Robert J. Harper II, Salvador Sarmiento, Daniel M. Schember. 1975. *The Current Status of U. S. Bilingual Education Legislation*. Arlington, VA: Center for Applied Linguistics.

Gellner, Ernst. 1964. *Thought and Change*. Chicago: University of Chicago Press.

Gelman, R. and M. Shatz. n. d. Rule-governed Variation in Children's Conversations. Unpublished MS. University of Pennsylvania.

Gerhart, Eugene C. 1954. Improving our legal writing. *American Bar Association Journal* 40: 1057–60.

Gerli, E. Michael, James E. Alatis, and Richard I. Brod, eds. 1978. *Language in American Life*. Washington, DC: Georgetown University Press.

Gilbert, Glenn G., ed. 1970. *Texas Studies in Bilingualism*. Berlin: Walter de Gruyter.

ed. 1971. *The German Language in America*. Austin, TX: University of Texas Press.

1972. *Linguistic Atlas of Texas German*. Austin, TX: University of Texas Press.

1977. Origin and present day location of German speakers in Texas: a statistical interpretation. In *Texas and Germany: crosscurrents*. Joseph Wilson, ed. Rice University Studies 63.3.

Gilbert, Glenn G. and Jacob Orstein, eds. 1978. *Problems in Applied Educational Sociolinguistics: readings on language and culture problems of United States ethnic groups*. The Hague: Mouton.

Glanz, Rudolf. 1956–7. German Jews in New York City in the 19th century. *YIVO Annual of Jewish Social Science* 11: 9–38.

Glazer, Nathan and Daniel Patrick Moynihan. 1970. *Beyond the Melting Pot: The Negroes, Puerto Ricans, Jews, Italians, and Irish of New York City*. 2nd edn. First published 1963. Cambridge: MIT Press.

1975. Introduction. In *Ethnicity: theory and experience*. N. Glazer and D. P. Moynihan, eds. Cambridge, MA: Harvard University Press.

Gluckman, Max. 1969. Concepts in the comparative study of tribal law. In *Law in Culture and Society*. Laura Nader, ed. Chicago: Aldine.

Goddard, Ives. 1977. Some early examples of American Indian Pidgin English from New England. *International Journal of American Linguistics* 43: 37–41.

1978. A further note on Pidgin English. *International Journal of American Linguistics* 44: 73.

Goffman, Erving. 1971. *Relations in Public: microstudies of the public order*. Harmondsworth, Middlesex, England: Penguin Books.

Gokak, Vinayak Krishna. 1964. *English in India: its present and future*. Bombay: Asia Publishing House.
Gold, David L. 1972. Review of J. L. Rayfield, *The Languages of a Bilingual Community*. *Language Sciences* 29.
1974. Review of *For Max Weinreich on his Seventieth Birthday*. *Language Sciences* 31: 47–53.
1977a. Successes and failures in the standardization and implementation of Yiddish spelling and romanization. In *Advances in the Creation and Revision of Writing Systems*. J. A. Fishman, ed. The Hague: Mouton
1977b. Dzhudezmo. *Language Sciences* 47: 14–16.
In press a. Modern Hebrew. *Lebende Sprachen*.
In press b. Planning glottonyms for Jewish languages. In *Language Planning and Language Treatment: worldwide case studies*. E. Wood, ed. Special issue of *Word*.
Gonzales, Ambrose. 1969. *With Aesop Along the Black Border*. New York: Negro Universities Press.
Gonzales, Andrew B., ed. 1973. *Parangal kay Cecilio Lopez: essays in honor of Cecilio Lopez on his 75th birthday*. Special monograph issue 4 of *Philippine Journal of Linguistics*. Quezon City: Linguistics Society of the Philippines.
Gonzales, Andrew B., Teodoro Llamzon, and Fe Otanes, eds. 1973. *Readings in Philippine Linguistics*. Manila: Linguistics Society of the Philippines.
Goody, Jack. 1968. *Literacy in Traditional Societies*. Cambridge, England, and New York: Cambridge University Press.
Granda, Germán de. 1969. *Transculturación e interferencia lingüística en el Puerto Rico contemporáneo 1898–1968*. Spain: Ateneo Puertorriqueño.
Grant, Steven A. 1978. Language policy in the United States. *Newsletter of the American Council of Teachers of Foreign Languages*. 1–12.
Graves, Donald H. 1978a. *Balance the Basics: let them write*. New York: Ford Foundation.
1978b. The second R. *The National Elementary Principal* 57.4: 30–5.
Grebler, Leo, Joan W. Moore, and Ralph C. Guzman. 1970. *The Mexican-American People: the nation's second largest minority*. New York: The Free Press–Macmillan.
Greenberg, Joseph. 1953. Historical linguistics and unwritten languages. In *Anthropology Today*. A. L. Kroeber, ed. Missoula, MT: University of Montana Press.
1966. *Language Universals*. The Hague: Mouton.
Greenfield, Philip. 1973. Cultural conservatism as an inhibitor of linguistic change: a possible Apache Case? *International Journal of American Linguistics* 39: 98–104.
Grice, H. P. 1975. Logic and conversation. In *Syntax and Semantics, Vol. III: Speech Acts*. P. Cole and J. L. Morgan, eds. New York: Academic Press.
Grimsby, O. M. 1926. The Contribution of the Scandinavian and Germanic People to the Development of Montana. M. A. thesis, University of Montana.
Grissinger, S. E., L. W. Wolfe, and M. R. Cohen. 1973. A protocol for consultation with discharged patients about their medications. *Hospital Pharmacy* 8.6: 178–9, 182–3.
Grittner, Frank M. 1971. Pluralism in foreign language education: a reason for being. In *Britannica Review of Foreign Language Education*, Vol. III. D. L. Lange, ed. Chicago: Encyclopaedia Britannica.
Gudde, Erwin G. 1969. *California Place Names: the origin and etymology of current geographical names*. 3rd edn. Berkeley and Los Angeles: University of California Press.
Guerard, Albert L. 1922. *A Short History of the International Language Movement*.

London: T. Fisher Unwin.

Gumina, Deanna Paoli. 1977. The Italian Colony of San Francisco 1850 to 1930: La Colonia Italiana di San Francisco. Staten Island, NY: Center for Migration Studies.

Gumperz, John J. 1976a. Language, communication, and public negotiation. In *Anthropology and the Public Interest: fieldwork and theory*. P. Sanday, ed. New York: Academic Press.

1976b. The sociolinguistic significance of conversational code-switching. Papers on Language and Context, University of California, Berkeley.

1977. Sociocultural knowledge in conversational inference. In *Georgetown Round Table on Languages and Linguistics 1977*. M. Saville-Troike, ed. Washington, DC: Georgetown University Press.

1978. The conversational analysis of interethnic communication. In *Interethnic Communication*. E. L. Ross, ed. Proceedings of the Southern Anthropological Society. Auburn: University of Georgia Press.

1981. *Conversational Strategies*. New York: Academic Press.

Gumperz, John J. and Eduardo Hernández-Chavez. 1972. Bilingualism, bidialectalism and classroom interaction. In *Functions of Language in the Classroom*. C. Cazden, Vera John, and D. Hymes, eds. New York and London: Teachers College Press.

1975. Cognitive aspects of bilingual communication. In *El Lenguaje de los Chicanos: regional and social characteristics of language used by Mexican-Americans*. E. Hernández-Chavez, A. D. Cohen, and A. F. Beltramo, eds. Arlington, VA: Center for Applied Linguistics.

Gunther, John. 1947 *Inside U.S.A.* New York: Harper.

Haas, Mary R. 1944. Men's and women's speech in Koasati. *Language* 20: 142–9.

1969. *The Prehistory of Languages*. The Hague: Mouton.

1975. What is Mobilian? In *Studies in Southeastern Indian Linguistics*. J. M. Crawford, ed. Athens, GA: University of Georgia Press.

Habermas, J. 1971. *Knowledge and Human Interests*. Boston: Beacon Press.

1979. *Communication and the Evolution of Society*. Boston: Beacon Press.

Hage, Per and Wick R. Miller. n. d. "Eagle" = "Bird": a note on the structure and evolution of Shoshoni ethnoornithological nomenclature. Unpublished MS.

Hager, John. 1959. Let's simplify legal language. *Rocky Mountain Law Review* 32: 74–86.

Haggerty, R. and K. Roghmann. 1972. No compliance and self-medication. *Pediatric Clinics of North America* 19: 101–15.

Haiman, Mieczyslaw. 1974. *Polish Past in America, 1608–1865*. Chicago: Polish Museum of America.

Hall, Edward T. 1959. *The Silent Language*. New York: Doubleday.

1966. *The Hidden Dimension*. Garden City, NY: Anchor Books.

1977. *Beyond Culture*. New York: Doubleday.

Hall, Robert A., Jr. 1950. The African substratum in Negro English. *American Speech* 25: 51–4.

1966. *Pidgin and Creole Languages*. Ithaca, NY: Cornell University Press.

Hancock, Ian F. 1970. A provisional comparison of the English-based Atlantic creoles. In *Pidginization and Creolization of Languages*. D. Hymes, ed. Cambridge, England, and New York: Cambridge University Press.

Hannerz, Ulf. 1969. *Soulside: inquiries into ghetto culture and community*. New York: Columbia University Press.

Hansell, M. and C. Seabrook. 1978. Some conversational conventions of Black English.

In *Proceedings of the Fourth Annual Meeting of the Berkeley Linguistics Society.*
Berkeley, CA.

Hanson, Earl Parker. 1962. *Puerto Rico: ally for progress.* Princeton: D. Van Nostrand.

Hanzeli, Victor E. 1969. *Missionary linguistics in New France: a study of seventeenth-
and eighteenth-century descriptions of American Indian languages.* The Hague:
Mouton.

Harrington, John P. 1909. Notes on the Piro language. *American Anthropologist* 11:
563–94.

Haugen, Einar. 1966. *Language Conflict and Language Planning: the case of modern
Norwegian.* Cambridge: Harvard University Press.

1969. *The Norwegian Language in America: a study in bilingual behavior.* 2nd edn.
Bloomington, IN: Indiana University Press. First published in 2 vols. 1953.

Havard, Valery. 1880. The French half breeds of the Northwest. *Annual Report of the
Board of Regents of the Smithsonian Institution for 1879:* 309–27. Washington, DC:
U.S. Government Printing Office.

Havránek, Bohuslav and Milos Weingart. 1932. *Spisovna cestina a jazykova kultura.*
Prague: Melantrich.

Hawaii, State Department of Education. 1976. *Identification, Assessment, and Planning
System for Limited English Speakers (IAPS): a comprehensive plan, revised October 1, 1976.*

Hawgood, John A. 1940. *The Tragedy of German-America.* New York: Putnam.

Heath, Shirley Brice. 1976a. Colonial language status achievement: Mexico, Peru, and
the United States. In *Language and Sociology.* A. Verdoodt and R. Kjolseth, eds.
Louvain: Peeters.

1976b. Early American attitudes toward variation in speech: a view from social history
and sociolinguistics. Forum Lecture, LSA Institute.

1976c. A national language academy? Debate in the new nation. *International Journal
of the Sociology of Language* 11: 9–43.

1977. Language and politics in the United States. In *Georgetown University Round
Table on Languages and Linguistics 1977.* M. Saville-Troike, ed. Washington,
DC: Georgetown University Press.

1978. Bilingual education and a national language policy. In *Georgetown University
Round Table on Languages and Linguistics 1978.* J. E. Alatis, ed. Washington,
DC: Georgetown University Press.

1979. The context of professional languages: an historical overview. In *Georgetown
University Round Table on Languages and Linguistics 1979.* J. E. Alatis and G. R.
Tucker, eds. Washington, DC: Georgetown University Press.

1981. Toward an ethnohistory of writing in American education. In *Variation in Writing: functional and linguistic–cultural differences.* M. F. Whiteman, ed. Baltimore,
MD: Erlbaum.

In press. Ethnography in education: toward defining the essentials. In *Ethnography and
Education: children in and out of school.* P. Gilmore and A. A. Glatthorn, eds.
Philadelphia: University of Pennsylvania Press.

Forthcoming. *Ways with Words: Ethnography of communication, communities and
classrooms.*

Heizer, Robert F. 1978. ed., *Handbook of North American Indians,* gen. ed. W. C.
Sturtevant, Vol. III: *California.* Washington, DC: Smithsonian Institution.

Henripin, Jacques. 1968. *Tendances et facteurs de la fecondité au Canada.* Ottawa:
Bureau Fédéral de la Statistique.

Henzl, Věra M. 1975. Cultivation and Maintenance of Literary Czech by American Speakers. Ph.D. dissertation, Stanford University.

Hernández-Chavez, Eduardo. 1978. Language maintenance, bilingual education, and philosophies of bilingualism in the United States. In *Georgetown University Round Table on Languages and Linguistics 1978.* J. E. Alatis, ed. Washington, DC: Georgetown University Press.

Hernández-Chavez, Eduardo, Andrew D. Cohen, and Anthony F. Beltramo. 1975. *El Lenguaje de los Chicanos: regional and social characteristics of language used by Mexican-Americans.* Arlington, VA: Center for Applied Linguistics.

Hillocks, G., Jr. 1978. Books and bombs: ideological conflict and the schools–a case study of the Kanawha County book protest. *School Review* 86: 632–54.

Hoar, M. E. 1972. New roles for the hospital pharmacist. *Hospital Pharmacy* 7.7: 223–6.

Hoar, N. and M. E. Hoar. In press. PPI readability. *Drug Information and Clinical Pharmacy.*

Hoetker, J. and W. P. Ahlbrand, Jr. 1969. The persistence of the recitation. *American Educational Research Journal* 6: 145–67.

Hoijer, Harry. 1946. Introduction. *Linguistic structures of Native America. Viking Fund Publications in Anthropology* 6: 9–30. New York: Wenner-Gren Foundation.

Holmes, Abiel. 1804a. *A Memoir of the Moheagan Indians Written in the Year M. DCCC. IV.* Boston.

   1804b. Memoir of the Moheagan Indians. *Massachusetts Historical Society Collections,* first series 9: 75–99. Boston.

Holmes, Ruth Bradley and Betty Sharp Smith. 1976. *Beginning Cherokee.* Norman, OK: University of Oklahoma Press.

Hoover, M. 1978. Community attitudes toward Black English. *Language in Society* 7: 65–87.

Hornby, P. A. 1977. *Bilingualism: psychological, social, and educational implications.* New York: Academic Press.

Houts, P. L., ed. 1977. *The Myth of Measurability.* New York: Hart.

Howard, Joseph Kinsey. 1952. *Strange Empire: narrative of the Northwest.* New York: Morrow.

Hymes, Dell, ed. 1971. *Pidginization and Creolization of Language.* Cambridge, England, and New York: Cambridge University Press.

   1974. *Foundations of Sociolinguistics: an ethnographic approach.* Philadelphia: University of Pennsylvania Press.

International Institute of Columbia Teachers College. 1926. *A Survey of the Public Educational System in Puerto Rico.* New York: Columbia University.

Isaacs, Harold R. 1975. Basic group identity: the idols of the tribe. In *Ethnicity: theory and experience.* N. Glazer and D. P. Moynihan, eds. Cambridge: Harvard University Press.

Jacob, Henry. 1947. A Planned Auxiliary Language. London: Dennis Dobson.

Jaipaul, Rolf. 1973. Bilingual education programs in the United States: for assimilation or pluralism? In *Bilingualism in the Southwest.* P. R. Turner, ed. Tucson: University of Arizona Press.

Jensen, Vickie and Carol McLaren. 1976. *Quileute for Kids.* Quileute: Quileute Language Committee.

Jespersen, Otto. 1905. *Growth and Structure of the English Language.* Garden City, NY: Doubleday.

   1922. *Language, its Nature, Development, and Origin.* London: Allen and Unwin.

John, Elizabeth A. 1975. *Storms Brewed in Other Men's Worlds: the confrontation of Indians, Spanish, and French in the Southwest, 1540–1795.* College Station, TX: Texas A. and M. University Press.

Johnson, Gerald W. 1949. *Our English Heritage.* Philadelphia: J. P. Lippincott.

Johnson, Samuel V. 1977. *Chinook Jargon: a computer assisted analysis of variation in an American Indian pidgin.* Ann Arbor, MI: University of Michigan Microfilm.

   1980. Chinook jargon variation: towards the compleat Chinooker. *Issues in English Creoles: papers from the 1975 Hawaii conference.* R. R. Day, ed. Heidelberg: J. Groos Verlag.

Jones, Bessie and Bess Lomax Hawes. 1972. *Step it Down: games, plays, songs, and stories from the Afro-American heritage.* New York: Harper and Row.

Jones, Daniel. 1918. *An Outline of English Phonetics (OEP).* Cambridge, England: Heffer. Revised edn. 1956.

   1956. *Everyman's English Pronouncing Dictionary (EPD).* New York: Dutton.

Jones, Electa F. 1854. *Stockbridge, Past and Present; or, Records of an Old Mission Station.* Springfield, IL: Sam. Bowles.

Jones, Oakah L., Jr. 1979. *Los paisanos: Spanish settlers on the northern frontier of New Spain.* Norman, OK: Oklahoma University Press.

Jones, Richard Foster. 1965. *The Triumph of the English Language.* Stanford, CA: Stanford University Press.

Jones, William. 1906. An Algonquin Syllabary. In *Boas Anniversary Volume.* New York: G. E. Stechert and Co.

Jorgenson, Lloyd P. 1956. *The Founding of Public Education in Wisconsin.* Madison, WI: State Historical Society of Wisconsin.

Joyner, Charles W. 1977. Slave Folklife on the Waccamaw Neck: Antebellum Black culture in the South Carolina Low Country. Ph.D. dissertation, University of Pennsylvania.

Kachru, Braj B. 1965. The Indianness in Indian English. *Word* 21: 391–410.

   1966. Indian English: a study in contextualization. In *In Memory of J. R. Firth.* C. E. Bazell et al., eds. London: Longmans.

   1969. English in South Asia. In *Current Trends in Linguistics,* Vol. V. T. Sebeok, ed. The Hague: Mouton. Revised version in *Advances in the Study of Societal Multilingualism.* J. A. Fishman, ed. The Hague: Mouton.

   1973. Toward a lexicon of Indian English. In *Issues in Linguistics: papers in honor of Henry and Renee Kahane.* B. B. Kachru et al., eds. Urbana, IL: University of Illinois Press.

   1975. Lexical innovations in South Asian English. *International Journal of the Sociology of Language* 4: 55–94.

   1976a. Models of English for the Third World: White man's linguistic burden or language pragmatics? *TESOL Quarterly* 10: 221–39.

   1976b. Indian English: a sociolinguistic profile of a transplanted language. In *Dimensions of Bilingualism: theory and case studies.* B. B. Kachru, ed. Special issue of *Studies in Language Learning.* Urbana, IL: Unit for Foreign Language Study and Research, University of Illinois.

   1977. The new Englishes and old models. *English Language Forum* 15: 29–35.

   1978. Toward structuring code-mixing: an Indian perspective. In *Aspects of Sociolinguistics in South Asia.* B. B. Kachru and S. N. Sridhar, eds. Special issue of *International Journal of the Sociology of Language* 16.

   1979a. Code-mixing as a communicative strategy in India. In *Georgetown University*

Round Table on Languages and Linguistics 1978. J. E. Alatis, ed. Washington, DC: Georgetown University Press.

1979b.The Englishization of Hindi: language rivalry and language change. In *Linguistic Method: essays in honor of Herbert Penzl.* I. Rauch and G. Carr, eds. The Hague: Mouton.

1980. The pragmatics of non-native varieties of English. In *English for Cross-Cultural Communication.* L. Smith, ed. London: Macmillan.

Kahane, Henry and Renée Kahane. 1977. Virtues and vices in the American language: a history of attitudes. *TESOL Quarterly* 11: 185–202.

Kammer, Edward J. 1941. *A Socioeconomic Survey of the Marshdwellers of Four Southeastern Louisiana Parishes.* Washington, DC: Catholic University Press.

Kant, Julia G. 1969. Foreign language registrations in institutions of higher education. *Foreign Language Annals* 3: 247–304.

1970. Foreign language offerings and enrollments in public secondary schools. *Foreign Language Annals* 3: 400–76.

Katz, Linda F. 1974. The Evolution of the Pachuco Language and Culture. M. A. thesis, University of California, Los Angeles.

Keil, Charles. 1966. *Urban Blues.* Chicago: University of Chicago Press.

Kelson, Benjamin. 1950. The Jews of Montana. M. A. thesis, Montana State University.

Kenyon, John Samuel. 1924. *American Pronunciation.* Ann Arbor, MI: George Wahr.

1944. *A Pronouncing Dictionary of American English.* Springfield, MA: G. and C. Merriam.

Kephart, Horace, ed. 1915. *Captives Among the Indians.* New York: Outing Publishing.

Kessler, Carolyn. 1971. *The Acquisition of Syntax in Bilingual Children.* Washington, DC: Georgetown University Press.

Key, Mary Ritchie. 1972. Linguistic behavior of male and female. *Linguistics* 88: 15–31.

1975. *Male/Female Language.* Metuchen, NJ: Scarecrow Press.

Kiddle, Lawrence B. 1978. American Indian borrowings of Spanish Caballo. In *Papers on Linguistics and Child Language. Ruth Hirsch Weir Memorial Volume.* V. Honsa and M. J. Hardman-de-Bautista, eds. The Hague: Mouton.

Kimball, C. P. 1971. Medicine and dialects. *Annals of Internal Medicine* 74: 137–39.

Kirschenblatt-Gimblet, Barbara. 1974. The concept and varieties of narrative performance in East European Jewish culture. In *Explorations in the Ethnography of Speaking.* R. Bauman and J. Sherzer, eds. Cambridge, England, and New York: Cambridge University Press.

Kjolseth, Rolf. 1973. Bilingualist education programs in the United States: for assimilation or pluralism? In *Bilingualism in the Southwest.* P. R. Turner, ed. Tucson: University of Arizona Press.

Kloss, Heinz. 1966. *Excerpts from the National Minority Laws of the United States of America.* Honolulu: East–West Center.

1974. *Atlas of the 19th and 20th Century German–American Settlements.* Marburg, Germany: Elwert Verlag.

1977. *The American Bilingual Tradition.* Rowley, MA: Newbury House.

Kluger, Richard. 1975. *Simple Justice: the history of Brown vs. Board of Education and Black America's struggle for equality.* New York: Knopf.

Kluwin, Mary Bridget. Forthcoming. Coping with Language and Cultural Diversity: a study of changing language instruction policy from 1860 to 1930 in three American cities. Ph.D. dissertation, Stanford University.

Knapp, D. A., D. E. Knapp, and J. F. Engel. 1966. The public, the pharmacist, and self-medication. *Journal of the American Pharmaceutical Association* NS 6.9: 460–2.

Knappert, Jan. 1965. Language problems of the new nations in Africa. *African Quarterly* 5: 95–105.

Kochman, Thomas. 1971. Cross-cultural communication: contrasting perspectives, conflicting sensibilities. *The Florida FL Reporter,* Spring/Fall, 9: 3–18.

ed. 1972. *Rappin' and Stylin' Out: communication in urban Black America.* Urbana, IL: University of Illinois Press.

1979. *Boasting and Bragging "Black" and "White".* Working Papers in Sociolinguistics 58. Austin, Texas: Southwest Educational Development Laboratory.

Kohn, S. D. 1977. The case of the missing curriculum reform movement. *The National Elementary School Principal* 57: 12–17.

1978. In the wintertime, snakes carbonate. *The National Elementary School Principal* 57.4: 14–19.

Korsch, B. M. and V. F. Negrete. 1972. Doctor–patient communication. *Scientific American* 227: 66–74.

Korsch, B. M., E. K. Gozzi, and V. Francis. 1968. Gaps in doctor–patient communication: doctor–patient interaction and patient satisfaction. *Pediatrics* 42: 855–71.

Krapp, George Philip. 1919. *Pronunciation of Standard English in America.* New York: Oxford University Press.

Krauss, Michael E. 1973. Eskimo–Aleut. In *Current Trends in Linguistics,* Vol. X. T. A. Sebeok, ed. The Hague: Mouton.

Kreidler, Charles W. 1957. A Study of the Influence of English on the Spanish of Puerto Ricans in Jersey City, New Jersey. Ph.D. dissertation, University of Michigan.

Kroeber, Alfred L. and George W. Grace. 1960. *The Sparkman Grammar of Luiseno.* University of California Publications in Linguistics 16. Berkeley and Los Angeles.

Kroskrity, Paul V. 1978. Inferences from Spanish Loanwords in Arizona Tewa. *Anthropological Linguistics* 20: 340–50.

Kurath, Hans. 1939–43. *Linguistic Atlas of New England.* 3 vols. bound as 6. Reprinted 3 vols. New York: AMS. 1972.

Kurath, Hans and Raven I. McDavid, Jr. 1961. *The Pronunciation of English in the Atlantic States.*Ann Arbor: University of Michigan Press.

Kurath, Hans et al. 1949. *A Word Geography of the Eastern United States.* Ann Arbor: University of Michigan Press.

1979. *Linguistic Atlas of the Middle and South Atlantic States.* Chicago: University of Chicago Press.

Labov, William. 1964. Stages in the acquisition of Standard English. In *Social Dialects and Language Learning.* R. W. Shuy, ed. Champaign, IL: National Council of Teachers of English.

1966. *The Social Stratification of English in New York City.* Washington, DC: Center for Applied Linguistics.

1970. *The Study of Nonstandard English.* Champaign, IL: National Council of Teachers of English.

1972a. *Language in the Inner City: studies in the Black English Vernacular.* Philadelphia: University of Pennsylvania Press.

1972b. The logic of nonstandard English. In *Language in the Inner City.* Philadelphia: University of Pennsylvania Press.

1972c. *Sociolinguistic Patterns.* Philadelphia: University of Pennsylvania Press.

Labov, William and David Fanshel. 1977. *Therapeutic Discourse: psychotherapy as conversation*. New York: Academic Press.

Labov, William, D. Cohen, C. Robins, and J. Lewis. 1968. *A Study of the Non-Standard English of Negro and Puerto Rican Speakers in New York City*. Report on Co-perative Research Project 3288. New York: Columbia University.

Laird, Charlton. 1970. *Language in America*. Englewood Cliffs, NJ: Prentice-Hall.

Lakoff, Robin. 1973a. Language and woman's place. *Language in Society* 2: 45–79.

  1973b. The logic of politeness: or, minding your P's and Q's. In *Papers from the 9th Regional Meeting of the Chicago Linguistic Society*. Chicago: Linguistics Depart-ment, University of Chicago.

  1975. *Language and Woman's Place*. New York: Harper and Row.

Lancaster, Hal. 1977. Rising tide. Poor Mexicans flood into U.S. to seek jobs, deluging border patrol. *The Wall Street Journal*, September, 19.1: 18.

Lane, George S. 1935. Note on Louisiana-French: the Negro-French dialect. *Language* 11: 5–16.

Lange, Dale L., ed. 1972. Foreign language education: a reappraisal. *ACTFL Review* 4.

Language Policy Task Force (LPTF) 1978a. *Language Policy and the Puerto Rican Community*. New York: Centro de Estudios Puertorriqueños. First published *Bi-lingual Review* 5.1: 2.

  1978b. *LPTF Papers presented at Conference of LPTF, June 1978*. New York: Centro de Estudios Puertorriqueños.

  1978c. *Language Attitudes in the New York Puerto Rican Community*. Final Report for Ford Foundation. New York: Centro de Estudios Puertorriqueños.

Lavandera, Beatriz R. 1978. The variable component in bilingual performance. In *Georgetown University Round Table on Languages and Linguistics 1978*. J. E. Alatis, ed. Washington, DC: Georgetown University Press.

Lawton, David. 1971. The question of creolization in Puerto Rican Spanish. In *Pidginization and Creolization of Languages*. D. Hymes, ed. New York: Cam-bridge University Press.

Le Jeune, Paul. 1897. Brief relation of the journey to New France made in the month of April last by Father leJeune, of the Society of Jesus. In *The Jesuit Relations and Allied Documents: travels and explorations of the Jesuit missionaries in New France 1610–1791*. R. G. Thwaites, ed. Cleveland, OH: The Burrows Brothers Company.

Leap, William L., ed. 1977. *Studies in Southwestern Indian English*. San Antonio, TX: Trinity University Press.

Lee, Rose Hum. 1947. The Growth and Decline of Chinese Communities in the Rocky Mountain Region. Ph.D. dissertation, University of Chicago.

Leecham, Douglas and Robert A. Hall. 1955. American Indian Pidgin English: attesta-tions and grammatical peculiarities. *American Speech* 30: 163–71.

Leibowitz, Arnold H. 1969. English literacy; legal sanction for discrimination. *Notre Dame Lawyer* 45.1: 7–67.

  1970. English literacy: legal sanction for discrimination. *Revista Juridica de la Universidad de Puerto Rico* 39: 313–400.

  1971. *Educational Policy and Political Acceptance: the imposition of English as the language of instruction in American schools*. Washington, DC: ERIC/CAL.

  1976. Language and the law: the exercise of power through official designation of language. In *Language and Politics*. W. M. O'Barr and J. F. O'Barr, eds. The Hague: Mouton.

Leiby, June. 1976. *Beneath the Mask: life with the Hutterites*. Big Timber, MT: Griggs.

Lein, Laura and Donald Brenneis. 1978. Children's disputes in three speech communities. *Language in Society* 7: 299–323.

Lescarbot, Marc. 1907. *The History of New France . . . with an English translation, notes and appendices by W. L. Grant . . . and an Introduction by H. P. Biggar.* Toronto: The Champlain Society.

Levine, Lawrene W. 1977. *Black Culture and Black Consciousness: Afro-American folk thought from slavery to freedom.* London and New York: Oxford University Press.

Lewis, E. Glyn. 1972. *Multilingualism in the Soviet Union.* The Hague: Mouton.

1976. Bilingualism and bilingual education: the Ancient World to the Renaissance. In *Bilingual Education: an international sociological perspective.* J. A. Fishman, ed. Rowley, MA: Newbury House.

Liberman, P. and A. J. Swartz. 1972. Prescription dispensing to the problem patient. *American Journal of Hospital Pharmacy* 29: 163–6.

Lieber, Francis n.d. Notebooks on Language. Manuscript Collection. Huntington Library, San Marino, CA.

Lieberson, Stanley. 1966. Language questions in censuses. *Sociological Inquiry* 36: 262–79.

1970. *Language and Ethnic Relations in Canada.* New York: Wiley.

Lieberson, S. and T. J. Curry. 1971. Language shift in the United States: some demographic clues. *International Migration Review* 5: 125–37.

Lieberson, S., G. Dalto, and M. E. Johnston. 1975. The course of mother tongue diversity in nations. *American Journal of Sociology* 81: 34–61.

Lightfoot, Keith. 1973. *The Philippines.* New York: Praeger.

Ligouri, S. 1977. Patient package inserts: an overview. *The Apothecary* 89: 22–4, 46–8.

1978. A quantitative assessment of the readability of PPIs. *Drug Intelligence and Clinical Pharmacy* 12: 712–16.

Lind, E. A. and W. M. O'Barr. 1979. The social significance of speech in the courtroom. In *Language and Social Psychology.* H. Giles and R. St. Clair, eds. Oxford: Blackwell.

Lind, E. A., B. Erickson, J. Conley, and W. M. O'Barr. 1978. Social attributions and conversational style in trial testimony. *Journal of Personality and Social Psychology* 36: 1558–67.

Linn, L. S. and G. D. Lawrence. 1978. Requests made in community pharmacies. *American Journal of Pharmacy* 68.5: 492-3.

Livingston, Arthur. 1918. La Mercia Sanemagogna. *Romanic Review* 9: 206–26.

Llamzon, Teodoro A. 1969. *Standard Filipino English.* Manila: Ateneo University Press.

Loftus, Elizabeth. 1974. Reconstructing memory: the incredible eye-witness. *Psychology Today* 8.2: 117–19.

Loftus, Elizabeth and John Palmer. 1974. Reconstruction of automobile destruction: an example of the interaction between language and memory. *Journal of Verbal Learning and Verbal Behavior* 13: 585–9.

Lohr, O. 1962. *Deutschland und Übersee.* Herrenalb: Erdmann.

Lomax, Alan. 1950. *Mister Jelly Roll.* Berkeley: University of California Press.

Long, John K. 1904. Voyages and travels of an Indian interpreter and trader, describing the manners and customs of the North American Indians; with an account of the posts situated on the river Saint Lawrence, Lake Ontario, etc. April 10, 1760–Spring, 1782. In *Early Western Travels 1748–1846,* Vol. II, R. G. Thwaites, ed. Cleveland, OH: Arthur Clark.

Lopata, Helena Z. 1976. *Polish Americans: status competition in an ethnic community.* Englewood Cliffs, NJ: Prentice-Hall.

Lopez, Adalberto and James Petras, eds. 1974. *Puerto Rico and Puerto Ricans: studies in history and society*. New York: Halsted Press.

Lopez, Celio. 1930. A contribution to our language problem. *The Philippine Social Science Review* 3: 2.

Lourie, M. A. and N. F. Conklin. 1978. *A Pluralistic Nation: the language issue in the United States*. Rowley, MA: Newbury House.

Love, D. W., H. J. Wiese, and C. L. Parker. 1978. Continuing education in factors affecting communication. *American Journal of Pharmaceutical Education* 42.3: 304–7.

Lyra, Franciszek. 1962. English and Polish in Contact. Ph.D. dissertation, Indiana University, Bloomington.

Ma, Roxana and Eleanor Herasimchuk. 1971. The linguistic dimensions of a bilingual neighborhood. In *Bilingualism in the Barrio*. J. A. Fishman., R. L. Cooper, R. Ma et al., eds. Bloomington, IN: Indiana University Press.

MacCurdy, Raymond R. 1948a. The Spanish Dialect of St. Bernard Parish. Ph.D. Dissertation, University of North Carolina, Chapel Hill.

1948b. Spanish riddles from St. Bernard Parish. *Louisiana Southern Folklore Quarterly* 12: 129–35.

1949. Spanish folklore from St. Bernard Parish, Louisiana, Parts I and II. *Southern Folklore Quarterly* 13: 180–91.

1950. *The Spanish Dialect in St. Bernard Parish, Louisiana*. University of New Mexico Publications in Language and Literature 6. Albuquerque, NM: University of New Mexico Press.

1975. *Los "isleños" de la Luisiana: supervivencia de la lengua y folklore canarios*. Anuario de Estudios Atlánticos 21. Madrid: Gráficas Uguina.

Macías, Reynaldo F. 1979. Language choice and human rights in the United States. In *Georgetown University Round Table on Languages and Linguistics 1979*, J. E. Alatis and G. R. Tucker, eds. Washington, DC: Georgetown University Press.

Mackey, William F. and Albert Verdoodt. 1975. *The Multinational Society*. Rowley, MA: Newbury House.

Maddenn, E. E., Jr. 1973. Evaluation of outpatient pharmacy patient counseling. *Journal of the American Pharmaceutical Association* 13.8: 437–43.

Magner, Thomas F. 1972. *Introduction to the Croatian and Serbian Language*. State College, PA: Singidunum Press.

1976. The melting pot and language maintenance in South Slavic immigrant groups. *General Linguistics* 16: 59–67.

Major, Mabel and T. M. Pearce. 1972. *Southwest Heritage: a literary history with bibliographies*. 3rd edn. Albuquerque, NM: University of New Mexico Press.

Malahy, B. 1966. The effect of instruction and labeling on the number of medication errors made by patients at home. *American Journal of Hospital Pharmacy* 23: 283–92.

Mallery, Garrick. 1881. Sign Language among North American Indians compared with that among other peoples and deaf-mutes. In *First Annual Report of the Bureau of Ethnology, Smithsonian Institution*. Washington, DC: U.S. Government Printing Office.

Malone, Michael P. and Richard B. Roeder. 1976. *Montana: a history of two centuries*. Seattle: University of Washington Press.

Marckwardt, Albert H. 1958. *American English*. London and New York: Oxford University Press.

Marckwardt, Albert H. and R. Quirk. 1964. *A Common Language: British and American English*. London: British Broadcasting Corporation.

Marckwardt, Albert H. et al. 1976–8. Linguistic Atlas of the North-Central States. Published as Chicago MS in *Cultural Anthropology Series* 38: 200–8.

Marlos, Litsa and Ana Celia Zentella. 1978. A quantified analysis of code switching by four Philadelphia Puerto Rican adolescents. *Pennsylvania Review of Linguistics* 3: 46–57.

Mathesius, Vilém. 1947. *Čeština a obecný jazykozpyt*. Prague: Melantrich.

Mathews, M. M. 1931. *The Beginnings of American English: essays and comments*. Chicago: University of Chicago Press.

   1951. *Dictionary of Americanisms on Historical Principles*. Chicago: University of Chicago Press.

Mathieson, M. 1975. *The Preachers of Culture: a study of English and its teachers*. London: Allen and Unwin.

Mathiot, Madeleine. 1962. Noun class and folk taxonomy in Papago. *American Anthropologist* 64: 340–50.

Mazrui, Ali A. 1975. *The Political Sociology of the English Language: an African perspective*. The Hague: Mouton.

McDavid, Raven I. Jr. 1958. American English dialects. In *The Structure of American English*. W. N. Francis, ed. New York: Ronald Press.

   1979a. *Dialects in Culture*. W. Kretzschmar, ed. University, AL: University of Alabama Press.

   1979b. *Varieties of American English*. Anwar Dil, ed. Stanford: Stanford University Press.

McDavid, Raven I. and Virginia McDavid. 1971. The relationship of the speech of American Negroes to the speech of Whites. In *Black–White Speech Relationships*. W. Wolfram and N. H. Clarke, eds. Arlington, VA: Center for Applied Linguistics.

McDavid, Raven I., Raymond K. O'Cain, and George T. Dorrill. 1978. The Linguistic Atlas of the Middle and South Atlantic States. *Special Libraries Association Geography and Map Division. Bulletin* 113: 17–23.

McDermott, John Francis. 1965. The French in the Mississippi Valley. Urbana, IL: University of Illinois Press.

   ed. 1969. *Frenchmen and French Ways in the Mississippi Valley*. Urbana, IL: University of Illinois Press.

McGregor, G. P. 1971. *English in Africa*. London: Heinemann Educational Books.

McMurtrie, Douglas C. and Albert H. Allen. 1930. *Jotham Meeker Pioneer Printer of Kansas with a bibliography of the known issues of the Baptist Mission Press at Shawanoe, Stockbridge, and Ottawa, 1834–1854*. Chicago: Eyncourt Press.

McRae, Kenneth D. 1964. *Switzerland: example of cultural coexistence*. Toronto: Canadian Institute of International Affairs.

McWilliams, Carey. 1949. *North from Mexico: the Spanish-speaking people of the United States*. Philadelphia: J. P. Lippincott. Reprinted New York: Greenwood Press. 1968.

   1973. Introduction. In *America is in the Heart*. Carlos Bulosan, author. Seattle, WA: University of Washington Press.

Mechanic, D. 1972. Some psychologic factors affecting the presentation of bodily complaints. *New England Journal of Medicine* 286: 1132–9.

Mehan, H. 1979. *Learning Lessons*. Cambridge, MA: Harvard University Press.

Melendy, H. Brett. 1972. *The Oriental Americans*. New York: Twayne Publishers.

1976. Filipinos in the United States. In *Counterpoint: perspectives on Asian America*. Los Angeles: UCLA Asian American Studies Center.

1977. *Asians in America: Filipinos, Koreans, and East Indians*. Boston: G. K. Hall.

Mellinkoff, David. 1963. *The Language of the Law*. Boston: Little, Brown.

Mencken, H. L. 1919. *The American Language*. New York: Knopf.

1921. *The American Language*. Rev. edn. New York: Knopf.

1923. *The American Language*. 3rd edn. New York: Knopf.

1936. *The American Language*. 4th edn. New York: Knopf.

1945. *The American Language. Supplement I*. New York: Knopf.

1948. *The American Language. Supplement II*. New York: Knopf.

1977. *The American Language*. One-volume abridged edn. R. I. McDavid, Jr., ed. New York: Knopf.

Mengarini, Gregorio. 1877. *A Dictionary of the Kalispel or Flathead Indian Language*. St. Ignatius, MT: St. Ignatius Print. Also in *Indian Language Collection: the Pacific Northwest tribes*. Oregon Province of the Society of Jesus. Microfilm edition. Spokane, WA: Gonzaga University.

1970. *Grammatica Linguae Selicae: a Selish or Flathead grammar*. New York: AMS Press. First published 1861. Also in *Indian Language Collection: the Pacific Northwest tribes*. Oregon Province of the Society of Jesus. Microfilm edition. Spokane, WA: Gonzaga University.

Merriam, H. G. 1943. Ethnic Settlement of Montana. *The Pacific Historical Review* 12: 157–68.

Meyerstein, Goldie P. 1959. Selected Problems of Bilingualism among Immigrant Slovaks. Ph.D. dissertation, University of Michigan, Ann Arbor.

Michelson, Truman. 1927. Fox linguistic notes. In *Festschrift Meinhof Sprachwissenschaftliche und Andere Studien*. Hamburg: Kommissionsverlag von L. Friederichsen.

Milán, William G. 1976. The influence of bilingualism on the evolution of American urban Spanish: Puerto Rican speech in New York City, a case in point. Paper presented at the Chicano-Riqueño Lecture Series, Indiana University, Bloomington.

1978. Toward a Comprehensive Language Policy for a Desegregated School System: reassessing the future of bilingual education. MS available from the National Institute of Education.

Miller, Casey and Kate Swift. 1976. *Words and Women*. New York: Doubleday Anchor.

Miranda, Edward J. 1977. The Italian-American: who, what, where, when, why. *Identity* 11–16.

Mishkin, Bernard. 1940. *Rank and Warfare Among the Plains Indians*. Monograph 3. Seattle: American Ethnological Society.

Mitchell, Henry H. 1970. *Black Preaching*. Philadelphia: J. P. Lippincott.

Mitchell-Kernan, Claudia. 1971. *Language Behavior in a Black Urban Community*. Monograph 2 of the Language-Behavior Research Laboratory. Berkeley, CA.

1972a. On the status of Black English for native speakers: an assessment of attitudes and values. In *Functions of Language in the Classroom*. C. B. Cazden, V. P. John, and D. Hymes, eds. New York: Teachers College Press.

1972b. Signifying and marking: two Afro-American speech acts. In *Directions in Sociolinguistics*. J. Gumperz and D. Hymes, eds. New York: Holt, Rinehart, and Winston.

Mitchell-Kernan, Claudia and Keith T. Kernan. 1975. Children's insults: America and Samoa. In *Sociocultural Dimensions of Language Use*. M. Sanches and B. G. Blount, eds. New York: Academic Press.

1977. Pragmatics of directive choice among children. In *Child Discourse*. S. Ervin-Tripp and C. Mitchell-Kernan, eds. New York: Academic Press.

Mizrahi, Maurice. 1970. The French-speaking communities in the United States. In *Bilingual Schooling in the United States*, Vol. II. T. Andersson and M. Boyer, eds. Washington, DC: U.S. Government Printing Office.

Moffett, J. and B. J. Wagner. 1976. *Student-centered Language Arts and Reading: a handbook for teachers*. 2nd edn. Boston: Houghton-Mifflin.

Mooney, James. 1900. *Myths of the Cherokee, Part 1. 19th Annual Report of the Bureau of American Ethnology. Smithsonian Institute*. Washington, DC: U.S. Government Printing Office.

Morgan, Raleigh, Jr. 1959. Structural sketch of Saint Martin Creole. *Anthropological Linguistics* 1.8: 20–4f.

1964. Saint Martin Creole and genetic relationships. In *Studies in Language and Linguistics*. A. H. Marckwardt, ed. Ann Arbor, MI: The English Language Institute, University of Michigan.

1970. Dialect levelling in non-English speech of Southwest Louisiana. In *Texas Studies in Bilingualism*. G. G. Gilbert, ed. Berlin: Walter de Gruyter.

1975. Playing dead thrice: Louisiana Créole animal tale. *Revue de Louisiana* 4: 23–32.

Morris, E. E. 1898. *Austral English*. London: Macmillan.

Morse, Reverend Jedidiah. 1822. *A Report to the Secretary of War of the United States on Indian Affairs .´. .* New Haven, CT: S. Converse.

Morton, Robert A. 1941. Challenge made to Beardsley's plan for plain and simple legal syntax. *Journal of the State Bar of California* 16: 103–6.

Morvillo, Anthony. 1895. A Dictionary of the Perce Language. In *Indian Language Collection: The Pacific Northwest tribes*. Oregon Province of the Society of Jesus. Microfilm edition. Spokane, WA: Gonzaga University.

Mukherjee, Meenakshi. 1971. *The Twice-Born Fiction: themes and techniques of the Indian novel in English*. New Delhi and London: Heinemann.

Muñoz, Alfredo N. 1971. *The Filipinos in America*. Los Angeles, CA: Mountainview.

Nader, Laura. 1965. The anthropological study of law. *American Anthropologist* 67: 3–32.

Nash, Rose. 1970. Spanglish: language contact in Puerto Rico. *American Speech* 45: 223–33.

National Center for Education Statistics (NCES). 1978a. *The Educational Disadvantage of Language-Minority Persons in the United States, Spring 1976*. Bulletin, July 26, 1978, NCES 78–121, ERIC/CAL.

1978b. *Geographic Distribution, Nativity, and Age Distribution of Language Minorities in the United States, Spring 1976*. Bulletin, August 22, 1978, NCES 78–134, ERIC/CAL.

1978c. *Place of Birth and Language Characteristics of Persons of Hispanic Origin in the United States, Spring 1976*. Bulletin, October 20, 1978, NCES 78–135, ERIC/CAL.

1979. *Place of Birth and Language Characteristics of Persons of Chinese, Japanese, Korean, Pilipino, and Vietnamese Origin in the United States, Spring 1976*. Bulletin, May 21, 1979, NCES 79–144, ERIC/CAL.

The National Council of Teachers of English (NCTE). 1961. *The National Interest and the Teaching of English*. Champaign, IL: NCTE.

National Institute of Education. 1975. Spanish–English Bilingual Education in the United States: current issues, resources, and recommended funding priorities for research. Unpublished MS.

National Puerto Rican Task Force on Educational Policy (NPTFEP). 1977. *Toward a*

Language Policy for Puerto Ricans in the United States: an agenda for community involvement. New York: NPTFEP.

Navarro, Tomás. 1966. *El Español en Puerto Rico.* Río Piedras, PR: Editorial Universitaria.

Nee, Victor and Brett duBarry Nee. 1974. *Longtime Californ'.* Boston: Houghton-Mifflin.

Negrón de Montilla, Aida. 1975. *Americanization in Puerto Rico and the Public School System 1900–1930.* San Juan, Universidad de Puerto Rico: Editorial Universitaria.

Nelkin, D. 1977. *Science Textbook Controversies and the Politics of Equal Time.* Cambridge: MIT Press.

Nelli, Humbert. 1967. Italians in urban America: a study in ethnic adjustment. *International Migration Review* 1: 38–55.

Newman, Edwin. 1974. *Strictly Speaking: Will America be the death of English?* New York: Bobbs-Merrill.

Newman, Stanley. 1955. Vocabulary levels: Zuñi sacred and slang usage. *Southwestern Journal of Anthropology* 11: 345–54.

1958. *Zuñi Dictionary.* Indiana University Research Center in Anthropology, Folklore, and Linguistics 6. Bloomington, IN.

Newport, E. L. 1976. Motherese: the speech of mothers to young children. In *Cognitive Theory,* Vol. II. N.J. Castella, D. B. Pisoni, and G. R. Potts, eds. Hillsdale, NJ: Lawrence Erlbaum.

Newport, E. L., H. Gleitman, and L. R. Gleitman. 1977. Mother, I'd rather do it myself: some effects and non-effects of maternal speech style. In *Talking to Children: language input and acquisition.* C. E. Snow and C. A. Ferguson, eds. Cambridge, England, and New York: Cambridge University Press.

Nichols, John. 1974. Notes on a Traditional Potawatomi Writing System. Unpublished MS. Wisconsin Native American Languages Project, The University of Wisconsin, Milwaukee.

Nichols, Patricia C. 1976. Linguistic Change in Gullah: sex, age, and mobility. Ph.D. dissertation, Stanford University.

1978. Black women in the rural South: conservative and innovative. *International Journal of the Sociology of Language* 17: 45–54.

Nicodemus, Lawrence. 1975. *Snchitsu'umshtsn: the Coeur D'Alene language.* Albuquerque, NM: Southwest Language Associates.

Nihalani, P., R. K. Tongue, and P. Hosali. 1978. *Indian and British English: a handbook of usage and pronunciation.* New Delhi: Oxford University Press.

Norell, Irene P. 1976. *Literature of the Filipino-Americans in the United States: selected and annotated bibliography.* San Francisco, CA: R & E Associates.

Novak, Michael. 1977. *The Rise of the Unmeltable Ethnics: politics and culture in the seventies.* New York: Macmillan.

O'Barr, William M. and John M. Conley. 1976. When a juror watches a lawyer. *Barrister* 3: 8–11, 33.

O'Barr, William M. and E. A. Lind. In press. Ethnography and experimentation – partners in legal research. In *Perspectives in Law and Psychology,* Vol. II: *The Jury, Judicial, and Trial Processes.* B. D. Sales, ed. New York: Plenum.

O'Barr, William M. and Jean F. O'Barr, eds. 1976. *Language and Politics.* The Hague: Mouton.

O'Barr, William M., J. M. Conley, and E. A. Lind. 1976. Manipulation of speech styles in an American trial courtroom. In *Proceedings of the 1975 Temple University*

Conference on Culture and Communication. R. Chelfen, ed. Philadelphia: Temple University Department of Anthropology.

Odo, Carol. 1970. English patterns in Hawaii. *American Speech* 45: 234–9.

Ohannessian, Sirapi, Charles A. Ferguson, and Edgar C. Polomé, eds. 1975. *Language Surveys in Developing Nations: papers and reports on sociolinguistic surveys.* Arlington, VA: Center for Applied Linguistics.

Okara, Gabriel. 1963. African speech . . . English words. *Transition* 10: 13–18.

Oregon Province of the Society of Jesus. 1976. *Indian Language Collection: the Pacific Northwest tribes.* Microfilm edition. Spokane, WA: Gonzaga University.

Ornstein, Jacob. 1975. Sociolinguistics and the study of Spanish and English language varieties and their use in the U.S. Southwest. In *Three Essays on Linguistic Diversity in the Spanish-speaking World.* J. Ornstein, ed. The Hague: Mouton.

1976. A cross-disciplinary sociolinguistic investigation of Mexican-American bilinguals/biculturals at a U.S. border university: language and social parameters. *La linguistique* 12: 131–45.

Osuna, Juan Jose. 1949. *A History of Education in Puerto Rico.* Río Piedras: Editorial de la Universidad de Puerto Rico.

Pane, Remigio U. 1970. Present Status of Italian studies in the United States and Canada. *Modern Language Journal* 54: 507–23.

1975. Doctoral dissertations on the Italian-American experience completed in the U.S. and Canada 1908–1974. *International Migration Review* 9: 545–56.

Paredes, Americo. 1966. El Folklore de los grupos de origen Mexicano en Estados Unidos. *Folklore Americano* 14: 146–63.

Parker, William Riley. 1961a. *The National Interest and Foreign Languages.* 3rd edn. Department of State Publication 6389. International Organization and Conference Series IV, UNESCO 30. Washington, DC: U.S. Government Printing Office.

1961b. *The National Interest and the Teaching of English as a Second Language.* Champaign, IL: National Council of Teachers of English.

Parlee, Mary Brown. 1979. Conversational politics. *Psychology Today* 12: 48–56.

Partridge, Eric and John W. Clark. 1951. *British and American English since 1900.* New York: Philosophical Library.

Pascasio, Emy M., ed. 1977. *The Filipino Bilingual: studies on Philippine bilingualism and bicultural education.* Quezon City: Ateneo de Manila University Press.

Patterson, Orlando. 1975. Context and choice in ethnic allegiance: a theoretical framework and Caribbean study. In *Ethnicity: theory and practice.* N. Glazer and D. P. Moynihan, eds. Cambridge, MA: Harvard University Press.

Paulston, R. G. 1976. Ethnic revival and educational conflict in Swedish Lapland. *Comparative Educational Review* 20: 179–92.

Pearce, T. M. ed. 1965. *New Mexico Place Names: a geographical dictionary.* Albuquerque, NM: University of New Mexico Press.

Pederson, Lee A. et al. Forthcoming. *Linguistic Atlas of the Gulf States.*

Pérez Sala, Paulino. 1973. *Interferencia lingüística del inglés en el español hablado en Puerto Rico.* Hato Rey, PR: Inter-American University Press.

Perlman, Alan M. 1973. Grammatical Structure and Style Shift in Hawaiian Pidgin and Creole. Ph.D. dissertation, University of Chicago.

Peterkin, Julia. 1970. *Collected Short Stories.* F. Durham, ed. Columbia, SC: University of South Carolina Press.

Pfaff, Carol. 1975. Constraints on code switching. Paper presented at Linguistic Society of America.

Pfeiffer, Anita B. 1975. Developing a bilingual curriculum. In *Proceedings of the First Inter-American Conference on Bilingual Education*. R. Troike and N. Modiano, eds. Arlington, VA: Center for Applied Linguistics.

Phelan, John Leddy. 1959. *The Hispanization of the Philippines: Spanish aims and Filipino responses 1565–1700*. Madison, WI: University of Wisconsin Press.

Philbrick, Frederick A. 1949. *Language and the Law: the semantics of forensic English*. New York: Macmillan.

Philips, S. U. 1972. Acquisition of rules for appropriate speech usage. In *The Functions of Language in the Classroom*. C. B. Cazden, V. P. John, and D. Hymes eds. New York: Teachers College Press.

Phillips, June K. 1977. *The Language Connection: from the classroom to the world*, Vol. IX. The ACTFL Foreign Language Education Series. Skokie, IL: National Textbooks.

Phillips, J. R. 1973. Syntax and vocabulary of mother's speech to young children. *Child Development* 44: 182–5.

Pickering, John. 1816. *A Vocabulary, Or Collection of Words and Phrases which have been supposed to be peculiar to the United States of America*. Also in *The Beginnings of American English: essays and comments*. M. M. Mathews, ed. Chicago: University of Chicago Press. 1931.

Pilling, James C. 1891. *Bibliography of the Algonquian Languages*. Smithsonian Institution, Bureau of Ethnology Bulletin 13. Washington, DC.

Pitt, Leonard. 1970. *The Decline of the Californios: a social history of the Spanish-speaking Californians, 1846–1890*. Berkeley and Los Angeles: University of California Press.

Pittenger, J. 1977. Big Schools, big problems. *Harvard Graduate School of Education Association Bulletin* 21: 13–16.

Pizzo, Anthony P. 1968. *Tampa Town, 1824–1886: The Cracker Village with a Latin Accent*. Miami, FL: Hurricane House.

Platt, J. T. 1975. The Singapore English speech continuum and basilect 'Singlish' as a 'Creoloid'. *Anthropological Linguistics* 17: 363–74.

    1976. *The sub-varieties of Singapore English: their sociolectal and functional status*. In *The English Language in Singapore*. W. Crewe, ed. Singapore: Eastern University Press.

Poplack, Shana. 1977. The notion of the plural in Puerto Rican Spanish: competing constraints on /s/ deletion. In *Quantitative Analyses of Linguistic Structure*. W. Labov, ed. New York: Academic Press.

    1978a. Quantitative analysis of a functional and formal constraint on code switching. Paper presented at the National Conference on Chicano and Latino Discourse Behavior, Educational Testing Service, Princeton, NJ, April 18, 1978.

    1978b. Dialect acquisition among Puerto Rican bilinguals. *Language in Society* 7: 89–103.

Postal, Paul M. 1964. Boas and the development of phonology: comments based on Iroquoian. *International Journal of American Linguistics* 30: 269–80.

Pousada, Alicia. 1979. Translation and linguistic minorities. In *Georgetown University Round Table on Languages and Linguistics 1979*. J. E. Alatis and G. R. Tucker, eds. Washington, DC: Georgetown University Press.

Powell, John Wesley. 1891. *Indian Linguistic Families of America North of Mexico. 7th Annual Report, Bureau of American Ethnology*. Washington, DC: U.S. Government Printing Office.

Powers, Stephen. 1877. Tribes of California. *Contributions to North American Ethnology* 3: 1–635.

Prator, Clifford H. 1950. *Language Teaching in the Philippines*. Manila: United States Educational Foundation in the Philippines.

Prezzolini, Giuseppe. 1939. La lingua della "Giobba." *Lingua Nostra* 1: 121–2.

Prince, John Dyneley. 1905. A tale in the Hudson River Indian language. *American Anthropologist* 7: 74–84.

1912. An ancient New Jersey Indian jargon. *American Anthropologist* 14: 508–24.

Prucha, Francis Paul, ed. 1973. *Americanizing the American Indians*. Cambridge, MA: Harvard University Press.

Pulte, William and Durbin Feeling. 1975. Outline of Cherokee grammar. In *Cherokee–English Dictionary*. W. Pulte, ed. Tahlequah: Cherokee Nation of Oklahoma.

Pyles, Thomas. 1971. *The Origin and Development of the English Language*. 2nd edn. New York: Harcourt Brace Jovanovich.

Quirk, Randolph. 1962. *The Uses of English*. London: Longmans.

1972. *English Language and Images of Matter*. London and New York: Oxford University Press.

Quirk, Randolph, et al. 1972. *A Grammar of Contemporary English*. London: Longmans.

Rabaya, Violet. 1971. Filipino Immigration: the creation of a new social problem. In *Roots: an Asian reader*. Amy Tachiki et al., eds. Los Angeles: UCLA Asian American Studies Center.

Racelis, Maria and Geronima Pecson. 1959. *Tales of the American Teachers in the Philippines*. Manila: Carmelo and Bauermann.

Radin, Paul. 1920. *The Autobiography of a Winnebago Indian*. Berkeley, CA: University of California Press.

1935. *The Italians of San Francisco: their adjustment and acculturation*. Monograph 1, in 2 pts. Abstract from the S.E.R.A. Project. *Cultural Anthropology*: 44–54.

1954 *The Evolution of an American Indian Prose Epic, a study in comparative literature, Pt. 1*. Ethnographical Museum, Basel, Switzerland.

von Raffler Engel, Walburga. 1953. Studies in Italian–English Bilingualism. Ph.D. dissertation, Indiana University.

1961. Investigation of Italo-American bilinguals. *Zeitschrift für Phonetik* 14: 127–30.

Ramchand, Kenneth. 1973. The language of the master? In *Varieties of Present-day English*. R. W. Bailey and J. L. Robinson, eds. New York: Macmillan.

Ramos, Teresita V. 1971. *Tagalog Structure*. Honolulu: University of Hawaii Press.

Ramson, W. S. 1966. *Australian English: an historical study of vocabulary 1788–1898*. Canberra: Australian National University Press.

ed. 1970. *English Transported: essays on Australasian English*. Canberra: Australian National University Press.

Ransom, Jay E. 1941. Aleut semaphore signals. *American Anthropologist* 43: 422–7.

1945. Writing as a medium of acculturation among the Aleut. *Southwestern Journal of Anthropology* 1: 333–44.

Rao, G. S. 1954. *Indian Words in English: a study in Indo-British cultural and linguistic relations*. London and New York: Oxford University Press.

Read, Allen Walker. 1936. American projects for an academy to regulate speech. *Publications of the Modern Language Association* 51: 1141–79.

Reed, Carroll E. 1977. *Dialects of American English*. Amherst, MA: University of Massachusetts Press.

Reed, David W. et al. Forthcoming. *Linguistic Atlas of California and Nevada.*

Reinecke, John E. 1969. *Language and Dialect in Hawaii: a sociolinguistic history to 1935.* Stanley M. Tsuzaki, ed. Honolulu: University of Hawaii Press.

Reinecke, John E. and Stanley M. Tsuzaki, eds. 1977. *The Carrier Pidgin.* Honolulu: Social Sciences and Linguistics Institute, University of Hawaii.

Reinecke, John E., Stanley M. Tsuzaki, David De Camp, Ian F. Hancock, and Richard E. Wood, eds. 1975. A *Bibliography of Pidgin and Creole Languages.* Honolulu: University of Hawaii Press.

Remick, H. 1971. The Maternal Environment of Linguistic Development. Ph.D. Dissertation, University of California, Davis.

Resnick, D. P. and L. B. Resnick. 1977. The nature of literacy: an historical exploration. *Harvard Educational Review* 47: 370–85.

Rhodes, Richard. 1977. French Cree: a case of borrowing. In *Actes du Huitième Congrès des Algonquinistes.* Ottawa: Carleton University Press.

Rich, Andrea. 1974. *Interracial Communication.* New York: Harper and Row.

Robinson, Cecil. 1969. *With the Ears of Strangers: the Mexican in American literature.* Tucson, AZ: University of Arizona Press.

Rolle, Andrew F. 1966. The Italian moves westward. *Montana: the magazine of western history* 16.1: 13–24.

  1968. *The Immigrant Upraised: Italian adventurers and colonists in an expanding America.* Norman, OK: University of Oklahoma Press.

  1972. *The American Italians: their history and culture.* Belmont, CA: Wadsworth Publishing Co.

Rosario, Rubén del. 1969. Un libro de Granda. *Ateneo* 6: 99–105.

  1970. *La Lengua de Puerto Rico.* Río Piedras, PR: Editorial Cultural.

Rosenberg, Bruce A. 1970. *The Art of the American Folk Preacher.* London and New York: Oxford University Press.

Ross, Alexander. 1849. *Adventures of the First Settlers on the Oregon or Columbia River.* London: Smith, Elder.

Rouček, Joseph S. 1968. *The Czechs and Slovaks in America.* 2nd edn. Minneapolis: Lerner.

Rus, Jan. 1973. One court, two cultures: rhetorical strategy and cultural interference in a changing Maya community. Paper presented at the annual meeting of the American Anthropological Association.

Saito, Shiro. 1973. *Philippine Ethnography: a critically annotated and selected bibliography.* Honolulu: University of Hawaii Press.

  1977. *Filipinos Overseas: a bibliography.* Staten Island, NY: Center for Migration Studies.

Sales, B. D., A. Elwork, and J. J. Alfini. 1977. Improving comprehension for jury instructions. In *Perspectives in Law and Psychology,* Vol I: *The Criminal Justice System.* B. D. Sales, ed. New York: Plenum.

Samarin, William J. 1968. Lingua francas of the world. In *Readings in the Sociology of Language.* J. A. Fishman, ed. The Hague: Mouton.

Sanchez, R. 1972. Nuestra circunstancia lingüística. *El Grito* 6. 1: 45–74.

  1974. A Generative Study of Two Spanish Dialects. Ph.D. dissertation, University of Texas, Austin.

Sanders, Irwin T. and Ewa T. Morawska. 1975. *Polish-American Community Life: a survey of research.* Boston: Boston University.

Sankoff, D. and Rejean Lessard. 1975. Vocabulary richness: a sociolinguistic analysis. *Science* 190: 689.

Santiago, Isaura. 1978. *A Community's Struggle for Equal Educational Opportunity: Aspira vs. Board of Education*. Princeton, NJ: Office for Minority Education.

Sapir, Edward. 1929. Central and North American languages. In *Encyclopedia Britannica*. 14th edn. London: Encyclopedia Britannica Co.

Sapir, Edward and Morris Swadesh. 1946. American Indian grammatical categories. *Word* 2: 103–112.

Savard, J. G. and R. Vigneault, eds. 1975. *Multilingual Political Systems: problems and solutions*. Québec: Laval University Press.

Saville-Troike, M. 1976. *Foundations for Teaching English as a Second Language: theory and method*. Englewood Cliffs, NJ: Prentice-Hall.

Scanpresence. 1977. *Action Conference on the Scandinavian Presence in America*. Minneapolis, MN: Scanpresence.

Scarlett, Marie R. 1976. Su única enfermedad era una barrera del idioma. *Registered Nurse* 39: 69–72.

Schachter, Paul and Fe Otanes. 1972. *Tagalog Reference Grammar*. Berkeley, CA: University of California Press.

Schaechter, Mordkhe. 1969. The 'hidden standard': a study of competing influences in standardization. In *Field of Yiddish: third collection*. M. Herzog et al., eds. The Hague: Mouton.

    1975. [The Yivo and Yiddish]. *Yidishe shprakh*. New York. 34: 2–22.

    1977. Four schools of thought in Yiddish language planning. *Michigan Germanic Studies* 3: 34–66.

Schegloff, Emanuel A. 1968. Sequencing in conversational openings. *American Anthropologist* 70: 1075–95.

    1973. Recycled turn beginnings: a precise repair mechanism in conversation's turn taking organization. Paper presented in the series Language in the Context of Space, Time, and Society, Summer Institute of Linguistics sponsored by the Linguistic Society of America, University of Michigan, July.

Schegloff, Emanuel A. and Harvey Sacks. 1973. Opening up closings. *Semiotica* 8: 289–327.

Schelfen, A. E. 1964. Significance of posture in communication systems. *Psychiatry* 27: 316–31.

Schermerhorn, R. A. 1970. *Comparative Ethnic Relations: a framework for theory and research*. New York: Random House.

    1972. Towards a general theory of minority groups. Cited in A. Verdoodt. The differential impact of immigrant French speakers on indigenous German speakers: a case study in the light of two theories. In *Advances in the Sociology of Language*, Part II. J. A. Fishman, ed. The Hague: Mouton.

Schmitt, Alfred. 1951. *Die Alaska-Schrift und ihre Schriftgeschichtliche Bedeutung*. Marburg: Simons.

Searle, J. R. 1969. *Speech Acts*. Cambridge, England, and New York: Cambridge University Press.

Sey, K. A. 1973. *Ghanaian English: an exploratory survey*. London: Macmillan.

Shatz, M. and R. Gelman. 1973. *The Development of Communication Skills: modifications in the speech of young children as a function of listener*. Society for Research in Child Development Monographs 38.5.

Shaughnessy, M. P. 1977. Errors and Expectations: a guide for the teacher of basic writing. New York: Oxford University Press.

Shenkin, B. N. 1973. Giving the patient his medical record: a proposal to improve the system. *New England Journal of Medicine* 289: 688–92.

Shepherd, Susan C. 1975. Words of Spanish Origin in Some Southwestern American Indian Languages and their Significance in Terms of Historical Contact and Language Maintenance. Unpublished MS, Stanford University.

Shipley, E. S., C. S. Smith, and L. R. Gleitman. 1969. A study in the acquisition of language: free responses to commands. *Language* 45: 322–42.

Shopen, Timothy. 1980. *Standards and Dialects in English*. Cambridge, MA: Winthrop Publishers.

Shores, David L. 1972. *Contemporary English: change and variation*. Philadelphia: J. P. Lippincott.

Shuy, Roger W. 1967. *Discovering American Dialects*. Champaign, IL: National Council of Teachers of English.

    1973. The study of vernacular Black English as a factor in educational change. *Research in the Teaching of English* 7: 297–311.

    1974. Communication problems in the cross-cultural medical interview. In Papers of the Second Annual Conference on Psychosomatic Obstetrics and Gynecology. D. Mosley, ed. Mimeo. Key Biscayne, FL.

    1976. The medical interview: problems in communication. *Primary Care* 3: 365–86.

    1978. Learning to talk like teachers. Paper presented at the Annual Meeting of the American Educational Research Association. Toronto, April, 1978.

Shuy, Roger W. and R. W. Fasold. 1973. *Language Attitudes: current trends and prospects*. Washington, DC: Center for Applied Linguistics.

Shuy, Roger, Walt Wolfram, and William K. Riley. 1967. *A Study of Social Dialects in Detroit*. Report on project 6-1347. Washington, DC: Office of Education.

Sibayan, Bonifacio. 1974. Language policy, language engineering, and literacy in the Philippines. In *Advances in Language Planning*. J. A. Fishman, ed. The Hague: Mouton.

    1975. Survey of language use and attitudes towards language in the Philippines. In *Language Surveys in Developing Nations*. S. Ohannessian, C. A. Ferguson, and E. C. Polomé, eds. Arlington, VA: Center for Applied Linguistics.

    1978. Bilingual education in the Philippines: strategy and structure. In *Georgetown University Round Table on Languages and Linguistics 1978*. J. E. Alatis, ed. Washington, DC: Georgetown University Press.

Siegrist, J. 1977. Empirische Untersuchungen zu Kommunikationsprozessen bei Visiten. *Österreichische Zeitschrift für Soziologie* 3: 4.

Silver, Brian. 1974. The impact of urbanization and geographical dispersion on the linguistic russification of Soviet nationalities. *Demography* 11.

Silverstein, Michael. 1972. Chinook jargon: language contact and the problem of multilevel generative systems. *Language* 48, Part I: 378–406, Part II: 596–625.

Simon, H. A. and M. Barenfeld. 1969. Information processing analysis of perceptual processes in problem solving. *Psychological Review* 76: 473–83.

Simon, Paul. 1977. Battling linguistic chauvinism. *Change Magazine* 9.

Simoncini, Forrest. 1959. The San Francisco Italian dialect: a study. *Orbis* 8: 342–54.

Sledd, James and Wilma R. Ebbit. 1962. *Dictionaries and that Dictionary*. Chicago: Scott, Foresman.

Smith, A. G. 1966. *Communication and Culture: readings in the codes of human interaction*. New York: Holt, Rinehart, and Winston.

Smith, Arthur L. 1973. *Transracial Communication*. Englewood Cliffs, NJ: Prentice-Hall.

Smith, Huron H. 1933. Ethnobotany of the Forest Potawatomi Indians. *Public Museum of* the City of Milwaukee, Bulletin 7.1: 1–230.

Smith, Larry, ed. 1980. *English for Cross-Cultural Communication*. London: Macmillan.

Smith, M. Estellie. 1968. The Spanish-speaking population of Florida. In *Spanish-Speaking People of the United States*. J. Helm, ed. Proceedings of the 1968 Annual Spring Meeting of the American Ethnological Society, Detroit. Seattle: University of Washington Press.

Snow, C. E. 1972. Mothers' speech to children learning language. *Child Development* 43: 549–65.

Sodo, Eva. 1977. *Glimpses of History from the Pages of Italian-American Newspapers in San Francisco*. Columbus: The Publication of the Columbus Celebration, 1977.

Spencer, John, ed. 1963. *Language in Africa*. Cambridge, England, and New York: Cambridge University Press.

1971a. *The English Language in West Africa*. London: Longmans.

1971b. Colonial language policies and their legacies. In *Current Trends in Linguistics, Vol. VII: Linguistics in sub-Saharan Africa*. T. A. Sebeok, ed. The Hague: Mouton.

Spencer, Robert F. 1947. Spanish loanwords in Keresan. *Southwestern Journal of Anthropology* 3: 130–46.

Spencer, Robert F., Jesse D. Jennings et al. 1977. *The Native Americans*. New York: Harper and Row.

Spicer, Edward H. 1943. Linguistic aspects of Yaqui acculturation. *American Anthropologist* 45: 410–26.

1961. Yaqui. In *Perspectives in American Indian Culture Change*. Chicago: University of Chicago Press.

Spicer, K. 1974. Notes for a speech. In *Bilingualism, Biculturalism and Education*. S. T. Carey, ed. Edmonton, Alberta: University of Alberta.

Spolsky, Bernard, ed. 1972. *The Language Education of Minority Children*. Rowley, MA: Newbury House.

Spolsky, Bernard and Robert Cooper, eds. 1977. *Frontiers in Bilingual Education*. Rowley, MA: Newbury House.

eds. 1978. *Case Studies in Bilingual Education*. Rowley, MA: Newbury House.

Spurlin, Paul M. 1976. The Founding Fathers and the French language. *The Modern Language Journal* 60: 85–97.

Stack, Carol. 1976. *All Our Kin*. New York: Harper and Row.

Stefánsson, Vilhjalmur. 1909. The Eskimo trade jargon of Herschel Island. *American Anthropologist* 11: 217–32.

1913. *My Life with the Eskimo*. New York: Macmillan.

Steiner, Edward A. 1916. *Nationalizing America*. New York: Fleming H. Revell Co.

Stewart, George R. 1967. *Names On the Land: a historical account of place-naming in the United States*. 3rd edn. Boston: Houghton-Mifflin. First published 1945.

1970. *American Place-Names: a concise and selective dictionary for the continental United States*. London and New York: Oxford University Press.

Stewart, William A. 1967. Sociolinguistic factors in the history of American Negro dialects. *Florida Foreign Language Reporter* 5: 11–29.

1968. Continuity and change in American Negro dialects. *Florida Foreign Language Reporter* 6.2: 3–14.

1970. Sociopolitical issues in the linguistic treatment of Negro dialect. *Georgetown Round Table on Languages and Linguistics*. Washington, DC: Georgetown University Press.

Strevens, Peter. 1972. *British and American English*. London: Collier-Macmillan.

1977. *New Orientations in the Teaching of English*. London and New York: Oxford University Press.

Stubbs, M. 1976. *Language, Schools, and Classrooms*. London: Methuen.

Sturtevant, W. C., gen. ed. Forthcoming. *Handbook of North American Indians*, Washington, DC: Smithsonian Institution.

Susman, Amelia. 1940. The Winnebago Syllabary. MS. Boas Collection, Library of the American Philosophical Society. Philadelphia.

1943. The Accentual System of Winnebago. Ph.D. dissertation, Columbia University.

Swadesh, Morris. 1960. On interhemisphere linguistic connections. In *Culture in History: essays in honor of Paul Radin*. S. Diamond, ed. New York: Columbia University Press.

Swift, Jonathan. 1907. A proposal for correcting, improving and ascertaining the English tongue (1712). In *The Prose Works of Jonathan Swift*, Vol XI: *Literary Essays*. T. Scott, ed. London: Bell.

Szasz, Margaret. 1974. *Education and the American Indian: the road to self-determination, 1928–1973*. Albuquerque, NM: University of New Mexico Press.

Tachiki, Amy, Eddie Wong, and Franklin Odo, eds. 1971. *Roots: an Asian American Reader*. Los Angeles: UCLA Asian American Studies Center.

Tannen, Deborah. 1979. What's in a frame? Surface evidence for underlying expectations. In *New Directions in Discourse Processing*. R. O. Freedle, ed. Norwood, NJ: Ablex.

Taylor, Allan R. 1975. Nonverbal communications systems in Native North America. *Semiotica* 13: 329–74.

Teeter, Karl V. 1971. The main features of Malecite-Passamaquoddy grammar. In *Studies in American Indian Languages Dedicated to Mary R. Haas*. J. Sawyer, ed. University of California Publications in Linguistics 65.

Teitelbaum, Herbert and R. J. Hiller. 1977a. Bilingual education: the legal mandate. *Harvard Educational Review* 47: 138–72.

1977b. *The Legal Perspective*, Vol. III: *Bilingual Education: current perspectives*. Arlington, VA: Center for Applied Linguistics.

Teschner, Richard V., Garland D. Bills, and Jerry R. Craddock. 1975. *Spanish and English of United States Hispanos: a critical, annotated, linguistic bibliography*. Arlington, VA: Center for Applied Linguistics.

1977. Current research on the language(s) of U.S. Hispanos. *Hispania* 60: 347–58.

Thomason, Sarah Grey. 1976. On interpreting 'The Indian Interpreter'. Paper presented at the Annual Meetings of the Linguistic Society of America.

Thompson, R.M. 1974 Mexican American language loyalty and the validity of the 1970 census. *International Journal of the Sociology of Language* 2: 6–18.

Thorne, Barrie and Nancy Henley, eds. 1975. *Language and Sex: differences and dominance*. Rowley, MA: Newbury House.

Thorne, Barrie, Nancy Henley, and Sheris Kramarae, eds. 1980. *Language and Sex: differences and dominance*. 2nd edn. Rowley, MA: Newbury House.

Timm, L. A. 1975. Spanish–English code switching: el porque and how not to. *Romance Philology* 28: 473–82.

Tisch, Joseph Le Sage. 1959. *French in Louisiana*. New Orleans: A. F. Laborde.

Todd, Loreto. 1974. *Pidgins and Creoles*. London: Routledge and Kegan Paul.

Tofani, Maurice L. 1951. A Linguistic Approach to the Acculturation of Italians in New York City. M. A. Thesis, Columbia University.

Tomkins, William. 1929. *Universal Indian Sign Language of the Plains Indians of North America*. San Diego: William Tomkins.

Tongue, Ray. 1974. *The English of Singapore and Malaysia*. Singapore: Eastern Universities Press.

Townsend, H. E. R. and E. Brittan. 1972. *Organization in Multiracial Schools*. Windsor, England: N.F.E.R. Publishing Co.

Toynbee, Arnold J. 1934–54. *A Study of History*. 10 vols. London: Royal Institute of International Affairs. Reprinted London and New York: Oxford University Press. 1962.

Trager, George L. 1944. Spanish and English loanwords in Taos. *International Journal of American Linguistics* 10: 144–58.

1967. The Tanoan settlement of the Rio Grande area: a possible chronology. In *Studies in Southwestern Ethnolinguistics*. D. Hymes and W. Bittle, eds. The Hague: Mouton.

Trager, George L. and Felicia Harben. 1958. *North American Indian Languages: classification and maps*. Studies in Linguistics Occasional Papers 5. Buffalo, NY: SUNY.

Traugott, Elizabeth. 1976. Pidgins, creoles, and the origins of vernacular Black English. In *Black English: a seminar*. D. S. Hamison and T. Trabasso, eds. Hillsdale, NJ: Erlbaum.

Traugott, Elizabeth and Mary L. Pratt. 1980. *Linguistics and Its Uses in Literary Analysis: an introduction*. New York: Harcourt, Brace, Jovanovich.

Trejo, Arnulfo D. 1968. *Diccionario etimológico latinoamericano del léxico de la delincuencia*. Mexico, D. F.: UTEHA.

Trudgill, Peter. 1974. *Sociolinguistics: an introduction*. Harmondsworth, Middlesex, England: Penguin Books.

Tully, Marjorie F. and Juan B. Rael. 1950. *An Annotated Bibliography of Spanish Folklore in New Mexico and Southern Colorado*. University of New Mexico Publications in Language and Literature 3. Albuquerque, NM: University of New Mexico Press.

Turano, Anthony M. 1932. The speech of Little Italy. *American Mercury* 26: 356–9.

Turner, George W. 1966. *The English Language in Australia and New Zealand*. London: Longmans.

Turner, Lorenzo Dow. 1945. Notes on the sounds and vocabulary of Gullah. *Publications of the American Dialect Society* 3.

1949. *Africanisms in the Gullah Dialect*. Chicago: University of Chicago Press.

UCLA Asian American Studies Center. 1976. *Letters in Exile: an introductory reader on the history of Pilipinos in America*. Los Angeles: UCLA AA Studies Center.

Umiker-Sebeok, D. Jean, and Thomas A. Sebeok. 1978. *Aboriginal Sign Languages of the Americas and Australia*. New York: Plenum Press.

U.S. Bureau of the Census. 1943. *Sixteenth Census of the United States 1940: population, nativity, and parentage of the White population: mother tongue*. Washington, DC: U.S. Government Printing Office.

1966. *U.S. Census of Population: 1960*. Final Report PC(2)-1E: *Mother tongue of the foreign born*. Washington, DC: U.S. Government Printing Office.

1971a. *Characteristics of the Population by Ethnic Origin: November 1969*. Current Population Reports, P-20, No. 221. Washington, DC: U.S. Government Printing Office.

1971b. *Persons of Spanish Origin in the United States: November 1969*. Current

Population Reports, P-20, No. 213. Washington, DC: U.S. Government Printing Office.

1972. *Public Use Samples of Basic Records from the 1970 Census: description and technical documentation*. Washington, DC: U.S. Government Printing Office.

1973a. *Census of Population: 1970*, Vol. I: *Characteristics of the Population: state reports*. Washington, DC: U.S. Government Printing Office.

1973b. *Census of Population: 1970*. Subject Reports. Final Report PC(2)-1A: *National Origin and Language*. Washington, DC: U.S. Government Printing Office.

1973c. *Census of Population: 1970*. Subject Reports. Final Report PC(2)-1F: *American Indians*. Washington, DC: U.S. Government Printing Office.

1973d. *Detailed Characteristics of the Population, Table 142: mother tongue of the population by nativity, parentage, and race*. Washington, DC: U.S. Government Printing Office.

1973e. *Persons of Spanish Ancestry. 1970 Census of Population*, PC(SI)-30. Washington, DC: U.S. Government Printing Office.

1973f. *Persons of Spanish Origin in the United States: March 1972 and 1971*. Current Population Reports, P-20, No. 250. Washington, DC: U.S. Government Printing Office.

1973g. *Population and Housing Inquiries in U.S. Decennial Censuses, 1790–1970*. Working Paper No. 39. Washington, DC: U.S. Government Printing Office.

1974. *Accuracy of Data for Selected Population Characteristics as Measured by Reinterviews. Census of Population and Housing: 1970*. Evaluation and Research Programs, PHC(E)-9. Washington, DC: U.S. Government Printing Office.

1976. *Bureau of the Census Pocket Data Book*. Washington, DC: U.S. Government Printing Office.

U.S. Commission on Civil Rights. 1972. *Mexican American Educational Study, Report V*. Washington, DC: U.S. Government Printing Office.

1974. *Counting the Forgotten: the 1970 census count of persons of Spanish speaking background in the United States*. Washington, DC: U.S. Government Printing Office.

1976. *Puerto Ricans in the Continental United States: an uncertain future*. Washington, DC: U.S. Government Printing Office.

U.S. General Accounting Office. 1976. *Bilingual Education: an unmet need*. Washington, DC: U.S. Government Printing Office.

U.S. Immigration and Naturalization Service. 1975. *Annual Report of the Immigration and Naturalization Service for the Year Ended June 30, 1975*. Washington, DC: U.S. Government Printing Office.

Valdés Fallis, Guadalupe. 1976. Social interaction and code switching patterns: a case study of Spanish/English alternation. In *Bilingualism in the Bicentennial and Beyond*. G. Keller, R. V. Teschner, and S. Vierra, eds. Jamaica, NY: Bilingual Press.

1978a. Code-switching and language dominance: some initial findings. *General Linguistics* 18: 90–104.

1978b. *Language in Education: theory and practice*. Vol. IV: *Code-Switching and the Classroom Teacher*. Arlington, VA: Center for Applied Linguistics.

1980. Code-switching as a deliberate verbal strategy. In *Discourse Processes: advances in research and theory*. R. Freedle, ed. Norwood, NJ: Ablex Publishing Co.

Valdés Fallis, Guadalupe and Rodolfo García Moya, eds. 1976. *Teaching Spanish to the Spanish-speaking: theory and practice*. San Antonio, TX: PISE Series, Trinity University.

Valdés Fallis, Guadalupe and Richard V. Teschner. 1978. *Español escrito: primer curso para hispano-hablantes bilingües*. New York: Charles Scribner's Sons.

Valdés Fallis, Guadalupe, Anthony G. Lozano, and Rodolfo García Moya, eds. 1981. *Teaching Spanish to the Hispanic Bilingual: issues, aims, and methods*. New York: Teachers College Press.

Valdman, Albert, ed. 1977. *Pidgin and Creole Linguistics: present state and current trends*. Bloomington, IN: Indiana State University Press.

Valenti, Paul. 1976. *A Brief History of the Italian Bilingual Education in the City of New York*. New York: Office of Bilingual Education, Board of Education.

Vallangca, Roberto V. 1977. *Pinoy: the first wave*. San Francisco: Strawberry Hill Press.

Van Riper, William Robert, et al. Forthcoming. *Linguistic Atlas of Oklahoma*.

Varela de Cuéllar, Beatriz. 1974. La influencia del Inglés en los Cubanos de Miami y Nueva Orleans. *El Español Actual* 26: 16–25.

Varo, Carlos. 1971. *Consideraciones antropológicas y políticas en torno a la enseñanza de "Spanglish" en Nueva York*. Río Piedras, PR: Ediciones Librería Internacional.

Vaughn, Herbert H. 1926a. Italian and its dialects as spoken in the U.S. *American Speech* 1: 431–5.

1926b. Italian dialects in the United States. *American Speech* 2: 13–18.

Vecoli, Rudolph J. 1978. The coming of age of the Italian Americans: 1945–1974. *Ethnicity* 5: 119–147.

Velasquez, G. J. 1973. Evaluation of a Bilingual/Bicultural Education Program. Ph.D. dissertation, United States International University.

Velikonja, Joseph. 1970. Italian immigrants in the United States in the sixties. In *The Italian Experience in the United States*. S. M. Tomasi and M. H. Engel, eds. Staten Island, NY: Center for Migration Studies.

Vera Cruz, Philip. 1971. Interview. In *Roots: an Asian American reader*. A. Tachiki et al., eds. Los Angeles: UCLA Asian American Studies Center.

Villagra, Gaspar Perez de. 1610. *Historia de la Nueva México*. Alcalá de Henares, Spain: Luis Martinez Grande.

Voegelin, C. F., F. M. Voegelin, and Noel W. Schutz. 1967. The language situation in Arizona as part of the Southwest culture area. In *Studies in Southwestern Ethnolinguistics*. D. Hymes, ed. The Hague: Mouton.

Voorhis, Paul. 1972. Mesquakie and Kickapoo Standard Orthography. MS.

Wagenheim, Kal. 1970. *Puerto Rico: a profile*. New York: Praeger.

Waggoner, Dorothy. 1976. Results of the Survey of Languages. Supplement to the July 1975 Current Population Survey. Paper presented to the Fifth Annual Bilingual–Bicultural Education Conference in San Antonio, Texas.

1978. Non-English language background persons: three U.S. surveys. *TESOL Quarterly* 13: 247–62.

n.d. Language and Demographic Characteristics of the U.S. Population with Potential Need for Bilingual and Other Special Educational Programs, July 1975. Unpublished MS, available from ERIC/CAL.

Waitzkin, H. and J. D. Stoeckle. 1972. The communication of information about illness: clinical, sociological, and methodological considerations. *Advances in Psychosomatic Medicine* 8: 180–215.

1976. Information control and the micropolitics of health care: summary of an ongoing research project. *Social Science and Medicine* 10: 263–76.

Waitzkin, H. and B. Waterman. 1974. *The Exploitation of Illness in Capitalist Society*. Indianapolis, IN: Bobbs-Merrill.

Walker, Willard. 1974. The Winnebago syllabary and the generative model. *Anthropological Linguistics* 16: 393–414.

———. 1975. Cherokee. In *Studies in Southeastern Indian Languages*. J. M. Crawford, ed. Athens, GA: University of Georgia Press.

Ward, Jack H. 1971. *A Bibliography of Philippine Linguistics and Minor Languages*. Data Paper No. 83. Southeast Asia Program, Department of Asian Studies, Southeast Asia Series No. 20. Center for International Studies, Ohio University.

Ward, Martha Coonfield. 1971. *Them Children: a study in language learning*. New York: Holt, Rinehart, and Winston.

Washburn, Wilcomb E. 1975. *The Indian in America*. New York: Harper.

Webb, John T. 1976. A Lexical Study of Caló and Non-Standard Spanish in the Southwest. Ph.D. dissertation, University of California, Berkeley.

Webster, Noah. 1789. *Dissertations on the English Language*. Boston: Isaiah Thomas.

Weinreich, Max. 1979. *History of Yiddish*. 4 vols. Chicago: University of Chicago Press and Yivo Institute for Jewish Research.

[Weinreich, Max]. 1964. *For Max Weinreich on his Seventieth Birthday: studies in Jewish language, literature and society*. The Hague: Mouton.

Weinreich, Uriel. 1971. Yiddish. In *Encylopaedia Judaica*. Jerusalem: Macmillan Co.

Wertheimer, A. I., E. Shafter, and R. M. Cooper. 1973. More on the pharmacist as a drug consultant: three case studies. *Drug Intelligence and Clinical Pharmacy* 7: 58–61.

West, La Mont, Jr. 1960. *The Sign Language: an analysis*. Ann Arbor, MI: University Microfilms.

Whatley, Elizabeth. Forthcoming. *Child Discourse in the Black Community*.

White, John K. 1962. On the revival of printing in the Cherokee language. *Current Anthropology* 3: 511–14.

Whitten, Norman E. and John F. Szwed. 1970. *Afro-American Anthropology: contemporary perspectives*. New York: The Free Press.

Whorf, Benjamin Lee. 1936. The punctual and segmental aspects of verbs in Hopi. *Language* 12: 127–31.

Williams, Roger. 1973. *A Key into the Language of North America*. Detroit, MI: Wayne State University Press. First published 1643.

Williams, Stanley T. 1955. *The Spanish Background of American Literature*. 2 vols. New Haven, CT: Yale University Press.

Williamson, Juanita and Virginia Burke, eds. 1971. *A Various Language*. New York: Holt, Rinehart, and Winston.

Willke, I. 1975. Schooling of immigrant children in West Germany, Sweden, England: the educationally disadvantaged. *International Review of Education* 21: 357–82.

Wilson, H. H. 1940. *A Glossary of Judicial and Revenue Terms and of Useful Words Occurring in Official Documents, Relating to the Administration of the Government of British India*. Calcutta. First published 1885.

Wolf, Leon. 1968. *Little Brown Brother*. Manila: Erehwon Publishing House.

Wolfram, Walt. 1969. *A Sociolinguistic Description of Detroit Negro Speech*. Urban Linguistic Series No. 5. Washington, DC: Center for Applied Linguistics.

———. 1973. Review of *Black English* by J. L. Dillard. *Language* 49: 670–9.

———. 1974. *Sociolinguistic Aspects of Assimilation: Puerto Rican English in New York City*. Arlington, VA: Center for Applied Linguistics.

Wolfram, Walt and Donna Christian. 1976. *Appalachian Speech*. Arlington, VA: Center for Applied Linguistics.

Wolfram, Walt and Ralph W. Fasold. 1974. *Social Dialects in American English.* Englewood Cliffs, NJ: Prentice-Hall.

Wright, Louis B. 1943. Thomas Jefferson and the Classics. *Proceedings of the American Philosophical Society* 87: 223–33.

Yabes, Leopoldo. 1967. Developing a national language for the Philippines. In *The Modernization of Languages in Asia.* S. T. Alisjahbana, ed. Kuala Lumpur: The Malaysia Society of Asian Studies.

Yngve, Victor. 1970. On getting a word in edgewise. In *Papers from the Sixth Regional Meeting of the Chicago Linguistic Society.*

Yoder, C. 1976. Diglossia Within the Old Order Amish Speech Community of Lancaster, Pennsylvania. Unpublished MS, University of Pittsburgh.

Young, Virginia Heyer. 1970. Family and childhood in a southern Negro community. *American Anthropologist* 72: 269–88.

Younger, Irving. 1976. In praise of simplicity. *American Bar Association Journal* 62: 632–4.

Yule, Henry N. and A. C. Burnell. 1886. *Hobson-Jobson: a glossary of colloquial Anglo-Indian words and phrases, and of kindred terms, etymological, historical, geographical, and discursive.* London: J. Murray. Reprinted 1903.

Zallio, A. G. 1927. The Piedmontese dialects in the United States. *American Speech* 2: 501–5.

Zborowski, M. 1952. Cultural components of response to pain. *Journal of Social Issues* 8: 16–30.

Zentella, Ana Celia. 1973. The linguistic repercussions of colonialism on the languages of Puerto Rico. Paper delivered at American Anthropological Association Meeting, New Orleans, November 28.

1978. *Code Switching and Interactions Among Puerto Rican Children.* Sociolinguistic Working Paper 50. Austin, TX: Southwest Educational Development Laboratory.

1981. Ta bien, you could answer me en cualquier idioma: code switching in New York Puerto Rican bilingual classrooms. In *Latino Language and Communicative Behavior.* R. Duran, ed. Norwood, NJ: Ablex.

Zeydel, Edwin H. 1964. The teaching of German in the United States from colonial times to the present. *The German Quarterly* 37: 315–92. Also in *Reports of Surveys and Studies in the Teaching of Modern Foreign Languages.* New York: Modern Language Association.

Zirkel, Perry A. 1973. Puerto Rican parents: an educational survey. *Integrated Education* 11: 20–6.

Zisa, Charles A. 1970. *American Indian Languages: classifications and list.* Arlington, VA: ERIC Clearinghouse for Languages and Linguistics, Center for Applied Linguistics.

Zola, I. K. 1966. Culture and symptoms: an analysis of patients presenting complaints. *American Sociological Review* 31: 615–31.

Index

Notes: Page numbers in bold type indicate reference to chapters, and substantial parts thereof. Page numbers in italic type refer to tables and figures.